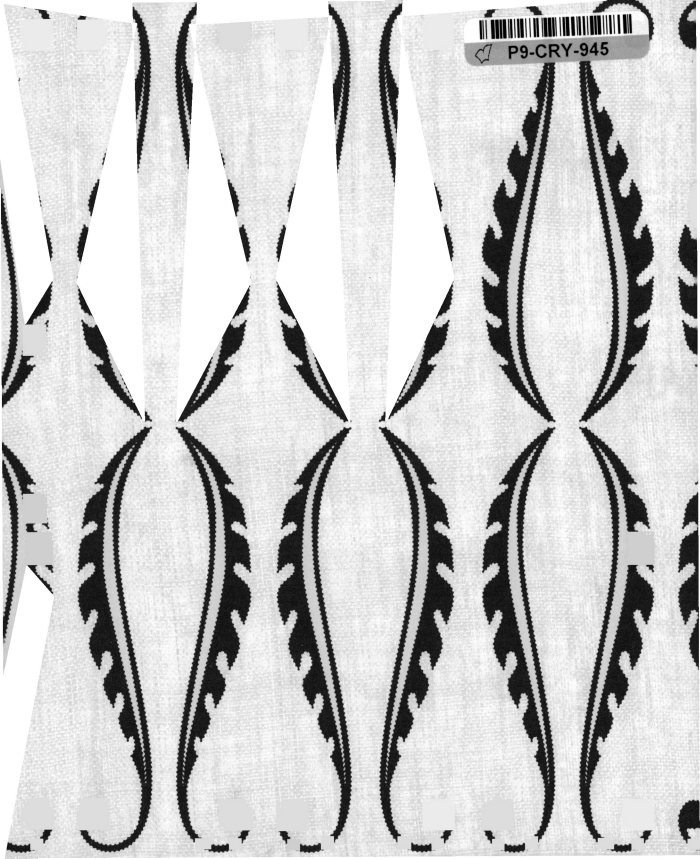

Southern Living 1001 WAYS TO COOK SOUTHERN

Southern Living 1001 WAYS TO COOK SOUTHERN

The ultimate treasury of Southern classics—
fresh flavors, wholesome ingredients, quick cooking techniques,
and beloved food traditions

ISBN-13: 978-0-8487-3311-7
ISBN-10: 0-8487-3311-8
Library of Congress Number: 2009925692

Oxmoor House, Inc.
VP, Publishing Director: Jim Childs
Editorial Director: Susan Payne Dobbs
Brand Manager: Daniel Fagan
Senior Editor: Rebecca Brennan
Managing Editor: Laurie Herr

1001 Ways To Cook Southern
Editor: Susan Hernandez Ray
Project Editor: Vanessa Lynn Rusch
Senior Designer: Melissa Jones Clark
Director, Test Kitchen: Elizabeth Tyler Austin
Assistant Director, Test Kitchen: Julie Christopher
Test Kitchen Professionals: Allison E. Cox, Julie Gunter,
    Kathleen Royal Phillips, Catherine Crowell Steele, Ashley T. Strickland
Photography Director: Jim Bathie
Senior Photo Stylist: Kay E. Clarke
Associate Photo Stylist: Katherine Eckert Coyne
Senior Production Manager: Greg Amason

Contributors
Editors: Vicki Poellnitz, Elizabeth Taliaferro
Copy Editor: Donna Baldone
Proofreaders: Jasmine Hodges, Rhonda Richards
Indexer: Mary Ann Laurens
Writer: Deborah Lowery
Interns: Christine Taylor Davis, Georgia Dodge, Perri K. Hubbard,
    Allison Leigh Sperando

Southern Living®
Executive Editor: Scott Jones
Food Editor: Shannon Sliter Satterwhite
Senior Writer: Donna Florio
Senior Food Editors: Shirley Harrington, Mary Allen Perry
Senior Recipe Editor: Ashley Leath
Assistant Recipe Editor: Ashley Arthur
Test Kitchen Director: Lyda Jones Burnette
Assistant Test Kitchen Director: Rebecca Kracke Gordon
Test Kitchen Specialists/Food Styling: Marian Cooper Cairns,
    Vanessa McNeil Rocchio
Test Kitchen Professionals: Norman King, Pam Lolley, Angela Sellers
Senior Photographers: Ralph Anderson, Jennifer Davick
Photographer: Beth Dreiling Hontzas
Senior Photo Stylist: Buffy Hargett

To order additional publications, call 1-800-765-6400 or
    1-800-491-0551

For more books to enrich your life, visit oxmoorhouse.com
To search, savor, and share thousands of recipes, visit myrecipes.com

CONTENTS

Dear Friends,

As part of our tradition to share our beloved recipes, we invite you to enjoy one of the most comprehensive food collections *Southern Living* has published. But, it's much more than a cookbook. In addition to over 1000 intrinsically Southern recipes, discover lighthearted commentary detailing cultural influences, enduring Southern restaurant finds, and fiery food debates. Plus, get an insider's look at the essential ingredients, equipment, and techniques that make up the heart and soul of every Southern kitchen.

Generations of home cooks have passed down their favorite recipes, full of warm memories. After sampling tens of thousands of recipes for over 40 years, this collection pulls together the best-of-the-best. Many recipes are flagged with tags identifying them as *Southern Lights*, *Casual Gatherings*, *Quick*, *Family Favorite*, *Make Ahead*, *For Kids*, *Freeze It*, and *Test Kitchen Favorite*, which you can search using our index. And we've included all of our very favorites like melt-in-your-mouth Orange Rolls on page 146, the favorite Aunt Mary's Pot Roast on page 507, and the refreshing Tomato and Watermelon Salad on page 740.

Many of our classic Southern recipes come with a mini article called *Taste of the South* that explains just what makes them Southern. Examples include Pimiento Cheese, Macaroni and Cheese, and Pineapple Upside Down Cake—just to name a few. In addition, *Seasonal Gatherings* menus are strategically placed throughout the book to help you plan get-togethers with family and friends. And, be sure not to miss the *Inspirations* found in each chapter that provide simple ideas for your tastes and table.

Our food staff's knowledge is legendary. Throughout this book we share their no-fail techniques and favorite tips for cooking success. Handy step-by-step tips and how-to boxes make cooking traditional Southern recipes foolproof. Beautiful full-page photography scattered throughout the pages inspires the cook and leads to perfect results.

So, welcome your friends and family to your Southern table with some of our classic recipes guaranteed to nurture the soul.

Scott Jones
Executive Editor

ESSENTIAL SOUTHERN KITCHEN BASICS

"No one who cooks, cooks alone. Even at her most solitary, a cook in the kitchen is surrounded by generations of cooks past, the advice and menus of cooks present, the wisdom of cookbook writers."

—Laurie Colwin

THAT SOUTHERNERS MUST HAVE

Well-Seasoned Cast-Iron Skillet

A regional icon, the versatile cast-iron skillet can stand in for a sandwich press, a pizza stone, a baking dish, or a sauté pan. From frying catfish to baking cornbread, you can do just about anything with it.

When it comes to cooking with your cast-iron skillet, the more seasoned it is, the better. Seasoning is the process of oiling and heating cast iron to protect its porous surface from moisture. The oil is absorbed, creating a rustproof nonstick surface. Generally, you need to season your pan only once before using it. Now, you can buy cast-iron skillets preseasoned, so they're ready to cook with the day you bring them home. But for tradition's sake, we recommend seasoning it yourself.

How to Season a Cast-Iron Skillet

1. Using a stiff scrub brush, wash with dish soap and hot water; rinse, and dry thoroughly.

2. Spread a thin layer of solid shortening or vegetable oil over both the interior and exterior surfaces of the cookware, including the handle and the underside of any lids.

3. Place the cookware upside down on a rack in an aluminum foil-lined broiler pan. Bake at 350° for 1 hour. Turn off the oven, leaving the door closed, and allow the cookware to cool completely before removing.

4. You will need to repeat the procedure several times to darken the color of the cookware from brown to black, but it's ready to use after this first seasoning. Once seasoned, never use harsh detergents to clean it or put it in the dishwasher. Wash with a stiff brush under hot running water; dry immediately, and rub with a thin coating of vegetable oil. Store in a cool, dry place with a folded paper towel between the lid and the cookware to allow the air to circulate and prevent rust.

{ Southernism }

No kitchen south of the Mason-Dixon Line would be complete without that heavy black skillet. The secret to down-home Southern cooking, cast-iron cookware is not only affordable, it's also virtually indestructible, which could explain the tradition of passing down a skillet like you would a family heirloom.

Cast-iron cookware has been the touchstone of Southern food and hospitality for generations, creating perfectly fried chicken and cornbread so crisp you can hear it crackle when cut.

The most treasured pieces of cast-iron cookware are those well-seasoned windfalls we're fortunate enough to inherit from a doting aunt or a much-loved grandmother. With proper care, cast iron will last for years. Even that rare flea market find, splattered with rust, can be scoured with a steel-wool soap pad and re-seasoned.

Norman King
Test Kitchen Professional

One of my favorite memories is when I learned the importance of a heavy stockpot while making my first gumbo. The patient teacher stood by my side instructing me to "first make a roux, and you want it to be the color of the Mississippi River." Now, only in the South would you know exactly what he was talking about! Eventually, the wonderful aroma of a full pot of gumbo filled my kitchen, and my love affair with my trusty stockpot had begun.

Pam Lolley
Test Kitchen Professional

A Heavy Stockpot

Take a look around most Southern kitchens and you're bound to find at least one good heavy stockpot. Ever since Native Americans began sharing their secrets for one-pot cooking with settlers, Southerners have found ways to turn a pot of stew into a party. In fact, most Southern states have their own specialty soup or stew. Kentucky's burgoo made of meat and vegetables is similar to the Brunswick stew claimed by Georgia and Virginia. Instead of wild game, today the meat is chicken, pork, or beef. In South Carolina, Frogmore or Beaufort stew pots are full of potatoes, smoked sausage, ears of corn, and shrimp. North Carolina's muddle is fish or chicken, potatoes, and seasonings. And, of course, Louisiana has gumbo and jambalaya.

When it comes to buying a good stockpot, buy the best pot you can afford. Choose a pot with a heavy gauge (thickness) and sturdy construction—one that won't warp, dent, or scorch. Look for one with a thick bottom, tight-fitting lid, and heat-resistant handles that are securely attached.

Stock Basics

• Use a narrow and deep stockpot to prevent excessive evaporation during cooking.
• Start with cold water to cover ingredients. Bring stock slowly just to a boil; cook at a simmer.
• Never rush a stock by boiling it.
• Simmer stock partially covered.
• Never add salt to stock as it simmers. The long simmering time will concentrate the salt and ruin the resulting stock.

CHICKEN BROTH

makes 10 cups

prep: 10 min.   cook: 1 hr., 30 min.

This recipe makes a large quantity. Freeze in an airtight container up to three months and thaw as needed.

6   lb. chicken pieces
2½ qt. water
3   celery ribs with leaves, cut in half
2   onions, quartered
2   fresh thyme sprigs or ½ teaspoon dried thyme
1   bay leaf
1½ tsp. salt
¾   tsp. pepper

1. Combine first 6 ingredients in a large stockpot. Bring to a boil; cover, reduce heat, and simmer 1½ hours. Add salt and pepper.
2. Line a large wire-mesh strainer with a double layer of cheesecloth; place in a large bowl. Remove chicken; reserve for another use. Pour broth through strainer, discarding vegetables and herbs. Cover broth, and chill thoroughly. Skim and discard solidified fat from top of broth.
3. Store broth in a tightly covered container in the refrigerator up to 3 days, or freeze up to 3 months. Thaw and use as directed in recipes that call for chicken broth.

A Box Grater

Creamy grits, mashed potatoes, pimiento cheese, cornbread, biscuits, and that all-time favorite, macaroni-and-cheese casserole, are Southern staples that appeal to the kid in all of us. What a list of Southern soul food traditions if there ever was one. And, for the most part, all incorporate cheese. In fact, most Southerners can find a way to add cheese to just about anything. The prepackaged, store-bought varieties simply won't do, either. For the real deal, a true Southern cook will lovingly grate a block of cheese by hand with a box-style grater, thus ensuring the most scrumptious results.

A good box-style grater gives you a choice of hole sizes—a different size on each side. Use the smaller holes for grating hard cheese, such as Parmesan, and the larger holes for shredding soft cheese, such as Cheddar. You can also use your box grater to shred other foods such as carrots, potatoes, and chocolate, just to name a few.

Marian likes her pimiento cheese spicy, so she makes the Spicy Roasted Red Bell Pepper Pimiento Cheese using the largest holes on the box grater to shred the cheese faster. She serves it with crackers, a drop of Sriracha (hot chili sauce), and Wickles pickles.

SPICY ROASTED RED BELL PEPPER PIMIENTO CHEESE

makes 4 cups   prep: 25 min.

Use the largest holes on a box grater to shred cheese in a snap.

1¼ cups mayonnaise
½   (12-oz.) jar roasted red bell peppers, drained and chopped
2   tsp. finely grated onion
2   tsp. coarse-grained mustard
½   tsp. ground red pepper
2   (10-oz.) blocks sharp white Cheddar cheese, shredded
Freshly ground black pepper to taste
Assorted crackers

1. Stir together first 5 ingredients until well blended; stir in cheese and black pepper to taste. Serve with assorted crackers. Store in the refrigerator in an airtight container up to 4 days.

A quality box grater is a true essential in every Southern kitchen. My mother advised me well when building my kitchen necessities post college. Her advice: Choose a grater that is 100% stainless steel and doesn't have plastic attachments or parts. The plastic will eventually break or get lost over the years, and stainless steel should last a lifetimetrust me. She was right; more than a decade later, I'm still making the best pimiento cheese with that same one we picked out together.

Marian Cooper Cairns
Test Kitchen Specialist/
Food Styling

When I first had an apartment, I took a Mason jar that was left over from a *Southern Living* photo shoot home with me and left it in my kitchen. I grabbed it one day when I made my first turkey dinner. I shook four ingredients and water together to make gravy. And now I use it for salad dressing, to shake up gelatin, for my son to rinse off his paint brushes when doing water colors, and to store leftover pancake batter…shake the next day and pour. I also use it to make cocktail sauce to take to the beach and to shake up quick marinades. I love this Mason jar!

Vanessa McNeil Rocchio
Test Kitchen Specialist/Food Styling

Mason Jar

Southerners have always loved to garden, and Mason jars are handy for preserving the fruits of their harvest. Mason jars are especially useful tools for canning all things Southern such as strawberry jam, peach preserves, and pickled cucumbers. But that's just the beginning.

Mason jars can be used at the Southern table for serving specialties such as sweet tea or holding a flower arrangement. Mason jars are great for mixing—in fact, about a half century ago, blenders were sold with Mason jars in the package. Blenders were originally made to fit Mason jars so that you could use the blender to chop and blend things such as nuts and whipped cream and then easily store them. They're also great containers for storing homemade mixes for cookies, brownies, pancakes, and other favorites. A Mason jar is a great tool for creating one of our favorite dressings.

LEMON-HERB DRESSING WITH MINT AND TARRAGON

makes about ¾ cup   prep: 10 min.

This dressing is a favorite in summer salads.

⅓   cup canola oil
3   Tbsp. chopped fresh mint
1   Tbsp. chopped fresh tarragon
1   Tbsp. honey mustard
1   tsp. lemon zest
¼   cup fresh lemon juice
1   tsp. salt
½   tsp. dried crushed red pepper

1. Combine all ingredients in a Mason jar; shake until blended.

Lemon-Herb Dressing With Chives and Tarragon: Substitute chopped fresh chives for mint. Proceed with recipe as directed.

Lemon-Herb Dressing With Basil: Substitute ⅓ cup chopped fresh basil for mint and tarragon. Proceed with recipe as directed. Season with salt to taste.

{ *Southernism* }

This Southern staple has been around for a long time, since it was developed and patented by tinsmith John L. Mason in 1858. Prior to the Mason jar, food was preserved either in tin cans or glass jars that had a flat tin top that was sealed with wax, which easily came loose and allowed for bacteria to grow in the jar. The invention revolutionized canning in homes across the South.

A Mighty Mixer

A heavy-duty stand mixer can be a Southern cook's best friend. This gem comes equipped with a basic set of attachments: wire whisk, dough hook, and paddle. These are used for mixing, kneading, whipping, and beating or creaming ingredients. KitchenAid and other brands of heavy-duty mixers are good for mixing large amounts and heavy batters such as cookie or bread dough. The bowls are generally large, so they can handle hefty amounts of batter or dough. Best of all, they do most of the work for you, so they're great for all kinds of things such as making big batches of holiday goodies.

Mixing It Up

Each attachment has a unique function. The dough hook (left) makes quick work of mixing and kneading yeast breads. The wire whisk attachment (center) is terrific for whipping egg whites or cream as well as emulsifying homemade mayonnaise and salad dressing. The flat paddle attachment is used for general mixing, including beating together butter and sugar and mixing cake batter and cookie dough. This is the attachment you'll want to use when making a pound cake or the cookies at right.

LEMON BUTTER COOKIES

**makes about 4 dozen (2¼-inch) or
2 dozen (3¼-inch) cookies**
prep: 30 min.   bake: 12 min. per batch
cool: 25 min.

Rebecca uses her mighty mixer to create one of our favorite cookie recipes.

1   cup butter, softened
1   tsp. lemon zest
1   cup powdered sugar
2   cups all-purpose flour
¼   tsp. salt
Parchment paper

1. Preheat oven to 325°. Beat butter and zest at medium speed with a heavy-duty electric stand mixer until creamy. Gradually add sugar, beating well.
2. Combine flour and salt; gradually add to butter mixture, beating until blended. Shape dough into a disc.
3. Roll dough to ⅛-inch thickness on a lightly floured surface. Cut with a 2¼- or 3¼-inch heart-shaped cutter; place ½ inch apart on parchment paper-lined baking sheets.
4. Bake at 325° for 12 to 14 minutes or until edges are lightly browned. Cool on baking sheets 5 minutes. Transfer to wire racks; cool completely (about 20 minutes).

I pulled into my mom's driveway just the other day with my niece and KitchenAid stand mixer in tow—a gift from her and my father while I was studying in Charleston in culinary school. That mixer still hums like a champ. Although I don't keep it on the counter all of the time, each time I reach for it, it's like becoming reacquainted with an old childhood friend. You may not have seen each other in a long while, but you always seem to pick up right where you left off from the visit before—seamlessly. Whether mixing cookie dough for my husband and his 6th grade students or taking an afternoon to mix and bake fresh loaves of sandwich bread with my sweet mom and niece, I know I can always depend on my tried and true Mercedes of mixers to get the job done and have loads of fun and laughs along the way.

**Rebecca Kracke Gordon
Assistant Test Kitchen Director**

techniques

How To Fry Anything

While many Southerners have cherished memories of grandmother's cooking that revolved around fried chicken and other fried favorites, some folks have several concerns about frying. Here are some of the reasons that frying can be intimidating and some tips that will hopefully change your mind about frying.

"The hot oil splatters."

HINT: Make sure your pots and pans are completely dry before adding oil. One little drop of water can explode just to escape the heat. Pat dry whatever you're frying (i.e. chicken, pork, shrimp) before dredging in flour or dipping in batter. Water is the enemy! You can also use a splatter guard.

"I can't tell if it's done."

HINT: Use a thermometer to heat the oil to the correct temperature and to test for doneness. When frying dense things such as chicken breast or thighs, Angela will pierce each piece with a fork or skewer to allow the hot oil to penetrate the flesh.

Use heavy-bottomed pots and pans, including cast-iron skillets. These allow the oil to heat evenly and help maintain a constant temperature. Add a few extra pieces just for testing. (You deserve it!) And, chicken floats when it's done.

"Fried food is greasy."

HINT: If fried properly and at the correct temperature, the food absorbs very little oil. If you want, you can press each fried item between two layers of paper towels to soak up any extra flavor (we meant fat!), or you can just enjoy fried items with a big green healthy salad. It really cuts down on the guilt.

"The smell can be overpowering at times."

HINT: Open at least two windows (for air circulation), use your ceiling fans, turn on the exhaust over the stove, and light scented candles. Also wipe down cabinets and countertops after frying. This is what Angela does, and it really helps. But, then again, who doesn't love the alluring smell of fried food?

{ *Southernism* }

Fried okra, fried green tomatoes, fried chicken, chicken-fried steak, fried pies—all these dishes have starred on family and company tables since the earliest days of the South. It has been said that Southerners will fry just about anything. And why not? Nothing is quite as delicious as a crispy, golden outside that covers a warm and flavorful goodness on the inside.

There are two types of people in the world: People that fry and people that don't. I'm happy to say that I love to fry. Unfortunately, it's not something that my diet will allow me to do often, but whenever I decide to treat myself to crunchy, crispy, juicy chicken, I fry it.

**Angela Sellers
Test Kitchen Professional**

My first foray into baking was a disaster that quickly became a fond family memory. Only my father ate the end result: dense little patties of ecru-colored batter—a cross between miniature cakes and hockey puck cookies. I stuck to it though, gradually improved, and, after awhile, I felt the pull of that famous Southern dessert: the quintessential pound cake.

For my first attempt, I was prepared for failure. So I picked a recipe that had the best chance of being edible: the Dark Chocolate Pound Cake from our December 2007 issue.

Now, almost three years later, I've made this cake so many times I've lost count. It's never failed me, and I have this one recipe to thank for giving me the push I needed to conquer the South's beloved desserts.

Ashley Leath
Senior Recipe Editor

Making Pound Cake

Nothing beats the rich, buttery flavor of a homemade pound cake. Originally made with a pound each of butter, sugar, eggs, and flour, creative cooks have, over time, come up with countless variations, such as replacing a portion of the butter with cream cheese or a few of the eggs with sour cream and leavening.

The most extraordinary thing about these pound cakes is how easy they are to prepare. You can bake them days ahead of time and store them in the pantry, or place them in large zip-top freezer bags and store in the freezer for up to two months.

Here are some insider tips for turning out a perfect pound cake.

• Carefully read through the entire recipe, and prepare any special ingredients, such as chopped fruits or toasted nuts, before starting to mix the batter.

• Use name-brand ingredients. Store brands of sugar are often more finely ground than name brands, yielding more sugar per cup, which can cause the cake to fall. Store brands of butter may contain more liquid fat or flours more hard wheat, making the cake heavy.

• Measure accurately. Extra sugar or leavening causes a cake to fall; extra flour makes it dry.

• For maximum volume, have ingredients at room temperature. We like to pre-measure our ingredients and assemble them in the order listed. That way, if interrupted, we're less likely to make a mistake.

• Beat softened butter (and cream cheese or vegetable shortening) at medium speed with an electric mixer until creamy. This can take from 1 to 7 minutes, depending on the power of your mixer. Gradually add sugar, continuing to beat until light and fluffy. These steps are so important because they whip air into the cake batter so it will rise during baking.

• Add the eggs, one at a time, beating just until the yellow disappears. Overbeating the eggs may cause the batter to overflow the sides of the pan when baked or create a fragile crust that crumbles and separates from the cake as it cools.

• Grease cake pans with solid vegetable shortening, such as Crisco, and always dust with flour.

• Use an oven thermometer to check your oven's temperature for accuracy.

• Place the cake pan in the center of the oven, and keep the door closed until the minimum baking time has elapsed. If the cake requires more baking, gently close the oven door as soon as possible after testing to prevent jarring and loss of heat—both can cause a cake to fall if it's not completely done.

• Test for doneness by inserting a long wooden pick into the center of the cake. It should come out clean, with no batter clinging to it.

Making Pralines

From Texas to Georgia, Southerners love pralines. These rich patty-shaped caramel-flavored candies are made with sugar, cream, butter, and pecans. After cooking, the praline mixture is beaten with a wooden spoon just until the mixture begins to thicken; then it's quickly dropped in mounds onto wax paper.

Pralines are best made when the weather is dry, because humidity tends to make them grainy. If your mixture becomes too stiff to spoon into mounds, just stir a few drops of hot water into the mixture, and then work quickly. You can also try returning the mixture to the cooktop and heating gently, stirring just until the mixture is no longer dry. Turn to page 275 for one of our favorite praline recipes.

Equipment Needed:

A heavy saucepan: In general, candy mixtures usually triple in volume as they cook, so you'll need pans large enough to allow the praline mixture to boil without boiling over. Aluminum pans are a good choice, because they conduct heat more evenly than stainless steel.

A wooden spoon: Long-handled wooden spoons are preferred for candy making, because wooden spoons don't hold heat like metal spoons.

Candy thermometer: A candy thermometer allows you to cook to a precise temperature and doneness stage. Buy one that's clearly marked and has an adjustable clip so that it can be attached to the side of the pan during cooking.

{ *Southernism* }

This delectable Louisiana brittle candy dates back to 1750. Originally the patty-shaped, fudgelike delicacy was made with almonds—the preferred nut of the French—and was considered an aid to digestion at the end of a meal. However, the Creoles quickly found a better alternative in the abundant pecan and replaced the white sugar with brown. Today it's considered one of the paramount sweets in the South, particularly in Texas and Louisiana. In New Orleans, it used to be a tradition for young women to make pralines before going to a ball and then enjoy them with friends (and beaux) at their homes afterward.

Plunge an iconic ingredient of the South—pecans—into a hot, buttery brown sugar mixture, and you're moments away from enjoying a classic praline. Pronunciation of the word praline all depends on the region you live in or are visiting. To some it's "PRAY-leen"; to others it's "PRAH-leen." A good rule of thumb is to say it the way the locals do.

Making them isn't difficult, it just requires some patience, stirring, and your full attention. Before you start cooking, have a partner lined up to help quickly drop the mixture on wax paper before it hardens, and mute your cell phone (seriously!).

A candy thermometer is essential to avoid pralines that are too soft from undercooking or too crumbly from overcooking. When beating the praline mixture, use a wooden spoon, and notice when the mixture starts to feel heavier and the color becomes lighter. Those changes indicate it's ready to drop.

Shirley Harrington
Senior Food Editor

Iced tea and Southerners go hand in hand. It's the drink most of us have grown up with, and it's that standard that we use to compare each batch we taste. Of course, the way we grew up drinking it is the way it should be. You can accessorize it all you want, but my drink of choice is pure and simple: tea, sugar, and water. I can still remember the pitcher my mother made the tea in every night. Some say lemon is a must and then there's the company-is-comin' version—mint. There are purists that say there is only one way to make tea, but if you ask any Southerner, you'll hear enough methods to fill volumes. One thing we would all agree on though—our way is surely the best.

Lyda Jones Burnette
Test Kitchen Director

Making Iced Tea

K nown as the signature drink of the region, a tall glass of iced tea in the South goes with just about every event—church suppers, family meals, ladies luncheons, and it's just perfect for porch sitting on a sizzling summer day. It's so easy to make and feeds a thirsty crowd. Typically in the North, iced tea begins with a powdered ingredient from a tin can, but not in the South. Beginning with tea bags and allowing for a bit of steep time are two important elements in getting the perfect pitcher of iced tea.

Our Test Kitchen has a favorite recipe and few secrets to making a batch of this Southern specialty.

• Instead of icing a glass of tea with ice cubes, use tea frozen in an ice cube tray so that when the ice melts, the tea won't be too watery.
• Fresh mint sprigs, lemon slices, lime wedges, and fresh citrus slices all make nice garnishes for a glass of iced tea.
• Teas made with no-calorie sweeteners (versus sugar) tend to become sweeter when stored.

Perhaps it's fitting that South Carolina was the first place in the United States where tea was grown and the only place where it was ever produced commercially. And, the oldest sweet tea recipe in print can be traced to a community cookbook published in 1879 titled *Housekeeping in Old Virginia* by Marion Cabell Tyree. It states:

After scalding the teapot, put into it one quart of boiling water and two teaspoonfuls green tea. If wanted for supper, do this at breakfast. At dinner time, strain, without stirring, through a tea strainer into a pitcher. Let it stand till tea time and pour into decanters, leaving the sediment in the bottom of the pitcher. Fill the goblets with ice, put two teaspoonfuls granulated sugar in each, and pour the tea over the ice and sugar. A squeeze of lemon will make this delicious and healthful, as it will correct the astringent tendency.

SOUTHERN SWEETENED TEA

makes 1 gal.   prep: 5 min.   steep: 10 min.
pictured on page 79

6   cups water
4   family-size tea bags
1   to 1¾ cups sugar

1. Bring 6 cups water to a boil in a saucepan; add tea bags. Boil 1 minute; remove from heat. Cover and steep 10 minutes. Remove tea bags, squeezing gently.
2. Add sugar, stirring until dissolved. Pour into a 1-gallon pitcher, and add enough water to fill pitcher. Serve over ice.

Pot Likker

There's a wide range of opinion around the region on the best way to cook Pot Likker. Executive Editor Scott Jones, an expert on the subject, starts his Pot Likker soup by sautéing carrots, onions, and garlic before deglazing with a little white wine. He then adds red pepper flakes, a smoked ham hock or two, chicken broth, and greens. At this point, the stage is set—time and gentle simmering work their magic. When the greens are tender, he strains the broth through a fine-mesh strainer and chills it overnight. He pulls the meat off the hocks, stirring half into the greens and reserving the other half for the consommé. The next day, he skims off the fat before reheating. When everything's ready to go, he places a hearty pinch of shredded pork in the bottom of a bowl, then ladles on the pot likker. Crumble in a little leftover jalapeno-pepper Jack cornbread and, as Scott's mema used to say, he's in hog heaven.

One thing that Southerners do seem to agree on is that the most important equipment needed to simmer the perfect pot of Pot Likker is a Dutch oven. You likely have one if you purchased a set of cookware or received one as a wedding present. But most Dutch ovens can be purchased individually. Just be sure to choose one with a good heavy bottom for even heat distribution.

Hands down, the *Southern Living* staff agrees that one of our favorite recipes for this soothing soup is on page 884. We even have an express version you can try if you don't have all day to simmer the soup. But, one thing is for certain, be sure to prepare it with the Cornbread Croutons that accompany the soup for an unbelievable treat.

{ *Southernism* }

There's nothing quite so cozy as a pot of soup or stew bubbling away on the stove. Of all the wonderful soups prepared in the region, there's perhaps none quite as Southern as Pot Likker Soup made from such ingredients as smoked ham hocks and fresh collard greens that spend the entire day simmering in a Dutch oven. The soup actually comes from the delicious broth of the greens as it cooks. Collard greens, indeed a Southern staple, grow in poor soil and are actually found in spots in the region where little else thrives. The soup is said to have originated in the South among slaves who used the leftover juice from the greens from the plantation house. Little did these owners know that they were throwing out the most nutritious—and delicious—part of their pot of greens.

Greens have always been a part of my life. From an early age, my family's Sunday and holiday gatherings always included a mess of greens—be it collards, mustards, turnips, or any combination of the three.

Today, the curative and culinary powers of this rich ham-scented broth are legendary in my house. And once the first frost hits, few things make me happier than a big soup bowl full of my famous pot likker consommé. (Call it my Southern update on the refined French soup).

Scott Jones
Executive Editor

ingredients
THAT SOUTHERNERS PERFECTED

Bacon

Everything's better with bacon. That's always been the Southern train of thought. Wrap it around appetizers or a steak, chop it up and use it to season stove-cooked veggies, sprinkle crisp pieces over salads, slap slices on sandwiches, lay strips over game meat as it cooks to keep the lean meat moist, or use the drippings to bake cornbread. Bacon has been a staple in the South for centuries, because it was easily smoked and cured for long storage and hogs were plentiful. From maple-cured to hickory-smoked, the savory flavor of bacon is one that can't be matched. Despite the health revolution, bacon hasn't lost its place in Southern cuisine. It's still a breakfast staple and a popular item on upscale menus. Leaner versions with less salt help Southerners satisfy the craving to bring home the bacon without guilt.

BROWN SUGAR BACON

makes 10 servings   prep: 5 min.   cook: 38 min.
stand: 2 min.

10 slices thick-cut bacon (14 ounces)
½ cup firmly packed dark brown sugar

1. Preheat oven to 350°. Arrange bacon in a single layer on a wire cooling rack in an aluminum foil-lined jelly-roll or broiler pan. Coat bacon with brown sugar.
2. Bake at 350° for 38 to 40 minutes or until done. Let stand 2 to 3 minutes or until sugar is set.

{ *Southernism* }

"Streak of lean" or bacon was traditionally used to flavor vegetable dishes, especially turnip greens, green beans, cabbage, and cornbread. In fact, it often is used today too.

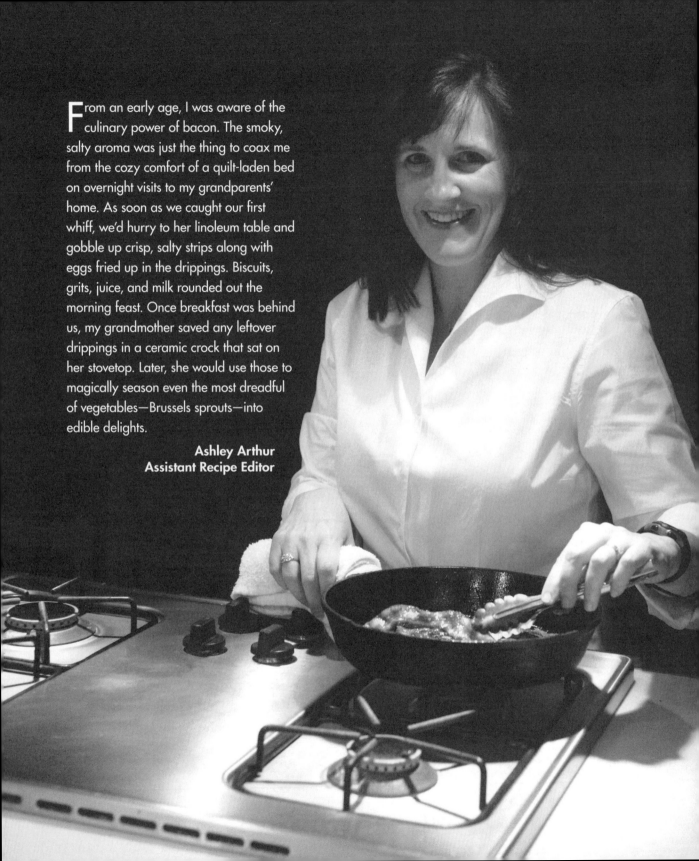

From an early age, I was aware of the culinary power of bacon. The smoky, salty aroma was just the thing to coax me from the cozy comfort of a quilt-laden bed on overnight visits to my grandparents' home. As soon as we caught our first whiff, we'd hurry to her linoleum table and gobble up crisp, salty strips along with eggs fried up in the drippings. Biscuits, grits, juice, and milk rounded out the morning feast. Once breakfast was behind us, my grandmother saved any leftover drippings in a ceramic crock that sat on her stovetop. Later, she would use those to magically season even the most dreadful of vegetables—Brussels sprouts—into edible delights.

Ashley Arthur
Assistant Recipe Editor

If you're a traditional Southern cook who regularly makes biscuits, cornbread, and fried chicken, then you likely always have buttermilk in your refrigerator. Even if you don't cook that way, you should keep some of the creamy, tangy liquid on hand for adding a touch of tenderness or tartness to recipes. Stir it into mayonnaise and add garlic and herbs for a great salad dressing. Use it as the liquid in cornbread, even if you start with a mix. Or try it in sherbets—it balances the sweetness beautifully. But by all means, try it.

Donna Florio
Senior Writer

Buttermilk

We'll let you in on a Southern secret—tart, creamy buttermilk is our Test Kitchen's favorite surprise ingredient. With flecks of butter punctuating its smooth texture, buttermilk as a beverage lacks a certain appeal. But as an ingredient, it's a Southern superstar. It enhances baked goods, adds richness to gravies, and offers a creamy base for salad dressings. Want light, tender biscuits or cake layers? Substitute buttermilk for some of the milk. Need a good soaking liquid for that chicken you're planning to fry or bake? Buttermilk not only boosts the flavor and tenderizes the meat, but it also helps the breading cling to the chicken.

A Not-So-Buttery Product

Though buttermilk seems richer and creamier than regular milk, it actually contains the same fat content as the whole, low-fat, and nonfat milks from which it is made. Originally, it was the liquid that remained after churning butter. Today's commercial buttermilk is made by adding lactic acid to pasteurized, homogenized milk, causing it to thicken and sour. (The process is similar to the one used to make sour cream and yogurt.) Some producers add a few flecks of butter for color and richness. The acid makes buttermilk a prized ingredient in baked goods—it tenderizes them and lends depth of flavor. It also makes this milk a long-lasting staple that will keep in the refrigerator for up to a week past its sell-by date.

BUTTERMILK DROP BISCUITS

makes 15 biscuits   prep: 20 min.   bake: 12 min.

Use a ¼ cup ice-cream scoop or lightly greased ¼ cup dry measuring cup to drop evenly sized biscuits.

3½ cups self-rising flour
2¼ tsp. baking powder
2¼ tsp. sugar
¼　cup shortening
¼　cup butter, chilled and cut into pieces
1½ cups buttermilk*
1　Tbsp. butter, melted

1. Preheat oven to 500°. Combine first 3 ingredients in a large bowl until well blended. Cut in shortening and butter with a pastry blender or a fork until crumbly. Add buttermilk, stirring just until dry ingredients are moistened.
2. Drop dough by ¼ cupfuls onto an ungreased baking sheet. Brush lightly with melted butter.
3. Bake at 500° for 12 to 15 minutes or until golden.

* Nonfat buttermilk may be substituted.

Note: We used White Lily Self-Rising Flour.

Pecans

Perhaps the most iconic ingredient on the Southern dessert table is the pecan. While they're good for eating, pecans are most prized for their contribution to a variety of cakes, pies, and cookies as well as to many meat and vegetable dishes.

A member of the hickory family, the pecan tree is the only major nut tree native to the U.S. During precolonial times, pecan trees were typically found in central North America and the river valleys of Mexico. It wasn't until after the Civil War that they began to flourish across the Southern states. Today, Georgia is the country's top producer of pecans, and Albany, Georgia—home to more than 600,000 pecan trees—is the official pecan capital of the world.

With its smooth, oval, tan and brown shell, each pecan contains two deeply crinkled lobes of golden brown nutmeat. Its sweet and delicate, yet rich and buttery flavor lends itself to an array of Southern dishes, including pralines, sweet potato casserole, and the ever-popular pecan pie.

Early American settlers preferred pecans not only for their great taste, but also because they were easier to shell than other nut species. Believe it or not, there are more than 1,000 varieties of pecans, and many are named for Native American tribes, including Cheyenne, Mohawk, Sioux, Choctaw, and Shawnee.

SWEET-AND-SPICY PECANS

makes 1 cup prep: 5 min. soak: 10 min. bake: 10 min.

These delicious treats add great flavor to Chef Franklin Bigg's famous Baby Blue Salad.

¼ cup sugar
1 cup warm water
1 cup pecan halves
2 Tbsp. sugar
1 Tbsp. chili powder
⅛ tsp. ground red pepper

1. Preheat oven to 350°. Stir together ¼ cup sugar and warm water until sugar dissolves. Add pecans; soak 10 minutes. Drain; discard liquid. Combine 2 tablespoons sugar, chili powder, and red pepper. Add pecans; toss to coat. Place pecans in a single layer on a lightly greased baking sheet. Bake at 350° for 10 minutes or until golden brown, stirring once.

{ *Southernism* }

Whether it's pronounced pih-KAHN pie, pih-KAN pie, or even PEE-kan pie may still be up for debate, but the verdict is in on the palatability. It's 100% delicious and 100% Southern. Of the many varieties of nut pies that appear on Southern tables, the pecan pie is probably the most popular.

I must confess: I was never a fan of pecans until adulthood. Perhaps my disgruntled attitude stemmed from a childhood chore of having to pick bagfuls of them from my yard, where two very large pecan trees resided. Unfortunately, I tried a raw nut and was instantly turned off. I vowed to never go near another pecan again. No cookie, brownie, or piece of fudge could make me change my mind. But the boycott quickly ended the day I tasted a toasted one. It was the Baby Blue Salad at Franklin's Gourmet restaurant in Birmingham, Alabama, that changed my taste buds forever—fresh greens, sweet strawberries, chunky blue cheese, and, of course, toasted pecans. I soon realized after all these years that it wasn't the pecans' fault. They just needed a little love in the oven, making them irresistibly fragrant and crisp.

Shannon Sliter Satterwhite
Food Editor

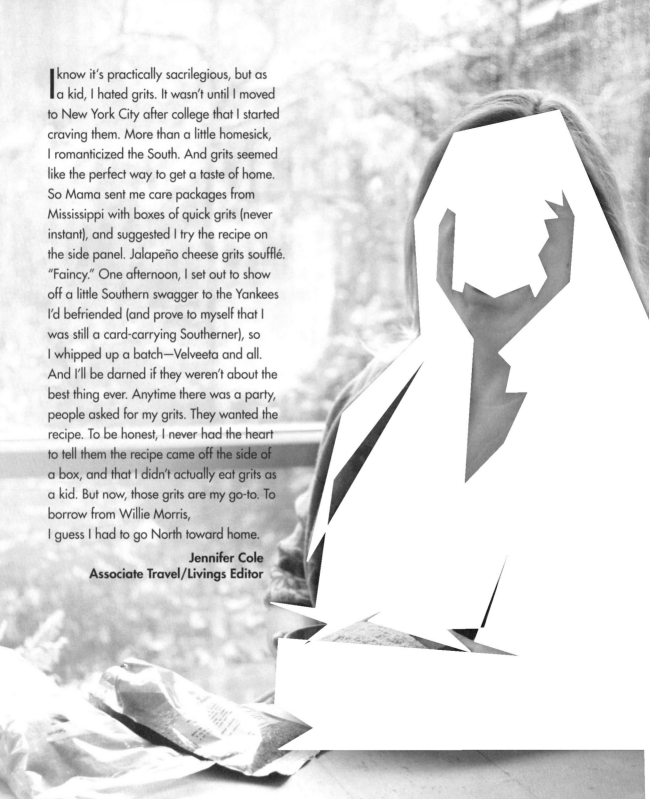

I know it's practically sacrilegious, but as a kid, I hated grits. It wasn't until I moved to New York City after college that I started craving them. More than a little homesick, I romanticized the South. And grits seemed like the perfect way to get a taste of home. So Mama sent me care packages from Mississippi with boxes of quick grits (never instant), and suggested I try the recipe on the side panel. Jalapeño cheese grits soufflé. "Faincy." One afternoon, I set out to show off a little Southern swagger to the Yankees I'd befriended (and prove to myself that I was still a card-carrying Southerner), so I whipped up a batch—Velveeta and all. And I'll be darned if they weren't about the best thing ever. Anytime there was a party, people asked for my grits. They wanted the recipe. To be honest, I never had the heart to tell them the recipe came off the side of a box, and that I didn't actually eat grits as a kid. But now, those grits are my go-to. To borrow from Willie Morris, I guess I had to go North toward home.

Jennifer Cole
Associate Travel/Livings Editor

Grits

Through the years grits have been the workhorse of the Southern table. They've been around the South for a long time. Grits can be traced back to 1607 when the colonists first landed in Jamestown, Virginia, and were offered a boiled corned dish by the Native Americans. The Low Country, in particular, has been serving shrimp and grits for ages.

Confusion abounds over what grits actually are. Commercially produced grits are made from ground, degerminated, dried white or yellow corn kernels that have been soaked in a solution of water and lye. The only grits for purists are produced by the old-fashioned method of stone grinding with a water-turned stone. These grits retain a more natural texture and rich flavor. Stone-ground grits are sometimes labeled as "speckled heart" because the remaining germ—or heart of the kernel—looks like a tiny black fleck.

At their most basic appearance, grits are cooked quickly in water and seasoned with salt and pepper. At their best, grits are luxuriously rich when cooked slowly in broth or whipping cream.

HOT TOMATO GRITS

makes 6 servings   prep: 10 min.   cook 28 min.

Grits go beyond breakfast these days. Let them replace rice or pasta.

2 bacon slices, chopped
2 (14½-oz.) cans chicken broth
½ tsp. salt
1 cup uncooked quick-cooking grits
2 large tomatoes, peeled and chopped
2 Tbsp. canned chopped green chiles
1 cup (4 oz.) shredded Cheddar cheese
Garnishes: chopped fresh parsley,
**   shredded Cheddar cheese (optional)**

1. Cook bacon in a heavy saucepan over medium-high heat 8 to 10 minutes or until crisp. Remove bacon, reserving drippings in pan. Drain bacon on paper towels.
2. Gradually add chicken broth and salt to hot drippings in pan; bring to a boil. Stir in grits, tomatoes, and green chiles; return to a boil, stirring often. Reduce heat, and simmer, stirring often, 15 to 20 minutes.
3. Stir in Cheddar cheese until melted. Top with chopped bacon. Garnish, if desired. Serve immediately.

[*Southernism*]

The ultimate comfort food, grits act as a foundation for flavorful items such as gravy, hash, or over-easy eggs. However, in the past decade or so, grits have experienced a renaissance, appearing on upscale dinner menus with the likes of shrimp, beef, and a host of herbs and cheeses.

Summer Berries

Strawberries

You know spring is here when you take that first bite into a plump, juicy strawberry. Enjoy the freshest berries while you can—the season peaks in May.

select: Choose brightly colored berries that still have their green caps attached. If fully ripe, they should have a potent strawberry fragrance.

store: Store (in a single layer if possible) in a moisture-proof container in the refrigerator for three or four days.

prepare: Do not wash or remove the hulls until you're ready to use the strawberries. Use an egg slicer to cut strawberries into uniform slices to use in a recipe for garnishing.

Blackberries

Purplish-black in color, the plump blackberry has a sweet, tangy flavor when ripe. Blackberries are sometimes called bramble berries because they grow wild on bramble vines along rural roadsides from May through August.

select: When buying fresh blackberries, select plump, well-colored berries with hulls detached. If hulls are still intact, the berries were picked too early.

store: Like most berries, fresh blackberries are best stored in the refrigerator. They will keep up to a week. Choose a wide, shallow bowl to store berries, and cover with plastic wrap to keep them from drying out.

prepare: Just before you use your blackberries, rinse them under cold water. For the best flavor, allow the berries to come to room temperature.

Blueberries

A blueberry is a tiny, round, deep purplish-blueberry with a tiny star-shaped cap. The delicate orbs have a refreshing, frosty appearance and a mild, sweet flavor.

select: Pick plump, juicy berries with a bloom that have no trace of mold or discoloration. Look for firm, uniformly sized berries with deep color and no hulls or stems. Hulls and stems are a sure sign berries were picked too soon.

store: If eating blueberries within 24 hours of picking, store them at room temperature; otherwise, keep them refrigerated in a moisture-proof container up to three days.

prepare: Wash berries just before using them.

No one planted the blackberries I picked as a kid growing up in the South Carolina Lowcountry. They grew wild along the edges of woods, on the banks of ditches, and at abandoned homesites. Just as the weather would begin to warm, their white flowers would open. Sweet-scented and five-petaled, they courted buzzing bees and spawned daydreams of lazy days ahead. Those flowers were my harbinger of freedom: no school, no shoes, and no schedules.

About when the hydrangeas bloomed, the first blackberries were ready for picking. Turning from red to black, the berries ripened. My patience was tested by Mother Nature as she converted water and sun into sugar. "Not until they're plump," Grandmamma would urge. "Not until they're plump." Each day, I'd ride my purple Schwinn to check, Cool Whip container in hand. At first, none would make it home. I'd gorge on what was ready, feeding the rest to Chester, our cocker spaniel. As the days grew hotter, my bowl overflowed. Two or three trips ensured a proper cobbler. I'd watch through the oven window as the crisp and buttery dessert bubbled. That jammy fragrance that laced the air during cooking is still a favorite scent. My brothers and I would beg for the cobbler hot out of the oven, but Mama would always make us wait. "Let it set. It will taste even better," she'd promise. "It will taste even better."

Rebecca Bull Reed
Associate Garden Editor

APPETIZERS & BEVERAGES

"They say that you may always know the grave of a Virginian as, from the quantity of julep he has drunk, mint invariably springs up where he has been buried." ——Frederick Marryat

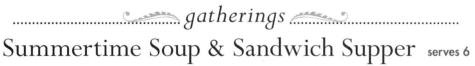

Summertime Soup & Sandwich Supper serves 6

Blue Cheese Thumbprints
Garden Salad With Tarragon-Mustard Vinaigrette (page 712)
Red Pepper-and-Pear Soup (page 878)
Magnolia Cream Cheese Brownies (page 307)

BLUE CHEESE THUMBPRINTS

makes about 5 dozen   prep: 15 min.   chill: 2 hr.   bake: 15 min. per batch

Cheese straws are like deviled eggs—every Southern cook wants to make great ones. This tasty snack pairs well with soups or salads, or can go solo with a glass of Champagne or beer.

2 (4-oz.) packages crumbled blue cheese	3 Tbsp. poppy seeds
½ cup butter, softened	¼ tsp. ground red pepper
1⅓ cups all-purpose flour	⅓ cup cherry preserves

1. Preheat oven to 350°. Beat blue cheese and butter at medium speed with an electric mixer until fluffy. Add flour, poppy seeds, and red pepper, beating just until combined. Roll dough into ¾-inch round balls; cover and chill 2 hours.

2. Arrange balls on ungreased baking sheets, and press thumb into each ball of dough, leaving an indentation.

3. Bake at 350° for 15 minutes or until golden. Transfer to wire racks to cool completely. Place about ¼ tsp. preserves in each indentation.

Blue Cheese Crisps: Combine ingredients for dough as directed. Shape dough into 2 (9-inch-long) logs. Wrap each log in plastic wrap, and chill 2 hours. Cut each log into ¼-inch-thick slices, and place on ungreased baking sheets. Bake at 350° for 10 to 12 minutes or until golden brown. Transfer to wire racks to cool completely. Omit cherry preserves. Store crisps in an airtight container up to 1 week.

CHEDDAR CHEESE STRAWS

makes about 10 dozen   prep: 30 min.   bake: 12 min per batch

Savory and rich with just a bit of a peppery bite, cheese straws are great party snacks. They're especially easy to make and travel well. If you don't have a heavy-duty stand mixer, you can use a handheld mixer. Just divide the ingredients in half, and work with two batches.

1½ cups butter, softened
1   (1-lb.) block sharp Cheddar cheese, shredded
1½ tsp. salt

1   to 2 tsp. ground red pepper
½   tsp. paprika
4   cups all-purpose flour

1. Preheat oven to 350°. Beat first 5 ingredients at medium speed with a heavy-duty stand mixer until blended. Gradually add flour, beating just until combined.

2. Use a cookie press with a star-shaped disk to shape mixture into long ribbons, following manufacturer's instructions, on parchment paper-lined baking sheets. Cut ribbons into 2-inch pieces.

3. Bake at 350° for 12 minutes or until lightly browned. Remove to wire racks to cool.

Cheese Wafers: Combine ingredients as directed; chill dough 2 hours. Shape dough into 4 (8-inch-long) logs; wrap each in plastic wrap, and chill 8 hours. Cut each log into ¼-inch-thick slices; place on parchment paper-lined baking sheets. Bake at 350° for 13 to 15 minutes or until lightly browned. Remove to wire racks to cool. Store in an airtight container 1 week.

[make ahead]

Our Best Cheese Straw Tips

• Shred your own cheese; it's stickier and blends better than preshredded cheese.

• Refrigerate unbaked dough between batches to keep wafers from spreading too thin when baked.

• Store baked cheese straws in an airtight container for 1 week. Store unbaked dough in the fridge for 1 week or in the freezer for 1 month.

• Bake stored cheese straws in the oven at 350° for 3 to 4 minutes to make them crispy again.

• Bake on parchment paper to yield the best results; one sheet can be used multiple times.

PECAN-CORNMEAL SHORTBREADS

makes 2½ dozen   prep: 17 min.   chill: 1 hr.   bake: 25 min.

Serve these nutty, mildly spiced bites alongside cheese and fresh fruit for a light appetizer.

¾   cup butter, softened
1½   cups all-purpose flour
½   cup cornmeal
2   Tbsp. sugar
½   tsp. salt

¼   tsp. ground red pepper
1   large egg, lightly beaten
½   cup chopped pecans
30   pecan halves

1. Beat butter at medium speed with an electric mixer until creamy. Add flour and next 5 ingredients, beating at low speed until blended. Stir in chopped pecans. Wrap dough with plastic wrap; chill 1 hour.

2. Preheat oven to 350°. Shape dough into 2 (9-inch-long) logs. Wrap in plastic wrap, and chill 1 hour. Cut dough into ½-inch-thick slices. Place rounds on lightly greased baking sheets; top each round with a pecan half.

3. Bake at 350° for 25 minutes or until lightly browned; remove to wire racks, and let cool completely.

HONEY-NUT SNACK MIX

makes 9½ cups   prep: 6 min.   cook: 5 min.   bake: 30 min.

4   cups crisp oat cereal squares
1½   cups uncooked regular oats
1½   cups coarsely chopped pecans
1½   tsp. ground cinnamon
¼   tsp. salt

½   cup butter
½   cup firmly packed light brown sugar
½   cup honey
1   (6-oz.) package sweetened dried cranberries (about 1½ cups)

1. Preheat oven to 325°. Combine first 5 ingredients in a large bowl; set aside.

2. Combine butter, brown sugar, and honey in a small saucepan over low heat, stirring until butter melts and sugar dissolves. Pour butter mixture over cereal mixture, stirring to coat. Spread in a single layer on a lightly greased aluminum foil-lined 15- x 10-inch jelly-roll pan.

3. Bake at 325° for 20 minutes, stirring once. Stir in cranberries, and bake 10 more minutes. Spread snack mix immediately on wax paper; cool. Store in an airtight container.

[make ahead]

SUGARED NUTS

makes 5 cups   prep: 5 min.   cook: 22 min.

These nuts are good sprinkled over a salad, garnishing a dessert, or as a stand-alone snack.

1   large egg white
4   cups pecan halves, walnut halves, or
    whole almonds

1   cup sugar

1. Preheat oven to 350°. Whisk egg white in a large bowl until foamy; stir in pecans, coating well. Stir in sugar, coating well. Spread pecan mixture in a single layer on a lightly greased 15- x 10-inch aluminum foil-lined jelly-roll pan.
2. Bake at 350° for 10 minutes. Stir gently with a wooden spoon; bake 10 to 12 more minutes or until sugar is light golden brown. Remove from oven, and cool completely on pan. Store in an airtight container up to 5 days.

CARIBBEAN CASHEWS

makes: 2 cups   prep: 5 min.   bake: 22 min.

Orange zest adds a fresh citrus note to these simple spiced nuts.

1½ tsp. butter
2   cups lightly salted whole cashews

2   tsp. grated orange zest
2   tsp. Caribbean jerk seasoning

1. Preheat oven to 350°. Heat butter in an 8-inch cake pan in oven for 2 to 3 minutes or until melted; stir in nuts and remaining ingredients, tossing to coat.
2. Bake at 350° for 20 minutes, stirring occasionally.
3. Arrange cashews in a single layer on wax paper, and let cool. Store in an airtight container.

Note: We tested with McCormick Caribbean Jerk Seasoning.

[make ahead]

[make ahead]

BAKED PITA CHIPS

makes about 5 dozen prep: 10 min. bake: 12 min.

1 (8-oz.) package 4-inch pita rounds
Olive oil cooking spray

1½ tsp. coarsely ground kosher salt

1. Preheat oven to 350°. Separate each pita into 2 rounds. Cut each round into 4 wedges. Arrange in a single layer on ungreased baking sheets. Coat with olive oil cooking spray, and sprinkle evenly with 1½ tsp. kosher salt.
2. Bake at 350° for 12 to 15 minutes or until golden and crisp.

Note: We tested with Toufayan Mini Pitettes.

PECAN-SWISS PENNIES

makes about 6½ dozen prep: 15 min. chill: 10 hr. bake: 10 min. per batch

To easily cut the logs into slices, use a long piece of dental floss. Place the floss under the dough ¼ inch from end of roll. Cross ends of floss over top of roll; slowly pull ends to cut through dough.

¾ cup butter, softened
2 cups all-purpose flour
1 (8-oz.) block Swiss cheese, grated
½ cup pecans, finely chopped

3 Tbsp. honey-Dijon mustard
¾ tsp. salt
Kosher salt (optional)

1. Beat butter at medium speed with a heavy-duty stand mixer until fluffy. Add flour and next 4 ingredients, beating just until combined. Cover and chill 2 hours.
2. Shape dough into 2 (8-inch-long) logs; wrap each log in plastic wrap, and chill 8 hours.
3. Preheat oven to 350°. Cut each log into ¼-inch-thick slices, and place on parchment paper-lined baking sheets. Sprinkle evenly with kosher salt, if desired.
4. Bake at 350° for 10 to 12 minutes or until lightly browned. Transfer to wire racks to cool completely.

CITRUS PARTY OLIVES

makes 6 servings   prep: 20 min.   chill: 8 hr.   stand: 30 min.

4   garlic cloves, chopped
½   cup olive oil
1   Tbsp. orange zest
2   tsp. lemon zest
⅓   cup fresh orange juice
3   Tbsp. fresh lemon juice

1½   tsp. chopped fresh rosemary
1   tsp. coarse salt
½   tsp. freshly ground pepper
4   (6-oz.) cans ripe pitted black olives, drained
Garnish: fresh rosemary sprigs

1. Stir together first 10 ingredients in a large bowl.
2. Cover and chill at least 8 hours. Let stand 30 minutes at room temperature before serving. Garnish, if desired. Serve with a slotted spoon.

[make ahead]

MARINATED MOZZARELLA

makes about 4 cups   prep: 20 min.   chill: 8 hr.   **pictured on page 73**

For a big crowd, double all the ingredients in this recipe except the black pepper and garlic powder. For those strong flavors, use one-and-a-half times the amount called for.

3   (8-oz.) blocks mozzarella cheese
1   (8.5-oz.) jar sun-dried tomatoes, drained and halved
½   cup olive oil
3   Tbsp. finely chopped fresh flat-leaf parsley
1   tsp. garlic powder
1   tsp. onion powder

½   tsp. dried oregano
½   tsp. dried Italian seasoning
¼   tsp. salt
¼   tsp. freshly ground pepper
Garnish: flat-leaf parsley sprigs or fresh rosemary stems

1. Cut blocks of cheese into 1-inch cubes. Arrange cheese cubes and tomato halves in an 8-inch square baking dish.
2. Whisk together ½ cup olive oil, chopped parsley, and next 6 ingredients; pour evenly over cheese cubes. Cover and chill at least 8 hours or up to 24 hours. Transfer mixture to a serving plate. Garnish with fresh flat-leaf parsley sprigs, or spear tomato halves and cheese cubes with short rosemary stems, if desired. Drizzle with marinade, if desired.

[make ahead]

CORN-AND-FIELD PEA DIP

makes 8 cups   prep: 10 min.   chill: 8 hr.

2   (15.8-oz.) cans field peas with snaps, rinsed
and drained

2   (11-oz.) cans white shoepeg corn, drained

2   (10-oz.) cans diced tomato and green chiles

1   (14½-oz.) can diced tomatoes

5   green onions, diced

1   (16-oz.) bottle zesty Italian dressing

2   garlic cloves, minced

1   Tbsp. finely chopped fresh parsley

1. Stir together all ingredients. Cover and chill 8 hours. Drain before serving. Serve dip with corn chips.

CUCUMBER DIP

makes 3 cups   prep: 20 min.   chill: 9 hr.

This no-cook dip doubles as a delicious sandwich spread.

5   small cucumbers, unpeeled

½   cup rice vinegar

1   tsp. kosher salt

1   tsp. garlic salt, divided

2   (8-oz.) packages cream cheese, softened

½   cup mayonnaise

2   tsp. chopped fresh chives

Garnish: fresh chives

Pita chips

1. Grate cucumbers into a medium bowl. Toss with rice vinegar, salt, and ½ tsp. garlic salt. Cover and chill 8 hours. Drain cucumber mixture well, pressing between paper towels.
2. Beat cream cheese, mayonnaise, and remaining ½ tsp. garlic salt at medium speed with an electric mixer 1 to 2 minutes or until smooth. Stir in cucumber mixture and chives. Cover and chill at least 1 hour. Garnish, if desired. Serve with pita chips.

Most people think about garden projects only when they see a strawberry jar. These versatile pots, though, can fill a host of uses. We wowed guests by turning one into a serving piece for crisp veggies with a great dip. Try it this weekend.

Fresh Buttermilk-Herb Dip

makes about 1½ cups   prep: 10 min.   chill: 30 min.

Whisk together 1¼ cups mayonnaise, 6 Tbsp. buttermilk, 2 Tbsp. fresh lemon juice, 1 Tbsp. chopped fresh chives, 1 Tbsp. chopped fresh parsley, ¼ tsp. salt, and freshly ground pepper to taste in a medium bowl. Cover and chill 30 minutes. Place a 2-gal. zip-top plastic bag in the center of an 18-inch-tall glazed strawberry jar; fill to top with ice, and seal. Nestle a ramekin on ice in top opening of jar. Fill ramekin with dip. Arrange assorted vegetable sticks, such as carrots, celery, and bell peppers, in side pockets of jar, and serve.

SPICY WHITE CHEESE DIP

makes about 8 cups   prep: 8 min.   cook: 3 hr.

To prevent the bottom of the cheese dip from burning, we recommend cooking on the LOW setting and holding on the WARM setting when serving.

1 small onion, diced	½ tsp. ground cumin
2 garlic cloves, minced	½ tsp. coarsely ground black pepper
2 (10-oz.) cans diced tomatoes and green chiles	2 lb. white American deli cheese slices, torn
¾ cup milk	Assorted tortilla and corn chips

1. Place first 7 ingredients in a 6-qt. oval slow cooker. Cover and cook on LOW 3 hours, stirring gently every hour. Stir before serving. Serve with assorted tortilla and corn chips.

To Make Ahead and Freeze: Spoon into quart-size freezer containers, and freeze up to 1 month. Thaw overnight in the refrigerator. Microwave at HIGH, stirring every 60 seconds until thoroughly heated.

[*freeze it*]

Restaurant Tyler

We know there's no place quite like the South—and this Mississippi-born chef admits it took seeing the world to appreciate plump local blackberries, pecans from just down the road, the sweet potatoes of tiny Vardaman ("Sweet Potato Capital of the World"), and the comfort of a Southern accent. Chef Ty Thames's whole background whirls together on the plate: a touch of Vermont here (culinary school), a notable dollop of Italy there (a Michelin-rated inn near Parma), and sophistication throughout (The Ritz-Carlton and other top Washington, D.C., spots). The fusion of elements comes together best in the sweet potato gnocchi, lush with homegrown sweet potatoes and braised wild boar sausage, topped off with truffle sauce, wild mushrooms, and Lazy Magnolia Southern Pecan beer. The flavors of the South and elsewhere blend quietly, without fanfare. Ty returns to his roots with catfish and crawfish; he overnights fish from Honolulu for the same menu. It's all about bringing fine dining to Starkville. "I was looking for a place where I could highlight Mississippi the way I wanted to," he says. "And I've found it here."

100 East Main Street
Starkville, MS 39759
www.restauranttyler.com or (662) 324-1014

LAYERED SPICY BLACK BEAN DIP

makes 8 servings   prep: 10 min.

Arrange thinly sliced jalapeño peppers on one-half of this no-fuss appetizer for guests that can stand the heat.

1   (8-oz.) package cream cheese, softened
1   (16-oz.) jar spicy black bean dip
½   (8-oz.) package shredded Mexican
    cheese blend

Toppings: sliced green onions, chopped tomatoes,
    sliced black olives
Assorted tortilla and corn chips

1. Layer cream cheese, dip, and cheese in a 1-qt. serving dish. Add toppings; serve with chips.

Note: We tested with Desert Pepper Trading Company Spicy Black Bean Dip.

WARM TURNIP GREEN DIP

makes 4 cups   prep: 15 min.   cook: 15 min.   broil: 4 min.

Transfer the dip to a 1- or 2-quart slow cooker set on WARM so guests can enjoy this creamy dip throughout your party. To make it spicier, serve your favorite brand of hot sauce on the side.

5   bacon slices, chopped
½   sweet onion, chopped
2   garlic cloves, chopped
¼   cup dry white wine
1   (16-oz.) package frozen chopped turnip
    greens, thawed

12 oz. cream cheese, cut into pieces
1   (8-oz.) container sour cream
½   tsp. dried crushed red pepper
¼   tsp. salt
¾   cup freshly grated Parmesan, divided

1. Preheat oven to broil. Cook bacon in a Dutch oven over medium-high heat 5 to 6 minutes or until crisp; remove bacon, and drain on paper towels, reserving 1 Tbsp. bacon drippings in Dutch oven.

2. Sauté onion and garlic in hot drippings 3 to 4 minutes. Add wine, and cook 1 to 2 minutes, stirring to loosen particles from bottom of Dutch oven. Stir in turnip greens, next 4 ingredients, and ½ cup Parmesan cheese. Cook, stirring often, 6 to 8 minutes or until cream cheese is melted and mixture is thoroughly heated. Transfer to a lightly greased 1½-qt. baking dish. Sprinkle evenly with remaining ¼ cup Parmesan cheese.

3. Broil 6 inches from heat 4 to 5 minutes or until cheese is lightly browned. Sprinkle evenly with bacon.

BAKED SPINACH-AND-ARTICHOKE DIP

makes 11 servings   prep: 10 min.   cook: 6 min.   bake: 15 min.

For easy entertaining, this dish can be assembled up to a day ahead. Store in an airtight container in the refrigerator, and then bake just before serving.

southern lights

2   (6-oz.) packages fresh baby spinach
1   Tbsp. butter
1   (8-oz.) package ⅓-less-fat cream cheese, softened
1   garlic clove, chopped
1   (14-oz.) can artichoke hearts, drained and chopped

½   cup light sour cream
½   cup shredded part-skim mozzarella cheese, divided
Fresh pita wedges or baked pita chips

1. Preheat oven to 350°. Microwave spinach in a large microwave-safe bowl at HIGH 3 minutes or until wilted. Drain spinach well, pressing between paper towels. Chop spinach.

2. Melt butter in a nonstick skillet over medium-high heat. Add cream cheese and garlic; cook 3 to 4 minutes, stirring constantly, until cream cheese melts. Fold in spinach, artichokes, sour cream, and ¼ cup mozzarella cheese; stir until cheese melts.

3. Transfer mixture to a 1-qt. shallow baking dish. Sprinkle with remaining ¼ cup mozzarella cheese.

4. Bake at 350° for 15 minutes or until hot and bubbly. Serve immediately with fresh pita wedges or baked pita chips.

Note: Thoroughly wash bagged spinach before using.

Per ¼ cup dip (not including pita wedges or baked pita chips): Calories 113; Fat: 7g (sat 4.7g, mono 0.5g, poly 0.1g); Protein 5.5g; Carb 8.5g; Fiber 2.4g; Chol 24mg; Iron 1mg; Sodium 340mg; Calc 71mg

DRESSED-UP SALSA

makes 2 cups   prep: 10 min.

test kitchen favorite

1   (24-oz.) jar chunky medium salsa
2½   Tbsp. fresh lime juice
3   Tbsp. chopped fresh cilantro

2   garlic cloves, minced
1   jalapeño pepper, seeded and chopped

1. Pulse all ingredients in a food processor or blender 3 to 4 times or until thoroughly combined.

Note: We tested with Pace Chunky Medium Salsa.

WATERMELON SALSA

makes about 3 cups   prep: 20 min.   **pictured on page 74**

This recipe doubles as a healthful and refreshing topping for grilled, baked, or broiled fish, shrimp, or chicken.

1½ tsp. lime zest
¼ cup fresh lime juice (about 3 limes)
1 Tbsp. sugar
¾ tsp. ground black pepper
3 cups seeded and finely chopped watermelon
1 cucumber, peeled, seeded, and diced

2 jalapeño peppers, seeded and minced
¼ cup chopped red onion
¼ cup chopped fresh basil
½ tsp. salt
Tortilla chips

1. Whisk together first 4 ingredients in a large bowl. Add watermelon and next 4 ingredients, tossing gently to coat. Chill until ready to serve. Stir in salt just before serving. Serve with tortilla chips.

CORN-AND-AVOCADO SALSA

makes 4½ cups   prep: 25 min.   cook: 6 min.   chill: 30 min.

Serve with tortilla or corn chips. To add flavor without more heat, increase the fajita seasoning by ½ tablespoon.

4 cups fresh or frozen corn kernels
1 Tbsp. fajita seasoning
½ tsp. pepper
2 Tbsp. vegetable oil
1 red bell pepper, chopped
½ jalapeño pepper, seeded and chopped

½ cup chopped green onions
¼ cup fresh chopped cilantro
¼ cup fresh lime juice
2 Tbsp. orange juice
¾ tsp. salt
2 ripe avocados, diced

1. Sauté first 3 ingredients in hot oil in a large skillet over medium-high heat 6 to 8 minutes or until corn is slightly golden. Remove from heat; let cool.
2. Stir together corn mixture, bell pepper, and next 6 ingredients. Cover and chill at least 30 minutes. Stir in avocado just before serving.

Note: We tested with Badia Fajita Seasoning.

[test kitchen favorite]

[test kitchen favorite]

MARINATED BLACK-EYED PEAS

makes 5½ cups   prep: 15 min.   chill: 2 hr.

The original version of this recipe didn't contain corn or a jalapeño pepper. Pickled black-eyed peas, as it's referred to, is still commonly served alongside fresh summer vegetables.

[test kitchen favorite]

2 (16-oz.) cans black-eyed peas, rinsed and drained
⅔ cup olive oil
⅓ cup white wine vinegar
½ red onion, diced
1 garlic clove, minced

½ tsp. salt
½ tsp. pepper
1 (16-oz.) can whole kernel corn, drained
1 jalapeño pepper, minced
½ red bell pepper, chopped
Tortilla chips

1. Stir together all ingredients; cover and chill mixture at least 2 hours. Serve with tortilla chips.

taking sides

Does Caviar Come From Alabama, Tennessee, or Texas?

If you're thinking about those little bitty red, black, and gold fish eggs put on fancy crackers at ritzy parties, then you better skip this page. This fight is over a more substantial appetizer made of black-eyed peas.

Though it's not really caviar, it is just as pretty with bright red, green, and yellow peppers and red onions making the marinated black-eyed pea mixture a burst of color. Though it features the lowly black-eyed pea, often known as a "poor man's food," this spiced salsa, dip, or salad served with corn chips or crackers knows no social boundaries in the South.

It is basically the same whether it's called Texas, Cowboy, Alabama or LA (Lower Alabama) Caviar. But who really came up with it first? According to an article by *Dallas Morning News* writer, Joyce Saenze Harris, this Southern "caviar" was introduced in the 1950s by the food service director at Neiman Marcus in Dallas. Sounds like Texas might have an edge, folks. Alabama, Tennessee— what do you say to that?

TENNESSEE CAVIAR

makes 4 cups   prep: 10 min.   chill: 2 hr.

Instead of fish eggs, this Southern version of caviar features down-home veggies. Make it a day ahead for the best flavor.

1   (15.8-oz.) can black-eyed peas
1   (11-oz.) can yellow corn with red and green
    bell peppers
3   plum tomatoes, seeded and chopped
1   small sweet onion, chopped

1   cup hot picante sauce
¼   cup chopped fresh cilantro
2   garlic cloves, minced
2   Tbsp. fresh lime juice
Tortilla chips

[make ahead]

1. Rinse and drain peas and corn.
2. Stir together peas, corn, tomatoes, and next 5 ingredients in a serving bowl; cover and chill at least 2 hours. Serve with tortilla chips.

GUACAMOLE GRANADA

makes 8 to 10 servings   prep: 20 min.

4   large ripe avocados, halved
1   Tbsp. fresh lime juice
½   tsp. garlic salt
6   green onions, chopped
1   (4-oz.) can roasted diced green chiles, rinsed
    and drained (optional)

1   large pomegranate, divided
Garnish: pomegranate seeds
Tortilla chips

1. Scoop avocado pulp into a medium bowl, and mash into small chunks. Stir in lime juice, garlic salt, onions, and, if desired, green chiles. Set mixture aside.
2. Cut off crown of pomegranate. Using a small paring knife, score the outer layer of skin into sections.
3. Working with pomegranate fully submerged in a large bowl of water, break apart sections along scored lines. Roll out seeds with your fingers. (The seeds will sink to the bottom, while the white membrane will float to the top.) Remove and discard membrane with a slotted spoon. Pour seed mixture through a fine wire-mesh strainer. Reserve 3 Tbsp. seeds for garnish, if desired. Stir remaining seeds into avocado mixture. Sprinkle evenly with reserved seeds to garnish, if desired. Serve with tortilla chips.

TASTE OF THE SOUTH

Pimiento Cheese, barbecue, catfish, and grits— all examples of true Southern culinary icons. Yet despite their humble beginnings, the Dixie-born gems have become popular across the country. Enter pimiento cheese. A cookbook containing one true recipe, let alone the many regional variations such as adding paprika or jalapeño peppers, is almost impossible to find; favorite recipes survive by way of oral tradition. Therefore, the popularity of this unique spread remains largely confined to states below the Mason-Dixon Line, where it assumes its place as a Southern delicacy. "I've seldom met a nonSoutherner who knew what it was," says novelist and North Carolina native Reynolds Price. But once the unfamiliar have a chance to sample this concoction, Reynolds adds, "They take to it on contact."

So what is pimiento cheese? To the uninitiated, it's little more than grated cheese, chopped pimiento peppers, and a little mayonnaise. However, to those fans who rank pimiento cheese right next to cold fried chicken and deviled eggs as essentials at any proper country picnic, it's much more. To devotees, pimiento cheese becomes a must-have—elevating an ordinary grilled cheese to something heavenly and dramatically raising the bar on cheeseburgers and omelets.

Admirers agree that sharp Cheddar cheese is the mixture's backbone. High-quality mayonnaise, such as Hellmann's or Duke's, is also a given. But here's where the opinions begin to fork off. On the issue of texture, Southern cookbook author James Villas shares common questions such as should the cheese be grated or mashed? If grated, coarse or fine? If mashed, is the fork or the modern food processor the best tool?

In our search for the definitive blend, we asked Senior Food Editor Mary Allen Perry for her secret recipe. She agreed, but admitted, "My recipe was originally that of my great grandmother Kersh, who lived until she was 98 years old—slim, trim, and fearless of fat content."

Mary Allen drew upon childhood memories to record this fabulous formula. So, whether you use pimiento cheese to fill celery sticks or to spread on crackers or a slice of your favorite bread, you should feel confident with this terrific version and its variations.

PIMIENTO CHEESE

makes 4 cups   prep: 15 min.

Mary Allen's tip: Use a box grater to achieve both coarse-grated and finely shredded cheese.

1½ cups mayonnaise

1   (4-oz.) jar diced pimiento, drained

1   tsp. Worcestershire sauce

1   tsp. finely grated onion

¼   tsp. ground red pepper

1   (8-oz.) block extra-sharp Cheddar cheese, finely shredded

1   (8-oz.) block sharp Cheddar cheese, shredded

1. Stir together first 5 ingredients in a large bowl; stir in cheeses. Store in refrigerator up to 1 week.

Jalapeño-Pimiento Cheese: Add 2 seeded and minced jalapeño peppers.

Cream Cheese-and-Olive Pimiento Cheese: Reduce mayonnaise to ¾ cup. Stir together first 5 ingredients, 1 (8-oz.) package softened cream cheese, and 1 (5¾-oz.) jar drained sliced salad olives. Proceed with recipe as directed.

Pecan-Pimiento Cheese: Stir in ¾ cup toasted chopped pecans.

Baked Pimiento Cheese: Preheat oven to 350°. Stir together first 5 ingredients in a large bowl; stir in cheeses. Spoon mixture into a lightly greased 2-qt. or 11- x 7-inch baking dish. Bake at 350° for 20 minutes or until dip is golden and bubbly.

BACON-PIMIENTO CHEESE

makes 1 qt.   prep: 20 min.   cook: 5 min.

8   bacon slices

2   (8-oz.) blocks smoked Cheddar cheese, shredded

2   (8-oz.) blocks Cheddar cheese, shredded

1½ cups mayonnaise

1   (4-oz.) jar diced pimiento, drained

1   Tbsp. sugar

¼   tsp. salt

¼   tsp. pepper

1. Cook bacon in a skillet until crisp; remove bacon, drain on paper towels, and crumble.

2. Stir together bacon, cheeses, and remaining ingredients in a bowl. Serve immediately.

THREE-CHEESE PIMIENTO CHEESE

makes 3½ cups   prep: 15 min.

Because it travels well, pimiento cheese is wonderful for tailgating, potluck suppers, and picnics.

1 (8-oz.) package cream cheese	¼ tsp. ground chipotle chile pepper
1 (4-oz.) jar diced pimiento, drained	¼ tsp. salt
1 (5-oz.) jar pimiento cheese spread	Freshly ground pepper to taste
½ cup mayonnaise	3 cups (12 oz.) shredded sharp Cheddar
¼ tsp. garlic powder	cheese

1. Microwave cream cheese in a microwave-safe bowl at HIGH 1 to 1½ minutes or until melted and smooth, stirring at 30-second intervals. Stir in diced pimiento and next 6 ingredients.
2. Stir in Cheddar cheese. Serve immediately, or cover and chill up to 4 hours. Store in the refrigerator in an airtight container up to 4 days.

Note: We tested with Kraft Pimiento Spread.

SMOKY "PIMIENTO" CHEESE SANDWICHES

makes 7 servings   prep: 10 min.

Cut into smaller sandwiches for easy pickup.

1 (3-oz.) package cream cheese, softened	2 cups (8 oz.) shredded smoked Gouda cheese
½ cup mayonnaise	½ (8.5-oz.) jar sun-dried tomatoes in oil, drained
1 tsp. paprika	and chopped
¼ tsp. salt	14 bread slices (sourdough and dark wheat)
2 cups (8 oz.) shredded smoked Cheddar cheese	

1. Stir together cream cheese and next 3 ingredients in a large bowl until blended. Stir in shredded cheeses and sun-dried tomatoes until combined.
2. Spread cheese mixture on half of bread slices (about ⅓ cup on each); top with remaining bread slices.

MACARONI-AND-PIMIENTO CHEESE BITES

makes 5½ dozen prep: 25 min. cook: 7 min.
chill: 8 hr. fry: 4 min. per batch **pictured on page 78**

Wow family and friends with this easy, delicious appetizer—they make perfect party poppers. You can also bake the mixture in a casserole dish and use the breadcrumb coating as a crispy topping.

1	(8-oz.) package elbow macaroni	1	(8-oz.) block sharp Cheddar cheese, shredded
3	Tbsp. butter	1	(4-oz.) jar diced pimiento, drained
¼	cup all-purpose flour	¾	cup fine, dry breadcrumbs
2	cups milk	¾	cup freshly grated Parmesan cheese
1	tsp. salt	2	large eggs, lightly beaten
¼	tsp. ground red pepper	½	cup milk
⅛	tsp. garlic powder		Vegetable oil

1. Prepare pasta according to package directions.

2. Meanwhile, melt butter in a large skillet over medium heat. Gradually whisk in flour until smooth; cook, whisking constantly, 1 minute. Gradually whisk in 2 cups milk and next 3 ingredients; cook, whisking constantly, 3 to 5 minutes or until thickened. Stir in Cheddar cheese and pimiento until melted and smooth. Remove from heat, and stir in pasta.

3. Line a 13- x 9-inch pan with plastic wrap, allowing several inches to extend over edges of pan. Pour mixture into prepared pan. Cool slightly; cover and chill 8 hours. Remove macaroni mixture from pan, and cut into 1-inch squares.

4. Stir together breadcrumbs and Parmesan cheese in a shallow dish or pie plate. Whisk together eggs and ½ cup milk in another shallow dish or pie plate; dip macaroni bites in egg mixture, and dredge in breadcrumb mixture.

5. Pour oil to a depth of 1 inch in a large skillet; heat to 350°. Fry bites, in batches, 2 minutes on each side or until golden.

Golden Baked Macaroni and Pimiento Cheese: Preheat oven to 350°. Prepare recipe as directed through Step 2. Pour macaroni mixture into a lightly greased 13- x 9-inch baking dish; do not chill. Omit eggs and ½ cup milk. Stir together breadcrumbs and Parmesan cheese; sprinkle over mixture. Omit oil. Bake at 350° for 15 to 20 minutes or until golden and bubbly.

~inspirations for your taste~

Experience the unique taste of lemon figs—sweet with a little twang. They anchor one of the best appetizers we've eaten. Serve them with a cool drink.

Lemon Figs With Pecans and Feta

makes 6 servings   prep: 10 min.   broil: 2 min.

Peel stem end back from 6 lemon figs. Slice each fig into quarters, cutting to, but not through, bottom, leaving figs intact. Place them on a foil-lined baking sheet; drizzle evenly with 1 Tbsp. olive oil. Broil 6 inches from heat 2 to 3 minutes or until edges begin to brown. Sprinkle evenly with 2 Tbsp. chopped toasted pecans and 2 Tbsp. crumbled feta cheese. Add salt and freshly ground pepper to taste.

Note: Fresh figs are available during July and August. If you can't find lemon figs, look for Mission or Brown Turkey figs at your local grocery store or farmers market.

BEAN-AND-ROSEMARY BITES

makes 12 servings   prep: 10 min.   bake: 5 min.   cook: 5 min.

1 (8-oz.) French bread loaf
1 garlic clove, minced
½ tsp. fresh rosemary, minced
1 tsp. extra virgin olive oil
1 (16-oz.) can cannellini or great Northern beans,
   rinsed and drained

¼ tsp. lemon zest
¼ tsp. salt
⅛ tsp. dried crushed red pepper

1. Preheat oven to 375°. Cut bread into 12 (½-inch) slices. Place on baking sheet.

2. Bake at 375° for 5 to 7 minutes or until toasted.

3. Sauté garlic and rosemary in hot oil in a nonstick skillet over medium-high heat 2 minutes. Stir in beans and next 3 ingredients. Cook until thoroughly heated, stirring frequently and mashing beans partially to desired consistency.

4. Spread about 2½ Tbsp. bean mixture over each bread slice.

Per serving: Calories 83; Fat 0.8g (sat 0.1g, mono 0.3g, poly 0.1g); Protein 3.8g; Carb 15.6g; Fiber 1.6g; Iron 1.3mg; Sodium 16mg; Calc 50mg

[southern lights]

SAUTÉED SMOKED GOUDA CHEESE GRITS
WITH BLACK BEAN SALSA

makes 6 servings   prep: 20 min.   cook: 20 min.   chill: 3 hr.

casual gatherings

2	cups milk	
¾	cup quick-cooking grits, uncooked	
¾	cup chopped smoked Gouda cheese	
½	tsp. salt	
2	Tbsp. butter	
2	cups all-purpose flour	
2	Tbsp. salt	
2	tsp. black pepper	

1	cup beer
	Butter, Olive oil
	Black Bean Salsa
½	cup sour cream
1	medium tomato, seeded and diced
2	Tbsp. chopped fresh parsley
2	Tbsp. chopped green onions
12	fresh chives, cut into 1-inch pieces

1. Stir together milk and ¾ cup water in a 1½-qt. saucepan over medium-high heat; bring to a boil. Stir in grits, cheese, and ½ tsp. salt; cook, stirring constantly, 9 minutes or until thickened. Stir in 2 Tbsp. butter. Pour into a greased 11- x 7-inch baking dish. Cover; chill 3 hours or until firm.
2. Combine flour, 2 Tbsp. salt, and pepper in a shallow dish. Pour beer into a small bowl. Cut grits into 2-inch squares. Dip squares into beer; dredge in flour mixture; repeat twice.
3. Melt 1 Tbsp. butter in skillet over medium heat; stir in 1 Tbsp. oil. Cook grits squares, in batches, in hot mixture 5 minutes on each side or until golden, adding butter and oil as needed.
4. Arrange 3 grits squares in center of 6 individual serving plates. Spoon Black Bean Salsa over grits squares. Top with sour cream. Sprinkle with tomato, parsley, green onions, and chives.

Black Bean Salsa:

makes about 4½ cups   prep: 15 min.   cook: 3 min.

2	Tbsp. butter
1	medium onion, diced
2	garlic cloves, minced
2	(15-oz.) cans black beans, drained
⅔	cup picante sauce
2	medium tomatoes, seeded and diced

2	tsp. chili powder
1	tsp. salt
½	tsp. pepper
¼	tsp. ground cumin
3	Tbsp. chopped fresh parsley
3	Tbsp. chopped green onions

1. Melt butter in a saucepan over medium heat; add onion and garlic; sauté until tender. Stir in beans and next 6 ingredients; cook, stirring occasionally, 3 minutes. Stir in parsley and green onions.

ASSEMBLE-YOUR-OWN BARBECUE STACKS

makes 6 to 8 servings prep: 15 min. **pictured on page 77**

Inspired by a recipe from Teresa Todd of Dickson, Tennessee, we came up with this version. Expand toppings to include pickled okra or sliced jalapeño peppers.

2 lb. warm shredded barbecued chicken
   without sauce*

⅓ cup red barbecue sauce

Cornbread Griddle Cakes

Red barbecue sauce to taste

30 plum tomato slices (about 5 tomatoes)

White Barbecue Sauce Slaw

1 cup White Barbecue Sauce

Toppings: red onion slices, cracked pepper

1. Toss chicken in ⅓ cup red barbecue sauce.

2. Spoon barbecued chicken mixture evenly onto Cornbread Griddle Cakes. Drizzle each with red barbecue sauce to taste. Top each with 1 tomato slice. Spoon White Barbecue Sauce Slaw onto each tomato slice. Serve with White Barbecue Sauce and desired toppings.

* 2 lb. shredded barbecued beef or pork without sauce may be substituted.

Note: We tested with Stubb's Original Bar-B-Q Sauce.

Cornbread Griddle Cakes:

makes 30 (2-inch) cakes prep: 5 min. cook: 4 min. per batch

Don't get confused and buy a cornbread mix; it won't work in this recipe. If you're short on time, buy cornbread muffins from the deli. Split them in half from top to bottom and then use each half in place of one cake.

2 cups yellow self-rising cornmeal

1 cup all-purpose flour

1½ cups milk

⅓ cup butter, melted

2 large eggs, lightly beaten

1 Tbsp. sugar

¼ tsp. ground red pepper

1. Stir together all ingredients just until moistened. Pour 2 Tbsp. batter for each cake onto a hot, greased griddle or large nonstick skillet. Cook cakes 2 to 3 minutes or until tops are covered with bubbles and edges look dry and cooked; turn and cook other side (about 2 minutes).

Note: To make ahead, place cooked griddle cakes on baking sheets. Cover and chill up to 24 hours. To reheat, bake at 300° for 8 to 10 minutes. Serve immediately.

White Barbecue Sauce

makes 1½ cups   prep: 15 min.   chill: 1 hr.

Reserve 1 cup sauce for guests to drizzle over their assembled stacks. Use the remaining ½ cup to make White Barbecue Sauce Slaw.

1¼ cups mayonnaise	1 Tbsp. lemon juice
¼ cup horseradish	1 tsp. coarsely ground pepper
3 Tbsp. cider vinegar	¼ tsp. salt

1. Stir together all ingredients in a small bowl. Cover and chill at least 1 hour until ready to serve.

White Barbecue Sauce Slaw:

makes 6 to 8 servings   prep: 10 min.   chill: 1 hr.

1 (16-oz.) package shredded coleslaw mix with carrots	¼ cup chopped red onion
½ cup White Barbecue Sauce	½ tsp. salt

1. Combine coleslaw mix, ½ cup White Barbecue Sauce, red onion, and salt. Toss gently; cover and chill 1 hour.

GEORGIA-STYLE BOILED PEANUTS

makes 18 cups   prep: 5 min.   cook: 18 hr.

Southern boiled peanuts are easily made in your slow cooker.

2 lb. raw peanuts, in shell	¾ to 1 cup salt

1. Combine peanuts, salt and 12 cups water in a 5-or 6-qt. slow cooker. Cover and cook on HIGH 18 hours or until peanuts are soft. Drain peanuts before serving or storing. Store in zip-top plastic bags in refrigerator up to 2 weeks.

[make ahead]

PORK TENDERLOIN ON CORNMEAL BISCUITS

makes 24 servings   prep: 5 min.   broil: 5 min.   bake: 20 min.
stand: 15 min.   **pictured on page 75**

Let guests make their own—serve sliced pork on a platter with chutney and biscuits on the side.

4 (¾- to 1-lb.) pork tenderloins	Cornmeal Biscuits, halved
2 tsp. salt	Texas Cranberry Chutney
2 tsp. ground black pepper	Garnish: sliced green onions
2 Tbsp. olive oil	

1. Preheat oven to broil. Place pork in a lightly greased 15- x 10-inch jelly-roll pan; sprinkle with salt and pepper. Rub evenly with oil.

2. Broil 5½ inches from heat 5 minutes; reduce oven temperature to 450°, and bake 20 minutes or until a meat thermometer inserted into thickest portion registers 160°. Let stand 15 minutes before slicing. Cut into ¼-inch-thick slices (about 18 slices each).

3. Place pork slices evenly over Cornmeal Biscuit halves, and top evenly with Texas Cranberry Chutney. Garnish, if desired.

Cornmeal Biscuits

makes about 3 dozen   prep: 20 min.   bake: 13 min.

The butter needs to be cut into the flour evenly and finely, almost until you can't see any bits of butter. Large pieces of butter will melt and leak out of the biscuits.

4 cups self-rising flour	2 cups buttermilk
½ cup yellow cornmeal*	¼ cup milk
1 cup butter, cut up	

1. Preheat oven to 425°. Combine flour and cornmeal in a large bowl; cut in butter with a pastry blender or fork until crumbly. Add buttermilk, stirring just until dry ingredients are moistened.

2. Turn dough out onto a lightly floured surface; knead 2 to 3 times. Pat or roll dough to a ½-inch thickness, and cut with a 2-inch round cutter. Place on lightly greased baking sheets. Reroll remaining dough, and proceed as directed. Brush tops with milk.

3. Bake at 425° for 13 to 15 minutes or until golden.

* White cornmeal may be substituted.

Note: We tested with Pillsbury Self Rising Flour.

Texas Cranberry Chutney

makes 3 cups   prep: 5 min.   cook: 10 min.

2   (8-oz.) cans crushed pineapple
1   (16-oz.) can whole-berry cranberry sauce
¼   cup firmly packed brown sugar
½   tsp. ground ginger

¼   tsp. salt
1   to 2 jalapeño peppers, seeded and minced
3   green onions, chopped

1. Drain pineapple well; pat dry with paper towels.

2. Stir together pineapple and next 4 ingredients in a small saucepan over medium heat, and bring to a boil. Reduce heat to low, and simmer, stirring often, 5 minutes or until thickened. Remove from heat, and stir in jalapeño and green onions. Cover and chill until ready to serve.

inspirations for your taste

Try this tasty quesadilla with your favorite Cabernet Sauvignon for a fresh twist on wine and cheese. Our resident wine expert, Scott Jones, suggests Columbia Crest Cabernet Sauvignon.

Pecan-Havarti Quesadilla With Pear Preserves

makes 2 servings   prep: 5 min.   cook: 4 min.

Sprinkle 1 side of an 8-inch flour tortilla with ⅓ cup shredded Havarti cheese; top with 2 Tbsp. chopped, toasted pecans. Fold tortilla over filling. Coat a nonstick skillet with vegetable cooking spray, and cook quesadilla over medium-high heat for 2 minutes on each side or until cheese melts. Remove from heat, slice into wedges, and serve with pear preserves. Pair it with a glass of Cabernet Sauvignon.

Note: This recipe can be easily doubled or tripled to serve more.

TOMATO CHUTNEY CHEESECAKE

makes 18 to 20 appetizer servings   prep: 15 min.   chill: 8 hr.

This savory no-cook appetizer will bring rave reviews. And the best part— it's make ahead.

make ahead

4   (8-oz.) packages cream cheese, softened
    and divided
2   cups shredded Cheddar cheese
½   tsp. ground red pepper
4   or 5 green onions, finely chopped
⅔   cup red tomato chutney

1   to 2 Tbsp. milk
    Assorted raw vegetables
    Cornbread crackers
    Garnishes: chopped fresh chives or green onions,
        cherry tomato halves (optional)

1. Beat 3 packages cream cheese, Cheddar cheese, and red pepper at medium speed with an electric mixer until blended and smooth. Stir in green onions.

2. Spread half of cream cheese mixture into an 8-inch round cake pan lined with plastic wrap; spread top with tomato chutney, leaving a ½-inch border of cream cheese around outside edge. Spread remaining cream cheese mixture over chutney and cream cheese border. Cover and chill at least 8 hours or up to 24 hours.

3. Invert cheesecake onto a serving platter; remove plastic wrap. Stir together 1 Tbsp. milk and remaining 1 package cream cheese, stirring until spreading consistency and adding additional milk, if needed. Frost top and sides of cheesecake. Serve with vegetables and crackers. Garnish, if desired.

BEER-BATTER FRIED PICKLES

makes 8 to 10 servings   prep: 15 min.   fry: 3 min. per batch

We used Wickles brand sweet-hot sliced pickles in this recipe. These Alabama-produced pickles are sold nationwide, but you can also order them from www.wickles.com.

2   (16-oz.) jars dill pickle sandwich slices, drained
1   large egg
1   (12-oz.) can beer
1   Tbsp. baking powder

1   tsp. seasoned salt
1½ cups all-purpose flour
    Vegetable oil
    Spicy Ranch Dipping Sauce

1. Pat pickles dry with paper towels.

2. Whisk together egg and next 3 ingredients in a large bowl; add 1½ cups flour, and whisk until smooth.

3. Pour oil to a depth of 1½ inches into a large heavy skillet or Dutch oven; heat over medium-high heat to 375°.

4. Dip pickle slices into batter, allowing excess batter to drip off. Fry pickles, in batches, 3 to 4 minutes or until golden. Drain and pat dry on paper towels; serve immediately with Spicy Ranch Dipping Sauce.

Spicy Ranch Dipping Sauce

makes about 1 cup   prep: 10 min.

¾ cup buttermilk

½ cup mayonnaise

2 Tbsp. minced green onions

1 garlic clove, minced

1 tsp. hot sauce

½ tsp. seasoned salt

Garnish: seasoned salt (optional)

1. Whisk together all ingredients. Garnish, if desired. Store in an airtight container in refrigerator up to 2 weeks.

Perfect Pickles Step-by-Step

We sampled a variety of breadings and pickle flavors and shapes in our kitchens, but lengthwise-sliced dills with a light beer batter proved our favorite combination.

1. Pat the pickles dry before dipping in the batter so it will adhere evenly.

2. Keep the oil at a steady temperature by adding the pickles gradually.

GRITS-STUFFED GREENS

makes 6 appetizer servings   prep: 20 min.   cook: 25 min.   stand: 5 min.

Egg rolls have gone Southern! Assemble these up to a day ahead, and refrigerate. Just steam them for an extra 5 minutes when ready to serve.

southern lights

6   large fresh collard green leaves
1   cup 2% reduced-fat milk
1   cup low-sodium fat-free chicken broth
½   cup uncooked quick-cooking grits
¾   cup (3 oz.) shredded 2% sharp
      Cheddar cheese

1   Tbsp. butter
½   tsp. garlic salt
¼   tsp. pepper
Pepper sauce

1. Rinse collard greens. Trim and discard thick stems from bottom of collard green leaves (about 2 inches); place greens in a steamer basket over boiling water. Cover and steam 10 to 12 minutes or until greens are tender. Cool completely.

2. Bring milk and broth to a boil in a medium saucepan over medium-high heat. Gradually stir in grits. Cover, reduce heat to low, and simmer, stirring occasionally, 5 minutes or until grits are thickened. Remove from heat; stir in cheese and next 3 ingredients, stirring until cheese is melted. Let stand 5 minutes.

3. Place 1 collard leaf on a flat surface, and spread out sides. Spoon ⅓ cup grits toward bottom center of leaf. Fold 1 side of leaf over filling. Fold opposite side of leaf over filling. Beginning at 1 short side, roll up leaf tightly, jelly-roll fashion. Repeat with remaining collard leaves and grits.

4. Place bundles in a single layer in a steamer basket; steam, covered, 10 to 15 minutes or until thoroughly heated. Serve with pepper sauce.

Note: We tested with Louisiana Hot Peppers in Vinegar for pepper sauce.

Per serving: Calories 133; Fat 5.9g (sat 3.7g, mono 0.8g, poly 0.2g); Protein 6.3g; Carb 12.5g; Fiber 0.3g; Chol 18mg; Iron 0.6mg; Sodium 312mg; Calc 156mg

CHICKEN FINGERS WITH HONEY-HORSERADISH DIP

makes 8 servings   prep: 25 min.   cook: 18 min.

This recipe won our highest flavor rating. We think little and big kids will love it.

[southern lights]

16   saltine crackers, finely crushed

¼   cup pecans, toasted and ground

½   tsp. salt

½   tsp. pepper

2   tsp. paprika

4   (6-oz.) skinned and boned chicken breast halves

1   egg white

Vegetable cooking spray

Honey-Horseradish Dip

1. Preheat oven to 425°. Stir together first 5 ingredients.

2. Cut each breast half into 4 strips. Whisk egg white until frothy; dip chicken strips into egg white, and dredge in saltine mixture.

3. Place a rack coated with cooking spray in a broiler pan. Coat chicken strips on each side with cooking spray; arrange on pan.

4. Bake at 425° for 18 to 20 minutes or until golden brown. Serve with Honey-Horseradish Dip.

Per serving: Calories 204; Fat 4.4g (sat 0.7g, mono 2g, poly 1.1g); Protein 23g; Carb 17g; Fiber 1.7g; Chol 50mg; Iron 1.3mg; Sodium 429mg; Calc 61mg

Honey-Horseradish Dip

makes 1 cup   prep: 5 min.

½   cup plain nonfat yogurt

¼   cup coarse grained mustard

¼   cup honey

2   Tbsp. prepared horseradish

1. Stir together all ingredients.

CHICKEN POPPERS

makes 8 to 10 appetizer servings   prep: 30 min.   cook: 16 min.   **pictured on page 78**

Tasty Chicken Poppers and Southern Sweetened Tea (page 93) will make perfect traveling companions for your next picnic.

20 vanilla wafers, finely crushed
1½ tsp. seasoned salt
¾   tsp. ground red pepper
½   tsp. pepper
1⅓ cups all-purpose flour, divided
¼   cup milk

1   large egg
6   skinned and boned chicken breast halves,
    cut into 1½-inch pieces
1   cup canola or vegetable oil
Ranch dressing
Garnish: sliced green onions

1. Stir together first 4 ingredients and 1 cup flour. Stir together milk and egg.

2. Dredge chicken pieces in remaining ⅓ cup flour; dip in egg mixture; dredge in wafer mixture.

3. Pour oil in a large skillet; heat to 375°. Fry chicken pieces, in 4 batches, 2 to 3 minutes on each side or until done. Drain chicken on paper towels, and serve with Ranch dressing. Garnish, if desired.

CHICKEN-FRIED STEAK FINGERS WITH CREOLE MUSTARD SAUCE

makes 8 servings   prep: 17 min.   cook: 30 min.   chill: 4 hr.

2   tsp. Cajun seasoning
Basic Marinade
1   (2-lb.) flank steak
2   large eggs
2   Tbsp. hot sauce
1   cup all-purpose flour

½   cup fine, dry breadcrumbs
1   Tbsp. Cajun seasoning
¼   tsp. ground red pepper
Vegetable oil
Creole Mustard Sauce

1. Stir Cajun seasoning into Basic Marinade until blended.

2. Place flank steak in a zip-top plastic freezer bag; add marinade mixture. Seal and chill 3 hours, turning occasionally.

3. Remove steak from marinade, discarding marinade. Cut steak in half lengthwise; cut halves diagonally across the grain into ½-inch-thick strips.

4. Whisk together eggs and hot sauce. Combine flour and next 3 ingredients. Dip steak strips into egg mixture; dredge in flour mixture. Cover and chill 1 hour.

5. Pour oil to a depth of 4 inches in a Dutch oven; heat to 375°. Fry steak strips, in batches, 10 minutes or until golden. Serve with Creole Mustard Sauce.

Basic Marinade

makes 1¼ cups prep: 5 min.

1	small onion, diced	2	Tbsp. Worcestershire sauce
3	garlic cloves, minced	2	tsp. sugar
½	cup olive oil	1	tsp. salt
¼	cup lemon juice*	1	tsp. pepper

1. Stir together all ingredients.

* White wine vinegar may be substituted for lemon juice.

Southwestern Marinade: Substitute ¼ cup lime juice for lemon juice. Add 2 Tbsp. chopped fresh cilantro and 1 tsp. ground cumin.

Asian Marinade: Substitute ½ cup peanut oil for olive oil, ¼ cup rice wine vinegar for lemon juice, and 2 Tbsp. soy sauce for Worcestershire sauce. Add 1 tsp. grated fresh ginger.

Creole Mustard Sauce

makes about 1¼ cups prep: 5 min.

1	(8-oz.) container sour cream	1	tsp. Cajun seasoning
¼	cup Creole mustard	⅛	tsp. ground red pepper
1	Tbsp. cider vinegar		

1. Stir together all ingredients; chill.

SMOKY-HOT BUFFALO CHICKEN PIZZAS

makes 6 appetizer servings   prep: 10 min.   bake: 8 min.

Don't be intimidated by these homemade pizzas. The convenience of deli chicken and store-bought crusts makes this recipe a cinch. Hot sauce, blue cheese dressing, and Colby-Monterey Jack add enticing flavor.

{ southern lights }

2   cups diced deli-roasted chicken breast

3   Tbsp. chipotle hot sauce

1   tsp. butter, melted

8   Tbsp. low-fat blue cheese dressing, divided

2   (7-inch) prebaked pizza crusts

½   cup (2 oz.) shredded 2% Colby-Monterey Jack cheese blend

2   green onions, thinly sliced (optional)

1. Preheat oven to 450°. Stir together chicken, hot sauce, and butter in a microwave-safe bowl. Microwave at HIGH 45 seconds or until heated.

2. Spread 3 Tbsp. blue cheese dressing evenly over each pizza crust, leaving a 1-inch border around edges. Top evenly with chicken mixture. Sprinkle with cheese.

3. Bake directly on oven rack at 450° for 8 to 10 minutes or until crusts are golden and cheese is melted. Drizzle remaining 2 Tbsp. dressing evenly over pizzas; sprinkle with green onions, if desired. Cut each pizza into 3 wedges.

Note: We tested with Mama Mary's Gourmet Pizza Crusts. For a softer crust, bake pizza on a pizza pan or baking sheet.

Per serving: Calories 278; Fat 8.9g (sat 2.7g, mono 0.7g, poly 0.4g); Protein 20.9g; Carb 27.3g; Fiber 2.6g; Chol 48mg; Iron 0.8mg; Sodium 395mg; Calc 80mg

Marinated Mozzarella,
page 47

Watermelon Salsa,
page 53

Pork Tenderloin on Cornmeal
Biscuits, page 64

Tex-Mex Egg Rolls With
Creamy Cilantro
Dipping Sauce,
page 85

Assemble-Your-Own
Barbecue Stacks,
page 62

Macaroni-and-Pimiento
Cheese Bites, page 59

Chicken Poppers,
page 70

1990 Hot Chocolate
Deluxe, page 100

Pink Lemonade Cocktail,
page 95

Southern Sweetened Tea,
page 27

Frozen Cranberry
Margaritos, page 97

Cream Cheese-Banana-
Nut-Bread, page 118

Grannie's Cracklin' Cornbread,
page 126

Easy Three-Seed Pan Rolls,
page 142

Easy Homemade Biscuits,
page 107

Hot Cross Buns,
page 134

Peach-Oat Muffins,
page 112

Pimiento Cheese Rolls,
page 130

TEX-MEX EGG ROLLS WITH CREAMY CILANTRO DIPPING SAUCE

makes 28 egg rolls   prep: 40 min.   fry: 2 min. per batch   **pictured on page 76**

1 (5-oz.) package yellow rice
1 tsp. salt
1 lb. ground hot pork sausage
1 (15-oz.) can black beans, rinsed and drained
1 (14.5-oz.) can Mexican-style diced tomatoes, undrained
2 cups (8 oz.) shredded Monterey Jack cheese

6 green onions, finely chopped
1 (1.25-oz.) package taco seasoning
28 egg roll wrappers
1 large egg, lightly beaten
4 cups peanut oil
Creamy Cilantro Dipping Sauce
Garnish: fresh cilantro sprigs

1. Cook rice according to package directions, using 1 tsp. salt. Cool completely.

2. Cook sausage in a skillet over medium heat, stirring until it crumbles and is no longer pink; drain well. Let cool.

3. Stir together rice, sausage, black beans, and next 4 ingredients in a large bowl. Spoon about ⅓ cup rice mixture in center of each egg roll wrapper.

4. Fold top corner of wrapper over filling, tucking tip of corner under filling; fold left and right corners over filling. Lightly brush remaining corner with egg; tightly roll filled end toward the remaining corner, and gently press to seal.

5. Pour oil into a heavy Dutch oven; heat to 375°. Fry egg rolls, in batches, 2 to 3 minutes or until golden. Drain on wire rack over paper towels. Serve with Creamy Cilantro Dipping Sauce. Garnish, if desired.

Creamy Cilantro Dipping Sauce

makes 3 cups   prep 10 min.

For a beautiful presentation, cut top from 1 large red bell pepper, reserving top; remove and discard seeds and membrane, leaving pepper intact. Arrange bell pepper on a serving plate, and fill with sauce.

2 (10-oz.) cans Mexican-style diced tomatoes
1 (8-oz.) package cream cheese, softened
2 cups loosely packed fresh cilantro leaves (about 1 bunch)

1 cup sour cream
3 garlic cloves, minced

1. Process all ingredients in a food processor until smooth.

Appetizers & Beverages   **85**

TASTE OF THE SOUTH

Crab Cakes, it seems, are on restaurant menus everywhere from the East Coast to Kansas. Simpler eating establishments pay homage to the delicate crab flavor by serving their cakes plain or with a basic sauce. Upscale chefs serve them with a variety of accompaniments including pineapple salsa, tomato concassé, grainy mustard sauce, or fennel coleslaw.

However, fancy additions don't sit too well with crab lovers in Maryland and Virginia. They like their cakes the old-fashioned way—with plenty of crab and not too much else. Depending on whom you ask, "not too much else" may mean a modest amount of binder and the merest hint of seasoning, while others see onion, bell pepper, and plenty of Old Bay seasoning as crucial. Then there is the matter of form. Fat and fluffy cakes generally have minimal additions; dense and sturdy ones usually appeal to the heavy seasoning crowd.

FAIDLEY'S CRAB CAKES

makes 8 servings   prep: 15 min.   stand: 3 min.   chill: 1 hr.   cook: 6 min. per batch

This favorite recipe came to us from Fraidley's Seafood Market in Baltimore, Maryland.

½   cup mayonnaise

1   large egg, lightly beaten

1   Tbsp. Dijon mustard

1   Tbsp. Worcestershire sauce

½   tsp. hot sauce

1   lb. fresh lump crabmeat, drained

1   cup crushed saltines (about 20 crackers)

1   qt. vegetable oil

Tartar sauce (optional)

1. Stir together first 5 ingredients; fold in crabmeat and saltines. Let stand 3 minutes. Shape mixture into 8 patties. Place on a wax paper-lined baking sheet; cover and chill 1 hour.
2. Fry crab cakes, in batches, in hot oil in a large skillet over medium-high heat 3 to 4 minutes on each side or until golden. Drain on paper towels. Serve with tartar sauce, if desired.

Note: To sauté crab cakes, cook in 3 Tbsp. butter or oil in a large nonstick skillet 3 to 4 minutes on each side or until golden.

CRAB CAKES WITH LEMON RÉMOULADE

makes 4 servings   prep: 20 min.   chill: 1 hr.   cook: 30 min.

3   Tbsp. butter, divided
1   large red bell pepper, finely chopped
½   medium onion, finely chopped
1   cup saltine cracker crumbs (finely crushed)
½   cup mayonnaise
1   large egg, lightly beaten
2   tsp. Old Bay seasoning
2   tsp. Worcestershire sauce

¾   tsp. dry mustard
¼   tsp. hot sauce
1   lb. fresh lump crabmeat, drained and picked
1   Tbsp. vegetable oil
Lemon Rémoulade
Garnishes: mixed baby greens, lemon wedges,
     parsley sprigs (optional)

1. Melt 2 Tbsp. butter in a large nonstick skillet over medium heat; add bell pepper and onion, and sauté 10 minutes or until tender. Remove from heat; stir in cracker crumbs and next 6 ingredients. Gently stir in crabmeat. Shape mixture into 8 patties; cover and chill at least 1 hour or up to 24 hours.

2. Melt ½ Tbsp. butter with ½ Tbsp. oil in a large skillet over medium-high heat. Cook 4 crab cakes 4 to 5 minutes on each side or until golden. Drain on paper towels. Repeat procedure with remaining ½ Tbsp. butter, ½ Tbsp. oil, and crab cakes. Serve with Lemon Rémoulade; garnish, if desired.

Note: Handle the crabmeat as little as possible in order to keep the succulent lumps intact.

Lemon Rémoulade

makes about 2¼ cups   prep: 10 min.   chill: 30 min.

This sauce may also be used as a dip for boiled shrimp or steamed asparagus; add a little milk to make a tangy salad dressing.

2   cups mayonnaise
¼   cup Creole mustard
2   garlic cloves, pressed
2   Tbsp. chopped fresh parsley

1   Tbsp. fresh lemon juice
2   tsp. paprika
¾   tsp. ground red pepper

1. Whisk together all ingredients until blended. Cover and chill 30 minutes or up to 3 days.

EASY EGG ROLLS WITH SWEET-AND-SOUR ORANGE DIPPING SAUCE

makes 15 egg rolls   prep: 30 min.   cook: 15 min.   stand: 30 min.   fry: 2 min. per batch

[make ahead]

1 lb. hot ground pork sausage
1½ Tbsp. grated fresh ginger
2 garlic cloves, pressed
1 (10-oz.) bag shredded coleslaw mix

1 (16-oz.) package egg roll wrappers
Vegetable oil
Sweet-and-Sour Orange Dipping Sauce

1. Brown sausage in a large nonstick skillet over medium-high heat, stirring until it crumbles and is no longer pink. Drain excess grease, and pat dry with paper towels, if necessary. Return sausage to skillet. Stir in ginger and garlic; cook 1 minute. Add coleslaw mix, and cook, stirring occasionally, 3 minutes or until coleslaw mix is tender; let stand 30 minutes to cool.

2. Spoon ¼ cup sausage mixture in center of each egg roll wrapper. Fold top corner of each wrapper over filling; fold left and right corners over filling. Lightly brush remaining corner with water; tightly roll filled end toward remaining corner, and gently press to seal.

3. Pour vegetable oil to a depth of 2 inches into a wok or Dutch oven; heat to 375°. Fry, in batches, 2 to 3 minutes or until golden, turning once; drain on paper towels. Serve with Sweet-and-Sour Orange Dipping Sauce.

Note: Egg rolls can be assembled up to a day ahead. Place them in a single layer on a baking sheet, cover tightly with plastic wrap, and chill. Fry according to recipe instructions. Do not fry them ahead of time or fry and freeze.

Sweet-and-Sour Orange Dipping Sauce

makes 2 cups   prep: 5 min.   cook: 5 min.   stand: 30 min.

1 (18-oz.) jar orange marmalade
½ cup white vinegar

2 Tbsp. sugar
1 Tbsp. soy sauce

1. Bring all ingredients to a boil in a small saucepan over medium heat. Cook 2 to 3 minutes or until marmalade melts. Remove from heat, and let stand 30 minutes. Serve at room temperature. Cover and store in refrigerator up to 1 week.

Family New Year's Eve Celebration serves 16

Mini Roast Beef Sandwiches
*Chicken Fingers With Honey-Horseradish Dip (page 69)   **Warm Turnip Green Dip** (page 51)
Marinated Black-eyed Peas (page 54)   **Cheese and fruit tray**
Dark Chocolate Brownies (page 306)   **Cherry Pistachio Bark** (page 278)

*double recipe

MINI ROAST BEEF SANDWICHES

makes 16 servings   prep: 20 min.

1	(8-oz.) container cream cheese spread	¾	lb. thinly sliced deli roast beef
2	Tbsp. prepared horseradish	½	small red onion, thinly sliced
8	(4-inch) miniature pita rounds, cut in half	1	avocado, peeled and thinly sliced
4	to 6 large green leaf lettuce leaves, torn		

1. Stir together cream cheese and horseradish until well blended.
2. Spread cream cheese mixture evenly inside pita halves (about 2 tsp. each). Stuff pita halves evenly with lettuce, roast beef, onion slices, and avocado slices.

MINI BACON, TOMATO, AND BASIL SANDWICHES

makes 12 appetizer servings   prep: 15 min.

9	slices ready-to-serve bacon, halved	9	slices extra-thin white bread slices
½	cup shredded Parmesan cheese	3	plum tomatoes, sliced
⅓	cup mayonnaise	12	fresh basil leaves
1	garlic clove, minced		

1. Heat bacon according to package directions until crisp.
2. Stir together cheese, mayonnaise, and garlic. Spread mixture onto 1 side of each bread slice. Layer 3 bread slices, mayonnaise sides up, with 3 bacon slices each. Top with 1 bread slice, tomato slices, and basil. Top each with remaining bread slices, mayonnaise sides down. Cut into quarters.

[make ahead]

ROASTED CHICKEN DRUMETTES

makes 8 appetizer servings (24 pieces)   prep: 15 min.   bake: 38 min.

24 chicken drumettes

2 Tbsp. olive oil

2 tsp. sugar

1 tsp. salt

1 tsp. garlic powder

¼ tsp. pepper

⅓ cup Dijon mustard

3 Tbsp. fresh lemon juice

1 tsp. dried oregano

1. Preheat oven to 450°. Rinse chicken with cold water, and pat dry. Stir together oil and next 4 ingredients in a large bowl. Add chicken, tossing to coat. Arrange chicken in a single layer on a wire rack in an aluminum foil-lined jelly-roll pan. Bake at 450° for 30 to 35 minutes.

2. Combine mustard, lemon juice, and oregano. Remove pan from oven; add hot chicken to mustard mixture. Toss to coat. Drain and discard accumulated fat from pan. Place chicken in a single layer on rack in jelly-roll pan. Bake at 450° for 8 to 10 more minutes or until done.

MINI CAJUN BURGERS WITH EASY RÉMOULADE

makes 12 appetizer servings   prep: 20 min.   grill: 10 min.

1¼ lb. ground beef

½ lb. spicy Cajun sausage, finely chopped

2 tsp. Cajun seasoning

1 (14-oz.) package dinner rolls, split

Green leaf lettuce

Easy Rémoulade

1. Preheat grill to 350° to 400° (medium-high) heat. Combine ground beef and sausage in a large bowl. Shape mixture into 12 (2½-inch) patties, and place on a large baking sheet. Sprinkle patties evenly with Cajun seasoning. Cover and chill up to 1 day, if desired.

2. Grill, covered with grill lid, over 350° to 400° (medium-high) heat 5 minutes on each side or until no longer pink in center. Serve on split rolls with green leaf lettuce and Easy Rémoulade.

Easy Rémoulade

makes 1 cup   prep: 5 min.   chill: 30 min.

¾ cup light mayonnaise

2 Tbsp. Creole mustard

2 Tbsp. chopped fresh parsley

1. Combine all ingredients, stirring well. Cover and chill 30 minutes or up to 3 days.

One large pumpkin yields about 1 cup of seeds, but don't throw them out. Seasonand toast them instead.

Toasted Pumpkin Seeds

makes 1 cup   prep: 10 min.   bake: 20 min.

Preheat oven to 350°. Rinse 1 cup fresh pumpkin seeds; pat dry with paper towels. Toss seeds with 1 Tbsp. olive oil, 1 Tbsp. dried ground thyme, and 1½ tsp. kosher salt; place in a single layer on a lightly greased baking sheet. Bake at 350° for 20 to 25 minutes or until toasted. Serve on top of a salad, or just enjoy them as a yummy snack.

HOT ROAST BEEF PARTY SANDWICHES

makes 12 to 16 servings   prep: 20 min.   cook: 5 min.   bake: 20 min.

This is an updated version of a recipe that used ham, cheese, and mustard. Eyes lit up at our tasting table when these came out of the oven.

½ cup finely chopped walnuts

2 (9.25-oz.) packages dinner rolls

⅔ cup peach preserves

½ cup mustard-mayonnaise blend

¾ lb. thinly sliced deli roast beef, chopped

½ lb. thinly sliced Havarti cheese

Salt and pepper to taste (optional)

[*freeze it*]

1. Preheat oven to 325°. Heat walnuts in a small nonstick skillet over medium-low heat, stirring occasionally, 5 to 6 minutes or until lightly toasted.

2. Remove rolls from packages. (Do not separate rolls.) Cut rolls in half horizontally, creating 1 top and 1 bottom per package. Spread preserves on cut sides of top of rolls; sprinkle with walnuts. Spread mustard-mayonnaise blend on cut sides of bottom of rolls; top with beef and cheese. Sprinkle with salt and pepper to taste, if desired. Cover with top halves of rolls, preserves sides down, and wrap in aluminum foil.

3. Bake at 325° for 20 to 25 minutes or until cheese is melted. Slice into individual sandwiches.

Note: We tested with Rainbo Dinner Time Rolls, Hellmann's Dijonnaise Mustard, and Boar's Head Londonport Top Round Seasoned Roast Beef. To make ahead, prepare recipe as directed through Step 2; freeze up to 1 month. Thaw overnight in refrigerator; bake as directed in Step 3.

WATERMELON AGUA FRESCAS

makes about 5 cups prep: 10 min.

Maria Corbalan, owner of Taco Xpress in Austin, Texas, shared this refreshing recipe with us.

4   cups seedless watermelon, cantaloupe, or
    honeydew melon, cubed

¼   cup sugar
2   cups cold water

1. Process cubed seedless watermelon, cantaloupe, or honeydew melon and sugar in a blender until smooth, stopping to scrape down sides as needed. Pour mixture through a fine wire-mesh strainer into a pitcher, discarding solids. Stir in cold water. Cover and chill until ready to serve.

LEMONADE

makes 2½ qt. prep: 10 min. cook: 5 min.

Use 1 cup of sugar if you plan to serve lemonade with a simple syrup. To extract the most juice from lemons, microwave them at HIGH for about 15 seconds.

1   to 1½ cups sugar
1   Tbsp. lemon zest (about 2 lemons)

1½ cups fresh lemon juice (about 13 lemons)
7   cups ice water

1. Bring ½ cup water to a boil in a medium saucepan. Stir in sugar and lemon zest, stirring until sugar is dissolved; remove from heat. Stir in lemon juice and ice water.

Limeade: Substitute 1 Tbsp. lime zest for lemon zest and 1½ cups fresh lime juice for lemon juice, and proceed with recipe as directed. Garnish with lime slices and fresh mint sprigs. Pictured on back cover.

{quick}

HONEY-GINGER TEA

makes 1 cup prep: 2 min. steep: 10 min.

We like it with a touch of fresh lemon juice. This recipe also easily doubles or triples.

1 (1-inch) piece fresh ginger, peeled

1 regular-size green tea bag

1 Tbsp. fresh lemon juice

2 Tbsp. honey

1 cup boiling water

1. Grate ginger, using the large holes of a box grater, to equal 1 Tbsp. Squeeze juice from ginger into a teacup; discard solids. Place tea bag, lemon juice, and honey in teacup; add boiling water. Cover and steep 3 minutes. Remove and discard tea bag, squeezing gently.

Note: We tested with Twinings Green Tea.

BLACKBERRY SPRITZER

makes 2 servings prep: 5 min. freeze: 1 hr.

We found that you can turn blackberries into luscious ice cubes that will flavor a glass of water as they thaw. Try it to create a refreshing drink that looks—and tastes—like the essence of summer.

1   pt. fresh blackberries

2   (6-inch) wooden skewers

1   to 2 Tbsp. corn syrup

1   Tbsp. lime zest (about 2 limes)

2   (8.45-oz.) bottles sparkling water, chilled

Garnish: fresh mint sprigs (optional)

1. Thread fresh blackberries onto 6-inch wooden skewers. Freeze 1 hour.
2. Dip rims of glasses into corn syrup, and roll in lime zest.
3. Place frozen blackberry skewers in prepared glasses. Pour chilled sparkling water over skewers, and garnish, if desired.

inspirations for your table

WATERMELON COOLER

makes about 8 servings   prep: 30 min.   freeze: 8 hr.   stand: 15 min.

8   cups (½-inch) watermelon cubes
1½ cups ginger ale

1   (6-oz.) can frozen limeade concentrate

1. Place watermelon cubes in a single layer in an extra-large zip-top plastic freezer bag, and freeze 8 hours. Let stand at room temperature 15 minutes.

2. Process half each of watermelon, ginger ale, ⅓ cup water, and limeade concentrate in a blender until smooth; pour mixture into a pitcher. Repeat procedure with remaining half of ingredients; stir into pitcher, and serve immediately.

Honeydew Cooler: Substitute 8 cups (½-inch) honeydew melon cubes for watermelon cubes and 1 (6-oz.) can frozen lemonade concentrate for limeade concentrate; proceed as directed.

Per (1-cup) serving: Calories 102; Fat 0.2g (mono 0.1g, poly 0.1g); Protein 1g; Carb 25.9g; Fiber 0.7g; Iron 0.5mg; Sodium 7mg; Calc 15mg

Cantaloupe Cooler: Substitute 8 cups (½-inch) cantaloupe cubes for watermelon, and add 2 tsp. grated fresh ginger to mixture in blender. Proceed as directed.

Per (1-cup) serving: Calories 117; Fat 0.3g (sat 0.1g, poly 0.1g); Protein 1.4g; Carb 29g; Fiber 0.1g; Iron 0.5mg; Sodium 32mg; Calc 19mg

[*southern lights*]

WHITE GRAPE-AND-ORANGE COOLER

makes about 6½ cups   prep: 5 min.   cook: 3 min.   chill: 2 hr.

⅓ cup sugar

1 cup white grape juice

½ cup orange juice

1 (1-liter) bottle ginger ale, chilled

Ice

Garnish: orange slices

1. Bring sugar and 1 cup water to a boil over medium-high heat, and cook, stirring often, 3 minutes or until sugar dissolves. Remove from heat, and cool.

2. Stir in juices, and chill 2 hours. Stir in ginger ale just before serving. Serve over ice. Garnish, if desired.

[make ahead]

PINK LEMONADE COCKTAIL

makes 6 to 8 servings   prep: 5 min.   **pictured on page 78**

1 (12-oz.) can frozen pink lemonade concentrate, thawed

3 (12-oz.) bottles beer (not dark), chilled

¾ cup vodka, chilled

Ice

Garnishes: citrus slices

1. Stir together first 3 ingredients. Serve over ice. Garnish, if desired.

HURRICANE PUNCH

makes 8¼ cups   prep: 10 min.

Serve red beans and rice, king cake, and this simple punch for your own Mardi Gras festivities.

½ (64-oz.) bottle red fruit punch

½ (12-oz.) can frozen limeade concentrate, thawed

1 (6-oz.) can frozen orange juice concentrate, thawed

1⅔ cups light rum

1⅔ cups dark rum

Ice

1. Stir together all ingredients. Serve over ice.

Our Best Margarita Secrets

You can really enhance a margarita glass by adding a little salt to the rim. Here's how to do it with perfect results.

 **1.** Moisten the rim of the glass with a lime wedge. You can also use orange liqueur or other sticky juices that allow the salt to cling.

 **2.** Dip prepared rims in margarita salt or other coarse salt varieties. Substitute sugar for salt, if desired.

CLASSIC MARGARITA

makes 1 serving   prep: 10 min.

Make any size batch of this recipe and all the variations by simply multiplying the ingredient measurements by the desired number of servings. For larger batches, stir together all ingredients in a pitcher until powdered sugar is dissolved. Chill and serve over ice.

Fresh lime wedge (optional)

Margarita salt (optional)

Ice

⅓ cup fresh lime juice*

3   Tbsp. orange liqueur

2   Tbsp. tequila

⅓ to ½ cup powdered sugar

1. Rub rim of a chilled margarita glass with lime wedge, and dip rim in salt to coat, if desired.

2. Fill cocktail shaker half full with ice. Add lime juice, liqueur, tequila, and powdered sugar; cover with lid, and shake until thoroughly chilled. Strain into prepared glass. Serve immediately.

* ⅓ cup thawed frozen limeade concentrate may be substituted for fresh lime juice. Omit powdered sugar, and proceed with recipe as directed.

Note: We tested with Cointreau for orange liqueur and Jose Cuervo Especial for tequila.

Frozen Margarita: Combine lime juice, liqueur, tequila, and powdered sugar in a small pitcher or measuring cup; stir until powdered sugar is dissolved. Pour into a zip-top plastic freezer bag. Seal and freeze 8 hours. Let stand 5 minutes at room temperature before serving. Pour into prepared glass. Makes 1 serving.

Frozen Strawberry Margaritas: Process lime juice, liqueur, tequila, powdered sugar, 1 cup fresh or frozen strawberries**, and 1 cup crushed ice in a blender until slushy. Rub rim of 2 chilled margarita glasses with lime wedge, and dip rim in red decorator sugar to coat, if desired. Serve immediately in prepared glasses. Makes 2 servings.

** Your favorite fruit, such as watermelon, peaches, or berries, may be substituted.

Margarita Sunrise: Pour lime juice, liqueur, tequila, powdered sugar, and 3 Tbsp. orange juice over ice in a cocktail shaker. Cover with lid, and shake until thoroughly chilled. Strain into prepared glass. Add 3 Tbsp. club soda or lemon-lime soft drink for a little fizz, if desired. Top with 2 tsp. grenadine. Serve immediately. Makes 1 serving.

Melon Margarita: Substitute melon liqueur for orange liqueur. Proceed with recipe as directed. Makes 1 serving.

Note: We tested with Midori for melon liqueur.

FROZEN CRANBERRY "MARGARITOS"

makes 5 cups   prep: 5 min.   **pictured on page 80**

A mojito traditionally uses rum; here we use tequila instead, hence the fun title. Dip rims of glasses in lime juice and a mixture of equal parts kosher salt and sugar for a twist on salt-rimmed glasses.

1 (10-oz.) can frozen mojito mix	2 Tbsp. fresh lime juice
¾ cup tequila	Ice
¼ cup whole-berry cranberry sauce	Garnishes: rosemary sprig, cranberries
2 Tbsp. orange liqueur	

1. Combine first 5 ingredients in a blender. Fill blender with ice to 5-cup level, and process until smooth. Garnish, if desired, and serve immediately.

Note: We tested with Triple Sec for orange liqueur.

More Than One Way To Make a Mint Julep

As the most genteel of Southern beverages, the battle between bartenders on how to serve a mint julep the "correct" way can take a brutal turn. Should you bruise, smash, crush, shave, or twist in a towel? Here the answer lies in nostalgia, tradition, or just plain preference.

To say "Southern Mint Julep" would be redundant. After all, the super sweet, spearmint-infused drink is synonymous with the South, just as are magnolias, sweeping porches, and Tara. However, there is controversy as to the "proper" way to make the libation whose origins are claimed by Virginia, Maryland, Georgia, Kentucky, and Louisiana.

Though bourbon is the alcohol of choice today, history tells us that it was once rye whiskey in Virginia and Maryland, brandy in Louisiana, and corn whiskey (forerunner to bourbon) in Kentucky. Though Virginia wins out for the origin, Kentucky, the land of bourbon makers, has embraced the mint julep as its own and as the traditional drink of both famed Churchill Downs and the Kentucky Derby.

While some might cavalierly combine all ingredients—simple sugar syrup, fresh mint leaves, bourbon, and shaved ice—in a shaker to mix before serving, others are much more particular about the way the mint is handled. Some insist on gently bruising the leaves to leave a mere hint of its flavor. Others believe it must be crushed or "muddled" to give intense flavor. Then there are recipes like the one on the Maker's Mark Web site that call for a time-consuming process that includes soaking the leaves in bourbon and then twisting them in a towel to strain the essence into the sugar syrup.

Disagreement also abounds about the container for serving a mint julep. Those holding to nostalgia and ceremony use shaved ice-filled silver or pewter julep cups that are coated with the appropriate amount of cold sweat beads before the bourbon mixture is added. Included is a straw ending merely 1 inch above the lip so that the nose can inhale the mint fragrance. And to follow true tradition, the cup must be held only by the bottom and top edges of the cup. Or, as is more commonly accepted today, mint juleps are sometimes served in a crystal highball or an old-fashioned glass, also with a straw. Whether served in the traditional way or simply in a glass, both sides agree that a sprig of mint is the crowning touch.

Kentucky Derby Dinner Party serves 12

**Mint Julep
Classic Cola-Glazed Ham (page 542)
*Green Bean-and-New Potato Salad** (page 731)   **Buttered corn**
Savory Deviled Eggs (page 870)   **Easy Cheddar Biscuits** (page 109)
*Bourbon Chocolate Pecan Tarts** (page 642)

*double recipe   **triple recipe

MINT JULEP

makes 4 cups   prep: 35 min.

Whether you serve this Southern cocktail in silver cups or crystal highballs, make sure the vessels are chilled by refrigerating them at least 1 hour before serving.

2 **cups bottled spring water**	3 **cups loosely packed fresh mint leaves**
¾ **cup sugar**	2 **cups bourbon**

1. Bring first 3 ingredients to a boil in a large saucepan, stirring until sugar dissolves. Remove from heat. Cover sugar mixture, and steep 30 minutes.

2. Pour mixture through a wire-mesh strainer into a pitcher, discarding mint leaves. Cool. Stir in bourbon. Serve over crushed ice.

Our Best Julep Tips

• **Term to know:** "Muddle," to crush or mash ingredients with a spoon to release flavor. A bar tool called a "muddler" can be used instead of a spoon. Its shape reminds us of a mini baseball bat.

• **Use crushed ice,** and pack into the cup tightly to keep the drink very cold, causing the cup to frost evenly. (Hold the cup at the rim while making to avoid fingerprints on the frosted cup.)

• **To make crushed ice:** Fill a 1-gal. heavy-duty zip-top plastic freezer bag half full with ice; seal. Crush ice using a rolling pin or heavy skillet.

AUNT KAT'S CREAMY EGGNOG

makes 3 qt.   prep: 10 min.   cook: 30 min.   chill: 8 hr.

1 qt. milk	¾ cup to 1½ cups bourbon*
12 large eggs	1 Tbsp. vanilla extract
¼ tsp. salt	½ tsp. ground nutmeg, divided
1½ cups sugar	1 qt. whipping cream

1. Heat milk in a large saucepan over medium heat. (Do not boil.)

2. Beat eggs and salt at medium speed with an electric mixer until thick and pale; gradually add sugar, beating well. Gradually stir about one-fourth of hot milk into egg mixture; add to remaining hot milk, stirring constantly.

3. Cook over medium-low heat, stirring constantly, 25 to 30 minutes or until milk mixture thickens and reaches 160°.

4. Stir in bourbon, vanilla, and ¼ tsp. nutmeg. Remove from heat, and cool. Cover and chill at least 8 hours.

5. Beat whipping cream at medium speed with an electric mixer until soft peaks form. Fold whipped cream into milk mixture. Sprinkle with remaining ¼ tsp. nutmeg before serving.

* 1½ to 2 cups milk may be substituted for bourbon.

1990 HOT CHOCOLATE DELUXE

makes 5 cups   prep: 10 min.   cook: 6 min.   **pictured on page 78**

¼ cup boiling water	⅓ to ½ cup coffee liqueur
⅓ cup chocolate syrup	Garnish: marshmallows, shaved chocolate
4 cups milk	

1. Stir together boiling water and chocolate syrup in a medium saucepan; add milk, stirring until blended. Cook over medium heat 6 to 8 minutes or until thoroughly heated. Stir in liqueur. Garnish, if desired.

Note: We tested with Kahlúa.

HOT CHOCOLATE WITH ALMOND LIQUEUR

makes about 5 cups   prep: 10 min.   cook: 6 min.

Test Kitchen Professional Marian Cooper Cairns recommends heating your serving container with warm water so that it won't cool down the hot chocolate mixture when you add it.

¼ cup boiling water

⅓ cup chocolate syrup

4 cups milk

⅓ cup almond liqueur

[quick]

1. Stir together boiling water and chocolate syrup in a medium saucepan; add milk, stirring until blended. Cook over medium heat 6 to 8 minutes or until thoroughly heated. Remove from heat, and stir in liqueur.

Note: We tested with Amaretto Almond Liqueur.

MOCHA PUNCH

makes 4½ qt.   prep: 10 min.   freeze: 20 min.

1 qt. chocolate milk

4 cups strong brewed coffee, chilled

1 cup Kahlúa or other coffee liqueur*

1 (14-oz.) can sweetened condensed milk

1 qt. chocolate ice cream

1 qt. coffee ice cream

Semisweet chocolate shavings

1. Combine first 4 ingredients in a large freezer-proof bowl. Cover and freeze 20 minutes. Pour mixture into a large punch bowl. Scoop chocolate and coffee ice creams into punch; stir gently. Sprinkle with chocolate shavings.

* Substitute amaretto-flavored nondairy liquid creamer for Kahlúa, or increase coffee to 5 cups.

BREADS

"The North thinks it knows how to make cornbread, but this is a gross superstition. Perhaps no bread in the world is quite as good as Southern cornbread, and perhaps no bread in the world is quite as bad as the Northern imitation of it." —Mark Twain

HOMEMADE BISCUITS

makes 14 (2-inch) biscuits   prep: 10 min.   bake: 10 min.

Self-rising flour contains salt and baking powder, which can leave a bitter taste, so sprinkle all-purpose flour on the surface when rolling and shaping biscuits.

¼ **cup shortening**
2 **cups self-rising flour**

⅔ **cup milk**

1. Preheat oven to 475°.
2. Cut shortening into flour with a pastry blender or fork until crumbly. Add milk, stirring just until dry ingredients are moistened.
3. Turn dough out onto a lightly floured surface, and knead lightly 3 or 4 times. Pat or roll dough to ½-inch thickness; cut with a 2-inch round cutter, and place on a lightly greased baking sheet.
4. Bake at 475° for 10 to 12 minutes or until golden brown.

Sour Cream Biscuits: Substitute 1 (8-oz.) container sour cream for ⅔ cup milk. Proceed as directed.

Ham-and-Swiss Cheese Biscuits: Stir ⅔ cup finely chopped ham and ⅔ cup finely chopped Swiss cheese into the flour and shortening mixture; add milk, and proceed as directed.

BASIC BUTTERY BISCUITS

makes about 2 dozen   prep: 10 min.   bake: 7 min.

Rebecca Kracke Gordon of our Test Kitchen keeps a dozen or two of these tasty gems in the freezer for drop-in company.

2¼ **cups all-purpose baking mix**
⅓ **cup buttermilk**

6 **Tbsp. unsalted butter, melted and divided**

1. Preheat oven to 450°.
2. Stir together baking mix, buttermilk, and 5 Tbsp. melted butter just until blended.
3. Turn dough out onto a lightly floured surface, and knead 1 to 2 times. Pat to a ½-inch thickness; cut with a 1½-inch round cutter, and place on lightly greased baking sheets.
4. Bake at 450° for 7 to 9 minutes or until lightly browned. Brush tops evenly with remaining 1 Tbsp. melted butter.

Note: We tested with Bisquick all-purpose baking mix.

[make ahead]

To make ahead: Freeze unbaked biscuits on a lightly greased baking sheet 30 minutes or until frozen. Store in a large zip-top plastic freezer bag up to 3 months. Bake as directed for 8 to 10 minutes.

Cranberry-Orange-Glazed Biscuits: Decrease baking mix to 2 cups plus 2 Tbsp. Add ½ cup chopped dried cranberries to baking mix. Prepare dough, and bake as directed. Omit 1 Tbsp. butter for brushing biscuits after baking. Stir together 6 Tbsp. powdered sugar, 1 Tbsp. orange juice, and ¼ tsp. orange zest. Drizzle evenly over warm biscuits.

To make ahead: Freeze unbaked biscuits on a lightly greased baking sheet 30 minutes or until frozen. Store in a zip-top plastic freezer bag up to 3 months. Bake as directed for 8 to 10 minutes or until lightly browned. Proceed with recipe as directed.

Tender, Flaky Goodness

1. Cut softened butter into flour with a pastry blender or two forks just until cubes are coated with flour.
2. Using your hands, gently combine the flour and butter mixture until it resembles small peas and the dough is crumbly. It is crucial to use your hands in this step so that you can feel the texture of the dough.

3. Turn the dough out onto a heavily floured surface. Use floured hands to pat dough to a ½-inch thickness. Don't use a rolling pin here; this will prevent the dough from being overworked.

More Biscuit Tricks

• When cutting out biscuits, don't twist the cutters. Simply press down, and pull straight up. Twisting compresses and seals the edges and prevents biscuits from rising.
• We prefer the texture of biscuits prepared with White Lily flour because it is a soft winter wheat flour and yields a more tender product.

Who Says It's Not "Homemade"?

An unofficial e-mail poll of cooks across the South shows that there is some sharp debate about what constitutes a "homemade" recipe. Can you use a mix or not? Some say, "You bet!" and others say, "No way." What do you think?

The issue seems to bring out three schools of thought:

1. From the purists: If it isn't made from "scratch" it's not homemade.

2. From the fence-sitters: If you embellish a mix with extra ingredients, it's just "semi-homemade."

3. From contemporary thinkers: If it requires any cooking at all from your kitchen, then it's definitely "homemade." Cooks answering an e-mail poll rarely said simply "yes" or "no." Some, like Jo Anne Marsch of Indian Springs, Alabama, are firm in their opinion. "Are you kidding me?" she says. "If it's not ready to eat when I buy it from a store, it's homemade at this house!"

Cookbook author Holly Clegg, of Baton Rouge, Louisiana, agrees. "I consider a cake mix a baking convenience item just as you might purchase frozen vegetables or bagged lettuce. Using a mix would be more homemade than buying something from the bakery."

But Georgian Lisa Kelly says, "My personal opinion is that using a prefab mix of any kind would be cheating!" Standing with Lisa are cooks from North Carolina, Tennessee, and Alabama who maintain that "cooking from scratch" and "homemade" mean the same thing. And, that means that adding individual ingredients—flour, sugar, baking powder, salt—are what makes the recipe truly homemade.

Jon Ruetz of Jonesborough, Tennessee, concedes that this is a sticky issue and takes an academic approach by deferring to the dictionary, which he claims defines "homemade" as made at home rather than in a store. Furthermore, he says that if you get right down to it, what's the difference in adding a seasoning mix that's mixed for you when the flavor is the same if you put the mixture together yourself?

Those who can't decide use words such as semi-homemade, almost homemade, easy homemade, look-like homemade, and half-baked. Despite the spatulas poised for battle, it took Jennifer Novak, a Yankee with Southern roots, to point out that homemade also means the time and love that go into something. On that, surely all can agree.

EASY HOMEMADE BISCUITS

makes about 1½ dozen   prep: 10 min.   bake: 9 min.   **pictured on page 84**

⅓ cup butter, softened and cubed*

2¼ cups self-rising flour

1 cup buttermilk

3 Tbsp. melted butter

1. Preheat oven to 450°.

2. Cut softened butter into flour with a pastry blender or 2 forks just until butter cubes are coated with flour. Using your hands, gently combine until mixture resembles small peas. Stir in buttermilk with a fork just until blended. (Mixture will be wet.)

3. Turn dough out onto a generously floured surface, and pat to ½-inch thickness. Cut dough with a well-floured 2-inch round cutter, and place on lightly greased baking sheets.

4. Bake at 450° for 9 to 11 minutes or until lightly browned. Remove from oven, and brush warm biscuits with melted butter. Serve immediately.

* ⅓ cup shortening may be substituted.

Note: We tested with White Lily Self-Rising Flour.

Butter Tips

• Soften butter at room temperature for about 30 minutes. Test the softness of butter by gently pressing the top of the stick with your index finger. If an indentation remains but the stick of butter still holds its shape, it's perfectly softened.

• Butter that's too cold overworks the dough when cut in and yields a tough biscuit. Likewise, butter that's too soft coats the flour and prevents the pea-size pellets from forming, thus yielding a flat biscuit.

• Perfectly softenend butter combines with flour to form small pea-size pellets that distribute evenly throughout the dough and release steam during cooking. These steam pockets cause the biscuit to puff for a fluffy, tender product with melt-in-your-mouth butter flavor.

FRESH TOMATO BISCUITS

makes 10 biscuits   prep: 10 min.   cook: 12 min.

Possibly the only thing that could compete with the flavor of a summer-fresh tomato sandwich on soft white sandwich bread is a summer-fresh tomato sandwich on a biscuit. This recipe uses the shortcut of canned biscuits, but you can substitute your favorite homemade recipe, if you'd like.

¼   cup mayonnaise

¼   tsp. salt

¼   tsp. coarsely ground pepper

¼   cup shredded fresh basil

1   (16.3-oz.) can refrigerated flaky biscuits

2   medium tomatoes, thinly sliced

1. Preheat oven to 400°.

2. Combine first 4 ingredients. Set aside.

3. Press each biscuit into a 4-inch circle. Place biscuit circles on a lightly greased baking sheet.

4. Bake at 400° for 6 minutes. Spread each biscuit evenly with about 2 tsp. mayonnaise mixture. Top evenly with tomato slices. Bake at 400° for 6 more minutes or until mayonnaise mixture is bubbly. Serve immediately.

Note: We tested with Pillsbury Golden Layers Buttermilk Biscuits.

BLUE CHEESE BISCUITS

makes 1 dozen   prep: 10 min.   bake: 15 min..

2   cups self-rising flour

1   (8-oz.) container sour cream

½   cup butter, melted

1   (4-oz.) package crumbled blue cheese

1. Preheat oven to 425°.

2. Stir together all ingredients just until blended.

3. Turn dough out onto a lightly floured surface. Pat dough to a ¾-inch thickness; cut with a 2-inch round cutter. Place dough rounds on a lightly greased baking sheet.

4. Bake at 425° for 15 to 18 minutes or until lightly browned.

EASY CHEDDAR BISCUITS

makes about 1½ dozen   prep: 10 min.   bake: 9 min.

⅓ **cup butter, softened and cubed***
2¼ **cups self-rising flour**
1 **cup shredded Cheddar cheese**

1 **cup buttermilk**
3 **Tbsp. melted butter**

1. Preheat oven to 450°.
2. Cut softened butter into flour with a pastry blender or 2 forks just until butter cubes are coated with flour. Using your hands, add cheese, and gently combine until mixture resembles small peas. Stir in buttermilk with a fork just until blended. (Mixture will be wet.)
3. Turn dough out onto a generously floured surface, and pat to ½-inch thickness. Cut dough with a well-floured 2-inch round cutter, and place on lightly greased baking sheets.
4. Bake at 450° for 9 to 11 minutes or until lightly browned. Remove from oven, and brush warm biscuits with melted butter. Serve immediately.

*** ⅓ cup shortening may be substituted.

Note: We tested with White Lily Self-Rising Flour.

ALE BISCUITS

makes about 2 dozen   prep: 10 min.   bake: 8 min.

⅓ **cup butter, frozen**
2½ **cups all-purpose baking mix**

⅔ **cup lager beer**

1. Preheat oven to 450°.
2. Grate ⅓ cup frozen butter through large holes of a box cheese grater into 2½ cups baking mix, and toss to combine. Stir in ⅔ cup lager beer just until dry ingredients are moistened. (Dough will be thick.)
3. Spoon dough into lightly greased miniature muffin pans, filling completely full.
4. Bake at 450° for 8 to 10 minutes or until biscuits are golden brown.

Note: We tested with Shiner Bock Beer.

TASTE OF THE SOUTH

Buttermilk Biscuits Here's your chance to

make melt-in-your-mouth biscuits from scratch that are worth every delicious bite. Experienced cooks may be surprised by this unique recipe. We went against the norm of handling the dough with kid gloves and actually kneaded it 20 to 25 times. Plus, we cranked up the oven to 500°, instead of the usual 375° to 425° range, to bake them. See what you think.

FLUFFY BUTTERMILK BISCUITS

makes about 18 biscuits   prep: 20 min.   bake: 9 min.

We preferred this half shortening-half butter combination, but all of one (even margarine) works well too. If using margarine, use the higher fat varieties or ones labeled "for baking." Shake the carton of buttermilk before measuring.

3½ cups self-rising flour	¼ cup butter, chilled and cut into pieces
2¼ tsp. baking powder	1½ cups buttermilk
2¼ tsp. sugar	½ to 1 cup self-rising flour
¼ cup shortening	1 Tbsp. butter, melted

1. Preheat oven to 500°.

2. Combine first 3 ingredients until well blended. Cut in shortening and chilled butter with a pastry blender or a fork until crumbly. Add buttermilk, stirring just until dry ingredients are moistened.

3. Turn dough out onto a well-floured surface; sprinkle with ½ cup self-rising flour. Knead 20 to 25 times, adding up to ½ cup additional flour until dough is smooth and springy to touch.

4. Pat dough into a ¾-inch-thick circle (about 8½ inches round). Cut dough with a well-floured 2-inch round cutter, making 12 biscuits. Place on ungreased baking sheets. Knead remaining dough together 3 or 4 times; repeat procedure, making 6 more biscuits. Lightly brush tops with melted butter.

5. Bake at 500° for 9 to 11 minutes or until golden.

Note: We tested with White Lily Self-Rising Flour.

Rosemary Biscuits: Stir 2 to 3 tsp. chopped fresh rosemary into dry ingredients. Proceed as directed.

Parmesan-Pepper Biscuits: Stir ½ cup (2 oz.) grated Parmesan cheese and 2 tsp. coarsely ground pepper into dry ingredients. (Less flour will be required while kneading.) Proceed as directed.

Steps to Success

We share all our tricks to making the best biscuits.

• The dough will be very soft out of the bowl. Generously sprinkle dough and work surface with self-rising flour to get started. Flour your hands too.

• To knead, fold 1 side of dough over, push away, turn dough, and repeat 20 to 25 times (not minutes). Work in self-rising flour as needed to prevent dough from sticking to countertop or hands.

• Stop a couple of times during kneading to press the dough with your finger. When it springs back, stop kneading. Use

fingers to pat dough into an 8½-inch circle.

• A bench scraper makes fast work of transferring biscuits to ungreased baking sheets. You can reroll

the scraps once, and cut 6 additional biscuits. By the way, make sure to cut biscuits straight down. Twisting the cutter will seal the edges of the biscuit, reduce the rise, and cause them to bake lopsided rather than straight and tall. We discovered that cutting biscuits with a glass sealed the edges and reduced the amount of rise as well. (You need both ends open to allow air to exit as you press down.) Biscuit cutters are sold at the grocery store.

PEACH-OAT MUFFINS

makes 24 muffins   prep: 15 min.   bake: 20 min.   **pictured on page 84**

These muffins are loaded with many of the components of a well-rounded breakfast: fiber and whole grains from oats and bran cereal, good fats from pecans and canola oil, dairy from nonfat buttermilk, and fruit from dried peaches.

¼ cup chopped pecans

1¾ cups uncooked regular oats

1 cup sugar

½ cup canola oil

2 large eggs

1¼ cups all-purpose flour

1 tsp. baking soda

½ tsp. salt

1 cup peach nectar

1 cup nonfat buttermilk

5 cups wheat bran cereal

⅓ cup chopped dried peaches

1. Preheat oven to 375°.

2. Heat pecans in a small nonstick skillet over medium-low heat, stirring often, 2 to 4 minutes or until toasted.

3. Process oats in a food processor or blender, about 45 seconds or until finely ground.

4. Beat sugar and oil at medium speed with an electric mixer 1 minute. Add eggs, 1 at a time, beating until blended after each addition. (Mixture will be light yellow.)

5. Combine ground oats, flour, baking soda, and salt in a small bowl. Stir together peach nectar and buttermilk in a small bowl. Add oat mixture to sugar mixture alternately with peach mixture, beginning and ending with oat mixture. Stir until blended after each addition. Gently stir in bran flakes, dried peaches, and toasted pecans. Spoon batter evenly into lightly greased muffin cups, filling three-fourths full.

6. Bake at 375° for 20 minutes or until golden brown.

Note: Muffins may be frozen for up to 1 month. Heat in toaster oven or microwave at HIGH 30 seconds. We tested with Post Premium Bran Flakes cereal.

Per muffin: Calories 176; Fat 6.6g (sat 0.6g, mono 3.6g, poly 1.8g); Protein 3.5g; Fiber 2.5g; Chol 18mg; Iron 3mg; Sodium 18mg; Calc 21mg

[southern lights]

BLUEBERRY MUFFINS

makes 1 dozen   prep: 10 min.   bake: 15 min.

2   cups self-rising flour
½   cup sugar
1   cup milk

¼   cup vegetable oil
2   large eggs
1   cup fresh or frozen blueberries

1. Preheat oven to 400°.

2. Combine first 2 ingredients in a large bowl; make a well in center of mixture.

3. Whisk together milk, oil, and eggs until well blended. Add to flour mixture, and stir just until dry ingredients are moistened. Gently fold in blueberries. Spoon mixture into lightly greased muffin pans, filling two-thirds full.

4. Bake at 400° for 15 to 18 minutes or until golden brown.

CRANBERRY-ORANGE MUFFINS

makes 1 dozen   prep: 10 min.   bake: 15 min.

2   cups self-rising flour
¾   cup sweetened dried cranberries
½   cup sugar
1   Tbsp. orange zest

1   cup milk
¼   cup vegetable oil
2   large eggs

1. Preheat oven to 400°.

2. Combine first 4 ingredients in a large bowl; make a well in center of mixture.

3. Whisk together milk, oil, and eggs until well blended. Add to flour mixture, and stir just until dry ingredients are moistened.

4. Spoon mixture into lightly greased muffin pans, filling two-thirds full.

5. Bake at 400° for 15 to 18 minutes or until golden brown.

CINNAMON STREUSEL MUFFINS

makes 1 dozen   prep: 15 min.   bake: 18 min.   cool: 15 min.

These delicious muffins are an excellent way to add more fruit to your diet.

1 (15.2-oz.) package cinnamon streusel
   muffin mix

½ cup dried apple pieces
½ cup golden raisins

1. Preheat oven to 375°.

2. Prepare muffin mix batter according to package directions. Stir in apples and raisins. Place foil baking cups in muffin pans. Spoon batter into cups, filling two-thirds full.

3. Bake at 375° according to package directions.

Note: We tested with Betty Crocker Cinnamon Streusel Premium Muffin Mix.

SAUSAGE-CHEESE MUFFINS

makes 15 muffins   prep: 15 min.   bake: 20 min.

Five easy ingredients lend Sausage-Cheese Muffins big flavor with little work.

1   (1-lb.) package ground pork sausage
3   cups all-purpose baking mix

1½ cups (6 oz.) shredded Cheddar cheese
1   (10 ¾-oz.) can condensed cheese soup

1. Preheat oven to 375°.

2. Cook sausage in a large skillet, stirring until it crumbles and is no longer pink. Drain and cool.

3. Combine sausage, baking mix, and shredded cheese in a large bowl; make a well in center of mixture.

4. Stir together soup and ¾ cup water; add to sausage mixture, stirring just until dry ingredients are moistened. Spoon into lightly greased muffin pans, filling to top of cups.

5. Bake at 375° for 20 to 25 minutes or until lightly browned.

[*for kids*]

HAM-AND-BROCCOLI MUFFINS

makes 12 muffins   prep: 15 min.   bake: 18 min.   stand: 2 min.

Store muffins in zip-top plastic freezer bags for up to one month. For a quick snack, thaw the muffins at room temperature, or microwave them in damp paper towels at HIGH for 10 to 15 seconds.

1½ cups reduced-fat all-purpose baking mix
1   cup finely chopped cooked ham or
    Canadian bacon
2   cups (8 oz.) shredded 2% reduced-fat
    Cheddar cheese, divided

1   (10-oz.) package frozen chopped broccoli,
    thawed and well drained
½   cup fat-free milk
1   Tbsp. butter, melted
1   large egg, lightly beaten

1. Preheat oven to 425°.

2. Combine baking mix, chopped ham, 1¾ cups shredded cheese, and broccoli in a large bowl; make a well in center of mixture.

3. Stir together fat-free milk, melted butter, and lightly beaten egg until well blended; add to cheese mixture, stirring just until moistened. Place paper baking cups in muffin pans, and coat with cooking spray. Spoon batter into paper baking cups, filling three-fourths full. Sprinkle tops evenly with remaining ¼ cup cheese.

4. Bake at 425° for 18 minutes or until golden. Let stand 2 to 3 minutes before removing from pans.

Note: Substitute miniature muffin pans for regular pans, if desired. Bake at 425° for 14 minutes or until golden. Makes 2½ dozen miniature muffins.

Per muffin: Calories 166; Fat 7.5g (sat 4g, mono 0.9g, poly 0.2g); Protein 10.8g; Carb 13g; Fiber 0.9g; Chol 44mg; Iron 0.9mg; Sodium 364mg; Calc 171mg

southern lights

TASTE OF THE SOUTH

Sally Lunn Bread A cross between cake and bread, this old-fashioned delicacy deserves a place at today's dinner table.

Some of our Foods staff had never heard of Sally Lunn Bread when we proposed it for a column. But after trying it, the group was sold on the slightly sweet flavor, nice shape, and ease of this yeast bread from the colonial South. They also offered suggestions for additional ways to use this top-rated recipe: in a luscious tomato sandwich, for French toast, or as the base for croutons. Our Senior Food Editor Mary Allen Perry says, "Sally Lunn Bread is like grits—the flavor complements everything."

This recipe starts with an easy-to-make yeast batter. Eggs offer the yellow color and rich taste. Baking in a Bundt or tube cake pan lends the signature shape. And the bread is sturdy enough to serve with supper and sop up gravy.

Where does this versatile food get its name? We don't really know who Sally Lunn was. Some sources contend that she was a woman who sold bread in England. Other historians say the name may have come from the French words *soleil* (which means sun) and *lune* (which means moon). The bread has a top as golden as the sun and a bottom as pale as the moon. Some food historians believe that the Jamestown colonists made this bread to remind them of their home in England. The recipe shows up in old Southern cookbooks from that time period and beyond.

Whatever its origin, you can make this sweet treat today to enjoy its light, buttery goodness. When you do, smile and raise your cup to Sally Lunn.

SALLY LUNN BREAD

makes 12 to 16 servings prep: 10 min. stand: 5 min. rise: 1 hr., 50 min. bake: 35 min.

2 (¼-oz.) envelopes active dry yeast
½ cup warm water (100° to 110°)
1½ cups milk
¾ cup sugar
½ cup butter

1 tsp. salt
2 large eggs
5 cups all-purpose flour
Blackberry Butter (optional)

1. Combine yeast and ½ cup warm water in a 1-cup measuring cup; let stand 5 minutes.

2. Heat milk and next 3 ingredients in a saucepan over medium heat, stirring until butter melts. Cool to 100° to 110°.

3. Beat yeast mixture, milk mixture, and eggs at medium speed with an electric mixer until blended. Gradually add flour, beating at lowest speed until blended. (Mixture will be a very sticky, soft dough.)

4. Cover and let rise in a warm place (85°), free from drafts, 1 hour or until dough is doubled in bulk.

5. Stir dough down; cover and let rise in a warm place (85°), free from drafts, 30 minutes or until dough is doubled in bulk.

6. Stir dough down, and spoon into a well-greased, 10-inch Bundt pan or tube pan. Cover and let rise in a warm place (85°), free from drafts, 20 to 30 minutes or until dough is doubled in bulk.

7. Preheat oven to 350°.

8. Bake at 350° for 35 to 40 minutes or until golden brown and a wooden pick inserted into center of bread comes out clean. Remove from pan immediately. Serve bread with Blackberry Butter, honey, molasses, or jelly, if desired.

Blackberry Butter: Stir 2 to 3 Tbsp. seedless blackberry jam into ½ cup softened butter.

CREAM CHEESE-BANANA-NUT BREAD

makes 2 loaves   prep: 15 min.   bake: 1 hr.   cool: 40 min.   **pictured on page 81**

Speedy to mix, this batter bakes in loaves or muffin cups. Add any one of the toppings, and you'll go faint with pleasure after the first divine bite. Warm bread is yummy, but to get perfect slices, let the bread cool 30 minutes, and cut it with a serrated or an electric knife.

¾ cup butter, softened	½ tsp. baking soda
1 (8-oz.) package cream cheese, softened	½ tsp. salt
2 cups sugar	1½ cups mashed bananas (1¼ lb. unpeeled
2 large eggs	bananas, about 4 medium)
3 cups all-purpose flour	1 cup chopped pecans, toasted
½ tsp. baking powder	½ tsp. vanilla extract

1. Preheat oven to 350°. Beat butter and cream cheese at medium speed with an electric mixer until creamy. Gradually add sugar, beating until light and fluffy. Add eggs, 1 at a time, beating just until blended after each addition.

2. Combine flour and next 3 ingredients; gradually add to butter mixture, beating at low speed just until blended. Stir in bananas, pecans, and vanilla. Spoon batter into 2 greased and floured 8- x 4-inch loaf pans.

3. Bake at 350° for 1 hour or until a long wooden pick inserted in center comes out clean and sides pull away from pan, shielding with aluminum foil during last 15 minutes to prevent browning, if necessary. Cool bread in pans on wire racks 10 minutes. Remove from pans, and cool 30 minutes on wire racks before slicing.

Cream Cheese-Banana-Nut Muffins: To bake muffins, spoon batter evenly into 24 paper-lined muffin cups. Bake at 350° for 25 minutes or until a wooden pick inserted in center comes out clean. Cool in pans 10 minutes. Remove from pans, and cool completely on wire racks.

Orange-Pecan-Topped Cream Cheese-Banana-Nut Bread: Prepare bread batter as directed, and spoon into desired pans. Sprinkle 1 cup coarsely chopped, toasted pecans evenly over batter in pans. Bake as directed. Cool bread or muffins in pans 10 minutes; remove from pans to wire racks. Stir together 1 cup powdered sugar, 3 Tbsp. fresh orange juice, and 1 tsp. orange zest until blended. Drizzle evenly over warm bread or muffins, and cool 30 minutes on wire racks.

Toasted Coconut-Topped Cream Cheese-Banana-Nut Bread: Prepare and bake bread or muffins in desired pans. While bread is baking, stir together ¼ cup butter, ¼ cup granulated sugar, ¼ cup firmly packed brown sugar, and ¼ cup milk in a small saucepan over medium-high heat; bring to a boil, stirring constantly. Remove from heat. Stir in 1 cup sweetened flaked coconut; 1 cup chopped, toasted pecans; and 2 tsp. vanilla extract. Remove baked bread or muffins from oven, and immediately spread tops with coconut mixture. Preheat broiler. Broil 5½ inches from heat 2 to 3 minutes or just until topping starts to lightly brown. Cool in pans on wire racks 20 minutes. Remove from pans, and cool 30 minutes on wire racks before slicing.

Cinnamon Crisp-Topped Cream Cheese-Banana-Nut Bread: Prepare bread batter as directed, and spoon into desired pans. Stir together ½ cup firmly packed brown sugar; ½ cup chopped, toasted pecans; 1 Tbsp. all-purpose flour; 1 Tbsp. melted butter; and ⅛ tsp. ground cinnamon. Sprinkle mixture evenly over batter. Bake and cool as directed.

Peanut Butter Streusel-Topped Cream Cheese-Banana-Nut Bread: Prepare bread batter as directed, and spoon into desired pans. Combine ½ cup plus 1 Tbsp. all-purpose flour and ½ cup firmly packed brown sugar in a small bowl. Cut in ¼ cup butter and 3 Tbsp. creamy peanut butter with a pastry blender or fork until mixture resembles small peas. Sprinkle mixture evenly over batter in pans. Bake and cool as directed.

Toffee-Topped Cream Cheese-Banana-Nut Bread: Prepare bread batter as directed, and spoon into desired pans. Stir together 3 tablespoons melted butter, ⅓ cup plus 3 tablespoons all-purpose flour, ⅓ cup firmly packed light brown sugar, ¼ teaspoon ground cinnamon, and 2 (1.4-ounce) chocolate-covered toffee candy bars, finely chopped. Sprinkle evenly over batter in pans. Bake and cool as directed.

Banana Basics

The perfect bananas for this bread don't look so perfect. Let them get ripe, almost black, or very speckled. It takes a week to go from green to ready.

To hasten ripening, place in a paper bag with a bruised apple. Once ripe, refrigerate or freeze unpeeled bananas in zip-top plastic freezer bags; thaw before mashing. We tried to freeze mashed bananas, but once thawed, they were watery and not suitable to use. A 6-ounce unpeeled banana yields about ⅓ cup mashed banana.

APPLE BREAD

makes 2 (9-inch) loaves   prep: 20 min.   bake: 1 hr.

This recipe freezes beautifully. Just place in an airtight container or zip-top plastic freezer bag, and store in freezer up to one month.

1	(3-lb.) bag small apples (12 to 14 apples)	3	cups all-purpose flour
2	cups sugar	2	tsp. ground cinnamon
1	cup vegetable oil	1	tsp. baking soda
3	large eggs, lightly beaten	½	tsp. salt
2	tsp. vanilla extract	1	cup chopped pecans, toasted

1. Preheat oven to 350°.

2. Peel and finely chop enough apples to equal 3 cups. Set aside.

3. Stir together sugar and next 3 ingredients in a large bowl.

4. Stir together flour and next 3 ingredients; add to sugar mixture, stirring just until blended. (Batter will be stiff.) Fold in finely chopped apples and 1 cup pecans.

5. Divide batter evenly between 2 greased and floured 9- x 5-inch loaf pans. Bake at 350° for 1 hour or until a wooden pick inserted in center comes out clean. Remove from pans, and cool on wire racks.

CHEESY GRITS BREAD

makes 3 loaves   prep: 15 min.   cook: 10 min.   stand: 30 min.   rise: 1 hr., 45 min.
bake: 35 min.   cool: 10 min.

We added some of our own twists to reader Catherine Boettner's flavorful recipe.

2	cups milk	1	cup warm water (100° to 110°)
¾	cup quick-cooking grits, uncooked	¼	cup sugar
2	tsp. salt	2	(¼-oz.) envelopes rapid-rise yeast
1	(10-oz.) block white Cheddar cheese, shredded	5	to 6 cups bread flour

1. Bring milk to a boil in a large saucepan over medium heat; stir in grits, and cook, stirring often, 5 minutes (mixture will be very thick). Remove from heat; add salt and cheese, stirring until cheese is melted. Let stand 25 minutes, stirring occasionally.

2. Combine 1 cup warm water, sugar, and yeast in the mixing bowl of a heavy-duty stand mixer; let stand 5 minutes. Add grits mixture, beating at medium-low speed with the dough hook attachment until well blended.

3. Add 4 cups flour, 1 cup at a time, beating until blended after each addition and stopping to scrape down sides as necessary. Gradually add enough flour to make a stiff but slightly sticky dough. Dough will form a ball around mixer attachment. Shape dough into a ball with well-floured hands, and place in a well-greased bowl, turning to coat top. Cover and let rise in a warm place (85°), free from drafts, 1 hour or until doubled in bulk.

4. Punch dough down, and divide into thirds; shape each portion into a loaf. Place into lightly greased 9- x 5-inch loaf pans; cover and let rise in a warm place (85°), free from drafts, 45 minutes or until doubled in bulk.

5. Preheat oven to 350°.

6. Bake at 350° for 35 to 40 minutes or until golden. Let bread cool in pans on wire racks 10 minutes. Remove from pans, and cool completely on wire racks.

Note: We tested with Cracker Barrel Vermont Sharp-White Cheddar.

Bacon-Cheddar Grits Bread: (pictured on page 157) Prepare dough as directed. After dividing dough, roll each third into a 14- x 9-inch rectangle on a lightly floured surface. Sprinkle each dough rectangle evenly with ½ cup cooked, crumbled bacon and ¾ cup shredded sharp Cheddar cheese. Roll up, jelly-roll fashion, starting with each short side and ending at middle of dough. You will form 2 rolls per loaf. Place into prepared loaf pans; let rise, and bake as directed.

Tomato-Black Olive Grits Bread: Prepare dough as directed. After dividing dough, roll each third into a 14- x 9-inch rectangle on a lightly floured surface. Sprinkle each dough rectangle evenly with ½ cup julienne-cut sun-dried tomatoes with herbs in oil (drained and patted dry with paper towels) and ½ cup sliced black olives (drained and patted dry with paper towels). Roll up, jelly-roll fashion, starting with each short side and ending at middle of dough. You will form 2 rolls per loaf. Place into prepared loaf pans; let rise, and bake as directed.

Note: We tested with California Sun-Dry Sun-Dried Julienne Cut Tomatoes With Herbs.

Basil Pesto-Cheese Grits Bread: Prepare dough as directed. After dividing dough, roll each third into a 14- x 9-inch rectangle on a lightly floured surface. Spread ¼ cup prepared basil pesto evenly over each dough rectangle; sprinkle each with ¾ cup shredded mozzarella or crumbled goat cheese. Roll up, jelly-roll fashion, starting with each short side and ending at middle of dough. You will form 2 rolls per loaf. Place into prepared loaf pans; let rise, and bake as directed.

SKILLET CORNBREAD

makes 6 servings   prep: 10 min.   bake: 15 min.

A well-seasoned cast-iron skillet is a must for a golden brown crust. Turn the hot cornbread onto a plate, bottom side up, to preserve its crunchy texture.

2   to 3 tsp. bacon drippings
2   cups buttermilk
1   large egg
1¾ cups white cornmeal

1   tsp. baking powder
1   tsp. baking soda
1   tsp. salt

1. Preheat oven to 450°.
2. Coat bottom and sides of a 10-inch cast-iron skillet with bacon drippings; heat in a 450° oven.
3. Whisk together buttermilk and egg. Add cornmeal, stirring well. Whisk in baking powder, baking soda, and salt. Pour batter into hot skillet.
4. Bake at 450° for 15 minutes or until cornbread is golden.

PIMIENTO-CHEESE CORN STICKS

makes about 5 dozen   prep: 10 min.   cook: 8 min.

1½ cups white cornmeal mix
½   cup all-purpose flour
1   tsp. sugar
2   large eggs, lightly beaten

1½ cups buttermilk
1   cup (4 oz.) shredded Cheddar cheese
1   (7-oz.) jar drained diced pimiento

1. Preheat oven to 450°.
2. Combine first 3 ingredients; make a well in the center of mixture. Add eggs and remaining ingredients to cornmeal mixture, stirring just until moistened.
3. Place cast-iron miniature corn stick pans in oven; heat 5 minutes or until hot. Remove pans from oven, and coat with vegetable cooking spray. Spoon batter into hot pans.
4. Bake at 450° for 8 minutes or until golden brown. Remove from pans immediately.

taking sides

Cornbread and Controversy

Crisp or soft? White or yellow? Thick or thin? Sweet or not? Cornbread recipe versions across the South are as staunchly defended as the local football team or favorite barbecue joint.

There's only one way to make a good pan of cornbread, explains Clyde Garrison of northeast Tennessee, a fan of his wife's crispy cornbread. "Thin. Real thin," he says, demonstrating the thickness with his thumb and forefinger about an inch apart. And with no sugar, and no eggs. And baked in a hot cast-iron skillet to which butter and then the batter is added so the crust is super crispy and the insides are soft—just right for crumbling into a tall glass of milk to eat with a spoon.

This version is typical of the one usually baked for crumbling into milk, buttermilk, soups, and stews, though many replace the traditional bacon drippings with butter. Cornbread for cutting into wedges and serving at a meal usually has an egg or two, uses buttermilk rather than "sweet" milk, and still has absolutely NO sugar. Texans often stir in jalapenos and corn, and even cheese, for a southwestern version.

Food historians say Northerners are most likely to use yellow cornmeal while Southerners prefer white, and that sugar and flour are rarely found in truly Southern versions with a few exceptions. According to Crescent Dragonwagon's book, *Cornbread Gospels*, in parts of Virginia and in some African-American kitchens, cornbread recipes may have as much flour as cornmeal, are sweetened with sugar, and are often baked in (gasp!) a square pan. For most of the South, centuries of tradition dictate that cornbread should be baked in a round, well-seasoned cast-iron skillet, preferably handed down from a previous generation.

Just as traditional as the crispy crust is how the cornbread is served. In the mountain regions, it's a must with soup beans and long-cooked greens. All over the region summer tables spread with slices of cucumber, tomato, and onion call for cornbread in wedges or fried into individual corn pones, fritters, or cakes. And it's the rare family reunion, church supper, or barbecue dinner where this Southern staple doesn't crown the table…usually right next to a big pitcher of sweet iced tea.

CHEESE-AND-ONION CORNBREAD

makes 9 servings prep: 10 min. bake: 18 min.

Serve this crusty bread to round out comfort food main dishes such as pot roast, chili, or vegetable soup.

2 (6-oz.) packages buttermilk cornbread mix
1 cup shredded Cheddar-Monterey Jack cheese blend

¼ cup chopped green onion tops
1 Tbsp. butter
1⅓ cups milk

1. Preheat oven to 450°.

2. Combine buttermilk cornbread mix, cheese, and chopped green onions in a large bowl; set aside.

3. Heat butter in an 8-inch baking pan in a 450° oven 3 to 4 minutes or until melted and lightly browned. Tilt pan to coat bottom with melted butter.

4. Add milk to cornbread mixture, stirring just until blended. Pour batter into hot pan.

5. Bake at 450° for 18 to 20 minutes or until golden and cornbread pulls away from sides of pan.

Note: We tested with Martha White Buttermilk Cornbread Mix.

HONEY-SWEET CORNBREAD

makes 4 to 6 servings prep: 15 min. bake: 10 min.

This is a thin, crisp cornbread.

¾ cup plus 2 Tbsp. stone-ground cornmeal
6 Tbsp. all-purpose flour
2 tsp. baking powder
¼ tsp. baking soda
½ tsp. salt

¾ cup buttermilk
¼ cup canola oil
2 Tbsp. yaupon or other wildflower honey
1 large egg
1 tsp. canola oil

1. Preheat oven to 450°.

2. Combine first 5 ingredients in a bowl. Stir in buttermilk and next 3 ingredients until well blended.

3. Heat 1 tsp. oil in a 9-inch cast-iron skillet over medium-high heat. Pour batter into skillet.

4. Bake at 450° for 10 to 12 minutes or until golden brown.

VIDALIA ONION CORNBREAD

makes 8 servings   prep: 10 min.   cook: 7 min.   bake: 30 min.

Turn an ordinary package of cornbread mix into a deliciously moist homemade dish that's reminiscent of spoonbread.

¼ cup butter or margarine

1 large Vidalia or other sweet onion, chopped

1 (7.5-oz.) package cornbread mix

1 cup (4 oz.) shredded sharp Cheddar cheese, divided

1 cup sour cream

⅓ cup milk

1 large egg, beaten

¼ tsp. salt

¼ tsp. dried dill weed (optional)

1. Preheat oven to 450°.

2. Melt butter in a medium saucepan over medium-high heat. Add onion, and sauté 5 minutes or until tender. (Do not brown onion.) Remove pan from heat. Stir in cornbread mix, ½ cup cheese, next 4 ingredients, and, if desired, dill.

3. Coat an 8-inch square pan with cooking spray; pour mixture into pan.

4. Bake at 450° for 25 minutes. Sprinkle evenly with remaining ½ cup cheese, and bake 5 more minutes or until a wooden pick inserted into center comes out clean. Cool slightly before cutting into squares.

SWEET POTATO CORNBREAD

makes 6 servings   prep: 5 min.   bake: 20 min.

Be sure to use self-rising cornmeal mix, or your bread will be flat and hard.

2 cups self-rising cornmeal mix

¼ cup sugar

1 tsp. ground cinnamon

1½ cups milk

1 cup mashed cooked sweet potato

¼ cup butter, melted

1 large egg, beaten

1. Preheat oven to 425°.

2. Whisk together all ingredients, whisking just until dry ingredients are moistened. Spoon batter into a greased 8-inch cast-iron skillet or baking pan.

3. Bake at 425° for 20 to 25 minutes or until a wooden pick inserted in center comes out clean.

Note: We tested with White Lily Self-Rising Buttermilk Cornmeal Mix.

SUPER-MOIST CORNBREAD

makes 8 servings   prep: 10 min.   bake: 30 min.

You can bake this cornbread one day in advance. Allow it to cool completely; then wrap it tightly in aluminum foil or plastic wrap.

make ahead

⅓ cup butter

1 (8-oz.) container sour cream

2 large eggs, lightly beaten

1 (8-oz.) can cream-style corn

1 cup self-rising white cornmeal mix

1. Preheat oven to 400°.

2. Heat butter in a 9-inch cast-iron skillet in 400° oven 5 minutes or until butter melts.

3. Combine sour cream, eggs, and corn in a medium bowl. Whisk in cornmeal mix just until combined. Whisk in melted butter. Pour batter into skillet.

4. Bake at 400° for 30 minutes or until golden brown.

GRANNIE'S CRACKLIN' CORNBREAD

makes 8 to 10 servings   prep: 7 min.   cook: 25 min.   **pictured on page 82**

Cornbread falls in the quick bread category because it does not require rising time.

¼ cup butter

2 cups self-rising cornmeal

½ cup all-purpose flour

2½ cups buttermilk

2 large eggs, lightly beaten

1 cup cracklings*

1. Preheat oven to 425°.

2. Place butter in a 9-inch cast-iron skillet, and heat in a 425° oven 4 minutes.

3. Combine cornmeal and flour in a large bowl; make a well in center of mixture.

4. Stir together buttermilk, eggs, and cracklings; add to dry ingredients, stirring just until moistened. Pour over melted butter in hot skillet.

5. Bake at 425° for 25 to 30 minutes or until golden brown.

* 1 cup cooked, crumbled bacon (12 to 15 slices) may be substituted for cracklings.

Grannie's Cracklin' Cakes: Prepare batter as directed above; stir in ¼ cup butter, melted. Heat a large skillet coated with vegetable cooking spray over medium-high heat. Spoon about ¼ cup batter for each cake into skillet; cook, in batches, 2 to 3 minutes on each side or until golden.

TASTE OF THE SOUTH

Hush Puppies
A fish fry and barbecue staple, hush puppies are made from a six-ingredient batter, which is dropped by spoonfuls into hot oil to cook. You can make them yourself—we walk you through the steps with our tips and photos. So, how did they get their name? They were perhaps the original treat (aka bribe) for Fido. Legends tell how Southern fishermen and Civil War soldiers first made the golden nuggets from scraps just to toss to barking and begging dogs with the command to "Hush, puppy."

HUSH PUPPIES

makes 1½ dozen prep: 10 min. stand: 10 min. cook: 4 min. per batch

1 cup self-rising white cornmeal mix	1 large egg, lightly beaten
½ cup self-rising flour	½ cup milk or beer
½ cup diced onion	Vegetable oil
1 Tbsp. sugar	

1. Combine first 4 ingredients in a large bowl.

2. Add egg and milk to dry ingredients, stirring just until moistened. Let stand 10 minutes.

3. Pour oil to a depth of 2 inches into a Dutch oven; heat to 375°.

4. Drop batter by rounded tablespoonfuls into hot oil, and fry, in batches, 2 to 3 minutes on each side or until golden brown. Drain on a wire rack over paper towels; serve immediately.

Jalapeño Hush Puppies: Add 1 seeded, diced jalapeño to batter. Proceed with recipe as directed.

Note: Keep fried hush puppies warm in oven at 225° for up to 15 minutes. We tested with White Lily Self-Rising White Cornmeal Mix.

Old-Fashioned Fish Fry   serves 12

*Classic Fried Catfish (page 372)

*Peanutty Coleslaw (page 732)   Corn on the cob

*Mississippi Hush Puppies

Lemon-Almond Pound Cake (cakes 209)

*Southern Sweetened Tea (page 27)

*double recipe

MISSISSIPPI HUSH PUPPIES

makes 1½ dozen   prep: 5 min.   fry: 4 min. per batch   pictured on page 127

This is a favorite of The Catfish Institute in Belzoni, Mississippi. Beer makes this bread light and tangy.

1 cup self-rising cornmeal mix	½ cup diced onion
½ cup self-rising flour	½ cup chopped green bell pepper
1 Tbsp. sugar	1 jalapeño pepper, chopped
1 large egg	Vegetable oil
½ cup milk or beer	

1. Combine first 3 ingredients in a large bowl, and make a well in center of mixture.

2. Combine egg and next 4 ingredients, stirring well; add to dry ingredients, stirring just until moistened.

3. Pour oil to a depth of 3 inches into a Dutch oven or large saucepan; heat to 375°.

4. Drop batter by rounded tablespoonfuls into hot oil, and fry, in batches, 2 minutes on each side or until golden brown. Drain on paper towels; serve immediately.

Hush Puppies Start to Finish

These addictive bites of fried cornbread are so easy to make. Here's how.

1. The Batter: Stir 10 times around the bowl—just until the dry and liquid ingredients are barely combined together. Overmixing causes a tough texture.

2. The Pot: Use a pot that is at least 6 inches deep and fits the largest element on your cooktop. Our Test Kitchen had excellent results frying this recipe in both the 6-qt. Dutch oven shown in the photographs and in a deep cast-iron skillet. We also tried an electric deep-fat fryer with a temperature control dial and found that the batter stuck to the basket, and the temperature did not get hot enough to properly fry the hush puppies. So stick with the old-fashioned pot-on-a-stove method.

3. The Oil: A clean ruler placed in the pot can help you determine the line for a 2-to 3-inch depth of oil. (Don't skimp; the batter needs to submerge in the oil.) For

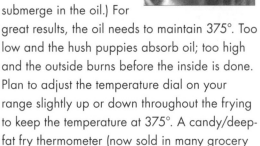

great results, the oil needs to maintain 375°. Too low and the hush puppies absorb oil; too high and the outside burns before the inside is done. Plan to adjust the temperature dial on your range slightly up or down throughout the frying to keep the temperature at 375°. A candy/deep-fat fry thermometer (now sold in many grocery stores for about $5) is a must.

4. The Drop: You can drop the batter using two soup-size spoons sprayed with vegetable cooking spray or a 1 tablespoon-measure ice-cream scoop.

5. The Flip: Sometimes hush puppies will flip themselves over. Use a slotted spoon or frying utensil, such as the one shown, to turn the rest.

6. The Finish: Hush puppies are usually done at the point you think they might need to cook longer—when the rough bumps or high spots are rich golden brown. Oil may be used for one

more fry job if stored properly. After all the hush puppies are cooked, let the oil cool thoroughly. To remove cooked particles, strain the oil through a fine wire-mesh strainer lined with cheesecloth or a coffee filter. Use a funnel to pour the oil into an empty vegetable oil bottle or a disposable plastic container with a lid. Label, date, and store in the fridge; use within one month.

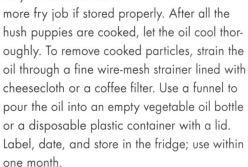

PIMIENTO CHEESE ROLLS

makes 1 dozen   prep: 15 min.   stand: 30 min.   bake: 20 min.   **pictured on page 84**

test kitchen favorite

1   (26.4-oz.) package frozen biscuits
All-purpose flour

2   cups Pimiento Cheese (page 57)

1. Arrange frozen biscuits, with sides touching, in 3 rows of 4 biscuits on a lightly floured surface. Let stand 30 to 45 minutes or until biscuits are thawed but cool to the touch.
2. Preheat oven to 375°.
3. Sprinkle thawed biscuits lightly with flour. Press biscuit edges together, and pat to form a 12- x 10-inch rectangle of dough; spread evenly with Pimiento Cheese.
4. Roll up, starting at 1 long end; cut into 12 (about 1-inch-thick) slices. Place 1 slice into each of 12 lightly greased 3-inch muffin pan cups.
5. Bake at 375° for 20 to 25 minutes or until golden brown. Cool slightly, and remove from pan.

Ham-and-Swiss Rolls: Omit Pimiento Cheese. Stir together ¼ cup each of softened butter, spicy brown mustard, and finely chopped sweet onion. Spread butter mixture evenly over 12- x 10-inch rectangle of thawed dough; sprinkle evenly with 1 cup each of shredded Swiss cheese and chopped cooked ham. Proceed with recipe as directed.

Sausage-and-Cheddar Rolls: Omit Pimiento Cheese. Spread ¼ cup softened butter evenly over 12- x 10-inch rectangle of thawed dough; sprinkle evenly with 1 cup each of shredded Cheddar cheese and cooked, crumbled sausage. Proceed with recipe as directed.

gatherings

Easter Lunch serves 8

Citrus Rosemary Turkey Breast (page 700)
*Thyme-Scented Green Beans With Smoked Almonds (page 845)
Garlic mashed potatoes
Buttery Dijon Deviled Eggs (page 871)   Spoon Rolls
Lemon-Coconut Cake (page 214)

*double recipe

SPOON ROLLS

makes 2 dozen rolls   prep: 15 min.   stand: 5 min.   bake: 20 min.

The batter can be made and stored in your refrigerator for up to one week, covered, for hot-from-the-oven rolls anytime.

1   (¼-oz.) envelope active dry yeast
1   tsp. sugar
2   cups lukewarm water (100° to 110°)
4   cups self-rising flour
¼   cup sugar
¾   cup butter, melted and cooled

1   large egg, lightly beaten
Pinch of salt
2   tsp. dried Italian seasoning
¼   tsp. garlic powder
Cooking spray for baking

[make ahead]

1. Preheat oven to 400°.

2. Combine first 3 ingredients in a large bowl; let mixture stand 5 minutes. Stir in flour and next 6 ingredients until blended. Spoon into muffin pans coated with baking spray, filling two-thirds full.

3. Bake at 400° for 20 minutes or until rolls are golden brown.

EASY YEAST ROLLS

makes 3 dozen   prep: 40 min.   stand: 5 min.   rise: 2 hr.   bake: 15 min.

2   (¼-oz.) envelopes active dry yeast
½   cup warm milk (100° to 110°)
1   cup milk
½   cup sugar
½   cup shortening, melted

2   large eggs, beaten
1   tsp. salt
5½ cups all-purpose flour
½   cup butter, melted and divided

1. Combine yeast and ½ cup warm milk in a 2-cup liquid measuring cup; let stand 5 minutes.
2. Combine yeast mixture, 1 cup milk, sugar, and next 3 ingredients in a large bowl. Gradually add 1 cup flour, stirring until smooth. Gradually stir in enough remaining flour to make a soft dough. Place in a well-greased bowl, turning to grease top of dough.
3. Cover and let rise in a warm place (85°), free from drafts, 1 hour or until doubled in bulk.
4. Turn dough out onto a floured surface; knead 5 or 6 times. Divide dough in half. Roll each dough portion on a lightly floured surface to ¼-inch thickness. Cut with a 2-inch round cutter. Brush rounds evenly with ¼ cup melted butter, and fold in half. Place rolls in 3 lightly greased 9-inch round cake pans.
5. Cover and let rise in a warm place (85°), free from drafts, 1 hour or until doubled in bulk.
6. Preheat oven to 375°.
7. Bake at 375° for 15 to 18 minutes or until golden. Brush with remaining ¼ cup melted butter.

HONEY YEAST ROLLS

makes 28 rolls   prep: 30 min.   stand: 1 hr., 5 min.   cook: 5 min.   rise: 2 hr.   bake: 10 min.

Tender, delectable Honey Yeast Rolls are best served warm from the oven and slathered with sweet honey butter.

¼   cup warm water (100° to 110°)
1   (¼-oz.) envelope active dry yeast
1   tsp. honey
1¾ cups milk
2   large eggs, at room temperature
½   cup butter, melted and cooled

⅓   cup honey
3   tsp. salt
6½ cups all-purpose flour, divided
½   cup butter, softened
¼   cup honey

1. Combine first 3 ingredients in a small bowl, and let stand 5 minutes or until mixture bubbles.
2. Meanwhile, heat milk in a saucepan over medium heat 3 to 5 minutes or until 100° to 110°.

[freeze it]

3. Stir together warm milk, eggs, and next 3 ingredients in bowl of a heavy-duty electric stand mixer, blending well. Add yeast mixture, stirring to combine. Gradually add 5 cups flour, beating at medium speed, using paddle attachment. Beat 3 minutes. Cover with plastic wrap, and let stand 1 hour.

4. Uncover dough, and add remaining 1½ cups flour, beating at medium speed 5 minutes. (Dough will be sticky.) Transfer to a lightly greased large mixing bowl. Cover with plastic wrap, and let rise in a warm place (85°), free from drafts, 1 hour or until doubled in bulk.

5. Punch down dough. Turn dough out on a well-floured surface, and roll into 28 (2½-inch) balls (about ¼ cup dough per ball). Place balls in 4 lightly greased 9-inch pans (7 balls per pan). Cover and let rise in a warm place (85°), free from drafts, 1 hour or until doubled in bulk.

6. Preheat oven to 400°.

7. Stir together ½ cup softened butter and ¼ cup honey.

8. Bake rolls at 400° for 10 to 12 minutes or until golden brown. Brush tops with honey butter. Serve with remaining honey butter.

Note: To freeze, place baked rolls in zip-top plastic freezer bags, and freeze up to two months. Let thaw at room temperature. Reheat, if desired.

Honey How-tos

- Coat your measuring cups and spoons with vegetable cooking spray to make it easy for honey to slide out when pouring.
- Store honey at room temperature. If it crystallizes, remove lid, and place in a container of hot water until crystals dissolve.
- When substituting honey for sugar in a recipe, reduce any liquid by ¼ cup and add a teaspoon of baking soda for each cup of honey used.
- Also reduce oven temperature by 25° to prevent overbrowning.

TASTE OF THE SOUTH

Hot Cross Buns We started our quest for the best bun with a quick Internet search. We found the verses to the nursery rhyme—"One a penny, Two a penny, Hot Cross Buns." Another site reminded us that they were sold by street vendors in the movie *Oliver*, based on Dickens's novel. One told of an English widow who baked them each Good Friday in hopes her lost sailor son would return home. And some accounts point to the buns as part of pagan rituals each spring. Many Southerners serve these buns during the Lenten season in recognition of the death and resurrection of Christ. Your family can decide what meaning to ascribe to this fine bread.

HOT CROSS BUNS

makes 20 buns   prep: 50 min.   cook: 5 min.   cool: 20 min.   rise: 2 hr.   bake: 15 min.

pictured on page 84

4 ½ to 5 cups all-purpose flour, divided
⅔ cup sugar
1   (¼-oz.) envelope rapid-rise yeast
1   tsp. salt
¾ tsp. ground nutmeg
½ tsp. ground cinnamon
1   cup milk
⅓ cup unsalted butter, cut up

2   large eggs
Vegetable cooking spray
⅔ cup currants
⅓ cup golden raisins
1   Tbsp. all-purpose flour
1   egg white, lightly beaten
Hint of Lemon Icing

1. Combine 2½ cups flour, sugar, and next 4 ingredients in the mixing bowl of a heavy-duty stand mixer, stirring well. Set aside.

2. Combine milk, ¼ cup water, and butter pieces in a saucepan; cook over medium heat, stirring constantly, just until butter melts. Cool 5 minutes (to 130°).

3. Pour milk mixture into flour mixture, and beat at low speed with dough hook attachment 2 minutes or until dry ingredients are moistened. Increase speed to medium; add eggs, 1 at

a time, beating just until yellow disappears after each addition. Beat 3 more minutes. Reduce speed to low, and gradually beat in enough remaining flour (up to 2½ cups) to make a soft dough (dough will be sticky). Beat at medium speed with dough hook attachment 5 minutes.

4. Scrape dough into a bowl coated with cooking spray, and lightly spray the top of the dough.

5. Cover and let rise in a warm place (85°), free from drafts, 1 hour. (Dough will almost double in bulk.) Punch dough down, and turn out onto a floured surface. Combine ⅔ cup currants, ⅓ cup raisins, and 1 Tbsp. flour, stirring to coat. Knead about one-fourth of fruit mixture at a time into dough until all fruit mixture is evenly dispersed.

6. Divide dough into 20 equal portions; shape each portion into a 2-inch ball. Evenly space dough balls on a parchment paper-lined 15- x 10-inch jelly-roll pan; cover and let rise in a warm place (85°), free from drafts, 1 hour or until doubled in bulk. Gently brush tops with beaten egg white.

7. Preheat oven to 375°.

8. Bake at 375° for 15 minutes or until buns are a deep golden brown and sound hollow when tapped. Cool buns 15 minutes in pan on a wire rack.

9. Spoon icing into a zip-top plastic freezer bag; snip a ¼-inch piece from corner of bag, and pipe an "X" on top of warm buns, forming a cross. Serve remaining icing with buns, if desired.

Hint of Lemon Frosting

makes ½ cup   prep: 5 min.

2   cups powdered sugar

1   Tbsp. butter

3   Tbsp. milk

½   tsp. grated lemon rind

¼   tsp. vanilla extract

1. Whisk together all ingredients.

Rising Success

• It's okay to let dough rise in a glass, metal, or pottery bowl. Spray the top of the dough with vegetable cooking spray to prevent the dough from drying out and crusting, which could inhibit rising.

• Your oven is the ideal warm, draft-free place for the dough. Heat the oven, and then turn it off. Allow oven to cool to 85° or below. Put dough in oven, along with a cup of hot water to add moisture and keep the dough soft. Leave on the oven light, and close the door.

DOUBLE WHAMMIE YEAST ROLLS

makes 1 dozen   prep: 25 min.   cook: 5 min.   stand: 5 min.   rise: 2 hr.   bake: 15 min.

This recipe was a finalist in the 2005 Southern Living Cook-Off. *The double whammy comes from using beer and potato buds in the recipe.*

⅔ cup sugar, divided

⅓ cup butter

1 cup milk

¼ cup dried instant potato buds

1¼ tsp. salt

2 (¼-oz.) envelopes active dry yeast

¼ cup beer, at room temperature

1 large egg, lightly beaten

4½ cups bread flour, divided

Butter (optional)

1. Remove and reserve 1 Tbsp. sugar. Cook remaining sugar, ⅓ cup butter, and next 3 ingredients in a medium saucepan over medium-low heat, stirring constantly, until butter melts. Cool to 110°.

2. Stir together yeast, beer, and reserved 1 Tbsp. sugar in a 2-cup liquid measuring cup; let stand 5 minutes.

3. Combine milk mixture and yeast mixture in a large bowl; stir in egg. Gradually stir in 4 cups flour to form a dough. (Dough will be very stiff.)

4. Turn dough out onto a lightly floured surface, and knead, adding additional flour (up to ½ cup) as needed, until smooth and elastic (about 6 to 8 minutes). Place in a bowl coated with cooking spray, turning to coat top of dough. Cover and let rise in a warm place (85°), free from drafts, 1 hour or until doubled in bulk.

5. Coat muffin pans with cooking spray. Punch dough down, and shape dough into 36 (1-inch) balls. Place 3 dough balls in each muffin cup. (Handle the dough as little as possible to prevent overkneading.) Cover and let rise in a warm place, free from drafts, 1 hour.

6. Preheat oven to 350°.

7. Bake at 350° for 15 to 18 minutes or until golden. Place a small pat of butter on top of each roll after baking 5 minutes, or brush with melted butter after baking, if desired.

ITALIAN BREAD

makes 1 loaf   prep: 15 min.   stand: 15 min.   rise: 30 min.   bake: 16 min.

A heavy-duty electric stand mixer with a dough hook makes this yeast bread extra easy. If you don't have a heavy-duty mixer, just mix the dough by hand, and knead on a lightly floured surface for 8 to 10 minutes.

1 (¼-oz.) envelope active dry yeast	2 to 3 cups bread flour
1 tsp. sugar	2 Tbsp. olive oil
1 cup warm water (100° to 110°)	1 tsp. salt

1. Combine yeast, sugar, and 1 cup warm water in bowl of a heavy-duty electric stand mixer; let stand 5 minutes. Add 2 cups flour, oil, and salt to bowl, and beat at low speed, using dough hook attachment, 1 minute. Gradually add additional flour until dough begins to leave the sides of the bowl and pull together. (**Note:** The dough will take on a "shaggy" appearance as the flour is being added. When enough flour has been added, the dough will look soft and smooth, not wet and sticky or overly dry with a rough surface.)

2. Increase speed to medium, and beat 5 minutes. Cover bowl of dough with plastic wrap, and let stand in a warm place (85°), free from drafts, 30 minutes or until doubled in bulk. Punch dough down, and let stand 10 minutes.

3. Preheat oven to 400°.

4. Turn dough out onto a lightly floured surface; shape dough into a 12-inch loaf, and place on a lightly greased baking sheet. Cut 3 (¼-inch-deep) slits across top of dough with a sharp paring knife. (The slits release interior steam and prevent the loaf from blowing apart at the side.)

5. Bake at 400° for 16 minutes or until golden brown. Cool on a wire rack.

Herbed Focaccia: Proceed with recipe as directed, shaping dough into a ball instead of a loaf. Roll dough into an 14- x 11-inch rectangle on a lightly greased baking sheet. Press handle of a wooden spoon into dough to make indentations at 1-inch intervals. Drizzle dough evenly with 1 Tbsp. olive oil; sprinkle evenly with 1 tsp. dried Italian seasoning. Bake at 475° for 12 to 15 minutes or until golden brown.

Pizza Crust: Proceed with recipe as directed, shaping dough into a ball instead of a loaf. Roll dough into an 14- x 11-inch rectangle on a lightly greased baking sheet. Drizzle with olive oil, or spread with pesto or pizza sauce, and sprinkle with desired toppings. Bake at 475° for 20 to 25 minutes.

PUMPERNICKEL BREAD

makes 1 loaf   prep: 20 min.   stand: 5 min.   rise: 30 min.   bake: 30 min.

Try this heavenly bread prepared as round loaves, mini rolls, or loaded with crunchy and chewy fillings.

1¾ cups warm water (100° to 110°)

1   (¼-oz.) envelope rapid-rise yeast

2   Tbsp. sugar

2   Tbsp. instant coffee granules

¼   cup molasses

4½ cups bread flour

1   cup rye flour

2   tsp. salt

Vegetable cooking spray

2   Tbsp. butter, melted

1. Preheat oven to 200°. Stir together first 3 ingredients in the mixing bowl of a heavy-duty electric stand mixer. Let stand 5 minutes.

2. Add coffee and next 4 ingredients to yeast mixture. Beat at low speed with dough hook attachment for 1 minute or until soft dough comes together. Beat at medium speed 4 minutes. (Dough will be slightly sticky.)

3. Turn dough out onto a lightly floured surface; shape dough into a 9- x 5-inch oval loaf. Place on a parchment paper-lined baking sheet; coat dough lightly with cooking spray, and cover loosely with plastic wrap. Turn oven off, and place loaf in oven. Let rise 30 minutes or until loaf is doubled in bulk. Remove loaf from oven. Remove and discard plastic wrap.

4. Preheat oven to 375°.

5. Bake bread for 30 to 35 minutes. Remove from oven, and brush with melted butter. Cool on wire rack.

German-Style Pumpernickel Rolls: Pat dough into a 10-inch square (½ inch thick). Cut into 2-inch squares. Roll into 1½-inch balls, and place on a parchment paper-lined baking sheet. Proceed with recipe as directed. Bake at 375° for 10 to 12 minutes or until lightly browned. Makes 25 rolls.

Walnut-Raisin Pumpernickel Boule: Add ¾ cup raisins (or golden raisins) and 1 cup coarsely chopped toasted walnuts to dough before mixing. Shape dough into a ball, and gently flatten into a 7-inch circle. Cut 3 slits in dough (¼ to ½ inch deep) with a sharp paring knife just before baking, if desired. Whisk together 1 egg white and 3 Tbsp. water in a small bowl; brush loaf with egg mixture. Bake at 375° for 38 minutes or until a wooden pick inserted in center comes out clean. Omit brushing on melted butter. Makes 1 loaf.

Sour-Rye Pumpernickel Bread: The Sour Starter gives this bold bread a subtle tangy flavor. Reduce water to 1 cup. Add 2 Tbsp. browning and seasoning sauce and 1 cup Sour Starter to dough; mix with dough hook attachment at medium-high speed with heavy duty stand mixer 5 minutes. Proceed with recipe as directed.

Note: We tested with Kitchen Bouquet sauce.

Sour Starter

Sourdough starters may be stored at room temperature indefinitely, as long as you "feed" the starter with water and flour. In fact, some sourdough starters are more than 20 years old.

3½ cups bread flour
1   cup rye flour

1   (¼-oz.) envelope active dry yeast

1. Whisk together bread flour, rye flour, yeast, and 8 cups water in a large bowl. Cover tightly with plastic wrap. Store at room temperature. You may use after 1 day at room temperature. Add 1 cup warm water, 1 cup bread flour, and ½ cup rye flour every other day. Discard unfed Sour Starter if you don't intend to use it after a few days. Makes 12 cups.

Rising Success

Letting the dough rise in a place that is warm enough—but not too warm—will ensure the best results for any yeast bread recipe. Try this tip from our Test Kitchen.

Place a cake pan filled with water on the bottom rack of the oven. Preheat oven to 200°. Turn off oven, and partially open door.

Let cool 20 minutes. Place loaves in oven on middle shelf, and let rise as directed with the oven door closed.

HONEY-OATMEAL WHEAT BREAD

makes 2 loaves, 12 slices per loaf   prep: 25 min.   stand: 5 min.   rise: 1 hr., 45 min.
bake: 30 min.   cool: 10 min.

This recipe makes two loaves, so freeze one after cooling to help it stay fresh longer. Slice first, if desired; then wrap the loaf in plastic wrap and aluminum foil, and place in a zip-top plastic freezer bag. Keep frozen for up to one month.

2	cups warm water (100° to 110°)	1	cup uncooked regular oats
3	Tbsp. molasses	1	Tbsp. salt
1	(¼-oz.) envelope active dry yeast	¼	cup honey
3	cups all-purpose flour, divided	3	Tbsp. olive oil
2½	cups whole wheat flour	6	Tbsp. all-purpose flour

1. Combine first 3 ingredients in a 2-cup glass measuring cup; let yeast mixture stand 5 minutes.

2. Combine 2 cups all-purpose flour, whole wheat flour, oats, and salt.

3. Beat yeast mixture, 1 cup all-purpose flour, honey, and olive oil at medium speed with a heavy-duty electric stand mixer until well blended. Gradually add whole wheat flour mixture, beating at low speed until a soft dough forms.

4. Turn out dough onto a well-floured surface, and knead 9 minutes, adding additional all-purpose flour (up to 6 Tbsp.) as needed. (Dough will be slightly sticky.) Place dough in a large bowl sprayed with vegetable cooking spray, turning to grease top of dough.

5. Cover bowl of dough with plastic wrap, and let dough rise in a warm place (85°), free from drafts, 1 hour or until doubled in bulk.

6. Punch down dough, and divide in half. Roll each portion into a 13- x 8-inch rectangle on a lightly floured surface. Roll up each dough rectangle, jelly-roll fashion, starting at 1 short side; pinch ends to seal. Place loaves, seam sides down, into 2 (8 ½- x 4 ½-inch) loaf pans sprayed with cooking spray.

7. Cover loosely with plastic wrap, and let rise in a warm place (85°), free from drafts, 45 minutes or until almost doubled in bulk. Remove and discard plastic wrap.

8. Preheat oven to 350°. Bake at 350° for 30 to 35 minutes or until loaves sound hollow when tapped and are golden. Cool in pans on wire racks 10 minutes. Remove loaves from pans; cool on wire racks.

Note: If you don't have a heavy-duty electric stand mixer, mix dough with a wooden spoon.

Per slice: Calories 150; Fat 2.4g (sat 0.3g, mono 1.4g, poly 0.4g); Protein 4g; Carb 29.2g; Fiber 2.4g; Iron 1.6mg; Sodium 297mg; Calc 14mg

SOUTHERN SODA BREAD

makes 2 loaves   prep: 15 min.   bake: 1 hr., 15 min.   cool: 1 hr., 10 min.

Southern Soda Bread is a twist on the Irish classic. Serve it warm from the oven with a cup of tea or to accompany a meal. We especially love it toasted and served with jam or honey butter.

[test kitchen favorite]

4½ cups all-purpose flour
⅔ cup sugar
4½ tsp. baking powder
1½ tsp. baking soda

1½ tsp. salt
3 cups buttermilk
3 large eggs, lightly beaten
4½ Tbsp. butter, melted

1. Preheat oven to 350°.

2. Whisk together first 5 ingredients in a large bowl. Make a well in center of mixture. Add buttermilk, eggs, and butter, whisking just until thoroughly blended. (Batter should be almost smooth.) Pour batter into 2 lightly greased 8½- x 4½-inch loaf pans.

3. Bake at 350° for 45 minutes. Rotate pans in oven, and shield with aluminum foil. Bake 30 to 35 minutes or until a long wooden pick inserted in center comes out clean. Cool in pans on a wire rack 10 minutes. Carefully run a knife along edges of bread to loosen from pans. Remove from pans, and cool completely on a wire rack (about 1 hour).

inspirations for your taste

Who says you can't have fresh-tasting bread in 20 minutes flat? Treat the whole family with "Mom's secret recipe" tonight.

Easy Garlic Rolls

makes 4 to 6 servings   prep: 10 min.   cook: 1 min.   bake: 7 min.

Preheat oven to 400°. Cut 4 artisan rolls in half horizontally. Melt ½ cup butter in a small saucepan over medium-low heat. Add 2 minced garlic cloves and ¼ to ½ tsp. dried Italian seasoning, and cook, stirring constantly, 1 to 2 minutes or until fragrant. Brush butter mixture on cut sides of bread. Place bread, cut sides up, on a lightly greased baking sheet. Bake 7 to 8 minutes or until lightly toasted.

Note: We tested with Chicago hard rolls from Publix. You could also use French bread rolls, a sliced French bread baguette, or any other small rolls from your grocery store.

ITALIAN BREAD KNOTS

makes 12 servings   prep: 5 min.   cook: 15 min.

2½ Tbsp. butter, melted

¼ tsp. dried Italian seasoning

1 (11-oz.) can refrigerated breadsticks

1 Tbsp. Parmesan cheese

1. Preheat oven to 350°.

2. Stir together melted butter and Italian seasoning until blended.

3. Unroll breadsticks. Separate each dough portion. Loosely tie each portion into a knot, and place, 1 inch apart, on an ungreased baking sheet. Brush evenly with butter mixture, and sprinkle with cheese.

4. Bake at 350° for 15 minutes or until breadsticks are golden.

EASY THREE-SEED PAN ROLLS

makes 9 rolls   prep: 10 min.   rise: 3 hr.   bake: 15 min.   **pictured on page 83**

The initial cost for these rolls is money well spent. You can make three scrumptious batches from the ingredients.

4 tsp. fennel seeds

4 tsp. poppy seeds

4 tsp. sesame seeds

9 frozen bread dough rolls

1 egg white, beaten

Melted butter

1. Combine first 3 ingredients in a small bowl. Dip dough rolls, 1 at a time, in egg white; roll in seed mixture. Arrange rolls, 1 inch apart, in a lightly greased 8-inch pan. Cover with lightly greased plastic wrap, and let rise in a warm place (85°), free from drafts, 3 to 4 hours or until doubled in bulk.

2. Preheat oven to 350°.

3. Uncover rolls, and bake at 350° for 15 minutes or until golden. Brush with melted butter.

Note: We tested with Rhodes White Dinner Rolls for frozen rolls.

Three-Seed French Bread: Substitute 1 (11-oz.) can refrigerated French bread dough for frozen bread dough rolls. Combine seeds in a shallow dish. Brush dough loaf with egg white. Roll top and sides of dough loaf in seeds. Place, seam side down, on a baking sheet. Bake and cut dough loaf according to package directions.

Use your favorite flavor of ice cream to make this fun bread. We started with vanilla and branched out to dozens of others—from delicately flavored strawberry to bold and earthy black walnut. We especially liked butter pecan and rum raisin. Premium ice creams yielded the richest taste and texture, but less expensive brands were also delicious in this recipe. We experimented with several low-fat ice creams, but we were disappointed with the results.

ICE-CREAM BREAD

makes 1 (8-inch) loaf   prep: 5 min.   bake: 40 min.

This two-ingredient bread is terrific any time of day. Pop it in the oven while you're preparing supper, or serve it for afternoon tea. If you are lucky enough to have leftovers, toast a few slices for breakfast, and serve with butter and jam.

1   **pt. (2 cups) ice cream, softened**   **1½ cups self-rising flour**

1. Preheat oven to 350°. Stir together ice cream and flour, stirring just until flour is moistened. Spoon batter into a greased and floured 8- x 4-inch loaf pan.
2. Bake at 350° for 40 to 45 minutes or until a wooden pick inserted in center of bread comes out clean. Remove from pan, and cool on a wire rack.

Note: Batter may also be divided evenly between 2 greased and floured 5- x 3-inch loaf pans. Bake at 350° for 20 minutes or until a wooden pick inserted in center of bread comes out clean.

quick

CORNBREAD CROUTONS

makes about 6 cups   prep: 10 min.   bake: 20 min.   cool: 10 min.

Blue cheese adds a delicious depth of flavor to these contemporary croutons. Make up to one month in advance, and store in an airtight container.

[*make ahead*]

1 cup all-purpose flour	1 large egg
1 cup yellow cornmeal	½ cup milk
1 Tbsp. sugar	¼ cup vegetable oil
2 tsp. baking powder	1 (4-oz.) container crumbled blue cheese
¼ tsp. salt	½ cup canned whole kernel corn, drained

1. Preheat oven to 400°.

2. Combine first 5 ingredients in a medium bowl.

3. Whisk together egg, milk, and oil. Stir egg mixture into flour mixture just until smooth; fold in blue cheese and corn. (Batter will be thick.) Spread mixture in an even layer (about 1 inch thick) in a greased 8-inch square pan.

4. Bake at 400° for 12 to 15 minutes or until golden brown. Cool in pan on a wire rack for 10 minutes. Remove cornbread from pan; place on rack to cool completely.

5. Cut cornbread into 1-inch cubes; place in a single layer on a baking sheet. Bake at 400° for 8 minutes, turning once after 4 minutes. Remove from oven, and let cool.

Kitchen Express Cornbread Croutons: Stir together 1 (6-oz.) package yellow cornbread mix, 1 large egg, and ⅔ cup milk. Fold in 1 (4-oz.) container crumbled blue cheese and ½ cup canned whole kernel corn, drained. Pour into a greased 8-inch square pan. Bake at 375° for 12 to 15 minutes or until golden brown. Cool in pan on a wire rack 10 minutes; remove from pan, and place on rack to cool completely. Cut cornbread into 1-inch cubes; place cubes in a single layer on a baking sheet. Bake at 400° for 8 minutes, turning once. Remove from oven; let cool.

CREOLE CROUTONS

makes about 8 cups   prep: 10 min.   cook: 30 min.

5   (1-inch-thick) white bread slices, cubed
¼   cup freshly grated Parmesan cheese

¼   cup butter, melted
½   Tbsp. Creole seasoning

1. Preheat oven to 300°.
2. Combine all ingredients in a large zip-top plastic freezer bag; seal bag, and shake to coat.
3. Arrange seasoned bread cubes in an even layer on an aluminum foil-lined baking sheet.
4. Bake at 300° for 30 minutes or until croutons are crisp and golden.

SWEET CROUTONS

makes 3 cups   prep: 5 min.   cook: 8 min.

These crunchy treats taste great in pumpkin soup, squash soup, or mixed in a salad.

4   cups French bread cubes
3   Tbsp. butter or margarine, melted

¼   cup sugar
½   tsp. ground cinnamon

1. Preheat oven to 375°.
2. Toss together bread cubes and melted butter. Combine sugar and cinnamon; add to bread cubes, tossing to coat. Spread in a single layer on a lightly greased baking sheet.
3. Bake at 375°, stirring occasionally, for 8 to 10 minutes or until golden brown.

Your family will definitely want to rise, shine, and dine when they smell these fresh rolls baking in the oven.

Easy Orange Rolls

makes 11 rolls   prep: 15 min.   bake: 25 min.

Preheat oven to 375°. Beat ½ (8-oz.) package softened cream cheese, ¼ cup firmly packed light brown sugar, and 1½ tsp. orange zest at medium speed with an electric mixer until smooth. Unroll 1 (11-oz.) can refrigerated French bread dough onto a lightly floured surface. Spread cream cheese mixture over dough, leaving a ¼-inch border. Sprinkle with 2 Tbsp. granulated sugar. Gently roll up dough, starting at 1 long side. Cut into 11 (1¼-inch) slices. Place slices in a lightly greased 8-inch round cake pan. Brush top of dough with 1 Tbsp. melted butter. Bake 25 to 30 minutes or until golden. Stir together ½ cup powdered sugar and 1 Tbsp. orange juice in a small bowl until smooth. Drizzle over hot rolls. Serve immediately.

Note: We tested with Pillsbury Crusty French Loaf.

ORANGE ROLLS

makes 24 servings   prep: 30 min.   stand: 5 min.   rise: 2 hr., 30 min.   bake: 20 min.   cool: 2 min.

The rolls need rising time, so plan this recipe for a weekend or a day off.

1 (¼-oz.) envelope active dry yeast	1 Tbsp. fresh lemon juice
1 tsp. sugar	4½ cups bread flour
¼ cup warm water (100° to 110°)	¼ tsp. ground nutmeg
½ cup butter, softened	¼ to ½ cup bread flour
½ cup sugar	Honey Topping
1 tsp. salt	1 cup coarsely chopped pecans (optional)
2 large eggs, lightly beaten	Fresh Orange Glaze
1 cup milk	

1. Combine first 3 ingredients in a 1-cup glass measuring cup; let stand 5 minutes.

2. Beat butter at medium speed with a heavy-duty electric stand mixer using the paddle attachment until creamy. Gradually add ½ cup sugar and salt, beating at medium speed until light and fluffy. Add eggs, milk, and lemon juice, beating until blended. Stir in yeast mixture.

3. Combine 4½ cups bread flour and nutmeg. Gradually add to butter mixture, beating at low speed 2 minutes or until well blended.

4. Turn dough out onto a surface floured with about ¼ cup bread flour; knead for 5 minutes, adding additional bread flour as needed. Place dough in a lightly greased large bowl, turning to grease top of dough. Cover and let rise in a warm place (85°), free from drafts, 1½ to 2 hours or until doubled in bulk.

5. Punch dough down; turn out onto a lightly floured surface. Divide dough in half. Divide 1 dough half into 12 equal pieces; shape each piece, rolling between hands, into a 7- to 8-inch-long rope. Wrap each rope into a coil, firmly pinching end to seal. Place rolls in a lightly greased 10-inch round cake pan. Repeat procedure with remaining dough half. Drizzle half of Honey Topping evenly over each pan of rolls.

6. Let rise, uncovered, in a warm place 1 hour or until doubled in bulk. Top evenly with pecans, if desired.

7. Preheat oven to 350°.

8. Bake at 350° for 20 to 22 minutes or until rolls are lightly browned. Cool rolls 2 minutes in pans. Spoon half of Fresh Orange Glaze evenly over each pan of warm rolls, and serve immediately.

Honey Topping

makes 1⅓ cups   prep: 5 min.

1⅓ cups powdered sugar
½ cup butter, melted

¼ cup honey
2 egg whites

1. Stir together all ingredients until smooth.

Fresh Orange Glaze

makes ¾ cup   prep: 10 min.

2 cups powdered sugar
2 Tbsp. butter, softened
2 tsp. orange zest

3 Tbsp. fresh orange juice
1 Tbsp. fresh lemon juice

1. Beat powdered sugar and butter at medium speed with an electric mixer until blended. Add remaining ingredients, and beat until smooth.

No food processor? No problem. You can make these the old-fashioned way—kneading them by hand.

To prepare the recipe without a food processor, omit Steps 1 and 2, and proceed as follows.

1. Stir together yeast, ½ cup warm water (100° to 110°), and 1 tsp. sugar in a 1-cup glass measuring cup; let stand 5 minutes.

2. Combine yeast mixture and ½ cup flour in a mixing bowl; stir vigorously until mixture is well blended. Gradually add mashed sweet potatoes, next 7 ingredients, and 4½ cups flour, stirring until well blended after each addition.

3. Turn dough out onto a well-floured surface, and knead in remaining ½ cup flour. Continue to knead until smooth and elastic (about 4 to 5 minutes). Proceed with recipe as directed, beginning with Step 3.

SWEET POTATO CINNAMON ROLLS

makes 12 rolls   prep: 30 min.   stand: 5 min   rise: 1 hr., 30 min.   bake: 17 min.
cool: 20 min.   **pictured on page 158**

You can make this dough the night before and let it rise overnight in the refrigerator. To prevent some of the Glaze from spilling over, put an aluminum foil-lined baking sheet on the rack below the pan while baking.

2 (¼-oz.) envelopes active dry yeast	½ cup sugar
½ cup warm water (100° to 110°)	¼ cup melted butter
1 tsp. sugar	2 Tbsp. orange zest
5½ cups all-purpose flour	1½ tsp. salt
1 cup mashed sweet potatoes	1 tsp. baking soda
1 large egg, lightly beaten	Filling
1 cup buttermilk	Glaze

1. Pulse first 3 ingredients in a large-capacity (11-cup) food processor 4 times or just until combined, using the metal blade. Remove metal blade, scraping yeast mixture into food processor bowl. Let stand 5 minutes.

2. Insert short plastic dough blade; add ½ cup flour to processor bowl, and process 2 minutes. Add mashed sweet potatoes, next 7 ingredients, and 4 cups flour; process 2 minutes. Add remaining 1 cup flour, and process 30 seconds or until a dough forms, coming together to hold a shape. (Dough will be sticky.)

3. Place dough in a large bowl coated with cooking spray. Cover with plastic wrap, and let rise in a warm place (85°), free from drafts, 1 hour to 1 hour and 30 minutes or until doubled in bulk.

4. Punch dough down. Turn dough out onto a well-floured surface, and roll into a 18- x 10-inch rectangle. Spread evenly with Filling, leaving a 1-inch border. Roll up dough, jelly-roll fashion, starting at 1 long side. Cut into 12 (1½-inch) slices, and arrange in a lightly greased 13- x 9-inch baking pan. Cover with plastic wrap, and let rise in a warm place (85°), free from drafts, 30 minutes.

5. Preheat oven to 400°.

6. Bake rolls at 400° for 10 minutes. Remove rolls from oven; drizzle about ½ cup Glaze slowly over rolls, starting at 1 edge of pan and drizzling in a circular pattern; let glaze soak in. Repeat procedure with remaining Glaze.

7. Bake rolls 7 to 10 more minutes or until lightly browned and a wooden pick inserted in center comes out clean.

8. Remove rolls from oven, and invert onto an aluminum foil-lined baking sheet. Invert again, glaze side up, onto a serving platter. Let cool 20 to 30 minutes. Serve warm.

Filling

makes 2½ cups   prep: 5 min.

¾ cup melted butter	1 cup chopped toasted pecans
2 cups firmly packed light brown sugar	2 Tbsp. ground cinnamon

1. Stir together all ingredients until blended.

Glaze

makes 1½ cups   prep: 10 min.   cook: 5 min.

1 cup firmly packed light brown sugar	½ cup whipping cream
⅓ cup light corn syrup	1 tsp. vanilla extract
¼ cup butter	

1. Stir together sugar, corn syrup, and butter in a small saucepan over medium heat. Bring to a light boil, stirring constantly. Remove from heat, and stir in cream and vanilla.

BREAKFAST & BRUNCH

"I've long said that if I were about to be executed and were given a choice of my last meal, it would be bacon and eggs." —James Beard

CREAM CHEESE SCRAMBLED EGGS

makes 4 to 6 servings   prep: 10 min.   cook: 6 min.

We used a heat-resistant spatula in preparing the eggs. A turning spatula will work too. This dish is great for Southern brunches—and also makes a tasty supper.

8 large eggs	1 Tbsp. butter
¼ cup milk	1 (3-oz.) package cream cheese, cut into cubes
½ tsp. salt	⅓ cup chopped fresh basil (optional)
½ tsp. pepper	Garnish: fresh basil sprigs

1. Whisk together first 4 ingredients.

2. Melt butter in a large nonstick skillet over medium heat; add egg mixture, and cook, without stirring, until eggs begin to set on bottom. Sprinkle cream cheese cubes evenly over egg mixture; draw a spatula across bottom of skillet to form large curds.

3. Cook until eggs are thickened but still moist. (Do not stir constantly.) Remove from heat. Stir in chopped basil before serving, if desired, and garnish, if desired.

Note: To lighten, substitute 2 cups egg substitute for eggs and 3 oz. light cream cheese for 3 oz. regular cream cheese. Proceed as directed.

Sausage-Egg Soft Tacos: Prepare Cream Cheese Scrambled Eggs as directed, substituting 1 seeded and chopped jalapeño pepper for chopped basil. Sprinkle 6 (8-inch) flour tortillas evenly with 1½ cups shredded colby-Jack cheese. Top one-half of each tortilla evenly with Cream Cheese Scrambled Eggs and 1 (16-oz.) package cooked, drained, and crumbled ground pork sausage. Sprinkle evenly with ½ cup shredded colby-Jack cheese. Fold tortillas over filling. Serve with sour cream and salsa. Makes 6 servings. Prep: 20 min., Cook: 15 min.

Best Scrambled Eggs

These creamy curds need no adornment other than seasoning. Take care not to stir them too much while they cook. Simply draw a heat-resistant spatula through egg mixture as it begins to set on the bottom, forming large curds. Continue until eggs are thickened but still moist; do not stir constantly, or they'll become dry and crumbly.

SAUSAGE-AND-SCRAMBLED EGG PIZZA

makes 8 servings   prep: 5 min   bake: 18 min.   cook: 16 min.

A jar of salsa and Mexican cheese blend add a Southwest flair to this sure-to-please recipe.

1 (13.8-oz.) can refrigerated pizza crust
1 lb. hot ground pork sausage
6 large eggs, lightly beaten
½ tsp. seasoned pepper

1 (16-oz.) jar salsa
1 (8-oz.) package shredded Mexican four-cheese blend
Sour cream (optional)

1. Preheat oven to 425°. Unroll refrigerated pizza crust, and press into a lightly greased 15- x 10-inch jelly-roll pan.

2. Bake at 425° for 6 to 8 minutes. Remove from oven, and set aside.

3. Brown ground sausage in a large nonstick skillet, stirring until it crumbles and is no longer pink. Drain and pat dry with paper towels; set aside. Wipe skillet clean.

4. Whisk together eggs and seasoned pepper. Cook in a lightly greased skillet over medium heat, without stirring, until eggs begin to set on bottom. Draw a spatula across bottom of skillet to form large curds. Continue cooking until eggs are thickened but still moist. (Do not stir constantly.) Remove skillet from heat.

5. Spoon and spread salsa evenly over partially baked crust; top evenly with sausage, scrambled eggs, and cheese.

6. Bake at 425° for 12 minutes or until crust is deep golden brown. Serve with sour cream, if desired.

Note: To lighten, substitute 1 (12-oz.) package reduced-fat ground pork sausage, and prepare as directed. Substitute 1½ cups egg substitute for eggs, and whisk together with seasoned pepper, ¼ tsp. hot sauce, and, if desired, ⅛ tsp. salt. Cook as directed. Substitute 1 (8-oz.) package reduced-fat Mexican four-cheese blend. Assemble and bake as directed. Serve with reduced-fat sour cream, if desired.

ENGLISH MUFFIN BREAKFAST STRATA

makes 8 servings prep: 20 min. chill: 8 hr. bake: 40 min. stand: 10 min.

This simple casserole is like a quiche, except it's held together with bread instead of a crust. Serve this with fruit for a tasty breakfast.

1 (16-oz.) package ground pork sausage

1 (12-oz.) package English muffins, split and buttered

1 (10-oz.) block sharp Cheddar cheese, shredded

1 (8-oz.) block mozzarella cheese, shredded

8 large eggs

1½ cups sour cream

1 (4-oz.) can chopped green chiles, drained

1. Cook sausage in a skillet, stirring until it crumbles and is no longer pink; drain on paper towels, and set aside.

2. Cut muffin halves into quarters, and arrange in an even layer in a lightly greased 13- x 9-inch baking dish.

3. Sprinkle half each of sausage, Cheddar cheese, and mozzarella cheese evenly over muffins.

4. Whisk together eggs, sour cream, and chiles in a large bowl; pour evenly over sausage and cheeses. Top with remaining sausage and cheeses. Cover and chill 8 hours.

5. Preheat oven to 350°.

6. Bake at 350° for 40 minutes. Let stand 10 minutes before serving.

SOUTHWEST BREAKFAST STRATA

makes 6 to 8 servings prep: 15 min. cook: 25 min. bake: 30 min.

This recipe received our highest rating. You can prepare it the night before and pop it in the oven just before breakfast. Let stand at room temperature 20 minutes before baking.

1 lb. mild ground pork sausage

1 small onion, chopped

½ green bell pepper, chopped

2 (10-oz.) cans diced tomatoes and green chiles

8 (10-inch) flour tortillas, torn into bite-size pieces

3 cups (12 oz.) shredded colby-Jack cheese blend

6 large eggs

2 cups milk

1 tsp. salt

½ tsp. pepper

1. Cook sausage in a large skillet over medium-high heat, stirring until it crumbles and is no longer pink. Drain and return to skillet.

2. Add chopped onion and bell pepper to sausage in skillet, and sauté over medium-high heat 5 minutes or until vegetables are tender. Stir in tomatoes and green chiles; reduce heat, and simmer 10 minutes.

make ahead

3. Layer half each of tortilla pieces, sausage mixture, and cheese in a lightly greased 13- x 9-inch baking dish. Repeat layers.

4. Whisk together eggs, milk, salt, and pepper; pour over layers in baking dish. Cover and chill up to 8 hours, if desired.

5. Preheat oven to 350°. Bake, lightly covered with aluminum foil, at 350° for 30 minutes or until golden and bubbly.

BRIE-AND-VEGGIE BREAKFAST STRATA

makes 8 to 10 servings   prep: 30 min.   cook: 10 min.   chill: 8 hr.   bake: 45 min.

pictured on page 160

1 large sweet onion, halved and thinly sliced	1 cup (4 oz.) shredded Parmesan cheese
1 large red bell pepper, diced	8 large eggs
1 large Yukon gold potato, peeled and diced	3 cups milk
2 Tbsp. olive oil	2 Tbsp. Dijon mustard
1 (8-oz.) Brie round*	1 tsp. seasoned salt
1 (12-oz.) package sourdough bread loaf, cubed	1 tsp. pepper

[make ahead]

1. Sauté first 3 ingredients in hot oil 10 to 12 minutes or just until vegetables are tender and onion slices begin to turn golden.

2. Trim and discard rind from Brie. Cut cheese into ½-inch cubes.

3. Layer a lightly greased 13- x 9-inch baking dish with half each of bread cubes, onion mixture, Brie cubes, and Parmesan cheese.

4. Whisk together eggs and next 4 ingredients; pour half of egg mixture evenly over cheeses. Repeat layers once. Cover and chill at least 8 hours or up to 24 hours.

5. Preheat oven to 350°.

6. Bake at 350° for 45 to 50 minutes or until lightly browned on top and set in center.

* 2 cups (8 oz.) shredded Swiss cheese may be substituted.

HAM-AND-BACON QUICHE

makes 6 to 8 servings   prep: 20 min.   bake: 1 hr.   cook: 10 min.   stand: 10 min.

When you need a meal that's family-friendly yet special enough for entertaining, try quiche. This version blends a familiar duo into one delicious dish and will be a popular addition to your recipe book.

1 (15-oz.) package refrigerated piecrusts	1 cup chopped cooked ham
1 egg white, lightly beaten	6 large eggs, lightly beaten
6 bacon slices	½ tsp. seasoning salt
½ cup chopped onion	½ tsp. pepper
1 cup sliced fresh mushrooms	2 cups (8 oz.) shredded Swiss cheese
1½ cups half-and-half	2 Tbsp. all-purpose flour

1. Fit 1 piecrust into a 9-inch deep-dish pie plate according to package directions; trim dough around edges of pie plate.

2. Place remaining piecrust on a lightly floured surface; cut desired shapes with a decorative 1-inch cookie cutter. Brush edge of piecrust in pie plate with beaten egg white; gently press dough shapes onto edge of piecrust. Pierce bottom and sides with a fork.

3. Preheat oven to 400°. Line piecrust with parchment paper or aluminum foil; fill piecrust with pie weights or dried beans.

4. Bake at 400° for 10 minutes. Remove weights and parchment paper; bake 5 more minutes, and set aside. Reduce oven temperature to 350°.

5. Cook bacon in a large skillet over medium-high heat until crisp. Remove bacon, and drain on paper towels, reserving 2 tsp. drippings in pan. Crumble bacon, and set aside.

6. Sauté chopped onion and mushrooms in hot drippings 3 to 4 minutes or until tender.

7. Stir together bacon, onion mixture, half-and-half, and next 4 ingredients in a large bowl. Combine cheese and flour; add to bacon mixture, stirring until blended. Pour mixture into crust.

8. Bake at 350° for 45 to 50 minutes or until a wooden pick inserted in center comes out clean. (Shield edges with aluminum foil to prevent excessive browning, if necessary.) Let stand 10 minutes before serving.

Bacon-Cheddar Grits Bread, page 121

Sweet Potato Cinnamon Rolls,
page 148

Cheddar Cheese Grits Casserole, page 181
and Sweet Apple Bacon, page 204

Mini Sausage-and-Egg
Casseroles, page 171

Gentlemen's Casserole,
page 173

Fresh Fruit Salad With Orange-
Ginger Syrup, page 203

Traditional Eggs Benedict,
page 174

Fresh Blueberry Pancakes,
page 196

Anniversary Cake,
page 218

Dark Chocolate Bundt Cake,
page 210

Shortcut Carrot Cake,
page 219

Buttery Pound Cake,
page 208

Skillet Pineapple Upside-Down Cake,
page 236

Hot Fudge Sundae
Cake Rolls, page 234

Mixed-Berry Angel Cakes With
Almond Sugar, page 233

Mississippi Mud Cake,
page 230

Brown Sugar-Pecan Coffee
Cake, page 255

MUSHROOM-SPINACH-SWISS QUICHE

makes 6 servings   prep: 20 min.   bake: 48 min.   cook: 15 min.   stand: 10 min.

½ (15-oz.) package refrigerated piecrusts

1 Tbsp. butter

1 (8-oz.) package fresh mushrooms, chopped

1 roasted red bell pepper, chopped

2 Tbsp. port wine or apple juice

1 cup half-and-half

3 large eggs

½ tsp. dried Italian seasoning

½ tsp. salt

¼ to ½ tsp. black pepper

⅛ tsp. ground red pepper

1 cup chopped fresh spinach

1 (5-oz.) package shredded Swiss cheese

1. Preheat oven to 400°. Unfold piecrust, and place on a lightly floured surface. Roll out to ⅛-inch thickness. Carefully place in a 9-inch pie plate. Fold edges under, and crimp.

2. Bake on lowest oven rack at 400° for 8 minutes. Cool.

3. Melt butter in a large skillet over medium-high heat. Add mushrooms and bell pepper; sauté 7 to 10 minutes or until tender. Stir in port; cook, stirring often, until liquid is absorbed.

4. Whisk together half-and-half and next 5 ingredients in a large bowl. Stir in mushroom mixture, spinach, and cheese. Pour into prepared crust.

5. Bake on lowest oven rack at 400° for 40 minutes or until set. Let stand 10 minutes.

Pretty Edges for a Quiche

Use one refrigerated piecrust for the bottom of the quiche, and make it pretty with the second one. On a lightly floured surface, cut desired shapes from the piecrust using a decorative 1-inch cookie cutter. Brush edge of piecrust in pieplate with beaten egg white. Gently press cut-outs onto edge of piecrust. You can actually dress up any piecrust with this technique.

SOUTHWEST BRUNCH CASSEROLE

makes 10 to 12 servings prep: 25 min. cook: 15 min. bake: 25 min.

Start the Chile-Cheese Sauce first, and then begin the casserole. We don't recommend egg substitute for this recipe. Pair this dish with your choice of fruit for a well-rounded meal.

[casusal gathering]

1 (16-oz.) package mild ground pork sausage
¼ cup chopped onion
12 large eggs, lightly beaten
Chile-Cheese Sauce
2 cups self-rising flour
⅓ cup vegetable oil
⅓ cup evaporated milk

1 large egg, lightly beaten
½ tsp. chili powder
1½ cups (6 oz.) shredded sharp
Cheddar cheese or Monterey Jack cheese with
   peppers
2 Tbsp. chopped fresh cilantro or parsley

1. Cook sausage and onion in a large nonstick skillet over medium-high heat, stirring until sausage crumbles and is no longer pink. Reduce heat to medium; add eggs, and cook, without stirring, until eggs begin to set on bottom. Gently stir to slightly break up eggs. Cook, stirring occasionally, until eggs are thickened but still moist. (Do not overstir, as this will form small, dry pieces.) Remove from heat; stir in Chile-Cheese Sauce. Spoon into a lightly greased 13- x 9-inch baking dish; set aside.

2. Preheat oven to 400°. Stir together flour and next 4 ingredients until a dough forms. Turn dough out onto a lightly floured surface; knead 3 or 4 times.

3. Roll dough into a 12-inch square; sprinkle evenly with shredded cheese and cilantro. Roll up, jelly-roll fashion, and cut into 12 (1-inch-thick) slices. Place dough slices over egg mixture, spacing evenly.

4. Bake at 400° for 25 to 30 minutes or until golden.

Kitchen Express: Prepare sausage, egg, and Chile-Cheese Sauce as directed; spoon into a lightly greased 13- x 9-inch baking dish. Top evenly with 12 frozen Southern-style biscuits. Bake at 400° for 25 to 30 minutes or until golden.

Note: We tested with Pillsbury Southern Style Oven Baked Biscuits, located in the freezer section of the supermarket.

Chile-Cheese Sauce

makes about 3 cups   prep: 10 min.   cook: 10 min.

2   Tbsp. butter
2½ Tbsp. all-purpose flour
2   cups milk
1   cup (4 oz.) shredded Cheddar cheese

1   (4.5-oz.) can chopped green chiles
½   tsp. salt
¼   tsp. pepper

1. Melt butter in a heavy saucepan over medium-low heat; add flour, whisking until smooth. Cook, whisking constantly, 1 minute. Increase heat to medium, and gradually add milk; cook, whisking constantly, until slightly thickened. Remove from heat; add cheese and remaining ingredients, stirring until cheese melts. Keep warm.

MINI SAUSAGE-AND-EGG CASSEROLES

makes 10 servings   prep: 20 min.   bake: 25 min.   **pictured on page 160**

8   (1½-oz.) sourdough bread slices, cut into
     ½-inch cubes
Vegetable cooking spray
1   (12-oz.) package fully cooked pork sausage
     patties, chopped
2½ cups 2% reduced-fat milk

4   large eggs
1   Tbsp. Dijon mustard
½   cup buttermilk
1   (10¾-oz.) can cream of mushroom soup
1   cup (4 oz.) shredded sharp Cheddar cheese

1. Preheat oven to 350°. Divide bread cubes evenly among 10 (8- to 10-oz.) ovenproof coffee mugs coated with cooking spray, placing in bottom of mugs. Top evenly with sausage. Whisk together 2½ cups milk, eggs, and Dijon mustard. Pour evenly over bread mixture in mugs.
2. Whisk together buttermilk and cream of mushroom soup. Spoon over bread mixture in mugs; sprinkle with Cheddar cheese. Place coffee mugs on a baking sheet.
3. Bake at 350° for 25 to 30 minutes or until casseroles are set and puffed. Serve immediately.

Note: Unbaked mugs of casserole can be covered with plastic wrap, then foil, and frozen up to 1 month. Thaw overnight in the refrigerator. Bake as directed.

Sausage-and-Egg Casserole: Omit coffee mugs. Arrange bread in 2 greased 8-inch square baking dishes or 1 greased 13- x 9-inch baking dish. Proceed as directed, increasing bake time to 1 hour or until casserole is set. **Note:** An unbaked casserole can be covered with plastic wrap, then foil, and frozen up to 1 month. Thaw overnight in the refrigerator. Bake as directed.

[*freeze it*]

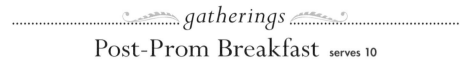

Post-Prom Breakfast serves 10

Sausage-Hash Brown Breakfast Casserole
Fresh strawberries, pineapple, and green grapes
Cinnamon-Pecan Coffee Cake (page 257)

SAUSAGE-HASH BROWN BREAKFAST CASSEROLE

makes 10 servings   prep: 30 min.   bake: 35 min.

We used frozen hash browns to streamline this breakfast or brunch favorite.

1 lb. mild ground pork sausage	½ tsp. pepper
1 lb. hot ground pork sausage	1 cup shredded Cheddar cheese
1 (30-oz.) package frozen hash browns	6 large eggs
1½ tsp. salt, divided	2 cups milk

1. Cook sausages in a large skillet over medium-high heat, stirring until sausage crumbles and is no longer pink. Drain well.
2. Prepare hash browns according to package directions, using ½ tsp. salt and pepper.
3. Stir together hash browns, sausage, and cheese. Pour into a lightly greased 13- x 9-inch baking dish.
4. Preheat oven to 350°.
5. Whisk together eggs, milk, and remaining 1 tsp. salt. Pour evenly over potato mixture.
6. Bake at 350° for 35 to 40 minutes.

GENTLEMEN'S CASSEROLE

makes 2 servings prep: 25 min. bake: 20 min. cook: 6 min. **pictured on page 161**

This recipe easily doubles to serve four. You can bake puff pastry shells the day before. Remove tops and reheat on a baking sheet at 350° for five minutes.

1 (10-oz.) package frozen puff pastry shells	Gruyère Cheese Sauce
1 Tbsp. butter	¼ cup grated Gruyère cheese
⅓ cup chopped cooked ham	Dash of paprika
1 Tbsp. chopped green onions	Garnish: chopped green onions (optional)
4 large eggs, lightly beaten	

1. Bake 4 pastry shells according to package directions. Reserve remaining pastry shells for another use.

2. Melt butter in a medium-size nonstick skillet over medium heat; add ham and green onions. Sauté 2 minutes or until green onions are tender. Add eggs, and cook, without stirring, 1 to 2 minutes or until eggs begin to set on bottom. Gently draw cooked edges away from sides of pan to form large pieces. Cook, stirring occasionally, 1 to 2 minutes or until eggs are thickened and moist. (Do not overstir.) Gently fold in Gruyère Cheese Sauce.

3. Spoon egg mixture into prepared pastry shells. Sprinkle with cheese and paprika. Garnish, if desired. Serve immediately.

Gruyère Cheese Sauce

makes about ¾ cup prep: 10 min. cook: 6 min.

You can make this up to two days ahead and store in the refrigerator. Reheat in a microwave-safe bowl at HIGH 1½ minutes, stirring halfway through.

¾ cup milk	½ cup grated Gruyère cheese
1 Tbsp. butter	¼ tsp. salt
1 Tbsp. all-purpose flour	⅛ tsp. pepper

1. Microwave milk in a 2-cup microwave-safe glass measuring cup at HIGH 1 minute.

2. Melt butter in a small heavy saucepan over medium heat; gradually whisk in flour. Cook 1 minute, whisking constantly. Gradually whisk in warm milk; cook over medium heat, whisking constantly, 3 to 5 minutes or until thickened and bubbly. Remove from heat; whisk in cheese, salt, and pepper.

TRADITIONAL EGGS BENEDICT

makes 2 servings   prep: 25 min.   cook: 10 min.   **pictured on page 162**

8   (½-oz.) Canadian bacon slices
Vegetable cooking spray
2   English muffins, split and toasted
4   large eggs, poached

Hollandaise Sauce
Coarsely ground pepper
Paprika

1. Cook bacon in a skillet coated with cooking spray over medium heat until thoroughly heated, turning once. Drain on paper towels.

2. Place 2 bacon slices on each muffin half. Top each with a poached egg, and drizzle evenly with Hollandaise Sauce. Sprinkle with pepper and paprika; serve immediately.

Hollandaise Sauce:

makes 1½ cups   prep: 5 min.   cook: 10 min.

4 large egg yolks
2 Tbsp. fresh lemon juice

1 cup butter, melted
¼ tsp. salt

1. Whisk yolks in top of a double boiler; gradually whisk in lemon juice. Place over hot water (do not boil). Add butter, ⅓ cup at a time, whisking until smooth; whisk in salt. Cook, whisking constantly, 10 minutes or until thickened and a thermometer registers 160°. Serve immediately.

WAFFLES BENEDICT

makes 4 servings   prep: 15 min.   stand: 5 min.   cook: 20 min.

Waffles for supper has been a Southern restaurant secret for a long time. You can substitute deli ham or country ham for the prosciutto.

2   cups all-purpose baking mix
1⅓ cups buttermilk
½   cup (2 oz.) shredded Parmesan cheese
2   Tbsp. vegetable oil
5   large eggs, divided
½   tsp. white vinegar

1   (0.9-oz.) envelope hollandaise sauce mix
1   Tbsp. lemon juice
¼   tsp. dried tarragon
8   thin prosciutto slices (about ¼ lb.)
Garnish: chopped fresh chives (optional)

[casual entertaining]

1. Stir together baking mix, next 3 ingredients, and 1 egg in a medium bowl until blended. Let batter stand 5 minutes.

2. Meanwhile, add water to a depth of 3 inches in a large saucepan. Bring to a boil; reduce heat, and maintain a light simmer. Add vinegar. Break remaining 4 eggs, and slip into water, 1 at a time, as close as possible to surface. Simmer 3 to 5 minutes or to desired degree of doneness. Remove with a slotted spoon. Trim edges, if desired.

3. Cook batter in a preheated, lightly greased waffle iron according to manufacturer's directions until golden.

4. Prepare hollandaise sauce according to package directions, adding lemon juice and tarragon.

5. Stack 2 waffles, and top with 2 prosciutto slices, 1 poached egg, and desired amount of hollandaise sauce. Garnish, if desired.

Note: We tested with Bisquick All-Purpose Baking Mix and Knorr Hollandaise Sauce Mix.

Poached Eggs

1. Add water to a large skillet, filling two-thirds full. Bring to a boil; reduce heat, and maintain at a light simmer. Break eggs into each of 4 (6-oz.) custard cups coated with cooking spray.

2. Place custard cups in simmering water in pan. Cover pan; cook 6 minutes.

3. Remove custard cups from water with tongs.

4. Carefully remove eggs from custard cups.

SOUTHERN-STYLE CHILES RELLENOS

makes 4 servings   broil: 5 min.   stand: 10 min.   prep: 30 min.   fry: 2 min. per batch

8   large fresh poblano or Anaheim chile peppers

Creamy Cheddar Grits

3   large eggs

½   cup whipping cream

1   cup all-purpose flour

1   cup yellow cornmeal

½   tsp. salt

Peanut oil

Country Ham Sauce

Garnishes: shredded Cheddar cheese, sliced green
      onions

1. Preheat oven to broil. Place peppers on an aluminum foil-lined baking sheet.

2. Broil 5 inches from heat about 5 minutes on each side or until peppers look blistered.

3. Place peppers in a bowl or zip-top plastic freezer bag; cover bowl with plastic wrap, or seal
bag. Let stand 10 minutes to loosen skins.

4. Peel peppers; carefully cut peppers lengthwise on side, leaving stems attached. Remove seeds.

5. Spoon Creamy Cheddar Grits into a large zip-top plastic freezer bag; seal. Snip a hole in 1
corner of bag; squeeze grits into peppers. Secure stuffed peppers with wooden picks, if desired.
Cover and chill until firm.

6. Combine eggs and whipping cream, stirring well.

7. Combine flour, cornmeal, and salt in a shallow dish; carefully dredge peppers in cornmeal
mixture, and dip into egg mixture. Dredge in cornmeal mixture again.

8. Pour oil to a depth of 1 inch into a large cast-iron or heavy skillet. Heat to 375°. Fry 2 peppers at a time, cut side up, 2 minutes, turning once. Drain on paper towels, and remove wooden
picks. Serve with Country Ham Sauce; garnish, if desired.

Creamy Cheddar Grits

makes 4 cups   prep: 5 min.   cook: 11 min.   cool: 10 min.

3   (10¾-ounce) cans condensed chicken broth,
      undiluted

½   cup whipping cream

1   cup uncooked quick-cooking grits

2   cups (8 ounces) shredded sharp Cheddar
      cheese

1. Combine chicken broth and cream in a large saucepan; bring to a boil. Stir in grits, and return
to a boil. Cover, reduce heat, and simmer 5 to 7 minutes. Stir in cheese. Cool 10 minutes.

Country Ham Sauce

makes 2½ cups   prep: 5 min.   cook: 12 min.

¼ cup butter

¼ cup all-purpose flour

1   (10¾-ounce) can condensed chicken broth, undiluted

¾ cup whipping cream

¼ cup chopped country ham

1   teaspoon freshly ground pepper

1. Melt butter in a heavy saucepan over low heat; add flour, stirring until smooth. Cook, stirring constantly, 3 to 5 minutes. Gradually add broth, cream, and ¼ cup water; cook over medium heat, stirring constantly with a whisk, until thickened and bubbly. Stir in ham and pepper.

Rellenos Around the South

When making chiles rellenos, think about what you have left over in your refrigerator. Use these flavorful regional fillings for personalizing the recipe for Southern-Style Chiles Rellenos.

You'll need about ½ cup filling per poblano pepper (which is mild to moderately hot in flavor) and ¼ cup filling per Anaheim (milder; closer in flavor to a bell pepper). Happy traveling through our delicious detours.

- **El Paso Rellenos (traditional):** ground beef or pork, raisins, olives, cinnamon, slivered almonds, garlic
- **Miami Rellenos:** stone crab and finely chopped Homestead tomatoes
- **New Orleans Rellenos:** red beans and rice
- **Kansas City Rellenos:** shredded barbecued beef and baked beans
- **Chesapeake Bay Rellenos:** blue crab and corn
- **Santa Fe Rellenos:** black beans, goat cheese, pine nuts, roasted red bell pepper
- **Breaux Bridge (Louisiana) Rellenos:** crawfish étoufée
- **Lafayette (Louisiana) Rellenos:** jambalaya

- **Chinatown (Washington, D.C.) Rellenos:** chicken-fried rice with sweet-and-sour sauce
- **Yazoo City (Mississippi) Rellenos:** catfish and wild rice
- **Memphis Rellenos:** rib meat, dry rub, and cornbread
- **Vidalia (Georgia) Rellenos:** ham and chopped Vidalia onions
- **Greensboro (North Carolina) Rellenos:** barbecued chicken with vinegar slaw
- **Austin Rellenos:** red bean chili and chipped onion
- **Key West Rellenos:** jerk pork and yellow rice
- **Louisville Rellenos:** pot roast and carrots

TASTE OF THE SOUTH

Cheese Grits
The topics in "Taste of the South" often generate intense discussions at our tasting table, and cheese grits proved no exception. We all agreed that this straightforward dish embodies the very definition of good old-fashioned, stick-to-your-ribs Southern food. The rest, however, was open to a little friendly debate. Following our standard procedure, we tested a number of recipes, which included everything from garlic to bacon, and just about every kind of cheese you can imagine. In the end, it was the unadorned but

extraordinarily delicious Two-Cheese Grits that won, hands down. The reason? The cheese. Specifically, sharp Cheddar and Monterey Jack. We found that the combination of tangy sharp Cheddar and mild Monterey Jack creates the perfect balance of creaminess and flavor. Here's why: The sharper the cheese, the less moisture it has. This is a good thing when sliced and eaten out of hand, but it's not so good when the cheese is heated. When sharp and extra-sharp Cheddar are melted, they can taste greasy and grainy. Enter Monterey Jack, whose high moisture content makes it just right for melting. When you try the recipe, you'll know why they're the perfect match.

TWO-CHEESE GRITS

makes 6 to 8 servings   prep: 10 min.   cook: 15 min.

1 tsp. salt

1¼ cups uncooked quick-cooking grits*

½ (8-oz.) block sharp Cheddar cheese, shredded (about 1 cup)

½ (8-oz.) block Monterey Jack cheese, shredded (about 1 cup)

½ cup half-and-half

1 Tbsp. butter

¼ tsp. pepper

1. Bring 5 cups water and salt to a boil in a medium saucepan over medium-high heat. Gradually whisk in grits; bring to a boil. Reduce heat to medium-low, and simmer, stirring

occasionally, 10 minutes or until thickened. Stir in Cheddar cheese and remaining ingredients until cheese is melted and mixture is blended. Serve immediately.

* Stone-ground grits may be substituted. Increase liquid to 6 cups, and increase cook time to 50 minutes.

Note: We tested with White Lily Quick Grits.

CREAMY CHEDDAR CHEESE GRITS

makes 8½ cups   prep: 10 min.   cook: 1 hr., 45 min.

This recipe goes with Hominy Grill's Shrimp and Grits on page 182.

4	Tbsp. butter	1	garlic clove, pressed
5	cups milk	1½	cups uncooked stone-ground white grits
2	tsp. salt	1	(10-oz.) block sharp white Cheddar cheese,
½	tsp. hot sauce		grated

1. Bring 2 Tbsp. butter, next 4 ingredients, and 5 cups water to a boil in a medium-size Dutch oven over medium-high heat. Gradually whisk in grits, and bring to a boil. Reduce heat to medium-low, and simmer, stirring occasionally, 1 ½ hours or until thickened. Stir in cheese and remaining 2 Tbsp. butter until melted. Serve immediately.

Quick-Cooking Creamy Cheddar Cheese Grits: Substitute 2 cups uncooked quick-cooking grits for stone-ground grits. Decrease water and milk to 4 ½ cups each. Prepare recipe as directed, cooking grits 10 to 15 minutes or until thickened.

MARGARET'S CREAMY GRITS

makes 12 cups   prep: 10 min.   cook: 22 min.

A former Test Kitchen director, Margaret Dickey, shared this recipe. We love the Southern kick the hot sauce adds to these grits.

8	cups half-and-half or whipping cream	1	(8-oz.) package cream cheese, cubed
1	tsp. salt	1	(12-oz.) package shredded sharp Cheddar cheese
½	tsp. granulated garlic		
½	tsp. pepper	1	tsp. hot sauce
2	cups uncooked quick-cooking grits		

1. Bring first 4 ingredients to a boil in a Dutch oven; gradually stir in grits. Return to a boil; cover, reduce heat, and simmer, stirring occasionally, 5 minutes or until thickened. Add cream cheese and remaining ingredients, stirring until cheese melts.

Grits Dictionary

Grits can be very different, depending on whether they're ground at a gristmill or purchased at the supermarket. This guide will help you with the different choices.

Hominy: Dried white or yellow corn kernels from which the hull and germ have been removed. It's sold dried or ready-to-eat in cans. When dried hominy is ground, it's called hominy grits. Grits are available in three grinds—fine, medium, and coarse.

Whole-ground or stone-ground grits: These grits are a coarse grind. You'll find stone-ground grits at gristmill gift shops and specialty food stores.

Quick and regular grits: The only difference between these types is in granulation. Quick grits are ground fine and cook in 5 minutes; regular grits are medium grind and cook in 10 minutes.

Instant grits: These fine-textured grits have been precooked and dehydrated. To prepare them, simply add boiling water.

Christmas Brunch serves 12

Praline Mustard-Glazed Ham (page 190)
Scrambled eggs   *Cheddar Cheese Grits Casserole
***Gingered Ambrosia** (page 202)
Sweet Potato Cinnamon Rolls (page 148)

*double recipe

CHEDDAR CHEESE GRITS CASSEROLE

makes 6 servings   prep: 15 min.   cook: 10 min.   bake: 35 min.   **pictured on page 159**

Cook and crumble six slices of bacon to sprinkle on top of the casserole after you pull it out of the oven, if desired.

4 cups milk	½ tsp. pepper
¼ cup butter	2 cups (8 oz.) shredded sharp Cheddar cheese
1 cup uncooked quick-cooking grits	¼ cup grated Parmesan cheese
1 large egg, lightly beaten	Garnish: parsley sprigs
1 tsp. salt	

1. Preheat oven to 350°. Bring milk just to a boil in a large saucepan over medium-high heat; gradually whisk in butter and grits. Reduce heat, and simmer, whisking constantly, 5 to 7 minutes or until grits are done. Remove from heat.

2. Stir in egg and next 3 ingredients. Pour into a lightly greased 11- x 7-inch baking dish. Sprinkle evenly with grated Parmesan cheese.

3. Bake, covered, at 350° for 35 to 40 minutes or until mixture is set. Serve immediately. Garnish, if desired.

{*family favorite*}

GRITS WITH GRILLED CHICKEN AND ONIONS

makes 6 to 8 servings   prep: 20 min.   cook: 1 hr., 12 min.   chill: 1 hr.

Grits are corn kernels that have been ground to a coarse, medium, or fine consistency. Stone-ground grits are considered coarsely ground.

2⅔ cups uncooked stone-ground grits

2   cups (8 oz.) shredded Cheddar cheese, divided

¼ cup butter, divided

1   tsp. salt, divided

¾ tsp. pepper, divided

2   large onions, cut into ½-inch slices

2   Tbsp. bourbon or apple juice

4   skinned and boned chicken breasts

½ cup barbecue sauce

1. Preheat grill to medium heat (300° to 350°). Rinse grits according to package directions. Bring 5⅓ cups water to a boil in a Dutch oven; gradually stir in grits. Reduce heat, and simmer, stirring occasionally, 25 minutes. Stir in ½ cup cheese, 2 Tbsp. butter, ½ tsp. salt, and ¼ tsp. pepper. Keep warm, or spread into a greased 11- x 7-inch baking dish; cover and chill at least 1 hour, and cut into 2-inch-square cakes.

2. Melt remaining 2 Tbsp. butter in a large skillet over medium heat; add onion, remaining ½ tsp. salt, and remaining ½ tsp. pepper. Cook, stirring often, 30 minutes or until onion is caramel colored. Add bourbon; cook, stirring constantly, 1 minute. Keep warm.

3. Grill chicken, uncovered, or cook in a skillet over medium heat 6 minutes on each side or until done. Cool slightly; shred. Stir together chicken and barbecue sauce. Top grits evenly with chicken mixture, onion, and remaining 1½ cups cheese.

HOMINY GRILL'S SHRIMP AND GRITS

makes 6 servings   prep: 30 min.   cook: 19 min.

2   lb. unpeeled, medium-size raw shrimp

2   Tbsp. all-purpose flour

5   bacon slices, chopped

1   (8-oz.) package sliced fresh mushrooms

3   garlic cloves, minced

⅓ cup fresh lemon juice

½ cup thinly sliced green onions

2   tsp. hot sauce

½ tsp. salt

Creamy Cheddar Cheese Grits (recipe on page 179)

[casual gathering]

1. Peel shrimp; devein, if desired. Toss shrimp with flour until lightly coated, shaking to remove excess.

2. Cook bacon in a medium skillet over medium-high heat 8 to 10 minutes or until crisp. Remove bacon, and drain on paper towels, reserving drippings in skillet.

3. Sauté mushrooms in hot drippings 4 minutes or just until mushrooms begin to release their liquid. Add shrimp, and sauté 3 to 3 ½ minutes or just until shrimp turn pink. Add garlic, and sauté 1 minute (do not brown garlic). Add lemon juice and next 3 ingredients; serve immediately over Creamy Cheddar Cheese Grits. Sprinkle with bacon.

SHRIMP-AND-GRITS BISCUITS

makes 48 brunch appetizers   prep: 30 min.   cook: 5 min.   cool: 15 min.   bake: 10 min.

1⅓ cups chicken broth

⅛ tsp. salt

⅓ cup uncooked quick-cooking grits

1 Tbsp. butter

⅛ tsp. pepper

¾ cup milk

3 cups all-purpose baking mix

1½ lb. large cooked shrimp, peeled and deveined

1 (3-oz.) package cream cheese

1 green onion, chopped

½ tsp. hot sauce

½ tsp. Old Bay seasoning

2 tsp. lemon juice

Garnishes: sliced green onions, barbecue sauce (optional)

1. Preheat oven to 425°. Bring chicken broth and salt to a boil in a saucepan over medium-high heat; add grits, and cook, stirring often, 5 minutes or until thickened. Add butter and pepper, stirring until butter melts. Remove from heat, and let cool 15 to 20 minutes.

2. Whisk milk into cooled grits; stir in baking mix until a soft dough forms. Turn dough out onto a lightly floured surface. Pat dough to a ½-inch thickness, and cut with a 2-inch round cutter. Place biscuits on lightly greased baking sheets.

3. Bake at 425° for 10 minutes or until biscuits are lightly browned.

4. Cut 24 shrimp in half lengthwise, and set aside.

5. Process cream cheese, next 4 ingredients, and remaining shrimp in a food processor until mixture is smooth, stopping to scrape down sides.

6. Split biscuits in half, and spread cut sides evenly with the shrimp puree, and top with remaining shrimp. Garnish, if desired.

GRILLADES AND GRITS

makes 4 servings   prep: 15 min.   cook: 28 min.

Our slimmed-down version of a New Orleans favorite is a well-balanced morning meal. It also doubles as a quick, good-for-you dinner option.

3   Tbsp. all-purpose flour
1   tsp. Creole seasoning, divided
1   lb. lean breakfast pork cutlets, trimmed
2   tsp. olive oil
1   cup finely diced onion

1   cup finely diced celery
½   cup finely diced green bell pepper
1   (14.5-oz.) can no-salt-added diced tomatoes
1   (14-oz.) can low-sodium fat-free chicken broth
Creamy Grits

1. Combine flour and ½ tsp. Creole seasoning in a shallow dish. Dredge pork in flour mixture.
2. Cook pork, in 2 batches, in ½ tsp. hot oil per batch in a large skillet over medium-high heat 2 minutes on each side or until done. Remove from skillet, and keep warm.
3. Add remaining 1 tsp. oil to skillet. Sauté diced onion, celery, and bell pepper in hot oil 3 to 5 minutes or until vegetables are tender. Stir in remaining ½ tsp. Creole seasoning. Stir in diced tomatoes and chicken broth, and cook 2 minutes, stirring to loosen particles from bottom of skillet. Simmer 15 to 18 minutes or until liquid reduces to about 2 Tbsp. Serve tomato mixture over Creamy Grits and pork.

Note: Nutritional analysis includes ½ cup Creamy Grits.

Per serving: Calories 371; Fat 10.3g (sat 3.1g, mono 5.2g, poly 1.1g); Protein 33.8g; Carb 36.1g; Fiber 3.4g; Chol 66mg; Iron 2.7mg; Sodium 350mg; Calc 149mg

Creamy Grits

makes 2 cups   prep: 5 min.   cook: 15 min.

1   (14-oz.) can low-sodium fat-free chicken broth
1   cup fat-free milk

½   cup uncooked quick-cooking grits

1. Bring broth and milk to a boil in a medium saucepan over medium-high heat; reduce heat to low, and whisk in ½ cup grits. Cook, whisking occasionally, 15 to 20 minutes or until creamy and thickened.

Per ½-cup serving: Calories 109; Fat 0.9g (sat 0.2g, mono 0.3g, poly 0.2g); Protein 5.8g; Carb 20g; Fiber 0.3g; Chol 1.2mg; Iron 1mg; Sodium 56mg; Calc 81mg

Reef

What lands on your plate at Reef depends a lot on the water temperature, the moon, how much sunlight the fish received during the day—and the catch local fishermen make available to Bryan Caswell's kitchen. It might be croaker or lesser-known sheepshead, tripletail, or triggerfish. "There are 15 to 20 species nobody ever uses," says the Houston-raised chef, a fisherman himself. "Our preparations don't change as much as the selection does." Bryan's devotion to local seafood, plus his Texas-Louisiana upbringing, figures largely on the menu: Grandmother Bertie B. Caswell's yeast rolls with jalapeño jelly, suggestions of Grandmother "Ma" Daigle's gumbo, grouper with collards and pot likker, corn pudding with grilled peach and salsa, and mussels steamed in Shiner Bock beer. It's local, heartfelt, and turning heads in Houston.

2600 Travis at McGowen
Houston, Texas 77006
www.reefhouston.com or (713) 526-8282.

BAKED GRITS AND GREENS

makes 8 to 10 servings   prep 20 min.   cook: 8 min.   bake: 30 min.

Prepare through Step 2 up to a day ahead; cover and chill. Remove from the fridge, add the buttered crushed croutons, and let stand 30 minutes before baking.

{ make ahead }

1   tsp. garlic salt

1   cup uncooked quick-cooking grits

⅓   cup finely chopped red onion

5   Tbsp. butter, divided

2   large eggs

1   (10-oz.) package frozen chopped spinach, thawed and drained

½   cups (6 oz.) shredded Parmesan cheese

½   cup bottled creamy Caesar dressing

½   tsp. freshly ground pepper

1¼   cups coarsely crushed garlic-flavored croutons

1. Preheat oven to 350°. Bring garlic salt and 4 cups water to a boil in a large saucepan over medium-high heat; gradually stir in grits. Reduce heat to medium, and cook, stirring often, 5 minutes or until thickened. Remove from heat, and stir in onion and 3 Tbsp. butter.

2. Whisk together eggs and next 4 ingredients in a large bowl. Stir about one-fourth of grits mixture gradually into egg mixture; add remaining grits mixture, stirring constantly. Pour into a lightly greased 13- x 9-inch baking dish.

3. Melt remaining 2 Tbsp. butter, and toss with coarsely crushed croutons; sprinkle over grits mixture.

4. Bake at 350° for 30 to 35 minutes or until mixture is set and croutons are golden brown.

Baked Grits and Greens With Bacon: Prepare recipe as directed, stirring 1 (3-oz.) package bacon bits into egg mixture.

Note: For testing purposes only, we used Oscar Mayer Real Bacon Bits.

inspirations for your taste

CREAMY PORK CHOPS

makes 4 to 6 servings   prep: 5 min.   cook: 17 min.

¼ cup all-purpose flour	1 (8-oz.) container sour cream
¾ tsp. salt, divided	2 Tbsp. sugar
½ tsp. pepper	⅛ tsp. ground cloves
8 pork breakfast chops	2 bay leaves
2 Tbsp. vegetable oil	1 Tbsp. chopped fresh parsley (optional)
¼ cup white vinegar	

1. Combine flour, ½ tsp. salt, and pepper. Dredge pork breakfast chops in flour mixture.

2. Cook pork chops in hot oil in a large skillet over high heat 5 minutes on each side or until golden. Remove pork chops from skillet.

3. Add vinegar, and cook 2 minutes, stirring to loosen particles from bottom of skillet. Stir in remaining ¼ tsp. salt, sour cream, and next 3 ingredients; simmer 5 minutes. Remove and discard bay leaves; pour sauce over pork chops. Sprinkle with parsley, if desired.

SMOKED CHOPS-AND-CHEESE OMELET

makes 4 servings   prep: 10 min.   cook: 15 min.

You know you're in the South when served smoked pork chops in your omelet. Use a heat-resistant spatula to flip the omelet over to cook on the second side. Keep cooked omelets warm on an ovenproof platter in a 250° oven.

1¼ cups chopped smoked pork chops (about 1 lb.)	¼ tsp. salt
2 small plum tomatoes, chopped	¼ tsp. pepper
2 Tbsp. finely chopped onion	4 tsp. butter, divided
6 large eggs	⅔ cup shredded Gouda cheese
1 Tbsp. chopped fresh parsley	

1. Cook chopped pork in an 8-inch nonstick omelet pan or a heavy skillet with sloped sides over medium-low heat 5 minutes or until thoroughly heated. Add tomatoes and onion, and cook, stirring often, until onion is tender. Remove pork mixture from pan; set aside. Wipe skillet clean with paper towels.

2. Whisk together eggs and next 3 ingredients.

3. Melt 1 tsp. butter in same skillet over medium heat. Pour one-fourth egg mixture into skillet. As egg mixture starts to cook, gently lift edges of omelet with a spatula, and tilt pan so uncooked portion flows underneath. Cook 1 to 2 minutes or until almost set. Flip omelet over.

4. Sprinkle 1 side of omelet with one-fourth each of cheese and reserved chopped pork mixture. Cook 1 minute or until cheese begins to melt. Slide filled side of omelet onto a plate, flipping remaining side of omelet over filling. Repeat procedure 3 times with remaining butter, egg mixture, cheese, and pork mixture. Serve immediately.

Note: We tested with Smithfield Smoked Pork Chops. You can substitute 1 (15-oz.) carton garden vegetable flavor egg substitute for eggs, parsley, salt, and pepper.

BAKED HAM WITH BOURBON GLAZE

makes 12 to 14 servings   prep: 10 min.   cook: 1 hr., 30 min.

1   cup honey
½   cup molasses
½   cup bourbon
¼   cup orange juice

2   Tbsp. Dijon mustard
1   (6- to 8-lb.) smoked ham half
Garnish: fresh herb sprigs

1. Preheat oven to 325°. Microwave honey and molasses in a 1-qt. microwave-safe dish at HIGH 1 minute; whisk to blend. Whisk in bourbon, orange juice, and mustard.

2. Remove skin and excess fat from ham, and place ham in a roasting pan.

3. Bake at 325° on lower oven rack for 1½ hours or until a meat thermometer inserted into thickest portion registers 140°, basting occasionally with honey mixture.

4. Bring drippings and remaining glaze to a boil in a small saucepan. Remove from heat, and serve with sliced ham. Garnish, if desired.

COFFEE-GLAZED HAM WITH RED EYE GRAVY

makes 10 to 12 servings   prep: 10 min.   cook: 2 hr., 30 min.   other: 10 min.

1   (8- to 10-lb.) bone-in, fully cooked smoked ham half
2   cups firmly packed light brown sugar

2   cups freshly brewed coffee
¼   cup heavy whipping cream
Garnishes: fresh herbs, kumquats (optional)

1. Remove skin from ham, if present, and trim fat to ¼-inch thickness. Place ham in a lightly greased broiler pan. Combine sugar and hot coffee in a medium bowl, stirring until sugar dissolves; pour over ham.

2. Bake at 350° for 2 ½ hours or until a meat thermometer inserted into thickest portion registers 140°, basting every 20 minutes. Transfer ham from pan to a serving platter. Cover and keep warm. Pour drippings into a 4-cup glass measuring cup; let stand 10 minutes. Pour off and discard fat; stir cream into remaining drippings. Serve gravy with ham. Garnish platter, if desired.

SAVORY HAM-AND-SWISS CASSEROLE

makes 8 servings   prep: 30 min.   cook: 5 min.   bake: 55 min.   cool: 20 min.

1	cup whipping cream	4	garlic cloves, pressed
2	Tbsp. butter	8	large eggs, divided
1	tsp. salt	2	cups chopped Praline-Mustard Glazed Ham
¼	tsp. pepper	6	green onions, chopped
⅔	cup uncooked quick-cooking grits	2	cups milk, divided
2	cups (8 oz.) shredded Swiss cheese, divided	3	cups all-purpose baking mix

1. Preheat oven to 350°. Bring 1⅔ cups water, whipping cream, butter, salt, and pepper to a boil in a medium saucepan; gradually stir in grits. Cover, reduce heat, and simmer, stirring occasionally, 5 to 7 minutes. Add ½ cup cheese and garlic, stirring until cheese melts; let mixture cool 10 to 15 minutes. Stir in 2 eggs, and pour into a lightly greased 13- x 9-inch baking dish.

2. Bake at 350° for 20 minutes; remove from oven. Increase oven temperature to 400°. Sprinkle remaining 1½ cups cheese, ham, and green onions evenly over grits crust. Whisk together remaining 6 eggs and ½ cup milk; pour into crust.

3. Stir together remaining 1½ cups milk and baking mix; pour over egg mixture, spreading to edge of dish with back of spoon.

4. Bake at 400° for 35 minutes. Cool 10 minutes, and cut into squares.

PRALINE-MUSTARD GLAZED HAM

makes 12 servings   prep: 10 min.   bake: 2 hr., 30 min.   stand: 10 min.   cook: 5 min.

Round out the meal with baked sweet potatoes, spinach salad, and pecan pie for dessert.

1	(7- to 8-lb.) bone-in smoked spiral-cut ham half	⅓	cup apple juice
1	cup maple syrup	¼	cup raisins
¾	cup firmly packed light brown sugar	1	cooking apple, thinly sliced
¾	cup Dijon mustard		

1. Preheat oven to 350°. Remove skin and excess fat from smoked ham; place ham in a lightly greased 13- x 9-inch pan.

2. Stir together maple syrup and next 3 ingredients. Pour mixture over ham.

3. Bake at 350° on lower oven rack 2 hours and 30 minutes or until a meat thermometer inserted into thickest portion registers 140°, basting every 20 minutes with glaze. Let ham stand 10 minutes. Remove from pan, reserving drippings. If desired, cool, cover, and chill ham.

4. Remove fat from drippings with a fat separator, and discard. Cover and chill drippings, if desired. Cook drippings, raisins, and apple slices in a saucepan over low heat 5 minutes. Serve warm sauce with ham.

HAM-AND-ASPARAGUS SANDWICHES

makes 4 servings   prep: 10 min.   broil: 1 min.

3   Tbsp. butter, softened

2   small garlic cloves, minced

1   (16-oz.) round bread loaf, split

¼   cup mayonnaise

16 Praline-Mustard Glazed Ham slices
     (previous recipe)

1   (10-oz.) package frozen asparagus spears,
     thawed

1   (6-oz.) package Muenster cheese slices

1   (6-oz.) package Swiss cheese slices

1. Preheat oven to broil. Stir together butter and garlic.

2. Spread butter mixture evenly over bottom half of bread. Spread mayonnaise evenly over top half of bread. Layer bottom half evenly with ham slices, asparagus, and cheese slices; place on a baking sheet.

3. Broil 2 inches from heat 1 minute or just until cheese melts. Top with remaining bread half.

PINEAPPLE-GLAZED HAM

makes about 25 (3½-oz.) servings   prep: 20 min.   chill: 8 hr.   cook: 2 hr.

To lower sodium, purchase a reduced-sodium ham and omit salt.

1   (10-lb.) smoked ham

3   Tbsp. whole cloves

1   (20-oz.) can crushed pineapple, undrained

2   cups pineapple juice

1½ cups firmly packed dark brown sugar

1   cup bourbon

½   tsp. salt

1. Preheat oven to 350°. Remove skin and excess fat from ham. Score ham in a diamond design, and insert cloves at 1-inch intervals. Place ham in an aluminum foil-lined roasting pan.

2. Stir together pineapple and next 4 ingredients; pour over ham. Cover and chill 8 hours.

3. Bake ham at 350° for 2 hours, basting every 30 minutes.

Per 3½-oz. serving: Calories 223; Fat 14g (sat 5g, mono 6.5g, poly 1.5g); Protein 18g; Carb 4.7g; Chol 51mg; Iron 0.8g; Sodium 996mg; Calc 9.5mg

[southern lights]

SHELLFISH CRÊPES IN WINE-CHEESE SAUCE

makes 12 servings prep: 1 hr. chill: 3 hr. stand: 30 min. bake: 20 min.

½ cup butter, divided

2 cups chopped cooked shrimp (about 1 lb.)

1 cup (8 oz.) fresh crabmeat

2 green onions, minced

¼ cup dry vermouth*

⅛ tsp. salt

¼ tsp. pepper

½ Tbsp. butter, melted

Wine-Cheese Sauce

Crêpes

2 cups (8 oz.) shredded Swiss cheese

Garnish: sliced green onions

1. Melt ¼ cup butter in a large skillet over medium-high heat. Add shrimp, crabmeat, and minced green onions, and sauté for 1 minute. Stir in vermouth, salt, and pepper. Bring mixture to a boil, and cook 7 minutes or until most of liquid is absorbed. Remove mixture from heat, and set aside.

2. Drizzle ½ Tbsp. melted butter into a 13- x 9-inch baking dish. Stir 2 cups Wine-Cheese Sauce into shrimp mixture. Spoon about 3 Tbsp. shrimp mixture down center of each Crêpe.

4. Roll up, and place, seam side down, in prepared dish. Spoon remaining 2 cups Wine-Cheese Sauce over Crêpes. Sprinkle with Swiss cheese, and dot with remaining ¼ cup butter. Cover and chill for 3 hours. Let stand at room temperature 30 minutes. Preheat oven to 450°. Bake at 450° for 20 minutes or until thoroughly heated. Garnish, if desired.

Wine-Cheese Sauce

makes 4 cups prep: 10 min. cook: 10 min.

¼ cup cornstarch

¼ cup milk

⅓ cup dry vermouth*

3 cups whipping cream

¼ tsp. salt

¼ tsp. pepper

2 cups (8 oz.) shredded Swiss cheese

1. Whisk together cornstarch and milk in a small bowl.

2. Bring vermouth to a boil in a large skillet, and cook until vermouth is reduced to 1 Tbsp. Remove from heat, and whisk in cornstarch mixture. Add whipping cream, salt, and pepper; cook over medium-high heat, whisking constantly, 2 minutes or until mixture comes to a boil. Boil 1 minute or until mixture is thickened. Add Swiss cheese; reduce heat, and simmer, whisking constantly, 1 minute or until sauce is smooth.

* Clam juice may be substituted for vermouth.

Crêpes

makes 2 dozen   prep: 8 min.   chill: 1 hr.   cook: 30 min.

4	**large eggs**
2	**cups all-purpose flour**
¼	**cup butter, melted**

1	**cup cold water**
1	**cup cold milk**
½	**tsp. salt**

[make ahead]

1. Process all ingredients in a blender or food processor until smooth, stopping to scrape down sides. Cover and chill 1 hour.

2. Place a lightly greased 8-inch nonstick skillet over medium heat until skillet is hot.

3. Pour 3 Tbsp. batter into skillet; quickly tilt in all directions so batter covers bottom of skillet.

4. Cook 1 minute or until crêpe can be shaken loose from skillet. Turn crêpe, and cook about 30 seconds. Repeat procedure with remaining batter. Stack crêpes between sheets of wax paper.

Note: To make ahead, prepare crêpes as directed, and freeze up to one month. Casserole may be prepared one day ahead; cover and chill. Let stand at room temperature 30 minutes before baking; proceed as directed.

How to Make Crêpes

Making crêpe batter is quick and easy. It's important to cover the batter and let it rest, chilled, for 1 hour.

1. Simply combine all the ingredients, and blend to make the batter. A blender or food processor will help you make a smooth batter.

3. The edges of the crêpe should be crisp, and the center will come loose if you gently shake the pan. This means the crêpe is ready to flip.

2. Add the batter to the center of the pan, and gently tilt the pan in a circular motion, allowing batter to reach the sides of the pan.

4. Crêpes will keep for up to five days if you stack them between layers of wax paper and chill them. You can freeze them for up to one month.

SPOONBREAD WITH SIMPLE CHORIZO

makes 8 servings   prep: 20 min.   cook: 5 min.   stand: 20 min.   bake: 25 min.

This hearty Texas twist on a classic Southern side features chorizo, a spicy Mexican sausage. Chorizo is also terrific in scrambled eggs and tacos.

[casual gathering]

Simple Chorizo

2   cups cornmeal

4   cups milk

2   garlic cloves, minced

¼   cup butter

1½ tsp. salt

4   large eggs, separated

2   tsp. baking powder

1½ cups (6 oz.) shredded Monterey Jack cheese

1. Cook Simple Chorizo in a large skillet over medium-high heat, stirring until it crumbles and is no longer pink; drain well. Set aside.

2. Place cornmeal in a large bowl.

3. Heat milk and garlic in a heavy-duty saucepan over medium-high heat (do not boil). Pour hot milk mixture over cornmeal, stirring until smooth. Add butter and salt, stirring until well blended; let stand 20 minutes.

4. Preheat oven to 375°. Lightly beat egg yolks. Add yolks, baking powder, cheese, and Simple Chorizo to cornmeal mixture, stirring until blended.

5. Beat egg whites at high speed with an electric mixer until stiff peaks form. Fold egg whites gently into cornmeal mixture. Pour into a lightly greased 13- x 9-inch baking dish.

6. Bake at 375° for 25 to 30 minutes or until lightly browned.

Simple Chorizo

makes 1 lb.   prep: 5 min.

[freeze it]

1   lb. ground pork

1   garlic clove, minced

2   tsp. dried crushed red pepper

1½ tsp. ground cinnamon

1¼ tsp. salt

1   tsp. ground coriander

1   tsp. dried oregano

1. Combine all ingredients, stirring to combine. Store in refrigerator up to 3 days, or freeze up to 1 month.

BREAKFAST SAUSAGE QUESADILLAS

makes 6 servings   prep: 10 min.   cook: 34 min.

1   (12-oz.) package 97% fat-free ground pork sausage

Vegetable cooking spray

1   to 2 tsp. hot sauce

1   (15-oz.) container Southwestern-flavored egg substitute

1½ cups (6 oz.) shredded reduced-fat Mexican cheese blend

6   (10-inch) whole wheat or white flour tortillas

½   cup nonfat sour cream

3   green onions, chopped

Salsa (optional)

1. Cook sausage in a large nonstick skillet coated with cooking spray over medium-high heat 10 minutes or until sausage crumbles and is no longer pink. Drain sausage, and pat dry with paper towels. Return to skillet, and stir in hot sauce; set aside.

2. Cook egg substitute in a large skillet coated with cooking spray over medium-high heat without stirring 1 to 2 minutes or until it begins to set on bottom.

3. Draw a spatula across bottom of skillet to form large curds. Cook 3 to 4 minutes or until thickened and moist. (Do not stir constantly.) Remove skillet from heat.

4. Spoon sausage, egg substitute, and cheese evenly over half of each tortilla. Fold in half, pressing gently to seal. Lightly coat both sides of tortillas with cooking spray.

5. Cook in a large skillet coated with cooking spray over medium-high heat, in 3 batches, 3 minutes on each side or until lightly browned and cheese is melted. Top evenly with sour cream, green onions, and, if desired, salsa. Serve immediately.

Note: We tested with Jimmy Dean 97% fat-free sausage and Egg Beaters Southwestern.

Per serving: Calories 288; Fat 9g (sat 4.1g, mono 0.7g, poly 1.3g); Protein 28g; Carb 25g; Fiber 2.2g; Chol 36.4mg; Iron 2.9mg; Sodium 828mg; Calc 289mg

PANCAKE MIX

makes 6 cups prep: 10 min.

Save money and add extra goodness to breakfast by making your own pancake mix. This recipe comes together in a snap. Once you try it, you'll be reminded that homemade doesn't have to be hard.

6 cups all-purpose flour

3 Tbsp. baking powder

2 tsp. baking soda

2 tsp. salt

1. Stir together all ingredients in a large bowl and store in a zip-top plastic freezer bag up to 6 weeks.

BASIC PANCAKES

makes 4 servings (about 15 pancakes) prep: 10 min. cook: 4 min. per batch

1½ cups Pancake Mix

1 Tbsp. sugar

1½ cups buttermilk

1 large egg, lightly beaten

1 Tbsp. vegetable oil

1. Combine Pancake Mix and sugar in a medium bowl.

2. Whisk together 1½ cups buttermilk, egg, and oil; add to dry ingredients, whisking just until lumps disappear.

3. Pour about ¼ cup batter for each pancake onto a hot, lightly greased griddle or large nonstick skillet. Cook pancakes 2 minutes or until tops are covered with bubbles and edges begin to look cooked; turn and cook 2 more minutes or until done.

Banana-Pecan Pancakes: Stir 1 chopped banana and ¼ cup toasted chopped pecans into batter; proceed as directed.

Fresh Blueberry Pancakes: Add ½ cup fresh blueberries to batter, and fold in gently. Pictured on page 163.

taking sides

A Case for Sweet Cane Syrup, Sorghum Syrup, and Molasses

For years folks have been confused about these Southern sweeteners that long have been sold at roadside stands, at festivals, from backyards, and in local grocery stores. Here's how to know the difference.

"I prefer sorghum molasses on my biscuits!" you may have heard someone say. Factually, molasses comes only from sugar cane. Sorghum syrup, made from only the sorghum grain, is tangier than molasses and comes in just one thickness and flavor.

On the other hand, sugarcane boiled down to a sweet syrup yields a molasses that's light colored and sweet after the first cooking, and dark and thicker after the second cooking. The dark version is the one Southerners love for baked beans and gingerbread. And, if there is a third cooking, the very thick, bitter-tasting, almost black syrup is called blackstrap molasses.

You'll find cane syrup or molasses farther South where the weather is hotter, as sugarcane dies after the first frost. But in the Southern Highlands of North Georgia, East Tennessee, Western North Carolina, and Kentucky, sorghum grows just fine in the temperate weather. Both syrups hold a strong place in Southern culture and were often used in the early days in place of refined sugar, which was expensive and hard to get.

Though the two syrups are often confused in name, true fans of either one claim they definitely know the difference. Sorghum maker Sharon Lykins of West Liberty, Kentucky, says there is no flavor confusion for her. "Sorghum has a real smooth taste," she says. "Molasses has more of a sharp taste that can give people heartburn."

In south Alabama, fifth generation cane syrup maker Joe Todd says he finds sorghum stronger and tarter than cane syrup. He also won't refer to his light, golden syrup as molasses. He bottles only the first cooking of syrup, and says if he boiled it a second time, then he would refer to the second cooking as molasses. "Around here, the only ones that make the thicker molasses are the sugar mills," he explains.

But what can you do with the sweet syrup besides pour it on a biscuit or pancakes? Joe says cane syrup is the original sweetener for pecan pie. "We also add a little bit to turnip or collard greens," he says. "And it's delicious in sweet potato soufflé."

SOUR CREAM-BLUEBERRY MORNING PANCAKES WITH WILD BLUEBERRY-AND-PEACH TOPPING

makes 14 pancakes   prep: 15 min.   cook: 4 min. per batch

Toss the warm peaches with the blueberry sauce, or leave them separate for a beautiful presentation.

[casual gathering]

1 cup all-purpose flour

¼ cup firmly packed light brown sugar

4 tsp. baking powder

¾ tsp. ground cinnamon

½ tsp. baking soda

¼ tsp. salt

2 large eggs, beaten

½ cup canola oil

½ cup 1% low-fat milk

½ cup sour cream

½ tsp. vanilla extract

1¼ cups crushed multigrain flakes and granola cereal with blueberries

Vegetable shortening

Wild Blueberry-and-Peach Topping

Whipped cream, fresh mint sprigs (optional)

Powdered sugar (optional)

1. Sift together first 6 ingredients in a large bowl. Whisk together beaten eggs and next 4 ingredients; stir in cereal. Add to flour mixture, stirring just until dry ingredients are moistened. (Batter will be thick.)

2. Pour about ¼ cup batter onto a hot (350°), greased griddle or a greased nonstick skillet over medium heat; spread batter into a circle with back of a spoon. Cook pancakes 2 minutes or until tops are covered with bubbles and edges look dry and cooked; turn and cook 2 to 3 minutes or until done. Top each serving evenly with Wild Blueberry-and-Peach Topping, and, if desired, whipped cream, mint sprigs, and powdered sugar.

Wild Blueberry-and-Peach Topping

makes 3 cups   prep: 5 min.   cook: 5 min.

½ cup sugar

1 Tbsp. cornstarch

2 cups blueberries

1 (24.5-oz.) jar sliced peaches, drained

1. Whisk together sugar, ¼ cup water, and cornstarch in a medium saucepan; stir in blueberries. Cook over medium-high heat, stirring constantly, until thickened and bubbly.

2. Heat peaches in a small saucepan over medium heat until warm. Stir into blueberry mixture, and serve immediately.

Note: We tested with Post Selects Blueberry Morning Cereal and Dole All Natural Sliced Peaches.

Imagine stepping out of your kitchen and picking your own fresh fruit. You can do just that by growing blueberries in a container—and it's not that hard.

Blueberry Harvest by the Door

If you can grow an azalea, you can succeed with a blueberry bush. Just look at your local nursery for a rabbiteye blueberry that's already bearing fruit. (Our favorites are Delite and Tifblue.) Plant it in a container filled with good soil and peat moss; then water it thoroughly. Be sure to place it in partial to full sun, and mulch well to retain moisture. Check daily during hot weather, because containers dry out quickly. Use an azalea fertilizer in the spring and fall. Not only will your blueberry bush look good year-round, providing bright fall color and great sculptural presence in winter, but you'll also be able to enjoy the sweet fruit for a month or so every summer.

Tip: Blueberries rank among the healthiest of foods. They are rich in antioxidants, such as vitamins C and E, and may reduce the risk of some kinds of cancer.

GUILTLESS FRENCH TOAST

makes 4 servings   prep: 10 min.   cook: 6 min.

8 egg whites	4 whole-grain bakery bread slices
¼ cup fresh orange juice	1 Tbsp. butter
1 Tbsp. vanilla extract	¼ cup maple syrup
1 tsp. ground cinnamon	Fresh blueberries, kiwi slices

1. Whisk together first 4 ingredients in a shallow dish. Dip bread slices in egg mixture, coating both sides.

2. Melt butter on a griddle or in a large nonstick skillet over medium heat. Place bread slices on hot griddle, and pour remaining egg mixture over bread slices. Cook 3 to 4 minutes on each side or until golden. Drizzle with maple syrup, and top with fruit.

Per serving: Calories 220; Fat 4.3g (sat 2.1g, mono 1.3g, poly 0.5g); Protein 10.8g; Carb 33.9g; Fiber 2.8g; Chol 8mg; Iron 1.7mg; Sodium 290mg; Calc 58mg

[southern lights]

OVERNIGHT OVEN-BAKED FRENCH TOAST

makes 8 servings   prep: 15 min.   chill: 8 hr.   bake: 45 min.

{ make ahead }

1	(16-oz.) French bread loaf
¼	cup butter, softened
4	large eggs
1	cup milk

¼	cup sugar
2	Tbsp. maple syrup
1	tsp. vanilla extract
½	tsp. salt

1. Cut bread loaf into about 10 (¾-inch-thick) slices.

2. Spread butter evenly over 1 cut side of each bread slice.

3. Arrange bread, butter side up, in an ungreased 13- x 9-inch baking dish.

4. Whisk together eggs and next 5 ingredients; pour over bread, pressing slices down. Cover and chill 8 hours.

5. Preheat oven to 350°. Remove bread slices from baking dish, and place on 2 lightly greased baking sheets.

6. Bake, uncovered, at 350° for 45 minutes or until golden.

CROISSANT FRENCH TOAST WITH FRESH STRAWBERRY SYRUP

makes 4 servings   prep: 15 min.   cook: 4 min. per batch

Although they're available almost year-round, May is the prime time for fresh strawberries.

4   large day-old croissants

¾   cup milk

2   large eggs

1   tsp. vanilla extract

2   Tbsp. butter

3   Tbsp. powdered sugar

Fresh Strawberry Syrup

Sweetened Whipped Cream (optional)

1. Slice croissants in half lengthwise.

2. Whisk together milk, eggs, and vanilla. Pour into a shallow dish. Dip croissant halves into egg mixture, coating well.

3. Melt 1 Tbsp. butter in a large nonstick skillet over medium heat. Add 4 croissant halves, and cook about 2 minutes on each side or until golden brown. Repeat procedure with remaining butter and croissant halves. Sprinkle with powdered sugar; top with Fresh Strawberry Syrup, and Sweetened Whipped Cream, if desired.

Fresh Strawberry Syrup

makes about 2 cups   prep: 10 min.   stand: 30 min.   cook: 5 min.

1   qt. fresh strawberries, sliced

½   cup sugar

¼   cup orange liqueur or orange juice

1   tsp. orange zest

1. Combine all ingredients in a saucepan, and let stand 30 minutes or until sugar dissolves. Cook over low heat, stirring occasionally, 5 minutes or until warm.

Sweetened Whipped Cream

makes about 1 cup   prep: 5 min.

½   cup whipping cream

1½ Tbsp. powdered sugar

1. Beat cream at medium speed with an electric mixer until soft peaks form. Add powdered sugar, beating until stiff peaks form.

GINGERED AMBROSIA

makes 6 to 8 servings   prep: 10 min.

6   large navel oranges
2   (20-oz.) cans pineapple chunks, drained
⅔   cup sweetened flaked coconut
¼   cup fresh mint leaves, cut into strips

2½ Tbsp. fresh lime juice
1½ Tbsp. grated fresh ginger
Garnish: fresh mint sprig

1. Peel and section oranges over a bowl, reserving juice. Combine orange sections, juice, and remaining ingredients; gently toss. Cover and chill until ready to serve. Garnish, if desired.

GRAND ORANGES AND STRAWBERRIES

makes 10 to 12 servings   prep: 30 min.   chill: 8 hr.

½   cup orange marmalade
1½ cups sparkling white grape juice, chilled
¼   cup orange liqueur

10 to 12 large navel oranges, peeled and sectioned
2   cups sliced fresh strawberries

1. Melt marmalade in a small saucepan over low heat, stirring constantly; remove from heat, and let cool slightly.
2. Stir together marmalade, white grape juice, and orange liqueur in a large serving dish or bowl until blended. Add orange sections, and gently stir. Cover and chill 8 hours.
3. Add strawberries to oranges in bowl, and gently stir. Serve with a slotted spoon.

Note: We tested with Grand Marnier for orange liqueur.

FRESH FRUIT SALAD WITH ORANGE-GINGER SYRUP

makes 8 to 10 servings   prep: 25 min.   **pictured on page 161**

1 large cantaloupe, cut into 2-inch cubes	1 pineapple, peeled, cored, and cut into
2 pt. fresh strawberries, halved	2-inch cubes
1 pt. fresh blueberries	Orange-Ginger Syrup

1. Combine cantaloupe, strawberries, blueberries, and pineapple in a large bowl. Serve with chilled Orange-Ginger Syrup.

Orange-Ginger Syrup

makes ¾ cup   prep: 10 min.   cook: 5 min.   stand: 15 min.   chill: 1 hr.

Make this citrusy-sweet syrup up to 3 days ahead. It's also tasty swirled into unsweetened iced tea.

1 cup sugar	2 tsp. orange zest
½ cup water	¼ tsp. lemon juice
2 Tbsp. chopped fresh ginger	

1. Cook all ingredients in a small saucepan over low heat until sugar dissolves. Bring to a boil; reduce heat, and simmer 1 minute.

2. Remove from heat; let stand 15 minutes. Remove and discard ginger and orange zest. Cool syrup; chill 1 hour or up to 3 days.

Note: Remove zest from an orange using a vegetable peeler or paring knife. Avoid the white, bitter pith as much as possible.

SPICED APPLES

makes 8 servings   prep: 10 min.   cook: 15 min.

½ cup butter	1½ cups sugar
8 large Granny Smith apples, peeled, cored, and sliced	1½ tsp. ground cinnamon
	½ tsp. ground nutmeg

1. Melt butter in a large skillet over medium-high heat; add apples and remaining ingredients. Sauté 15 to 20 minutes or until apples are tender.

SPICED APPLE-PECAN OATMEAL

makes 6 cups   prep: 10 min.   cook: 35 min.   stand: 10 min.

This oatmeal is cooked with equal parts of apple juice and fat-free milk for a creamy texture and lots of flavor.

2   Tbsp. chopped pecans
3   cups apple juice
3   cups fat-free milk
2   cups uncooked regular oats (not quick-cooking)

½   cup coarsely chopped dried apples
½   tsp. salt
2   Tbsp. cinnamon sugar
¼   tsp. vanilla extract

1. Cook pecans in a Dutch oven over medium-high heat, stirring constantly, 5 to 6 minutes or until toasted. Remove pecans, and wipe Dutch oven clean.

2. Bring juice, milk, and next 3 ingredients to a boil in Dutch oven over high heat; reduce heat to medium-low, and simmer, stirring occasionally, 20 minutes or until thickened. Remove from heat. Cover and let stand 10 minutes. Stir in cinnamon sugar, vanilla, and toasted pecans. Serve immediately.

Per 1-cup serving: Calories 275; Fat 3.6g (sat 0.4g, mono 1.5g, poly 1.1); Protein 9.2g; Carb 51.5g; Fiber 3.8g; Chol 2mg; Iron 1.3mg; Sodium 364mg; Calc 141mg

SWEET APPLE BACON

makes 16 slices   prep: 5 min.   cook: 45 min.   **pictured on page 159**

1   lb. thick bacon slices
¼   cup apple butter

2   Tbsp. dark brown sugar

1. Preheat oven to 350°. Arrange bacon in a single layer on rack in an aluminum foil-lined broiler pan.

2. Bake at 350° for 30 minutes. Turn slices; brush with apple butter, and sprinkle evenly with brown sugar.

3. Bake 15 to 20 more minutes or until bacon is lightly browned.

Mother was right—you should eat your breakfast.

• Studies show that eating breakfast improves your overall nutrition, ability to concentrate, and ability to maintain your weight.

• Aim to incorporate starch, fiber, and fat into your breakfast to maintain satiety throughout the morning.

BREAKFAST TURKEY SAUSAGE PATTIES

makes 8 servings   prep: 25 min.   chill: 8 hr.   cook: 12 min. per batch

Freshly grated apple adds a tangy flavor to this spicy turkey sausage. We used a Fuji apple, but any other sweet, crisp apple or pear would make a delicious substitute.

1 large Fuji apple	1¾ tsp. salt
2 garlic cloves, minced	½ tsp. dried crushed red pepper
1¼ lb. lean ground turkey	½ tsp. black pepper
½ cup chopped fresh parsley	1 large egg, beaten
¼ cup finely chopped fresh sage	2 tsp. olive oil

1. Peel and core apple; coarsely shred apple with a hand grater. Place in a wire-mesh strainer; drain well, pressing gently with paper towels.

2. Combine apple, garlic, and next 7 ingredients in a bowl; stir until blended. Shape mixture into 16 patties (about 2 Tbsp. each). Place patties on a wax paper-lined baking sheet. Cover and chill 8 hours or overnight.

3. Heat oil in a large nonstick skillet over medium heat. Cook patties, in batches, about 6 minutes on each side or until browned and done.

Note: Make patties ahead by wrapping in wax paper and heavy-duty aluminum foil and freezing up to 2 weeks. Thaw frozen patties overnight in the refrigerator, and cook as directed.

Per serving: Calories 139; Fat 7g (sat 1.6g, mono 1.1g, poly 0.2g); Protein 14g; Carb 4.5g; Fiber 0.8g; Chol 87mg; Iron 1.4g; Sodium 604mg; Calc 43.5g

[southern lights]

CAKES

"Vegetables are a must on a diet. I suggest carrot cake, zucchini bread, and pumpkin pie." —Jim Davis

BUTTERY POUND CAKE

makes 10 to 12 servings   prep: 15 min.   bake: 1 hr., 20 min.   cool: 15 min.   **pictured on page 166**

For a special dessert, serve toasted slices of this cake with vanilla ice cream, chocolate fudge sauce, and sliced fresh strawberries.

2	cups butter, softened	½	tsp. almond extract
3	cups sugar	4	cups all-purpose flour
6	large eggs	⅓	cup milk
1	tsp. vanilla extract		Toppings: chocolate sauce, sliced strawberries

1. Preheat oven to 325°. Beat butter and sugar at medium speed with an electric mixer until light and fluffy. Add eggs, 1 at a time, beating just until yellow disappears after each addition. Add extracts, beating just until blended. Gradually add flour, beating at low speed until combined. Add milk, beating until smooth. Pour batter into a greased and floured 12-cup Bundt pan.
2. Bake at 325° for 1 hour and 20 minutes or until a long wooden pick inserted in center of cake comes out clean. Cool in pan on a wire rack 15 minutes. Remove from pan; cool completely on wire rack. Serve with desired toppings.

GRANNY'S POUND CAKE

makes 10 to 12 servings   prep: 15 min.   bake: 1 hr., 15 min.   cool: 10 min.

1	cup butter, softened	1	tsp. salt
½	cup shortening	1	cup milk
3	cups granulated sugar	2	tsp. vanilla extract
5	large eggs		Powdered sugar
3	cups all-purpose flour		

1. Preheat oven to 325°. Beat butter and shortening at medium speed with an electric mixer until creamy. Gradually add granulated sugar, beating at medium speed until light and fluffy. Add eggs, 1 at a time, beating after each addition just until the yellow disappears.
2. Stir together flour and salt; add to butter mixture alternately with milk, beginning and ending with flour mixture. Beat at low speed just until blended after each addition. Beat in vanilla just until blended. Pour batter into a greased and floured 12-cup Bundt pan.
3. Bake at 325° for 1 hour and 15 minutes to 1 hour and 20 minutes or until a long wooden pick inserted in center of cake comes out clean. Cool in pan on a wire rack for 10 to 15 minutes. Remove from pan; cool completely on wire rack. Dust cake evenly with powdered sugar.

LEMON-ALMOND POUND CAKE

makes 10 to 12 servings prep: 20 min. bake: 1 hr., 40 min. cool: 10 min.

1 cup butter, softened	1 tsp. lemon extract
3 cups sugar	1 tsp. almond extract
6 large eggs	3 cups all-purpose flour
2 tsp. vanilla extract	1 (8-oz.) container sour cream

1. Preheat oven to 325°. Beat butter at medium speed with an electric mixer until creamy. Gradually add sugar, beating at medium speed until light and fluffy. Add eggs, 1 at a time, beating just until yellow disappears. Add extracts, beating just until blended.

2. Add flour to butter mixture alternately with sour cream, beginning and ending with flour. Beat batter at low speed just until blended after each addition. Pour batter into a greased and floured 12-cup tube pan.

3. Bake at 325° for 1 hour and 40 minutes or until a long wooden pick inserted in center of cake comes out clean. Cool in pan on a wire rack 10 to 15 minutes. Remove from pan; cool completely on wire rack.

CREAM CHEESE-COCONUT-PECAN POUND CAKE

makes 10 to 12 servings prep: 20 min. bake: 1 hr., 30 min. cool: 10 min.

1½ cups butter, softened	½ tsp. salt
1 (8-oz.) package cream cheese, softened	¼ cup bourbon
3 cups sugar	1½ tsp. vanilla extract
6 large eggs	1 cup chopped pecans, toasted
3 cups all-purpose flour	½ cup shredded coconut

1. Preheat oven to 325°. Beat butter and cream cheese at medium speed with an electric mixer until creamy. Gradually add sugar, beating at medium speed until light and fluffy. Add eggs, 1 at a time, beating just until yellow disappears.

2. Sift together flour and salt; add to butter mixture alternately with bourbon, beginning and ending with flour mixture. Beat batter at low speed just until blended after each addition. Stir in vanilla, pecans, and coconut. Pour batter into a greased and floured 12-cup tube pan.

3. Bake at 325° for 1 hour and 30 minutes to 1 hour and 35 minutes or until a long wooden pick inserted in center of cake comes out clean. Cool in pan on a wire rack 10 to 15 minutes. Remove from pan; cool completely on wire rack.

DARK CHOCOLATE BUNDT CAKE

makes 12 servings   prep: 20 min.   bake: 1 hr., 20 min.   cool: 45 min.   **pictured on page 165**

8   oz. semisweet chocolate, coarsely chopped

1   (16-oz.) can chocolate syrup

1   cup butter, softened

2   cups sugar

4   large eggs

2½ cups all-purpose flour

½   tsp. baking soda

¼   tsp. salt

1   cup buttermilk

1   tsp. vanilla extract

Garnishes: Wintry-White Icing (facing page),
    strawberry slices

1. Preheat oven to 325°. Melt chocolate in a microwave-safe bowl at HIGH for 30-second intervals until melted (about 1½ minutes total). Stir in chocolate syrup until smooth.

2. Beat butter at medium speed with an electric mixer until creamy. Gradually add sugar, beating at medium speed until light and fluffy. Add eggs, 1 at a time, beating just until blended after each addition.

3. Sift together flour, baking soda, and salt. Add to butter mixture alternately with buttermilk, beginning and ending with flour mixture. Beat at low speed just until blended after each addition. Stir in vanilla and melted chocolate just until blended. Pour batter into a greased and floured 14-cup Bundt pan.

4. Bake at 325° for 1 hour and 20 minutes or until a long wooden pick inserted in center comes out clean. Cool cake in pan on a wire rack 15 minutes; remove from pan to wire rack, and let cool 30 minutes or until completely cool. Garnish, if desired.

Bundt Success

• Cake recipes often yield different amounts of batter, so it's a good idea to double-check the size of your Bundt pan by filling it to the rim with cups of water. Depending on the brand, a 10-inch pan may hold 10, 12, or 14 cups. If you use a smaller pan than is called for in a recipe, fill the pan no more than one-half to two-thirds full. Refrigerate the remaining batter up to 1½ hours, return to room temperature, and bake as cupcakes or miniature loaf cakes.

• Beware of bright-colored silicone Bundt pans. The results tend to vary, but many buckle when heated and can bake unevenly, producing lopsided Bundt cakes that stick to the pan.

• To ensure that a Bundt cake releases easily from the pan, use a pastry brush to generously coat the inside with solid vegetable shortening. Then sprinkle with flour, tilting and tapping the pan to evenly cover all the narrow crevices. If the pan has a nonstick coating, vegetable cooking spray especially made for baking works equally well.

VANILLA BUTTER CAKE

makes 12 servings   prep: 20 min.   bake: 1 hr.   cool: 45 min.

1   cup butter, softened

2½ cups sugar

5   large eggs

3   cups all-purpose flour

1   tsp. baking powder

¼   tsp. salt

¾   cup half-and-half

1   Tbsp. vanilla extract

Garnishes: Wintry-White Icing, clear sparkling
           sugar, crushed peppermint candy

1. Preheat oven to 325°. Beat butter at medium speed with an electric mixer until creamy. Gradually add sugar, beating at medium speed until light and fluffy. Add eggs, 1 at a time, beating just until blended after each addition.

2. Sift together flour, baking powder, and salt. Add to butter mixture alternately with half-and-half, beginning and ending with flour mixture. Beat at low speed just until blended after each addition. Stir in vanilla. Pour into a greased and floured 12-cup Bundt pan.

3. Bake at 325° for 1 hour to 1 hour and 10 minutes or until a long wooden pick inserted in center of cake comes out clean. Cool in pan on a wire rack 15 minutes. Remove from pan to wire rack; cool 30 minutes or until completely cool. Garnish, if desired.

Wintry-White Icing

makes about ¾ cup   prep: 5 min.

2   cups powdered sugar

3   to 4 Tbsp. milk

1   tsp. vanilla extract

1. Stir together all ingredients until smooth.

HOLIDAY LANE CAKE

makes 12 servings   prep: 17 min.   bake: 15 min.   cool: 10 min.

A deliciously easy version of the bourbon-laced original, this cake is perfect for the beginner baker who wants to make a big impression. The traditional raisin filling is updated with a colorful mixture of candied cherries and sweetened dried cranberries; it's then trimmed with a candy bow and holly leaves, creating a dazzling centerpiece.

1 (18.25-oz.) package white cake mix	½ cup boiling water
3 large eggs	Holly Leaves
1¼ cups buttermilk	Assorted red candies
¼ cup vegetable oil	Candy Bow
Nutty Fruit Filling	Fruit-shaped candies (optional)
1 (7.2-oz.) package fluffy white frosting mix	White sugar crystals

1. Preheat oven to 350°. Beat first 4 ingredients at medium speed with an electric mixer 2 minutes. Pour into 3 greased and floured 8-inch round or square cake pans.

2. Bake at 350° for 15 to 20 minutes or until a wooden pick inserted in center comes out clean. Cool in pans on wire racks 10 minutes. Remove from pans, and cool completely on wire racks.

3. Spread Nutty Fruit Filling between layers. Set aside.

4. Beat frosting mix and ½ cup boiling water at low speed 30 seconds. Scrape down sides of bowl; beat at high speed 5 to 7 minutes or until stiff peaks form.

5. Spread frosting on top and sides of cake. Arrange Holly Leaves around top of cake to resemble a wreath. Arrange candies for berries, and place Candy Bow on wreath. Place fruit candies between leaves, if desired. Sprinkle cake with sugar crystals.

Nutty Fruit Filling

makes 3½ cups   prep: 16 min.

½ cup butter	1 cup chopped sweetened dried cranberries
8 egg yolks	1 cup sweetened flaked coconut
1 cup sugar	½ cup diced red or green candied cherries
1 cup chopped pecans, toasted	⅓ cup orange juice

1. Melt butter in a heavy saucepan over low heat. Whisk in egg yolks and sugar; cook, whisking constantly, 11 minutes or until mixture thickens. Stir in remaining ingredients. Cool.

Holly Leaves

makes 8 dozen   prep: 20 min.   stand: 11 hr.

1   (14-oz.) package green candy melts   Powdered sugar
⅓   cup light corn syrup

[make ahead]

1. Microwave candy melts in a glass bowl at MEDIUM (50% power), stirring once, 1 minute or until melted. Stir in corn syrup. Place in a zip-top plastic freezer bag; seal and let stand 8 hours.
2. Knead 2 to 3 minutes or until soft (about 12 times). Turn out onto a surface dusted with powdered sugar. Roll to ¹⁄₁₆-inch thickness. Cut with 1- and 2-inch holly leaf-shaped cutters. Score leaves with a knife. Place on wax paper over sides of an inverted cake pan for a curved shape. Let stand 3 to 4 hours. Store in an airtight container up to 3 days, if desired.

Candy Bow

makes 1 bow   prep: 25 min.   stand: 8 hr.

1 (14-oz.) package red candy melts   Powdered sugar
⅓ cup light corn syrup

[make ahead]

1. Microwave candy melts in a glass bowl at MEDIUM (50% power), stirring once, 1 minute or until melted. Stir in corn syrup. Place in a zip-top plastic bag; seal and let stand 8 hours.
2. Knead 2 to 3 minutes or until soft (about 12 times). Turn out onto a surface dusted with powdered sugar. Roll to ¹⁄₁₆-inch thickness. Cut into 6 (6- x ½-in.) strips and 1 (½-in.) square using a fluted pastry cutter.
3. Pinch ends of each strip together to form loops. Pinch ends of loops together to form a bow. Wrap ½-inch square around center of bow. Place bow on side of an inverted cake pan, and let stand until firm. Cut 2 (12- x ½-in.) strips; shape strips into streamers. Place streamers on sides of inverted cake pan, and let stand until firm. Store in an airtight container up to 3 days. Attach bow and streamers on outer edge of cake.

LEMON-COCONUT CAKE

makes 12 servings   prep: 30 min.   bake: 18 min.   cool: 10 min.

We spiked the filling with a couple of teaspoons of lemon zest.

1	cup butter, softened	1	tsp. vanilla extract
2	cups sugar		Lemon Filling
4	large eggs, separated		Cream Cheese Frosting
3	cups all-purpose flour	2	cups sweetened flaked coconut
1	Tbsp. baking powder		Garnishes: fresh rosemary sprigs, gumdrops
1	cup milk		

1. Preheat oven to 350°. Beat butter at medium speed with an electric mixer until fluffy; gradually add sugar, beating well. Add egg yolks, 1 at a time, beating until blended after each addition.
2. Combine flour and baking powder; add to butter mixture alternately with milk, beginning and ending with flour mixture. Beat at low speed until blended after each addition. Stir in vanilla.
3. Beat egg whites at high speed with electric mixer until stiff peaks form; fold one-third of egg whites into batter. Gently fold in remaining beaten egg whites just until blended. Spoon batter into 3 greased and floured 9-inch round cake pans.
4. Bake at 350° for 18 to 20 minutes or until a wooden pick inserted in center comes out clean. Cool in pans on wire racks 10 minutes; remove from pans, and cool completely on wire racks.
5. Spread Lemon Filling between layers. Spread Cream Cheese Frosting on top and sides of cake. Sprinkle top and sides with coconut. Garnish, if desired.

Lemon Filling

makes about 1⅔ cups   prep: 10 min.   cook: 5 min.

1	cup sugar	2	tsp. lemon zest
¼	cup cornstarch	⅓	cup fresh lemon juice
1	cup boiling water	2	Tbsp. butter
4	egg yolks, lightly beaten		

1. Combine sugar and cornstarch in a medium saucepan; whisk in 1 cup boiling water. Cook over medium heat, whisking constantly, until sugar and cornstarch dissolve (about 2 minutes). Gradually whisk about one-fourth of hot sugar mixture into egg yolks; add to remaining hot sugar mixture in pan, whisking constantly. Whisk in lemon zest, juice, and butter.

Cream Cheese Frosting

makes 3½ cups prep: 15 min.

1 (8-ounce) package cream cheese, softened
½ cup butter, softened

1 (16-ounce) package powdered sugar, sifted
1 teaspoon vanilla extract

1. Beat cream cheese and butter until fluffy. Gradually add powdered sugar, beating at low speed until blended; add vanilla, beating until blended.

GINGERBREAD CAKE WITH STOUT BUTTERCREAM

makes 12 servings prep: 15 min. bake: 35 min. cool: 1 hr., 10 min.

You'll need about 2 (12-oz.) bottles stout beer for this recipe.

2 (14.5-oz.) packages gingerbread cake mix
2 large eggs
2¾ cups stout beer, at room temperature, divided

½ cup butter, softened
1 (16-oz.) package powdered sugar
Garnishes: toasted pecans, rosemary sprigs

1. Preheat oven to 350°. Stir together gingerbread cake mix, eggs, and 2½ cups stout beer in a large bowl until combined. Pour batter evenly into 2 lightly greased 8-inch square pans.
2. Bake at 350° for 35 minutes or until a wooden pick inserted in center comes out clean. Cool in pans on a wire rack 10 minutes. Remove from pans, and let cool on wire rack 1 hour or until completely cool.
3. Beat softened butter at medium speed with an electric mixer until creamy. Gradually add powdered sugar and remaining ¼ cup stout beer, beating until blended after each addition. Beat 1 minute or until light and fluffy.
4. Spread stout buttercream between layers and on top of cake. Garnish, if desired.

Note: We tested with Betty Crocker Gingerbread Cake & Cookie Mix and Terrapin Wake-n-Bake Coffee Oatmeal Imperial Stout at one testing and Guinness Extra Stout beer at another.

{ freeze it }

inspirations for your taste

These are super easy. If your microwave has an "on" button, you can make them.

Strawberry Dips

prep: 5 min.

Melt chocolate in your microwave, give strawberries a quick dip, and then add a Southern touch by rolling them in chopped pecans.

CHOCOLATE TRUFFLE CAKE

makes 16 servings   prep: 53 min.   bake: 21 min.   cool: 10 min.

Wow your guests with this showy cake wrapped in a fence of rolled wafer cookies. Framing the cake with cookies is easy, fast, and fun.

[test kitchen favorite]

8 (1-oz.) semisweet chocolate baking squares, chopped	½ tsp. salt
1 cup butter, softened	1¾ cup buttermilk
1¾ cups sugar	Unsweetened cocoa
3 large eggs	Chocolate Truffle Filling
2 tsp. vanilla extract	Ganache
2⅔ cups all-purpose flour	2 (14-oz.) containers chocolate hazelnut rolled wafer cookies
1 tsp. baking soda	

1. Microwave chocolate in a mediumm glass bowl at HIGH 1 minute or until melted, stirring once.

2. Beat butter and sugar at medium speed with an electric mixer until fluffy. Add eggs, 1 at a time, beating just until yellow disappears. Add cooled chocolate and vanilla, beating until blended.

3. Combine flour, baking soda, and salt; add to butter mixture alternately with buttermilk, beginning and ending with flour mixture. Beat at low speed just until blended and after each addition.

4. Pour battter into 3 greased parchment paper-lined 9-inch round cake pans dusted with cocoa. Bake at 350° for 21 to 22 minutes or until a wooden pick inserted in center comes out clean. Cool in pan 10 minutes. Remove cake layers to wire racks; cool completely.

5. Spread Chocolate Truffle Filling between layers. Reserving ¼ cup Ganache, spread remaining Ganche on top and sides of cake. Break cookies into long pieces. Line sides of cake with cookies. Spoon reserved Ganache on top center of cake; place broken cookie pieces into mound of Ganache.

Chocolate Truffle Filling

makes 1¾ cups   prep: 5 min.   cook: 1 min.

4   (1-oz.) semisweet chocolate baking squares,
     chopped
6   Tbsp. butter

6   Tbsp. whipping cream
2½ cups powdered sugar, sifted

1. Microwave chocolate and butter at HIGH 1 minute, or until melted, stirring once. Stir in whipped cream. Gradually add powdered sugar, stirring until blended and smooth.

Ganache

makes 2 cups   prep: 6 min.   cook: 1 min.   cool: 5 min.

10 (1-oz.) semisweet chocolate baking squares,

½   cup whipping cream

1. Microwave chocolate and whipping cream in a medium glass bowl at HIGH 1 minute or until melted and smooth, stirring once.

Ganache

Ganache (gahn-AHSH) is a rich frosting made with chocolate and whipping cream.

- Ganache can be served warm, as a glaze.
- It can be cooled slightly and used as a filling for cakes, cookies, or tarts.

- After chilling for several hours, ganache becomes firm enough to shape into truffles.

ANNIVERSARY CAKE

makes 20 to 25 servings prep: 45 min. bake: 35 min. cool: 10 min. **pictured on page 164**

Nothing says celebration in the South like a tall cake spread with homemade frosting.

2 (18.25-oz.) packages white cake mix
  with pudding
2½ cups buttermilk
½ cup butter, melted
4 large eggs

2 Tbsp. lemon zest
1 Tbsp. vanilla extract
1 tsp. almond extract
Coconut Milk Frosting

1. Preheat oven to 350°. Grease and flour 2 (6-inch) and 2 (9-inch) round cake pans; set aside.
2. Beat first 4 ingredients at low speed with an electric mixer just until dry ingredients are moistened. Beat at medium speed 3 to 4 minutes or until batter is smooth.
3. Stir in lemon zest and extracts.
4. Spoon 1¾ cups batter into each 6-inch pan. Divide remaining batter evenly into 9-inch pans.
5. Bake at 350° for 35 to 40 minutes or until a wooden pick inserted in center comes out clean. Cool in pans on wire racks 10 minutes; remove layers from pans, and cool completely on wire racks.
6. Spread Coconut Milk Frosting between 9-inch layers and between 6-inch layers. Frost top and sides of 9-inch cake. Position 6-inch cake in center of 9-inch cake. Frost top and sides of 6-inch cake. Decorate with fresh flowers and ribbon.

Coconut Milk Frosting

makes 9 cups prep: 10 min.

1½ cups butter, softened
¼ tsp. salt
2 tsp. vanilla extract

½ tsp. almond extract
3 (16-oz.) packages powdered sugar
1 cup canned coconut milk

1. Beat first 4 ingredients at medium speed with an electric mixer until fluffy. Add powdered sugar to butter mixture alternately with coconut milk, beating until smooth.

Note: We tested with Pillsbury Moist Supreme Pudding in the Mix white cake mix.

SHORTCUT CARROT CAKE

makes 12 servings prep: 15 min. cook: 18 min. cool: 10 min. chill: 2 hr. **pictured on page 166**

If you have a sweet tooth but you're short on time, this cake takes just about 45 minutes to prepare, bake, and frost.

1   (26.5-oz.) package cinnamon streusel coffee
    cake mix
3   large eggs
⅓   cup vegetable oil
3   large carrots, finely grated

½   cup chopped pecans, toasted
1   cup sweetened flaked coconut
2   Tbsp. orange juice
Cream Cheese Frosting

1. Preheat oven to 350°. Grease 3 (8-inch) round cake pans. Line with wax paper; grease and flour pans.

2. Combine cake mix and streusel packet in a mixing bowl, reserving glaze packet. Add eggs, 1¼ cups water, and oil; beat at medium speed with an electric mixer 2 minutes. Stir in carrots, pecans, and coconut. Pour batter evenly into prepared pans.

3. Bake at 350° for 18 to 20 minutes. Cool in pans on wire racks 10 minutes. Remove from pans; place on racks.

4. Stir together reserved glaze and juice; brush evenly over warm cake layers. Cool completely on wire racks.

5. Spread Cream Cheese Frosting between layers and on top and sides of cake. Chill frosted cake at least 2 hours.

Cream Cheese Frosting

makes 5 cups prep: 10 min.

1   (8-oz.) package cream cheese, softened
1   (3-oz.) package cream cheese, softened
¾   cup butter, softened

7   cups powdered sugar
1   Tbsp. vanilla extract
3   to 4 Tbsp. milk

1. Beat cream cheese and butter at medium speed with an electric mixer until fluffy; gradually add powdered sugar, beating well. Stir in vanilla. Add milk, 1 Tbsp. at a time, until frosting reaches desired consistency.

Cabana

Simple food, simple thinking. Chef Brian Uhl looks at the small mound of fragrant vegetables on the plate at Cabana and pronounces them "squash casserole." No highfalutin title, no gussied-up nonsense from this classically trained chef.

Grilled trout arrives embellished with a smooth crab-corn ragoût. Grilled venison, with a coffee-cocoa rub and no gamy tinges, is complemented by a sweet potato-heirloom apple risotto. Here's our favorite: Tennessee Sliders, sweet potato biscuits with ham from Benton's (a Tennessee treasure featured by many top chefs), and house-made peach preserves. Before 10 p.m., this place concentrates on dinner; then it turns hip and clubby. Sit at traditional tables or cocoon in private, curtained cabanas that seat up to 12 and include MP3 hookups and flat-panel TVs. Just don't forget to eat. "It's casual Southern comfort food," says Brian. Put the emphasis on the word "comfort," and you'll be giving thanks.

1910 Belcourt Avenue, Nashville, Tennessee 37212; www.cabananashville.com or (615) 577-2262.

BASIC LAYER CAKE WITH RASPBERRY BUTTERCREAM FROSTING

makes 10 to 12 servings   prep: 20 min.   bake: 34 min.   cool: 1 hr., 10 min.   **pictured on back cover**

Add an additional ¼ tsp. vanilla extract if you do not have almond extract.

2 cups sugar

1 cup butter, softened

3 large eggs

1 tsp. vanilla extract

¼ tsp. almond extract

3 cups cake flour

1½ tsp. baking powder

¼ tsp. salt

1 cup buttermilks

Raspberry Buttercream Frosting

Garnishes raspberries, fresh mint sprigs

1. Preheat oven to 350°. Beat sugar and butter at medium speed with a heavy-duty electric stand mixer until creamy and fluffy (about 5 minutes). Add eggs, 1 at a time, beating until yellow disappears after each addition. Beat in vanilla and almond extracts.

2. Whisk together flour, baking powder, and salt in a small bowl; add to sugar mixture alternately with buttermilk, beginning and ending with flour mixture. Beat at medium-low speed just until blended after each addition. (Batter will be thick.)

4. Pour batter into 2 greased and floured 8-inch round (2-inch deep) cake pans, spreading to edges. Bake at 350° 34 to 38 minutes or until a wooden pick inserted in center comes out clean. Cool pans on a whiere rack 10 minutes. Remove from pans to wire rack, and cool completely (about 1 hour). Spread Raspberry Buttercream Frosting on top and sides of cake. Garnish, if desired.

Raspberry Buttercream Frosting

makes about 2½ cups   prep: 10 min.

½ cup butter, softened

½ cup fresh raspberries

1   tsp. vanilla extract

⅛ tsp. salt

1   (16-oz.) package powdered sugar

1. Beat first 4 ingredients at medium speed with an electric mixer until creamy.

2. Gradually add powdered sugar, beating at low speed until blended.

Note: Be sure to wash and thoroughly dry raspberries before adding to frosting

RED VELVET LAYER CAKE

makes 16 servings prep: 30 min. bake: 18 min. cool: 10 min.

We baked our cake layers in 6 (8-inch) disposable foil cake pans so that we could fill all the pans at once. This way, if you need to bake the cake layers in batches, the second batch will be ready to put in the oven as soon as the first one is done. To allow the heat to circulate for even baking, space pans at least 2 inches apart from one another and away from the inside walls of the oven. Although the pans are disposable, they can be washed and reused.

1 recipe Chocolate-Red Velvet Cake Batter
1½ recipes Cream Cheese Frosting

Garnishes: fresh mint sprigs, raspberry candies

1. Preheat oven to 350°. Spoon cake batter evenly into 6 greased and floured 8-inch round foil cake pans. Bake at 350° for 18 to 20 minutes or until a wooden pick inserted in center comes out clean.

2. Cool in pans on wire racks 10 minutes; remove from pans, and let cool completely on wire racks.

4. Spread Cream Cheese Frosting between layers and on top and sides of cake. Garnish, if desired.

Chocolate-Red Velvet Cake Batter

makes about 7 cups prep: 15 min.

1 cup butter, softened
2½ cups sugar
6 large eggs
3 cups all-purpose flour
3 Tbsp. unsweetened cocoa

¼ tsp. baking soda
1 (8-oz.) container sour cream
2 tsp. vanilla extract
2 (1-oz.) bottles red food coloring

1. Beat butter at medium speed with an electric mixer until creamy. Gradually add sugar, beating until light and fluffy. Add eggs, 1 at a time, beating just until blended after each addition.

2. Stir together flour, cocoa, and baking soda. Add to butter mixture alternately with sour cream, beating at low speed just until blended, beginning and ending with flour mixture. Stir in vanilla; stir in red food coloring. Use batter immediately.

[test kitchen favorite]

Cream Cheese Frosting

makes about 5 cups   prep: 15 min.

2 (8-oz.) packages cream cheese, softened

½ cup butter, softened

2 (16-oz.) packages powdered sugar

2 tsp. vanilla extract

1. Beat cream cheese and butter at medium speed with an electric mixer until creamy. Gradually add powdered sugar, beating until light and fluffy. Stir in vanilla extract.

Cake Troubleshooting

Use the following tips to help diagnose and correct any cake-baking problems.

If batter overflows:
- Overmixing
- Too much batter in pan

If cake falls:
- Oven not hot enough
- Undermixing
- Insufficient baking
- Opening oven door during baking
- Too much baking powder, soda, liquid, or sugar

If cake peaks in center:
- Oven too hot at start of baking
- Too much flour
- Not enough liquid

If cake sticks to pan:
- Cake cooking in pan too long
- Pan not properly greased and floured

If cake cracks and falls apart:
- Removing pan too soon

- Too much shortening, baking powder, baking soda, or sugar

If texture is heavy:
- Overmixing when adding flour and liquid
- Oven temperature is too low
- Too much shortening, sugar, or liquid

If texture is coarse:
- Inadequate mixing
- Oven temperature too low
- Too much baking powder or soda

If texture is dry:
- Overbaking
- Overbeating egg whites
- Too much flour, baking powder, or soda
- Not enough shortening or sugar

If crust is sticky:
- Insufficient baking
- Oven not hot enough
- Too much sugar

SO-EASY CHERRY-FUDGE CAKE

makes 12 to 15 servings   prep: 15 min.   bake: 27 min.   cool: 1 hr., 10 min.   cook: 5 min.

1	(18.25-oz.) package devil's food cake mix	1	cup sugar
1	(21-oz.) can cherry pie filling	⅓	cup milk
2	large eggs	5	Tbsp. butter
1	tsp. almond extract	1	cup semisweet chocolate morsels

1. Preheat oven to 350°. Beat first 4 ingredients at low speed with a heavy-duty electric stand mixer 20 seconds; increase speed to medium, and beat 1 minute. Pour batter into a greased and floured 13- x 9-inch pan.

2. Bake at 350° for 27 to 30 minutes or until a wooden pick inserted in center comes out clean. Cool cake in pan on a wire rack 10 minutes.

3. Bring sugar, milk, and butter to a boil in a heavy 2-qt. saucepan over medium-high heat, stirring occasionally; boil 1 minute. Remove from heat; stir in chocolate morsels until melted and smooth. Quickly spread frosting over warm cake. Cool completely (about 1 hour).

Note: We tested with Duncan Hines Moist Deluxe Devil's Food Cake Mix and Comstock Original Country Cherry Pie Filling or Topping.

HEAVENLY CANDY BAR CAKE

makes 12 servings   prep: 15 min.   cook: 5 min.   bake: 30 min.   cool: 1 hr., 10 min.

Crushed candy bars in every bite satisfy any sweet tooth.

9	fun-size or 21 mini chocolate-coated caramel and creamy nougat bars	1	tsp. salt
		1½	cups buttermilk
½	cup butter	½	tsp. baking soda
2	cups sugar	1	tsp. vanilla extract
1	cup shortening		Chocolate-Marshmallow Frosting
3	large eggs		Garnish: chopped frozen fun-size chocolate-coated
2½	cups all-purpose flour		caramel and creamy nougat bars (optional)

1. Preheat oven to 350°. Melt candy bars and butter in a heavy saucepan over low heat about 5 minutes, stirring until smooth. Set aside.

2. Beat sugar and shortening at medium speed with an electric mixer about 3 minutes or until well blended. Add eggs, 1 at a time, beating just until blended after each addition.

3. Combine flour and salt. Stir together buttermilk and baking soda. Gradually add flour mixture to sugar mixture, alternately with buttermilk mixture, beginning and ending with flour mixture. Beat at low speed just until blended after each addition. Stir in melted candy bar mixture and vanilla. Spoon batter into 3 greased and floured 9-inch cake pans.

4. Bake at 350° for 30 minutes or until a wooden pick comes out clean. Cool in pans on a wire rack 10 minutes; remove cakes from pans, and let cool completely on wire rack. Spread half of Chocolate-Marshmallow Frosting evenly between cake layers. Spread remaining frosting evenly over top and sides of cake. Garnish, if desired.

Note: We tested with Milky Way Bars.

Chocolate-Marshmallow Frosting

makes about 4½ cups   prep: 15 min.   cook: 5 min.

3 cups miniature marshmallows	6 oz. unsweetened chocolate, chopped
¾ cup butter, cut up	6 cups powdered sugar
¾ cup evaporated milk	1 Tbsp. vanilla extract

1. Melt first 4 ingredients in a 2-quart saucepan over medium-low heat, stirring constantly, 5 minutes or until mixture is smooth.

2. Transfer chocolate mixture to a large bowl. Place the bowl into a larger bowl filled with ice and water. Gradually add powdered sugar, beating at low speed with an electric mixer. Increase speed to medium-high, and beat 5 minutes or until frosting is cool, thick, and spreadable. Stir in vanilla. Use immediately.

CLASSIC COLA CAKE

makes 12 servings   prep: 8 min.   cook: 30 min.   cool: 10 min.

Don't make the frosting ahead—you need to pour it over the cake shortly after baking.

1 cup Coca-Cola	2 cups all-purpose flour
½ cup buttermilk	¼ cup unsweetened cocoa
1 cup butter, softened	1 tsp. baking soda
1¾ cups sugar	1½ cups miniature marshmallows
2 large eggs, lightly beaten	Coca-Cola Frosting
2 tsp. vanilla extract	Garnish: ¾ cup chopped pecans, toasted

1. Preheat oven to 350°. Combine Coca-Cola and buttermilk; set aside.

2. Beat butter at low speed with an electric mixer until creamy. Gradually add sugar; beat until blended. Add egg and vanilla; beat at low speed until blended.

3. Combine flour, cocoa, and soda. Add to butter mixture alternately with cola mixture, beginning and ending with flour mixture. Beat at low speed just until blended.

4. Stir in marshmallows. Pour batter into a greased and floured 13- x 9-inch pan. Bake at 350° for 30 to 35 minutes. Remove from oven; cool 10 minutes. Pour Coca-Cola Frosting over warm cake; garnish, if desired.

Coca-Cola Frosting

makes 2¼ cups prep: 5 min. cook: 5 min.

½ cup butter

⅓ cup Coca-Cola

3   Tbsp. unsweetened cocoa

1   (16-oz.) package powdered sugar

1   Tbsp. vanilla extract

1. Bring first 3 ingredients to a boil in a large saucepan over medium heat, stirring until butter melts. Remove from heat; whisk in sugar and vanilla.

taking sides

The Cola Debate

Next to sweet iced tea, this dark brown liquid is the South's choice for thirst quenching and even for cooking, whether you call it soda, pop, soft drink, or "Coke" (no matter what the brand).

More than 100 years ago, pharmacists, not cooks, brought us the most famous soft drinks in the South. Coca leaves and kola nuts were the source of Atlanta's hangover remedy, Coca-Cola. The first glass of Coca-Cola was sold at Jacob's Pharmacy for five cents a glass. Kola nuts and pepsin gave rise to North Carolina-born Pepsi, which was also invented by a pharmacist.

When sugar was scarce during the Depression, colas did more than quench thirst and cure headaches; they were used in cakes, frostings, glazes, and anything that needed sweetening.

The century-long history of both carbonated beverages in the South brings with it strong loyalties. Proving that the disagreement isn't just regional, one Georgia Internet blogger says, "I've always been a Pepsi girl in the Coke-Pepsi war. Pepsi beats Coke by a mile!" Carl Willis of Chattanooga, and a South Georgia native, disagrees. "Pepsi's just too sweet," he says. "The choice is definitely Coke!"

CHOCOLATE SHEET CAKE

makes 10 to 12 servings   prep: 20 min.   cook: 5 min.   bake: 30 min.

Make the icing five minutes before taking the cake out of the oven.

2   cups sugar
2   cups all-purpose flour
1   tsp. baking soda
1   tsp. ground cinnamon
⅛   tsp. salt
½   cup butter
½   cup shortening

¼   cup unsweetened cocoa
½   cup buttermilk
2   large eggs, lightly beaten
1   tsp. vanilla extract
Chocolate Icing
Vanilla ice cream (optional)

1. Preheat oven to 350°. Sift together first 5 ingredients in a large bowl.

2. Stir together butter, shortening, cocoa, and 1 cup water in a saucepan over medium-low heat, stirring constantly, 5 minutes or just until butter and shortening melt. Remove from heat; pour over sugar mixture, stirring until dissolved. Cool slightly.

3. Stir in buttermilk, eggs, and vanilla. Pour into a greased and lightly floured 15- x 10-inch jelly-roll pan.

4. Bake at 350° for 30 to 35 minutes. (Cake will have a fudgelike texture.) Spread Chocolate Icing over hot cake. Serve with vanilla ice cream, if desired.

Chocolate Icing

makes about 4 cups   prep: 5 min.   cook: 5 min.

½   cup butter
¼   cup unsweetened cocoa
6   Tbsp. milk

1   (16-oz.) package powdered sugar
1   tsp. vanilla
1   cup chopped pecans, toasted

1. Combine butter, cocoa, and milk in a saucepan. Cook over low heat 5 minutes or until butter melts. Cook over medium heat until bubbles appear on the surface. (It will not come to a rolling boil.) Remove from heat; gradually stir in sugar and vanilla. Beat at medium speed with an electric mixer until smooth and sugar dissolves, about 1 minute. Stir in pecans.

BLOND TEXAS SHEET CAKE

makes 12 servings   prep: 15 min.   cook: 15 min.   cool: 2 hr.

Here's a spin on the beloved chocolate Texas Sheet Cake. To serve as large triangles, cut cake into 5- x 5-inch squares, and then cut squares corner to corner.

1   (18.25-oz.) package white cake mix
1   cup buttermilk
⅓   cup butter, melted

4   egg whites
¼   tsp. almond extract
    Caramel-Pecan Frosting

1. Preheat oven to 350°. Beat together first 5 ingredients at low speed with an electric mixer 2 minutes or until blended. Pour batter into a greased 15- x 10-inch jelly-roll pan.
2. Bake at 350° for 15 to 20 minutes or until a wooden pick inserted in center comes out clean. Cool in pan on a wire rack 2 hours.
3. Prepare Caramel-Pecan Frosting. Pour immediately over cooled cake in pan, and spread quickly to cover cake.

Note: We tested with Pillsbury Moist Supreme Premium Classic White Cake Mix.

Caramel-Pecan Frosting

makes 3 cups   prep: 10 min.   bake: 6 min.   cook: 10 min.

1   cup chopped pecans
½   cup butter
1   cup light brown sugar
⅓   cup buttermilk

2   cups powdered sugar
½   tsp. vanilla extract
¼   tsp. almond extract

1. Preheat oven to 350°. Place chopped pecans in a single layer in a shallow pan.
2. Bake at 350° for 6 minutes or until lightly toasted.
3. Bring butter and brown sugar to a boil in a 3½-qt. saucepan over medium heat, whisking constantly (about 2 minutes). Remove from heat, and slowly whisk in buttermilk.
4. Return mixture to heat, and bring to a boil. Pour into bowl of a heavy-duty electric stand mixer. Gradually add powdered sugar and vanilla and almond extracts, beating at medium-high speed until smooth (about 1 minute). Stir in pecans. Use immediately.

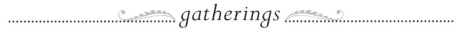

Decoration Dinner on the Grounds serves 12

*Picnic Fried Chicken (page 658)

*Broccoli Slaw (page 733)   Buttered new potatoes

Tomato and sweet onion slices

Bakery rolls

Mississippi Mud Cake

*double recipe

MISSISSIPPI MUD CAKE

makes 15 servings   prep: 15 min.   bake: 36 min.   pictured on page 168

When it comes to desserts at Assistant Test Kitchen Director Rebecca Kracke Gordon's house, sweeter is always better, and her mom's ooey-gooey cake definitely fits the description.

1 cup chopped pecans	4 large eggs
1 cup butter	1 tsp. vanilla extract
4 oz. semisweet chocolate, chopped	¾ tsp. salt
2 cups sugar	1 (10.5-oz.) bag miniature marshmallows
1½ cups all-purpose flour	Chocolate Frosting
½ cup unsweetened cocoa	

1. Preheat oven to 350°. Place pecans in a single layer on a baking sheet.

2. Bake at 350° for 8 to 10 minutes or until toasted.

3. Microwave 1 cup butter and semisweet chocolate in a large microwave-safe glass bowl at HIGH 1 minute or until melted and smooth, stirring every 30 seconds.

4. Whisk sugar and next 5 ingredients into chocolate mixture. Pour batter into a greased 15- x 10-inch jelly-roll pan.

5. Bake at 350° for 20 minutes. Remove from oven, and sprinkle evenly with miniature marsh-mallows; bake 8 to 10 more minutes or until golden brown. Drizzle warm cake with Chocolate Frosting, and sprinkle evenly with toasted pecans.

[casual gatherings]

Chocolate Frosting

makes about 2 cups   prep: 10 min.   cook: 5 min.

½ **cup butter**

⅓ **cup unsweetened cocoa**

⅓ **cup milk**

1 **(16-oz.) package powdered sugar**

1 **tsp. vanilla extract**

1. Stir together first 3 ingredients in a medium saucepan over medium heat until butter is melted. Cook, stirring constantly, 2 minutes or until slightly thickened; remove from heat. Beat in powdered sugar and vanilla at medium-high speed with an electric mixer until smooth.

Mississippi Mud Cupcakes: Prepare pecans and Mississippi Mud Cake batter as directed. Spoon batter evenly into 24 paper-lined muffin cups. Bake at 350° for 20 minutes or until puffed. Sprinkle evenly with 2 cups miniature marshmallows, and bake 5 more minutes or until golden. Remove from oven, and cool cupcakes in muffin pans 5 minutes. Remove cupcakes from pans, and place on wire rack. Drizzle warm cakes evenly with 1¼ cups Chocolate Frosting, and sprinkle with toasted pecans. Reserve remaining ¾ cup frosting for another use. **Note:** To serve remaining Chocolate Frosting over pound cake or ice cream, microwave reserved ¾ cup Chocolate Frosting in a medium-size microwave-safe glass bowl at HIGH 15 seconds or until warm.

Kitchen Express Mississippi Mud Cake: Prepare pecans as directed. Substitute 2 (17.6-oz.) packages fudge brownie mix for batter. Prepare mix according to package directions; pour batter into a greased 15- x 10-inch jelly-roll pan. Bake at 350° for 25 minutes. Remove from oven, and top with marshmallows; bake 8 to 10 more minutes. Proceed as directed. **Note:** We tested with Duncan Hines Chocolate Lover's Double Fudge Brownie Mix.

Test Kitchen Tips

• Be sure to grease pans with shortening, because butter may not release the cake from the pan as easily.

• Dough containing sticky ingredients, such as marshmallows and toffee bits, are best baked on parchment paper-lined baking sheets.

• Allow the last bits of unmelted chocolate to stand briefly in microwave-safe glass bowl before stirring until completely smooth.

COCONUT SHEET CAKE

makes 12 servings   prep: 15 min.   cook: 40 min.   freeze: 30 min.

Cream of coconut can be found in the ethnic food or drink mixers section of supermarkets.

3 large eggs	½ tsp. vanilla extract
1 (8-oz.) container sour cream	1 (18.25-oz.) package white cake mix
1 (8.5-oz.) can cream of coconut	Coconut-Cream Cheese Frosting

1. Preheat oven to 325°. Beat eggs at high speed with an electric mixer 2 minutes. Add sour cream, ⅓ cup water, and next 2 ingredients, beating well after each addition. Add cake mix, beating at low speed just until blended. Beat at high speed 2 minutes. Pour batter into a greased and floured 13- x 9-inch baking pan.

2. Bake at 325° for 40 to 45 minutes or until a wooden pick inserted in center comes out clean. Cool cake in pan on a wire rack. Cover pan with plastic wrap, and freeze cake 30 minutes. Remove from freezer.

3. Spread Coconut-Cream Cheese Frosting on top of chilled cake. Cover and store in refrigerator.

Note: If desired, cake can be baked in a greased and floured 15- x 10-inch jelly-roll pan for 30 to 32 minutes or until a wooden pick inserted in center comes out clean. Makes 15 servings.

Coconut-Cream Cheese Frosting

makes 4 cups   prep: 10 min.

1 (8-oz.) package cream cheese, softened	1 tsp. vanilla extract
½ cup butter, softened	1 (16-oz.) package powdered sugar, sifted
3 Tbsp. milk	1 (7-oz.) package sweetened flaked coconut

1. Beat cream cheese and butter at medium speed with an electric mixer until creamy; add milk and vanilla, beating well. Gradually add sugar, beating until smooth. Stir in coconut.

Frosting Facts

• For the smoothest frosting, freeze cake for at least 30 minutes; then frost. Freeze layers right on the wire rack. If you're not using them right away, wrap frozen layers well in plastic wrap.

• Brush off excess crumbs from top and sides of cooled cake layers before you begin frosting. Use a pastry brush or your fingers to do this.

MIXED-BERRY ANGEL CAKES WITH ALMOND SUGAR

makes 32 cupcakes   prep: 25 min.   chill: 1 hr.   bake: 15 min.   **pictured on page 168**

1 (8-oz.) package fresh strawberries (about 1 cup), sliced	⅔ cup sugar
1 pt. fresh blueberries (about 1 cup)	¾ tsp. almond extract
1 (6-oz.) package fresh raspberries (about 1 cup)	1 (1-lb.) package angel food cake mix
	Frozen whipped topping, thawed

1. Toss together berries. Stir together sugar and almond extract; sprinkle over berries, tossing to coat. Cover; chill 1 hour. Preheat oven to 350°. Prepare cake mix according to package directions.
2. Place paper baking cups in muffin pans; spoon batter into cups, filling two-thirds full. Bake, 1 muffin pan at a time, at 350° for 15 minutes or until lightly browned. Remove cupcakes from pans to wire racks; cool.
3. Cut cupcakes in half horizontally; spoon 1 Tbsp. berry mixture on bottom halves, and cover with tops. Spoon 1 Tbsp. berry mixture on top halves; dollop with whipped topping. Serve immediately.

CHOCOLATE ANGEL FOOD CAKES

makes 2 (15- x 10-inch) cakes   prep: 20 min.   bake: 15 min.   cool: 10 min.   chill: 30 min.

If you don't have 2 jelly-roll pans, use 2 (15- x 10 ¼-inch) disposable foil pans.

1   (16-oz.) package angel food cake mix   ⅔   cup powdered sugar
¼   cup unsweetened cocoa

1. Preheat oven to 325°. Line 2 (15- x 10-inch) jelly-roll pans with parchment or wax paper. Prepare angel food cake mix batter according to package directions, adding unsweetened cocoa. Pour evenly into prepared pans.

2. Bake at 325° for 15 to 20 minutes or until a wooden pick inserted in center comes out clean. Cool in pans on wire racks 10 minutes. (If baking cakes in 1 oven, bake on middle 2 racks for 10 minutes; then switch places, and continue baking for 5 to 10 minutes.)

3. Sift ⅔ cup powdered sugar evenly over 2 (24- x 18-inch) pieces heavy-duty aluminum foil.

4. Loosen edges of cakes from pans. Invert each slightly warm cake onto a prepared foil piece. Carefully remove parchment paper, and discard. Place a cloth towel on top of each cake. Starting at 1 long side, roll up foil, cake, and towel together.

5. Chill rolled cakes 30 minutes or until completely cool. Unroll cakes, and remove towels. (Keep each cake on foil piece.)

HOT FUDGE SUNDAE CAKE ROLLS

makes 10 to 12 servings   prep: 20 min.   freeze: 8 hr.   **pictured on page 168**

This recipe makes two cakes, so you'll have one for now and one for later.

1   recipe Chocolate Angel Food Cakes (recipe   1   (16-oz.) container frozen whipped topping,
     at right)   thawed
½   gal. vanilla ice cream, softened   **Garnishes: grated chocolate, maraschino cherries**
1   (10-oz.) jar maraschino cherries, drained and   **Hot Fudge Sauce**
     chopped

1. Bake, roll, and chill cakes as directed. Remove towels.

2. Spread half of ice cream over top of 1 prepared cake on foil piece, leaving a 1-inch border; sprinkle with half of chopped cherries, and roll up, jelly-roll fashion, ending seam side down. Wrap cake roll with foil piece, sealing at both ends. Place in freezer. Repeat procedure with remaining ice cream, cherries, and prepared cake on foil piece.

3. Freeze cake rolls at least 8 hours or until firm. Unwrap and frost each evenly with whipped topping. Serve immediately, or freeze cake roll 1 hour or until whipped topping is firm; rewrap with foil, and freeze until ready to serve. Garnish, if desired, and serve with Hot Fudge Sauce.

Hot Fudge Sauce

makes 3½ cups   prep: 5 min.   cook: 10 min.

5 (1-oz.) semisweet chocolate baking squares	1 cup evaporated milk
½ cup butter	1 (16-oz.) package powdered sugar

1. Stir together chocolate baking squares and butter in a heavy saucepan over medium-low heat, whisking constantly until melted. Whisk in evaporated milk until blended. Gradually whisk in powdered sugar; stir constantly until blended and smooth, and simmer 1 minute. Serve warm. Sauce may be stored in an airtight container in the refrigerator up to 2 weeks.

PEANUT BUTTER SURPRISE CUPCAKES

makes 10 to 12 servings   prep: 20 min.   bake: 18 min.   cool: 5 min.

¾ cup butter, softened	½ tsp. salt
2 cups granulated sugar	1 cup buttermilk
3 large eggs	1 tsp. vanilla extract
1 cup creamy peanut butter	24 milk chocolate kisses
2 cups all-purpose flour	Confectioners sugar
1 tsp. baking soda	

1. Preheat oven to 375°. Beat butter at medium speed with an electric mixer until creamy. Gradually add granulated sugar, beating until light and fluffy. Add eggs, 1 at a time, beating after each addition. Add peanut butter, beating until smooth.
2. Combine flour, baking soda, and salt; add to peanut butter mixture alternately with buttermilk, beginning and ending with flour mixture. Beat at low speed just until blended after each addition. Stir in vanilla extract.
3. Spoon 2 Tbsp. batter into each of 24 paper baking cups in muffin pans. Place 1 chocolate kiss on its side in center of batter in each cup. Top evenly with remaining batter (about 2 Tbsp. in each cup), covering chocolate kisses.
4. Bake at 375° for 18 to 20 minutes or until golden brown. Let cool in pans on wire racks 5 minutes. Remove from pans, and cool on wire racks. Dust with confectioners sugar. Serve warm or at room temperature.

[for kids]

Pineapple Upside-Down Cake

Our sweet memories of Pineapple Upside-Down Cake go back to childhood. We counted ourselves lucky if we were able to retrieve a portion of the softened pineapple that stuck to the bottom of the skillet. These morsels only increased our anticipation for the time when a real slice would come accompanied by a dollop of sweetened cream.

This Southern delight is noted for being baked in a cast-iron skillet. Our Test Kitchen's skillets got a workout as we tested recipes in search of the all-time best. The cake that wowed us came from *My Mother's Southern Desserts* by James and Martha Pearl Villas (William Morrow Cookbooks, 1998). The gooey pineapple and cherries coated with a buttery brown sugar glaze were scrumptious. But it was the cake base that tasted like no other—light and tender. The pineapple juice helped add volume and flavor, while the egg whites folded into the batter lightened it. If you're short on time, check out our express version, which uses a cake mix.

When inverting the cake, make sure the plate is larger than the skillet to catch additional fruit juices. You may be fortunate enough to sneak a bite of sticky topping and crumbs hot from the skillet.

SKILLET PINEAPPLE UPSIDE-DOWN CAKE

makes 8 to 10 servings   prep: 20 min.   bake: 45 min.   cool: 30 min.   **pictured on page 167**

¼ cup butter	¾ cup granulated sugar
⅔ cup firmly packed light or dark brown sugar	¾ cup all-purpose flour
1 (20-oz.) can pineapple slices, undrained	⅛ tsp. salt
9 maraschino cherries	½ tsp. baking powder
2 large eggs, separated	Whipped cream or vanilla ice cream (optional)

1. Preheat oven to 325°. Melt butter in a 9-inch cast-iron skillet. Spread brown sugar evenly over bottom of skillet. Drain pineapple, reserving ¼ cup juice; set juice aside. Arrange

pineapple slices in a single layer over brown sugar mixture, and place a cherry in center of each pineapple ring; set skillet aside.

2. Beat egg yolks at medium speed with an electric mixer until thick and lemon-colored; gradually add granulated sugar, beating well.

3. Heat reserved pineapple juice in a small saucepan over low heat. Gradually add juice mixture to the yolk mixture, beating until blended.

4. Combine flour, salt, and baking powder; add dry ingredients to the yolk mixture, beating at low speed with electric mixer until blended.

5. Beat egg whites until stiff peaks form; fold egg whites into batter. Spoon batter evenly over pineapple slices.

6. Bake at 325° for 45 to 50 minutes. Cool cake in skillet 30 minutes; invert cake onto a serving plate. Serve warm or cold with whipped cream or ice cream, if desired.

Express Pineapple Upside-Down Cake: Follow original recipe directions for first 4 ingredients. Substitute 1 (9-oz.) package golden yellow cake mix for next 5 ingredients. Prepare cake mix according to package directions, substituting ½ cup pineapple juice for ½ cup water. Spoon batter over prepared pineapple slices as directed. Bake at 350° for 20 to 25 minutes or until a wooden pick inserted in center comes out clean. **Note:** We tested with Jiffy Golden Yellow Cake Mix.

Step-by-Step Pineapple Upside-Down Cake

1. Sprinkle brown sugar over melted butter in skillet.

2. Place whole pineapple slice in skillet center; arrange 10 pieces around it.

3. Place remaining pineapple pieces around sides of skillet.

4. Pour batter over fruit; bake.

PRALINES-AND-CREAM CHEESECAKE

makes 8 servings   prep: 15 min.   bake: 25 min.   stand: 10 min.   chill: 3 hr.

We loved one of our favorite cheesecakes so much that we wanted to lighten it . . . no one will know that it's light unless you tell them.

2 (8-oz.) packages ⅓-less-fat cream cheese, softened	½ cup toffee bits
½ cup sugar	1 (6-oz.) reduced-fat graham cracker crust
½ tsp. vanilla extract	8 Tbsp. reduced-fat whipped topping
2 egg whites	8 tsp. caramel syrup
1 large egg	8 tsp. toffee bits

1. Preheat oven to 325°. Beat first 3 ingredients at medium speed with an electric mixer until blended. Add egg whites, 1 at a time, beating just until blended. Add egg, beating just until blended. Stir in ½ cup toffee bits. Pour into graham cracker crust.

2. Bake at 325° for 25 minutes or until edges of cheesecake are set and center is almost set. Turn off oven; let cheesecake stand in oven 10 minutes. Remove from oven, and cool completely on a wire rack. Cover and chill at least 3 hours. Serve each slice with 1 Tbsp. whipped topping, 1 tsp. caramel syrup, and 1 tsp. toffee bits.

Note: We tested with Heath Bits 'O Brickle Toffee Bits.

Per serving: Calories 401; Fat: 21.8g; (sat 10.8g; mono 0.20g; poly 0.1g); Protein: 8.9g; Chol: 72mg; Iron: 0.5mg; Sodium: 459mg; Calc: 45mg

Bake Cheesecakes Like a Pro

• Let the cream cheese stand at room temperature at least one hour to soften.

• Never beat cheesecake batter at high speed—that increases the chances of cracks on top.

• Use a knife dipped in hot water to cut the cake. Wipe off the knife after each cut. Or put the cake in the freezer until almost frozen. It will cut cleanly.

• If a cheesecake cracks when it comes out of the oven, cover it with a topping. It still tastes great.

RED VELVET CHEESECAKE

makes 8 to 10 servings   prep: 20 min.   bake: 1 hr., 25 min.   stand: 1 hr.   chill: 8 hr.

The cheesecake's deep red filling and snowy topping is wonderfully dramatic. Fresh mint sprigs add a pop of Christmas color.

1½ cups chocolate graham cracker crumbs
¼ cup butter, melted
1   Tbsp. granulated sugar
3   (8-oz.) packages cream cheese, softened
1½ cups granulated sugar
4   large eggs, lightly beaten
3   Tbsp. unsweetened cocoa
1   cup sour cream
½ cup buttermilk

2   tsp. vanilla extract
1   tsp. white vinegar
2   (1-oz.) bottles red liquid food coloring
1   (3-oz.) package cream cheese, softened
¼ cup butter, softened
2   cups powdered sugar
1   tsp. vanilla extract
Garnish: fresh mint sprigs (optional)

1. Preheat oven to 325°. Stir together graham cracker crumbs, melted butter, and 1 Tbsp. granulated sugar; press mixture into bottom of a 9-inch springform pan.

2. Beat 3 (8-oz.) packages cream cheese and 1½ cups granulated sugar at medium-low speed with an electric mixer 1 minute. Add eggs and next 6 ingredients, mixing on low speed just until fully combined. Pour batter into prepared crust.

3. Bake at 325° for 10 minutes; reduce heat to 300°, and bake for 1 hour and 15 minutes or until center is firm. Run knife along outer edge of cheesecake. Turn oven off. Let cheesecake stand in oven 30 minutes. Remove cheesecake from oven; cool in pan on a wire rack 30 minutes. Cover and chill 8 hours.

4. Beat 1 (3-oz.) package cream cheese and ¼ cup butter at medium speed with an electric mixer until smooth; gradually add powdered sugar and 1 tsp. vanilla, beating until smooth. Spread evenly over top of cheesecake. Remove sides of springform pan. Garnish, if desired.

PEACH-CARAMEL CHEESECAKE

makes 12 to 15 servings   prep: 25 min.   bake: 1 hr.   stand: 30 min.   chill: 8 hr.

2   cups crushed shortbread cookies
    (about 28 cookies)
3   Tbsp. butter, melted
4   (8-oz.) packages cream cheese, softened
¾   cup sugar
4   large eggs
1   tsp. vanilla extract
¼   tsp. almond extract (optional)

1   (5-oz.) jar caramel topping
3   Tbsp. whipping cream
½   cup chopped fresh peaches (about 1 small
    ripe peach)
5   cups thinly sliced fresh peaches (about
    5 medium-size ripe peaches)
1   (12-oz.) jar peach preserves

1. Preheat oven to 350°. Combine cookie crumbs and butter; press into bottom and up sides of a greased 10-inch springform pan.

2. Bake at 350° for 8 minutes or until lightly browned. Cool on a wire rack. Reduce oven temperature to 325°.

3. Beat cream cheese at high speed with an electric mixer until creamy, and gradually add sugar, beating well. Add eggs, 1 at a time, beating after each addition. Stir in vanilla and, if desired, almond extract. Pour mixture into prepared crust.

4. Stir together caramel topping and cream in a large glass bowl, and microwave at HIGH 1 to 2 minutes, stirring once. Stir in chopped peaches.

5. Add peach mixture to cream cheese mixture, swirling gently.

6. Bake at 325° for 50 minutes or until cheesecake is almost set. Turn off oven, and let cheesecake stand in oven, with door partially open, 30 minutes. Remove from oven, and gently run a knife around edge of cheesecake to loosen. Cool on a wire rack. Cover and chill at least 8 hours. Release sides of pan; arrange sliced peaches over cheesecake.

7. Microwave peach preserves in a glass bowl at HIGH 1 to 2 minutes or until melted, stirring once. Pour preserves through a wire-mesh strainer into a bowl, and brush over sliced peaches.

Cream Cheese Mints,
page 279

Salty Chocolate-Pecan Candy,
page 262

Classic Peanut Brittle,
page 270 and Popcorn
Peanut Brittle, page 271

popcorn
peanut
Brittle

Classic
Peanut
Brittle

Buckeye Balls,
page 267

Thumbprint Cookies,
page 289

Hot-Spiced Bourbon Balls,
page 268

From back to front:
White Chocolate-Covered Pretzel Cookies,
Cranberry-White Chocolate Cookies,
Nutty Peanut Butter-Chocolate Chip Cookies,
and Turtle Cookies, page 281

Fruit-Filled Cookies and Snowflake Cookies,
page 297

Honey-Pecan Shortbread,
page 311

Blackberry-Lemon
Squares, page 298

S'more Puffs,
page 369

Sugar-and-Spice Fruit Tamales,
page 350

250

Macadamia
Nut Crème Brûlée, page 321

English Rice Pudding,
page 322

Fig-Walnut Pudding,
page 337

IRISH STRAWBERRY-AND-CREAM CHEESECAKE

makes 10 to 12 servings   prep: 20 min.   bake: 1 hr., 5 min.   stand: 15 min.   chill: 8 hr.

1 cup graham cracker crumbs	2 tsp. vanilla extract
3 Tbsp. butter, melted	¼ cup Irish cream liqueur
3 Tbsp. sugar	4 large eggs
4 (8-oz.) packages cream cheese, softened	1¼ cups sour cream, divided
1 cup sugar	3 Tbsp. strawberry preserves
3 Tbsp. all-purpose flour	Garnish: whole strawberries (optional)

1. Preheat oven to 325°. Stir together first 3 ingredients; press mixture into bottom of a lightly greased 9-inch springform pan.

2. Bake crust at 325° for 10 minutes. Cool on a wire rack. Reduce oven temperature to 300°.

3. Beat cream cheese, 1 cup sugar, and 3 Tbsp. flour at medium speed with an electric mixer until smooth. Gradually add vanilla and Irish cream liqueur, beating just until blended. Add eggs, 1 at a time, beating at low speed just until blended after each addition. Add ¾ cup sour cream, beating just until blended.

4. Pour half of batter into prepared crust. Dollop strawberry preserves over batter; gently swirl batter with a knife to create a marbled effect. Top with remaining batter.

5. Bake at 300° for 55 minutes or until edges of cheesecake are set. (Center of cheesecake will not appear set.) Turn off oven; let cheesecake stand in oven 15 minutes. Remove cheesecake from oven; gently run a knife around edge of cheesecake to loosen. Cool completely on a wire rack. Cover and chill 8 hours.

6. Release and remove sides of pan. Spread remaining ½ cup sour cream evenly over top of cheesecake; garnish, if desired.

Note: We tested with Baileys Irish Cream.

PASSOVER CHEESECAKE

makes 10 to 12 servings   prep: 15 min.   cook: 45 min.   chill: 8 hr.

Matzo is a flat, brittle bread made from only flour and water and baked without leavening. Find it on the ethnic food aisle of your local supermarket.

¾ cup crushed matzo
¼ cup butter, melted
¼ cup sugar
3   (8-oz.) packages cream cheese, softened

1   cup sugar
3   large eggs
½ tsp. lemon zest
1   Tbsp. fresh lemon juice

1. Preheat oven to 375°. Stir together first 3 ingredients. Press mixture into bottom and 1 inch up sides of a lightly greased 9-inch springform pan.
2. Beat cream cheese at medium speed with an electric mixer until smooth. Gradually add 1 cup sugar, beating until blended.
3. Add eggs, 1 at a time, beating until blended after each addition. Beat in lemon zest and juice. Pour mixture into prepared crust.
4. Bake at 375° for 45 minutes or until set. Remove cheesecake from oven; cool on a wire rack. Cover and chill 8 hours. Gently run a knife around edge of cheesecake, and release sides of pan.

CHOCOLATE-CHERRY SURPRISE CHEESECAKE

makes 10 to 12 servings   prep: 30 min.   cook: 5 min.   cool: 5 min.   bake: 1 hr., 30 min.
stand: 15 min.   chill: 8 hr.

This cheesecake has a scrumptious homemade fudge brownie crust.

½ cup butter
4   (1-oz.) unsweetened chocolate baking squares
2¼ cups sugar, divided
5   large eggs
¼ cup milk
2   tsp. vanilla extract, divided
1   cup all-purpose flour
½ tsp. salt

3   (8-oz.) packages cream cheese, softened
½ cup sour cream
2   (1-oz.) semisweet chocolate baking squares, melted
1   cup canned cherry pie filling
Toppings: canned cherry pie filling, sweetened whipped cream, milk chocolate kisses

1. Preheat oven to 325°. Melt butter and unsweetened chocolate squares in a 3-qt. heavy saucepan over low heat, stirring constantly. Remove from heat, and cool 5 minutes. Stir in 1½ cups sugar. Add 2 eggs, 1 at a time, blending well after each addition. Add milk and 1 tsp. vanilla. Add flour and salt, stirring until well blended. Spread mixture evenly into a lightly greased 9-inch springform pan.

2. Bake at 325° for 25 minutes. Remove from oven, and cool in pan on a wire rack. Reduce oven temperature to 300°.

3. Beat cream cheese and remaining ¾ cup sugar at medium speed with an electric mixer until smooth. Add remaining 1 tsp. vanilla, beating just until blended. Add remaining 3 eggs, 1 at a time, beating at low speed just until blended after each addition. Add sour cream and melted semisweet chocolate squares, beating just until blended.

4. Spoon cherry pie filling evenly over prepared crust. Pour chocolate cheesecake mixture over cherry pie filling.

5. Bake at 300° for 1 hour and 5 minutes to 1 hour and 10 minutes or until edges of cheesecake are set. (Center of cheesecake will not appear set.) Turn oven off; let cheesecake stand in oven 15 minutes. Remove cheesecake from oven; gently run a knife around edge of cheesecake to loosen. Cool completely on a wire rack. Cover and chill 8 hours. Release and remove sides of pan; serve with desired toppings.

BROWN SUGAR-PECAN COFFEE CAKE

makes 12 servings   prep: 15 min.   bake: 25 min.   **pictured on page 168**

This recipe received our Test Kitchen's highest rating.

2	cups all-purpose flour	1	tsp. baking soda
2	cups firmly packed light brown sugar	3	Tbsp. granulated sugar
¾	cup butter, cubed	1	tsp. ground cinnamon
1	cup sour cream	1	cup chopped pecans
1	large egg, lightly beaten		

1. Preheat oven to 350°. Stir together flour and brown sugar in a large bowl. Cut ¾ cup butter into flour mixture with a pastry blender or 2 forks until crumbly. Press 2¾ cups crumb mixture evenly on the bottom of a lightly greased 13- x 9-inch pan.

2. Stir together sour cream, egg, and baking soda; add to remaining crumb mixture, stirring just until dry ingredients are moistened. Stir together granulated sugar and cinnamon. Pour sour cream mixture over crumb crust in pan; sprinkle evenly with cinnamon mixture and pecans.

3. Bake at 350° for 25 to 30 minutes or until a wooden pick inserted into center comes out clean.

CHOCOLATE-CREAM CHEESE COFFEE CAKES

makes about 24 servings prep: 30 min.   cook: 45 min.

1⅓ cups all-purpose flour

½ cup firmly packed brown sugar

½ cup cold butter, cut up

1 cup chopped pecans

1 (8-oz.) package cream cheese, softened

¼ cup granulated sugar

1 Tbsp. flour

1 large egg

1 tsp. vanilla extract, divided

Chocolate Velvet Cake Batter

1 cup powdered sugar

2 Tbsp. milk

1. Preheat oven to 350°. Stir together 1⅓ cups flour and brown sugar in a small bowl. Cut butter into flour mixture with a pastry blender or 2 forks until crumbly; stir in pecans. Set aside.

2. Beat cream cheese at medium speed with an electric mixer until smooth; add granulated sugar and 1 Tbsp. flour, beating until blended. Add egg and ½ tsp. vanilla, beating until blended.

3. Spoon Chocolate Velvet Cake Batter evenly into 2 greased and floured 9-inch springform pans. Dollop cream cheese mixture evenly over cake batter, and gently swirl through cake batter with a knife. Sprinkle reserved pecan mixture evenly over cake batter.

4. Bake at 350° for 45 minutes or until set. Cool on a wire rack.

5. Whisk together powdered sugar, milk, and remaining ½ tsp. vanilla. Drizzle evenly over tops of coffee cakes.

Chocolate Velvet Cake Batter

makes about 8½ cups prep: 15 min.

The addition of hot water at the end of this recipe makes an exceptionally moist cake.

1½ cups semisweet chocolate morsels

½ cup butter, softened

1 (16-oz.) package light brown sugar

3 large eggs

2 cups all-purpose flour

1 tsp. baking soda

½ tsp. salt

1 (8-oz.) container sour cream

1 cup hot water

2 tsp. vanilla extract

1. Melt semisweet chocolate morsels in a microwave-safe bowl at HIGH for 30-second intervals until melted (about 1½ minutes total time). Stir until smooth.

2. Beat butter and brown sugar at medium speed with an electric mixer, beating about 5 minutes or until well blended. Add eggs, 1 at a time, beating just until blended after each addition. Add melted chocolate, beating just until blended.

3. Sift together flour, baking soda, and salt. Gradually add to chocolate mixture alternately with sour cream, beginning and ending with flour mixture. Beat at low speed just until blended after each addition. Gradually add 1 cup hot water in a slow, steady stream, beating at low speed just until blended. Stir in vanilla.

CINNAMON-PECAN COFFEE CAKE

makes 10 to 12 servings   prep: 15 min.   chill: 8 hr.   bake: 55 min.   stand: 10 min.

1 cup sugar	½ cup butter, melted
1 Tbsp. ground cinnamon	1 cup chopped pecans
1 (25-oz.) package frozen roll dough	Brown Sugar Glaze

1. Combine sugar and cinnamon.

2. Dip rolls in butter, and roll in sugar mixture. Arrange rolls in a well-greased 10-inch tube pan; sprinkle with nuts. Cover and chill 8 hours.

3. Preheat oven to 325°. Pour Brown Sugar Glaze over dough.

4. Bake at 325° for 55 minutes or until done. Let stand 10 minutes. Invert onto a serving plate, and drizzle glaze in pan.

Note: We tested with Rich's Enriched Homestyle Roll Dough.

Brown Sugar Glaze

makes about ¾ cup   prep: 5 min.

½ cup whipping cream	1 tsp. ground cinnamon
½ cup firmly packed brown sugar	

1. Beat whipping cream at high speed with an electric mixer until soft peaks form; stir in brown sugar and cinnamon.

Mardi Gras Dinner   serves 6

Fresh grapes and strawberries
Shrimp and Andouille Sausage With Asiago Grits (page 405)
Mixed salad greens with bottled vinaigrette
Traditional King Cake
Pralines (page 275)

TRADITIONAL KING CAKE

makes 2 cakes (about 18 servings each)   prep: 30 min.   cook: 10 min.   stand: 5 min.
rise: 1 hr., 20 min.   bake: 14 min.   cool: 10 min.

This recipe uses bread flour, which makes for a light, airy cake. You still get tasty results with all-purpose flour—the cake will just be more dense.

1 (16-oz.) container sour cream	6 to 6½ cups bread flour*
⅓ cup sugar	⅓ cup butter, softened
¼ cup butter	½ cup sugar
1 tsp. salt	1½ tsp. ground cinnamon
2 (¼-oz.) envelopes active dry yeast	Creamy Glaze
½ cup warm water (100° to 110°)	Purple-, green-, and gold-tinted sparkling sugar
1 Tbsp. sugar	sprinkles
2 large eggs, lightly beaten	

1. Cook first 4 ingredients in a medium saucepan over low heat, stirring often, until butter melts. Set aside, and cool mixture to 100° to 110°.

2. Stir together yeast, ½ cup warm water, and 1 Tbsp. sugar in a 1-cup glass measuring cup; let stand 5 minutes.

3. Beat sour cream mixture, yeast mixture, eggs, and 2 cups flour at medium speed with a heavy-duty electric stand mixer until smooth. Reduce speed to low, and gradually add enough remaining flour (4 to 4½ cups) until a soft dough forms.

4. Turn dough out onto a lightly floured surface; knead until smooth and elastic (about 10 minutes). Place in a well-greased bowl, turning to grease top.

5. Cover and let rise in a warm place (85°), free from drafts, 1 hour or until doubled in bulk.

6. Punch down dough, and divide in half. Roll each portion into a 22- x 12-inch rectangle. Spread ⅓ cup softened butter evenly on each rectangle, leaving a 1-inch border. Stir together ½ cup sugar and cinnamon, and sprinkle evenly over butter on each rectangle.

7. Roll up each dough rectangle, jelly-roll fashion, starting at 1 long side. Place 1 dough roll, seam side down, on a lightly greased baking sheet. Bring ends of roll together to form an oval ring, moistening and pinching edges together to seal. Repeat with second dough roll.

8. Cover and let rise in a warm place (85°), free from drafts, 20 to 30 minutes or until doubled in bulk.

9. Bake at 375° for 14 to 16 minutes or until golden. Slightly cool cakes on pans on wire racks (about 10 minutes). Drizzle Creamy Glaze evenly over warm cakes; sprinkle with colored sugars, alternating colors and forming bands. Let cool completely.

Cream Cheese-Filled King Cake: Prepare each 22- x 12-inch dough rectangle as directed. Omit ⅓ cup softened butter and 1½ tsp. ground cinnamon. Increase ½ cup sugar to ¾ cup sugar. Beat ¾ cup sugar; 2 (8-oz.) packages cream cheese, softened; 1 large egg; and 2 tsp. vanilla extract at medium speed with an electric mixer until smooth. Spread cream cheese mixture evenly on each dough rectangle, leaving 1-inch borders. Proceed with recipe as directed.

* 6 to 6½ cups all-purpose flour may be substituted.

Creamy Glaze

makes 1½ cups   prep: 5 min.

3	cups powdered sugar	
3	Tbsp. butter, melted	
2	Tbsp. fresh lemon juice	

¼	tsp. vanilla extract
2	to 4 Tbsp. milk

1. Stir together first 4 ingredients. Stir in 2 Tbsp. milk, adding additional milk, 1 tsp. at a time, until spreading consistency.

CANDIES & COOKIES

"Think what a better world it would be if we all, the whole world, had cookies and milk about three o'clock every afternoon and then lay down on our blankets for a nap." —Robert Fulghum

SALTY CHOCOLATE-PECAN CANDY

makes 1¾ lb.   prep: 10 min.   bake: 13 min.   chill: 1 hr.   **pictured on page 242**

This candy will soften slightly while at room temperature.

1 cup pecans, coarsely chopped
3 (4-oz.) bars bittersweet chocolate baking bars

3 (4-oz.) white chocolate baking bars
1 tsp. coarse sea salt*

1. Preheat oven to 350°. Place pecans in a single layer on a baking sheet.
2. Bake at 350° for 8 to 10 minutes or until toasted. Reduce oven temperature to 225°.
3. Line a 17- x 12-inch jelly-roll pan with parchment paper. Break each chocolate bar into 8 equal pieces. (You will have 48 pieces total.) Arrange in a checkerboard pattern in jelly-roll pan, alternating white and dark chocolate. (Pieces will touch.)
4. Bake at 225° for 5 minutes or just until chocolate is melted. Remove pan to a wire rack. Swirl chocolates into a marble pattern using a wooden pick. Sprinkle evenly with toasted pecans and salt.
5. Chill 1 hour or until firm. Break into pieces. Store in an airtight container in refrigerator up to 1 month.

* ¾ tsp. kosher salt may be substituted.

Note: We tested with Ghirardelli 60% Cacao Bittersweet Chocolate Baking Bars and Ghirardelli White Chocolate Baking Bars.

VELVETY PECAN CANDY

makes about 3 dozen (about 3 lb.)   prep: 10 min.   bake: 8 min.   chill: 2 hr.

The South's favorite nut shines in these treats. They are so tasty no one will believe that they're also oh-so easy.

3 cups coarsely chopped pecans
Wax paper
1½ lb. vanilla or chocolate candy coating,
    coarsely chopped

1 (14-oz.) can sweetened condensed milk
¼ tsp. salt
1 tsp. vanilla extract

1. Preheat oven to 350°. Bake pecans in a single layer in a shallow pan 8 to 10 minutes or until toasted and fragrant.
2. Line a 15- x 10-inch jelly-roll pan with wax paper. Lightly grease wax paper.

You say PEE-cans, I say pah-KAHNS….You say PRAY-leens, I say PRAH-leens….

Southerners are often lumped together by the way they talk, but when it comes to pecans and pralines, pronunciation identifies one's roots.

"What a silly question," says an Atlanta-bred woman. "It's pah-KAHNS!" No, no, no, says a man from South Alabama, who says he eats only "PEE-cans."

When the word war escalates, the pah-KAHN sayers will remind the other side that a PEE-can is a container people used to put beside the bed when outhouses were in use. The comeback from those in the deeper South who tend to prefer PEE-can is that only Yankees say pah-KAHNS—and the definition of Yankee would be anyone who grew up north of the "Macon (as in Macon, Georgia)-Dixon" line. Then they remind pah-KAHN sayers that Mitchell County, Georgia, is the PEE-can capital of the world, where PEE-can wood came from that was used in the Olympic torch that was carried through Atlanta in 1996. And, if the people in the PEE-can capital of the world say it that way, it must be official. That's about as bad as it gets, but the word war continues, often splitting families.

Those who say PEE-can are just as likely to get in another word war over the pronunciation of "praline." Says Virginian Kathy Milburn, "I was raised in New Orleans, where the pralines are king. And THEY pronounce it PRAH-lines there, so I do too."

In Birmingham, Anita Skelton, a teacher of nonEnglish-speaking students, tells her pupils that you eat pah-KAHNS and PRAY-leens and both are delicious! Certainly, this is a war that will never be won. So perhaps the best way to keep all Southerners happy is simply to keep their mouths full of pecans and pralines. There's no disagreement on taste!

3. Microwave candy coating, sweetened condensed milk, and salt in a 2-qt. microwave-safe bowl at HIGH 3 to 5 minutes, stirring at 1-minute intervals. Stir until smooth. Stir in vanilla and pecans. Spread in an even layer in prepared pan. Cover and chill 2 hours or until set.
4. Turn candy out onto cutting board, and cut into squares. Store, covered, at room temperature.

DIVINITY CANDY WITH SUGARED MARASCHINO CHERRIES

makes 5 dozen   prep: 30 min.   stand: 16 hr.

1 (7.2-oz.) package home-style fluffy white
   frosting mix
½ cup boiling water
⅓ cup light corn syrup
2 tsp. vanilla extract

1 (16-oz.) package powdered sugar
1½ cups chopped pecans, toasted
Sugared Maraschino Cherries and Mint Sprigs
   (3 recipes) or 60 toasted pecan halves

1. Place first 4 ingredients in a 4-qt. mixing bowl. Beat at low speed with a heavy-duty electric mixer 1 minute or until mixture is blended. Beat mixture at high speed 3 to 5 minutes or until stiff peaks form. Gradually add powdered sugar, beating at low speed until blended. Stir in chopped pecans.

2. Drop mixture by rounded tablespoonfuls onto wax paper. Press tip of a lightly greased wooden spoon handle into center of each candy, making an indentation. Let stand 8 hours; remove to wire racks, and let stand 8 more hours or until bottom of candy is firm. Place 1 cherry or pecan half in each indentation just before serving. Store in airtight containers.

Sugared Maraschino Cherries and Mint Sprigs

makes 20 cherries   prep: 45 min.   stand: 2 hr.

16 to 20 maraschino cherries with stems,
   rinsed and well drained
16 fresh mint sprigs, rinsed

1⅓ cups powdered sugar
1 Tbsp. meringue powder
½ cup sugar

1. Place cherries and mint on paper towels, and let stand until completely dry.

2. Beat powdered sugar, ⅓ cup water, and meringue powder at medium speed with an electric mixer 2 to 3 minutes or until smooth and creamy.

3. Brush cherries with meringue mixture, using a small paintbrush; sprinkle with sugar, and place on a wire rack. Let stand 2 to 3 hours or until dry.

SIMPLY HEAVEN FUDGE

makes about 64 pieces   prep: 10 min.   cook: 12 min.

A candy thermometer simplifies the process of bringing the sugar, evaporated milk, and butter to the soft-ball stage. Make sure the thermometer isn't touching the bottom of the pot, and be sure to read the temperature at eye level. Soft-ball stage (234°) is a candy-making term. Drop a small amount of boiling mixture (in this recipe, the sugar, milk, and butter combination) into a glass cup of cold water. When it forms a soft ball that flattens as you remove it from the water, you've reached the soft-ball stage.

1⅔ cups sugar	2 cups miniature marshmallows
⅔ cup evaporated milk	1½ cups semisweet chocolate morsels
2 Tbsp. butter	2 tsp. vanilla extract

1. Bring first 3 ingredients to a boil in a large heavy saucepan over medium heat; boil, stirring constantly, until a candy thermometer registers 234° (about 7 minutes).

2. Remove from heat; stir in marshmallows and chocolate morsels until smooth. Stir in 2 tsp. vanilla.

3. Pour into a buttered 8-inch square pan; cool completely. Cut into 1-inch squares.

Roasted Pecan Fudge: Preheat oven to 450°. Soak 2½ cups pecan halves in water to cover 20 minutes; drain well. Sprinkle 2 Tbsp. salt evenly over the bottom of a 15- x 10-inch jelly-roll pan. Arrange pecans in a single layer in pan; sprinkle evenly with 2 more Tbsp. salt. Place pecans in hot oven, and turn off oven. Let stand in oven 1 hour and 30 minutes. Toss pecans in a strainer to remove excess salt. Coarsely chop pecans, and cool. Prepare Simply Heaven Fudge as directed, stirring in chopped pecans with vanilla. Makes about 64 pieces. Prep: 15 min.; Soak: 20 min.; Stand: 1 hr., 30 min.

MAMA'S FUDGE

makes about 20 (1-inch) pieces prep: 10 min.   cook: 20 min.   cool: 25 min.

Here's the old-fashioned way to make fudge. "My grandmother, Ruth Pilgrim, taught my mother, Anne Kracke, how to make this fudge, and my mother taught me," says Rebecca Kracke Gordon of the Test Kitchen. She adds that this decadent goodie is a staple gift during the holidays for teachers, neighbors, and friends.

2 cups sugar	¼ tsp. salt
⅔ cup milk	3 Tbsp. butter
¼ cup unsweetened cocoa	1 tsp. vanilla extract
1 Tbsp. corn syrup	

1. Stir together sugar, milk, cocoa, corn syrup, and salt in a 2-qt. saucepan. Bring mixture to a boil over medium-high heat, and cook until a candy thermometer registers 240°. Remove mixture from heat; add butter, and let melt. (Do not stir.) Let cool 10 to 15 minutes or until pan is cool to the touch. Stir in vanilla.

2. Beat mixture with an electric mixer at medium-low speed 2 to 3 minutes or until mixture begins to lose its gloss. Working quickly, pour fudge onto a buttered 11- x 7-inch platter. Let cool 15 minutes. Cut into 1-inch pieces.

MICROWAVE CHOCOLATE FUDGE

makes 3 dozen squares prep: 5 min.   cook: 5 min.   chill: 8 hr.

The milk chocolate morsels give this fudge a Tootsie Roll-like flavor.

3 cups milk chocolate morsels	¼ cup butter, cut into pieces
1 (14-oz.) can sweetened condensed milk	

1. Combine all ingredients in a 2-qt. glass bowl. Microwave chocolate mixture at MEDIUM (50% power) 5 minutes, stirring at 1½-minute intervals. Pour into a greased 8-inch square dish. Cover and chill 8 hours; cut into 1½-inch squares. Store in refrigerator.

Halloween Open House serves 24

*Layered Spicy Black Bean Dip (page 51)
Pork Tenderloin on Cornmeal Biscuits (page 64)
Assorted cheeses and grapes
Broccoli florets, cherry tomatoes, and carrot sticks with Ranch dip
Luscious Lemon Squares (page 298)   Buckeye Balls

*double recipe

BUCKEYE BALLS

makes 7 dozen   prep: 1 hr.   chill: 10 min.   **pictured on page 244**

With only five ingredients, these candies are simple to make and taste divine.

1   (16-oz.) jar creamy peanut butter
1   cup butter, softened
1½ (16-oz.) packages powdered sugar

2   cups (12 oz.) semisweet chocolate morsels
2   Tbsp. shortening

1. Beat peanut butter and butter at medium speed with an electric mixer until blended. Gradually add powdered sugar, beating until blended.

2. Shape into 1-inch balls; chill 10 minutes or until firm.

3. Microwave chocolate and shortening in a microwave-safe 2-qt. glass bowl at HIGH 1½ minutes or until melted, stirring twice.

4. Dip each ball in chocolate mixture until partially coated; place on wax paper to harden. Store in an airtight container.

PEANUT BUTTER BONBONS

makes about 7 dozen   prep: 1 hr.   chill: 1 hr.

[*make ahead*]

1   (18-oz.) jar creamy or chunky peanut butter

1   cup butter, softened

1½ cups finely crushed graham cracker crumbs

4   cups powdered sugar

1½ cups finely chopped roasted peanuts

1. Beat peanut butter and butter at medium speed with an electric mixer until creamy; add graham cracker crumbs, beating until blended. Gradually add powdered sugar, beating at low speed until blended. Shape into 1-inch balls, and roll in peanuts. Cover and chill 1 hour. Store in refrigerator.

HOT-SPICED BOURBON BALLS

makes 30 balls   prep: 35 min.   bake: 8 min.   chill: 1 hr.   **pictured on page 245**

[*make ahead*]

1   cup coarsely chopped pecans

1¼ cups powdered sugar, divided

2   Tbsp. unsweetened cocoa

½   tsp. salt

¼   tsp. ground cinnamon

¼   tsp. ground nutmeg

½   tsp. ground red pepper (optional)

¼   cup bourbon

2   Tbsp. sorghum*

60 vanilla wafers, finely crushed
    (about 2 cups plus 2 Tbsp.)

1. Preheat oven to 350°. Place pecans in a single layer in a shallow pan. Bake at 350° for 8 to 10 minutes or until toasted.

2. Sift together 1 cup powdered sugar, next 4 ingredients, and, if desired, ground red pepper. Stir together bourbon and sorghum. Gradually add powdered sugar mixture to bourbon mixture, stirring until blended. Stir in vanilla wafers and toasted pecans; stir 1 minute. (Place a small amount of mixture in palm of hand, and make a fist around mixture, testing to be sure dough will hold its shape. If not, continue to stir in 20-second intervals.)

3. Shape into 1-inch balls. Roll balls in remaining ¼ cup powdered sugar; place on a wax paper-lined baking sheet. Chill 1 hour or until slightly firm. Store in an airtight container in refrigerator up to 1 week.

* Molasses, honey, or cane syrup may be substituted.

Note: We tested with Hershey's Dutch Processed Cocoa at one tasting and Hershey's Unsweetened Cocoa at another. They were equally tasty.

YUM-RUM BALLS

makes about 4 dozen   prep: 40 min.   cook: 10 min.   chill: 3 hr.

For a great gift, nestle a Yum-Rum Ball in a coffee scoop to give to an early riser. Protect it by tucking it in a clear cellophane bag or covering it with plastic wrap.

1   (14-oz.) can sweetened condensed milk
3   cups semisweet chocolate morsels
3   Tbsp. dark rum

½   cup chocolate cookie crumbs
½   cup powdered sugar

1. Cook sweetened condensed milk and chocolate morsels in a heavy saucepan over medium heat, stirring often, until chocolate morsels melt.

2. Remove from heat, and stir in rum. Pour into a lightly greased 8-inch square pan. Cover and chill 3 hours or until firm.

3. Shape mixture into 1¼-inch balls; roll in chocolate cookie crumbs and then in powdered sugar. Place balls in miniature paper baking cups, if desired. Store in an airtight container in the refrigerator up to 1 week.

[make ahead]

CHOCOLATE-COFFEE SNOWBALLS

makes about 4 dozen   stand: 5 min.   prep: 20 min.

These takeoffs on bourbon balls are better the day after they're made.

⅓   cup coffee liqueur
2   Tbsp. light corn syrup
1   tsp. instant coffee granules
1   (9-oz.) package chocolate wafer cookies, finely crushed

¾   cup sifted powdered sugar
¾   cup chopped almonds, toasted
Powdered sugar

1. Combine liqueur, corn syrup, and instant coffee granules; let mixture stand 5 minutes. Stir until granules dissolve.

2. Combine cookie crumbs, ¾ cup powdered sugar, and chopped almonds; stir well. Pour coffee mixture over crumb mixture, stirring well.

3. Shape into 1-inch balls; roll in powdered sugar twice to coat well. Store in an airtight container up to 1 week.

Note: We tested with Kahlúa for coffee liqueur.

[make ahead]

TASTE OF THE SOUTH

Peanut Brittle
Southerners love peanuts. There are many ways to eat these nutty bites, but they are perhaps at their best in peanut brittle. These recipes will surprise you with their ease and remind you of why you fell for peanuts in the first place. Betsy Owens, executive director of Virginia-Carolina Peanut Promotions, sums up their robust flavor best: "It's like the aroma of brewing coffee and sizzling bacon. They taste and smell so good, there's no turning back."

CLASSIC PEANUT BRITTLE

makes 1 lb.   prep: 15 min.   **pictured on page 243**

You can make this sweet crunch of a candy on the cooktop or in the microwave. Choose a sunny, dry day to make this candy. It's sensitive to humidity. Store it in an airtight tin to keep the candy crisp and crunchy, not sticky to the touch.

1 cup sugar	2 Tbsp. butter
½ cup light corn syrup	1 tsp. baking soda
⅛ tsp. salt	2 tsp. vanilla extract
1 cup dry-roasted or shelled raw peanuts	

1. Combine first 3 ingredients in a large glass bowl. Microwave on HIGH 5 minutes, add peanuts, and microwave 2 more minutes with 1,000-watt microwave. Microwave 4 more minutes if using a 700-watt microwave. Stir in remaining ingredients.

2. Pour into a buttered 15- x 10-inch jelly-roll pan; shake pan to spread thinly. Cool until firm, and break into pieces. Store in an airtight container.

Cooktop Brittle: Cook first 3 ingredients in a medium-size heavy saucepan over medium heat, stirring constantly, until mixture starts to boil. Boil without stirring 5 minutes or until a candy thermometer reaches 310°. Add peanuts, and cook 2 to 3 more minutes or to 280°.

(Mixture should be golden brown.) Remove from heat, and stir in butter and remaining ingredients. Pour mixture onto a metal surface or into a shallow pan. Allow to stand 5 minutes or until hardened. Break into pieces. Prep: 5 min., Cook: 7 min., Stand: 5 min.

Pecan Brittle: Substitute 1 cup chopped pecans for peanuts.

Chocolate-Dipped Peanut Brittle: Prepare Classic Peanut Brittle as directed. Melt 2 (2-oz.) chocolate candy coating squares; dip peanut brittle pieces into melted chocolate. Place on wax paper, and let harden.

Popcorn Peanut Brittle: Prepare Classic Peanut Brittle as directed. Stir in 1 cup popped popcorn before pouring into pan. Pictured on page 243.

Step-by-Step Cooktop Brittle

1. Start with a heavy non-aluminum saucepan to encourage even cooking and prevent the mixture from overbrowning. Combine sugar, corn syrup, and salt. Attach the thermometer to side of pan. Boil without stirring until the mixture reaches 310°.

2. Add peanuts, and cook until thermometer reads 280°. Look for a rich golden-brown color. Remove from heat, and add butter, soda, and vanilla.

3. Grease the pan ahead of time with softened butter. Immediately pour mixture into a shallow pan. Don't pour onto wax paper or plastic wrap—these items can't take the heat.

4. Spread thinly. Cool. Break candy into pieces with your hands, or use a rolling pin.

ALMOND BRITTLE

makes about 1 lb.   prep: 5 min.   cook: 15 min.   stand: 30 min.

Start with a heavy nonaluminum saucepan to ensure even cooking and to prevent the mixture from overbrowning.

Butter

3   Tbsp. butter

1¼ cups whole almonds

1   cup sugar

½   tsp. baking soda

1. Line a baking sheet or 15- x 10-inch jelly-roll pan with aluminum foil; grease foil with butter. Set pan aside.

2. Melt 3 Tbsp. butter in a small skillet over medium heat. Add almonds, and cook, stirring constantly, 2 minutes. Remove from heat.

3. Cook sugar and ¼ cup water in a small heavy saucepan over medium-high heat, stirring constantly, until mixture starts to boil. (Use a small brush dipped in cold water to brush down sugar crystals that cling to sides of pan.) Boil without stirring about 10 minutes or until a candy thermometer reaches 310° (hard-crack stage). (Mixture should be golden.) Remove from heat, and stir in almond mixture and baking soda.

4. Pour mixture immediately onto prepared baking sheet, spreading mixture quickly into an even layer with a metal spatula. Allow to stand 30 minutes or until hardened. Break into pieces. Store in an airtight container.

MICROWAVE PECAN BRITTLE

makes 1 lb.   prep: 15 min.

1   cup sugar

½   cup light corn syrup

⅛   tsp. salt

1   cup chopped pecans

2   Tbsp. butter

1   tsp. baking soda

2   tsp. vanilla

1. Combine first 3 ingredients in a large glass bowl. Microwave on HIGH 5 minutes, add pecans, and microwave 2 more minutes with 1,000-watt microwave. Microwave 4 more minutes if using a 700-watt microwave. Stir in remaining ingredients.

2. Pour into a buttered 15- x 10-inch jelly-roll pan; shake pan to spread thinly. Cool until firm, and break into pieces. Store in an airtight container.

MILDRED'S TOFFEE

makes about 1½ lb.   prep: 10 min.   cook: 20 min.   chill: 1 hr.

Former Assistant Test Kitchen Director James Schend says that his grandmother's toffee recipe is almost as easy as boiling water.

1½ cups chopped toasted pecans, divided

1   cup sugar

1   cup butter

1   Tbsp. light corn syrup

1   cup semisweet chocolate morsels

[make ahead]

1. Spread 1 cup pecans into a 9-inch circle on a lightly greased baking sheet.

2. Bring sugar, butter, corn syrup, and ¼ cup water to a boil in a heavy saucepan over medium heat, stirring constantly. Cook until mixture is golden brown and a candy thermometer registers 290° to 310° (about 15 minutes). Pour sugar mixture over pecans on baking sheet.

3. Sprinkle with morsels; let stand 30 seconds. Spread melted morsels over top; sprinkle with remaining ½ cup chopped pecans. Chill 1 hour. Break into bite-size pieces. Store in an airtight container.

Bourbon-Pecan Toffee: Substitute ¼ cup bourbon for ¼ cup water. Proceed as directed.

Almond Toffee: Substitute 1 cup chopped toasted slivered almonds for 1 cup chopped pecans to sprinkle on baking sheet. Substitute ½ cup toasted sliced almonds for ½ cup chopped pecans to sprinkle over chocolate. Proceed as directed.

MICROWAVE PEANUT TOFFEE

makes 1 lb.   prep: 20 min.

¾   cup finely chopped unsalted peanuts, divided

½   cup butter

1   cup sugar

1   cup peanut butter-and-milk chocolate morsels

1. Spread ½ cup chopped peanuts into a 9-inch circle on a lightly greased baking sheet.

2. Coat top 2 inches of a 2½-qt. glass bowl with butter; place remaining butter in bowl. Add sugar and ¼ cup water. (Do not stir.) Microwave at HIGH 8 minutes or just until mixture begins to turn light brown; pour over peanuts on baking sheet.

3. Sprinkle with chocolate morsels; let stand 1 minute. Spread melted morsels evenly over peanut mixture, and sprinkle with remaining ¼ cup chopped peanuts. Chill until firm. Break into bite-size pieces. Store in an airtight container.

TASTE OF THE SOUTH

Pralines Few confections are so readily identified with the South as pralines—irresistible nuggets made of caramel and pecans. Different Southern cooks swear by a variety of recipes with or without brown sugar or baking soda; with evaporated milk, buttermilk, or half-and-half; and dropped large or small. We tasted them all before determining our favorite recipe, a combination of white and brown sugars and evaporated milk.

Pralines aren't difficult to make, but they can be tricky. The requirements are plenty of stirring, patience, and careful attention. Two big questions usually come up during preparation: when to remove the candy mixture from the heat and when to stop beating and start spooning. (You're allowed to enlist an extra set of hands at this stage.)

If the mixture gets too hot, the candy will be dry and crumbly. If it isn't cooked long enough, the mixture will be runny and sticky.

One trick we learned after making several batches in our Test Kitchen is to remove it from the heat at about 232°. The mixture will continue to climb to the required temperature (236°). A candy thermometer gives the best temperature reading and takes out most of the guesswork. We like to use two thermometers for accuracy.

Beat the mixture with a wooden spoon just until it begins to thicken. You'll feel the mixture become heavier, and its color will become lighter. Often the last few pralines that you spoon will be thicker and less perfectly shaped than the first, but they'll still be just as good. The candy tastes the best if eaten within a day or two; pralines become sugary and gritty with age. Be sure to store them in an airtight container (a metal tin works well).

If your pralines don't turn out right the first time, don't despair. Simply create a new dessert. Crumble and fold them into softened vanilla ice cream. Or, if they're too soft, scrape up the mixture, chill it, and roll it into 1-inch balls. Then dip the balls into melted chocolate to make truffles. If the candy mixture hardens in the pot, break it into pieces and sprinkle it over hot apple pie, cheesecake, or ice cream. Practice helps. And believe us, these Southern delicacies are well worth the effort.

PRALINES

makes about 2½ dozen   prep: 10 min.   cook: 30 min.

1½ cups sugar

1½ cups firmly packed brown sugar

1 cup evaporated milk

¼ cup butter

2 cups pecan halves, toasted

1 tsp. vanilla extract

1. Bring sugars and milk to a boil in a Dutch oven, stirring often. Cook over medium heat, stirring often, 11 minutes or until a candy thermometer registers 228° (thread stage).
2. Stir in butter and pecans; cook, stirring constantly, until candy thermometer registers 236° (soft ball stage).
3. Remove from heat; stir in vanilla. Beat with a wooden spoon 1 to 2 minutes or just until mixture begins to thicken. Quickly drop by heaping tablespoonfuls onto buttered wax paper or parchment paper; let stand until firm.

AFTER-THE-DANCE PRALINES

makes 20 pralines   prep: 10 min.   stand: 8 hr.

This beloved Louisiana confection got its name from the tradition of young women in New Orleans making them before going to a ball and then enjoying them with friends (and beaux) at their homes afterward.

1 cup firmly packed light brown sugar

1 egg white, beaten

1½ cups chopped pecans, lightly toasted

1. Preheat oven to 400°.
2. Stir together brown sugar and beaten egg white, and fold in chopped pecans.
3. Drop by heaping tablespoonfuls onto a heavy-duty aluminum foil-lined baking sheet.
4. Turn off oven; place baking sheet in oven, and let pralines stand 8 hours in oven.

SOFT-AND-CHEWY CARAMELS

makes 64 pieces   prep: 5 min.   cook: 20 min.   stand: 3 hr.

These rich candies are more tender than their store-bought cousins.

1   cup butter
1   (16-oz.) package light brown sugar

1   (14-oz.) can sweetened condensed milk
1   cup light corn syrup

1. Line an 8-inch square baking pan with foil, extending foil over edges of pan. Generously coat foil with vegetable cooking spray; set aside.

2. Melt 1 cup butter in a 3-qt. saucepan over low heat. Stir in brown sugar, condensed milk, and corn syrup until smooth. Bring mixture to a boil. Cook over medium heat, stirring often, until a candy thermometer registers 235°.

3. Remove mixture from heat; stir by hand 1 minute or until mixture is smooth and no longer bubbling. Quickly pour mixture into prepared pan; let stand 3 hours or until cool.

4. Lift foil and caramel out of pan. Cut caramels into 1-inch pieces with a buttered knife. Wrap each piece with plastic wrap.

COCONUT-MACADAMIA CARAMELS

makes 1½ lb.   prep: 10 min.   cook: 45 min.   cool: 3 hr.

Butter your knife to ease cutting.

1   cup sugar
⅔   cup light corn syrup
1   tsp. honey
1½ cups half-and-half, divided

½   cup sweetened flaked coconut
½   cup chopped macadamia nuts
1   Tbsp. minced dried pineapple
1   tsp. vanilla extract

1. Cook first 3 ingredients and ½ cup half-and-half in a large heavy saucepan over low heat, stirring constantly, until sugar dissolves. Cover and cook over medium-low heat 2 to 3 minutes to wash down sugar crystals from sides of pan.

2. Uncover and cook, stirring constantly, until a candy thermometer registers 242° (firm ball stage). Add ½ cup half-and-half, and cook over medium heat, stirring constantly, 12 minutes or until candy thermometer returns to 242°. Repeat procedure with remaining ½ cup half-and-half. Stir in flaked coconut and remaining ingredients.

3. Pour into a buttered 9-inch square pan. Cool and cut into 1½-inch logs; wrap individually in wax paper.

CHOCOLATE-CHERRY CORDIAL TRUFFLES

makes 2 dozen   prep: 1 hr., 50 min   chill: 2 hr   cook: 10 min.   **pictured on page 244**

⅓ **cup dried cherries**
¼ **cup cherry brandy**
2 **cups (12 oz.) semisweet chocolate morsels**
4 **egg yolks**

⅓ **cup butter**
⅓ **cup sifted powdered sugar**
¼ **tsp. cherry extract**
8 **(2-oz.) chocolate candy coating squares**

1. Stir together dried cherries and cherry brandy; let stand 1 hour.
2. Melt chocolate morsels in a heavy saucepan over low heat, stirring until smooth. Remove from heat.
3. Beat egg yolks at medium speed with an electric mixer until thick and pale. Gradually stir about one-fourth of melted chocolate into yolks; add to remaining chocolate, stirring constantly. Cook over medium heat, stirring constantly, 6 minutes or until a candy thermometer registers 160°. Remove from heat; add dried cherry mixture, butter, sugar, and extract, stirring until butter melts and mixture is blended. Chill 1 hour.
4. Shape cherry mixture into 1-inch balls. Cover and chill 1 hour.
5. Place coating in top of a double boiler; bring water to a boil. Reduce heat to low; cook, stirring constantly, until coating melts. Remove from heat, leaving coating over hot water. Dip balls in coating; place on wax paper. Let stand until firm. Store in refrigerator.

make ahead

RASPBERRY-FUDGE TRUFFLES

makes 6 dozen   prep: 30 min.   cook: 5 min.   chill: 2 hr.   freeze: 1 hr.

Use a sturdy wooden pick to dip well-chilled or frozen balls.

[make ahead]

2 cups (12 oz.) semisweet chocolate morsels	1½ cups vanilla wafer crumbs
2 (8-oz.) packages cream cheese, softened	10 (2-oz.) chocolate candy coating squares
1 cup seedless raspberry preserves	3 (1-oz.) white chocolate squares
2 Tbsp. raspberry liqueur	1 Tbsp. shortening

1. Microwave chocolate morsels in a 4-cup glass measuring cup at HIGH 1½ to 2½ minutes or until melted, stirring every 30 seconds.

2. Beat cream cheese at medium speed with an electric mixer until smooth. Add melted chocolate, preserves, and liqueur, beating until blended. Stir in crumbs; cover and chill 2 hours.

3. Shape mixture into 1-inch balls; cover and freeze 1 hour or until firm.

4. Microwave chocolate coating in a 4-cup glass measuring cup at HIGH 1½ to 2½ minutes or until melted, stirring every 30 seconds. Dip balls in coating; place on wax paper.

5. Place white chocolate and shortening in small zip-top plastic freezer bag; seal. Submerge in hot water until chocolate melts; knead until smooth. Snip a tiny hole in 1 corner of bag, and drizzle mixture over truffles. Let stand until firm. Store in refrigerator or freezer, if desired.

CHERRY-PISTACHIO BARK

makes 3½ lb.   prep: 10 min.   cook: 10 min.   chill: 1 hr.

Lightly grease cutter with cooking spray to make cutting easier.

[make ahead]

1¼ cups dried cherries	6 (2-oz.) vanilla candy coating squares
2 (12-oz.) packages white chocolate morsels	1¼ cups chopped red or green pistachios

1. Microwave cherries and 2 Tbsp. water in a small glass bowl at HIGH 2 minutes; drain.

2. Melt chocolate and candy coating in a heavy saucepan over low heat. Remove from heat; stir in cherries and pistachios. Spread into a wax paper-lined 15- x 10-inch jelly-roll pan.

3. Chill 1 hour or until firm. Cut with a 3-inch heart-shaped cookie cutter. Store in airtight container.

CREAM CHEESE MINTS

makes 8 dozen   prep: 1 hr., 10 min.   stand: 4 hr.   **pictured on page 241**

Freeze in layers of wax paper in an airtight container.

1 **(8-oz.) package cream cheese**	½ **tsp. peppermint extract**
¼ **cup butter, softened**	6 **drops red liquid food coloring (optional)**
1 **(2-lb.) package powdered sugar**	**Powdered sugar**

1. Cook cream cheese and butter in a saucepan over low heat, stirring constantly, until smooth. Gradually stir in package of powdered sugar; stir in extract. If desired, divide mixture into 2 portions; stir 2 drops coloring into 1 portion and remaining 4 drops coloring into second portion, if desired.

2. Shape mixture into 1-inch balls. Dip a 2-inch round cookie stamp or bottom of a glass into powdered sugar. Press each ball to flatten. Let stand, uncovered, 4 hours or until firm. Freeze, if desired.

COLA CANDY

makes 2 dozen   prep: 15 min.   chill: 30 min.

3½ **cups vanilla wafer crumbs**	½ **cup cola soft drink***
2 **cups powdered sugar**	2 **Tbsp. butter, melted**
1 **cup chopped pecans**	**Cola Frosting**

1. Stir together first 5 ingredients; shape mixture into 1-inch balls. Cover and chill at least 30 minutes.

2. Dip balls in Cola Frosting; chill until ready to serve.

* Your favorite dark soft drink may be substituted.

Cola Frosting

makes 1½ cups   prep: 5 min.

¾ **cup powdered sugar**	¼ **cup butter, softened**
¼ **tsp. vanilla extract**	2 **to 3 Tbsp. cola soft drink**

1. Stir together all ingredients.

When Assistant Test Kitchen Director Rebecca Kracke Gordon stirs up one of her special creations, the whole Food staff comes running. Crisp and buttery, rich and gooey, big batch or small—one versatile recipe for All-Time Favorite Chocolate Chip cookies delivers them all.

• Store cookie dough in an airtight container or a zip-top plastic freezer bag, and chill up to three days or freeze up to six months.

• For slice-and-bake cookies, shape dough into logs, wrap in parchment paper, and place in zip-top plastic freezer bags. Allow frozen dough to thaw overnight in the refrigerator.

• Another option is to use a small ice cream scoop to shape dough into balls; place on a baking sheet, and freeze until firm. Transfer frozen balls to a zip-top plastic freezer bag. Remove as needed and bake right from the freezer, allowing two or three minutes extra baking time.

ALL-TIME FAVORITE CHOCOLATE CHIP COOKIES

makes about 5 dozen   prep: 30 min.   bake: 10 min. per batch   cool: 15 min.

Bake 10 minutes for a soft and chewy cookie or up to 14 minutes for a crisp cookie.

¾ cup butter, softened
¾ cup granulated sugar
¾ cup firmly packed dark brown sugar
2 large eggs
1½ tsp. vanilla extract

2¼ cups plus 2 Tbsp. all-purpose flour
1 tsp. baking soda
¾ tsp. salt
1½ (12-oz.) packages semisweet chocolate morsels
Parchment paper

1. Preheat oven to 350°. Beat butter and sugars at medium speed with a heavy-duty electric stand mixer until creamy. Add eggs and 1½ tsp. vanilla, beating until blended.

2. Combine flour, baking soda, and salt in a small bowl; gradually add to butter mixture, beating just until blended. Beat in morsels just until combined. Drop by tablespoonfuls onto parchment paper-lined baking sheets.

3. Bake at 350° for 10 to 14 minutes or until desired degree of doneness. Remove to wire racks, and cool completely (about 15 minutes).

{test kitchen favorite}

Flavor Cravings: All sorts of goodies can be added to this recipe to create other signature cookies. Here are a few of our staff favorites.

Chocolate Chip-Pretzel Cookies: Prepare recipe as directed, beating in 2 cups coarsely crushed pretzel sticks with morsels.

Cranberry-White Chocolate Cookies: Substitute 1 (12-oz.) package white chocolate morsels, 1 (6-oz.) package sweetened dried cranberries, and 1 cup pistachios for chocolate morsels. Proceed as directed. Pictured on page 246.

White Chocolate-Covered Pretzel Cookies: Prepare recipe as directed, beating in 1 (7-oz.) bag white chocolate-covered mini pretzel twists, coarsely crushed, with morsels. Pictured on page 246.

Almond-Toffee Cookies: Substitute 6 (1.4-oz.) chopped chocolate-covered toffee candy bars and 1½ cups toasted slivered almonds for chocolate morsels. Proceed as directed.

Turtle Cookies: Substitute 1 (7-oz.) package milk chocolate-caramel-pecan clusters, coarsely chopped, and 1 (12-oz.) package dark chocolate morsels for semisweet chocolate morsels. Proceed as directed. **Note:** We tested with Nestlé Turtles. Pictured on page 246.

Nutty Peanut Butter-Chocolate Chip Cookies: Decrease salt to ½ tsp. Decrease morsels to 1 (12-oz.) package. Add 1 cup creamy peanut butter with butter and sugars, and add 1 cup lightly salted peanuts with morsels. Increase flour to 2½ cups plus 2 Tbsp. Proceed as directed. (Dough will look a little moist.) Pictured on page 246.

SEVEN-MINUTE CHOCOLATE COOKIES

makes 4 dozen cookies   prep: 10 min.   cook: 5 min.   bake: 7 min. per batch

¼ cup butter	1 tsp. vanilla extract
1 (12-oz.) package semisweet chocolate morsels	1 cup all-purpose flour
1 (14-oz.) can sweetened condensed milk	1 cup chopped pecans

1. Preheat oven to 350°. Combine butter, chocolate morsels, and condensed milk in a heavy saucepan. Cook over low heat, stirring constantly, 5 minutes or until chocolate morsels are melted. Remove from heat. Stir in vanilla and flour until well blended. Fold in pecans.
2. Drop immediately by level tablespoonfuls onto lightly greased baking sheets.
3. Bake at 350° for 7 to 10 minutes. Cool on baking sheets; remove to wire racks to cool completely.

PEANUT BUTTER-TOFFEE TURTLE COOKIES

makes 3 dozen   prep: 25 min.   bake: 10 min. per batch   cool: 16 min.

Traditional turtle candy calls for chocolate, caramels, and pecan halves to be molded into the shape of a turtle. For these cookies, traditional turtle candy flavors are teamed with creamy peanut butter for a Southern touch.

⅔ cup creamy peanut butter

½ cup unsalted butter, softened

½ cup granulated sugar

½ cup firmly packed light brown sugar

1 large egg

2 cups all-purpose baking mix

⅔ cup toffee bits

⅔ cup coarsely chopped peanuts

⅔ cup milk chocolate morsels

10 oz. vanilla caramels

2 to 3 Tbsp. whipping cream

½ tsp. vanilla extract

Pecan halves

⅔ cup milk chocolate morsels

1. Preheat oven to 350°. Beat first 4 ingredients at medium speed with an electric mixer until creamy. Add egg, beating until blended. Add baking mix, beating at low speed just until blended. Stir in toffee bits, chopped peanuts, and ⅔ cup chocolate morsels.

2. Drop dough by rounded tablespoonfuls onto ungreased baking sheets; flatten dough with hand.

3. Bake at 350° for 10 to 12 minutes or until golden brown. Cool on baking sheets 1 minute; remove to wire racks to cool completely.

4. Microwave caramels and 2 Tbsp. cream in a microwave-safe bowl at HIGH 1 minute; stir. Continue to microwave at 30-second intervals, stirring until caramels melt and mixture is smooth; add additional cream, if necessary. Stir in vanilla. Spoon mixture onto tops of cookies; top with pecan halves.

5. Microwave ⅔ cup chocolate morsels in a microwave-safe bowl at HIGH 1 minute and 15 seconds or until melted and smooth, stirring at 30-second intervals. Transfer to a 1-qt. zip-top plastic freezer bag; cut a tiny hole in 1 corner of bag. Pipe melted chocolate over cookies by squeezing bag.

Cookie Swap Party serves 12

Baked Spinach-and-Artichoke Dip (page 52)
*Layered Cornbread-and-Turkey Salad (page 737)
Grand Oranges and Strawberries (page 202)
Sampler of cookies guests bring to the swap

*double recipe

MISSISSIPPI MUD COOKIES

makes about 3 dozen   prep: 25 min.   bake: 10 min. per batch

Just like the banks of the Mississippi River, these cookies are ooey, gooey, and chocolate brown. The original Mississippi mud cake is thought to have been created by World War II-era cooks who found a way to use available ingredients to make a dense chocolate cake. Marshmallows pressed into the dough make these cookies just as dense and sweet as the famous cake.

1 cup semisweet chocolate morsels	1 tsp. baking powder
½ cup butter, softened	½ tsp. salt
1 cup sugar	1 cup chopped pecans
2 large eggs	½ cup milk chocolate morsels
1 tsp. vanilla extract	1 cup plus 2 Tbsp. miniature marshmallows
1½ cups all-purpose flour	

1. Preheat oven to 350°. Microwave semisweet chocolate morsels in a small microwave-safe glass bowl at HIGH 1 minute or until smooth, stirring every 30 seconds.

2. Beat butter and sugar at medium speed with an electric mixer until creamy; add eggs, 1 at a time, beating until blended after each addition. Beat in vanilla and melted chocolate.

3. Combine flour, baking powder, and salt; gradually add to chocolate mixture, beating until well blended. Stir in chopped pecans and ½ cup milk chocolate morsels.

4. Drop dough by heaping tablespoonfuls onto parchment paper-lined baking sheets. Press 3 marshmallows into each portion of dough.

5. Bake at 350° for 10 to 12 minutes or until set. Remove to wire racks to cool completely.

[test kitchen favorite]

GIANT OATMEAL-SPICE COOKIES

makes about 2½ dozen   prep: 20 min.   bake: 12 min. per batch

1½ cups all-purpose flour
1   tsp. ground cinnamon
½   tsp. salt
½   tsp. baking soda
½   tsp. ground ginger
¼   tsp. ground allspice
⅛   tsp. ground cloves

1   cup butter, softened
1   (16-oz.) package dark brown sugar
2   large eggs
1   tsp. vanilla extract
3   cups quick-cooking oats
1   cup chopped pecans, toasted
½   cup raisins (optional)

1. Preheat oven to 350°. Stir together first 7 ingredients.
2. Beat butter and sugar at medium speed with an electric mixer until fluffy. Add eggs and vanilla, beating until blended. Gradually add flour mixture, beating at low speed until blended.
3. Stir in oats, chopped pecans, and if desired, raisins.
4. Drop dough by ¼ cupfuls onto lightly greased baking sheets; lightly press down dough.
5. Bake, in batches, at 350° for 12 to 14 minutes. (Cookies should not be brown around the edges, and centers will not look quite done.) Cool slightly on baking sheets. Remove to wire racks; cool completely.

CRISPY PRALINE COOKIES

makes 2 dozen   prep: 10 min.   cook: 13 min. per batch   cool: 16 min.

½   cup butter, softened
1   cup firmly packed dark brown sugar
1   large egg

1   tsp. vanilla extract
1   cup all-purpose flour
1   cup chopped pecans

1. Preheat oven to 350°. Beat butter and sugar at medium speed with an electric mixer until creamy; add egg, beating just until blended. Add vanilla, and mix well.
2. Gradually add flour, beating just until blended. Stir in pecans.
3. Drop dough by tablespoonfuls onto parchment paper-lined baking sheets.
4. Bake at 350° for 13 to 15 minutes. Cool on baking sheets 1 minute, then remove to racks to cool completely.

Crispy Praline-Chocolate Chip Cookies: Add 1 cup semisweet chocolate morsels, and bake as directed.

SMOKY MOUNTAIN SNOWCAPS

makes 3½ dozen   prep: 25 min.   bake: 10 min. per batch

Most Southerners get excited about a few flakes in the sky, but the highest elevations of the Great Smoky Mountains of Tennessee and North Carolina get an average snowfall of 69 inches each winter. Reminiscent of the white-dusted mountain peaks, these cookies, with white chocolate and a dusting of powdered sugar, are as sweet as snowfall on a school day in the South. Toasted walnuts and nutmeg give them a nice crunch and spicy flavor.

6   oz. white chocolate, chopped
¾   cup butter, softened
1   cup sugar
3   large eggs
1   tsp. vanilla extract
3½ cups all-purpose flour

1   tsp. baking powder
¾   tsp. salt
⅛   tsp. ground nutmeg
1½ cups chopped walnuts, toasted
½   cup powdered sugar

1. Preheat oven to 350°. Melt white chocolate in a small saucepan over low heat, stirring until chocolate is smooth.

2. Beat butter and 1 cup sugar at medium speed with an electric mixer 5 minutes or until fluffy. Add eggs, 1 at a time, beating until blended after each addition. Add vanilla, beating well. Add melted chocolate, and beat 30 seconds.

3. Combine flour and next 3 ingredients; add to butter mixture, beating until blended. Stir in walnuts.

4. Drop dough by heaping tablespoonfuls onto lightly greased baking sheets.

5. Bake at 350° for 10 to 12 minutes or until edges are lightly browned. Remove to wire racks to cool completely. Sprinkle with powdered sugar. Freeze up to 1 month in an airtight container, if desired.

freeze it

What's Your Peanut Preference?

Because the only peanuts destined for boiling are those freshly dug, it makes sense that folks right next to the fields in south Georgia and south Alabama think boiled green goobers are superior to the dry, roasted kind.

Southerners are split in opinion as to whether the soggy-skinned boiled nuts with a chewy treasure inside are better than crunchy dried and roasted (some say parched) nuts. No matter what your favorite, iconic homemade signs announcing "P-Nuts" cover Dixie like the dew from summer through fall months. Look for the treats, usually in tiny brown paper bags, at roadside stands, flea markets, and county fairs.

Most in the Deep South, like Don Koehler of the Georgia Peanut Commission in Tifton, says there's no question about it. "I'd rather eat boiled peanuts than sleep," he says emphatically. "They've got this amazing pea texture. And peeling them gives you something to do while you're eating!" The South Carolina governor agreed when he signed a law making boiled peanuts the official state snack.

DOUBLE CHOCOLATE CHUNK-PEANUT COOKIES

makes 28 cookies   prep: 20 min.   bake: 15 min. per batch

Chunky peanut butter and dry-roasted peanuts make these chocolate cookies irresistible. A dash of cinnamon gives them an unexpected flavor. They are easy to make, and the balls of dough bake into nice round shapes just perfect for your next cookie swap.

½ cup butter, softened	1 tsp. ground cinnamon
½ cup shortening	1 cup unsalted dry-roasted peanuts
1 cup chunky peanut butter	1 (11.5-oz.) package chocolate chunks
⅓ cup unsweetened cocoa, sifted	1 cup granulated sugar
1½ tsp. baking soda	1 cup firmly packed brown sugar
1 tsp. baking powder	2 large eggs
½ tsp. salt	2 cups all-purpose flour

1. Preheat oven to 375°. Beat butter and shortening at medium speed with an electric mixer until creamy; add chunky peanut butter and sugars, beating well. Add eggs, beating until blended.

2. Combine flour and next 5 ingredients. Add to butter mixture, beating well.

3. Stir in peanuts and chocolate chunks.

4. Shape dough into 2-inch balls (about 2 Tbsp. for each cookie). Place 2 inches apart on ungreased baking sheets, and flatten cookies slightly.

5. Bake at 375° for 12 to 15 minutes or until lightly browned. Cool cookies on baking sheets for 1 to 2 minutes, and remove cookies to wire racks to cool completely.

EASIEST PEANUT BUTTER COOKIES

makes about 30 cookies   prep: 20 min.   bake: 15 min. per batch

The dough freezes well, so keep a batch on hand to bake whenever you need a pick-me-up.

1 cup peanut butter

1 cup sugar

1 large egg

1 tsp. vanilla extract

1. Preheat oven to 325°.

2. Stir together all ingredients in a large bowl until combined; shape dough into 1-inch balls. Place balls 1 inch apart on ungreased baking sheets, and flatten gently with tines of a fork. Bake at 325° for 15 minutes or until golden brown. Remove to wire racks to cool.

Variations: Evenly press 1 cup of your desired addition, such as chocolate morsels, chocolate-coated toffee bits, or chopped peanuts, onto the top of prepared cookie dough on baking sheets; bake as directed.

Peanut Butter-and-Chocolate Cookies: Divide peanut butter cookie dough in half. Stir 2 melted semisweet chocolate baking squares into half of dough. Shape doughs into 30 (1-inch) half peanut butter, half chocolate-peanut butter balls. Flatten gently with a spoon. Proceed as directed.

make ahead

COCOA-ALMOND BISCOTTI

makes 2 dozen   prep: 20 min.   bake: 38 min.   cool: 5 min.

Biscotti are elegantly sliced, intensely crunchy Italian cookies, perfect for dunking into a cup of hot coffee. Enjoy them for breakfast or dessert.

½   cup butter, softened

1   cup sugar

2   large eggs

1½ Tbsp. Kahlúa or other coffee liqueur

2½ cups all-purpose flour

1½ tsp. baking powder

¼   tsp. salt

3   Tbsp. Dutch process cocoa or regular unsweetened cocoa

1   (6-oz.) can whole almonds

1. Preheat oven to 350°. Beat butter and sugar in a large bowl at medium speed with an electric mixer until creamy. Add eggs, beating well. Mix in liqueur.

2. Combine flour and next 3 ingredients; add to butter mixture, beating at low speed until blended. Stir in almonds.

3. Divide dough in half; using floured hands, shape each portion into a 9- x 2-inch log on a lightly greased baking sheet.

4. Bake at 350° for 28 to 30 minutes or until firm. Cool on baking sheet 5 minutes. Remove to a wire rack to cool.

5. Cut each log diagonally into ¾-inch-thick slices with a serrated knife, using a gentle sawing motion. Place slices on ungreased baking sheets. Bake 5 minutes. Turn cookies over, and bake 5 to 6 more minutes. Remove to wire racks to cool completely.

BLACK-EYED SUSANS

make 8 dozen   prep: 20 min.   bake: 8 min.   chill: 30 min.

½   cup butter, softened

½   cup granulated sugar

½   cup firmly packed brown sugar

1   cup creamy peanut butter

1   large egg

1½ Tbsp. warm water

1   tsp. vanilla extract

1½ cups all-purpose flour

½   tsp. salt

½   tsp. baking soda

½   cup semisweet chocolate morsels

1. Preheat oven to 350°. Beat butter and sugars at medium speed with an electric mixer until light and fluffy. Add peanut butter and next 3 ingredients, beating well.

2. Combine flour, salt, and baking soda. Add to butter mixture, beating until blended.

{ freeze it }

3. Use a cookie gun fitted with a flower-shaped disc to make cookies, following manufacturer's instructions. Place cookies on lightly greased baking sheets. Place a chocolate morsel in the center of each cookie.

4. Bake at 350° for 8 minutes or until lightly browned. Remove to wire racks to cool. Chill 30 minutes. Freeze up to 1 month, if desired.

THUMBPRINT COOKIES

makes 3½ dozen   prep: 35 min.   chill: 1 hr.   bake: 15 min. per batch

These cookies have a bit of crunch from the finely chopped pecans, sweetness from the almond extract, and richness from the butter. But it's the thumbprint impressions on top that give them a personal touch. Strawberry and peach jams make beautiful jewel-colored fillings, but you can use other Southern favorite jams, such as blackberry, muscadine, or apple. They're the perfect cookies to make with the kids—let them make the thumbprints and choose the filling.

1 cup butter, softened	¼ tsp. salt
¾ cup sugar	1¼ cups finely chopped pecans
2 large eggs, separated	¼ cup strawberry jam
1 tsp. almond extract	¼ cup peach jam
2 cups all-purpose flour	

1. Beat butter at medium speed with an electric mixer until creamy; gradually add sugar, beating well. Add egg yolks and almond extract, beating until blended.

2. Combine flour and salt; add to butter mixture, beating at low speed until blended. Cover and chill dough 1 hour.

3. Preheat oven to 375°. Shape dough into 1-inch balls. Lightly beat egg whites. Dip each dough ball in egg white; roll in pecans. Place 2 inches apart on ungreased baking sheets. Press thumb in each dough ball to make an indentation.

4. Bake at 350° for 15 minutes. Cool 1 minute on baking sheets, and remove to wire racks to cool completely. Press centers again with thumb while cookies are still warm; fill center of each cookie with jam.

CLASSIC SUGAR COOKIES

makes 20 cookies   prep: 25 min.   chill: 1 hr.   cook: 8 min. per batch

Cut this dough into a variety of your favorite shapes. The dippable glaze will transform the cookies into works of art almost too pretty to eat.

1   cup butter, softened
1   cup granulated sugar
1   large egg
1   tsp. vanilla extract

3   cups all-purpose flour
¼   tsp. salt
Glaze
1   (3.25-oz.) jar coarse sparkling sugar

1. Beat butter at medium speed with an electric mixer until creamy. Gradually add granulated sugar, beating well. Add egg and vanilla, beating well. Combine flour and salt. Gradually add to butter mixture, beating until blended. Divide dough in half. Cover; chill 1 hour.

2. Preheat oven to 350°. Roll each portion of dough to ¼-inch thickness on a lightly floured surface. Cut with desired cookie cutters. (We used flower and starfish cutters.) Place on lightly greased baking sheets.

3. Bake at 350° for 8 to 10 minutes or until edges of cookies are lightly browned. Cool cookies 1 minute on baking sheets, and remove to wire racks to cool completely.

4. Dip cookies in Glaze, and sprinkle, while wet, with sparkling sugar.

Glaze

makes 1⅓ cups   prep: 5 min.

1   (16-oz.) package powdered sugar
6   Tbsp. warm water

Liquid food coloring (optional)

1. Stir together powdered sugar and warm water using a wire whisk. Divide mixture, and tint with food coloring, if desired; place in shallow bowls for ease in dipping cookies.

Follow our Test Kitchen's hints and tips for great cookies every time:

• Always bake cookies in a preheated oven unless a recipe specifies otherwise.

• Grease the baking sheet only if directed. Many cookie recipes contain enough fat that greasing the baking sheet isn't necessary.

• If you do grease the sheet, don't worry about regreasing between batches.

• Place dough on a cool baking sheet; if you spoon dough onto a hot baking sheet, the dough will spread too quickly and the cookies will be flat.

• For the best results, bake only one pan of cookies at a time, placing the pan in the center of the oven.

MOLASSES-SPICE CRINKLES

makes 3 dozen prep: 15 min. chill: 1 hr. bake: 9 min. per batch

For centuries Southerners have treasured their jars of molasses—the cooked-down sugar cane mixture that is thick, brown, and sticky with a sharp and tangy flavor. From the hills of Tennessee to the plains of Georgia, the syrup was a table condiment for drizzling on biscuits and pancakes, or stirring into desserts.

¾ cup shortening	¼ tsp. salt
1 cup granulated sugar	1 tsp. ground ginger
1 large egg	1 tsp. ground cinnamon
¼ cup molasses	½ tsp. ground nutmeg
2 cups all-purpose flour	¼ tsp. ground cloves
1 tsp. baking powder	¼ tsp. ground allspice
1 tsp. baking soda	1 cup sparkling sugar

1. Beat shortening at medium speed with an electric mixer until fluffy. Gradually add 1 cup granulated sugar, beating well. Add egg and molasses; beat well.

2. Combine flour and next 8 ingredients, stirring well. Add one-fourth of flour mixture at a time to shortening mixture, beating at low speed after each addition until blended. Cover and chill 1 hour.

3. Preheat oven to 375°. Shape dough into 1-inch balls, and roll in sparkling sugar. Place 2 inches apart on ungreased baking sheets.

4. Bake at 375° for 9 to 11 minutes. (Tops will crack.) Remove to wire racks to cool completely.

GINGER-OATMEAL SORGHUM COOKIES

makes 3 dozen   prep: 30 min.   bake: 8 min. per batch

4	cups all-purpose flour	1	cup butter, melted
1	Tbsp. baking soda	1	cup sorghum
1½	tsp. salt	1	cup chopped walnuts
4	cups quick-cooking oats	2	Tbsp. hot water
1¼	cups sugar	2	large eggs, lightly beaten
1½	tsp. ground ginger	½	cup sugar
1½	cups raisins		

1. Preheat oven to 375°. Combine first 7 ingredients in a large bowl; add butter and next 4 ingredients, stirring until blended.

2. Shape dough into 36 (2½-inch) balls. Place 2 inches apart on lightly greased baking sheets; flatten each to ¼-inch thickness. Brush tops with 1 to 2 Tbsp. water, and sprinkle with sugar.

3. Bake at 375° for 8 to 10 minutes or until lightly browned.

RAISIN-OATMEAL COOKIES

makes 2 dozen   prep: 10 min.   chill: 8 hr.   bake: 12 min. per batch

1	cup butter, softened	2	tsp. ground cinnamon
1	cup granulated sugar	3	cups uncooked regular oats
1	cup firmly packed brown sugar	1	cup raisins
2	large eggs	1	cup chopped pecans
2	cups self-rising flour		

1. Beat first 3 ingredients at medium speed with an electric mixer until fluffy. Add eggs, beating until blended. Gradually add flour and cinnamon, beating at low speed until blended. Stir in oats, raisins, and pecans. Cover and chill dough 8 hours.

2. Preheat oven to 400°. Divide dough into 2 equal portions. Roll each portion into a 12-inch log. Cut each log into 1-inch-thick slices. Place slices on ungreased baking sheets.

3. Bake at 400° for 12 minutes or until golden brown; remove to wire racks to cool.

GINGERBREAD SNOWFLAKE COOKIES

makes 8 cookies   prep: 1 hr.   chill: 1 hr.   bake: 12 min. per batch

Royal Icing dries rapidly. Work quickly, keeping extra icing covered tightly at all times.

1 cup butter, softened	1½ Tbsp. ground ginger
1 cup sugar	½ tsp. ground allspice
1½ tsp. baking soda	1½ tsp. ground cinnamon
1 cup molasses	**Royal Icing**
5 cups all-purpose flour	White sparkling sugar (optional)
¼ tsp. salt	

1. Beat butter and sugar at medium speed with an electric mixer until fluffy.

2. Stir together ¼ cup water and soda until dissolved; stir in molasses.

3. Combine flour and next 4 ingredients. Add to butter mixture alternately with molasses mixture, beginning and ending with flour mixture. Shape mixture into a ball; cover and chill 1 hour.

4. Preheat oven to 350°. Roll to ¼-inch thickness on a lightly floured surface. Cut with a 7½-inch snowflake cookie cutter. Place 2 inches apart on parchment paper-lined baking sheets. Cut out designs in snowflakes using ¼- to ½-inch cutters, and remove.

5. Bake at 350° for 12 to 15 minutes. Remove to wire racks to cool.

6. Spoon icing into a small zip-top plastic freezer bag. Snip a tiny hole in 1 corner of bag; pipe around edges of cookies. Sprinkle icing with sparkling sugar, if desired.

Note: Sparkling sugar can be found at cake decorating stores and kitchen shops.

Royal Icing

makes about 3 cups   prep: 5 min.

1 (16-oz.) package powdered sugar	6 to 8 Tbsp. warm water
3 Tbsp. meringue powder	

1. Beat all ingredients at low speed with an electric mixer until blended. Beat at high speed 4 minutes or until stiff peaks form. If needed, add warm water, ¼ tsp. at a time, until desired consistency.

Note: Meringue powder can be found at crafts stores and cake decorating stores. Purchase cookie cutters, or cut out your own design.

SWEDISH HOLIDAY COOKIES

makes about 5 dozen prep: 20 min. chill: 8 hr. bake: 8 min. per batch cool: 5 min.

1 cup butter, softened
¾ cup sugar
1½ Tbsp. dark molasses
2 tsp. ground cinnamon
½ tsp. ground cardamom

1 tsp. baking powder
2½ cups all-purpose flour
2 egg whites, lightly beaten
Sugar

1. Beat butter at medium speed with an electric mixer until creamy. Add ¾ cup sugar, beating until smooth. Add molasses, cinnamon, and cardamom, beating until blended.
2. Combine 1 Tbsp. water and baking powder, stirring until baking powder is dissolved; add to butter mixture. Gradually add flour to butter mixture, beating until blended. Cover; chill 8 hours.
3. Preheat oven to 375°. Turn dough out onto a lightly floured surface; roll to ¼-inch thickness. Cut with a 2-inch round or other desired shape cutter. Place 2 inches apart on lightly greased baking sheets. Brush evenly with egg white, and sprinkle with sugar.
4. Bake at 375° for 8 minutes or until lightly browned. Cool on baking sheets 5 to 6 minutes. Remove to wire racks to cool completely.

VICTORIAN CHRISTMAS TEA CAKES

makes about 6 dozen prep: 1 hr. chill: 8 hr. cook: 4 min. per batch

1 cup butter, softened
1½ cups sugar
2 large eggs
¼ cup milk
4 cups all-purpose flour
½ tsp. salt

¼ tsp. baking soda
2 tsp. baking powder
1 tsp. ground cinnamon
1 tsp. ground nutmeg
1 cup currants
Powdered sugar

1. Beat butter and 1½ cups sugar at low speed with an electric mixer until creamy. Add eggs, 1 at a time, beating until blended after each addition. Add milk, beating until blended. Add flour and next 6 ingredients, beating until blended. Cover and chill dough 8 hours.
2. Divide dough into fourths. Roll 1 portion to ¼-inch thickness on a lightly floured surface. Cut with a 1½-inch round cookie cutter or very small glass. Repeat procedure with remaining portions.

3. Cook, in batches, on a hot, lightly greased electric griddle or lightly greased skillet over low heat, 2 to 3 minutes on each side or until golden. Remove to wire racks, and sprinkle warm tea cakes with powdered sugar. Cool slightly and serve, or cool completely and store in wax paper-lined airtight containers.

Note: Tea cakes may also be baked on lightly greased baking sheets at 350° for 10 minutes or until cookies are golden.

GINGERBREAD BOYS

makes about 6 dozen   prep: 30 min.   chill: 8 hr.   bake: 8 min. per batch   cool: 1 min.

You can freeze these cookies for several months in airtight containers.

1 cup butter	5 cups all-purpose flour
1 cup sugar	1½ tsp. baking soda
½ tsp. salt	1 Tbsp. ground ginger
1 cup molasses	1 tsp. ground cinnamon
2 Tbsp. white vinegar	1 tsp. ground cloves
1 large egg	

1. Beat butter at medium speed with an electric mixer until creamy; gradually add sugar and salt, beating well. Add molasses, vinegar, and egg, beating at low speed just until blended.
2. Combine flour and next 4 ingredients; add to butter mixture, beating at low speed until blended. Cover and chill 8 hours.
3. Preheat oven to 375°. Divide dough into fourths. Roll each portion to a ⅛-inch thickness on a floured surface. Cut with a 3-inch gingerbread-boy cookie cutter. Place on lightly greased or parchment paper-lined baking sheets.
4. Bake at 375° for 8 minutes. Cool on pans 1 minute (this allows cookies to lift easily off pan); remove to wire racks to cool. Decorate as desired.

{ freeze it }

MiLa

You can tell a lot from the bread basket. That's where surprises begin at MiLa, a recent entry on the New Orleans comeback scene. You start here with two miniature cast-iron skillets, one with a creamy, I-want-the-recipe lima bean puree and the other a luxurious butter crusted with sea salt—both accompanying sweet potato rolls and a softly textured shallot corn-bread. Those are just the first of the clean and different foods emerging from the kitchen of Slade Rushing and Allison Vines-Rushing on this (or any) day.

The couple blends Southern roots and New York training in a next-step cuisine for the Big Easy. Not Cajun, not Creole, devoid of heavy creams, sauces, and other maskings. "New Orleans food traditionally has an overindulgence of rich items—crab, oysters, and hollandaise on one plate—but our food is about purification," says Slade. "We want you to taste the vegetable just picked yesterday." The ever-evolving menu features New Orleans-style Barbecue Lobster, Sweet Tea Brined Rotisserie Duck, and various Gulf fish, all deftly sweeping past predictable. "It's approachable," says Allison of the simple ingredients woven into unique combinations.

817 Common Street
New Orleans, Louisiana 70112
(in the Renaissance Pere Marquette Hotel)
www.milaneworleans.com or (504) 412-2580.

FRUIT-FILLED COOKIES

makes 3 dozen   prep: 30 min.   stand: 10 min.   chill: 30 min.
bake: 18 min. per batch.   cool: 5 min.   **pictured on page 247**

We loved Sherry Salo's unique yeast cookie dough so much that we made a variation called
Snowflake Cookies.

3	cups all-purpose flour	½	cup warm milk (100° to 110°)
1	Tbsp. sugar	1	large egg, lightly beaten
½	tsp. salt	½	tsp. vanilla extract
1	cup butter, cut into pieces		Powdered sugar
1	(¼-oz.) envelope active dry yeast	1	(12-oz.) can apricot or cherry dessert filling

1. Stir together first 3 ingredients. Cut butter into flour mixture with a pastry blender or 2 forks until crumbly.

2. Whisk together yeast and warm milk. Let stand 10 minutes. (Mixture does not foam.) Stir in egg and vanilla. Add milk mixture to flour mixture, stirring until dry ingredients are moistened. Divide dough into fourths; wrap each portion in plastic wrap, and chill 30 minutes.

3. Preheat oven to 350°. Roll each portion of dough to ⅛-inch thickness on a flat surface lightly dusted with powdered sugar. Cut into 3-inch squares. Spoon 1 heaping teaspoonful of apricot or cherry dessert filling in center of each square.

4. Fold 2 opposite corners to center, slightly overlapping. Place on parchment paper-lined baking sheets.

5. Bake at 350° for 18 to 20 minutes or until lightly golden. Cool cookies on baking sheet 5 minutes. Remove to wire racks, and let cool completely. Sprinkle cookies with powdered sugar before serving.

Note: We tested with Solo Filling for Pastries, Cakes, and Desserts.

Snowflake Cookies: Omit dessert filling. Prepare and roll out dough as directed. Cut dough with a 3¾-inch snowflake-shaped cookie cutter. Place on parchment paper-lined baking sheets. Sprinkle with sparkling sugar. Bake at 350° for 10 minutes or until lightly golden. Cool cookies as directed. Makes about 5 dozen. Prep: 20 min., Stand: 10 min., Chill: 30 min., Bake: 10 min. per batch. Pictured on page 247.

LUSCIOUS LEMON SQUARES

makes 2 dozen   prep: 20 min.   bake: 55 min.   cool: 1 hr.

2¼ cups all-purpose flour, divided

½   cup powdered sugar

1   cup cold butter, cut into pieces

4   large eggs

1½ cups granulated sugar

2   tsp. lemon zest

½   cup fresh lemon juice

1   tsp. baking powder

¼   tsp. salt

Powdered sugar

Garnish: lemon zest curls

1. Preheat oven to 350°. Line bottom and sides of a 13- x 9-inch pan with heavy-duty aluminum foil, allowing 2 to 3 inches to extend over sides; lightly grease foil.

2. Pulse 2 cups flour, ½ cup powdered sugar, and 1 cup butter in a food processor 5 to 6 times or until mixture is crumbly. Press mixture onto bottom of prepared pan.

3. Bake at 350° on an oven rack one-third up from bottom of oven 25 minutes or just until golden brown.

4. Whisk together eggs and next 3 ingredients in a large bowl until blended. Combine baking powder, salt, and remaining ¼ cup flour; whisk into egg mixture until blended. Pour lemon mixture into prepared crust.

5. Bake at 350° on middle oven rack 30 to 35 minutes or until filling is set. Let cool in pan on a wire rack 30 minutes. Lift from pan onto wire rack, using foil sides as handles, and let cool 30 minutes or until completely cool. Remove foil, and cut into 24 (2-inch) squares; sprinkle with powdered sugar. Garnish, if desired.

Blackberry-Lemon Squares: Prepare recipe as directed through Step 4. Pulse 2 cups fresh blackberries and ½ cup granulated sugar in a food processor 3 to 4 times or until blended. Transfer mixture to a small saucepan. Cook over medium-low heat, stirring often, 5 to 6 minutes or until thoroughly heated. Pour through a fine wire-mesh strainer into a bowl, gently pressing blackberry mixture with back of a spoon; discard solids. Drizzle over lemon mixture in pan. Proceed with Step 5. Garnish with fresh mint and blackberries, if desired. Pictured on page 249.

CITRUS BARS

makes 2 dozen   prep: 15 min.   bake: 48 min.   cool: 1 hr.

Be sure to bake bar cookies in the size pan indicated; otherwise, the baking time and the texture of the bars may vary.

1 cup butter, softened	1 tsp. finely grated orange zest
2¼ cups all-purpose flour, divided	4 large eggs, beaten
½ cup powdered sugar	1 tsp. baking powder
1¾ cups granulated sugar	¼ tsp. salt
⅓ cup fresh lemon juice	1 Tbsp. powdered sugar
⅓ cup fresh orange juice	Garnish: orange and lemon rind strips

1. Preheat oven to 350°. Beat butter at medium speed with an electric mixer until creamy; add 2 cups flour and ½ cup powdered sugar. Beat until mixture forms a smooth dough. Press mixture into a lightly greased 13- x 9-inch baking pan.

2. Bake at 350° for 20 to 22 minutes or until lightly browned.

3. Whisk together remaining ¼ cup flour, granulated sugar, and next 6 ingredients; pour over baked crust.

4. Bake at 350° for 28 to 30 minutes or until set. Cool in pan on wire rack. Sprinkle evenly with 1 Tbsp. powdered sugar, and cut into bars. Garnish, if desired.

KEY LIME SQUARES WITH MACADAMIA CRUST

makes: 2 dozen   prep: 25 min.   bake: 20 min.   stand: 3 min.   chill: 8 hr.

For a cooling summer dessert, you won't go wrong with this bar cookie variation of the classic Key lime pie. Found in the southernmost tip of Florida, key limes are small, yellow, and have a tarter flavor than other lime varieties. Macadamias contribute to the perfect crust for this creamy filling.

2	cups all-purpose flour	1	envelope unflavored gelatin
½	cup firmly packed light brown sugar	2	Tbsp. Key lime juice
⅔	cup chopped macadamias	1	(14-oz.) can sweetened condensed milk
6	Tbsp. butter, cubed	1	tsp. lime zest
½	tsp. salt		2½ cups whipping cream, whipped
¾	cup granulated sugar		Garnish: Key lime zest
½	cup Key lime juice		

1. Preheat oven to 350°. Process first 5 ingredients in a food processor until finely ground. Press mixture into a greased aluminum foil-lined 13- x 9-inch pan, allowing foil to extend over edges of pan.

2. Bake at 350° for 20 minutes or until golden. Cool on a wire rack.

3. Heat granulated sugar and ½ cup Key lime juice over low heat, stirring until sugar dissolves. Remove from heat, and set aside.

4. Sprinkle gelatin over 2 Tbsp. Key lime juice in a medium bowl; stir gelatin mixture, and let stand 3 to 5 minutes.

5. Add hot mixture to gelatin mixture, stirring until gelatin dissolves. Whisk in sweetened condensed milk and 1 tsp. lime zest.

6. Place bowl in a larger bowl filled with ice; whisk mixture 10 minutes or until partially set.

7. Fold in whipped cream. Pour over prepared crust; cover and chill 8 hours. Use foil to lift out of pan. Peel foil away, and cut into squares. Garnish, if desired.

PEACH-PECAN BARS

makes 15 bars   prep: 10 min.   bake: 41 min.   cook: 3 min.   cool: 20 min.

These bars can be served right out of the oven, but we liked them better after they sat overnight. Store in an airtight container up to five days.

¾ **cup chopped pecans**
1 **(16.5-oz.) package refrigerated sugar cookie dough**

1 **cup peach preserves**
2 **tsp. cornstarch**
Powdered sugar

make ahead

1. Preheat oven to 350°. Place pecans in a single layer in a shallow pan.

2. Bake at 350°for 8 to 10 minutes or until lightly toasted, stirring once after 5 minutes.

3. Divide cookie dough into 3 equal pieces, and press evenly onto bottom of a lightly greased 11- x 7-inch baking dish. Sprinkle evenly with pecans, pressing into dough.

4. Bake at 350°for 25 minutes or until edges are golden brown.

5. Bring peach preserves and cornstarch to a boil in a small saucepan. Boil 1 minute, stirring constantly. Pour preserve mixture evenly over warm crust.

6. Bake at 350°for 8 minutes. Remove pan from oven, and cool on a wire rack 20 minutes. Sprinkle evenly with powdered sugar, and cut into bars. Serve immediately or at room temperature.

Note: We tested with Pillsbury Create 'n Bake Sugar Refrigerated Cookie Dough.

PECAN PIE SQUARES

makes about 28 squares   prep: 20 min.   cook: 5 min.   bake: 45 min.

Pecan pie in cookie-size squares—that's what you'll get when you make this recipe. As a classic Southern dessert synonymous with Georgia, Louisiana, and Texas, pecan pie makes an appearance in most Southern cookbooks. The original version came about when Karo corn syrup was introduced in the early 1900s, and several states lay claim to this version. In this bar cookie version, honey replaces the syrup for the gooey filling cradled in a shortbread-style crust.

2 cups all-purpose flour	½ cup honey
⅔ cup powdered sugar	⅔ cup butter
¾ cup butter, softened	3 Tbsp. whipping cream
½ cup firmly packed brown sugar	3½ cups coarsely chopped pecans

1. Preheat oven to 350°. Sift together flour and powdered sugar. Cut in ¾ cup softened butter using a pastry blender or fork just until mixture resembles coarse meal. Pat mixture on bottom and 1½ inches up sides of a lightly greased 13- x 9-inch baking dish.

2. Bake at 350° for 20 minutes or until edges are lightly browned. Cool. Bring brown sugar, honey, ⅔ cup butter, and whipping cream to a boil in a saucepan over medium-high heat. Stir in pecans, and pour hot filling into prepared crust.

3. Bake at 350° for 25 to 30 minutes or until golden and bubbly. Cool in pan on a wire rack before cutting into 2-inch squares.

TURTLE SQUARES

makes 4 dozen   prep: 10 min.   bake: 12 min.   chill: 30 min.

1 (12-oz.) package vanilla wafers	1 cup pecan pieces
¾ cup butter, melted	1 (12¼-oz.) jar caramel topping
1 (12-oz.) package semisweet chocolate morsels	

1. Preheat oven to 350°. Place vanilla wafers in a large zip-top plastic freezer bag; crush with a rolling pin to fine crumbs.

2. Stir together vanilla wafer crumbs and butter; press into bottom of a 13- x 9-inch baking dish. Sprinkle with morsels and pecans. Drizzle with caramel topping.

3. Bake at 350° for 12 to 15 minutes. Cool in pan on a wire rack. Chill 30 minutes. Cut into 1½-inch squares.

OATMEAL CARMELITAS

makes 24 to 30 carmelitas   prep: 25 min.   bake: 30 min.

Caramels, chocolate morsels, and pecans combine for a melt-in-your-mouth treat.

2   cups all-purpose flour
2   cups uncooked quick-cooking oats
1½ cups firmly packed light brown sugar
1   tsp. baking soda
¼   tsp. salt
1   cup butter, melted

1   (12-oz.) package semisweet chocolate morsels
½   cup chopped pecans or walnuts, toasted
     (optional)
1   (14-oz.) package caramels
⅓   cup half-and-half

1. Preheat oven to 350°. Stir together first 5 ingredients in a large mixing bowl. Add butter, stirring until mixture is crumbly. Reserve half of mixture (about 2¾ cups). Press remaining half of mixture into bottom of a greased aluminum foil-lined 13- x 9-inch pan, allowing foil to extend over edges of pan. Sprinkle with chocolate morsels and, if desired, pecans.

2. Microwave caramels and ⅓ cup half-and-half in a microwave-safe bowl at MEDIUM (50% power) 3 minutes. Stir and microwave at MEDIUM 1 to 3 more minutes or until mixture is smooth. Let stand 1 minute. Pour over chocolate morsels. Sprinkle with reserved crumb mixture.

3. Bake at 350° for 30 minutes or until light golden brown. Cool in pan on a wire rack. Use foil to lift out of pan. Peel foil away, and cut into squares.

DEATH-BY-CARAMEL SQUARES

makes 2 dozen   prep: 24 min.   bake: 1 hr., 5 min.

These showy brownies are nice and tall, with pockets of soft caramel. They are wicked enough on their own; but for an over-the-top dessert, add a scoop of vanilla ice cream and a drizzle of caramel sauce. Find dulce de leche with other ethnic ingredients or on the baking aisle.

3	cups firmly packed light brown sugar	1	tsp. baking powder
2	cups unsalted butter, melted	½	tsp. baking soda
3	large eggs, lightly beaten	¾	tsp. salt
1	Tbsp. vanilla extract	6	(2.07-oz.) chocolate-coated caramel-peanut
4	cups all-purpose flour		nougat bars, chopped
1	cup uncooked regular oats	1	(14-oz.) can dulce de leche

1. Preheat oven to 325°. Combine first 4 ingredients in a large bowl; stir well. Combine flour and next 4 ingredients. Add to butter mixture, stirring just until blended. Fold in chopped candy bars.

2. Spoon batter into a greased aluminum foil-lined 13- x 9-inch pan coated with cooking spray, allowing foil to extend over edges of pan. (Pan will be very full.) Spoon dollops of dulce de leche over batter; swirl slightly into batter with a knife.

3. Bake at 325° for 1 hour and 5 minutes. Cool in a pan on a wire rack. (This may take several hours.) Use foil to lift uncut brownies out of pan. Peel foil away, and cut into squares.

Note: We tested with Snickers caramel-peanut nougat bars.

AMARETTO-WALNUT BROWNIES

makes 15 brownies   prep: 15 min.   bake: 42 min.
cool: 1 hr.   stand: 4 hr.   cook: 5 min.

1 cup coarsely chopped walnuts	¼ cup instant cocoa mix
½ cup almond liqueur	1⅔ cups all-purpose flour
1 cup butter	1 Tbsp. vanilla extract
8 (1-oz.) unsweetened chocolate baking squares	⅛ tsp. salt
5 large eggs	Amaretto Frosting
3⅓ cups sugar	

1. Preheat oven to 350°. Place walnuts in a single layer in a shallow pan.

2. Bake at 350° for 7 to 8 minutes or until toasted. Let cool 15 minutes. Place walnuts and liqueur in a large bowl, and let stand 4 hours. Drain, reserving liqueur for Amaretto Frosting.

3. Melt butter and chocolate baking squares in a heavy saucepan over low heat.

4. Beat eggs, sugar, and cocoa mix at medium-high speed with an electric mixer 8 minutes. Gradually add butter mixture, beating at low speed until blended. Gradually add flour, vanilla, and salt, beating until blended. Stir in walnuts. Pour into a lightly greased aluminum foil-lined 13- x 9-inch pan.

5. Bake at 350° for 35 to 45 minutes. Cool on a wire rack 45 minutes or until cool. Spread brownies with frosting, and cut into squares.

Amaretto Frosting

makes: 2½ cups   prep: 10 min.

½ cup butter, softened	¼ cup unsweetened cocoa
5 cups sifted powdered sugar	4 to 6 Tbsp. reserved almond liqueur

1. Beat butter at medium-high speed with an electric mixer until creamy; add sugar, cocoa, and 4 Tbsp. liqueur, beating until fluffy and adding remaining 2 Tbsp. liqueur, if necessary, for desired consistency.

Personalized brownies make the perfect treat to take to a party—especially if you start with a mix.

Monogrammed Jumbo Brownies

makes 1 dozen prep: 20 min. bake: 30 min. cool: 45 min. stand: 45 min.

Prepare and bake 1 (21-oz.) package fudge brownie mix according to directions for a 13- x 9-inch pan. Let cool in pan on a wire rack for 45 minutes. Stir together ½ cup butter, ⅓ cup milk, and 5 Tbsp. unsweetened cocoa over low heat, stirring constantly, 5 minutes or until butter melts and mixture is blended. Remove from heat, and beat in 1 (16-oz.) package powdered sugar at low speed with an electric mixer until smooth; spread frosting evenly over prepared brownies. Let stand 45 minutes or until frosting is firm. Cut into 12 equal squares. Tint ½ (16-oz.) container ready-to-spread vanilla frosting with desired shade of food coloring gel. Spoon frosting mixture into a small zip-top plastic freezer bag. Snip a hole in 1 corner of the bag. Pipe desired monogram on each brownie.

• You can find small letter-shaped cookie cutters at crafts stores to use as templates. Simply imprint letter on iced surface; then pipe over the imprint.

• If you don't have time to monogram, pick up a box of alphabet-shaped cookies to use as a topping.

DARK CHOCOLATE BROWNIES

makes 4 dozen prep: 15 min. bake: 30 min.

1 cup butter	4 large eggs
1 (8-oz.) package bittersweet baking chocolate squares	1 Tbsp. vanilla extract
	1½ cups chopped walnuts or pecans, toasted
2 cups (12 oz.) semisweet chocolate morsels, divided	1 cup all-purpose flour
	½ tsp. salt
2 cups sugar	

1. Preheat oven to 350°. Microwave butter, bittersweet chocolate, and 1 cup semisweet chocolate morsels in a 4-qt. microwave-safe bowl at HIGH 1½ to 2 minutes or until chocolate is melted, stirring mixture every 30 seconds. Whisk in sugar, eggs, and vanilla.

2. Toss together walnuts, 1 Tbsp. flour, and remaining 1 cup chocolate morsels. Stir remaining flour and salt into sugar mixture. Stir in walnut mixture. Spread batter into a greased 13- x 9-inch pan.

3. Bake at 350°for 30 to 40 minutes or until edges begin to pull away from pan. (A wooden pick inserted in center will not come out clean.) Cool on a wire rack. Cut into 1½-inch squares.

Dark Chocolate Bourbon Brownies: Substitute 1 Tbsp. bourbon for vanilla extract, and proceed as directed.

MAGNOLIA CREAM CHEESE BROWNIES

makes 1½ dozen   prep: 15 min.   cook: 2 min.   bake: 40 min.

4   (1-oz.) unsweetened chocolate baking squares
4   (1-oz.) semisweet chocolate baking squares
⅓   cup butter
2   (3-oz.) packages cream cheese, softened
¼   cup butter, softened
2   cups sugar, divided
6   large eggs
1   tsp. vanilla extract

2   Tbsp. all-purpose flour
1½ cups (9 oz.) semisweet chocolate morsels, divided
2   tsp. vanilla extract
1   cup all-purpose flour
1   tsp. baking powder
1   tsp. salt

1. Preheat oven to 325°. Microwave first 3 ingredients in a 1-qt. glass bowl at HIGH 2 minutes or until melted, stirring once. Cool and set aside.

2. Beat cream cheese and ¼ cup butter at medium speed with an electric mixer until creamy; gradually add ½ cup sugar, beating well.

3. Add 2 eggs, 1 at a time, beating until blended. Stir in 1 tsp. vanilla. Fold in 2 Tbsp. flour and ½ cup chocolate morsels; set aside.

4. Beat remaining 4 eggs in a large bowl at medium speed with an electric mixer. Gradually add remaining 1½ cups sugar, beating well. Add melted chocolate mixture and 2 tsp. vanilla extract; beat mixture until well blended.

5. Combine 1 cup flour, baking powder, and salt; fold into chocolate batter until blended, and stir in remaining 1 cup chocolate morsels.

6. Reserve 3 cups chocolate batter; spread remaining batter evenly in a greased 13- x 9-inch pan. Pour cream cheese mixture over batter. Top with reserved 3 cups batter, and swirl mixture with a knife.

7. Bake at 325° for 40 to 45 minutes. Cool and cut brownies into squares.

PRALINE-PECAN BROWNIES

makes 32 brownies   prep: 15 min.   bake: 35 min.

To easily remove and cut brownies, line the pan with greased and floured heavy-duty aluminum foil, allowing several inches to extend over sides. After baking and cooling, lift the block of brownies from the pan using the foil. Press the foil sides down, and cut.

4	(1-oz.) unsweetened chocolate baking squares	1	tsp. vanilla extract
1	cup butter, softened	1	cup semisweet chocolate morsels
2	cups sugar		Chocolate Glaze
4	large eggs	2	cups coarsely chopped Pralines (recipe on
1	cup all-purpose flour		page 275)

1. Preheat oven to 350°. Microwave chocolate squares in a microwave-safe bowl at MEDIUM (50% power) 1½ minutes, stirring at 30-second intervals until melted. Stir until smooth.
2. Beat butter and sugar at medium speed with an electric mixer until light and fluffy. Add eggs, 1 at a time, beating just until blended after each addition. Add melted chocolate, beating just until blended.
3. Add flour, beating at low speed just until blended. Stir in vanilla and chocolate morsels. Spread batter into a greased and floured 13- x 9-inch pan.
4. Bake at 350° for 35 to 40 minutes or until center is set. Cool completely on wire rack. Spread uncut brownies evenly with Chocolate Glaze; sprinkle evenly with 2 cups chopped Pralines. Cut into squares.

Chocolate Glaze

makes 1⅓ cups   prep: 10 min.   cook: 5 min.

1	cup (6 oz.) semisweet chocolate morsels	¼	cup milk
3	Tbsp. butter	1½	cups powdered sugar

1. Whisk together first 3 ingredients in a heavy saucepan over low heat, and cook, whisking constantly, 5 minutes or until butter and chocolate melt. Remove pan from heat; whisk in powdered sugar until smooth and spreading consistency.

CHOCOLATE CHIP CHEESECAKE BARS

makes 1 dozen   prep: 15 min.   bake: 38 min.   chill: 4 hr.

Take these festive bars to your next gathering—you can make them ahead of time and transport them easily.

1	cup all-purpose flour	3	large eggs
⅓	cup firmly packed light brown sugar	⅓	cup sour cream
¼	cup butter, softened	½	tsp. vanilla extract
3	(8-oz.) packages cream cheese, softened	1	(12-oz.) package semisweet chocolate
¾	cup granulated sugar		mini morsels, divided

1. Preheat oven to 350°. Beat first 3 ingredients at medium-low speed with an electric mixer until combined. Increase speed to medium, and beat until well blended and crumbly. Pat mixture into a lightly greased 13- x 9-inch pan.

2. Bake at 350° for 13 to 15 minutes or until lightly browned.

3. Beat cream cheese at medium speed with electric mixer until creamy. Gradually add granulated sugar, beating until well blended. Add eggs, 1 at a time, beating at low speed just until blended after each addition. Add sour cream, vanilla, and 1 cup chocolate morsels, beating just until blended. Pour over baked crust.

4. Bake at 350° for 25 minutes or until set. Cool in pan on a wire rack.

5. Microwave remaining chocolate morsels in a 2-cup glass measuring cup on HIGH 1 minute, stirring after 30 seconds. Stir until smooth. Transfer to a 1-qt. zip-top plastic freezer bag; cut a tiny hole in 1 corner of bag. Pipe melted chocolate over cheesecake by gently squeezing bag. Cover and chill at least 4 hours; cut into bars.

MILLIONAIRE SHORTBREAD

makes about 3 dozen squares or 6 dozen triangles prep: 15 min. bake: 18 min.
cook: 29 min. chill: 45 min.

This recipe came from Fairfield Grocery employee Jane and her husband's good friend, Dr. Anne Peters of Edinburgh, Scotland. It uses white rice flour, which gives the shortbread a crispy texture. You can substitute all-purpose flour for the rice flour.

1½ cups butter, softened and divided

2 cups all-purpose flour

¾ cup white rice flour*

½ cup granulated sugar

Cooking spray for baking

1 (14-oz.) can sweetened condensed milk

¼ cup light corn syrup

1 cup firmly packed light brown sugar

1½ cups semisweet chocolate morsels

1. Preheat oven to 350°. Pulse 1 cup butter, flours, and granulated sugar in a food processor 10 to 15 times or until crumbly. Press mixture evenly into a 15- x 10-inch jelly-roll pan coated with cooking spray for baking.

2. Bake at 350° for 18 to 20 minutes or until light golden brown.

3. Stir together remaining ½ cup butter, condensed milk, and corn syrup in a 2-qt. heavy saucepan over low heat 4 minutes or until butter is melted and mixture is blended. Add brown sugar, and cook, stirring constantly, 25 to 30 minutes or until caramel colored and thickened. Pour evenly over baked cookie in pan, and spread into an even layer. Chill 30 minutes or until caramel is set.

4. Microwave morsels in a small glass bowl at HIGH 1 minute or until almost melted. Stir until smooth. Spread over caramel layer in pan. (The chocolate layer will be thin.) Chill 15 minutes or until chocolate is firm. Cut into 2-inch squares; if desired, cut each square into 2 triangles.

* ¾ cup all-purpose flour may be substituted.

HONEY-PECAN SHORTBREAD

makes about 24 bars prep: 20 min. bake: 50 min. **pictured on page 248**

1 cup butter, softened
⅓ cup honey
2 Tbsp. brown sugar

1 tsp. vanilla extract
2½ cups all-purpose flour
¾ cup pecan halves, toasted and chopped

1. Preheat oven to 300°. Beat butter at medium speed with an electric mixer until fluffy; add honey, brown sugar, and vanilla, and beat until blended, stopping to scrape down sides. Gradually add flour, beating at low speed until blended. Stir in pecans.

2. Press dough evenly into bottom of an ungreased 9-inch square pan.

3. Bake at 300° for 55 to 65 minutes or until golden (begin checking for doneness at 50 minutes just in case your oven runs hot). Let cool in pan on a wire rack. Cut into bars. Store in an airtight container.

Note: This shortbread can also be baked in an ungreased 10-inch cast-iron skillet, if desired.

BLUEBERRY-PECAN SHORTBREAD SQUARES

makes 2 dozen prep: 20 min. bake: 53 min. cool: 2 hr.

¾ cup chopped pecans
2¼ cups all-purpose flour
½ tsp. salt
1 cup butter, softened
1½ cups powdered sugar

¼ tsp. vanilla extract
3 (4.4-oz.) containers fresh blueberries (about 2½ cups)
2 Tbsp. granulated sugar
1 tsp. lime zest

1. Preheat oven to 350°. Place pecans in a single layer in a shallow pan.

2. Bake at 350° for 8 minutes or until toasted.

3. Stir together pecans, flour, and salt in a bowl.

4. Beat 1 cup butter and 1½ cups powdered sugar at medium speed with a heavy-duty electric stand mixer 2 minutes or until pale and fluffy. Beat in ¼ tsp. vanilla. Gradually add flour mixture, beating at low speed 30 seconds after each addition until a dough forms and comes together to hold a shape.

5. Press 2 cups of dough in a thick layer onto bottom of a lightly greased 13- x 9-inch pan. Top evenly with fresh blueberries. Combine granulated sugar and lime zest, and sprinkle evenly over berries. Crumble remaining dough over berries. Bake at 350° for 45 to 50 minutes or until golden. Cool shortbread in pan on a wire rack 2 hours. Cut into squares before serving.

DESSERTS

"When I was a child and the snow fell, my mother always rushed to the kitchen and made snow ice cream and divinity fudge—egg whites, sugar and pecans, mostly. It was a lark then, and I always associate divinity fudge with snowstorms." —Eudora Welty

RICH BLACK-AND-WHITE PUDDING

makes 6 servings   prep: 20 min.   bake: 50 min.   chill: 8 hr.

3½ cups whipping cream, divided

5   (1-oz.) semisweet chocolate squares

6   egg yolks

½   cup sugar

1   tsp. vanilla extract

3   Tbsp. sugar

Grated semisweet chocolate

1. Preheat oven to 325°. Cook ½ cup whipping cream and chocolate in a heavy saucepan over low heat, stirring constantly, until chocolate melts and mixture is smooth. Pour into a large bowl. Set aside.

2. Whisk together 2 cups whipping cream, yolks, ½ cup sugar, and vanilla in a bowl until sugar dissolves and mixture is smooth.

3. Whisk 1 cup egg mixture into chocolate mixture until smooth. Cover and chill remaining egg mixture. Pour chocolate mixture into 6 (8-oz.) custard cups; place cups in a 13- x 9-inch pan. Add hot water to pan to a depth of ½ inch.

4. Bake at 325° for 30 minutes or until almost set. (Center will be soft.) Slowly pour remaining egg mixture evenly over custards; bake 20 to 25 more minutes or until set. Cool custards in water in pan on a wire rack. Remove from pan; cover and chill at least 8 hours.

5. Beat remaining 1 cup whipping cream at high speed with an electric mixer until foamy; gradually add 3 Tbsp. sugar, beating until stiff peaks form. Top custards with whipped cream; sprinkle with grated chocolate.

CHOCOLATE PUDDING

makes 5 cups   prep: 15 min.   cook: 10 min.

4   cups whipping cream

6   Tbsp. cornstarch

1   cup sugar

1   cup semisweet chocolate morsels

1   tsp. vanilla extract

1. Stir together 6 Tbsp. cream and cornstarch, stirring until a paste forms. Bring remaining cream to a simmer in a 2-qt. saucepan over medium heat. Stir in cornstarch mixture, sugar, chocolate morsels, and vanilla; cook, stirring constantly, until chocolate melts. Cook mixture, stirring often, 8 minutes or until thick and creamy.

[for kids]

DELTA VELVET PUDDING DESSERT

makes 10 to 12 servings   prep: 20 min.   bake: 18 min.   chill: 2 hr.

Debi Hochgertle from Lawrenceville, Georgia, picked up this recipe while in college at The University of Southern Mississippi.

½ cup butter, softened
1 cup all-purpose flour
1 cup finely chopped pecans, toasted
1 (8-oz.) package cream cheese, softened
1½ cups powdered sugar
1 (8-oz.) container frozen whipped topping, thawed

1 (3.4-oz.) package French vanilla instant pudding mix
1 (3.9-oz.) package chocolate instant pudding mix
3 cups milk
Toppings: whipped topping, toasted chopped pecans, toffee bits, shaved chocolate

1. Preheat oven to 350°. Cut butter into flour with a pastry blender or fork until crumbly; stir in 1 cup pecans. Press mixture into a 13- x 9-inch pan or baking dish.

2. Bake at 350° for 18 to 20 minutes or until lightly browned. Remove pan to wire rack to cool completely.

3. Beat cream cheese and powdered sugar at medium speed with an electric mixer until fluffy. Fold in whipped topping. Spread cream cheese mixture evenly over cooled crust.

4. Beat pudding mixes and milk in a large bowl at medium speed with an electric mixer 2 minutes. Pour evenly over cream cheese mixture in pan. Cover and chill 2 hours or up to 3 days. Serve pudding in individual bowls with desired toppings.

[make ahead]

inspirations for your taste

Quick & Tasty Banana Pudding

makes 1 serving   prep: 10 min.

Cut half of 1 small banana into slices; keep other half in the peel and save for another use. Layer 1 (5-oz.) glass with 1 Tbsp. thawed nondairy whipped topping, one-fourth of banana slices, 1 Tbsp. prepared vanilla pudding, another fourth of banana slices, and 1 vanilla wafer. Repeat layers. Dollop with 1 Tbsp. thawed nondairy whipped topping.

Note: We tested with Hunt's Snack Pack Vanilla Pudding. One (3.5-oz.) pudding cup yields 6 Tbsp. pudding.

RUM BANANA PUDDING

makes 10 to 12 servings   prep: 10 min.   cook: 6 min.   stand: 5 min.   bake: 8 min.

1½ cups milk	6 medium bananas, sliced
⅔ cup sugar	30 vanilla wafers
2 egg yolks	1 cup chopped toasted pecans
3 Tbsp. cornstarch	2 egg whites
3 Tbsp. light rum	⅛ tsp. cream of tartar
1 tsp. vanilla extract	2 Tbsp. sugar

1. Whisk together first 5 ingredients in a large saucepan over medium-low heat; cook, whisking constantly, 6 to 8 minutes or until thickened. Remove from heat, and stir in vanilla. Let stand 5 minutes. Gently stir bananas into pudding mixture.

2. Arrange 15 vanilla wafers in a single layer on bottom of a 1½-qt. baking dish; sprinkle ½ cup pecans evenly on vanilla wafers. Pour half of pudding mixture on top of pecans in dish. Repeat layers with remaining vanilla wafers, pudding, and ending with pecans.

3. Preheat oven to 400°.

4. Beat egg whites and ⅛ tsp. cream of tartar at high speed with an electric mixer until foamy. Add 2 Tbsp. sugar, 1 Tbsp. at a time, beating until soft peaks form and sugar dissolves (about 1 to 2 minutes). Spread meringue evenly over top of banana mixture, sealing edges.

5. Bake at 400° for 8 to 10 minutes or until golden brown.

BLASTIN' BANANA-BLUEBERRY PUDDING

makes 10 to 12 servings   prep: 10 min.   cook: 20 min.   stand: 10 min.   chill: 4 hr.

4 cups milk	1 (12-oz.) box vanilla wafers
4 egg yolks	4 large ripe bananas, sliced
1½ cups granulated sugar	2 cups frozen blueberries
⅓ cup all-purpose flour	1½ cups whipping cream
2 Tbsp. butter	3 Tbsp. powdered sugar
1 Tbsp. vanilla extract	

1. Whisk together first 4 ingredients in a large saucepan over medium-low heat. Cook, whisking constantly, 20 minutes or until thickened. Remove from heat; stir in butter and vanilla until butter melts. Let stand 10 minutes.

2. Arrange half of vanilla wafers evenly in a 13- x 9-inch baking dish; top with half of banana slices and half of blueberries. Spoon half of pudding mixture evenly over fruit. Repeat layers. Cover and chill 4 hours.

3. Beat whipping cream at high speed with an electric mixer until foamy; gradually add powdered sugar, beating until soft peaks form. Spread sweetened whipped cream evenly over chilled pudding. Serve immediately.

FREE-FORM STRAWBERRY CHEESECAKE

makes 6 servings   prep: 20 min.

Powdered sugar dissolves almost instantly when stirred into berries, while granulated sugar needs stand time. We chose powdered for this quick-to-put-together recipe.

2 cups fresh strawberries, sliced	1 Tbsp. lime juice
4 Tbsp. powdered sugar, divided	6 crisp gourmet cookies, crumbled
1½ cups ready-to-eat cheesecake filling	Garnishes: crisp gourmet cookies, lime slices
1 tsp. lime zest	

1. Stir together strawberries and 2 Tbsp. powdered sugar.

2. Stir together cheesecake filling, lime zest, lime juice, and remaining 2 Tbsp. powdered sugar.

3. Spoon cheesecake mixture into 6 (6-oz.) glasses or ramekins. Sprinkle with crumbled cookies. Top with strawberries. Garnish, if desired. Serve immediately.

Note: We tested with Philadelphia Ready-To-Eat Cheesecake Filling and Biscoff cookies.

test kitchen favorite

PERSIMMON PUDDING

makes 6 servings   prep: 20 min.   bake: 50 min.

2 cups persimmon pulp	½ tsp. baking soda
½ cup butter, melted	1 tsp. ground cinnamon
1 cup sugar	½ cup milk
2 large eggs	½ cup buttermilk
1 cup all-purpose flour	Cinnamon-Butter Sauce
1½ tsp. baking powder	

1. Preheat oven to 350°. Stir together first 4 ingredients until blended. Add flour and next 5 ingredients, stirring well (batter will not be smooth). Pour batter into a greased and floured 9-inch square pan.

2. Bake at 350° for 50 to 55 minutes. Serve with Cinnamon-Butter Sauce.

Cinnamon-Butter Sauce

makes 1½ cups   prep: 5 min.   cook: 6 min.

1 cup sugar	1 cup hot water
½ cup butter	1 tsp. cinnamon
2 Tbsp. all-purpose flour	

1. Cook first 4 ingredients in a saucepan over medium-high heat, stirring occasionally, 6 to 8 minutes or until thickened. Stir in cinnamon.

Persimmon Primer

The persimmon is one of winter's rare, delicious fruits. The Japanese persimmon is what most local markets carry. It's similar in appearance to a tomato and should be eaten when fully ripe. To enjoy it at its simplest, cut it in half, and scoop out the tangy flesh.

Choose fruit that is plump and soft with smooth, glossy skin. When ripe, persimmons will store in the refrigerator up to three days. Persimmons add flavor to custards and may be dried or canned.

Fulton Five

For the best meals in Charleston, eat where the locals go. To help find those spots for you, former Charlestonian and *Southern Living* Senior Writer Donna Florio shared one of her favorite spots. Fulton Five has served up northern Italian food for the past 13 years. Celadon-green walls and flattering light call for hushed, romantic conversations and big glasses of wine. The menu changes seasonally (visit their Web site for current listings), but one pasta offered year-round is the ragu alla Bolognese. Or try the filleto d'Espresso, a chocolate-rubbed filet served over whipped potatoes, asparagus, and a balsamic-veal jus. For dessert try the dense, slightly crunchy pistachio ice cream. Its near-gelato texture gives a perfect Italian finish to the dinner.

5 Fulton Street, Charleston, South Carolina, 29401; www.fultonfive.net or (843) 853-5555.

BASIC CRÈME BRÛLÉE

makes 5 servings   prep: 10 min.   bake: 45 min.   chill: 8 hr.   broil: 5 min.   stand: 5 min.

Crème brûlée is simply a custard wearing a brown sugar cap.

2 cups whipping cream	1 Tbsp. vanilla extract
5 egg yolks	½ cup firmly packed light brown sugar
½ cup sugar	Garnishes: fresh raspberries, fresh mint sprig

1. Preheat oven to 275°. Combine first 4 ingredients, stirring with a wire whisk until sugar dissolves and mixture is smooth. Pour mixture evenly into 5 (5- x 1-inch) round individual baking dishes; place dishes in a large roasting pan or a 15- x 10-inch jelly-roll pan. Prepare ½-inch water bath (see Brûlée Basics on facing page).

2. Bake at 275° for 45 to 50 minutes or until almost set. Cool custards in water in pan on a wire rack. Remove from pan; cover and refrigerate 8 hours or overnight.

3. Increase heat to broil. Sprinkle about 1½ Tbsp. brown sugar evenly over each custard; place custards in a jelly-roll pan.

4. Broil 5 inches from heat until brown sugar melts. Let stand 5 minutes to allow sugar to harden.

Note: All baking times are for 5- x 1-inch round individual baking dishes. As a general rule, to use 4-, 6-, or 8-oz. custard cups, bake for an additional 15 to 20 minutes. When the crème brûlée is done, the center will still be slightly liquid and a knife will not come out clean. The yield will vary with different size dishes: For 4-oz. cups you'll get 10 servings, for 6-oz. cups you'll get 7 servings, and for 8-oz. cups you'll get 4 servings.

Chocolate Crème Brûlée: Combine 4 (1-oz.) squares semisweet chocolate and ½ cup whipping cream from basic recipe in a small heavy saucepan; cook over low heat, stirring constantly until chocolate melts. Add remaining 1½ cups whipping cream; reduce vanilla to 1 tsp. Proceed as directed in basic recipe, baking for 55 minutes. To make a Chocolate-Raspberry version, place 8 to 10 fresh raspberries in each baking dish, add chocolate custard, and increase baking time to 1 hour and 5 minutes.

Berry Crème Brûlée: Place 8 to 10 fresh blackberries or raspberries in each baking dish; pour custard mixture over berries. Proceed as directed in basic recipe, baking for 45 minutes.

Double Raspberry Crème Brûlée: Reduce vanilla to 1 tsp.; add 1 additional egg yolk and 1½ Tbsp. raspberry liqueur to custard mixture. Place 8 to 10 fresh raspberries in each baking dish; pour custard mixture over berries. Proceed as directed in basic recipe, baking for 55 minutes.

Ginger Crème Brûlée: Reduce vanilla to 1 tsp.; add 2 Tbsp. grated fresh ginger to custard mixture. Proceed as directed in basic recipe, baking for 1 hour and 5 minutes.

White Chocolate-Macadamia Nut Crème Brûlée: Pictured on page 252. Combine 4 oz. white chocolate and ½ cup whipping cream from basic recipe in a small heavy saucepan; cook over low heat, stirring constantly until chocolate melts. Add remaining 1½ cups whipping cream; reduce vanilla to 1 tsp. Proceed as directed in basic recipe. Place 1 Tbsp. chopped macadamia nuts, toasted, in each baking dish, and pour custard over nuts. Bake as directed for 1 hour and 10 minutes. Pictured on page 252.

Almond Crème Brûlée: Reduce vanilla to 1 tsp.; add 1 additional egg yolk, 2 Tbsp. almond liqueur, and ¼ cup chopped toasted almonds to custard mixture. Proceed as directed in basic recipe, baking for 1 hour.

Brûlée Basics:

• Don't panic when you see the term water bath. A water bath is simply a roasting pan or jelly-roll pan filled with water. The water creates a cushion from the heat of the oven, allowing the custards to bake slowly without curdling.

• Don't burn yourself. Before you take the water bath out of the oven, remove some of the water with a basting bulb or a long-handled ladle.

• When you broil the brown sugar, get the crème brûlées as close to the heating element as possible. To do this, place an inverted roasting pan on the top shelf of the oven; then place the crème brûlées on a baking sheet on top of the roasting pan.

• An adventurous alternative to the broiler is a welding torch. Your dinner guests will think you have gone mad, but the torch gives the ultimate glassy crust. Torching is the professional chef's method of choice.

• Crème brûlée is an even more extraordinary dessert if the custard is cold and firm when you crack into the warm caramelized sugar topping. Here's the secret: Place the custards in a roasting pan filled with ice, and then broil them. The ice keeps the custards cold while the sugar melts.

• You can bake the crème brûlées ahead of time, but wait until just a few minutes before serving to caramelize the sugar. The caramelized sugar will begin to liquefy if the custards sit for more than an hour.

• We found that Dixie Crystals brand brown sugar works best for crème brûlées. It caramelizes evenly to a perfect golden brown.

• Don't waste your money on salamanders sold in gourmet catalogs and used for caramelizing the top of crème brûlées. They work like branding irons to melt the brown sugar. When we tried one, we ended up with burned—not caramelized—sugar.

CREAMY RICE PUDDING WITH PRALINE SAUCE

makes 6 to 8 servings prep: 15 min. cook: 50 min.

2 cups milk

1 cup uncooked extra long-grain white rice

½ tsp. salt

2¾ cups half-and-half, divided

4 egg yolks, beaten

½ cup sugar

1½ tsp. vanilla extract

20 caramels

½ cup chopped toasted pecans

1. Stir together first 3 ingredients and 2 cups half-and-half in a large saucepan. Cover and cook over medium-low heat, stirring often, 35 to 40 minutes or until rice is tender.

2. Whisk together egg yolks, ½ cup half-and-half, and sugar. Gradually stir about one-fourth of hot rice mixture into yolk mixture; stir yolk mixture into remaining hot mixture. Cook over medium-low heat, stirring constantly, until mixture reaches 160° and is thickened and bubbly (about 7 minutes). Remove from heat; stir in vanilla.

3. Stir together caramels and remaining ¼ cup half-and-half in a small saucepan over medium-low heat until smooth. Stir in pecans. Serve over rice pudding.

ENGLISH RICE PUDDING

makes 18 servings prep: 5 min. bake: 1 hr. **pictured on page 252**

3 cups cooked long-grain rice

2 cups hot milk

2 cups hot whipping cream

4 large eggs, lightly beaten

1½ cups sugar

1 cup raisins

1 tsp. vanilla extract

¼ tsp. salt

2 Tbsp. butter, cut up

¼ tsp. ground nutmeg

Garnish: lemon twist

Lemon Sauce (optional)

1. Preheat oven to 350°. Stir together first 8 ingredients until thoroughly blended. Pour into a greased 13- x 9-inch baking dish; dot with butter, and sprinkle evenly with nutmeg. Place dish in a large baking pan; add hot water to pan to a depth of 1 inch.

2. Bake at 350° for 1 hour or until lightly browned and set. Cool slightly, and cut into squares. Garnish, if desired. Serve with Lemon Sauce, if desired.

Lemon Sauce

makes 1½ cups prep: 5 min. cook: 6 min.

1 cup water

½ cup sugar

2 Tbsp. cornstarch

⅛ tsp. salt

1 Tbsp. butter or margarine

1 Tbsp. lemon zest

½ cup fresh lemon juice

1. Stir together first 4 ingredients in a small saucepan until smooth. Cook, stirring constantly, over medium heat 5 minutes or until thickened. Remove from heat, and stir in butter, zest, and lemon juice. Serve warm or cold.

OLD-FASHIONED RICE PUDDING

makes 6 servings prep: 20 min. cook: 25 min. stand: 15 min. chill: 2 hr.

This pudding is delicious served warm or cold.

1 (3.5-oz.) bag boil-in-bag rice

3 Tbsp. butter

1 (14½-oz.) can evaporated low-fat 2% milk, divided

⅓ cup sugar

¼ tsp. salt

½ cup dried cherries*

1 large egg

1½ tsp. vanilla extract

1½ tsp. ground cinnamon

1. Prepare rice according to package directions.

2. Stir together rice, butter, 1 cup evaporated milk, sugar, and salt in a medium saucepan, and cook, stirring often, over medium heat 20 minutes or until rice mixture is thick and creamy.

3. Place cherries in a small bowl; add boiling water to cover, and let stand 15 minutes. Drain.

4. Stir together egg and remaining evaporated milk until blended; gradually pour into hot rice mixture in pan, stirring constantly. Cook, stirring often, 5 minutes. Remove from heat; stir in vanilla and cherries. Sprinkle evenly with cinnamon. Serve warm, or cover and chill at least 2 hours.

* ½ cup raisins may be substituted.

SUMMER PUDDING

makes 4 servings   prep: 15 min.   stand: 2 hr.   bake 10 min.

Toasting the breadcrumbs is the only cooking that you'll do to prepare this refreshing and cool seasonal dessert.

2 cups fresh raspberries

1 cup fresh blackberries

1 cup quartered fresh strawberries

½ cup sugar

1 Tbsp. grated lemon rind

2 Tbsp. fresh lemon juice

½ tsp. vanilla extract

⅛ tsp. salt

2 Tbsp. raspberry or blackberry liqueur (optional)

1 lemon verbena sprig (optional)

½ tsp. crushed green peppercorns (optional)

2 cups day-old white bread slices, cut into ½-inch cubes

Garnishes: fresh blackberries, fresh blueberries, fresh strawberries

1. Preheat oven to 350°. Combine first 8 ingredients and, if desired, liqueur, lemon verbena, and peppercorns in a large nonaluminum bowl. Cover and let stand at room temperature at least 1½ hours.

2. Spread bread cubes evenly on a baking sheet; bake at 350° for 10 to 15 minutes or until toasted. Cool.

3. Stir bread into berry mixture, and let stand for 30 minutes. Remove lemon verbena, and discard.

4. Spoon pudding mixture into 4 (8-oz.) individual serving dishes. Garnish, if desired.

Note: We tested with Sara Lee Honey White Bakery Bread.

Brownie Tiramisù,
page 352

No-Cook Chocolate-Almond Ice Cream,
No-Cook Peach Ice Cream, and
No-Cook Strawberry Ice Cream,
page 363

Lemon Pie Dip, page 368

Cold Marinated Shrimp and
Avocados, page 392

Lemon-Basil Shrimp Salad, page 394

Shrimp and Andouille Sausage with Asiago Grits, page 405

Broiled Mahi-Mahi With Parsleyed Tomatoes, page 386

Spicy Catfish with Vegetables and Basil Cream, page 378

Catfish Pecan With Lemon-Thyme-Pecan Butter, page 374

Southern-Style Fish Tacos, page 379

Oysters Rockefeller, page 423

Southwest Fried
Oysters, page 408

Maryland Crab Cakes With
Creamy Caper-Dill Sauce,
page 426

Flank Steak Sandwiches With
Blue Cheese, page 453

Grilled Chicken With White
Barbecue Sauce, page 439

Grilled Sweet Chili Chicken With Mango-Cucumber Slaw, page 444

Rosemary Grilled Chicken Thighs, page 441

Mixed Grill With Cilantro Pesto, page 456

Molasses-Balsamic Pork Kabobs With Green Tomatoes and Plums, page 469

FIG-WALNUT PUDDING

makes 8 servings   prep: 20 min.   stand: 20 min.   cook: 5 min.
bake: 1 hr., 3 min.   **pictured on page 252**

Challah is a braided Jewish egg bread. You can substitute any braided loaf or soft French bread.

12 to 14 dried figs
8 to 10 (½-inch) challah bread slices
1 cup walnuts
2 cups milk
1 cup whipping cream
1 cup sugar, divided

6 large eggs
½ cup honey
2 Tbsp. vanilla extract
½ tsp. ground nutmeg
Pinch of ground cloves
Rum Sauce (optional)

1. Preheat oven to 500°. Place figs in a heat-proof bowl with boiling water to cover; let stand 20 minutes or until plump. Drain figs, and slice.

2. Place bread and walnuts in a 15- x 10-inch jelly-roll pan; bake at 500° for 3 to 4 minutes or until toasted. Remove from oven, and set aside. Reduce heat to 350°.

3. Heat milk, cream, and ¾ cup sugar in a medium saucepan over medium heat. (Do not boil.)

4. Whisk together eggs and next 4 ingredients in a large bowl; slowly whisk in milk mixture.

5. Layer half of bread and walnuts evenly in a lightly greased 11- x 7-inch baking dish or 10-inch pie plate, slightly overlapping slices; layer half of figs evenly over bread. Pour half of milk mixture evenly over figs. Repeat procedure with remaining bread, figs, and milk mixture. Press lightly with a spatula. Sprinkle walnuts and remaining ¼ cup sugar evenly over top.

6. Cover loosely with foil, leaving corners uncovered to brown edges (if using a pie plate, loosely cover with foil, allowing edges to brown).

7. Bake at 350° for 45 minutes or until set. Remove foil, and bake 15 more minutes. Serve pudding warm with Rum Sauce, if desired.

Rum Sauce

makes 1¼ cups   prep: 5 min.   cook: 10 min.

½ cup butter
⅓ cup firmly packed brown sugar
½ cup whipping cream

2 tablespoons rum
¼ teaspoon orange zest
Pinch of cloves

1. Melt butter and brown sugar in a heavy saucepan over low heat, stirring until smooth. Stir in remaining ingredients. Cook, stirring constantly, 10 minutes or until thickened.

POUND CAKE BANANA PUDDING

makes 10 to 12 servings   prep: 20 min.   cook: 15 min.   chill: 6 hr.   bake: 15 min.

This recipe is inspired by the one served at the famous Mrs. Wilkes' Dining Room in Savannah, Georgia. Look for pound cake in the frozen dessert case of the supermarket.

4 cups half-and-half	3 Tbsp. butter
4 egg yolks	2 tsp. vanilla extract
1½ cups sugar	1 (1-lb.) pound cake, cubed
¼ cup cornstarch	4 large ripe bananas, sliced
¼ tsp. salt	Meringue

1. Preheat oven to 375°. Whisk together first 5 ingredients in a saucepan over medium-low heat; cook, whisking constantly, 13 to 15 minutes or until thickened. Remove from heat; stir in butter and vanilla until butter melts. Layer half of pound cake cubes, half of bananas, and half of pudding mixture in a 3-qt. round baking dish. Repeat layers. Cover pudding, and chill 6 hours.
2. Spread Meringue over pudding.
3. Bake at 375° for 15 minutes or until golden brown.

Note: We tested with Sara Lee Family Size All Butter Pound Cake.

Meringue

makes about 3½ cups   prep: 10 min.

¼ cup sugar	4 egg whites
⅛ teaspoon salt	¼ teaspoon vanilla extract

1. Combine sugar and salt.
2. Beat egg whites and vanilla at high speed with an electric mixer until foamy. Add sugar mixture, 1 tablespoon at a time, and beat 2 to 3 minutes or until stiff peaks form and sugar dissolves.

BANANAS FOSTER BREAD PUDDING

makes 10 to 12 servings   prep: 15 min.   cook: 10 min.   bake: 45 min.   stand: 30 min.

Chef Don Boyd of Café Reconcile in New Orleans combines the classic flavors of rum and brown sugar, distinctive in the original Brennan's Restaurant recipe for Bananas Foster, to create this delicious bread pudding.

3   large eggs
½   cup whipping cream
1   cup granulated sugar
1   cup firmly packed brown sugar
¼   cup rum
1   Tbsp. banana extract

4   cups milk
¼   cup butter
1   (16-oz.) stale French bread loaf, cut into
    1-inch cubes
Bread Pudding Sauce

1. Preheat oven to 325°. Stir together first 6 ingredients in a large bowl.

2. Heat milk and butter in a large saucepan over medium-high heat until melted, stirring constantly. (Do not boil.)

3. Stir about one-fourth of hot milk mixture gradually into egg mixture; add to remaining hot milk mixture, stirring constantly.

4. Place bread cubes in a lightly greased 13- x 9-inch baking dish. Pour egg mixture evenly over bread. Press bread to absorb mixture.

5. Bake at 325° for 45 to 55 minutes. Remove from oven, and let stand 30 minutes before serving.

6. Serve with Bread Pudding Sauce.

Bread Pudding Sauce

makes 1¼ cups   prep: 5 min.   cook: 5 min.

½   cup butter
½   cup firmly packed brown sugar
¼   cup dark rum

½   teaspoon banana extract
2   bananas, sliced

1. Combine all ingredients in a saucepan over medium-high heat, and cook, stirring occasionally, 5 minutes. (Do not boil.) Remove from heat.

casual gatherings

Nutmeg

Freshly grated nutmeg provides a more intense flavor than the prepackaged variety and should be used immediately. You can use either a nutmeg grater or the smallest blade on a regular grater to grate whole nutmeg. Whole nutmeg, when it is stored in an airtight container, will keep for at least two to three years.

SPICED CARAMEL-APPLE BREAD PUDDING

makes 8 servings   prep: 20 min.   cook: 2 min.   chill: 1 hr.   bake: 45 min.

This dessert is significantly lower in sugar and fat than traditional versions. Drizzle with Toasted Pecan-Caramel Sauce, and indulge.

1   Granny Smith apple, peeled and chopped
½   tsp. ground cinnamon, divided
½   (16-oz.) Italian bread loaf, cut into bite-size pieces
Vegetable cooking spray
3   large eggs

1½   cups 2% reduced-fat milk
1   cup apple cider
¼   cup firmly packed brown sugar
1   tsp. vanilla extract
¼   tsp. ground nutmeg
Toasted Pecan-Caramel Sauce (recipe on page 822)

1. Sauté apple and ¼ tsp. cinnamon in a lightly greased skillet over medium-high heat 2 minutes or until tender. Stir together bread and apple in an 11- x 7-inch baking dish coated with cooking spray.
2. Whisk together eggs, milk, apple cider, brown sugar, vanilla, nutmeg, and remaining ¼ tsp. cinnamon; pour over bread mixture in baking dish. Cover and chill 1 hour.
3. Preheat oven to 350°. Bake bread mixture 45 to 50 minutes or until top is crisp and golden brown. Serve warm with Toasted Pecan-Caramel Sauce.

Per 1 serving bread pudding and 4½ tsp. Toasted Pecan-Caramel Sauce: Calories 299; Fat 7.2g (sat 2.1g, mono 2.9g, poly 1.5g); Protein 8.1g; Carb 51.6g; Fiber 1.4g; Chol 85mg; Iron 1.5mg; Sodium 241mg; Calc 146mg

{southern lights}

BERRY BREAD PUDDING WITH
VANILLA CREAM SAUCE

makes 10 servings   prep: 30 min.   stand: 50 min.   bake: 1 hr.

Make the sauce the day before, and reheat in the microwave. Assemble the bread pudding when the roast comes out of the oven, and bake it while you have dinner. This is a moist bread pudding.

1	(16-oz.) French bread loaf, cubed	1	tsp. ground cinnamon
1	cup frozen raspberries (do not thaw)	1	tsp. ground nutmeg
1	cup frozen blackberries (do not thaw)	1	tsp. vanilla extract
4	large eggs, lightly beaten	2	Tbsp. melted butter
2¾	cups milk	2	Tbsp. sugar
1	cup sugar		Vanilla Cream Sauce
¼	cup butter, melted		Garnishes: fresh raspberries, powdered sugar

1. Preheat oven to 350°. Arrange half of bread pieces in a lightly greased 11- x 7-inch baking dish. Arrange frozen berries in a single layer over bread. Top with remaining bread pieces.

2. Whisk eggs and next 6 ingredients until smooth. Slowly pour egg mixture over bread, pressing down with a wooden spoon until bread absorbs mixture. Let stand 20 minutes.

3. Bake, covered, at 350° for 30 minutes. Uncover, brush evenly with 2 Tbsp. melted butter; sprinkle evenly with 2 Tbsp. sugar, and bake 30 more minutes or until set. Remove from oven, and let stand 30 minutes. Serve with Vanilla Cream Sauce. Garnish, if desired.

Vanilla Cream Sauce

makes 2½ cups   prep: 10 min.   cook: 5 min.

2	cups whipping cream	½	cup butter
1	cup sugar	1	tsp. vanilla extract
2	Tbsp. all-purpose flour		

1. Stir together first 3 ingredients in a saucepan. Add butter, and cook, stirring constantly, over medium heat until butter is melted and mixture begins to boil. Cook, stirring constantly, 3 minutes or until mixture is slightly thickened. Remove from heat, and stir in vanilla. Serve warm.

Entertain neighbors and friends with this dessert-like drink.

Ultimate Alexander

makes 5 cups   prep: 5 min.

Process ¼ cup cold brewed coffee, 2 pts. coffee ice cream, ½ cup brandy, and ½ cup chocolate syrup in a blender until smooth, stopping to scrape down sides. Pour mixture into glasses, and garnish with sweetened whipped cream, chocolate curls, and milk chocolate sticks, if desired. Serve immediately.

Note: We tested with Hershey's Milk Chocolate Sticks.

BROWN SUGAR BREAD PUDDING WITH CRÈME ANGLAISE

makes 9 servings   prep: 30 min.   stand: 10 min.   bake: 30 min.   **pictured on page 252**

We prefer fresh French bread from the bakery to achieve the crispiest top and softest center. Save the egg yolks from the separated eggs for the Crème Anglaise.

4   egg whites
1   large egg
1¼ cups 2% reduced-fat milk
¾   cup evaporated fat-free milk
½   cup firmly packed light brown sugar
1   tsp. ground cinnamon
¼   tsp. ground nutmeg
⅛   tsp. salt
⅛   tsp. ground allspice

2   tsp. vanilla extract
1   (12-oz.) French bread loaf, cut into 1-inch cubes
    (about 8 cups)
4   tsp. light brown sugar
½   Tbsp. butter, cut into small pieces
¼   cup sliced almonds, toasted
Crème Anglaise
Garnish: cinnamon sticks (optional)

1. Preheat oven to 350°. Whisk together egg whites and egg in a medium bowl until blended. Whisk in reduced-fat milk and next 7 ingredients.

2. Arrange bread cubes in an 8-inch square pan coated with cooking spray. Pour egg mixture evenly over bread. Sprinkle evenly with 4 tsp. brown sugar, butter, and almonds. Press down gently on bread cubes, and let stand 10 minutes.

[southern lights]

3. Bake at 350° for 30 to 35 minutes or until a knife inserted in center comes out clean. Serve warm with 2 Tbsp. chilled Crème Anglaise per serving. Garnish, if desired.

Per 1 serving bread pudding and 2 Tbsp. Crème Anglaise: Calories 261; Fat 6g (sat 2g, mono 2.6g, poly 0.9g); Protein 10.2g; Carb 39.6g; Fiber 1.6g; Chol 81mg; Iron 1.4mg; Sodium 363mg; Calc 183mg

Crème Anglaise

makes 2 cups   prep: 10 min.   cook: 8 min.   chill: 4 hr.

We prepared our Crème Anglaise with milk instead of heavy cream to reduce the fat and calories. So expect a slightly thinner consistency but the same delicious flavor. Store leftover sauce in an airtight container in the refrigerator up to 1 week, and serve over fresh berries.

1¾ cups 2% reduced-fat milk	1 tsp. vanilla extract
⅓ cup sugar	2 Tbsp. bourbon
4 egg yolks	

1. Heat milk in a medium saucepan over medium heat just until bubbles and steam appear (do not boil). Remove from heat.

2. Whisk together sugar and egg yolks in a medium bowl until blended. Gradually add heated milk to egg yolk mixture, whisking constantly. Return mixture to saucepan. Cook over medium heat, whisking constantly, 6 minutes or until mixture thinly coats the back of a spoon. Pour mixture into a bowl. Stir in vanilla. Place plastic wrap directly on surface of mixture, and chill at least 4 hours. (Mixture will thicken slightly as it cools.) Stir in bourbon before serving.

Per 2 Tbsp.: Calories: 47; Fat 1.6g (sat 0.7g, mono 0.6g, poly 0.2g); Protein 1.6g; Carb 5.6g; Chol 53mg; Iron 0.1mg; Sodium 15mg; Calc 38mg

CROISSANT BREAD PUDDING

makes 6 to 8 servings   prep: 30 min.   cook: 2 min.   stand: 10 min.   chill: 1 hr.   bake: 1 hr.

9	large croissants		3	cups heavy cream
¼	cup bourbon		2	Tbsp. vanilla extract
⅓	cup golden raisins		⅛	tsp. salt
8	large eggs			Bourbon Sauce
1½	cups sugar			

1. Slice croissants in half lengthwise; tear bottom halves of croissants into small pieces.

2. Heat bourbon in a small saucepan over low heat; stir in raisins. Remove from heat, and let stand for 10 minutes. Layer croissant pieces evenly in a lightly greased 13- x 9-inch baking dish. Sprinkle with raisins. Place croissant tops, crust sides up, over mixture.

3. Whisk together eggs and sugar. Whisk in cream, vanilla, and salt. Slowly pour mixture over croissant tops; press bread to absorb liquid. Cover; chill 1 hour.

4. Preheat oven to 350°.

5. Place dish into a larger pan. Pour hot water into larger pan, filling half full.

6. Bake at 350° for 45 minutes or until set. Cover with aluminum foil, and bake 15 more minutes. Remove from oven, and remove dish from water pan. Serve pudding warm with Bourbon Sauce.

Bourbon Sauce

makes 1½ cups   prep: 15 min.

2	tsp. cornstarch		¼	cup sugar
1	cup whipping cream		2	Tbsp. bourbon

1. Stir together cornstarch and 2 tablespoons water.

2. Bring cream and sugar to a boil in a heavy saucepan. Reduce heat to low, and whisk in cornstarch mixture until cream mixture thickens. Remove from heat, and stir in bourbon.

OLD-FASHIONED BREAD PUDDING

makes 8 servings prep: 15 min. bake: 35 min.

One spoonful will tell you why this received our highest rating.

1 (16-oz.) day-old French bread loaf, cubed	1 cup raisins
2 (12-oz.) cans evaporated milk	1½ cups sugar
1 cup water	5 Tbsp. vanilla extract
6 large eggs, lightly beaten	¼ cup butter, cut up and softened
1 (8-oz.) can crushed pineapple, drained	Bourbon Sauce
1 large Red Delicious apple, grated	

1. Preheat oven to 350°. Combine first 3 ingredients; stir in eggs, blending well. Stir in pineapple and next 4 ingredients. Stir in butter, blending well. Pour mixture into a greased 13- x 9-inch baking dish.

2. Bake at 350° for 35 to 45 minutes or until set. Serve with Bourbon Sauce

Bourbon Sauce

makes 1½ cups prep: 2 min. cook: 13 min.

3 Tbsp. butter	2 Tbsp. bourbon
1 Tbsp. all-purpose flour	1 Tbsp. vanilla extract
½ cup sugar	1 tsp. nutmeg
1 cup whipping cream	

1. Melt butter in a small saucepan; whisk in flour, and cook 5 minutes. Stir in sugar and whipping cream; cook 3 minutes. Stir in bourbon, vanilla, and nutmeg, and simmer 5 minutes.

BROWNIE TRIFLE

makes 16 to 18 servings prep: 25 min. bake: 20 min. chill: 8 hr.

1 (19.8-oz.) package fudge brownie mix

¼ cup coffee liqueur (optional)

1 (3.9-oz.) package chocolate fudge instant pudding mix

1 (8.7-oz.) package toffee-flavored candy bars, crushed

1 (12-oz.) container frozen whipped topping, thawed

1. Prepare brownie mix according to package directions in a 13- x 9-inch pan. Prick tops of warm brownies at 1-inch intervals with a wooden pick, and brush with coffee liqueur, if desired. Crumble into small pieces.

2. Prepare pudding mix according to package directions, omitting chilling.

3. Place half of crumbled brownies in bottom of a 3-qt. trifle bowl; top with half each of pudding, candy bars, and whipped topping. Repeat layers. Cover and chill at least 8 hours.

Note: We tested with Kahlúa for coffee liqueur.

GEORGIA PEACH TRIFLE

makes 8 servings prep: 15 min. chill: 2 hr., 5 min. **pictured on page 251**

1 (3.4-oz.) package vanilla instant pudding mix

2 cups milk

6 large fresh peaches, peeled and sliced

3 Tbsp. granulated sugar

½ (20-oz.) package pound cake

⅓ cup bourbon

1 cup whipping cream

2 Tbsp. powdered sugar

½ cup sliced almonds, toasted

1. Prepare pudding mix according to package directions, using 2 cups milk. Cover and chill 5 minutes.

2. Toss sliced peaches with granulated sugar.

3. Cut pound cake into ½-inch slices. Place half of cake slices on bottom of a trifle dish or deep bowl; drizzle evenly with half of bourbon. Spoon half of peach mixture evenly over cake slices. Spread half of pudding over peaches. Repeat with remaining cake slices, bourbon, peach mixture, and pudding. Cover and chill at least 2 hours.

4. Beat whipping cream at medium speed with an electric mixer until foamy; gradually add powdered sugar, beating until soft peaks form. Spread whipped cream over trifle; sprinkle with almonds.

TROPICAL RUM TRIFLE

makes 10 to 12 servings prep: 45 min. chill: 1 hr., 50 min.

Make the Coconut Cream Custard first; while it's chilling, prepare the remaining ingredients.

2   mangoes, peeled and cut into ½-inch cubes*
1   (20-oz.) can pineapple chunks in syrup, undrained
⅓   cup coconut-flavored rum
1   (10.75-oz.) frozen pound cake, thawed and thinly sliced
2   bananas, sliced
Coconut Cream Custard

1⅓   cups sweetened flaked coconut, toasted
⅔   cup chopped macadamia nuts, toasted
1   cup whipping cream
¼   cup powdered sugar
¼   tsp. vanilla extract
Garnishes: mango, star fruit, toasted coconut, toasted macadamia nuts (optional)

1. Stir together first 3 ingredients in a bowl. Cover and chill 20 minutes.

2. Remove fruit from bowl with a slotted spoon, reserving syrup mixture.

3. Brush pound cake slices with syrup mixture. Arrange half of slices in bottom of a 4-qt. bowl or trifle bowl. Top with half each of mango mixture, banana slices, Coconut Cream Custard, coconut, and macadamia nuts. Repeat layers.

4. Beat whipping cream until foamy; gradually add sugar, beating until soft peaks form. Add vanilla; beat until blended. Spread evenly over top of trifle. Cover and chill 1½ hours. Garnish, if desired.

Note: We tested with Malibu Caribbean Rum With Natural Coconut Flavor.

* 1 (24-oz.) jar refrigerated mango, drained and cut into ½-inch cubes, may be substituted.

Coconut Cream Custard

makes 4 cups prep: 10 min. cook: 3 min. chill: 1 hr.

1   cup sugar
⅓   cup cornstarch
2   cups milk

1   (14-oz.) can coconut milk
6   egg yolks

1. Whisk together all ingredients in a heavy saucepan. Bring to a boil over medium heat, whisking constantly; boil, whisking constantly, 1 minute or until thickened. Remove from heat. Place pan in ice water; whisk custard occasionally until cool.

2. Cover and chill 1 hour.

MOCHA CHARLOTTES

makes 8 servings   prep: 20 min.   stand: 7 min.   cook: 5 min.   chill: 8 hr.

For a quick version of this dessert, line pretty cups with ladyfingers, fill with chocolate ice cream, and top with whipped cream.

1	envelope unflavored gelatin	1½ tsp. instant coffee granules	
¼	cup cold water	2	tsp. vanilla extract
½	cup granulated sugar	1½ cups whipping cream, divided	
2	large eggs	2	(3-oz.) packages ladyfingers, split
1	cup milk	3	Tbsp. powdered sugar
⅓	cup semisweet chocolate morsels	Garnish: 8 (3-inch) cinnamon sticks (optional)	

1. Sprinkle gelatin over ¼ cup cold water; stir and let stand 1 minute. Set gelatin mixture aside.

2. Beat granulated sugar and eggs at medium speed with an electric mixer 2 to 3 minutes or until thick and pale.

3. Heat milk in a large saucepan over low heat. Gradually add about one-fourth of hot milk to egg mixture; add to remaining hot milk, stirring constantly. Cook over low heat, stirring constantly, 4 to 5 minutes or until mixture coats the back of a spoon. Remove from heat; stir in gelatin mixture until gelatin dissolves.

4. Whisk in chocolate morsels, coffee granules, and vanilla until coffee granules dissolve and chocolate melts.

5. Pour mixture into a metal bowl; place bowl over ice, and let stand, stirring often, 6 to 8 minutes or until cold and slightly thickened.

6. Beat 1 cup whipping cream at high speed with an electric mixer until soft peaks form, and gradually fold into coffee mixture.

7. Line each of 8 teacups with 6 ladyfinger halves, placing rounded sides of ladyfingers against edge of each cup. Spoon custard evenly into cups; cover and chill 8 hours.

8. Beat remaining ½ cup whipping cream and powdered sugar until soft peaks form. Top custards with whipped cream; garnish, if desired.

TELIA'S TEA CAKES AND FRESH STRAWBERRIES

makes 6 servings   prep: 15 min.   chill: 3 hr.   stand: 30 min.   bake: 10 min.

This recipe makes a large batch of dough. You can freeze tightly wrapped dough or baked tea cakes up to six weeks.

1 cup butter, softened	3½ cups self-rising flour
2½ cups sugar, divided	3 cups sliced fresh strawberries
3 large eggs	1 cup whipping cream, whipped
1 tsp. vanilla extract	Garnish: fresh mint leaves (optional)

1. Beat butter at medium speed with an electric mixer until creamy; gradually add 2 cups sugar, beating well. Add eggs, 1 at a time, beating after each addition. Stir in vanilla. Gradually add flour, beating at low speed until blended after each addition.

2. Divide dough in half. Roll each portion into a 12-inch log; wrap in plastic wrap, and chill at least 3 hours.

3. Sprinkle remaining ½ cup sugar over strawberries. Let stand 30 minutes.

4. Preheat oven to 350°.

5. Cut logs into ½-inch-thick slices; place 1 inch apart on greased baking sheets.

6. Bake at 350° for 10 minutes or until edges begin to brown. Remove to wire racks to cool.

7. Place 1 tea cake on each serving plate; top each cake with ¼ cup strawberries. Place another tea cake over strawberries, and top with ¼ cup strawberries and a dollop of whipped cream. Garnish, if desired.

[test kitchen favorite]

SUGAR-AND-SPICE FRUIT TAMALES

makes about 14 tamales prep: 45 min. soak: 1 hr. cook: 35 min.
stand: 5 min. **pictured on page 250**

Most folks think of these steamed bundles of goodness as strictly savory, usually filled with pork or chicken. But Sylvia Calvano of Hoover, Alabama, recalls her mother's dessert tamales. "My mom was born and raised in Mexico, so tamales were always an important part of our Christmas celebration," Sylvia says. "I love this sweeter, fruit-filled version that she made for our family and to share with the neighborhood."

18 dried corn husks
⅔ cup vegetable shortening
1½ cups corn masa mix
3 Tbsp. light brown sugar
1 tsp. baking powder
1 tsp. ground cinnamon
½ tsp. salt
½ cup warm milk

½ cup canned pumpkin
1 (20-oz.) can crushed pineapple in heavy
   syrup, drained
½ cup raisins, chopped
Kitchen string
Vanilla Sauce
Mexican Chocolate Sauce

1. Soak corn husks in hot water to cover 30 minutes. Separate husks, and continue soaking 30 more minutes. Drain husks, and pat dry. Tear 4 smallest husks into 14 strips.

2. Beat shortening at medium speed with a heavy-duty electric stand mixer 2 minutes. Combine masa and next 4 ingredients. Gradually beat masa mixture into shortening. Beat shortening mixture 2 minutes, scraping down sides of bowl as needed.

3. Gradually add warm milk to shortening mixture, beating at medium speed just until blended and scraping down sides as needed. Add pumpkin, and beat at medium speed 3 minutes. Cover dough with plastic wrap.

4. Using hands lightly coated with masa mix, spread about 2 Tbsp. dough into a 3- x 4-inch rectangle on right side of 1 husk, leaving a ½-inch border on right side and a 2-inch border from narrow bottom end of husk.

5. Spoon about 1 Tbsp. pineapple down center of dough. Sprinkle with about 1½ tsp. raisins. Roll up husk, rolling left side over right, enclosing pineapple mixture and raisins completely in dough. Fold bottom narrow end up and over, and secure with husk strips or kitchen string. Repeat procedure with remaining corn husks, dough, pineapple, and raisins.

6. Place 2 tamales side by side, seam sides inward and open ends facing same direction. Tie tamales together with kitchen string, securing bundles at top above dough. Repeat procedure with remaining tamales.

7. Arrange tamale bundles, open ends up, in a steamer basket over boiling water in a large Dutch oven. Cover and steam 35 minutes, adding more boiling water as needed. Remove tamales from Dutch oven, and let stand 5 minutes. Serve with Vanilla Sauce and Mexican Chocolate Sauce.

Note: We tested with Masa Brosa Harina de Maiz Instant Corn Masa.

Vanilla Sauce

makes about 1 cup   prep: 10 min.   cook: 5 min.

¾ cup whipping cream
½ cup firmly packed light brown sugar
½ tsp. ground cinnamon
⅛ tsp. ground nutmeg

Pinch of salt
1 vanilla bean, split lengthwise
1 Tbsp. butter

1. Combine whipping cream and next 4 ingredients in a small saucepan. Carefully scrape seeds from vanilla bean into saucepan. Add vanilla bean to saucepan, and cook mixture over medium heat, whisking constantly, until smooth (about 2 minutes). Reduce heat to medium-low. Cook, whisking constantly, 2 to 3 minutes or until thickened.
2. Remove saucepan from heat. Carefully remove vanilla bean. Stir in butter until melted. Serve immediately. Store sauce in an airtight container in refrigerator up to 5 days.

Note: To reheat, warm sauce in a small saucepan over low heat, stirring in 1 to 2 tsp. whipping cream as needed to thin sauce.

Mexican Chocolate Sauce

makes about 1½ cups   prep: 5 min.   cook: 3 min.

2 (4.4-oz.) packages Mexican chocolate, broken into pieces
¾ cup whipping cream

2 tsp. light brown sugar
Pinch of salt
1 Tbsp. butter

1. Combine chocolate, whipping cream, brown sugar, and salt in a small saucepan. Cook, whisking occasionally, over low heat until mixture is smooth and chocolate is melted (about 3 minutes). Remove from heat. Whisk in butter until melted. Serve immediately.

Note: We tested with Nestlé Abuelita Marqueta Mexican Chocolate.

BROWNIE TIRAMISÙ

makes 12 servings   prep: 25 min.   bake: 40 min.   cool: 1 hr., 10 min.   **pictured on page 326**

Mascarpone gives the topping a special flavor, but an equal amount of softened cream cheese may be substituted. Almond liqueur makes a delicious substitute for coffee liqueur.

½ cup chopped pecans
⅓ cup coffee liqueur
⅓ cup strong brewed coffee
1½ (4-oz.) semisweet chocolate bars, divided
¾ cup butter
2¼ cups sugar, divided

3 large eggs
1 cup all-purpose flour
1 (8-oz.) container mascarpone cheese
1 tsp. vanilla extract
1 cup whipping cream

1. Preheat oven to 350°. Arrange pecans in a single layer on a baking sheet, and bake 5 to 7 minutes or until lightly toasted and fragrant.

2. Stir together coffee liqueur and coffee.

3. Coarsely chop 1 chocolate bar. Microwave coarsely chopped chocolate and butter in a large microwave-safe bowl at MEDIUM (50% power) 1 to 1½ minutes or until melted and smooth, stirring at 30-second intervals. Whisk in 2 cups sugar and eggs, whisking until blended; stir in flour, stirring just until blended. Spoon batter into a lightly greased 11- x 7-inch pan.

4. Bake at 350° for 35 minutes or until center is set. Remove from oven, and cool in pan on a wire rack 10 minutes. Pierce brownie multiple times using the tines of a fork. Pour coffee mixture over brownie. Let cool on a wire rack 1 hour or until completely cool.

5. Whisk together remaining ¼ cup sugar, mascarpone cheese, and vanilla in a large bowl. Beat whipping cream at medium speed with an electric mixer until stiff peaks form. Fold whipped cream into mascarpone mixture.

6. Crumble half of brownies; divide evenly among 6 (8-oz.) glasses. Spoon half of mascarpone cheese mixture over brownies. Repeat procedure with remaining brownies and mascarpone cheese mixture.

7. Chop remaining half of chocolate bar into thin shreds. Sprinkle chocolate and pecans over mascarpone cheese mixture. Serve immediately, or cover and chill up to 24 hours.

Note: We tested with Kahlúa for coffee liqueur.

DECADENT S'MORES TIRAMISÙ

makes 6 servings   prep: 40 min.   cook: 6 min.   chill: 6 hr., 15 min.   broil: 30 sec.   cool: 10 min.

14 graham cracker sheets

½ cup cold whipping cream

1 tsp. vanilla extract

3 egg yolks

½ cup sugar

1 (8-oz.) package cream cheese, softened

2 Tbsp. orange liqueur*

1 cup brewed espresso or double-strength coffee, at room temperature

2 (1.55-oz.) milk chocolate candy bars, chopped

2 cups miniature marshmallows

1 tsp. unsweetened cocoa

Garnish: 6 fresh mint sprigs (optional)

1. Break each graham cracker sheet into 4 equal pieces along perforations. Remove and reserve 2 graham cracker pieces.

2. Beat whipping cream and vanilla at high speed with an electric mixer until soft peaks form. Cover and chill.

3. Meanwhile, bring a small amount of water to a boil in a medium saucepan over medium heat. Whisk together egg yolks and sugar in a medium-size stainless steel bowl. Place metal bowl with egg mixture over boiling water in saucepan, making sure bottom of bowl does not touch boiling water. Whisk egg mixture constantly, over boiling water, 6 to 7 minutes or until a candy thermometer registers 165°. (Mixture should be thick, pale, and hot to the touch.) Transfer to a small bowl; cover and chill 15 minutes or until cool.

4. Beat cream cheese at medium speed 30 seconds or until creamy. Gradually add cooled egg mixture and orange liqueur, beating until smooth. Gently fold in whipped cream mixture.

5. Place espresso in a shallow dish or bowl. Quickly dip 18 graham cracker pieces, 1 at a time, into espresso, and place in an 8-inch square baking dish to cover bottom. (Make certain that you use a broiler-proof baking dish.) Spread one-third of cream cheese mixture evenly over crackers. Repeat layers twice. Sprinkle with chopped chocolate, and top with marshmallows.

6. Broil 5 inches from heat 30 seconds to 1 minute or until marshmallows are puffed and golden. Let cool 10 minutes. Dust with cocoa. Cover and chill at least 6 hours or up to 24 hours.

7. Break each reserved graham cracker piece into thirds. Insert 1 corner of 1 graham cracker piece into top of each serving. Garnish, if desired. Serve tiramisù cold.

* 2 Tbsp. milk may be substituted.

LIGHTENED TIRAMISÙ

makes 10 servings   prep: 15 min.   cook: 30 min.   chill: 2 hr.

This rich yet light-textured dessert is best when chilled at least 2 hours to allow all the flavors to become well acquainted. Our changes from the original version resulted in a savings of more than 270 calories.

½ cup granulated sugar
1 cup whipping cream, divided
2 cups fat-free milk
½ cup egg substitute
2 egg yolks
1 Tbsp. all-purpose flour
½ vanilla bean, split
1 (8-oz.) package fat-free cream cheese, softened

1 (8-oz.) package reduced-fat cream cheese, softened
½ cup brewed espresso or dark-roast coffee
3 Tbsp. Marsala
3 (3-oz.) packages ladyfingers
3 Tbsp. powdered sugar
1 Tbsp. unsweetened cocoa

1. Stir together sugar, ½ cup whipping cream, milk, and next 4 ingredients in a heavy saucepan. Cook over medium heat, stirring constantly, 30 minutes or until thickened. Cool mixture completely. Discard vanilla bean. Whisk in cream cheeses.

2. Stir together espresso and Marsala. Layer one-fourth ladyfingers in a trifle bowl or large clear bowl; brush with espresso mixture. Top with one-fourth cream cheese mixture. Repeat 3 times with remaining ladyfingers, coffee mixture, and cream cheese mixture.

3. Beat remaining ½ cup whipping cream at high speed with an electric mixer until foamy; gradually add powdered sugar, beating until soft peaks form. Spoon over cream cheese mixture, and sprinkle with cocoa. Cover and chill 2 hours.

Note: To prepare espresso, stir together ¾ cup hot water and ⅓ cup ground espresso or dark-roast coffee. Let stand 5 minutes; pour through a wire-mesh strainer lined with a coffee filter into a glass measuring cup, discarding coffee grounds. Makes ¾ cup.

This may also be prepared in a 13- x 9-inch dish, layering ladyfingers brushed with coffee mixture and cream cheese mixture. Spread with whipped cream mixture.

Per serving: Calories 345; Fat 16.6g (sat 9.5g, mono 4.3g, poly 1.1g); Protein 12.3g; Carb 35g; Fiber 0.4g; Chol 182mg; Iron 1.4mg; Sodium 325mg; Calc 166mg

EASY TIRAMISÙ

makes 8 servings prep: 20 min. chill: 8 hr.

1 (16-oz.) package mascarpone cheese*

1¼ cups whipping cream

¼ cup powdered sugar

1½ tsp. vanilla extract

1 cup brewed espresso

2 Tbsp. dark rum

2 (3-oz.) packages ladyfingers

4 (1-oz.) bittersweet chocolate squares, grated

1. Beat first 4 ingredients at high speed with an electric mixer 30 seconds or just until blended.

2. Stir together espresso and rum.

3. Arrange 1 package ladyfingers in bottom of a 3-qt. bowl or trifle dish; brush with half of espresso mixture. Layer half of mascarpone cheese mixture over ladyfingers; sprinkle with half of grated chocolate. Repeat layers. Cover and chill 8 hours.

* 2 (8-oz.) packages cream cheese, softened; ⅓ cup sour cream; and ¼ cup whipping cream, beaten until blended, may be substituted for 16 oz. mascarpone cheese.

inspirations for your taste

Celebrate summer with this creamy, dreamy treat.

Strawberry-Blueberry Shortcake Ice-Cream Sandwiches

makes 10 servings prep: 10 min. stand: 10 min.

Combine 1 lb. fresh strawberries, sliced, with 2 cups fresh blueberries; sprinkle with 3 Tbsp. sugar, and toss. Let stand 10 minutes. Spoon evenly over 10 miniature ice-cream sandwiches, and dollop with ½ (8-oz.) container thawed whipped topping.

Note: Add an additional pound of fresh strawberries, sliced, for the blueberries to make a strawberry shortcake version.

Summer Supper serves 6

Flank Steak Sandwiches With Blue Cheese (page 453)
French Fries (page 865)
Fruit salad
Watermelon Sorbet

....

WATERMELON SORBET

makes about ½ gal.   prep: 15 min.   cook: 5 min.   chill: 2 hr.   freeze: about 1 hr.

1   cup sugar
4   cups seeded, chopped watermelon

¼   cup lime juice

1. Bring 3 cups water and sugar just to a boil in a medium saucepan over high heat, stirring until sugar dissolves. Remove from heat. Cool.

2. Process sugar syrup and watermelon, in batches, in a blender until smooth. Stir in lime juice. Cover and chill 2 hours.

3. Pour mixture into the freezer container of a 1-gal. ice-cream maker, and freeze according to manufacturer's instructions.

Grapefruit Sorbet: Substitute 3 cups fresh grapefruit juice and 1 tsp. chopped fresh mint for watermelon and lime juice. Proceed as directed.

Pineapple Sorbet: Substitute 2 cups chopped pineapple for watermelon and lime juice. Strain and discard pulp after processing mixture in blender, if desired. Proceed as directed.

Lemon Sorbet: Substitute ½ cup fresh lemon juice and 2 tsp. lemon zest for watermelon and lime juice. Proceed as directed.

Orange Sorbet: Substitute 3 cups fresh orange juice and 2 tsp. orange zest for watermelon and lime juice. Proceed as directed.

Strawberry Sorbet: Substitute 5 cups fresh or frozen strawberries and 2 Tbsp. lemon juice for watermelon and lime juice. Proceed as directed.

[freeze it]

Cantaloupe Sorbet: Substitute 4 cups chopped cantaloupe for watermelon and lime juice. Proceed as directed.

Cherry Sorbet: Substitute 1 (6-oz.) can frozen lemonade concentrate, prepared, and 1 (16-oz.) jar maraschino cherries for watermelon and lime juice. Strain and discard pulp, if desired. Proceed as directed.

Raspberry Sorbet: Substitute 5 cups fresh or frozen raspberries for watermelon and lime juice. Proceed as directed.

WARM BLACKBERRY SAUCE OVER MANGO SORBET

makes 6 servings   prep: 10 min.   cook: 5 min.

A small cookie scoop, available at discount stores, will let you portion the sorbet accurately, giving your guests just a little something sweet after the meal.

2 pt. fresh blackberries, halved	½ tsp. ground ginger
¼ cup sugar	1 pt. mango sorbet
2½ tsp. orange zest	6 gingersnaps, crushed

1. Stir together first 4 ingredients in a saucepan over medium heat; cook, stirring constantly, 5 minutes or until thoroughly heated. Serve over sorbet; sprinkle with gingersnaps.

Note: We tested with Häagen-Dazs Mango Sorbet.

Per serving: Calories 184; Fat 1.2g (sat 0.2g, mono 0.4g, poly 0.4g); Protein 1.8g; Carb 44g; Fiber 5.9g; Iron 1.1mg; Sodium 47mg; Calc 35mg

Sweet Sorbet Success

Unlike its cousins ice cream and sherbet, sorbet is made without cream or eggs, so it's the perfect little pick-me-up for the dog days of summer. Sugar is the key to creating a good sorbet—too little sugar and the crystals will be too big, too much sugar and the sorbet will be slushy. Make sure you select the ripest, most fragrant fruits available to add even more punch. Cover leftover sorbet in plastic wrap (directly on the surface), and store in a plastic container in the freezer for up to two weeks.

TASTE OF THE SOUTH

Buttermilk Though buttermilk seems richer and creamier than regular milk, it actually contains the same fat content as the whole, low-fat, and nonfat milks from which it is made. Originally it was the liquid that remained after churning the butter. Today's commercial buttermilk is made by adding lactic acid to pasteurized, homogenized milk, causing it to thicken and sour. (The process is similar to the one used to make sour cream and yogurt.) Some producers add a few flecks of butter for color and richness. The acid makes buttermilk a prized ingredient in baked goods—it tenderizes and lends depth of flavor. It also makes this milk a long-lasting staple that will keep in the refrigerator for up to a week past its sell-by date.

STRAWBERRY-BUTTERMILK SHERBET

makes about 4½ cups   prep: 15 min.   chill: 1 hr.   freeze: 2 hr.

2   cups fresh strawberries*
2   cups buttermilk
1   cup sugar

1   tsp. vanilla extract
Garnish: fresh mint sprigs

1. Process strawberries in a food processor or blender 30 seconds or until smooth, stopping to scrape down sides. Pour strawberry puree through a fine wire-mesh strainer into a large bowl, pressing with back of a spoon. Discard solids. Add buttermilk, sugar, and vanilla to puree; stir until well blended. Cover and chill 1 hour.
2. Pour strawberry mixture into freezer container of a 1½-qt. electric ice-cream maker, and freeze according to manufacturer's instructions. (Instructions and times may vary.) Garnish, if desired.

* 1 (16-oz.) package frozen strawberries, thawed, may be substituted.

VANILLA ICE CREAM WITH FRUIT BLEND

makes about ½ gal.   prep: 10 min.   cook: 15 min.   cool: 10 min.   chill: 8 hr.

Serve this soft right out of the ice-cream maker's container, or freeze it for a firmer consistency.

3 large eggs	1 cup whipping cream
1½ cups sugar	1 Tbsp. vanilla extract
2 Tbsp. all-purpose flour	1 recipe Mixed Berry Blend or
½ tsp. salt	Nectarine-and-Toasted Almond Blend
4 cups 2% reduced-fat milk	(page 360)

1. Beat eggs at medium speed with an electric mixer until frothy. Stir together sugar, flour, and salt until well blended. Gradually add sugar mixture to eggs, beating until thickened. Gradually add milk, beating until blended.

2. Cook egg mixture in a Dutch oven over medium-low heat, stirring constantly, 15 to 20 minutes or until a candy thermometer registers 170°. (Mixture should be thick enough to coat a spoon.)

3. Fill a large bowl or pan with ice; place Dutch oven in ice, and stir occasionally 10 to 15 minutes until custard is completely cool. Transfer mixture to an airtight container; cover and chill 8 hours. Stir in whipping cream, vanilla, and desired fruit blend.

4. Pour mixture into freezer container of a 1-gal. electric ice-cream maker, and freeze according to manufacturer's instructions. (Instructions and freezing times will vary.)

Mixed Berry Blend

makes 4 cups   prep: 10 min.   chill: 2 hr.

4 cups fresh strawberries, quartered	1 cup sugar
2 cups fresh raspberries	

1. Process all ingredients in a food processor 30 to 45 seconds. Transfer mixture to a large bowl; cover and chill at least 2 hours.

Nectarine-and-Toasted Almond Blend

makes about 4 cups   prep: 15 min.   chill: 2 hr.   cook: 4 min.

Like peaches, nectarines can be placed in a paper bag to speed ripening.

5	cups peeled nectarine slices, (about 2¾ lb.)	¾	cup slivered almonds
1	cup sugar	¾	tsp. salt
2	Tbsp. butter		

1. Process nectarines and sugar in a food processor 30 to 45 seconds. Transfer to a large bowl; cover and chill 2 hours.

2. Melt butter over medium-low heat in a medium skillet; add almonds and salt. Cook almonds, stirring frequently, 3 to 5 minutes or until toasted and golden. Pour nut mixture through a fine wire-mesh strainer, shaking to remove excess butter and salt. Stir almonds into nectarine mixture; cover and chill until ready to use.

PEACH-CINNAMON ICE CREAM

makes 6 to 8 servings   prep: 20 min.   cook: 20 min.   chill: 4 hr.   freeze: 25 min.

Peach nectar is a sweet, intensely flavored drink that's usually found on the international food aisle, with the fruit juices, or with cocktail mixes.

4	cups peeled, diced fresh peaches (about 3 lb.)	1	cup half-and-half
1	cup peach nectar	1	tsp. lemon juice
½	cup sugar	½	tsp. ground cinnamon
3	egg yolks		Garnish: sliced fresh peaches (optional)
4	cups milk		

1. Combine first 3 ingredients in a medium bowl. Process peach mixture, in batches, in a food processor until smooth, stopping to scrape down sides. Set aside.

2. Whisk together yolks and milk in a heavy saucepan over medium heat; cook, stirring constantly, 20 minutes or until mixture thickens and coats a spoon. Do not boil.

3. Remove from heat; whisk in peach mixture, half-and-half, lemon juice, and ground cinnamon. Cover and chill 4 hours.

4. Pour mixture into freezer container of a 6-qt. electric ice-cream maker. Freeze according to manufacturer's instructions. (Instructions and times will vary.) Garnish, if desired.

Note: We tested with a White Mountain 6-Quart Electric Ice Cream Freezer.

[test kitchen favorite]

VANILLA ICE MILK

makes about 12 (½-cup) servings   prep: 10 min.   freeze: 20 min.

½ cup sugar

2½ Tbsp. fat-free, sugar-free vanilla instant
    pudding mix

2 cups 2% reduced-fat milk

1 (12-oz.) can evaporated fat-free milk

½ cup egg substitute

2 tsp. vanilla extract

1. Combine sugar and pudding mix in a large bowl. Gradually whisk in milk and remaining ingredients.

2. Pour milk mixture into freezer container of a 1½-qt. electric ice-cream maker, and freeze according to manufacturer's instructions. (Instructions and times will vary.)

CARAMEL-CASHEW ICE CREAM

makes about 1 qt.   prep: 10 min.   freeze: 6 hr.

Only four ingredients are needed to prepare this simple, creamy ice cream.

2 cups whipping cream

1 (14-oz.) can sweetened condensed milk

½ cup butterscotch-caramel topping

1 cup salted cashews, chopped

Toppings: butterscotch-caramel topping,
    chopped cashews

[*quick*]

1. Beat whipping cream at high speed with an electric mixer until stiff peaks form.

2. Stir together sweetened condensed milk and ½ cup butterscotch-caramel topping in a large bowl. Fold in whipped cream and 1 cup cashews. Place in an airtight container; freeze 6 to 8 hours or until firm. Serve with desired toppings.

Tips for Great Ice Cream

Here are a few tricks for getting the best results making homemade ice cream.

• Chill the liquid ice-cream mixture 30 minutes before churning to ensure a smoother texture.

• To facilitate speedy freezing, place the freshly churned ice cream (in the freezing container from your ice-cream maker) directly into the freezer. Freeze for 15 minutes, add any stir-ins, and then transfer to an airtight container; refreeze.

• Freeze ice cream 8 hours or longer for the best texture. Allow to stand at room temperature 30 minutes to 1 hour before serving.

• Customize with stir-ins: Add 1 cup chopped toasted nuts, chocolate chips, crushed cream-filled chocolate sandwich cookies, or toasted coconut to your favorite variation.

NO-COOK VANILLA ICE CREAM

makes 1 qt.   prep: 5 min.   chill: 30 min.   freeze: 1 hr., 15 min.

Several years ago, concerns about egg safety prompted us to cook any ice-cream base that used fresh eggs. Not to worry; this recipe doesn't use eggs. Instead, the mixture gets incredible richness from sweetened condensed milk. Use our basic vanilla ice cream as a base, and try every delicious flavor.

1   (14-oz.) can sweetened condensed milk

1   (5-oz.) can evaporated milk

2   Tbsp. sugar

2   tsp. vanilla extract

2   cups whole milk

1. Whisk all ingredients in a 2-qt. pitcher or large bowl until blended. Cover and chill for 30 minutes.

2. Pour milk mixture into freezer container of a 1-qt. electric ice-cream maker, and freeze according to manufacturer's instructions. (Instructions and times will vary.)

3. Remove container with ice cream from ice-cream maker, and place in freezer 15 minutes.

4. Transfer to an airtight container; freeze until firm, about 1 to 1½ hours.

Note: We tested with a Rival 4-Quart. Durable Plastic Bucket Ice Cream Maker and a Cuisinart Automatic Frozen Yogurt-Ice Cream & Sorbet Maker.

No-Cook Chocolate Ice Cream: Omit sugar, vanilla, and whole milk. Add 2 cups whole chocolate milk and ⅔ cup chocolate syrup. Proceed as directed. Makes 1 qt.

No-Cook Chocolate-Almond Ice Cream: Pictured on page 327. Prepare No-Cook Chocolate Ice Cream as directed. Remove container with ice cream from ice-cream maker, and place in freezer. Freeze 15 minutes. Stir ¾ cup toasted sliced almonds into prepared ice cream. Place in an airtight container; freeze until firm. Makes 1¼ qt.

No-Cook Turtle Ice Cream: Prepare No-Cook Vanilla Ice Cream as directed. Stir ¼ cup caramel sauce into prepared ice cream. Remove container with ice cream from ice-cream maker, and place in freezer. Freeze 15 minutes. Microwave ½ cup semisweet chocolate morsels and 1 tsp. shortening in a microwave-safe glass bowl at HIGH 1 minute. Stir until smooth. Place ¾ cup toasted chopped pecans on a parchment paper-lined baking sheet. Drizzle pecans with melted chocolate. Freeze 5 minutes. Break into bite-size pieces. Stir chocolate-and-pecan pieces into ice cream. Place in an airtight container; freeze until firm. Makes 1½ qt.

No-Cook Fig-Mint Ice Cream: Prepare No-Cook Vanilla Ice Cream as directed. Remove container with prepared ice cream from ice-cream maker, and place in freezer. Freeze 15 minutes. Stir together 2 cups chopped peeled fresh figs, ¼ cup fresh lemon juice, 2 Tbsp. sugar, and 2 tsp. chopped fresh mint. Stir mixture into prepared ice-cream mixture. Place in an airtight container; freeze until firm. Makes 1½ qt.

Note: We used Black Mission Figs; any fresh figs in season should work, including green figs.

No-Cook Peach Ice Cream: Pictured on page 327. Omit vanilla and sugar, and reduce whole milk to 1¼ cups. Process 4 peeled, sliced medium-size fresh ripe peaches or 1 (15.25-oz.) can peaches in light syrup, drained, with 2 Tbsp. sugar; ¼ cup fresh lemon juice; and ¼ tsp. salt in a blender or food processor until smooth. Stir into milk mixture with ¾ cup peach nectar. Proceed as directed. Makes 1½ qt.

No-Cook Strawberry Ice Cream: Pictured on page 327. Omit vanilla, and reduce whole milk to 1½ cups. Process 1 (16-oz.) container fresh strawberries or 1 (16-oz.) package thawed frozen strawberries, 2 Tbsp. lemon juice, and ¼ tsp. salt in a blender or food processor until smooth. Stir into milk mixture. Proceed as directed. Makes 1½ qt.

No-Cook Coconut Ice Cream: Omit vanilla and sugar, and reduce whole milk to ½ cup. Whisk 1 (13.5-oz.) can coconut milk, 2 Tbsp. fresh lemon juice, and ¼ tsp. salt into milk mixture. Proceed as directed. Serve ice cream with toasted coconut, shaved chocolate, or chopped macadamia nuts. Makes 1 qt.

Note: To make a tropical sundae, top coconut ice cream with sliced bananas, mango slices, and pineapple chunks.

⚬⚬⚬inspirations for your taste ⚬⚬⚬

As temperatures climb, everybody yearns for that perfect icy snack. Here it is: a good-for-you frozen concoction that will excite any taste bud.

Raspberry-Banana-Yogurt Freezer Pops

makes 10 pops   prep: 10 min.   cook: 5 min.   chill: 30 min.   freeze: 6 hr.

Process 1 cup low-fat vanilla yogurt and 1 banana in a blender 30 seconds or until smooth. Bring 3 cups fresh or frozen raspberries and ½ cup honey to a boil in a medium saucepan over medium-high heat; reduce heat to low, and simmer 5 minutes. Pour mixture through a fine wire-mesh strainer into a bowl, using back of spoon to squeeze out juice and pulp. Discard skins and seeds. Cover and chill raspberry mixture 30 minutes. Pour yogurt mixture evenly into 10 (2-oz.) pop molds. Top with raspberry mixture, and swirl, if desired. Top with lid of pop mold, and insert craft sticks, leaving 1½ to 2 inches sticking out of pop. Freeze 6 hours or until sticks are solidly anchored and pops are completely frozen.

Tip: For a different taste, substitute 3 cups fresh or frozen blueberries or halved strawberries.

KEY LIME FROZEN YOGURT

makes 12 servings   prep: 5 min.   freeze: 30 min.

Serve with fresh raspberries or blackberries, pressed between graham crackers or gingersnaps, or on its own for a tangy treat.

1 (32-oz.) container whole milk French vanilla yogurt	1 (14-oz.) can fat-free sweetened condensed milk
	½ cup Key lime juice

1. Whisk together all ingredients in a large bowl until well blended. Pour mixture into freezer container of a 1½-qt. electric ice-cream maker, and freeze according to manufacturer's instructions. (Instructions and times will vary.) Cover and freeze until desired firmness.

Note: We tested with Stonyfield Farm Organic Whole Milk French Vanilla Yogurt and Nellie & Joe's Famous Key West Lime Juice.

Per ½-cup serving: Calories 178; Fat 2.7g (sat 1.7g); Protein 5.6g; Carb 32.8g; Fiber 1g; Chol 12mg; Sodium 75mg; Calc 211mg

[southern lights]

BLUEBERRY-LIME GRANITA

makes 7 servings   prep: 15 min.   freeze: 8 hr.   stand: 5 min.   **pictured on page 325**

Blueberries contain powerful antioxidants that help combat disease and fight aging.

2   **cups blueberries**
½   **cup sugar***
½   **tsp. lime zest**

2   **tsp. fresh lime juice**
3   **cups diet lemon-lime soft drink, chilled**
Garnish: lime zest twists

1. Process blueberries in a food processor or blender until smooth, stopping to scrape down sides. Add sugar, lime zest, and lime juice; process until well blended. Pour into an 11- x 7-inch baking dish. Stir in soft drink. Cover and freeze 8 hours. Remove from freezer; let stand 5 minutes.

2. Chop mixture into large chunks, and place in food processor in batches; pulse 5 to 6 times or until mixture is smooth. Serve immediately, or freeze until ready to serve. Garnish, if desired.

*   ½ cup of no-calorie sweetener (such as Splenda) may be substituted.

Per 1-cup serving: Calories 80; Fat 0.1g; Protein 0.3g; Carb 20.4g; Fiber 1g; Iron 0.1mg; Calc 3mg

Per 1-cup serving with no-calorie sweetener: Calories 25; Fat 0.1g; Protein 0.3g; Carb 6.2g; Fiber 1g; Iron 0.1mg; Calc 3mg

WARM COOKIE SUNDAES

makes 6 servings   prep: 5 min.   bake: 25 min.   cool: 5 min.

We liked the cookie cups soft, but for a crisper cookie, increase the bake time.

6   **packaged ready-to-bake peanut butter cookie dough rounds with mini peanut butter cups**

Vanilla ice cream
Toppings: hot fudge sauce, whipped cream, chopped peanuts

1. Preheat oven to 350°. Place each cookie dough round into a lightly greased 8-oz. ramekin or individual soufflé dish.

2. Bake at 350° for 25 to 30 minutes or until cookies are lightly browned. Let cool 5 minutes. Scoop vanilla ice cream into each ramekin, and top sundaes with desired toppings. Serve immediately.

Note: We tested with half of an 18-oz. package of Pillsbury Ready To Bake Peanut Butter Cup Cookies.

WAFFLE TACO SUNDAES

makes 8 servings prep: 15 min. freeze: 1 hr., 30 min.

8 round frozen waffles

1 qt. chocolate ice cream

½ cup miniature marshmallows

Maraschino cherries, candy sprinkles

1. Microwave 8 round frozen waffles, in 2 batches, in a single layer at HIGH 1 to 2 minutes or just until warm. Gently fold each waffle in half to form a taco; place in an 11- x 7-inch baking dish, pressing waffles together to hold shape. Stir together 1 qt. chocolate ice cream, softened, and ½ cup miniature marshmallows. Freeze 30 minutes.

2. Spoon ice cream evenly into waffles; cover and freeze 1 hour or until firm. Drizzle with fudge sauce, and top with maraschino cherries and candy sprinkles.

JOHN'S BANANAS FOSTER

makes 6 to 8 servings prep: 10 min. cook: 5 min.

This recipe is a favorite of former Southern Living *editor John Floyd. Working quickly, pre-scoop ice cream into a large bowl, and store scoops in the freezer to make serving easy. If you don't have countertops that accommodate a hot skillet, just move the skillet to an unlit burner on your stovetop before igniting.*

4 medium-size ripe bananas

½ cup butter

1 cup firmly packed brown sugar

¼ cup banana liqueur

½ cup rum

Vanilla ice cream

1. Cut bananas in half crosswise; cut each half in half lengthwise. Melt butter in a large skillet over medium-high heat; add brown sugar, and cook, stirring constantly, 2 minutes.

2. Add bananas to skillet, and remove from heat. Stir in liqueur and rum, and carefully ignite the fumes just above mixture with a long match or long multipurpose lighter. Let flames die down.

3. Return skillet to heat, and cook 3 to 4 minutes or until bananas are soft and curl slightly. Remove from heat. Serve banana mixture immediately over vanilla ice cream.

BANANAS FOSTER GRATIN

makes 4 servings   prep: 10 min.   cook: 4 min.   bake: 10 min.

Get all the flavor without the flaming in this version of the famous dessert.

¼ cup firmly packed light brown sugar

1 Tbsp. dark rum

¼ tsp. ground cinnamon

2 tsp. butter

4 medium-size ripe bananas

1 almond biscotti, crushed (about ⅓ cup)

Vanilla ice cream

1. Preheat oven to 450°. Stir together first 3 ingredients in a 10-inch skillet over medium heat; bring to a boil. Reduce heat to medium-low, and simmer, stirring constantly, 2 minutes. Remove from heat, and stir in butter.

2. Slice bananas diagonally. Add to brown sugar mixture in skillet, tossing to coat.

3. Spoon banana mixture evenly into 4 lightly greased (1- to 1½-cup) gratin dishes or a shallow lightly greased 1-qt. baking dish.

4. Bake at 450° for 10 minutes or until bubbly. Remove from oven, and sprinkle evenly with biscotti crumbs. Serve warm with vanilla ice cream.

BRANDY-VANILLA CHEESECAKE DIP

makes 3 cups   prep: 5 min.

Refrigerated cheesecake filling is sold in a tub near the cream cheese. It is fully cooked and ready to use. Serve this incredibly easy but equally impressive dessert dip with sliced pears, apricots, cherries, strawberries, and assorted cookies.

1 (24.2-oz.) container ready-to-eat cheesecake
   filling

5 Tbsp. brandy

1 tsp. vanilla extract

1. Stir together all ingredients. Cover and chill until ready to serve.

Note: We tested with Philadelphia Ready-To-Eat Cheesecake Filling.

Orange Cheesecake Dip: Prepare recipe as directed, substituting ¼ cup orange marmalade, melted, and 2 tsp. orange zest for brandy and vanilla.

Rum-Almond Cheesecake Dip: Prepare recipe as directed, substituting 3 to 5 tsp. spiced rum and ½ tsp. almond extract for brandy and vanilla.

LEMON PIE DIP

makes 8 to 10 servings prep: 5 min. chill: 2 hr. **pictured on page 327**

Serve this treat as a finger-friendly snack or casual dessert. Simply hollow out lemon halves for a fun presentation.

1   (14-oz.) can sweetened condensed milk   Graham cracker sticks, fresh strawberries
½   cup fresh lemon juice

1. Whisk together condensed milk and lemon juice in a bowl until blended, and chill 2 hours. Serve with graham cracker sticks and fresh strawberries.

Note: We tested with Honey Maid Grahams Cinnamon Sticks.

CARAMEL DIP

makes about 2 cups prep: 5 min. cook: 5 min.

Store this dip in an airtight container in the refrigerator. Simply reheat in the microwave for 1 minute or until hot, stirring at 20-second intervals.

½   cup butter   2   cups coarsely chopped pecans, toasted
1   (8-oz.) container sour cream   (optional)
1   (16-oz.) package light brown sugar   Apple, pear, or other fruit slices

1. Cook first 3 ingredients over low heat in a 3-qt. saucepan, stirring constantly, 5 minutes or until mixture is smooth.
2. Stir in pecans, if desired. Serve with fruit slices.

PEANUT BUTTER DIP

makes about 2 cups prep: 5 min.

1½ cups plain low-fat yogurt   ¼   cup maple syrup
½   cup creamy peanut butter

1. Stir together all ingredients until well blended. Serve immediately, or store in an airtight container in the refrigerator up to 5 days.

Per ¼-cup seving: Calories 150; Fat 8.9g (sat 2.1g, mono 4g, poly 2.2g); Protein: 6.5g; Carb 13g; Fiber 0.9g; Chol 2.8mg; Iron 0.5mg; Sodium 108mg; Calc 97mg

TOFFEE-APPLE DIP

makes about 3 cups   prep: 5 min.

One recipe makes enough dip for six large apples or pears. To prevent the cut fruit from turning brown, soak the slices for an hour in canned pineapple juice.

1 (8-oz.) package cream cheese, softened
1 (8-oz.) package toffee bits
¾ cup firmly packed light brown sugar

½ cup granulated sugar
1 tsp. vanilla extract
Sliced apples or pears

1. Stir together all ingredients until well blended. Serve immediately, or store in an airtight container in the refrigerator up to 5 days. Serve with apple or pear slices.

SWEET DIP WITH COOKIES AND FRUIT

makes 6 servings   prep: 10 min.   chill: 1 hr.   stand: 30 min.

4 oz. cream cheese, softened
3 Tbsp. butter
1 Tbsp. plain or vanilla yogurt
½ tsp. orange zest

2½ Tbsp. powdered sugar
Assorted cookies
Assorted berries
Dark chocolate squares

1. Beat first 4 ingredients at medium-high speed with an electric mixer until smooth. Gradually add sugar, beating until creamy. Cover and chill at least 1 hour or up to 3 days. Let stand at room temperature 30 minutes before serving. Serve with cookies, berries, and chocolate.

S'MORE PUFFS

makes 12 puffs   prep: 5 min.   bake: 8 min.   cool: 5 min.   **pictured on page 249**

Watch the little ones—the center of the marshmallow will still be warm after the 5-minute cooling time. Chocolate kisses will soften but not melt.

12 round buttery crackers
12 milk chocolate kisses

6 large marshmallows, cut in half

1. Preheat oven to 350°. Place crackers on a baking sheet. Top each with 1 milk chocolate kiss and 1 marshmallow half, cut side down. Bake at 350° for 8 minutes or just until marshmallows begin to melt. Let cool on a wire rack 5 minutes.

FISH & SHELLFISH

"If I go down for anything in history, I would like to be known as the person who convinced the American people that catfish is one of the finest eating fishes in the world." —Willard Scott

TASTE OF THE SOUTH

Fried Catfish Members of our Food staff have a tough time arriving at a consensus when it comes to the Southern delicacy of fried catfish. We tried a variety of techniques, from soaking catfish overnight to combining the best ingredients from several different recipes. We found 4- to 6-ounce, thin-cut, farm-raised fillets easy to manage in the skillet, and they curl up when cooked, giving great eye appeal. (If you purchase frozen fillets, place them in a colander with a pan underneath, and thaw in the refrigerator overnight; otherwise, keep them in the coldest part of your refrigerator, and use within two days.) In searching for the perfect fried catfish recipe, Test Kitchen director Lyda Jones Burnette has the answer—cornmeal. It offers a crunchy texture without a greasy taste. Catfish opinions aside, we all agree our choices for side dishes are hush puppies, baked beans, and coleslaw. As for condiments, a dab of ketchup and tartar sauce and a squeeze of lemon are high on our list.

CLASSIC FRIED CATFISH

makes 6 servings   prep: 15 min.   cook: 5 min.

Add a splash of hot sauce or a squeeze of lemon to these crispy fillets.

¾ cup yellow cornmeal	¼ tsp. garlic powder
¼ cup all-purpose flour	6 (4- to 6-oz.) farm-raised catfish fillets
2 tsp. salt	¼ tsp. salt
1 tsp. ground red pepper	Vegetable oil

1. Combine first 5 ingredients in a large shallow dish. Sprinkle fish with ¼ tsp. salt; dredge in cornmeal mixture, coating evenly.

2. Pour oil to a depth of 1½ inches into a deep cast-iron skillet; heat to 350°. Fry fish, in batches, 5 to 6 minutes or until golden; drain on paper towels.

FRONT-PORCH FRIED CATFISH

makes 10 servings   prep: 10 min.   cook: 3 min.

Frying becomes second nature if you follow a few guidelines. First, select an oil with a high smoke point, such as peanut oil. Next, use a deep-fat thermometer to maintain an accurate temperature. When the oil is hot enough, the cooking process seals the outside of the fish to lock in flavor and moisture. Fry in batches to prevent the oil temperature from dropping too low.

1   cup all-purpose flour
1   Tbsp. salt
2   tsp. black pepper
2   tsp. ground red pepper
2½ cups cornmeal mix
1   Tbsp. garlic powder

2   Tbsp. dried thyme
10 (6- to 8-oz.) farm-raised catfish fillets,
    cut into strips
1   cup buttermilk
Peanut oil

1. Combine first 4 ingredients in a shallow dish.
2. Combine cornmeal, garlic powder, and thyme in a zip-top plastic freezer bag.
3. Dredge catfish fillets in flour mixture, and dip in buttermilk, allowing excess to drip off.
4. Place catfish fillets in cornmeal mixture; seal bag, and shake to coat.
5. Pour oil to a depth of 1½ inches into a large cast-iron or other heavy skillet; heat to 360°.
6. Fry catfish fillets, in batches, 3 minutes or until golden. Drain on paper towels, and serve immediately.

Frying Tips

Try these tips from our Test Kitchen.

• Remove excess moisture from fish before dredging.
• Keep one hand clean for dredging and the other hand available for frying.
• Use a large Dutch oven or deep cast-iron skillet to keep the hot oil from popping out.
• Don't overcrowd the skillet; fry, in batches, two fillets at a time. Bring remaining oil back to the proper temperature before frying the next batch.

• Remove fish from skillet with a wide, slotted, curved spoon.
• To keep warm, place fried fish on a wire rack with an aluminum foil-lined pan underneath; place in a 250° oven. For a crisp texture, do not cover fillets.
• For more information visit www.catfishinstitute.com.

QUICK PAN-FRIED CATFISH

makes 4 servings   prep: 15 min.   cook: 6 min.

Fish generally cooks 10 minutes per inch of thickness. If the catfish you buy is thicker, it will take longer to cook. Just lower the temperature slightly.

¾ cup all-purpose baking mix

½ cup yellow cornmeal

1 Tbsp. Old Bay seasoning

4 (4- to 6-oz.) catfish fillets

Ranch dressing

Lemon wedges

1. Combine first 3 ingredients in a shallow bowl.

2. Pat catfish fillets dry with paper towels; brush both sides of each fillet evenly with Ranch dressing. Dredge in cornmeal mixture; lightly press cornmeal mixture onto fillets.

3. Cook catfish in hot vegetable oil in a large nonstick skillet over medium-high heat 3 to 5 minutes on each side or until fish flakes with a fork. Serve immediately with lemon wedges.

Note: We tested with Bisquick for all-purpose baking mix.

CATFISH PECAN WITH LEMON-THYME-PECAN BUTTER

makes 8 servings   prep: 25 min.   cook: 28 min.   pictured on page 330

Keep the cooked fish warm in a low oven for up to 30 minutes.

1½ cups pecan halves, divided

¾ cup all-purpose flour

1½ tsp. Creole seasoning, divided

1 large egg

1 cup milk

8 (6-oz.) catfish, flounder, redfish, or bass fillets

1 cup butter, divided

2 large lemons, halved

1 Tbsp. Worcestershire sauce

6 large fresh thyme sprigs

Kosher salt and pepper to taste

Garnish: lemon slices (optional)

1. Process ¾ cup pecans, flour, and 1 tsp. Creole seasoning in a food processor until finely ground; place pecan mixture in a large shallow bowl, and set aside.

2. Whisk together egg and milk in a large bowl, and set aside.

3. Sprinkle both sides of fillets evenly with remaining ½ tsp. Creole seasoning.

4. Dip catfish fillets in egg mixture, draining off excess; dredge fillets in pecan mixture, coating both sides, and shake off excess.

5. Melt 2 Tbsp. butter in a large nonstick skillet over medium heat until butter starts to bubble. Place 2 fillets in skillet, and cook 2 to 3 minutes on each side or until golden. Drain on a wire rack in a jelly-roll pan, and keep warm in a 200° oven. Wipe skillet clean, and repeat procedure with remaining fillets.

6. Wipe skillet clean. Melt remaining ½ cup butter in skillet over high heat; add remaining ¾ cup pecans, and cook, stirring occasionally, 2 to 3 minutes or until toasted. Squeeze juice from lemon halves into skillet; place halves, cut sides down, in skillet. Stir in Worcestershire sauce, thyme, salt, and pepper, and cook 30 seconds or until thyme wilts and becomes very aromatic. Remove and discard lemon halves and wilted thyme.

7. Place fish on a serving platter; spoon pecan mixture over fish. Garnish, if desired.

CRISPY OVEN-FRIED CATFISH

makes 4 servings   prep: 10 min.   chill: 20 min.   bake: 30 min.

1 cup low-fat buttermilk	½ tsp. salt
4 (6-oz.) catfish fillets	3 cups cornflakes cereal, crushed
2½ tsp. salt-free Creole seasoning	Lemon wedges

1. Place 1 cup low-fat buttermilk in a large zip-top plastic freezer bag; add 4 (6-oz.) catfish fillets, turning to coat. Seal and chill 20 minutes, turning once.

2. Preheat oven to 425°. Remove catfish fillets from buttermilk, discarding buttermilk. Sprinkle catfish fillets evenly with Creole seasoning and salt.

3. Place crushed cornflakes in a shallow dish. Dredge catfish fillets in cornflakes, pressing cornflakes gently onto each fillet. Place fillets on a rack coated with cooking spray in a roasting pan.

4. Bake catfish fillets at 425° for 30 to 35 minutes or until fish flakes with a fork. Serve catfish fillets immediately with lemon wedges.

Note: We tested with The Spice Hunter Cajun Creole Salt Free Seasoning Blend.

Calories 321; Fat 13.1g (sat 3.1g, mono 6.2g, poly 2.7g); Protein 28.6g; Fiber 1.2g; Chol 81mg; Iron 5.3mg; Sodium 472mg; Calc 36mg

CARIBBEAN CATFISH WITH SPICY ISLAND SWEET POTATOES

makes 6 servings   prep: 30 min.   cook: 21 min.   broil: 6 min.

7 Tbsp. fresh lime juice, divided	1 tsp. adobo sauce from can
6 Tbsp. dark molasses	1 tsp. ground cumin
2 Tbsp. lite soy sauce	½ tsp. salt
2 Tbsp. minced fresh ginger	Black pepper to taste
¼ tsp. ground allspice	1½ Tbsp. canola oil
⅛ tsp. ground red pepper	½ cup minced green onions
3 garlic cloves, minced	6 catfish fillets (about 2¼ lb.)
2 lb. sweet potatoes, peeled and shredded (about 3 medium potatoes)	Cooking spray
	Salt to taste
1 tsp. minced canned chipotle peppers in adobo sauce	2½ Tbsp. minced fresh cilantro
	Garnish: fresh cilantro sprigs

1. Bring 6 Tbsp. lime juice, molasses, and next 5 ingredients to a boil in a small heavy saucepan over medium heat. Reduce heat to medium low, and simmer, stirring occasionally, 15 minutes or until mixture is reduced to ½ cup; cool.

2. Sauté sweet potatoes, next 4 ingredients, and black pepper to taste in a large nonstick skillet in hot oil 6 to 7 minutes or just until tender. (Do not brown.) Stir in green onions and remaining 1 Tbsp. lime juice. Remove from heat; cover with foil to keep warm.

3. Preheat oven to broil. Place catfish fillets on a broiler pan coated with cooking spray; season fillets with salt.

4. Broil 6 inches from heat 3 minutes; brush molasses mixture evenly on fillets, and broil 3 to 5 minutes or just until fish flakes with a fork.

5. Spoon sweet potato mixture evenly onto 6 serving plates; top each with 1 fillet. Sprinkle evenly with minced cilantro. Garnish, if desired.

Note: Analysis does not include added salt to taste.

Calories 314; Fat 8.7g (sat 1.5g, mono 3.5g, poly 2.6g); Protein 30g; Fiber 2.6g; Chol 99mg; Iron 3.8mg; Sodium 517mg; Calc 156mg

SOUTH BY SOUTHWEST CATFISH WITH GUACAMOLE AÏOLI

makes 6 servings   prep: 20 min.   fry: 10 min. per batch

2   cups crushed tortilla chips
2   large eggs
⅛   tsp. ground coriander
6   catfish fillets (about 3 lb.)
Canola oil

Guacamole Aïoli
1   (10-oz.) can diced tomatoes and green chiles, drained
Garnish: fresh cilantro sprigs

1. Place crushed chips in a large shallow bowl. Whisk together eggs, 1 Tbsp. water, and coriander in a large bowl. Pat catfish fillets dry with paper towels. Dip fillets in egg mixture, coating completely; dredge in crushed chips, coating evenly.

2. Pour oil to a depth of 1½ inches in a large skillet; heat to 350°. Fry catfish in hot oil, in batches, 5 minutes on each side. Drain on paper towels.

3. Spoon ¼ cup Guacamole Aïoli on each of 6 serving plates; top with catfish fillets. Drizzle evenly with remaining Guacamole Aïoli, and sprinkle with diced tomatoes and green chiles. Garnish, if desired.

Guacamole Aïoli

makes about 3 cups   prep: 15 min.

2   large avocados
⅓   cup fresh lime juice
1   cup mayonnaise
1   (8-oz.) package cream cheese, softened

1   Tbsp. minced garlic
1   tsp. freshly ground black pepper
¼   tsp. salt
⅓   cup chopped fresh cilantro

1. Cut avocados in half. Scoop pulp into a medium bowl; mash into large chunks with a fork. Add lime juice and next 5 ingredients.

2. Process avocado mixture with a handheld immersion blender or electric mixer until smooth; stir in chopped cilantro. Cover and chill until ready to serve.

CAJUN-BAKED CATFISH

makes 4 servings   prep: 10 min.   bake: 30 min.

For a twist, substitute 1 Tbsp. lemon pepper for 1 Tbsp. Cajun seasoning.

2 cups cornmeal	2 Tbsp. Cajun seasoning
2 tsp. salt	1 to 2 tsp. seasoned salt
1 Tbsp. pepper	¼ cup butter, melted
8 (3- to 4-oz.) catfish fillets	Garnish: lemon wedges

1. Preheat oven to 400°. Combine first 3 ingredients. Dredge catfish fillets in cornmeal mixture; place fillets, skin sides down, on a greased baking sheet.

2. Combine Cajun seasoning and seasoned salt; sprinkle over fillets. Drizzle with butter.

3. Bake at 400° for 30 minutes or until golden and fish flakes with a fork. Garnish, if desired.

SPICY CATFISH WITH VEGETABLES AND BASIL CREAM

makes 4 servings   prep: 25 min.   cook: 25 min.   **pictured on page 330**

This recipe, developed by our Test Kitchen, shows the versatility and creativity of sautéing.

3 Tbsp. butter, divided	½ cup all-purpose flour
1 (16-oz.) package frozen whole kernel corn, thawed	¼ cup yellow cornmeal
1 medium onion, chopped	1 Tbsp. Creole seasoning
1 medium-size green bell pepper, chopped	4 (6- to 8-oz.) catfish fillets
1 medium-size red bell pepper, chopped	⅓ cup buttermilk
¾ tsp. salt	1 Tbsp. vegetable oil
¾ tsp. pepper	½ cup whipping cream
	2 Tbsp. chopped fresh basil

1. Melt 2 Tbsp. butter in a large skillet over medium-high heat. Add corn, onion, and peppers; sauté 6 to 8 minutes or until tender. Stir in salt and pepper; spoon onto serving dish, and keep warm.

2. Combine flour, cornmeal, and Creole seasoning in a large shallow dish. Dip fillets in buttermilk, and dredge in flour mixture.

3. Melt remaining 1 Tbsp. butter with oil in skillet over medium-high heat. Cook fillets, in batches, 2 to 3 minutes on each side or until golden. Remove and arrange over vegetables.

4. Add cream to skillet, stirring to loosen particles from bottom of skillet. Add chopped basil, and cook, stirring often, 1 to 2 minutes or until thickened. Serve sauce with fillets and vegetables.

CATFISH JEZEBEL

makes 4 servings   prep: 5 min.   bake: 20 min.

¼ cup orange marmalade	1 tsp. spicy brown mustard
¼ cup ketchup	1 Tbsp. Creole seasoning
1 Tbsp. horseradish sauce	4 (6-oz.) catfish fillets

1. Preheat oven to 425°. Stir together first 4 ingredients, and set aside.
2. Sprinkle Creole seasoning evenly over catfish. Place fish in an aluminum foil-lined roasting pan.
3. Bake at 425° for 20 minutes or until fish flakes with a fork. Serve with marmalade mixture.

SOUTHERN-STYLE FISH TACOS

makes 4 servings   prep: 20 min.   fry: 2 min. per batch   **pictured on page 331**

3 large limes, divided	Canola oil
4 (6-oz.) catfish fillets, cut into 1-inch-thick strips	8 (6-inch) corn or flour tortillas, warmed
1½ cups yellow cornmeal	1 cup thinly shredded green cabbage
2 Tbsp. dried parsley flakes	1 cup thinly shredded red cabbage
2 Tbsp. paprika	Refrigerated creamy Ranch dressing
2 tsp. ground red pepper	Bottled salsa
2 tsp. lemon pepper	Toppings: ripe avocado slices, seeded and diced
2 tsp. salt	tomatoes, chopped fresh cilantro
1 tsp. garlic powder	

1. Squeeze juice of 1 lime over fish. Combine cornmeal and next 6 ingredients in a large zip-top plastic freezer bag. Pat fish dry with paper towels, and place in bag, shaking to coat.
2. Pour oil to a depth of 1½ inches in a large deep skillet; heat to 325°. Fry catfish, in batches, in hot oil 2 to 3 minutes or until crispy and golden brown. Drain on paper towels.
3. Place catfish in warmed tortillas; top evenly with cabbage, desired amount of salad dressing, salsa, and toppings. Cut remaining 2 limes into wedges, and serve with tacos.

MINI CATFISH CAKES

makes 6 appetizer servings prep: 20 min. cook: 6 min. per batch

Make the catfish mixture up to one day ahead before forming into patties, if desired. Find panko on the Asian aisle or with breadcrumbs at your supermarket.

1 lb. catfish fillets	½ tsp. salt
1¼ cups Japanese breadcrumbs (panko)*	¼ tsp. fresh cracked black pepper
3 green onions, minced	¼ cup vegetable oil
2 large eggs, beaten	Caper-Dill Sour Cream
½ cup finely chopped red bell pepper	Garnish: fresh dill sprigs

1. Chop catfish into ¼-inch pieces. Combine catfish, ¾ cup breadcrumbs, and next 5 ingredients; gently stir until well blended. Shape mixture into 12 patties (about ¼ cup each). Dredge patties in remaining ½ cup breadcrumbs.
2. Cook patties, in batches, in hot oil in a large nonstick skillet over medium heat 3 to 4 minutes on each side or until golden; drain on paper towels. Serve with Caper-Dill Sour Cream; garnish with fresh dill sprigs.

* 1¼ cups fresh breadcrumbs may be substituted.

Caper-Dill Sour Cream

makes about 1 cup prep: 5 min.

1 (8-oz.) container sour cream	2 tsp. lemon juice
3 Tbsp. chopped, drained capers	Salt and pepper to taste
1 Tbsp. chopped fresh dill	

1. Stir together all ingredients. Serve as a dip with sliced cucumbers and pita chips, or Mini Catfish Cakes.

Note: Topping can be made up to two days in advance. Store, covered, in refrigerator.

GREEK SNAPPER ON THE GRILL

makes 12 servings   prep: 15 min.   grill: 15 min.

Accompany this recipe with red rice and slaw. A hollowed lemon half makes a clever container for Dot's Tartar Sauce.

12 (8-oz.) snapper or grouper fillets
¼ cup olive oil
1 Tbsp. Greek seasoning

24 (¼-inch-thick) lemon slices
Dot's Tartar Sauce

1. Preheat grill to 350° to 400° (medium-high) heat. Rub fish fillets with oil; sprinkle evenly with Greek seasoning. Top each fillet with 2 lemon slices.
2. Place a large piece of lightly greased heavy-duty aluminum foil over grill cooking grate. Arrange fish on foil.
3. Grill fillets, covered with grill lid, 15 minutes or until fish flakes with a fork. Serve with Dot's Tartar Sauce.

Note: We tested with Cavender's All-Purpose Greek Seasoning.

Dot's Tartar Sauce

makes 1½ cups   prep: 10 min.

1 cup mayonnaise
2 Tbsp. dill pickle relish
2 Tbsp. drained capers
2 Tbsp. chopped fresh chives
1 Tbsp. chopped fresh tarragon

1 Tbsp. Dijon mustard
2 tsp. fresh lemon juice
¼ tsp. pepper
Garnish: chopped fresh chives

1. Stir together first 8 ingredients until blended. Cover and chill until ready to serve. Garnish, if desired.

BROILED GROUPER

makes 6 servings prep: 10 min. broil: 10 min.

2 lb. grouper fillets

½ cup grated Parmesan cheese

1 Tbsp. butter, softened

3 Tbsp. reduced-fat mayonnaise

3 Tbsp. chopped green onions

1 garlic clove, pressed

¼ tsp. salt

Dash of hot sauce

1. Place fillets in a single layer in a lightly greased 13- x 9-inch pan.
2. Stir together cheese and next 6 ingredients; spread over fillets.
3. Broil 5½ inches from heat 10 minutes or until lightly browned and fish flakes with a fork.

Note: Do not broil on the top rack, or the topping may burn before the fish is done.

BLACKENED FISH

makes 6 servings prep: 5 min. cook: 24 min.

Chef Paul Prudhomme created this dish in the 1980s. This makes a lot of spicy smoke, so it's best to cook it outside over a burner or on a stove with a strong exhaust fan.

6 (6- to 8-oz.) redfish, grouper, or catfish fillets
   (about ½ inch thick)

1 cup unsalted butter, melted

2 Tbsp. blackened fish seasoning

Lemon wedges

1. Dip fillets in melted butter. Sprinkle 1 tsp. seasoning evenly over both sides of each fillet. Press seasoning into fish, and place on wax paper.
2. Heat a large cast-iron skillet over medium-high heat 10 minutes or until smoking. Place 2 fillets in the skillet, and cook 4 minutes on each side or until lightly charred. Transfer fillets to a serving dish; cover and keep warm. Drain butter from skillet, and carefully wipe clean with paper towels.
3. Heat skillet 5 minutes or until smoking. Place 2 fillets in skillet, and repeat cooking procedure. Repeat with remaining 2 fillets. Serve with lemon wedges.

Note: We tested with Chef Paul Prudhomme's Magic Seasoning Blends Blackened Redfish Magic for seasoning.

COASTAL BEND REDFISH WITH SHRIMP AND CRAB

makes 4 servings   prep: 35 min.   cook: 7 min.

½ lb. unpeeled, large raw shrimp
1 cup Beurre Blanc
⅓ cup tomato puree
1 tsp. sugar
1 tsp. garlic salt
2 shallots, minced
1 small jalapeño pepper, seeded and minced
¼ cup olive oil, divided
2 plum tomatoes, peeled, seeded, and diced
½ lb. fresh jumbo lump crabmeat

4 (6- to 8-oz.) redfish or red snapper fillets, skinned
1 tsp. salt
1 tsp. pepper
12 asparagus spears, cooked
8 small carrots, sliced and cooked
2 zucchini, sliced and cooked
2 large plum tomatoes, seeded and chopped
½ cup grated fontina cheese
Garnish: fresh chopped cilantro

1. Preheat oven to broil. Peel shrimp, and devein, if desired; chop, and set aside.

2. Whisk together Beurre Blanc and next 3 ingredients.

3. Sauté shallots and jalapeño in 2 Tbsp. hot oil in a large skillet over medium heat 1 minute. Add shrimp, and cook 1 minute or just until shrimp turn pink. Add diced tomato; sauté 30 seconds. Stir in crabmeat and Beurre Blanc mixture; keep warm.

4. Brush fillets with remaining 2 Tbsp. olive oil; sprinkle with salt and pepper. Place on a broiling rack in a roasting pan.

5. Broil 4 inches from heat 2 minutes on each side or until fish flakes with a fork. Remove to a serving platter. Arrange asparagus and next 3 ingredients around fillets; sprinkle with cheese. Serve with shrimp mixture; garnish, if desired.

Beurre Blanc

makes 2 cups   prep: 5 minutes   cook: 35 minutes

¾ cup dry white vermouth
2 shallots, minced
2 Tbsp. white wine vinegar
¾ cup whipping cream

½ cup butter, cut up
1 Tbsp. fresh lemon juice
½ tsp. salt
⅛ tsp. ground white pepper

1. Bring first 3 ingredients to a boil in a small saucepan; cook 15 minutes or until liquid is reduced to ¼ cup. Stir in cream, and cook 10 minutes or until reduced to ⅓ cup.

2. Reduce heat, and whisk in butter, 1 Tbsp. at a time; cook, whisking constantly, 5 minutes or until sauce thickens. Stir in lemon juice, salt, and pepper.

SEWEE PRESERVE'S SEAFOOD SALAD

makes 8 servings   prep: 20 min.   broil: 10 min.   chill: 1 hr.

Our Food staff decided this tasty recipe was worth the splurge to buy the crabmeat. Reserve the juice from the capers for the vinaigrette.

1 lb. unpeeled cooked medium-large shrimp	½ cup chopped red onion
1 (1-lb.) skinless flounder or grouper fillet	¼ cup finely chopped dill pickle
2 tsp. olive oil	2 Tbsp. drained capers
¼ tsp. salt	Dill Vinaigrette
¼ tsp. pepper	Watercress
1 lb. fresh lump crabmeat, drained and picked	

1. Peel and devein shrimp; set aside.

2. Preheat oven to broil. Place fillet on a lightly greased rack in a broiler pan. Brush fillet with olive oil, and sprinkle evenly with salt and pepper. Broil 5 inches from heat 10 to 13 minutes or until fish flakes with a fork. Remove from pan, and cool.

3. Break cooled fish into large pieces, and place in a large bowl. Add shrimp, crabmeat, and next 3 ingredients; toss gently to combine. Drizzle with Dill Vinaigrette; toss gently to coat.

4. Cover and chill at least 1 hour. Arrange seafood mixture on watercress.

Dill Vinaigrette

makes about ¾ cup   prep: 10 min.

¼ cup red wine vinegar	2 Tbsp. minced dill pickle
¼ cup olive oil	2 tsp. liquid from jarred capers
2 Tbsp. fresh lemon juice	¾ tsp. salt
2 Tbsp. finely chopped sweet onion	¾ tsp. coarsely ground black pepper
2 Tbsp. minced fresh dill	½ tsp. sugar

1. Whisk together all ingredients. Cover and chill

SPICY SKILLET FISH

makes 6 servings prep: 10 min. chill: 30 min. cook: 10 min.

2 garlic cloves

1 (2-inch) piece fresh ginger, peeled and chopped
   (about 2 Tbsp. chopped)

½ cup chopped fresh cilantro

1 small jalapeño pepper, seeded

1 tsp. salt

½ tsp. ground paprika

½ tsp. ground turmeric

½ tsp. ground coriander

2 tsp. vegetable oil

2 lb. catfish, grouper, or flounder fillets
   (about 6 fillets)

2 Tbsp. vegetable oil

Fresh lemon or lime wedges (optional)

1. Process first 9 ingredients in a food processor until finely chopped.

2. Spread 2 tsp. spice mixture over both sides of each fillet. Cover and chill 30 minutes.

3. Cook fish, in batches, in hot vegetable oil in a large nonstick skillet over medium-high heat 5 minutes on each side or until fish flakes with a fork. Serve with fresh lemon or lime wedges, if desired.

PAN-SEARED TROUT WITH ITALIAN-STYLE SALSA

makes 6 servings prep: 5 min. cook: 2 min. per batch

6 (6-oz.) trout fillets

¾ tsp. salt

½ tsp. freshly ground pepper

4 Tbsp. olive oil, divided

Italian-Style Salsa

1. Sprinkle fillets with salt and pepper. Cook 3 fillets in 2 Tbsp. hot oil in a large nonstick skillet over medium high heat 1 to 2 minutes on each side or until fish flakes with a fork. Repeat with remaining fillets and oil. Top with salsa. Serve immediately.

Italian-Style Salsa

makes 2 cups prep: 10 min.

4 plum tomatoes, chopped

½ small red onion, finely chopped

12 kalamata olives, pitted and chopped

2 garlic cloves, minced

2 Tbsp. chopped fresh parsley

1 Tbsp. balsamic vinegar

1 Tbsp. olive oil

2 tsp. drained capers

¼ tsp. salt

¼ tsp. freshly ground pepper

1. Stir together all ingredients in a medium bowl. Cover and chill until ready to serve.

BROILED MAHI-MAHI WITH PARSLEYED TOMATOES

makes 6 servings   prep: 15 min.   cook: 13 min.   broil: 8 min.   pictured on page 330

2 medium onions, sliced	2 garlic cloves, chopped
2 Tbsp. olive oil	½ tsp. salt, divided
2 tomatoes, seeded and chopped	½ tsp. pepper, divided
2 Tbsp. chopped fresh parsley	6 (6- to 8-oz.) mahi-mahi fillets
¼ cup white wine	1 (4-oz.) package crumbled feta cheese
1 Tbsp. tomato paste	Garnish: lemon slices

1. Preheat oven to broil. Sauté sliced onions in hot olive oil over medium-high heat 8 minutes or until tender. Add chopped tomatoes, next 4 ingredients, and ¼ tsp. each of salt and pepper. Simmer, stirring occasionally, 5 minutes. Set onion-and-tomato mixture aside.
2. Place fish in a single layer on a lightly greased rack in an aluminum foil-lined broiler pan; sprinkle with remaining ¼ tsp. each of salt and pepper.
3. Broil 5 inches from heat 8 minutes or until fish flakes with a fork.
4. Spoon onion-and-tomato mixture evenly onto a platter; top with fish fillets. Sprinkle evenly with crumbled feta cheese, and garnish, if desired.

PEPPERED TUNA WITH MUSHROOM SAUCE

makes 6 servings   prep: 15 min.   cook: 20 min.

If you can't find fresh tuna, frozen tuna steaks will work just fine; just be sure to thaw before using. Look for plum sauce on the ethnic food aisle of the supermarket.

3 Tbsp. butter	2 Tbsp. vegetable oil
1 cup sliced fresh mushrooms	6 (6-oz.) tuna steaks (about 1½ inches thick)
¾ cup plum sauce	1 Tbsp. freshly ground multicolored peppercorns
¼ cup lite soy sauce	or 2 tsp. freshly ground black pepper
1 tsp. ground ginger	

1. Melt butter in a large skillet over medium-high heat until lightly browned. Add mushrooms; sauté 4 to 7 minutes or until lightly browned and tender. Stir in plum sauce, soy sauce, and ginger. Bring to a boil, reduce heat, and simmer, stirring often, 3 to 4 minutes. Keep warm.
2. Heat oil in a large nonstick skillet over medium-high heat. Sprinkle tuna evenly with pepper, and cook 4 minutes on each side (rare) or to desired degree of doneness. Serve with warm mushroom sauce.

BAKED SALMON WITH CARIBBEAN FRUIT SALSA

makes 8 servings   prep: 5 min.   chill: 2 hr.   bake: 20 min.

1   (3-lb.) whole skinless salmon fillet
1   Tbsp. Caribbean jerk seasoning*
1½ Tbsp. olive oil

Caribbean Fruit Salsa
Garnish: lime wedges

1. Place salmon fillet in a roasting pan; sprinkle evenly on 1 side with jerk seasoning. Drizzle with oil. Cover and chill 2 hours.

2. Preheat oven to 350°. Bake salmon at 350° for 20 to 25 minutes or until fish flakes with a fork. Serve with Caribbean Fruit Salsa. Garnish, if desired.

* Substitute Jamaican jerk seasoning, if desired. Caribbean jerk seasoning has a hint of sweetness.

Caribbean Fruit Salsa

makes 5 cups   prep: 20 min.   chill: 2 hr.

This salsa's also great as an appetizer served with tortilla chips.

1   mango (about ½ lb.), peeled and diced*
1   papaya (about ½ lb.), peeled and diced*
1   medium-size red bell pepper, diced
1   medium-size green bell pepper, diced
1   cup diced fresh pineapple

1   small red onion, diced
3   Tbsp. chopped fresh cilantro
2   Tbsp. fresh lime juice
1   Tbsp. olive oil

1. Stir together all ingredients. Cover and chill at least 2 hours.

* Substitute 1 cup each diced, refrigerated jarred mango and papaya, if desired.

SHRIMP SALAD

makes about 2½ cups   prep: 20 min.

1   lb. Boiled Shrimp

¼   cup minced celery

2   Tbsp. minced onion

1¼   cups Dipping Sauce for Shrimp

1   head iceberg lettuce, shredded

3   to 4 tomatoes, cut into wedges

Garnish: chopped fresh chives

1. Peel shrimp, and devein, if desired. Coarsely chop shrimp, and place in a bowl.

2. Stir together celery, onion, and Shrimp Sauce. Add shrimp, and toss. Serve over iceberg lettuce with tomato wedges. Garnish, if desired.

Boiled Shrimp

makes 6 to 8 servings   prep: 5 min.   cook: 5 min.   stand: 10 min.

Save 1 lb. of these shrimp to make the salad. Enjoy the rest with Dipping Sauce for Shrimp.

2   (3-oz.) packages boil-in-bag shrimp-and-crab boil

1   large lemon, halved

1   small onion

3   Tbsp. salt

4   lb. unpeeled large raw shrimp

1. Bring 4 qt. water, shrimp-and-crab boil, lemon, onion, and salt to a boil in a large Dutch oven over high heat. Cover and boil 3 to 4 minutes. Add shrimp; remove from heat. Cover and let stand 10 minutes. (Shrimp will turn pink, and shells will loosen slightly.) Drain, discarding lemon, onion, and boil bags.

Note: We tested with Zatarain's Shrimp & Crab Boil.

Dipping Sauce for Shrimp

makes about 2½ cups   prep: 10 min.

2   cups mayonnaise

6   Tbsp. ketchup

4   tsp. yellow mustard

4   tsp. lemon juice

2   tsp. Worcestershire sauce

1   tsp. garlic powder

1. Whisk together all ingredients.

Frozen Cooked Shrimp

We decided to try a few bags of the frozen cooked shrimp that are already peeled and deveined as a substitute for recipes that call for boiled shrimp. Such a convenience product is a great idea for last-minute appetizers or salads, but regardless of the brand we chose or how closely we followed the package directions, the shrimp always tasted slightly rubbery.

Our Test Kitchen solved the problem by putting the frozen shrimp in a large strainer or colander, lowering it into boiling water for 2 to 3 minutes, and then immediately plunging it into a large bowl of ice water to stop the cooking process. Once the shrimp were cold, we simply lifted the strainer, allowing the water to drain back in the bowl. This process afforded the convenience of peeled and deveined frozen cooked shrimp with a texture like fresh. For extra flavor, add your favorite seasoning blend to the water before bringing it to a boil.

CINCO DE MAYO SHRIMP COCKTAIL

makes 6 servings   prep: 35 min.   cook: 5 min.

Jalapeño peppers and lime juice add a twist to this tasty appetizer.

4 plum tomatoes, coarsely chopped	½ tsp. salt (optional)
½ red onion, sliced	¼ tsp. chili powder
¼ cup chopped fresh cilantro	¼ tsp. pepper
1 jalapeño pepper, seeded	30 unpeeled, large raw shrimp
2 garlic cloves	1 large avocado, diced
¼ cup fresh lime juice	Garnish: lime slices
2 tsp. sugar	Lime-flavored tortilla chips

1. Process first 10 ingredients in a blender or food processor until smooth, stopping to scrape down sides. Cover and chill sauce up to 1 week.

2. Bring 6 cups water to a boil; add shrimp, and cook 2 to 3 minutes or just until shrimp turn pink. Drain and rinse with cold water. Chill up to 24 hours, if desired.

3. Peel shrimp, leaving tails on; devein, if desired.

4. Stir avocado into sauce; spoon sauce evenly into 6 chilled martini glasses or small bowls.

5. Arrange 5 shrimp around edge of each glass; garnish, if desired. Serve with lime-flavored tortilla chips.

test kitchen favorite

SOUTHERN SHRIMP COCKTAILS

makes 12 servings   prep: 15 min.

Have the seafood market steam shrimp to save time, or follow our easy instructions below. Serve the shrimp, okra, and breadsticks on a platter around a bowl of the sauce, or make individual cocktails. Use 4-oz. votive candleholders, shot glasses, cordial glasses, or mini-martini glasses.

12 unpeeled, jumbo cooked shrimp

Rémoulade Sauce

12 whole pickled okra

12 very thin crispy breadsticks, broken in half

Garnish: grape tomato slices

1. Peel shrimp, leaving tails on; devein, if desired.

2. Spoon 1 heaping Tbsp. of Rémoulade Sauce evenly into each of 12 individual serving glasses. Place 1 shrimp, 1 whole pickled okra, and 2 breadstick halves in each glass. Garnish, if desired. Serve immediately.

Note: To cook shrimp at home, bring 3 qt. water to a boil in a large Dutch oven. Cut 2 lemons in half, and squeeze juice into boiling water; add squeezed lemon halves to water. Add 1 tsp. pepper, 1 tsp. salt, and 2 bay leaves. Return to a boil over medium-high heat. Add 1 to 2 lb. unpeeled, jumbo raw shrimp, and cook 3 minutes or just until shrimp turn pink; drain. Plunge shrimp into ice water to stop the cooking process; drain. Cover and chill.

Rémoulade Sauce

makes 2 cups   prep: 10 min.   chill: 1 hr.

You can make this sauce three days ahead.

1½ cups mayonnaise

4   green onions, sliced

3   Tbsp. chopped fresh parsley

3   Tbsp. Creole mustard

1½ Tbsp. lemon juice

1   garlic clove, pressed

1½ tsp. horseradish

1   tsp. paprika

1. Stir together all ingredients; cover and chill 1 hour.

inspirations for your taste

SHRIMP SULLIVAN'S ISLAND

makes 18 appetizer servings   prep: 45 min.   cook: 10 min.   chill: 12 hr.

2 lemons, cut in half
5 lb. unpeeled, medium-size raw shrimp
3 medium-size sweet onions, thinly sliced
3 (14-oz.) cans quartered artichoke hearts, drained
2 cups olive oil

1¾ cups cider vinegar
1 (3.5-oz.) jar capers, undrained
¼ cup Worcestershire sauce
1 tsp. salt
½ to 1 tsp. hot sauce
Garnish: chopped fresh parsley

1. Bring 10 qt. water to a boil in a 12-qt. stockpot over medium-high heat; squeeze lemon halves over water, and add squeezed halves to water in stockpot. Add shrimp, and cook 3 minutes or just until shrimp turn pink. Drain and rinse with cold water to stop the cooking process.
2. Peel shrimp; devein, if desired.
3. Layer shrimp, onions, and artichoke hearts in 2 (13- x 9-inch) baking dishes.
4. Stir together olive oil and next 5 ingredients; pour evenly over shrimp mixture. Cover and chill at least 12 hours or up to 48 hours, stirring occasionally. Garnish, if desired, and serve with a slotted spoon.

COLD MARINATED SHRIMP AND AVOCADOS

makes 8 appetizer servings   prep: 20 min.   chill: 1 hr.   **pictured on page 328**

If making this ahead, get all the ingredients (except the avocados) ready to combine; place in individual zip-top plastic freezer bags, and store in the refrigerator. Once you arrive at your destination, peel and chop the avocados; gently stir together up to 2 hours before serving, and chill.

{ make ahead }

1 lb. large peeled cooked shrimp	2 Tbsp. chopped red onion
2 medium avocados, chopped	Lime Vinaigrette
1 cup fresh corn kernels	Garnishes: fresh cilantro leaves, red onion slices
¼ cup chopped fresh cilantro	(optional)

1. Combine first 5 ingredients. Gently stir in Lime Vinaigrette to coat. Cover and chill at least 1 hour. Garnish, if desired.

Lime Vinaigrette

makes about ¾ cup   prep: 5 min.

½ cup fresh lime juice	½ tsp. salt
¼ cup honey	¼ tsp. pepper
1 garlic clove, pressed	⅓ cup olive oil

1. Whisk together first 5 ingredients. Gradually whisk in ⅓ cup olive oil until blended.

CITRUS-MARINATED SHRIMP WITH LOUIS SAUCE

makes 10 to 12 appetizer servings   prep: 35 min.   cook: 5 min.   chill: 25 min.

2 lemons, halved	½ cup fresh lime juice
2 limes, halved	1 lemon, sliced
½ orange, halved	1 orange, sliced
1 Tbsp. dried crushed red pepper	1 lime, sliced
4 lb. unpeeled, large raw shrimp	1 grapefruit, sliced
2 cups fresh orange juice	1 tsp. dried crushed red pepper
2 cups grapefruit juice	Lettuce leaves
2 cups pineapple juice	Louis Sauce
½ cup fresh lemon juice	Garnish: citrus fruit slices (optional)

1. Combine lemon halves, next 3 ingredients, and salted water to cover in a Dutch oven. Bring to a boil; add shrimp, and cook 2 to 3 minutes or just until shrimp turn pink. Plunge shrimp into ice water to stop the cooking process; drain.

2. Peel shrimp, leaving tails on. Devein, if desired.

3. Combine orange juice and next 9 ingredients in a large shallow dish or zip-top plastic freezer bag. Add shrimp, cover or seal, and chill 25 minutes. Drain off liquid. Serve shrimp over lettuce leaves with Louis Sauce. Garnish, if desired.

Louis Sauce

makes 3 cups   prep: 10 min.

This sauce can be prepared a day ahead.

1 (12-oz.) jar chili sauce	1½ tsp. Greek seasoning
2 cups mayonnaise	1½ tsp. Worcestershire sauce
2 Tbsp. grated onion	¼ tsp. ground red pepper
2 Tbsp. lemon zest	½ tsp. hot sauce
3 Tbsp. lemon juice	Garnish: lemon zest
1 Tbsp. prepared horseradish	

1. Stir together all ingredients. Cover and chill until ready to serve. Garnish, if desired.

make ahead

LEMON-BASIL SHRIMP SALAD

makes 8 servings   prep: 20 min.   chill: 8 hr.   **pictured on page 329**

Don't skip the lemon zest and juice in the marinade; that's what makes this recipe extra-special. These shrimp also make a terrific appetizer. Both the shrimp and dressing can all be made a day ahead.

{make ahead}

3 lb. unpeeled, cooked large shrimp	Lemon Marinade
1 large red onion, sliced	½ cup chopped fresh basil
1 red bell pepper, sliced	16 cups salad greens
1 yellow bell pepper, sliced	Fresh Lemon Vinaigrette

1. Peel shrimp, and devein, if desired. Place shrimp and next 4 ingredients in a large zip-top plastic freezer bag. Seal and chill 8 hours or up to 24 hours, turning bag occasionally. Stir in basil 1 hour before serving. Drain and discard marinade just before serving.

2. Divide greens evenly between serving bowls; arrange drained shrimp mixture evenly over lettuce. Serve with Fresh Lemon Vinaigrette.

Lemon Marinade

makes about 2½ cups   prep: 10 min.

1 cup vegetable oil	2 Tbsp. hot sauce
1 cup red wine vinegar	2 Tbsp. Dijon mustard
2 Tbsp. lemon zest	2 garlic cloves, pressed
¼ cup fresh lemon juice	½ tsp. salt
3 Tbsp. sugar	

1. Whisk together all ingredients in a bowl.

Note: To prepare ahead, store in an airtight container in the refrigerator up to 1 week. Bring to room temperature, and whisk before using.

Fresh Lemon Vinaigrette

makes about ¾ cup   prep: 5 min.

¼ cup fresh lemon juice

1 tsp. Dijon mustard

1 large garlic clove, pressed

¼ tsp. salt

¼ tsp. freshly ground black pepper

½ cup vegetable oil

1. Whisk together first 5 ingredients. Gradually add oil in a slow, steady stream, whisking until blended.

Note: To prepare ahead, store in an airtight container in the refrigerator up to 1 week. Bring to room temperature, and whisk before serving.

GALATOIRE'S SHRIMP RÉMOULADE

makes 12 appetizer servings   prep: 15 min.   chill: 6 hr.

This recipe, created by Chef Ross Eirich of Galatoire's in New Orleans, is a favorite starter at the restaurant.

4 celery ribs, coarsely chopped

4 green onions, coarsely chopped

1 small onion, chopped (about ½ cup)

¾ cup flat-leaf parsley

½ cup red wine vinegar

½ cup ketchup

½ cup tomato purée

½ cup Creole mustard

1 Tbsp. prepared horseradish

1 tsp. Worcestershire sauce

1 cup plus 2 Tbsp. vegetable oil

2 tsp. paprika (optional)

2 lb. cooked large raw shrimp, peeled and deveined

Lettuce leaves

1. Pulse first 4 ingredients in a food processor until finely chopped. Add vinegar and next 5 ingredients, and process until well blended and smooth, stopping to scrape down sides. With processor running, pour oil in a slow, steady stream, processing until blended. Stir in paprika, if desired.

2. Cover and chill 6 to 8 hours.

3. Stir chilled sauce; pour over shrimp, gently tossing to coat. Serve on lettuce leaves.

Max's Grille

Этhis perennial local favorite is stylish but casual and welcoming. Roasted red pepper hummus arrives at your table with a basket of breads as you work your way through the menu. Salads are large and lovely, but we chose the full-flavored Crispy-Duck Tacos—a meal in themselves. Pulled duck in a chili-lime barbecue sauce was cradled in crisp taco shells. The filling was salty but the overall combination pleasing. More to our taste was the special—Snapper Français—a very fresh piece of fish perfectly sautéed and served with red potatoes in an arugula broth.

404 Plaza Real, Boca Rotan, Florida 33432
www.maxsgrille.com or (561) 368-0080.

PEANUT SHRIMP SALAD WITH BASIL-LIME DRESSING

makes 4 servings   prep: 20 min.   cook: 6 min. per batch.

test kitchen favorite

3   green onions, white and light green parts only

20 unpeeled, uncooked, raw or frozen
    jumbo shrimp

1   cup Japanese breadcrumbs (panko)

½   cup dry-roasted salted peanuts

1   Tbsp. cornstarch

1   tsp. red curry powder

1   large egg, lightly beaten

2   Tbsp. peanut oil

3   cups mixed baby salad greens

1   cup diced English cucumber

1   cup peeled, diced mango

½   cup mung bean sprouts

¼   cup loosely packed fresh mint leaves

Basil-Lime Dressing

¼   cup dry-roasted salted peanuts, chopped

1. Cut green onions into 2-inch-long thin strips.

2. If frozen, thaw shrimp according to package directions. Peel shrimp; devein, if desired.

3. Pulse breadcrumbs and next 3 ingredients in a food processor 5 times or until mixture resembles fine crumbs. Transfer mixture to a shallow dish or pie plate.

4. Dip shrimp in egg; dredge in breadcrumb mixture.

5. Cook shrimp in hot oil in a large nonstick skillet over medium-high heat 3 minutes on each side or until golden.

6. Gently toss together green onions, salad greens, next 4 ingredients, and 2 Tbsp. Basil-Lime Dressing in a large bowl. Arrange salad on 4 individual plates; top each with 5 shrimp. Sprinkle with ¼ cup peanuts, and drizzle with remaining dressing. Serve immediately.

Basil-Lime Dressing

makes ½ cup   prep: 10 min.

½   cup loosely packed fresh basil leaves

¼   cup fresh lime juice

2   Tbsp. peanut oil

1   Tbsp. fish sauce

1   Tbsp. sugar

1   tsp. Asian garlic-chili sauce

1   tsp. grated fresh ginger

1   garlic clove, minced

1. Process all ingredients in a food processor 20 seconds or until blended.

GREEK SHRIMP PASTA SALAD

makes 4 to 6 servings prep: 20 min. cook: 10 min. chill: 1 hr.

½ (16-oz.) package rotini pasta

¼ cup lemon juice

1 Tbsp. Greek seasoning

3 Tbsp. mayonnaise

½ tsp. minced garlic

¼ tsp. sugar

¼ cup olive oil

½ lb. peeled cooked medium shrimp

1 cup chopped tomatoes (1 large tomato)

¼ cup chopped red onion

1 (2.5-oz.) can sliced ripe black olives, drained

2 Tbsp. chopped parsley

Lettuce leaves (optional)

1. Cook pasta according to package directions. Rinse. Drain well, and set aside.

2. Whisk together lemon juice and next 4 ingredients. Gradually add oil in a slow, steady stream, whisking until blended. Cover and chill until ready to use.

3. Combine cooked pasta, shrimp, and next 4 ingredients in large bowl. Drizzle with vinaigrette, tossing to coat. Cover and chill 1 hour. Serve on lettuce-lined plate, if desired.

SHRIMP AND PASTA WITH CREOLE CREAM SAUCE

makes 4 to 6 servings prep: 10 min. cook: 18 min.

1½ lb. unpeeled, medium-size raw shrimp*

2 tsp. Creole seasoning

12 oz. uncooked penne pasta

2 Tbsp. butter

4 green onions, sliced

2 garlic cloves, minced

1½ cups whipping cream

1 tsp. hot sauce

¼ cup chopped fresh parsley

½ cup (2 oz.) freshly grated Parmesan cheese

1. Peel shrimp, and devein, if desired. Toss shrimp with Creole seasoning; set aside.

2. Prepare pasta according to package directions; drain. Keep warm.

3. Melt butter in a large skillet over medium-high heat; add shrimp, and cook, stirring constantly, 5 minutes or just until shrimp turn pink. Remove shrimp from skillet. Add green onions and garlic to skillet; sauté 2 to 3 minutes or until tender. Reduce heat to medium; stir in cream and hot sauce. Bring to a boil; reduce heat, and simmer, stirring constantly, 8 to 10 minutes or until sauce is slightly thickened. Stir in shrimp and parsley. Toss with pasta. Sprinkle evenly with cheese. Serve immediately.

* 1½ lb. frozen shrimp, thawed, may be substituted.

ASIAN SHRIMP WITH PASTA

makes 6 servings   prep: 25 min.   cook: 8 min.

It may seem like a lot of ingredients, but you'll make this often, so keep these items on hand.

1   lb. unpeeled, medium-size raw shrimp

1   (9-oz.) package refrigerated angel hair pasta

¼   cup lite soy sauce

¼   cup seasoned rice wine vinegar

2   tsp. sesame oil

6   green onions, chopped

1   cup frozen sweet green peas, thawed

¾   cup shredded carrots

1   (8-oz.) can sliced water chestnuts, drained

¼   cup chopped fresh cilantro

2   Tbsp. minced fresh ginger

2   garlic cloves, minced

1   tsp. vegetable oil

2   Tbsp. fresh lime juice

½   tsp. freshly ground pepper

2   Tbsp. chopped unsalted dry-roasted peanuts

1. Peel shrimp, and devein, if desired. Set shrimp aside.

2. Prepare pasta according to package directions, omitting salt and fat. Drain and place in a large bowl or on a platter.

3. Stir together soy sauce, vinegar, and sesame oil. Drizzle over pasta. Add green onions and next 4 ingredients to pasta; toss.

4. Sauté ginger and garlic in hot vegetable oil 1 to 2 minutes. (Do not brown.) Add shrimp, lime juice, and pepper; cook 3 to 5 minutes or just until shrimp turn pink. Add shrimp mixture to pasta mixture, and toss. Sprinkle with nuts. Serve immediately.

Calories 292; Fat 6.2g (sat 0.9g, mono 2.1g, poly 2.3g); Protein 24g; Fiber 4.7g; Chol 146mg; Iron 4.5mg; Sodium 517mg; Calc 81mg

BIG EASY BARBECUE SHRIMP

makes 6 servings   prep: 10 min.   cook: 5 min.   bake: 25 min.

Bay leaves are an integral seasoning in Cajun and Creole cooking. However, when left whole, as in this recipe, discard them before serving the dish.

3	lb. unpeeled, large raw shrimp	2	Tbsp. Old Bay seasoning
¾	cup butter	1	Tbsp. dried Italian seasoning
¼	cup Worcestershire sauce	2	Tbsp. Asian garlic-chili sauce
¼	cup ketchup	2	tsp. hot sauce
3	bay leaves	1	(16-oz.) French baguette, sliced
2	lemons, sliced		

1. Preheat oven to 325°. Spread shrimp in a shallow aluminum foil-lined broiler pan or disposable aluminum roasting pan.

2. Stir together butter and next 8 ingredients in a saucepan over low heat until butter melts; pour mixture over shrimp.

3. Bake at 325° for 25 minutes, stirring and turning shrimp after 10 minutes. Serve with French bread.

Note: We tested with A Taste of Thai Garlic Chili Pepper Sauce, which is found on the international or Asian foods aisle of the supermarket.

TEXAS BEST FRIED SHRIMP

makes 18 servings   prep: 40 min.   fry: 3 min. per batch

Make sure your bread is at least a day or two old before you process it; this will give you perfectly dry breadcrumbs. This recipe feeds a small army, so feel free to halve it and the sauces.

1	(16-oz.) loaf day-old very thin white bread slices	1	large egg
		2	cups all-purpose flour
5	lb. frozen shrimp, thawed		Canola oil
2	cups half-and-half		Red Sauce
¾	cup sugar		Tartar Sauce

1. Process day-old bread slices, in batches, in a food processor or blender until medium-fine crumbs. Set aside.

2. Peel shrimp, leaving tails on. Butterfly shrimp by making a deep slit lengthwise down the back from the large end to the tail, cutting to, but not through, the inside curve of shrimp. Remove vein. Pat shrimp dry with paper towels; set aside.

3. Whisk together half-and-half, sugar, and egg until sugar dissolves.

4. Dredge shrimp in flour; shake off excess, and dip in egg mixture. Coat with breadcrumbs, and arrange on baking sheets.

5. Pour oil to a depth of 3 inches into a Dutch oven; heat to 300°. Fry shrimp, in batches, 3 minutes; drain on wire racks over paper towels. Serve with Red Sauce and Tartar Sauce.

Red Sauce

makes about 4 cups   prep: 10 min.

2 cups chili sauce	3 Tbsp. fresh lemon juice
2 cups ketchup	3 Tbsp. grated fresh horseradish*

1. Whisk together all ingredients; chill, if desired.

* 3 Tbsp. prepared horseradish may be substituted.

Tartar Sauce

makes about 6 cups   prep: 10 min.

4 cups mayonnaise	2 Tbsp. dried parsley flakes
1½ cups finely chopped onion	¾ tsp. hot sauce
¾ cup sweet pickle relish	1 tsp. Worcestershire sauce
⅓ cup plus 1 Tbsp. fresh lemon juice	

1. Whisk together all ingredients; chill until ready to serve.

CITRUS SHRIMP TACOS

makes 6 to 8 servings   prep: 25 min.   chill: 10 min.   grill: 6 min.

Soak wooden skewers in water at least 30 minutes before grilling to keep them from burning.

2   lb. unpeeled, large raw shrimp
20   (12-inch-long) skewers
2   Tbsp. Southwest seasoning
3   garlic cloves, minced
⅓   cup lime juice
3   Tbsp. lemon juice

16   (8-inch) soft taco-size flour tortillas, warmed
1   head iceberg lettuce, finely shredded
1   head radicchio, finely shredded
Southwest Cream Sauce
Grilled Corn Salsa
Garnish: fresh cilantro leaves

1. Peel shrimp; devein, if desired. Thread shrimp onto skewers.

2. Coat cold cooking grate of grill with cooking spray, and place on grill. Preheat grill to 350° to 400° (medium-high) heat. Combine Southwest seasoning and garlic in a long shallow dish; add lime juice, lemon juice, and shrimp, turning to coat. Cover and chill 10 minutes. Remove shrimp from marinade, discarding marinade.

3. Grill shrimp, 2 to 3 minutes on each side or just until shrimp turn pink. Remove shrimp from skewers. Serve in warm tortillas with next 4 ingredients. Garnish, if desired.

Note: We tested with Emeril's Southwest Seasoning.

Southwest Cream Sauce

makes about 2 cups   prep: 10 min.

1   (16-oz.) container sour cream
1   garlic clove, minced
2   Tbsp. finely chopped red onion
1   tsp. chili powder
½   tsp. ground cumin

½   tsp. ground red pepper
¼   tsp. salt
2   Tbsp. chopped fresh cilantro
2   Tbsp. fresh lime juice

1. Whisk together first 7 ingredients. Whisk in cilantro and lime juice until smooth. Cover and chill until ready to serve.

Grilled Corn Salsa

makes about 6 cups   prep: 25 min.   grill: 15 min.   cool: 15 min.   stand: 30 min.

3 ears fresh corn, husks removed

Cooking spray

1 tsp. salt

½ tsp. pepper

3 medium tomatoes, seeded and chopped

2 jalapeño peppers, seeded and minced

2 (15-oz.) cans black beans, rinsed and drained

¾ cup chopped fresh cilantro

⅓ cup fresh lime juice

2 Tbsp. chopped fresh mint

2 avocados

1. Preheat grill to 350° to 400° (medium-high) heat. Lightly coat corn cobs with cooking spray. Sprinkle with salt and pepper.

2. Grill corn, covered with grill lid, 15 to 20 minutes or until golden brown, turning every 5 minutes. Remove from grill; cool 15 minutes.

3. Hold each grilled cob upright on a cutting board; carefully cut downward, cutting kernels from cob. Discard cobs; place kernels in a large bowl. Gently stir in tomatoes and next 5 ingredients. Cover and chill until ready to serve, if desired.

4. If chilled, let corn mixture stand at room temperature 30 minutes. Peel and chop avocados; toss with corn mixture just before serving.

Seafood Savvy

It's easy to buy the right seafood if you know what to look for. Follow these guidelines for picking it fresh.

• Purchase seafood from a reputable market or grocery store. Observe how it is stored: Seafood is best packed on ice.

• Choose shrimp that are slightly firm in texture, avoiding those that are soft and limp. Make sure the shells are tightly attached. Watch out for any dark spots, which probably mean that the shrimp are past their peak.

• Buy shrimp one day before you plan to serve it. This will give you time to peel and, if desired, devein the shrimp in advance.

• Avoid crab and shrimp that smell fishy. Fresh seafood should not have a strong odor.

CROOK'S CORNER SHRIMP AND GRITS

makes 4 servings   prep: 30 min.   cook: 40 min.

The late Bill Neal has influenced young chefs across the South, and diners still enjoy his inspired recipes at this landmark restaurant in Chapel Hill. Executive chef Bill Smith has added some creative touches to the menu, but Shrimp and Grits is still a Crook's Corner Classic.

[*test kitchen favorite*]

1   (14-oz.) can chicken broth
¾   cup half-and-half
¾   tsp. salt
1   cup uncooked regular grits
¾   cup shredded Cheddar cheese
¼   cup grated Parmesan cheese
2   Tbsp. butter
½   tsp. hot sauce
¼   tsp. white pepper
3   bacon slices
1   lb. medium-size raw shrimp, peeled and deveined

¼   tsp. black pepper
⅛   tsp. salt
¼   cup all-purpose flour
1   cup sliced mushrooms
½   cup chopped green onions
2   garlic cloves, minced
½   cup low-sodium fat-free chicken broth
2   Tbsp. fresh lemon juice
¼   tsp. hot sauce
Lemon wedges

1. Bring 2 cups water, broth, half-and-half, and salt to a boil in a medium saucepan; gradually whisk in grits. Reduce heat, and simmer, stirring occasionally, 10 minutes or until thickened. Add Cheddar cheese and next 4 ingredients. Keep warm.

2. Cook bacon in a large skillet until crisp; remove bacon, and drain on paper towels, reserving 1 Tbsp. drippings in skillet. Crumble bacon, and set aside.

3. Sprinkle shrimp with pepper and salt; dredge in flour.

4. Sauté mushrooms in hot drippings in skillet 5 minutes or until tender. Add green onions, and sauté 2 minutes. Add shrimp and garlic, and sauté 2 minutes or until shrimp are lightly brown. Stir in chicken broth, lemon juice, and hot sauce, and cook 2 more minutes, stirring to loosen particles from bottom of skillet.

5. Serve shrimp mixture over hot cheese grits. Top with crumbled bacon, and serve with lemon wedges.

SHRIMP AND ANDOUILLE SAUSAGE WITH ASIAGO GRITS

makes 6 servings   prep: 25 min.   cook: 19 min.   **pictured on page 330**

1½ lb. unpeeled, medium-size raw shrimp

1   Tbsp. butter

½   lb. andouille sausage, diced

¾   cup whipping cream

⅓   cup chicken broth

⅓   cup dry white wine

½   cup freshly grated Asiago or Parmesan cheese

¼   tsp. ground white pepper

Asiago Grits

Garnish: chopped fresh chives

1. Peel shrimp; devein, if desired.

2. Melt butter in a large skillet over medium-high heat; add sausage; cook, stirring constantly, 5 minutes or until lightly browned. Add shrimp, and cook, stirring constantly, 3 to 5 minutes or just until shrimp turn pink. Remove shrimp and sausage mixture from skillet.

3. Add cream, broth, and wine to skillet; cook over medium heat, stirring constantly, 5 minutes or until slightly thickened. Stir in cheese and pepper; cook, stirring constantly, 6 to 8 minutes or until cheese is melted. Stir in shrimp and sausage mixture. Serve over Asiago Grits. Garnish, if desired.

Asiago Grits

makes 6 servings   prep: 5 min.   cook: 20 min.

2   (14-oz.) cans chicken broth

¾   cup uncooked quick-cooking grits

½   (8-oz.) container chive-and-onion cream cheese

½   cup freshly grated Asiago or Parmesan cheese

¼   tsp. ground white pepper

1. Bring chicken broth to a boil in a medium saucepan over medium-high heat; gradually whisk in grits. Cover, reduce heat to medium-low, and simmer, stirring occasionally, 12 to 15 minutes or until thickened. Add cheeses and pepper, stirring until melted.

Lowcountry Supper serves 12

Frogmore Stew
Crusty French bread
Rum Banana Pudding (page 316)

FROGMORE STEW

makes 12 servings   prep: 10 min.   cook: 30 min.

¼ cup Old Bay seasoning

4 lb. small red potatoes

2 lb. kielbasa or hot smoked link sausage,
   cut into 1½-inch pieces

6 ears fresh corn, halved

4 lb. unpeeled, large raw shrimp

Old Bay seasoning (optional)

Cocktail sauce

1. Bring 5 qt. water and ¼ cup Old Bay seasoning to a rolling boil in a large covered stockpot.
2. Add potatoes; return to a boil, and cook, uncovered, 10 minutes.
3. Add sausage and corn, and return to a boil. Cook 10 minutes or until potatoes are tender.
4. Add shrimp to stockpot; cook 3 to 4 minutes or until shrimp turn pink. Drain. If desired, serve with Old Bay seasoning and cocktail sauce.

SCALLOPS IN ORANGE-BUTTER SAUCE

makes 4 servings   prep: 10 min.   cook: 22 min.

For a golden crust, pat scallops dry before searing, and cook in a very hot skillet.

1 (16-oz.) package vermicelli

5 Tbsp. butter, softened and divided

12 large sea scallops (about 1½ lb.)

½ tsp. kosher salt

¼ tsp. pepper

1 Tbsp. olive oil

6 Tbsp. fresh orange juice

6 Tbsp. dry white wine

½ tsp. orange zest

Garnish: shredded fresh basil

1. Cook vermicelli according to package directions; drain, toss with 2 Tbsp. butter, and keep warm.
2. Rinse scallops, and pat dry with paper towels; sprinkle with kosher salt and pepper.

3. Melt 1 Tbsp. butter with 1½ tsp. olive oil in a large skillet over medium-high heat; add 6 scallops, and cook 2 to 3 minutes on each side or until golden. Remove from skillet, cover loosely with aluminum foil, and keep warm. Repeat procedure with 1 Tbsp. butter and remaining 1½ tsp. oil and 6 scallops.

4. Combine orange juice and wine in a small saucepan; cook over medium-high heat 10 minutes or until mixture is reduced by half. Remove from heat; stir in orange zest and remaining 1 Tbsp. butter. Divide vermicelli among 4 plates; top with scallops and sauce. Garnish, if desired.

FRIED BACON-WRAPPED OYSTERS

makes 6 to 8 servings   prep: 30 min.   cook: 2½ min. per batch

1   cup all-purpose flour

1   tsp. salt

1   tsp. pepper

2   pt. fresh oysters (about 46), rinsed and drained

23   bacon slices, cut in half

Peanut oil

[test kitchen favorite]

1. Combine first 3 ingredients in a shallow dish. Dredge oysters in flour mixture. Wrap each oyster with a bacon piece, and secure with a wooden pick. Pour peanut oil to a depth of 1 inch in a deep cast-iron skillet or Dutch oven; heat to 350°.

2. Fry oysters, in batches, 2½ to 3 minutes or until bacon is cooked. Drain on paper towels. Serve immediately.

But Are Oysters Safe?

Cooked oysters are generally safe to eat. Raw oysters, though, can harbor a variety of ills, among them Norwalk virus, which causes stomach upset and hepatitis (though such occurrences are extremely rare). A naturally occurring bacteria, *Vibrio vulnificus*, has caused serious illness and death in a number of people.

The seafood industry has come up with different ways to treat raw oysters to kill the bacteria called post-harvest processing or PHP. Oysters can be frozen, treated with hydrostatic pressure, or pasteurized. Oysters treated this way are designated virtually bacteria-free by the FDA. If you are concerned about eating raw ones, ask your seafood market to order post-harvest processed oysters. In a restaurant, ask if the oysters have been post-harvest processed. If not, order cooked oysters instead.

SOUTHWEST FRIED OYSTERS

makes 4 to 6 servings   prep: 20 min.   chill: 2 hr.   fry: 3 min. per batch   **pictured on page 333**

Selects are fairly large shucked oysters—the perfect size for frying.

2   pt. fresh Select oysters, drained
2   cups buttermilk
1   cup all-purpose flour
½   cup yellow cornmeal
1   Tbsp. paprika
1½ tsp. garlic powder
1½ tsp. dried oregano
1½ tsp. ground red pepper
½   tsp. dry mustard

½   tsp. salt
½   tsp. ground black pepper
Vegetable oil
½   cup melted butter
½   cup hot sauce
2   Tbsp. fresh lemon juice
Ranch dressing
Celery sticks

1. Combine oysters and buttermilk in a large shallow dish or zip-top plastic freezer bag. Cover or seal, and chill at least 2 hours. Drain oysters well.

2. Combine flour and next 8 ingredients. Dredge oysters in flour mixture, shaking off excess.

3. Pour oil to a depth of 1 inch in a Dutch oven; heat to 370°.

4. Fry oysters, in batches, 3 minutes or until golden. Drain on paper towels.

5. Stir together melted butter, hot sauce, and lemon juice. Pour butter mixture evenly over hot fried oysters. Serve oysters with Ranch dressing and celery sticks.

Fried Buffalo Oysters: Prepare Southwest Fried Oysters as directed, omitting the chili powder. Stir together ½ cup melted butter, ½ cup hot sauce, and 2 Tbsp. fresh lemon juice. Pour butter mixture evenly over hot fried oysters. Serve oysters with Ranch dressing and celery sticks.

Pimiento Cheese-Stuffed
Burgers, page 446

Tabb's Barbecue Pork,
page 464

Big "D" Smoked Baby Back Ribs,
page 460

Grilled Lamb Chops With
Lemon-Tarragon Aïoli and
Orange Gremolata,
page 470

Grilled Peaches Jezebel,
page 482

Potato-Stuffed
Grilled Bell Peppers,
page 481

Grilled Romaine Salad With Buttermilk-Chive Dressing, page 476

Beef Tenderloin With Five-Onion Sauce, page 487

Grilled Rib-eye Steaks, page 454

Aunt Mary's Pot Roast, page 507

414

Grilled Steaks Balsamico,
page 505

Beef-and-Sausage Meatloaf With Chunky
Red Sauce on Cheese Toast, page 516

Skillet Pepper Steak amd Rice, page 508

417

Osso Bucco, page 523

Crown Pork Roast,
page 533

Ham Steak With Orange Glaze, page 543

Italian Meatballs, page 521

GRILLED OYSTERS WITH PAUL'S COCKTAIL SAUCE

makes 2 dozen oysters   prep: 5 min.   grill: 20 min.

2   dozen fresh oysters (in the shell)   Paul's Cocktail Sauce

1. Preheat grill to 300° to 350° (medium) heat. Grill oysters, covered with grill lid, 20 minutes or until oysters open. Serve with Paul's Cocktail Sauce.

Paul's Cocktail Sauce

makes 1½ cups   prep: 10 min.   chill: 30 min.

1   (12-oz.) jar chili sauce   2   tsp. Worcestershire sauce
½   cup cider or white vinegar   1   tsp. lemon juice
2   tsp. pepper

1. Stir together all ingredients. Cover and chill 30 minutes.

SCALLOPED OYSTERS

makes 8 servings   prep: 15 min.   chill: 8 hr.   stand: 30 min.   bake: 30 min.

1   qt. fresh oysters, undrained   1   cup butter, melted
2½ sleeves rectangle buttery crackers   1½ cups half-and-half
    (about 66 crackers), crushed   1   tsp. Worcestershire sauce
1   tsp. salt   ½   tsp. freshly ground pepper

1. Drain oysters, reserving ½ cup oyster liquor (liquid from oyster container).
2. Place cracker crumbs in a large bowl; sprinkle evenly with salt. Drizzle butter over crumbs, tossing to combine.
3. Whisk together ½ cup reserved oyster liquor, half-and-half, and Worcestershire sauce.
4. Place one-third crumb mixture evenly in the bottom of a 2-qt. baking dish; top with half of oysters. Sprinkle with ¼ tsp. pepper. Pour half of cream mixture evenly over oysters. Repeat layers, ending with crumb mixture.
5. Cover and chill at least 8 hours.
6. Preheat oven to 350°. Let stand at room temperature 30 minutes before baking. Bake at 350° for 30 minutes or until bubbly.

Note: We tested with Keebler Club Original crackers.

Oysters Rockefeller
There is much ado over the original recipe for Oysters Rockefeller. We do know that it was invented by Jules Alciatore, the second-generation proprietor of Antoine's restaurant in New Orleans. We don't know, however, what exactly went into the original dish—just that there was a wealth of bright green herbs and it was rich, like John D. Rockefeller himself.

In restaurants today, we find a host of impostors, such as oysters masked in Parmesan cheese, parading around with pale artichoke hearts, or cavorting with anchovy paste.

These variations, although often delicious, are not the true taste of Oysters Rockefeller. A true Rockefeller is bold and strong with freshly blended ingredients including parsley, celery leaf, and fennel bulb. The addition of anise-flavored liqueur such as Pernod only enhances the green herbaceous flavor.

Over the years, there has also been the spinach versus watercress debate for this dish. We prefer, when in season, the edgy bite of crisp watercress. But if you favor spinach and no celery leaves or tarragon and no chervil, trust your taste buds and use what you like. When making these baked bivalves, it is most important to choose the freshest oysters and the freshest herbs available.

Our version of Oysters Rockefeller, adapted from a wealth of provocative recipes, rated very highly in our Test Kitchen. It seems that this classic Southern taste, which has incited such debate, must be worth trying at least once.

OYSTERS ROCKEFELLER

makes 4 to 6 servings   prep: 45 min.   cook: 21 min.   **pictured on page 332**

A true Rockefeller recipe is bold and strong with freshly blended ingredients.

1   cup unsalted butter, divided
½   cup chopped flat-leaf parsley
¼   cup chopped green onions
¼   cup fennel bulb, chopped
1   tsp. chopped fresh chervil or tarragon
2   to 3 chopped celery leaves
2   cups watercress or baby spinach leaves
⅓   cup fine, dry breadcrumbs

2   Tbsp. anise-flavored liqueur
¼   tsp. salt
¼   tsp. pepper
⅛   to ¼ tsp. hot sauce
½   (4-lb.) box rock salt
2   dozen fresh oysters on the half shell
Rock salt
Garnish: lemon wedges

1. Preheat oven to 450°. Melt 3 Tbsp. butter in a skillet over medium-high heat; add parsley and next 4 ingredients. Sauté 2 to 3 minutes. Add watercress, and cook 2 to 3 minutes or until wilted. Cool.

2. Pulse parsley mixture in a food processor with the remaining 13 Tbsp. butter, breadcrumbs, and liqueur until smooth, stopping to scrape down sides.

3. Add salt, pepper, and hot sauce.

4. Fill pie pans or a large baking sheet with 2 lb. rock salt. Dampen salt slightly, and arrange oysters on the beds of salt.

5. Top each oyster with a spoonful of the parsley mixture.

6. Bake at 450° about 12 to 15 minutes or until lightly browned and bubbly. Serve on a bed of rock salt, and garnish, if desired.

Note: We tested with Pernod for anise liqueur.

TOPLESS OYSTERS

makes 4 to 6 servings   prep: 55 min.

Your guests have a choice of three sauces to spoon onto the oysters.

2   fresh kumquats

¼   cup fresh lime juice

1   tsp. grated fresh ginger

¼   cup rice vinegar

1½ tsp. lite soy sauce

1   shallot, minced

2   dozen fresh oysters (in the shell)

Fresh Tomato Salsa

Lemon wedges

1. Bring 2½ cups water to a boil in a small saucepan. Reduce heat, and add kumquats; simmer 1 minute or until tender. Drain; let cool. Remove seeds, and cut kumquats into thin slices.

2. Combine kumquats, lime juice, and ginger, tossing gently to coat. Set aside.

3. Stir together vinegar, soy sauce, and shallot.

4. Scrub oyster shells, and open, discarding tops. Arrange shell bottoms (containing oysters) over crushed ice on a serving platter. Serve with kumquat sauce, vinegar sauce, Fresh Tomato Salsa, and lemon wedges.

Fresh Tomato Salsa

makes 1½ cups   prep: 5 min.

3   plum tomatoes, peeled, seeded, and diced

2   Tbsp. chopped fresh cilantro

1   Tbsp. minced onion

1   to 2 tsp. minced jalapeño pepper

1   tsp. fresh lime juice

⅛   tsp. salt

1. Combine all ingredients in a small bowl.

CRAB, AVOCADO, AND TOMATO MARTINI

makes 6 servings prep: 15 min.

[quick]

¼ cup rémoulade sauce
¼ cup cocktail sauce
2 Tbsp. gin
½ tsp. lemon pepper
½ garlic clove, chopped
¼ tsp. salt
1 medium avocado, peeled and chopped
   into ½-inch cubes

1 medium tomato, peeled, seeded, and chopped
   into ½-inch cubes
1 lb. fresh lump crabmeat, drained and picked
12 pimiento-stuffed Spanish olives or cocktail
   onions

1. Process first 6 ingredients in a food processor or blender 15 seconds or until blended. Remove and reserve 3 Tbsp. rémoulade sauce mixture. Stir together remaining rémoulade sauce mixture, avocado, and tomato in a medium bowl.

2. Place half of crabmeat in 6 martini glasses. Top evenly with avocado mixture and remaining half of crabmeat. Drizzle each evenly with reserved 3 Tbsp. rémoulade sauce mixture (about 1½ tsp. each). Spear 2 stuffed olives onto a wooden pick, and place in a glass; repeat with remaining stuffed olives. Serve immediately.

WEST INDIES SALAD

makes 3½ cups prep: 15 min. chill: 8 hr.

This recipe is worth the splurge. Saltiness varies with crabmeat and other seafood, so adjust the amount of salt to suit your taste.

[make ahead]

1 lb. lump crabmeat, picked
1 medium-size sweet onion, diced
½ cup vegetable oil
⅓ cup cider vinegar
½ cup ice cubes

¾ tsp. salt
½ tsp. pepper
Assorted crackers
Garnish: fresh chopped parsley

1. Toss together first 7 ingredients gently. Cover and chill at least 8 hours or up to 48 hours. Serve with assorted crackers, and garnish, if desired.

MARYLAND CRAB CAKES WITH CREAMY CAPER-DILL SAUCE

makes 14 cakes   prep: 30 min.   cook: 30 min.   chill: 1 hr.   **pictured on page 333**

2   lb. fresh lump crabmeat*

½   cup minced green onion

½   cup minced red bell pepper

1   Tbsp. olive oil

½   cup Italian-seasoned breadcrumbs

1   large egg, lightly beaten

½   cup mayonnaise

1   Tbsp. fresh lemon juice

1½ tsp. Old Bay seasoning

½   tsp. pepper

Dash of Worcestershire sauce

2   Tbsp. butter

Lemon wedges

Creamy Caper-Dill Sauce

Garnish: fresh dill sprigs (optional)

1. Rinse, drain, and flake crabmeat, being careful not to break up lumps, and remove any bits of shell. Set crabmeat aside.

2. Sauté green onion and bell pepper in hot olive oil in a large nonstick skillet 8 minutes or until tender.

3. Stir together green onion mixture, breadcrumbs, egg, and next 5 ingredients. Gently fold in crabmeat. Shape mixture into 14 (2½-inch) cakes (about ⅓ cup for each cake). Place on an aluminum foil-lined baking sheet; cover and chill at least 1 hour or up to 8 hours.

4. Melt butter in a large nonstick skillet over medium heat. Add crab cakes, and cook, in 2 batches, 4 to 5 minutes on each side or until golden. Drain on paper towels. Serve with a squeeze of lemon and Creamy Caper-Dill Sauce. Garnish, if desired.

* Regular crabmeat may be substituted for lump.

Creamy Caper-Dill Sauce

makes 1¼ cups   prep: 10 min.

¾   cup mayonnaise

½   cup sour cream

¼   tsp. lemon zest

2   Tbsp. fresh lemon juice

1   Tbsp. drained capers

2   tsp. chopped fresh dill

1   tsp. Dijon mustard

¼   tsp. salt

¼   tsp. pepper

1. Stir together all ingredients. Cover and chill up to 3 days.

CRAB CAKES WITH SWEET WHITE CORN-AND-TOMATO RELISH

makes 8 servings   prep: 20 min.   cook: 6 min. per batch

6 Tbsp. butter, divided	1 Tbsp. Dijon mustard
1 small sweet onion, chopped	1 Tbsp. Worcestershire sauce
2 garlic cloves, minced	¼ tsp. salt
1 lb. fresh lump crabmeat, drained and picked	¼ tsp. pepper
3 cups soft breadcrumbs, divided	¼ tsp. hot sauce
¼ cup mayonnaise	1 tsp. lemon juice
1 large egg, lightly beaten	Sweet White Corn-and-Tomato Relish
2 Tbsp. chopped fresh parsley	

1. Melt 2 Tbsp. butter in a large skillet over medium heat; add onion and garlic, and sauté until tender. Remove from heat; stir in crabmeat, 2 cups breadcrumbs, and next 9 ingredients.

2. Shape mixture into 8 patties; dredge in remaining 1 cup breadcrumbs.

3. Melt 2 Tbsp. butter in a large skillet over medium-high heat; cook 4 crab cakes 3 to 4 minutes on each side or until golden. Drain on paper towels. Repeat procedure with remaining 2 Tbsp. butter and crab cakes. Serve with Sweet White Corn-and-Tomato Relish immediately, or cover and chill up to 4 hours.

Sweet White Corn-and-Tomato Relish

makes 3 cups   prep: 15 min.   cook: 1 min.   chill: 3 hr.

4 ears fresh sweet white corn	½ tsp. salt
2 large tomatoes, peeled and chopped	½ tsp. pepper
3 green onions, sliced	¼ tsp. garlic salt
2 Tbsp. lemon juice	⅛ tsp. hot sauce
1 Tbsp. olive oil	

1. Cook corn in boiling water to cover 1 minute; drain and cool. Cut kernels from cobs.

2. Stir together corn, tomato, and remaining ingredients; cover and chill 3 hours.

Note: We tested with Silver Queen for sweet white corn.

CRAB-AND-SCALLOP CAKES

makes 8 servings   prep: 30 min.   chill: 2 hr.   cook: 6 min.

This make-ahead dish is great for a party. The day before, mix and shape the cakes, and make the sauces. Sauté the cakes one hour before the party; cover and keep warm in a 200° oven.

[make ahead]

1	lb. bay scallops, drained	3	medium tomatoes, peeled, seeded, and diced
⅓	cup whipping cream	2	lb. fresh lump crabmeat, drained and picked
1	large egg	2	Tbsp. butter
1	tsp. Old Bay seasoning		Red Pepper Sauce
½	tsp. salt		Yellow Pepper Sauce
¼	tsp. pepper		Garnishes: parsley sprigs, lemon wedges (optional)
6	green onions, thinly sliced		

1. Process scallops in a food processor until chopped. Add cream and next 4 ingredients; process until combined, stopping to scrape down sides.

2. Combine scallop mixture, onions, and tomato; gently fold in crabmeat. Cover and chill at least 2 hours.

3. Shape mixture into 8 patties (about ⅓ cup each).

4. Melt butter in a large skillet over medium-high heat; add cakes, and cook, in batches, 3 to 4 minutes on each side or until golden. Serve with Red Pepper Sauce and Yellow Pepper Sauce; garnish, if desired.

Red Pepper Sauce

makes 1 cup   prep: 10 min.   cook: 30 min.

2	large red bell peppers, coarsely chopped	¼	teaspoon salt
1	cup whipping cream		

1. Combine all ingredients in a saucepan over medium heat; cover and simmer 30 minutes.

2. Process mixture in a blender or food processor until smooth. Pour puree through a wire-mesh strainer into a bowl. Serve warm.

Yellow Pepper Sauce: Substitute 2 large yellow bell peppers for red bell peppers.

STEAMED BLUE CRABS

makes 1 dozen prep: 10 min.   cook: 35 min.

¼ cup plus 2 Tbsp. Old Bay seasoning

¼ cup plus 2 Tbsp. coarse salt

3 Tbsp. coarse salt

3 Tbsp. pickling spice

2 Tbsp. celery seeds

1 Tbsp. dried crushed red pepper (optional)

White vinegar

12 live hard-shell blue crabs

Lemon butter

1. Combine first 5 ingredients, and, if desired, crushed red pepper; set aside.

2. Combine water and vinegar in equal amounts to a depth of 1 inch in a very large pot with a lid; bring to a boil. Place a rack in pot over boiling liqud; arrange half of crabs on rack. Sprinkle with half of seasoning miture. Top with remaining crabs, and sprinkle with remaining seasoning mixture.

3. Cover tightly, and steam 20 to 25 minutes or until crabs turn bright red. Rinse with cold water, and drain well. Serve crabs hot or cold with Lemon Butter.

Lemon Butter

makes 1¼ cups prep: 4 min.

1 cup butter

½ cup lemon juice

1. Melt butter over low heat; fat will rise to the top, and milk solids will sink to the bottom. Skim off white froth that appears on top. Then strain off the clear, yellow butter, keeping back the sediment of milk solids. Add lemon juice, stirring well. Chill until ready to serve; then reheat.

FRIED SOFT-SHELL CRABS

makes 1 dozen   prep: 40 min.   stand: 15 min.   cook: 20 min.

When crabs are in their molting state, they shed their hard outer shell, leaving a soft shell, which is entirely edible.

12 fresh soft-shell crabs

3 large eggs

½ tsp. ground black pepper

1½ cups yellow cornmeal

1 cup all-purpose flour

2 tsp. baking powder

1 tsp. salt

½ tsp. ground black pepper

½ tsp. garlic powder

⅛ tsp. ground red pepper

Vegetable oil

1. To clean crabs, remove spongy gills that lie under the tapering poings on either side of back shell. Place crabs on back, and remove the small piece at lower part of shell that terminates in a point (the apron). Wash crabs thoroughly; drain well.

2. Combine eggs and ½ tsp. black pepper in a large shallow dish. Add crabs, turning to coat. Let stand 10 minutes.

3. Combine cornmeal and next 6 ingredients. Remove crabs from egg mixture, and dredge in cornmeal mixture. Let stand 5 minutes., dredge in cornmeal mixture again.

4. Pour oil to a depth of ½ inch into a large heavy skillet or an electric skillet; heat oil to 375°. Fry crabs 2 minutes on each side or until browned. Drain; serve immediately.

Crawfish Eatin' 101

For those unfamiliar with the "art" of eating crawfish, here is a quick primer on dealing with these delicious little crustaceans.

1. Begin by snapping apart the head and the tail.

2. If you're not a big fan of the crawfish head, you can toss the head aside, and then peel the tail by working your thumbs down the sides of the hard shell to release the sweet meat.

3. For the true crawfish lover, the renowned sucking of the head gives full access to the fiery concoction of spices and fat.

CRAWFISH BOIL

makes 5 lb.   prep: 1 hr.   cook: 55 min.   stand: 30 min.

The longer you allow the cooked crawfish to soak, the more flavorful and spicy they become.

10	bay leaves	1	Tbsp. dried crushed red pepper
1	cup salt	1	Tbsp. black peppercorns
¾	cup ground red pepper	1	tsp. whole cloves
¼	cup whole allspice	4	celery ribs, quartered
2	Tbsp. mustard seeds	3	medium onions, halved
1	Tbsp. coriander seeds	3	garlic bulbs, halved crosswise
1	Tbsp. dill seeds	5	lb. crawfish

1. Bring 1½ gal. water to a boil in a 19-qt. stockpot over high heat. Add bay leaves and next 12 ingredients to water. Return to a rolling boil.

2. Reduce heat to medium, and cook, uncovered, 30 minutes.

3. Add crawfish. Bring to a rolling boil over high heat; cook 5 minutes.

4. Remove stockpot from heat; let stand 30 minutes. (For spicier crawfish, let stand 45 minutes.)

5. Drain crawfish. Serve on large platters or newspaper.

casual gatherings

CRAWFISH JAMBALAYA

makes 4 to 6 servings prep: 15 min. cook: 55 min.

1 cup uncooked long-grain rice	1 (14.5-oz.) can stewed tomatoes, undrained
2 cups chicken broth	1 tsp. Cajun seasoning
¼ cup butter	1 lb. frozen crawfish tails, thawed, rinsed, and
1 medium onion, chopped	drained
½ cup chopped green bell pepper	1 cup chopped green onions
½ cup chopped celery	⅛ tsp. pepper
4 garlic cloves, minced	Garnish: chopped green onions

1. Cook rice according to package directions, substituting 2 cups chicken broth for water; set aside.

2. Melt butter in a Dutch oven over medium-high heat; sauté onion, bell pepper, and celery 8 minutes or until vegetables are tender. Add garlic; sauté 1 minute.

3. Stir in stewed tomatoes and Cajun seasoning; reduce heat to low, and simmer, uncovered, 15 to 20 minutes. Add crawfish tails, and cook 5 minutes. Stir in 1 cup chopped green onions, cooked rice, and pepper. Garnish, if desired.

TRADITIONAL CRAWFISH ÉTOUFFÉE

makes 6 servings prep: 25 min. cook: 50 min.

Tradition, in this case, means you stir up a rich buttery roux as the base for this classic.

1 cup uncooked long-grain rice	6 Tbsp. all-purpose flour
10 Tbsp. butter, divided	2¾ cups chicken broth
1 lb. frozen cooked peeled crawfish tails,	¼ cup chopped green onions
thawed and drained	2 Tbsp. chopped fresh parsley
1 medium onion, chopped	1 Tbsp. salt-free Cajun seasoning
1 green bell pepper, chopped	¼ tsp. salt
3 celery ribs, chopped	¼ tsp. ground red pepper
4 garlic cloves, minced	

1. Prepare rice according to package directions.

2. Melt 4 Tbsp. butter in a large Dutch oven over medium-high heat; add crawfish, and cook 5 minutes or until thoroughly heated. Remove crawfish, and keep warm.

[freeze it]

3. Add onion, bell pepper, and celery to Dutch oven. Cook over medium-high heat 8 minutes or until tender. Add garlic, and cook 1 minute. Remove vegetables, and keep warm.

4. Melt remaining 6 Tbsp. butter in Dutch oven over medium heat. Add flour, and cook, stirring constantly, 20 minutes or until caramel colored. Reduce heat to low, and gradually stir in chicken broth and next 5 ingredients. Cook over medium heat 10 minutes or until slightly thickened. Stir in vegetables and crawfish; cook 5 minutes. Serve with rice.

Note: To freeze, divide étouffée evenly into 3 (1-qt.) zip-top plastic freezer bags. Freeze up to 1 month. Thaw in refrigerator overnight. Remove from freezer bag, and warm in saucepan, stirring until thoroughly heated. Each bag contains about two servings.

QUICK CRAWFISH ÉTOUFFÉE

makes 6 servings   prep: 20 min.   cook: 21 min.

Forgo the roux in this quick étouffée by stirring in a can of cream of mushroom soup as a thickener.

1   cup uncooked long-grain rice

¼   cup butter

1   large onion, chopped

1   green bell pepper, chopped

4   celery ribs, chopped (about 1 cup)

4   garlic cloves, minced

1   (10¾-oz.) can cream of mushroom soup

1   (14.5-oz.) can chicken broth

1   Tbsp. salt-free Cajun seasoning

⅛   to ¼ tsp. ground red pepper

1   lb. frozen cooked peeled crawfish tails, thawed and drained

¼   cup chopped green onions

3   Tbsp. chopped fresh parsley

1. Prepare rice according to package directions.

2. Melt butter in a large cast-iron skillet or Dutch oven over medium heat. Add onion and next 3 ingredients; cook, stirring constantly, 8 minutes.

3. Stir together soup and chicken broth. Add to vegetable mixture. Stir in Cajun seasoning and ground red pepper.

4. Cook over medium-low heat 10 minutes, stirring occasionally. Stir in crawfish, green onions, and parsley; cook 3 minutes or until hot. Serve over rice.

Note: To freeze, divide étouffée evenly into 3 (1-qt.) zip-top plastic freezer bags. Freeze up to 1 month. Thaw in refrigerator overnight. Remove from freezer bag, and warm in a saucepan, stirring until thoroughly heated. Each bag contains about two servings.

GRILLING

"The summer picnic gave the ladies a chance to show off their baking hands. On the barbecue pit, chickens and spareribs sputtered in their own fat and a sauce whose recipe was guarded in the family like a scandalous affair." —Maya Angelou

GRILLED STUFFED PEPPERS

makes about 24   prep: 25 min.   grill: 6 min.

This method and cooking time work equally as well with jalapeños, but we found the heat level of those peppers to be too unpredictable for everyone to enjoy.

2   pt. miniature sweet peppers
12 to 14 hickory-smoked bacon slices
1   (8-oz.) container buttery garlic-and-herb
      spreadable cheese

8   (5- x 3-inch) disposable aluminum loaf pans

1. Preheat grill to 350° to 400° (medium-high) heat. Cut ½ inch from stem end of each pepper. Remove and discard seeds and membranes.
2. Cut bacon slices in half crosswise. Microwave, in 2 batches, at HIGH 90 seconds or until bacon is partially cooked.
3. Spoon cheese into a 1-qt. zip-top plastic freezer bag. (Do not seal.) Snip 1 corner of bag to make a small hole. Pipe cheese into cavity of each pepper, filling almost full.
4. Place 1 bacon half over cut side of each pepper, securing with a wooden pick.
5. Carefully cut 3 (1-inch) holes in bottom of each loaf pan. Turn pans upside down; place peppers, cut sides up, in holes in pans.
6. Grill peppers, in pans, covered with grill lid, 6 to 8 minutes or until bottoms of peppers are charred and bacon is crisp.

Note: To make ahead, prepare recipe as directed through Step 4. Cover and chill peppers 4 hours. Proceed with recipe as directed.

BACON-WRAPPED MUSHROOMS WITH HONEY-BARBECUE SAUCE

makes 8 appetizer servings   prep: 15 min.   cook: 3 min.   grill: 8 min.

24 small fresh mushrooms
12 bacon slices

1   cup Honey-Barbecue Sauce

1. Preheat grill to 350° to 400° (medium-high) heat. Wash mushrooms thoroughly. Cut bacon slices in half crosswise, and microwave, in 2 batches, at HIGH 1½ to 2 minutes or until bacon is partially cooked. Pat dry with paper towels. Wrap each mushroom with a bacon slice, and secure with wooden picks. Dip wrapped mushrooms into Honey-Barbecue Sauce.

2. Grill mushrooms (using a grill basket, if necessary), covered with grill lid, 4 to 5 minutes on each side or until bacon is crisp and thoroughly cooked.

Honey-Barbecue Sauce

makes about 2¾ cups prep: 10 min. cook: 20 min.

Cover and store leftover sauce in the refrigerator up to 1 week.

2	cups ketchup	2	Tbsp. white vinegar
1	cup dry white wine	2	Tbsp. lemon juice
⅓	cup honey	1	Tbsp. Worcestershire sauce
1	small onion, diced	1	tsp. hot sauce
2	garlic cloves, minced	¼	tsp. salt
1	Tbsp. dried parsley flakes		

1. Bring all ingredients to a boil in a large saucepan; reduce heat, and simmer, stirring often, 15 to 20 minutes or until slightly thickened.

SMOKY VEGETABLE GUACAMOLE

makes 4 cups prep: 15 min. grill: 16 min.

4	small avocados, peeled and seeded	1	large sweet onion, cut into ¾-inch-thick slices
3	Tbsp. fresh lime juice	6	large shallots, peeled
½	cup light sour cream	2	jalapeño peppers
2	Tbsp. balsamic vinegar	2	Tbsp. olive oil
½	tsp. salt		Tortilla chips
1	large red bell pepper, seeded and quartered		

1. Preheat grill to 350° to 400° (medium-high) heat. Mash avocados and lime juice together in a medium bowl. Stir in sour cream, vinegar, and salt. Chill.
2. Brush vegetables with oil, and place in a grill basket, if desired.
3. Grill vegetables, without grill lid, 8 minutes on each side. Remove vegetables; cool. Remove seeds from jalapeño peppers. Chop vegetables; stir into avocado mixture. Cover and chill, if desired. Serve with tortilla chips.

[make ahead]

Nothing—repeat, nothing—tastes better in the summertime than fresh grilled corn on the cob. Just cook up your favorite variety, and then flavor it with one of our tasty butters.

Lemon-Basil Butter

makes ½ cup   prep: 5 min.

Stir ½ cup softened butter, 2 tsp. finely chopped fresh basil, 2 tsp. lemon zest, and salt and pepper to taste.

Parmesan-Parsley Butter

makes ½ cup   prep: 8 min.

Stir ½ cup softened butter, ½ cup freshly grated Parmesan cheese, 2 Tbsp. chopped fresh parsley, and salt and pepper to taste.

ROASTED POBLANO CHILE CON QUESO

makes 3½ cups   prep: 20 min.   cook: 17 min.   stand: 10 min.

3 fresh poblano peppers	1 (8-oz.) loaf pasteurized prepared cheese
2 fresh red Anaheim peppers	product, cubed
1 large onion, minced	½ cup half-and-half
2 garlic cloves, minced	Tortilla chips
2 Tbsp. olive oil	Garnish: chopped red Anaheim peppers (optional)
2 cups (8 oz.) shredded Monterey Jack cheese	

1. Preheat grill to 350° to 400° (medium-high) heat. Grill poblano and Anaheim peppers, without grill lid, 5 to 7 minutes or until peppers look blistered, turning often.
2. Place peppers in a zip-top plastic freezer bag; seal and let stand 10 minutes to loosen skins. Peel peppers; remove and discard seeds. Slice peppers into thin strips.
3. Sauté onion and garlic in hot oil in a large skillet over medium-high heat. Add pepper strips, and cook 2 minutes or until tender; reduce heat to low. Add cheeses and half-and-half, stirring until cheese is melted. Serve warm with tortilla chips. Garnish, if desired.

Note: We tested with Velveeta for cheese product.

GRILLED CHICKEN WITH WHITE BARBECUE SAUCE

makes 5 servings   prep: 15 min.   chill: 4 hr.   grill: 16 min.   **pictured on page 335**

1 Tbsp. dried thyme	½ tsp. salt
1 Tbsp. dried oregano	½ tsp. pepper
1 Tbsp. ground cumin	10 chicken thighs (about 3 lb.)*
1 Tbsp. paprika	White Barbecue Sauce
1 tsp. onion powder	

1. Combine first 7 ingredients. Rinse chicken, and pat dry; rub mixture evenly over chicken. Place chicken in a zip-top plastic freezer bag. Seal and chill 4 hours. Remove chicken from bag, discarding bag.

2. Preheat grill to 350° to 400° (medium-high) heat. Grill, covered with grill lid, 8 to 10 minutes on each side or until a meat thermometer inserted into thickest portion registers 170°. Serve with White Barbecue Sauce.

* 4 chicken leg quarters (about 3 lb.) may be substituted for chicken thighs. Increase cooking time to 20 to 25 minutes on each side.

White Barbecue Sauce

makes 1¾ cups   prep: 10 min.   chill: 2 hr.

Developed by Test Kitchen Professional Pam Lolley, this versatile sauce received our highest rating and is also good over baked potatoes or as a condiment for burgers.

1½ cups mayonnaise	1 Tbsp. spicy brown mustard
¼ cup white wine vinegar	1 tsp. sugar
1 garlic clove, minced	1 tsp. salt
1 Tbsp. coarse ground pepper	2 tsp. horseradish

1. Stir together all ingredients until well blended. Store in an airtight container in refrigerator up to 1 week.

GRILLED CHICKEN WITH ORANGE-JALAPEÑO GLAZE

makes 5 servings   prep: 15 min.   grill: 16 min.

Boneless chicken thighs may be used; grill about 4 to 5 minutes on each side.

Orange-Jalapeño Glaze	½ tsp. salt
10 skinned chicken thighs (about 3 lb.)	½ tsp. pepper

1. Preheat grill to 350° to 400° (medium-high) heat. Reserve 1 cup Orange-Jalapeño Glaze.
2. Rinse chicken, and pat dry. Sprinkle evenly with salt and pepper. Brush chicken lightly with remaining ⅔ cup Orange-Jalapeño Glaze.
3. Grill, covered with grill lid, 8 to 10 minutes on each side or until a meat thermometer inserted into thickest portion registers 170°, basting each side with reserved 1 cup glaze during last few minutes.

Orange-Jalapeño Glaze

makes 1⅔ cups   prep: 15 min.   cook: 20 min.

2 cups orange juice	1 Tbsp. olive oil
3 medium jalapeño peppers, seeded and finely chopped	3 Tbsp. maple syrup
	1 tsp. salt
4 garlic cloves, minced	½ tsp. ground ginger
3 Tbsp. orange zest	½ tsp. pepper

1. Stir together all ingredients in a medium saucepan; bring to a boil over medium-high heat. Reduce heat to medium, and cook, stirring often, 15 minutes or until reduced by half.

ROSEMARY GRILLED CHICKEN THIGHS

makes 4 to 6 servings   prep: 10 min.   chill: 1 hr.   grill: 10 min.   stand: 10 min.   **pictured on page 336**

For a tasty alternative, try these with our quick Honey Mustard Sauce (below).

1 **garlic clove, pressed**	½ **tsp. pepper**
1 **Tbsp. olive oil**	1½ **lb. skinned and boned chicken thighs****
2 **Tbsp. Dijon mustard**	½ **lemon**
2 **Tbsp. honey**	**Sautéed Garlic Spinach**
1 **tsp. salt**	**Two-Cheese Grits**
1 **tsp. chopped fresh rosemary***	

1. Combine first 7 ingredients in a large zip-top plastic freezer bag, squeezing bag to combine ingredients. Add chicken, turning to coat, and seal bag. Chill 1 to 24 hours.

2. Preheat grill to 350° to 400° (medium-high) heat. Remove chicken from marinade, discarding marinade. Grill chicken, covered with grill lid, 5 to 7 minutes on each side. Transfer chicken to a large piece of aluminum foil. Squeeze juice from lemon over chicken; fold foil around chicken, covering chicken completely. Let stand 10 minutes. Serve with Sautéed Garlic Spinach and Two-Cheese Grits.

* Fresh thyme, cilantro, or oregano may be substituted.

** 1½ lb. skinned and boned chicken breasts may be substituted.

Rosemary Grilled Pork Tenderloin: Omit chicken thighs. Substitute 2 lb. pork tenderloin, and grill as directed 8 to 10 minutes on each side. Proceed with recipe as directed. Makes 4 to 6 servings; Prep: 10 min., Chill: 1 hr., Grill: 16 min., Stand: 10 min.

Sautéed Garlic Spinach: Heat 1 tsp. olive oil in a nonstick skillet over medium-high heat. Sauté 1 pressed garlic clove in hot oil 30 seconds. Add 1 (10-oz.) bag fresh spinach, thoroughly washed, to skillet, and cook 2 to 3 minutes or until spinach is wilted. Sprinkle with salt and pepper to taste. Serve spinach with slotted spoon or tongs. Makes 4 servings; Prep: 5 min., Cook: 4 min.

Two-Cheese Grits: Bring 4 cups water and 1 tsp. salt to a boil in a 3-qt. saucepan. Whisk in 1 cup uncooked quick-cooking grits; reduce heat to medium-low, and cook 5 to 6 minutes or until tender. Remove from heat, and stir in 1 cup (4 oz.) shredded Cheddar cheese, ½ cup (2 oz.) shredded Parmesan cheese, and 2 Tbsp. butter. Sprinkle with pepper to taste. Makes 4 servings; Prep: 5 min., Cook: 10 min.

Honey Mustard Sauce: Stir together ½ cup mayonnaise, 2 Tbsp. Dijon mustard, and 2 Tbsp. honey. Makes about ¾ cup; Prep: 5 min.

inspirations for your taste

HERB-GRILLED CHICKEN

makes 4 servings   prep: 10 min.   grill: 12 min.

We've concocted a simple, healthful recipe to start your season of outdoor cooking. Choose your favorite fresh herb to enhance the flavor of grilled chicken. Remove the herb sprig before serving, or leave it as a garnish. Our top herb picks included fresh dill, basil, sage, rosemary, flat-leaf parsley, thyme, tarragon, and oregano.

4 (4- to 6-oz.) skinned and boned chicken breasts	1 tsp. pepper
2 Tbsp. olive oil	Fresh herb sprigs
1 tsp. salt	Fresh spinach

1. Preheat grill to 350° to 400° (medium-high) heat. Rub chicken breasts evenly with 2 Tbsp. olive oil; sprinkle with salt and pepper. Cut a small slit at 1 end of each chicken breast; tuck end of 1 fresh herb sprig into each slit, laying sprigs over top of chicken. Grill chicken breasts, covered with grill lid, 6 to 7 minutes on each side or until done. If desired, remove and discard herb sprigs. Serve chicken over fresh spinach.

Note: Herbs will char a little because the sprigs will be next to the grate, but the result is a pretty and rustic look.

taking sides

The Great (Sweet) (Iced) Tea Controversy

Two surefire ways to let people know you weren't raised in the South: 1. Declare the tea to be "too sweet." 2. Give the waitress a confused look when she asks if your tea should be "sweet or un." (translation for Yankees reading this: "sweet or unsweetened tea?")

True story. An Alabama teenager settled in at a restaurant in Vermont. When the waitress appeared, he asked for sweet iced tea. She promptly brought him a glass of ice, a cup of hot tea, and sugar. One sip of the concoction and he reacted, well, as most teenage boys do when they taste something unpalatable. (You get the picture.) While mopping the table, the mother explained the difference in Southern sweet tea and tea that you get, um, elsewhere. In other words, never order sweet tea unless you're in a state where barbecue restaurants are plentiful and easily found. The teenager's response? "Mama, take me home!" he wailed, echoing the sentiments of many misplaced Southerners.

It's easy to understand how sweet iced tea came about in the South. First, the summers always have been hot. Second, ice boxes and the rise of refrigeration made it easy to make the tea cold. Third, rationing of sugar during World War II encouraged creative and thrifty Southern cooks to add sugar to the tea while hot, so it

took less sugar to make the tea sweet. The supersaturated elixir soon became a Southern staple and the undisputed drink with barbecue and fried chicken, and at fish fries, family reunions, and church suppers. That's because Southern gatherings are usually big, and large quantities can be made quickly and inexpensively.

Though some health-conscious Southerners have taken to drinking their tea without sugar, it's wise to specify that to the waitress when eating out. If you ask for tea in most restaurants in the region, you're likely to get it iced and sweet. Besides fussing with the Yankees when they claim the tea's too sweet, Southerners still have battles to wage among themselves. Whose sweet tea is best? Milo's Famous Sweet Tea from Birmingham? Or tea from Pal's, a famous burger stand in East Tennessee? Every Southerner can argue that the best tea is found at their favorite local spot. Of course, you can always end the debate in a civil way with an unarguable, politically correct answer to where the best tea is found: "My mama's."

GRILLED SWEET CHILI CHICKEN WITH MANGO-CUCUMBER SLAW

makes 4 servings   prep: 15 min.   grill: 12 min.   **pictured on page 336**

½ cup sweet chili sauce

3 Tbsp. orange juice

2 Tbsp. honey

1 Tbsp. lite soy sauce

1 tsp. minced jalapeño pepper*

1 tsp. minced fresh ginger

Vegetable cooking spray

4 boneless, skinless chicken breasts

Mango-Cucumber Slaw

2 Tbsp. chopped roasted peanuts (optional)

1. Whisk together first 6 ingredients in a small bowl until blended. Reserve half of sweet chili sauce mixture.

2. Coat cold cooking grate with cooking spray, and place on grill. Preheat grill to 350° to 400° (medium-high) heat. Lightly spray chicken with cooking spray, and place on cooking grate. Grill chicken 6 minutes on each side or until done, basting with sweet chili sauce mixture during last few minutes on each side.

3. Divide Mango-Cucumber Slaw among 4 serving plates, topping each with 1 chicken breast. Drizzle with reserved half of sweet chili sauce mixture; if desired, sprinkle with roasted peanuts.

* 1 tsp. sambal oelek may be substituted for minced jalapeño. Sambal oelek is an Indonesian chili sauce that can be found on the ethnic food aisle of the supermarket.

Note: We tested with Maggi Taste of Asia Sweet Chili Sauce.

Mango-Cucumber Slaw

makes about 7 cups   prep: 20 min.   chill: 1 hr.

3 cups thinly sliced napa cabbage

2 cups thinly sliced red cabbage

1 ripe mango, peeled and cut into thin strips

½ cucumber, peeled, seeded, and cut into thin strips

½ small sweet onion, thinly sliced

½ small red bell pepper, thinly sliced

1 carrot, shredded

¼ cup fresh cilantro

3 Tbsp. rice vinegar

2 Tbsp. fresh lime juice

3 Tbsp. vegetable oil

1 Tbsp. sweet chili sauce

2 tsp. sugar

1 tsp. toasted sesame oil

1. Combine first 8 ingredients in a large bowl. Whisk together vinegar and next 5 ingredients until sugar dissolves. Pour over cabbage mixture, and toss to coat. Cover and chill 1 hour.

MOLE-RUBBED CHICKEN WITH CONFETTI CORN RELISH

makes 4 servings   prep: 10 min.   grill: 10 min.

While mole chicken maybe Mexican, corn relish is purely Southern. The two make a colorful and tasty combination.

2 Tbsp. light brown sugar	½ tsp. cracked black pepper
1½ tsp. chili powder	¼ tsp. ground cinnamon
1½ tsp. garlic powder	4 (5-oz.) skinned and boned chicken breasts
1½ tsp. unsweetened cocoa	**Confetti Corn Relish**
½ tsp. coarse-grain salt	Garnish: fresh cilantro sprigs (optional)

1. Coat cold cooking grate with cooking spray, and place on grill. Preheat grill to 350° to 400° (medium-high) heat.

2. Stir together first 7 ingredients in a small bowl until well blended. Place chicken in a shallow dish; add brown sugar mixture, and turn chicken to coat, pressing mixture into chicken.

3. Place chicken on cooking grate, and grill, covered with grill lid, 5 to 6 minutes on each side or until done. (Meat thermometer should read 165° when inserted into thickest portion of breast.)

4. Place chicken on a serving platter. Spoon Confetti Corn Relish over top of and around chicken. Garnish, if desired.

Confetti Corn Relish

makes about 2½ cups   prep: 15 min.   cook: 5 min.

1 Tbsp. unsalted butter	1 jalapeño pepper, seeded and minced
½ cup diced sweet onion	½ tsp. salt
1 cup fresh corn kernels	¼ tsp. cracked black pepper
1 cup diced red bell pepper	2 Tbsp. chopped fresh cilantro

1. Melt butter in a large skillet over medium heat. Add onion, and sauté 2 to 3 minutes or just until onion begins to turn golden. Stir in corn and next 4 ingredients; sauté 1 to 2 minutes or until vegetables are crisp-tender. Remove from heat, and stir in cilantro.

PIMIENTO CHEESE-STUFFED BURGERS

makes 4 servings   prep: 15 min.   chill: 30 min.   grill: 14 min.   **pictured on page 409**

Purchase pimiento cheese from your favorite deli, or make your own. This recipe is easy to increase for a crowd. Just prepare one recipe at a time to ensure the seasonings are correct.

2 lb. ground chuck	Hamburger buns
1 tsp. freshly ground black pepper	Toppings: tomato slices, red onion slices, lettuce
1⅓ cups prepared pimiento cheese, divided	leaves, mustard, mayonnaise, ketchup
1 tsp. salt	

1. Combine ground beef and pepper in a large bowl until blended. (Do not overwork meat mixture.) Shape mixture into 8 (4-inch) patties; spoon 1½ Tbsp. pimiento cheese in center of each of 4 patties. Top with remaining 4 patties; pressing edges to seal. Cover and chill at least 30 minutes. Sprinkle evenly with salt.

2. Preheat grill to 350° to 400° (medium-high) heat. Grill, covered with grill lid, 7 to 8 minutes on each side or until beef is no longer pink. Serve on buns with desired toppings and remaining pimiento cheese.

BARBARA'S BIG JUICY BURGERS

makes 10 servings   prep: 20 min.   grill: 14 min.

Shape into 12 patties for smaller, quarter-pound burgers.

1 (11.5-oz.) can lightly tangy vegetable juice	1½ tsp. salt
3 white sandwich bread slices, torn into pieces	1 tsp. pepper
3 lb. ground chuck or ground round	10 hamburger buns
1 large egg	Vegetable cooking spray

1. Preheat grill to 350° to 400° (medium-high) heat. Microwave vegetable juice in glass bowl at HIGH 1 minute. Add bread pieces; let cool.

2. Combine, using hands. Combine vegetable juice mixture, ground chuck, and next 3 ingredients. Shape into 10 patties.

3. Grill patties, covered with grill lid, 6 to 8 minutes on each side or until beef is no longer pink.

4. Spray cut sides of buns with cooking spray; place buns, cut sides down, on grill rack; grill 2 minutes or until lightly browned. Serve hamburgers on buns.

BEEF BURGERS WITH DILL PICKLE RÉMOULADE

makes 6 servings   prep: 15 min.   cook: 10 min.

1   lb. lean ground beef

½   lb. ground pork sausage

⅓   cup grated carrot

¼   cup finely chopped onion

2   Tbsp. chopped fresh parsley

2   Tbsp. dill pickle relish

2   Tbsp. Dijon mustard

¼   tsp. salt

¼   tsp. pepper

Vegetable cooking spray

Dill Pickle Rémoulade

6   seeded hamburger buns, split and lightly toasted

6   Swiss cheese slices

6   cooked bacon slices

Toppings: green leaf lettuce, sliced ripe tomatoes, thin Vidalia onion slices

1. Combine first 9 ingredients in a large bowl. Shape into 6 patties.

2. Cook patties over medium heat in a large skillet or on a griddle coated with cooking spray 5 to 7 minutes on each side or until patties are done.

3. Spread Dill Pickle Rémoulade evenly on cut sides of each bun half; layer bottoms with meat patties, cheese slices, bacon slices, and desired toppings. Top with top halves of buns.

Dill Pickle Rémoulade

makes ¾ cup   prep: 5 min.

½   cup mayonnaise

¼   cup dill pickle relish, drained

1   Tbsp. Dijon mustard

¼   tsp. paprika

1. Stir together all ingredients until blended; cover and chill until ready to serve.

TASTY TURKEY BURGERS

makes 4 servings   prep: 15 min.   grill: 12 min.

1 lb. ground turkey

½ cup Italian-seasoned breadcrumbs

1 large egg, beaten

¼ cup finely chopped green bell pepper

1 Tbsp. minced dried onion

½ tsp. salt

½ tsp. freshly ground pepper

2 Tbsp. Fresh Herb Marinade

4 hamburger buns

Herb-Grilled Onion Rings

Toppings: spicy mustard, shaved Parmesan cheese

1. Preheat grill to 350° to 400° (medium-high) heat. Combine first 7 ingredients. Shape mixture into 4 equal-size patties.

2. Grill, covered with grill lid, 5 to 6 minutes on each side or until no longer pink in center, basting each side occasionally with Fresh Herb Marinade.

3. Grill buns, cut sides down, 2 minutes or until toasted. Serve burgers on buns with Herb-Grilled Onion Rings and desired toppings.

Classic Burgers: Substitute 1 lb. ground chuck for ground turkey. Prepare recipe as directed.

HERB-GRILLED ONION RINGS

makes 4 servings   prep: 5 min.   grill: 8 min.

2 large Vidalia onions

4 Tbsp. Fresh Herb Marinade, divided

1. Preheat grill to 350° to 400° (medium-high) heat. Cut each onion into ½-inch-thick slices. Brush slices evenly with 2½ Tbsp. Fresh Herb Marinade.

2. Grill, covered with grill lid, 4 to 6 minutes on each side or until tender, basting once with remaining marinade.

Fresh Herb Marinade

makes about ⅓ cup   prep 10 min.

¼ cup vegetable oil

2 Tbsp. balsamic vinegar

1½ Tbsp. chopped fresh cilantro

1 Tbsp. chopped fresh rosemary

½ tsp. kosher salt

Freshly ground pepper to taste

1. Stir together first 5 ingredients in a small bowl. Season with pepper to taste.

- Premarinated meats and poultry offer a speedy solution for last-minute suppers. Low in fat, rubs and seasoning blends also add fast flavor and help seal in juices.
- Pair vegetables and fruit with similar cook times, such as bell pepper and summer squash, and keep the pieces uniform in size. If you'd like to add potatoes or carrots, parboil them first until almost done but still firm.
- Tightly packed skewers take longer to grill, so leave a small amount of space between each piece to ensure quick, even cooking.

SPICY THAI CHICKEN KABOBS

makes 4 to 6 servings   prep: 20 min.   chill: 8 hr.   soak: 30 min.   grill: 12 min.

Stir up a superfast peanut sauce, and marinate the chicken before you head out for the day. The remaining ingredients can be quickly put together when you get home from work.

½ cup creamy peanut butter

½ cup lite soy sauce

¼ cup firmly packed light brown sugar

1 Tbsp. lime zest

1 tsp. dried crushed red pepper

1½ lb. skinned and boned chicken breasts, cut into 1-inch pieces

8 (12-inch) wooden or metal skewers

1 bunch green onions, cut into 2-inch pieces

1 large red bell pepper, cut into 1-inch pieces

1 large yellow bell pepper, cut into 1-inch pieces

32 fresh snow peas

16 basil leaves

1. Whisk together first 5 ingredients and ½ cup water in a large shallow dish or zip-top plastic freezer bag; reserve ¾ cup. Add chicken to dish, turning to coat. Cover or seal, and chill 8 hours, turning occasionally.

2. Soak wooden skewers in water 30 minutes.

3. Preheat grill to 350° to 400° (medium-high) heat. Remove chicken from marinade, discarding marinade. Thread chicken, onions, and next 4 ingredients alternately onto wooden skewers, leaving ¼ inch between pieces.

4. Grill kabobs, covered with grill lid, 6 to 8 minutes on each side or until done. Remove from grill, and baste with reserved ¾ cup marinade.

Spicy Thai Pork Kabobs: Substitute 1 (1.5-lb.) package pork tenderloin, trimmed, for chicken. Proceed with recipe as directed.

Lakehouse Cookout serves 8

*Beef Tenderloin Shish Kabobs

Hot cooked rice

Mango-Cucumber Slaw (page 444)   **Toasted barbecue bread**

Blackberry Cobbler (page 636)

*double recipe

BEEF TENDERLOIN SHISH KABOBS

makes 4 servings   prep: 20 min.   chill: 2 hr.   grill: 10 min.

½ cup dry sherry or beef broth

¼ cup olive oil

2 Tbsp. soy sauce

1 garlic clove, minced

¼ tsp. pepper

1 lb. beef tenderloin steaks or boneless top
   sirloin steaks, cut into 1-inch cubes

8 large mushrooms

1 red bell pepper, cut into 1-inch pieces

8 cherry tomatoes

2 small onions, quartered

1 green bell pepper, cut into 1-inch pieces

1. Combine first 5 ingredients in a shallow dish or a large zip-top freezer plastic bag; add steak and remaining ingredients. Cover or seal, and chill 2 hours, turning steak occasionally.

2. Preheat grill to 350° to 400° (medium-high) heat. Remove steak and vegetables from marinade, discarding marinade. Thread onto 4 (12-inch) skewers.

3. Grill kabobs, covered with grill lid, 5 to 7 minutes on each side or until desired degree of doneness.

BEEF BRISKET WITH TEXAS BARBECUE SAUCE

makes 6 to 8 servings   prep: 15 min.   chill: 8 hr.   grill: 4 hr.

1 cup vegetable oil	¾ tsp. paprika
1 cup cider vinegar	1 (3-lb.) beef brisket, trimmed
¼ cup Worcestershire sauce	Texas Barbecue Sauce
1 bay leaf, crumbled	Garnishes: fresh thyme sprigs, grilled
1¼ tsp. seasoned salt	red onions (optional)
2¼ tsp. pepper	

1. Combine first 4 ingredients in a shallow dish or large zip-top plastic freezer bag.

2. Combine seasoned salt, pepper, and paprika; rub into brisket. Place brisket in marinade.

3. Cover or seal; chill 8 hours, turning occasionally.

4. Prepare a hot fire by placing 2 pieces of oak or 10 hickory chunks at front and back of grill, piling charcoal in the center. Let burn until coals are white.

5. Remove brisket from marinade, discarding marinade. Rake coals to 1 side of grill; place meat on other side. Grill, covered, over indirect heat 3 to 4 hours.

6. Brush both sides of brisket with 1 cup Texas Barbecue Sauce; cook 1 hour, basting with sauce. Serve with remaining sauce. Garnish, if desired.

Texas Barbecue Sauce

makes 3 cups   prep: 10 min.   cook: 10 min.

2 cups ketchup	1 Tbsp. seasoned salt
½ cup cider vinegar	1 Tbsp. brown sugar
½ cup Worcestershire sauce	1½ tsp. chili powder
1 small onion, grated	1½ tsp. pepper
¼ cup butter	1 small bay leaf

1. Bring all ingredients to a boil in a large saucepan. Reduce heat, and simmer, stirring occasionally, 10 minutes. Remove and discard bay leaf from sauce before serving.

MARINATED LONDON BROIL

makes 6 to 8 servings   prep: 5 min.   chill: 24 hr.   grill: 24 min.   stand: 10 min.

For the juiciest flavor, pull this hearty cut of beef off the grill before it reaches medium (155°). It will continue to cook as it stands.

1   (12-oz.) can cola soft drink
1   (10-oz.) bottle teriyaki sauce

1   (2½- to 3-lb.) London broil

1. Combine cola and teriyaki sauce in a shallow dish or large zip-top plastic freezer bag; add London broil. Cover or seal, and chill 24 hours, turning occasionally.
2. Remove London broil from marinade, discarding marinade.
3. Preheat grill to 350° to 400° (medium-high) heat. Grill, covered with grill lid, 12 to 15 minutes on each side or to desired degree of doneness. Let stand 10 minutes; cut diagonally across the grain into thin slices.

SMOKED PRIME RIB

makes 8 to 10 servings   prep: 25 min.   soak: 1 hr.   grill: 6 hr.   stand: 15 min.

When it comes to beef, it's hard to beat prime rib. And when cooked on a smoker, the results redefine delicious.

Hickory wood chunks
4   garlic cloves, minced
1   Tbsp. salt
2   Tbsp. coarsely ground pepper
1   Tbsp. dried rosemary

1   tsp. dried thyme
1   (6-lb.) beef rib roast
1½ cups dry red wine
1½ cups red wine vinegar
½   cup olive oil

1. Soak wood chunks in water 1 hour. Prepare smoker according to manufacturer's directions, bringing internal temperature to 225° to 250°; maintain temperature for 15 to 20 minutes. Drain wood chunks, and place on coals.
2. Combine minced garlic and next 4 ingredients, and rub garlic mixture evenly over beef roast.
3. Stir together dry red wine, red wine vinegar, and olive oil; set wine mixture aside.
4. Place beef roast in center on lower cooking grate. Gradually pour wine mixture over beef roast. Cover with smoker lid.
5. Smoke beef roast, maintaining temperature inside smoker between 225° and 250°, for 6 hours or until a meat thermometer inserted into thickest portion of beef roast registers 145° (medium) Remove beef roast from smoker, and let stand 15 minutes before slicing.

[test kitchen favorite]

FLANK STEAK SANDWICHES WITH BLUE CHEESE

makes 6 servings prep: 20 min. grill: 22 min. stand: 10 min. **pictured on page 334**

2   large sweet onions

4   Tbsp. olive oil, divided

½   tsp. salt

½   tsp. freshly ground pepper

3   red bell peppers

6   (2- to 3-oz.) ciabatta or deli rolls, split

5   oz. soft ripened blue cheese

1½   cups loosely packed arugula

Herb-Marinated Flank Steak

6   Tbsp. mayonnaise

1. Preheat grill to 400° to 450° (high) heat. Cut onion into ¼-inch-thick slices. Brush with 1 Tbsp. olive oil, and sprinkle with ¼ tsp. salt and ¼ tsp. pepper. Cut bell peppers into 1-inch-wide strips. Place pepper strips in a large bowl, and drizzle with 1 Tbsp. olive oil. Sprinkle with remaining ¼ tsp. salt and ¼ tsp. pepper; toss to coat.

2. Grill onion and bell pepper strips, covered with grill lid, over 400° to 450° (high) heat 7 to 10 minutes on each side or until lightly charred and tender.

3. Brush cut sides of rolls with remaining 2 Tbsp. olive oil, and grill, cut sides down, without grill lid, over 400° to 450° (high) heat 1 to 2 minutes or until lightly browned and toasted.

4. Spread blue cheese on cut sides of roll bottoms; top with arugula, bell pepper strips, steak, and onion. Spread mayonnaise on cut sides of roll tops. Place roll tops, mayonnaise sides down, on top of onion, pressing lightly.

Herb-Marinated Flank Steak

makes 6 servings prep: 15 min. chill: 30 min. grill: 18 min. stand: 10 min.

½   small sweet onion, minced

3   garlic cloves, minced

¼   cup olive oil

2   Tbsp. chopped fresh basil

1   Tbsp. chopped fresh thyme

1   Tbsp. chopped fresh rosemary

1   tsp. salt

½   tsp dried crushed red pepper

1¾   lb. flank steak

1   lemon, halved

1. Place first 8 ingredients in a 2-gal. zip-top plastic bag, and squeeze bag to combine. Add steak; seal bag, and chill 30 minutes to 1 hour and 30 minutes. Remove steak from marinade, discarding marinade.

2. Preheat grill to 400° to 450° (high) heat. Grill steak, covered with grill lid, 9 minutes on each side or to desired degree of doneness. Remove from grill; squeeze juice from lemon over steak. Let stand 10 minutes. Cut across the grain into thin slices.

Easy Father's Day Dinner serves 6

Grilled Rib-eye Steaks

Baked potatoes   *Tangy Feta Dressing Over Iceberg (page 714)

Herb-Topped Bread (page 130)

Homemade peach ice cream

*double recipe

GRILLED RIB-EYE STEAKS

makes 6 servings   prep: 5 min.   stand: 20 min.   grill: 10 min.   **pictured on page 414**

6   (1-inch-thick) boneless rib-eye steaks

3   tsp. steak seasoning

3   Tbsp. butter, softened

1. Let steaks stand at room temperature 15 to 20 minutes. Rub steaks evenly with steak seasoning.

2. Preheat grill to 300° to 350° (medium) heat. Grill, covered with grill lid, 2½ minutes. Using tongs, turn each steak at a 60-degree angle, and grill 2½ more minutes. Flip steaks, and grill 2½ minutes. Turn steaks at a 60-degree angle, and grill 2½ more minutes (medium-rare) or to desired degree of doneness.

3. Remove steaks from grill, and brush evenly with butter. Let stand 5 minutes.

Note: We tested with McCormick Grill Mates Montreal Steak Seasoning.

BEEF GORGONZOLA

makes 6 servings   prep: 10 min.   cook: 40 min.   grill: 10 min.   stand: 10 min.

2   Tbsp. butter

1   medium onion, thinly sliced

1   (8-oz.) package sliced fresh mushrooms

1   pt. whipping cream

4   oz. crumbled Gorgonzola cheese

6   (6-oz.) beef tenderloin fillets

¾   tsp. salt

¼   tsp. pepper

Garnish: crumbled Gorgonzola cheese (optional)

1. Preheat grill to 350° to 400° (medium-high) heat. Melt butter in a large skillet over medium-high heat; add onion, and cook, stirring often, 6 to 8 minutes or until tender. Add mushrooms, and cook, stirring often, 5 minutes. Reduce heat to medium, and cook 5 more minutes or until mushrooms are tender.

2. Bring whipping cream to a boil in a medium saucepan over medium heat. Reduce heat to low, and simmer, stirring often, 15 minutes or until slightly thickened.

3. Whisk crumbled cheese into whipping cream, and cook, whisking often, over medium heat 4 minutes or until cheese is melted. Stir in onion mixture. Keep warm.

4. Sprinkle fillets with salt and pepper. Grill fillets, covered with grill lid, 5 to 8 minutes on each side or to desired degree of doneness. Remove from grill, and let stand 10 minutes. Serve with warm cheese sauce. Garnish, if desired.

Note: To make recipe on an indoor grill pan, prepare as directed through Step 3. Heat a non-stick grill pan over medium-high heat. Sprinkle fillets with salt and pepper. Cook fillets 4 to 5 minutes on each side or to desired degree of doneness. Proceed with recipe as directed.

STRIP STEAK WITH ROSEMARY BUTTER

makes 4 servings   prep: 15 min.   chill: 1 hr.   grill: 6 min.

½ cup butter, softened	1½ Tbsp. olive oil
1 Tbsp. fresh rosemary	2 garlic cloves, minced
2 tsp. lemon zest, divided	1 tsp. pepper
Salt and pepper to taste	½ tsp. salt
1 Tbsp. dried Italian seasoning	4 (6-oz.) beef strip steaks (½ inch thick)

1. Stir together butter, rosemary, 1 tsp. lemon zest, and salt and pepper to taste. Cover and chill until ready to serve.

2. Combine Italian seasoning and next 4 ingredients in a small bowl. Stir in remaining 1 tsp. lemon zest. Rub mixture over steaks. Cover and chill 1 hour.

3. Preheat grill to 350° to 400° (medium-high) heat. Grill steaks, covered with grill lid, 3 to 4 minutes on each side or to desired degree of doneness. Serve with butter.

Keep the Grill Ready

A clean grill invites spur-of-the-moment use. We suggest you clean it immediately after each use. It's a lot easier task at this point and requires less elbow grease to get the job done.

- Remove racks from grill, and scrape off stuck-on particles using a stiff grill brush or scouring pad. Racks may still be slightly warm.
- Clean racks with hot soapy water; rinse and dry thoroughly.
- Coat racks with vegetable cooking spray or oil.
- Clean out the firebox.
- Replace racks, and cover with grill lid.

MIXED GRILL WITH CILANTRO PESTO

makes 8 servings   prep: 5 min.   grill: 29 min.   stand: 5 min.   **pictured on page 336**

4 (1½-inch-thick) center-cut bone-in pork chops
4 (6-oz.) beef tenderloin fillets
   (about 2 inches thick)
Kosher salt

Pepper
Cilantro Pesto
Garnishes: fresh cilantro sprigs, rosemary sprigs,
   chives (optional)

1. Preheat grill to 350° to 400° (medium-high) heat. Sprinkle pork chops and beef fillets evenly with desired amount of salt and pepper.

2. Grill chops 8 to 10 minutes on each side or until done. Grill fillets 8 to 10 minutes. Turn fillets over, and cook 5 more minutes or to desired degree of doneness. Remove chops and fillets from grill, and let stand 5 minutes. Serve with Cilantro Pesto. Garnish, if desired.

Cilantro Pesto

makes about ¾ cup   prep: 10 min.

½ cup loosely packed fresh cilantro leaves
½ cup loosely packed fresh flat-leaf parsley
2 garlic cloves
¼ cup (1 oz.) freshly grated Parmesan cheese

2 Tbsp. pumpkin seeds, toasted
¼ tsp. salt
¼ cup olive oil

1. Pulse first 6 ingredients in a food processor 10 times or just until chopped. Drizzle olive oil over mixture, and pulse 6 more times or until a coarse mixture forms. Cover and chill until ready to serve.

ZESTY GRILLED PORK CHOPS

makes 6 servings   prep: 10 min.   grill: 6 min.

2   tsp. Creole seasoning

2   tsp. ground cumin

2   tsp. garlic powder

2   medium-size yellow squash, cut lengthwise into ¼-inch-thick slices

2   medium zucchini, cut lengthwise into ¼-inch-thick slices

2   Tbsp. olive oil, divided

6   (1¼-inch-thick) bone-in pork chops

1. Preheat grill to 400° (high) heat. Combine first 3 ingredients in a small bowl.

2. Toss squash and zucchini with 1 Tbsp. oil in a large bowl; sprinkle vegetables with 1 tsp. Creole mixture.

3. Stir remaining 1 Tbsp. oil into remaining Creole mixture. Rub evenly on pork chops.

4. Grill vegetables and pork chops 3 minutes on each side or until pork is done.

BOURBON-GLAZED PORK CHOPS

makes 6 servings   prep: 10 min.   chill: 30 min.   grill: 10 min.

½   cup firmly packed light brown sugar

3   Tbsp. Dijon mustard

2   Tbsp. soy sauce

2   Tbsp. bourbon

½   tsp. salt

¼   tsp. pepper

6   (1-inch-thick) bone-in pork chops

1. Preheat grill to 350° to 400° (medium-high) heat. Stir together first 6 ingredients in a shallow dish or large zip-top plastic freezer bag; add pork chops. Cover or seal, and chill 30 minutes, turning once.

2. Remove pork from marinade, reserving marinade.

3. Grill pork, covered with grill lid, about 10 to 12 minutes or until a meat thermometer inserted into thickest portion registers 160°, turning once.

4. Bring reserved marinade to a boil in a small saucepan, and cook, stirring occasionally, 2 minutes. Pour over chops before serving.

SAUCY PORK CHOPS WITH ORANGE SLICES

makes 4 servings   prep: 10 min.   chill: 30 min.   grill: 22 min.   stand: 5 min.

Sweet orange marmalade is slightly less bitter than traditional orange marmalade. Either works fine in this recipe. If your chops are thinner than ours, reduce the grilling time.

4   (1¼-inch-thick) bone-in pork rib chops or loin chops*

½   cup orange juice

2   tsp. soy sauce

¼   tsp. dried crushed red pepper

1   tsp. salt

¾   tsp. black pepper

¼   cup sweet orange marmalade

½   cup bottled barbecue sauce

4   (¼-inch-thick) orange slices

1. Preheat grill to 350° to 400° (medium-high) heat. Pierce pork chops with a fork several times on each side. Combine pork chops and next 3 ingredients in a large shallow dish or large zip-top plastic freezer bag. Cover or seal, and chill for 30 minutes.

2. Remove chops from marinade, discarding marinade. Sprinkle chops evenly with salt and black pepper.

3. Stir together marmalade and barbecue sauce in a small bowl. Brush 1 side of pork chops evenly with half of marmalade mixture.

4. Grill chops, marmalade mixture side up and covered with grill lid, 10 minutes. Turn pork chops, and brush evenly with remaining half of marmalade mixture. Grill 10 minutes or until done. Remove chops from grill, and let stand 5 minutes.

5. Grill orange slices, covered with grill lid, over medium-high heat 1 minute on each side. Serve with pork chops.

* 4 (1¼-inch-thick) boneless pork loin chops may be substituted. Reduce grilling time to 8 minutes on each side or until done.

Note: We tested with Jack Daniel's Original No. 7 Recipe Barbecue Sauce.

PORK TACOS WITH PINEAPPLE SALSA

makes 8 servings prep: 30 min.   cook: 6 min.   stand: 10 min.

1 Tbsp. curry powder
½ tsp. garlic powder
¼ tsp. salt
¼ tsp. freshly ground pepper
⅛ tsp. ground red pepper

6 (4-oz.) boneless pork loin chops, trimmed
   Vegetable cooking spray
   Pineapple Salsa
8 (8-inch) fat-free flour tortillas, warmed

1. Preheat grill to 350° to 400° (medium-high) heat. Combine curry powder and next 4 ingredients; sprinkle over pork chops. Coat pork evenly with cooking spray.
2. Grill, covered with grill lid, 3 to 4 minutes on each side or until done. Let stand 10 minutes. Coarsely chop pork.
3. Serve with Pineapple Salsa and warm tortillas.

Pineapple Salsa

makes 2 cups prep: 15 min.

¼ cup orange juice
2 Tbsp. lemon juice
1 Tbsp. honey
¼ tsp. salt

¼ tsp. ground pepper
2 cups chopped fresh pineapple
2 Tbsp. chopped fresh cilantro
¼ small red onion, chopped

1. Whisk together ¼ cup orange juice and next 4 ingredients. Stir in pineapple, cilantro, and onion.

Per taco: Calories 288; Fat 6g (sat 2g, mono 2.5g, poly 0.5g); Protein 24g; Fiber 4g; Chol 55mg; Iron 1.5mg; Sodium 417mg; Calc 25mg

BIG "D" SMOKED BABY BACK RIBS

makes 6 servings   prep: 30 min.   stand: 30 min.   soak: 30 min.
smoke: 5 hr.   **pictured on page 411**

When residents of Paul Bender's East Dallas neighborhood see and smell smoke billowing from behind his house, they don't call the fire department; they know he's cooking. His backyard is home to some of the best barbecue you'll put in your mouth.

3   slabs baby back pork ribs (about 6 lb.)
¼   cup lemon juice
¼   cup olive oil
6   Tbsp. Paul's Pork Ribs Rub

Hickory wood chunks
4   to 6 (12-oz.) bottles dark beer
2   cups Paul's Barbecue Sauce

1. Rinse and pat ribs dry. Remove thin membrane from back of ribs by slicing into it with a knife and then pulling. (This makes for more tender ribs and allows smoke and rub to penetrate meat better.)

2. Place lemon juice in a small bowl; add oil in a slow, steady stream, whisking constantly.

3. Coat ribs evenly with lemon juice mixture. Sprinkle meat evenly with Paul's Pork Ribs Rub, and rub into meat. Let stand at room temperature 30 minutes.

4. Soak wood chunks in water for at least 30 minutes.

5. Prepare smoker according to manufacturer's directions, substituting beer for water in water pan. Bring internal temperature to 225° to 250°, and maintain temperature for 15 to 20 minutes.

6. Drain wood chunks, and place on coals. Place rib slabs in a rib rack on upper cooking grate; cover with smoker lid.

7. Smoke ribs, maintaining the temperature inside smoker between 225° and 250°, for 4 hours and 30 minutes. Remove lid, baste with half of Paul's Barbecue Sauce, and, if necessary, add more beer to water pan. Cover with smoker lid, and smoke 30 more minutes. Cut meat into 3-rib sections, slicing between bones, and serve with remaining half of Paul's Barbecue Sauce.

Paul's Pork Ribs Rub

makes about 1¾ cups   prep: 5 min.

1 cup Greek seasoning
¼ cup garlic powder

¼ cup paprika
¼ cup firmly packed brown sugar

1. Combine all ingredients. Store in an airtight container.

Note: We tested with Cavender's All Purpose Greek Seasoning.

Paul's Chicken Rub: Substitute 3 Tbsp. dried oregano for the brown sugar, and store in an airtight container. Makes about 1⅔ cups.

Paul's Barbecue Sauce

makes about 3½ cups   prep: 20 min.   cook: 20 min.

This barbecue sauce is so darn good that it will be a permanent condiment in your refrigerator. Make an extra batch, and store in an airtight container up to 3 weeks.

2 Tbsp. butter
1 Tbsp. olive oil
1 medium onion, finely chopped
½ green bell pepper, finely chopped
4 garlic cloves, minced
3 medium jalapeño peppers, seeded and minced
1 cup firmly packed brown sugar
1 cup cider vinegar
1 cup chili sauce

1 cup bottled barbecue sauce
1 Tbsp. dry mustard
1 Tbsp. paprika
3 Tbsp. fresh lemon juice
2 Tbsp. Worcestershire sauce
2 Tbsp. hot sauce
2 Tbsp. molasses
¼ tsp. salt

1. Melt butter with oil in a large Dutch oven over medium heat.
2. Add onion and next 3 ingredients, and sauté 5 to 6 minutes or until onion is tender.
3. Stir in brown sugar and remaining ingredients; bring to a boil. Reduce heat to medium-low, and simmer 10 minutes. Pour mixture through a wire-mesh strainer into a bowl, discarding solids.

taking sides

What's on the Side?

Barbecue side dishes can be as traditional as the meat or sauce. Once again, the region dictates what you're likely to find.

Most barbecue fans can agree on a few sides that are absolute "must-haves." The universally accepted accompaniments include coleslaw, potato salad, French fries or chips, baked beans, corn on the cob, and cornbread of some kind. Sweet iced tea is the undisputed beverage of choice.

But in South Carolina, you may get hash over rice and even some collard greens.

Hushpuppies come with North Carolina 'cue. In Texas, expect two slices of white bread, jalapeños, perhaps a slice of cheese, and down it all with beer or a Big Red soft drink. The baked beans there will be Southwest-spiced pintos, not the mustard and molasses-sweetened baked beans of the rest of the region. And, in Kentucky, burgoo is a must, just as Brunswick stew is a given in south Georgia.

BABY LOIN BACK RIBS

makes 3 to 4 servings   prep: 20 min.   chill 3 hr.   grill: 2 hr.

2   slabs baby loin back ribs (about 4 lb.)

3   Tbsp. Dry Spices

1   cup Basting Sauce

1   cup Sweet Sauce

1. Place ribs in a large, shallow pan. Rub Dry Spices evenly over ribs. Cover and chill 3 hours.
2. Light one side of grill, heating to 300° to 350° (medium) heat. Place food over unlit side, and grill, covered with grill lid, for 2 to 2½ hours, basting every 30 minutes with Basting Sauce and turning occasionally. Brush ribs with Sweet Sauce the last 30 minutes. Prepare a hot fire by piling charcoal or lava rocks on one side of grill, leaving other side empty. (For gas grill, light only one side.) Place food rack on grill. Arrange ribs over unlit side.
3. Grill ribs, covered with grill lid, over medium heat (300° to 350°) for 2 to 2½ hours, basting every 30 minutes with Basting Sauce and turning occasionally. Brush ribs with Sweet Sauce the last 30 minutes.

Note: Use remaining Dry Spices as a rub on pork or chicken.

Dry Spices

makes 6½ Tbsp.   prep: 5 min.

3	Tbsp. paprika	1	tsp. dry mustard
2	tsp. seasoned salt	1	tsp. ground oregano
2	tsp. garlic powder	1	tsp. ground red pepper
2	tsp. ground black pepper	½	tsp. chili powder

1. Combine all ingredients in a small bowl.

Basting Sauce

makes 4½ cups   prep: 5 min.   stand: 8 hr.

¼	cup firmly packed brown sugar	¼	cup Worcestershire sauce
1½	Tbsp. Dry Spices	½	tsp. hot sauce
2	cups red wine vinegar	1	small bay leaf
2	cups water		

1. Stir together all ingredients; cover and let stand 8 hours. Remove bay leaf. (Sauce is intended for basting ribs only.)

Sweet Sauce

make 1 qt.   prep: 10 min.   cook: 30 min.

1	cup ketchup	1	Tbsp. seasoned salt
1	cup red wine vinegar	1	Tbsp. paprika
1	(8-oz.) can tomato sauce	1	Tbsp. lemon juice
½	cup spicy honey mustard	1½	tsp. garlic powder
½	cup Worcestershire sauce	⅛	tsp. chili powder
¼	cup butter	⅛	tsp. ground red pepper
2	Tbsp. brown sugar	⅛	tsp. ground black pepper
2	Tbsp. hot sauce		

1. Bring all ingredients to a boil in a Dutch oven. Reduce heat, and simmer sauce, stirring occasionally, 30 minutes.

TABB'S BARBECUE PORK

makes 8 servings   prep: 30 min.   chill: 8 hr.   stand: 1 hr., 15 min.   soak: 1 hr.   smoke: 8 hr.

pictured on page 410

1	(6-lb.) bone-in pork shoulder roast (Boston butt)	Hickory wood chunks
1	cup Barbecue Rub	Apple juice

1. Trim fat on pork shoulder roast to about ⅛ inch thick.

2. Sprinkle pork evenly with Barbecue Rub; rub thoroughly into meat. Wrap pork tightly with plastic wrap, and chill 8 hours.

3. Discard plastic wrap. Let pork stand at room temperature 1 hour.

4. Soak hickory chunks in water 1 hour.

5. Prepare smoker according to manufacturer's instructions, bringing internal temperature to 225° to 250°; maintain temperature for 15 to 20 minutes.

6. Drain wood chunks, and place on coals. Place pork on lower cooking grate, fat side up.

7. Spritz pork with apple juice each time charcoal or wood chunks are added to the smoker.

8. Smoke pork roast, maintaining the temperature inside smoker between 225° and 250°, for 6 hours or until a meat thermometer inserted horizontally into thickest portion of pork registers 170°. Remove pork from smoker, and place on a sheet of heavy-duty aluminum foil; spritz with apple juice. Wrap tightly, and return to smoker, and smoke 2 hours or until thermometer inserted horizontally into the thickest portion of pork registers 190°. Remove pork from smoker, and let stand 15 minutes. Remove bone, and chop pork.

Barbecue Rub

makes about 3 cups   prep: 20 min.

1¼	cups firmly packed dark brown sugar	1	Tbsp. ground cumin
⅓	cup kosher salt	1	Tbsp. lemon pepper
¼	cup granulated garlic	1	Tbsp. onion powder
¼	cup paprika	2	tsp. dry mustard
1	Tbsp. chili powder	2	tsp. ground black pepper
1	Tbsp. ground red pepper	1	tsp. ground cinnamon

1. Combine all ingredients. Store in an airtight container.

taking sides

South's Best Barbecue

That's easy. Just don't express too strong of an opinion about religion. Or politics. Or football. Or, especially, barbecue.

Opinions about barbecue throughout the South are as many as the stars in the sky. But voices can rise and heads will shake when the conversation comes around to whose is the best. The great divide in preferences usually boils down to what was on the menu at a favorite barbecue joint near where one grew up, though most Southerners have learned to appreciate, even if they don't relish, other styles.

Regional preferences run strong, such as in Texas, where beef is king. In East Texas, ribs are likely found with the brisket, and the sauces are dark and sweet. German influence brings sausage, called "hot links," to the barbecue plate in Central Texas, along with brisket, though it's not hard to find pork, all smoked over oak. Mesquite smoke flavors barbecue farther west, where goat, or "cabrito," is common on the pit.

South Carolina, known for pulled pork, offers three styles of sauce. Mustard flavored is favored in mid- to lower Carolina, and vinegar-and-pepper sauce in the Lowcountry. Look for red tomato-based type in the Upstate area.

North Carolina is severely split. In the east, vinegar sauce with red and black pepper reigns over roasted whole hog pork chopped fine. In the west, Lexington- or Piedmont-style sweet sauce of ketchup and vinegar flavors smoky pork shoulders chopped or sliced. In Tennessee it's still pork—dry-rubbed ribs in Memphis, sweeter red sauces in the east, and near Nashville, it's easy to find a mayo-based white sauce for chicken.

Perhaps that's because Nashville's not too far from North Alabama, where white barbecue sauce with chicken became famous. The rest of Alabama, Georgia, and Mississippi offer mostly pork, but the sauces vary from red to vinegar to white, and sometimes all three are on the table so you can have your choice.

In Kentucky, tradition brings mutton to the pit alongside other meats, a holdover from the 1800s when sheep grazed there. Sassafras, hickory, and oak smoke season the meat served with a range of sauce flavors.

SLOW-GRILLED PORK WITH RANCH-BARBECUE SAUCE

makes 6 servings   prep: 15 min.   chill: 8 hr.   stand: 45 min.   grill: 3 hr., 30 min.

This recipe is for a two-burner gas grill.

1   (1-oz.) envelope Ranch dressing mix
1   (5-lb.) bone-in pork shoulder roast (Boston butt)
½   (16-oz.) bottle Creole butter injector sauce
    (with injector)

Ranch-Barbecue Sauce
Garnish: bread-and-butter pickle slices (optional)

1. Rub dressing mix evenly over roast. Inject butter sauce evenly into roast. Wrap tightly with plastic wrap, and place in a shallow dish or large zip-top plastic freezer bag; cover or seal and chill 8 hours. Let stand at room temperature 30 minutes before grilling. Remove plastic wrap.
2. Light one side of grill, heating to high heat (400° to 500°); leave other side unlit. Place roast, fat side up, over unlit side of grill, and grill, covered with grill lid, 3½ to 4½ hours or until meat thermometer inserted into thickest portion registers 185°. (Meat will easily pull away from bone.) Let stand 15 minutes. Coarsely chop, and serve with Ranch-Barbecue Sauce. Garnish, if desired.

Note: We tested with Cajun Injector Creole Butter Injectable Marinade.

Ranch-Barbecue Sauce

makes about 1¼ cups   prep: 5 min.   cook: 20 min.

1   (18-oz.) bottle barbecue sauce
1   (1-oz.) envelope Ranch dressing mix

¼   cup honey
½   tsp. dry mustard

1. Stir together all ingredients in a saucepan over medium-high heat; bring to a boil. Reduce heat, and simmer, stirring occasionally, 20 minutes.

Note: We tested with Stubb's Original Bar-B-Q Sauce.

JALAPEÑO GRILLED PORK

makes 8 servings   prep: 35 min.   chill: 8 hr.   grill: 40 min.

5	to 6 jalapeño peppers, divided
2	garlic cloves, minced
1	plum tomato, peeled, seeded, and diced
¼	cup lime juice

2	Tbsp. chopped fresh cilantro
1¼	tsp. salt, divided
1	(3-lb.) boneless pork loin roast
¼	cup butter

1. Preheat grill to 350° to 400° (medium-high) heat. Seed and chop 3 peppers. Stir together chopped pepper, next 4 ingredients, and ¼ tsp. salt.

2. Butterfly roast by making a lengthwise cut down center of 1 flat side, cutting to within ½ inch from left side; repeat procedure to right side. Open roast, and place between 2 sheets of heavy-duty plastic wrap; flatten to ½-inch thickness using a meat mallet or rolling pin. Spread pepper mixture over roast. Roll up, and tie at 1-inch intervals with string. Place, seam side down, in a lightly greased 11- x 7-inch baking dish; cover and chill 8 hours.

3. Seed and chip remaining 2 to 3 jalapeño peppers. Stir together peppers, butter, and remaining 1 tsp. salt.

4. Grill pork, covered, 40 minutes or until a meat thermometer inserted into thickest portion registers 160°, turning once and basting often with butter mixture. Slice and serve with gourmet greens.

GRILLED HONEY-MUSTARD PORK TENDERLOIN

makes 8 servings   prep: 10 min.   chill: 2 hr.   grill: 30 min.   stand: 10 min.

2½	lb. pork tenderloin
½	cup chopped fresh parsley
½	cup red wine vinegar
¼	cup olive oil
¼	cup honey

3	Tbsp. country-Dijon mustard
2	garlic cloves, minced
1	Tbsp. kosher salt
1½	tsp. coarsely ground pepper

1. Remove silver skin from tenderloin, leaving a thin layer of fat covering the tenderloin.

2. Stir together chopped parsley and next 7 ingredients until blended. Pour mixture into a large, shallow dish or zip-top plastic freezer bag; add pork, cover or seal, and chill at least 2 hours or up to 8 hours, turning occasionally. Remove pork, discarding marinade.

3. Preheat grill to 350° to 400° (medium-high). Grill tenderloin, covered with grill lid, 8 to 10 minutes on all sides or until a meat thermometer inserted into thickest portion registers 150° to 155°. Remove tenderloin from grill, and let stand 10 minutes before slicing.

{family favorite}

GRILLED PORK TENDERLOIN SALAD WITH ROASTED SWEET POTATOES

makes 6 servings   prep: 30 min.   bake: 20 min.   grill: 24 min.   stand: 10 min.

3   small sweet potatoes (about 1½ lb.)

2   tsp. olive oil

½   tsp. ground allspice

¼   tsp. ground red pepper

1½ tsp. salt, divided

1   (2-lb.) package pork tenderloin

½   tsp. freshly ground black pepper

8   cups gourmet mixed salad greens

1   (4-oz.) package crumbled feta cheese

½   small red onion, halved and sliced

¾   cup sweetened dried cranberries

½   cup sliced honey-roasted almonds

Raspberry Salad Dressing

1. Preheat oven to 450°. Peel sweet potatoes, and cut into ½-inch-thick wedges; toss with oil, allspice, red pepper, and ½ tsp. salt. Arrange potato wedges in a single layer on a lightly greased jelly-roll pan.

2. Bake at 450° on an oven rack one-third up from bottom of oven 10 minutes; turn potatoes, and bake 10 to 15 minutes or until crisp-tender. Remove from oven, and let cool.

3. Preheat grill to 350° to 400° (medium-high) heat. Sprinkle pork with ½ tsp. black pepper and remaining 1 tsp. salt. Grill pork, covered with grill lid, 6 to 8 minutes on all sides or until a meat thermometer inserted into thickest portion registers 150° to 155°. Remove pork from grill, and let stand 10 minutes. Cut diagonally into ½-inch-thick slices.

4. Toss together greens and next 4 ingredients in a large bowl; transfer to a serving platter, and top with sliced pork and sweet potatoes. Serve with Raspberry Salad Dressing.

Note: We tested with Sunkist Almond Accents Honey Roasted Flavored Sliced Almonds.

Raspberry Salad Dressing

makes about ¾ cup   prep: 5 min.

¼   cup white wine vinegar

2   Tbsp. raspberry preserves

1   Tbsp. honey

½   cup olive oil

1. Whisk together first 3 ingredients in a bowl until blended. Add olive oil in a slow, steady stream, whisking constantly, until blended.

MOLASSES-BALSAMIC PORK KABOBS WITH GREEN TOMATOES AND PLUMS

makes 4 to 6 servings   prep: 20 min.   soak: 30 min.   grill: 18 min.   **pictured on page 336**

8 (12-inch) wooden or metal skewers
1 (1.5-lb.) package pork tenderloin, trimmed and cut into 1½-inch pieces
4 large plums, quartered
2 medium-size green tomatoes, cut into eighths

2 medium-size red onions, cut into eighths
2 tsp. seasoned salt
2 tsp. pepper
½ cup molasses
¼ cup balsamic vinegar

1. Soak wooden skewers in water 30 minutes.

2. Preheat grill to 350° to 400° (medium-high). Thread pork and next 3 ingredients alternately onto skewers, leaving ¼ inch between pieces. Sprinkle kabobs with seasoned salt and pepper. Stir together molasses and vinegar.

3. Grill kabobs, covered with grill lid, over 350° to 400° (medium-high) heat 12 minutes, turning after 6 minutes. Baste kabobs with half of molasses mixture, and grill 3 minutes. Turn kabobs, baste with remaining half of molasses mixture, and grill 3 more minutes or until done.

Molasses-Balsamic Chicken Kabobs With Green Tomatoes and Plums: Substitute 1½ lb. skinned and boned chicken breasts for pork. Proceed with recipe as directed.

Molasses-Balsamic Turkey Kabobs With Green Tomatoes and Plums: Substitute 2 (¾-lb.) turkey tenderloins for pork. Proceed with recipe as directed.

Molasses-Balsamic Pork Kabobs With Green Apples and Peppers: Substitute 1 Granny Smith apple, cut into eighths, and 1 large red bell pepper, cut into 1-inch pieces, for plums and green tomatoes. Proceed with recipe as directed.

GRILLED LEG OF LAMB

makes 8 servings   prep: 15 min.   chill: 8 hr.   grill: 1 hr., 30 min.   stand: 30 min.

1   head garlic
1   (6- to 7-lb.) leg of lamb, trimmed
1   (750-milliliter) bottle dry red wine
¼   cup olive oil

1   Tbsp. dried oregano
1   Tbsp. dried rosemary
2   tsp. paprika

1. Peel garlic; cut 5 cloves into thin slices, and crush remaining cloves.

2. Make 1-inch-deep cuts into lamb, using a small paring knife; insert a garlic slice into each cut. Place lamb in a large shallow dish.

3. Combine crushed garlic, wine, and next 4 ingredients; reserve 1 cup wine mixture, and refrigerate. Pour remaining wine mixture over lamb; cover and refrigerate 8 hours or overnight, turning occasionally.

4. Remove lamb from marinade, discarding marinade.

5. Preheat grill to 250° to 300° (low) heat. Grill, covered with grill lid, for 1½ hours or until a meat thermometer inserted into thickest portion, not touching fat or bone, registers 145°, turning and basting with reserved wine mixture every 15 minutes. Remove from heat; cover and let stand 30 minutes.

GRILLED LAMB CHOPS WITH LEMON-TARRAGON AÏOLI AND ORANGE GREMOLATA

makes 4 servings   prep: 10 min.   stand: 20 min.   grill: 10 min.   **pictured on page 412**

At medium-rare, the meat will feel soft and slightly springy when pressed with tongs or your finger. Medium lamb will be slightly firm and springy. Lamb chops cooked beyond medium doneness may be tough and dry. Remember, the meat will continue to cook during the five-minute standing time.

8   (1½- to 2-inch-thick) lamb loin chops
     (about 2½ lb.)
2   Tbsp. olive oil
1   tsp. salt

½   tsp. freshly ground pepper
1   navel orange
Lemon-Tarragon Aïoli
Orange Gremolata

1. Preheat grill to 350° to 400° (medium-high) heat. Trim fat from edges of lamb chops to ⅛-inch thickness. Brush both sides of lamb evenly with olive oil. Sprinkle evenly with salt and pepper. Let stand 15 minutes.

2. Grill lamb chops, covered with grill lid, 4 to 5 minutes on each side (medium-rare) or to desired degree of doneness. Transfer lamb chops to a serving platter; cover loosely with aluminum foil, and let stand 5 minutes.

3. Cut orange into 8 wedges. Grill orange wedges, covered with grill lid, 1 to 2 minutes on each side or until grill marks appear. Serve lamb chops with grilled orange wedges, Lemon-Tarragon Aïoli, and Orange Gremolata.

Lemon-Tarragon Aïoli

makes about 1 cup   prep: 10 min.   chill: 30 min.

1 shallot, chopped	2 Tbsp. fresh lemon juice
¾ cup mayonnaise	1 tsp. fresh minced garlic
2 Tbsp. chopped fresh tarragon	1½ tsp. Dijon mustard

1. Process all ingredients in a blender until smooth; transfer to a small bowl. Cover and chill at least 30 minutes or up to 3 days.

Orange Gremolata

makes about ½ cup   prep: 10 min.

½ cup minced fresh flat-leaf parsley	⅛ tsp. salt
2 tsp. orange zest	Pinch of pepper
2 tsp. minced fresh garlic	

1. Combine all ingredients. Serve immediately, or cover and chill up to 3 days.

Get To Know Lamb

• Excellent quality lamb is available year-round now, not just in the spring. It's produced in America and also imported from Australia and New Zealand.

• Lamb is sold packaged fresh in a meat tray with plastic overwrap. Use lamb within two days of purchase, or freeze up to two months. It is also sold vacuum-sealed in heavy plastic wrapping. Store in fridge up to two weeks, or freeze. When you open a vacuum-sealed package you may detect a slight, unusual smell. This is normal and will dissipate in a few minutes.

• Thaw lamb as you would other frozen meals—overnight in the fridge. This method preserves juiciness, texture, and flavor.

RED PEPPER-PEACH GRILLED TURKEY

makes 8 servings   prep: 30 min.   grill: 3 hr.   stand: 10 min.

Allowing the turkey to stand for a full 10 minutes is important. If you slice it sooner, all of the juices will end up on the cutting board rather than redistributed back into the meat.

1 (8-lb.) turkey, thawed	13 bacon slices (about ¾ lb.)
1 Tbsp. vegetable oil	½ cup red pepper jelly
2 tsp. salt	½ cup peach preserves
½ tsp. pepper	Vegetable cooking spray

1. Coat cold cooking grate with cooking spray, and place on grill over a drip pan for indirect grilling. Light one side of grill, heating to high heat (400° to 500°). Remove giblets, neck, and gravy packet from turkey; reserve for another use, if desired.

2. Rinse turkey with cold water; pat dry. Cut turkey along both sides of backbone, separating backbone from the turkey. Remove and discard backbone. Clip off wing tips. Using your hands, press down center along breast until flattened. Rub evenly with oil, and sprinkle with salt and pepper. Wrap or cover turkey, breast side up, with bacon.

3. Combine red pepper jelly and peach preserves in a small bowl.

4. Place turkey, breast side up, over unlit side of grill, and grill 1½ hours. Rotate turkey 180°, turning side closest to heat source away from heat source, and grill 1½ hours or until a meat thermometer inserted into thickest portion registers 170°, basting with jelly mixture during last 45 minutes of cooking. Remove from grill, and let stand 10 minutes.

Note: Thaw turkey in the refrigerator for 2 to 3 days. Let stand at room temperature for 30 to 45 minutes before grilling to ensure even cooking. Meat and poultry thawed slowly in a refrigerator retain more moisture when cooked.

Grilling fish on cedar planks is so easy. Not only does the wood add smoky flavor to your dish, but the planks also prevent the fish from flaking and falling through the food grate. Soak the planks in water at least 8 hours beforehand to prevent burning. Keep a spray bottle of water handy for any flare-ups. Look for the planks in the grilling section of your grocery store, home-improvement center, or specialty kitchen or garden shop.

LEMON-GRILLED SALMON

makes 4 servings   prep: 15 min.   soak: 8 hr.   grill: 15 min.

2	(15- x 6-inch) cedar grilling planks	1	Tbsp. olive oil
3	Tbsp. chopped fresh dill	1	garlic clove, pressed
3	Tbsp. chopped fresh parsley	½	tsp. salt
2	tsp. lemon zest	¼	tsp. pepper
3	Tbsp. fresh lemon juice	4	(6-oz.) salmon fillets

1. Weigh down cedar planks with a heavier object in a large container. Add water to cover, and soak at least 8 hours.

2. Combine dill and next 5 ingredients; set aside.

3. Sprinkle salt and pepper evenly on salmon.

4. Remove cedar planks from water, and place planks on cooking grate on grill.

5. Preheat grill to 350° to 400° (medium-high) heat. Grill soaked planks, covered with grill lid, 2 minutes or until the planks begin to lightly smoke. Place 2 fillets on each cedar plank, and grill, covered with grill lid, 15 to 18 minutes or until fish flakes with a fork. Remove fish from planks to individual serving plates using a spatula. (Carefully remove planks from grill using tongs.) Spoon herb mixture over fish, and serve immediately.

Per serving: Calories 310; Fat 15.7g, (sat 2.4g, mono 6.6g, poly 5.3g); Protein 38.7g; Fiber 0.3g; Chol 107mg; Iron 1.8mg; Sodium 378mg; Calc 31mg

[southern lights]

GRILLED SALMON WITH HERB VINAIGRETTE

makes 4 servings   prep: 10 min.   cook: 5 min.   grill: 10 min.

You can substitute grouper, redfish, or tuna for salmon.

4	(8-oz.) salmon fillets	1	Tbsp. Dijon mustard
1	tsp. salt, divided	¼	tsp. sugar
½	tsp. pepper	1	Tbsp. each chopped fresh chives, parsley, and tarragon
2	shallots, minced		
½	cup olive oil, divided	⅛	tsp. dried crushed red pepper (optional)
2	Tbsp. white wine vinegar		Vegetable cooking spray

1. Coat cold cooking grate with cooking spray; place on grill. Preheat grill to 400° to 500° (high) heat. Sprinkle salmon evenly with ¾ tsp. salt and ½ tsp. pepper.

2. Sauté shallots in 1 Tbsp. hot oil over medium heat 5 minutes or until golden. Remove from heat.

3. Whisk together vinegar and mustard in a small bowl; whisk in remaining oil in a slow, steady stream until mixture is thickened and blended. Stir in shallots, remaining ¼ tsp. salt, sugar, herbs, and, if desired, crushed red pepper.

4. Place salmon on cooking grate, and grill 5 to 7 minutes on each side or to desired degree of doneness. Serve with vinaigrette.

GRILLED SHRIMP WITH BACON AND JALAPEÑOS

makes 8 servings   prep: 20 min.   soak: 30 min.   grill: 4 min.

If you're in a hurry, try the fully cooked bacon slices. Don't use flat, thin wooden picks—use thick, round ones.

16	thick, round wooden picks	¼	tsp. salt
16	unpeeled, large raw shrimp	⅛	tsp. black pepper
2	jalapeño peppers	8	thick-cut bacon slices, halved
2	Tbsp. olive oil		

1. Preheat grill to 350° to 400° (medium-high) heat. Soak round wooden picks in water 30 minutes.

2. Peel shrimp, leaving tails on; devein, if desired. Set shrimp aside.

3. Cut each pepper lengthwise into 8 pieces; remove seeds.

4. Toss together shrimp, jalapeño peppers, olive oil, salt, and black pepper in a bowl. Set aside.

5. Microwave bacon slices on HIGH 30 seconds.

6. Wrap 1 bacon slice half around 1 shrimp and 1 piece of jalapeño pepper. Secure with a wooden pick. Repeat procedure with remaining bacon slices, shrimp, and jalapeño pepper pieces.

7. Grill, without grill lid, 4 to 6 minutes or until shrimp turn pink, turning once.

GRILLED PARSLEYED SHRIMP AND VEGETABLES

makes 6 to 8 appetizer servings   prep: 15 min.   grill: 14 min.   chill: 8 hr.

The lemon halves placed in the bottom of the serving bowl add color and act as a strainer. The shrimp and veggies sit on top, while the marinade settles to the bottom of the bowl.

3	lb. unpeeled jumbo raw shrimp (16 to 20 count per lb.)	2	large red onions
2	lemons, halved	1	cup chopped fresh flat-leaf parsley
2	large yellow bell peppers	1	garlic clove, pressed
2	large green bell peppers	1	(16-oz.) bottle olive oil-and-vinegar dressing
			Garnish: fresh flat-leaf parsley sprigs (optional)

1. Preheat grill to 350° to 400° (medium-high) heat. Peel shrimp, leaving tails on; devein, if desired.

2. Squeeze juice from lemon halves to measure ¼ cup; set juice aside. Reserve and chill lemon halves for later use.

3. Grill shrimp, covered with grill lid, 2 to 3 minutes on each side or until shrimp turn pink. Place in a large bowl.

4. Cut each pepper into 4 large pieces; cut each onion horizontally into 3 large slices.

5. Grill vegetables, covered with a grill lid, 5 to 7 minutes on each side or until bell peppers look blistered and onions are crisp-tender; cut into 2-inch pieces. Add grilled vegetables, chopped parsley, and garlic to shrimp in bowl. Pour dressing and lemon juice over mixture, and stir to coat and combine. Cover and chill 8 hours or overnight.

7. Arrange reserved lemon halves in bottom of a deep serving bowl. Spoon marinated shrimp and vegetable mixture over top of lemon halves. Garnish, if desired.

Note: We tested with Newman's Own Olive Oil & Vinegar dressing.

GRILLED ROMAINE SALAD WITH BUTTERMILK-CHIVE DRESSING

makes 4 servings   prep: 10 min.   grill: 3 min.   **pictured on page 414**

Vegetable cooking spray or oil

4   bunches romaine hearts

1   red onion

1   to 2 Tbsp. olive oil

Buttermilk-Chive Dressing

Kosher salt to taste

Freshly ground pepper to taste

½   cup freshly shaved or shredded Parmesan cheese

1. Coat cold cooking grate of grill with cooking spray, or brush lightly with vegetable oil, and place on grill. Preheat grill to 300° to 350° (medium) heat.

2. Cut romaine hearts in half lengthwise, keeping leaves intact. Cut red onion crosswise into ½-inch slices, keeping rings intact; brush with olive oil, and set aside.

3. Place romaine halves, cut side down, on cooking grate. Grill, without grill lid, 3 to 5 minutes or until just wilted. If desired, rotate halves once to get crisscross grill marks. Brush warm romaine halves with Buttermilk-Chive Dressing, coating lightly.

4. Place 2 romaine halves on each of 4 salad plates. Sprinkle with salt and pepper to taste. Top each evenly with onion slices and freshly shaved Parmesan cheese. Serve immediately with remaining Buttermilk-Chive Dressing.

Buttermilk-Chive Dressing

makes 1¼ cups   prep: 5 min.

¾   cup buttermilk

½   cup mayonnaise

2   Tbsp. chopped fresh chives

1   Tbsp. minced green onion

1   garlic clove, minced

½   tsp. salt

¼   tsp. freshly ground pepper

1. Whisk together all ingredients. Cover; chill until ready to use.

HERBED SALAD WITH GRILLED
BALSAMIC VEGETABLES

makes 6 to 8 servings   prep: 15 min.

To prepare ahead, wash the greens, and spin them dry. Wrap in damp paper towels. Store in zip-top plastic freezer bags in the refrigerator.

8 cups mixed baby greens	3 Tbsp. chopped fresh basil
3 tomatoes, sliced	2 Tbsp. chopped fresh chives or green onions
Grilled Balsamic Vegetables	1 Tbsp. chopped fresh marjoram (optional)
½ cup pitted ripe black olives	½ cup crumbled feta or goat cheese
½ cup olive oil	⅓ cup refrigerated shredded Romano or Parmesan
3 Tbsp. balsamic vinegar	cheese

1. Place mixed greens on a large serving platter. Arrange tomato slices in center of platter over greens. Arrange Grilled Balsamic Vegetables and black olives around edge of platter over greens.
2. Whisk together olive oil and vinegar; drizzle over tomatoes and grilled vegetables. Sprinkle tomatoes evenly with basil, chives, and, if desired, marjoram. Top evenly with cheeses.

Grilled Balsamic Vegetables

makes 6 to 8 servings   prep: 25 min.   grill: 14 min.

4 medium-size fresh beets	¼ cup canola oil
2 large red bell peppers	1½ Tbsp. balsamic vinegar
2 small zucchini	½ tsp. salt
1 small eggplant	½ tsp. freshly ground pepper
1 large red onion	Crumbled goat cheese (optional)

1. Preheat grill to 350° to 400° (medium-high) heat. Trim stems from beets to 1 inch; cut into ½-inch-thick rounds. Cut bell peppers into 1-inch strips. Cut off ends of zucchini and eggplant; cut each lengthwise into ¾-inch-thick slices. Cut onion into ½-inch-thick rounds.
2. Whisk together oil and vinegar in a large bowl. Add cut vegetables, and sprinkle vegetables evenly with salt and pepper, tossing to coat.
3. Grill beets, covered with grill lid, 4 to 7 minutes on each side or until tender; grill bell peppers, zucchini, eggplant, and onion 3 to 5 minutes on each side or until crisp-tender. Cool beets slightly, and, if desired, peel. Sprinkle vegetables with goat cheese, if desired.

GRILLED SWEET POTATOES WITH CREAMY BASIL VINAIGRETTE

makes 6 servings   prep: 10 min.   cook: 12 min.   stand: 10 min.   grill: 12 min.

Vegetable cooking spray   Creamy Basil Vinaigrette
3   lb. sweet potatoes (about 4 to 5)

1. Coat cold cooking grate with cooking spray, and place on grill. Preheat grill to 350° to 400° (medium-high) heat. Bring potatoes and water to cover to a boil in a Dutch oven over high heat; reduce heat to medium-high, and cook 12 to 15 minutes or just until slightly tender. Drain. Plunge potatoes into ice water to stop the cooking process. Drain well. Let stand 10 minutes. Peel and cut into wedges.

2. Place potatoes on cooking grate, and grill, covered with grill lid, 6 to 7 minutes on each side or until grill marks appear. Drizzle potato wedges with Creamy Basil Vinaigrette, and serve immediately.

Per serving (including about 2½ Tbsp. vinaigrette): Calories 201; Fat 1g (sat 0.2g, poly 0.2g); Protein 4.8g; Fiber 6g; Iron 1.3mg; Sodium 352mg; Calc 111mg

Creamy Basil Vinaigrette

makes about 1 cup   prep: 10 min.

½   cup plain fat-free yogurt   ¼   cup red wine vinegar
2   Tbsp. chopped fresh basil   ½   tsp. salt
2   Tbsp. balsamic vinaigrette   ¼   tsp. pepper
2   Tbsp. honey

1. Whisk together all ingredients. Serve immediately, or cover and chill up to 8 hours. If chilling, let stand at room temperature 30 minutes before serving.

Note: We tested with Newman's Own Balsamic Vinaigrette.

Per 2½ Tbsp.: Calories 42; Fat 0.7g (sat 0.1g); Protein 1.3g; Fiber 0.1g; Iron 0.1mg; Sodium 288mg; Calc 44mg

GRILLED ONION SALAD

makes 4 servings   prep: 20 min.   chill: 2 hr.   grill: 10 min.

4	large sweet onions	1	tsp. salt
⅓	cup balsamic vinegar	8	cups mixed salad greens
2	Tbsp. walnut oil	¼	cup chopped fresh parsley
2	Tbsp. honey	¼	cup chopped pecans, toasted

1. Peel onions, leaving root end intact. Cut each onion vertically into quarters, cutting to within ½ inch of root end. Cut each quarter vertically into thirds. Place in a shallow dish.

2. Whisk together vinegar and next 3 ingredients. Pour over onions; cover and chill 2 hours.

3. Drain onions, reserving vinaigrette mixture.

4. Preheat grill to 350° to 400° (medium-high) heat. Grill onions, covered with grill lid, 10 to 15 minutes or until tender. Place each onion on 2 cups salad greens; drizzle with reserved vinaigrette. Sprinkle with parsley and pecans.

GRILLED TOMATOES

makes 8 servings   prep: 5 min.   grill: 4 min.

4	large tomatoes, cut in half crosswise	¼	cup chopped fresh basil
2	Tbsp. olive oil	½	tsp. salt
2	garlic cloves, minced	½	tsp. pepper

1. Brush cut sides of tomato halves with oil, and sprinkle evenly with garlic and remaining ingredients.

2. Preheat grill to 350° to 400° (medium-high) heat. Grill, covered with grill lid, about 2 minutes on each side. Serve immediately.

PORTOBELLO MUSHROOM BURGERS WITH CARROT-CABBAGE SLAW

makes 4 servings   prep: 10 min.   chill: 1 hr.   grill: 6 min.

[southern lights]

4 large portobello mushroom caps	¼ tsp. salt
¼ cup white balsamic vinegar	4 whole wheat hamburger buns
1 Tbsp. olive oil	Carrot-Cabbage Slaw

1. Scrape gills from mushroom caps with a spoon, if desired.

2. Combine vinegar, oil, and salt in a shallow dish or large zip-top plastic freezer bag; add mushrooms, turning to coat. Cover or seal, and chill 1 hour, turning occasionally. Remove mushrooms from marinade, discarding marinade.

3. Preheat grill to 350° to 400° (medium-high) heat. Grill mushrooms, covered with grill lid, 3 to 4 minutes on each side or until tender.

4. Serve mushrooms on buns with slaw.

Per serving (including ½ cup slaw): Calories 258; Fat 9g (sat 1.3g, mono 5.5g, poly 1.7g); Protein 6.5g; Fiber 6.5g; Iron 1.9mg; Sodium 535mg; Calc 73mg

Carrot-Cabbage Slaw

makes 4 servings   prep: 10 min.

For light dressings, we prefer to use white vinegars to prevent the vegetables from becoming discolored.

1 cup shredded carrot (about 2 large carrots)	1 Tbsp. chopped fresh mint
1 cup shredded red cabbage	1 Tbsp. olive oil
½ cup shredded jicama (about ½ small jicama)	1 Tbsp. honey
3 Tbsp. white balsamic vinegar	¼ tsp. salt

1. Stir together all ingredients. Cover and chill until ready to serve.

Per ½ cup: Calories 77; Fat 3.5g (sat 0.5g , mono 2.5g, poly 0.4g); Protein 0.7g; Fiber 2g; Iron 0.4mg; Sodium 174mg; Calc 20mg

POTATO-STUFFED GRILLED BELL PEPPERS

makes 8 servings prep: 25 min. bake: 1 hr., 30 min. cool: 15 min. grill: 18 min.

pictured on page 413

Think twice-baked potato, except the potato mixture is stuffed into a bell pepper half. The peppers roast and char on the bottom, imparting a wonderful sweet flavor, while the upper edges remain crisp-tender. Don't forget to bake the potatoes before the guests arrive.

4	large baking potatoes (about 3½ to 4 lb.)
4	large red bell peppers
1	(16-oz.) container sour cream
½	cup shredded Gouda cheese
¼	cup sliced green onions

3	Tbsp. butter
3	Tbsp. chopped fresh flat-leaf parsley
¾	tsp. salt
½	tsp. pepper
¼	tsp. paprika

1. Preheat oven to 450°. Pierce each potato 3 to 4 times with a fork, and place potatoes directly on oven rack.

2. Bake 1 hour and 30 minutes. Let cool slightly, about 15 minutes.

3. Cut bell peppers in half lengthwise, cutting through stems and keeping intact. Remove and discard seeds and membranes; rinse and pat dry. Set aside.

4. Preheat grill to 350° to 400° (medium-high) heat.

5. Cut baked potatoes in half. Scoop out pulp into a large bowl, discarding shells. Add sour cream and next 6 ingredients to pulp, blending well with a fork or potato masher.

6. Spoon potato mixture evenly into bell pepper halves. Sprinkle with paprika.

7. Grill peppers, covered with grill lid, 18 minutes or until peppers are blistered and potato mixture bubbles around edges. Serve immediately.

Note: We tried microwaving the potatoes, but the texture is mealy; baking is the best choice.

Grilled Stuffed Potatoes: Omit red bell peppers. Proceed with recipe as directed, reserving potato shells and spooning potato mixture into reserved potato shells. Grill as directed, or bake at 350° for 20 minutes or until thoroughly heated.

[casual gatherings]

CHILI-LIME GRILLED CORN

makes 8 servings   prep: 15 min.   stand: 1 hr.   grill: 25 min.

Soak corn husks in a cooler of water before grilling to prevent the husks from burning. After grilling, drain water, and put corn back into cooler for up to 20 minutes to keep warm until ready to serve.

8 ears fresh corn with husks
½ cup butter, softened
1 tsp. lime zest

1 tsp. fresh lime juice
Chili powder

1. Remove heavy outer husks from corn; pull back inner husks. Remove and discard silks. Pull husks over corn. Cover corn with water; let stand 1 hour.

2. Preheat grill to 300° to 350° (medium) heat. Stir together ½ cup softened butter, 1 tsp. lime zest, and 1 tsp. lime juice.

3. Drain corn, and pat dry.

4. Grill corn, without grill lid, 25 minutes or until tender, turning often. Remove corn from grill. Carefully pull back husks, and tie with a leftover husk or kitchen string. Spread with desired amount of butter mixture. Sprinkle corn evenly with desired amount of chili powder.

Note: Stir ½ tsp. chili powder into the butter mixture, if desired.

GRILLED PEACHES JEZEBEL

makes 6 servings   prep: 5 min.   grill: 6 min.   **pictured on page 412**

Horseradish adds a spicy bite to this simple and delicious favorite.

Vegetable cooking spray
¼ cup honey
2 tsp. Dijon mustard

1 tsp. horseradish
6 firm, ripe peaches, halved

1. Coat a cold cooking grate of grill with cooking spray, and place on grill. Preheat grill to 300° to 350° (medium) heat. Whisk together first 3 ingredients. Brush half of honey mixture evenly over cut sides of peaches.

2. Arrange peach halves, cut sides up, on cooking grate; grill, covered with grill lid, 3 minutes on each side or until tender and golden. Remove from grill, and brush cut sides of peaches evenly with remaining honey mixture.

[test kitchen favorite]

STRAWBERRY NAPOLEONS

makes 6 servings   prep 10 min.   grill: 2 min.

2   (5.3-oz.) containers plain fat-free yogurt
3   Tbsp. honey
1   (16-oz.) container fresh strawberries, sliced
2   Tbsp. sugar
4   frozen phyllo sheets, thawed

Vegetable cooking spray
1   tsp. sugar
Garnishes: mint sprigs, whole strawberries
      (optional)

1. Preheat grill to 300° to 350° (medium) heat. Stir together yogurt and honey; cover and chill yogurt sauce until ready to serve.

2. Combine strawberries and 2 Tbsp. sugar; cover and chill until ready to serve.

3. Place 1 phyllo sheet on a flat work surface. Coat with cooking spray, and sprinkle evenly with ¼ tsp. sugar. Top with 1 phyllo sheet; coat again with cooking spray, and sprinkle with ¼ tsp. sugar. Cut phyllo stack into thirds lengthwise; cut each in half, creating 6 even rectangular stacks. Repeat procedure with remaining phyllo sheets, cooking spray, and ½ tsp. sugar.

4. Grill phyllo stacks, without grill lid, 1 to 2 minutes on each side or until lightly browned.

5. Place 1 grilled phyllo stack on each of 6 serving plates; top evenly with half of strawberry slices. Drizzle evenly with half of yogurt sauce. Top each with 1 grilled phyllo stack. Top evenly with remaining strawberry slices and yogurt sauce. Garnish, if desired. Serve immediately.

Calories: 156; Fat 1.2g (sat 0.2g, mono 0.4g, poly 0.3g); Protein 5.3g; Fiber 2.2g; Chol 1mg; Iron 0.9mg; Sodium 118mg; Calc 117mg

MEATS

"I don't know what it is about food your mother makes for you, especially when it's something that anyone can make—pancakes, meatloaf, tuna salad—but it carries a certain taste of memory."

—Mitch Albom

Easy, Elegant Dinner serves 8

Rosemary-Thyme Rib Roast
Potato-Horseradish Gratin With Caramelized Onions (page 862)
Lanny's Salad With Candied Pumpkin Seeds (page 710)
Bakery rolls
Lemon-Coconut Cake (page 214)

ROSEMARY-THYME RIB ROAST

makes 8 to 10 servings   prep: 25 min.   bake: 3 hr.   stand: 15 min.

If you can't find a boneless rib roast, purchase a 6-lb. bone-in roast and have the butcher remove the bone for you.

1 Tbsp. salt	1½ cups dry red wine
2 Tbsp. coarsely ground pepper	1½ cups red wine vinegar
1 (4½-lb.) boneless beef rib roast	½ cup olive oil
4 garlic cloves, minced	Garnishes: fresh rosemary sprigs, fresh thyme
1 Tbsp. dried rosemary	sprigs (optional)
1 tsp. dried thyme	

1. Preheat oven to 250°. Combine salt and pepper; rub evenly over roast.

2. Brown roast on all sides in a large skillet over medium-high heat. Remove skillet from heat, and let roast cool slightly.

3. Combine garlic, dried rosemary, and dried thyme. Rub mixture evenly over roast; place on a lightly greased rack in an aluminum foil-lined roasting pan.

4. Stir together wine, vinegar, and oil. Gradually pour wine mixture over roast.

5. Bake at 250° for 2 hours; increase oven temperature to 350°, and bake 1 more hour, or until a meat thermometer inserted into thickest portion registers 145° (medium-rare) or to desired degree of doneness. Remove roast from oven, and let stand 15 minutes before slicing. Garnish, if desired.

BEEF TENDERLOIN WITH FIVE-ONION SAUCE

makes 8 servings   prep: 15 min.   cook: 30 min.   bake: 45 min.
stand: 10 min.   **pictured on page 414**

Buy a 5- to 6-lb. one, and ask your butcher to trim it to size. Serve this dish with mashed potatoes for a delicious Southern supper.

1 (3½-lb.) trimmed beef tenderloin	2 large red onions, sliced and separated
1½ tsp. salt, divided	into rings
1 tsp. pepper, divided	2 bunches green onions, chopped
2 Tbsp. canola oil	12 shallots, chopped
3 Tbsp. butter	5 garlic cloves, minced
2 large yellow onions, sliced and separated	½ cup cognac
into rings	½ cup beef broth

1. Preheat oven to 400°. Sprinkle tenderloin with ½ tsp. salt and ½ tsp. pepper. Secure with string at 1-inch intervals. Brown tenderloin on all sides in hot oil in a heavy roasting pan or oven-proof Dutch oven. Remove tenderloin, reserving drippings in pan.

2. Add butter to drippings, and cook over medium-high heat until melted. Add yellow and red onions, and sauté 5 minutes. Add green onions, shallots, and garlic, and sauté 10 minutes. Stir in cognac and broth; cook over high heat, stirring constantly, until liquid evaporates (about 5 minutes). Place tenderloin on top.

3. Bake, covered, at 400° for 45 minutes or until a meat thermometer inserted into thickest portion registers 145° (medium-rare). Remove tenderloin from roasting pan, reserving onion mixture in pan; cover tenderloin loosely, and let stand at room temperature 10 minutes.

4. Cook onion mixture over medium heat, stirring constantly, 3 to 5 minutes or until liquid evaporates. Stir in remaining 1 tsp. salt and remaining ½ tsp. pepper. Serve onion mixture with sliced tenderloin.

BOURBON-PEPPERED BEEF IN A BLANKET

makes 8 servings   prep: 25 min.   chill: 8 hr.   cook: 8 min.   bake: 13 min.

8 (6- to 8-oz.) beef tenderloin steaks
   (1½ inches thick)
2 leeks, chopped
¾ cup bourbon
¼ cup freshly cracked black pepper

1 lb. portobello mushrooms, thinly sliced
3 Tbsp. Worcestershire sauce
2 (8-oz.) cans refrigerated crescent rolls
1 egg white, lightly beaten
Garnish: fresh chives (optional)

1. Combine first 3 ingredients in a shallow dish or large zip-top plastic bag. Cover or seal, and chill 8 hours, turning occasionally.

2. Preheat oven to 375°. Remove steaks from marinade, reserving marinade. Press pepper evenly onto both sides of steaks.

3. Cook steaks in a large nonstick skillet over medium-high heat 4 to 5 minutes on each side. Set aside; cool completely.

4. Bring reserved marinade to a boil in a medium saucepan over medium heat. Stir in mushrooms and Worcestershire sauce; reduce heat, and simmer 10 minutes. Keep warm.

5. Unroll crescent rolls, and separate into 8 rectangles; press perforations to seal. Roll rectangles into 6-inch squares.

6. Place 1 steak in center of each pastry square. Bring corners of 1 pastry square to center, pinching to seal. Repeat with remaining steaks and pastry. Brush evenly with egg white.

7. Bake, seam side down, on a lightly greased rack in a broiler pan at 375° for 13 minutes.

8. Spoon warm sauce evenly onto serving plates; top with steaks. Garnish, if desired.

Note: Steaks and sauce can be prepared 1 day ahead. Follow the above directions up to baking the steaks. Remove steaks and sauce from refrigerator, and let stand 30 minutes before completing the recipe.

BEEF TENDERLOIN WITH
AVOCADO BÉARNAISE SAUCE

makes 8 to 10 servings   prep: 20 min.   chill: 1 hr.   bake: 50 min.   stand: 15 min.

1	(4-lb.) trimmed beef tenderloin	3	garlic cloves, minced
1½ tsp. salt		¼	cup minced fresh parsley
¾ tsp. freshly ground pepper		1	Tbsp. lemon zest
3	Tbsp. butter, softened		Avocado Béarnaise Sauce

1. Sprinkle tenderloin evenly with salt and pepper. Stir together butter and next 3 ingredients, and rub mixture over tenderloin. Cover and chill 1 to 2 hours. Place in an aluminum foil-lined 15- x 10-inch jelly-roll pan.

2. Preheat oven to 400°. Bake tenderloin at 400° for 50 minutes or until a meat thermometer inserted into thickest portion registers 145° (medium-rare). Remove from oven, and let stand 15 minutes. Serve with Avocado Béarnaise Sauce.

Avocado Béarnaise Sauce

makes about 3 cups   prep: 20 min.   cook: 8 min.

4	large shallots, diced	½	cup mayonnaise
¾	cup dry white wine	2	Tbsp. lemon juice
3	Tbsp. white wine vinegar	½	tsp. salt
2	tsp. dried tarragon	½	tsp. freshly ground pepper
4	small avocados, peeled, seeded, and chopped		

1. Cook first 4 ingredients in a small saucepan over medium-high heat 8 to 10 minutes or until liquid is reduced to about 2 Tbsp. Cool.

2. Process reduced mixture, avocado, and remaining ingredients in a blender or food processor until smooth, stopping to scrape down sides. Chill up to 2 days, if desired.

[*make ahead*]

RIB EYES WITH RED PEPPER-POLENTA FRIES AND CHILE CORN JUS

makes 8 servings prep: 45 min. grill: 10 min.

8 (10-oz.) rib-eye steaks	½ tsp. pepper
1 Tbsp. vegetable oil	Red Pepper-Polenta Fries
½ tsp. salt	Chile Corn Jus

1. Preheat grill to 350° to 400° (medium-high) heat. Rub steaks evenly with oil. Sprinkle with salt and pepper.

2. Grill steaks, covered with grill lid, 5 minutes on each side or to desired degree of doneness. Serve with Red Pepper-Polenta Fries and Chile Corn Jus.

Red Pepper-Polenta Fries

makes 8 servings prep: 20 min. cook: 14 min. chill: 2 hr.

1 Tbsp. butter	1½ cups yellow cornmeal, divided
1 small onion, diced	3 Tbsp. shredded Monterey Jack cheese
1 small red bell pepper, minced	1 Tbsp. chopped fresh cilantro
1 cup whipping cream	3 cups peanut oil
1 cup chicken broth	1 tsp. salt

1. Melt butter in a large skillet over medium-high heat; add onion and bell pepper, and sauté 3 minutes or until tender. Stir in whipping cream and broth, and bring to a boil. Add 1 cup cornmeal; cook, whisking often, 3 to 5 minutes or until mixture is very thick. Remove from heat. Stir in shredded cheese and cilantro.

2. Spoon polenta into a lightly greased 9- x 5-inch loaf pan. Chill 2 hours.

3. Cut polenta into ½-inch-thick slices; cut each slice into 4 strips. Sprinkle evenly with remaining ½ cup cornmeal.

4. Pour peanut oil into a Dutch oven, and heat to 375°. Add polenta strips, and fry, in batches, 3 minutes or until golden brown. Drain on paper towels. Sprinkle with salt.

Chile Corn Jus

makes 1 cup   prep: 15 min.   cook: 5 min.

1   ear fresh corn
2   plum tomatoes, diced
2   Tbsp. minced onion
¼   medium ancho chile, chopped
2   Tbsp. butter

¼   cup chicken broth
1   tsp. chopped fresh cilantro
¼   tsp. salt
¼   tsp. pepper

1. Cut corn kernels from cob.

2. Cook corn in a lightly greased skillet over medium-high heat 3 minutes. Stir in tomato and remaining ingredients. Reduce heat, and simmer 2 minutes.

BEEF WITH RED WINE SAUCE

makes 6 servings   prep: 15 min.   cook: 6 hr.

A bed of egg noodles absorbs the rich juices of this scrumptious main dish.

3   lb. boneless beef chuck roast, cut into
    1-inch pieces
1   medium onion, sliced
1   lb. fresh mushrooms, halved
1   (1.61-oz.) package brown gravy mix
1   (10½-oz.) can beef broth

1   cup red wine
2   Tbsp. tomato paste
1   bay leaf
Hot cooked egg noodles or rice
Garnish: chopped fresh parsley (optional)

1. Place first 3 ingredients in a 6-qt. slow cooker.

2. Whisk together gravy mix and next 3 ingredients; pour evenly over beef and vegetables. Add bay leaf.

3. Cover and cook on HIGH 6 hours. Remove and discard bay leaf. Serve beef over noodles. Garnish, if desired.

inspirations for your taste

This effortless side dish that pairs perfectly with a variety of meats starts with frozen mashed potatoes, but no one will believe it. That's because it tastes like twice-baked. The ingredient list is short, and the dish is ready in a snap.

Cheesy Ranch-and-Bacon Mashed Potatoes

makes 8 servings   prep: 5 min.   cook: 12 min.

Whisk together 1 (1-oz.) package Ranch dressing mix, 1 cup sour cream, and 1¾ cups milk in a large glass bowl. Stir in 1 (22-oz.) package frozen mashed potatoes. Microwave at HIGH 12 minutes, stirring every 4 minutes. Stir in 6 cooked and crumbled bacon slices and ½ cup shredded Cheddar cheese. Top with sliced green onions, if desired.

COFFEE-RUBBED STRIP STEAKS

makes 4 servings   prep: 10 min.   stand: 10 min.   cook: 20 min.

{family favorite}

2 (1-lb.) beef strip steaks, trimmed and halved	¼ cup minced onion
2 tsp. salt	¼ cup bourbon
1 Tbsp. ground coffee	1 cup brewed coffee
1 Tbsp. cracked pepper	2 Tbsp. butter
1 Tbsp. vegetable oil	Chopped fresh parsley (optional)

1. Preheat oven to 350°. Sprinkle both sides of steaks evenly with salt, and let stand 10 minutes.

2. Combine ground coffee and cracked pepper; rub both sides of steaks with coffee mixture.

3. Cook steaks in hot oil in a large nonstick ovenproof skillet over high heat 2 minutes or until well browned. Remove skillet from heat, and turn steaks.

4. Bake steaks in skillet, browned sides up, at 350° for 5 minutes or to desired degree of doneness. Remove steaks from skillet, and keep warm.

5. Sauté onion in skillet 2 minutes or until tender. Remove skillet from heat; stir in bourbon, and let stand 30 seconds. Return skillet to heat, and cook, stirring often, until liquid almost evaporates. Add brewed coffee, and cook, stirring often, over medium heat, 5 minutes or until liquid is reduced by half. Remove skillet from heat, and stir in butter until melted. Pour sauce over steaks; sprinkle with parsley, if desired, and serve immediately.

Pork Roast With Hopping John
Stuffing, page 538

Tortilla-Crusted Pork, page 534

Apple-Sage Stuffed Pork Chops, page 528

Citrus Glazed Ham,
page 543

Mushroom-and-Fresh
Parsley Noodles,
page 556

Tomato-Herb Pasta, page 547

Easy Lasagna, page 567

Two-Tomato
Linguine,
page 552

Chicken Scaloppine With
Spinach and Linguine,
page 551

Fire-Roasted Shrimp With Orzo,
page 558

Fantastic Foolproof
Smokey Jambalaya,
Page 595

Red Beans and Sausage,
page 592

Red Rice, page 594

Double Apple Pie With
Cornmeal Crust, page 607

Classic Chess Pie,
page 613

Pineapple Meringue
Pie, page 620

Bourbon-Chocolate-
Pecan Tarts, page 642

GRILLED STEAKS BALSAMICO

makes 4 servings prep: 15 min. chill: 2 hr. grill: 10 min. cook: 2 min. **pictured on page 415**

We served the cheese sauce in hollowed-out lemon halves.

⅔ cup balsamic vinaigrette

¼ cup fig preserves

4 (6- to 8-oz.) boneless beef chuck-eye steaks

1 tsp. salt

1 tsp. freshly ground pepper

1 (6.5-oz.) container buttery garlic-and-herb spreadable cheese

1. Process vinaigrette and preserves in a blender until smooth. Place steaks and vinaigrette mixture in a shallow dish or a large zip-top plastic freezer bag. Cover or seal, and chill at least 2 hours. Remove steaks from marinade, discarding marinade.

2. Preheat grill to 350° to 400° (medium-high) heat. Grill, covered with grill lid, 5 to 7 minutes on each side or until desired degree of doneness. Remove to a serving platter, and sprinkle evenly with salt and pepper; keep warm.

3. Heat cheese in a small saucepan over low heat, stirring often, 2 to 4 minutes or until melted. Serve cheese sauce with steaks.

Note: We tested with Alouette Garlic & Herbs Spreadable Cheese.

GRECIAN SKILLET RIB EYES

makes 2 to 4 servings prep: 5 min. cook: 10 min.

Early immigrants, particlarly European and African settlers, brought their heritage homestly cooking to this region to shape the oldest Southern food traditions. You'll find that influence in this this olive-feta-herb topping that works great on chicken and lamb too.

1½ tsp. garlic powder

1½ tsp. dried basil, crushed

1½ tsp. dried oregano, crushed

½ tsp. salt

⅛ tsp. pepper

2 (1-inch-thick) rib-eye steaks (1¾ to 2 lb.)

1 Tbsp. olive oil

1 Tbsp. fresh lemon juice

2 Tbsp. crumbled feta cheese

1 Tbsp. chopped kalamata or ripe olives

1. Combine first 5 ingredients; rub onto all sides of steaks.

2. Pour oil into a large nonstick skillet; place over medium heat until hot. Add steaks, and cook 10 to 14 minutes or to desired degree of doneness, turning once. Sprinkle with lemon juice; top with cheese and olives.

ITALIAN POT ROAST

makes 6 to 8 servings   prep: 35 min.   bake: 3 hr., 30 min.   cook: 13 min.

To make ahead, chill baked roast overnight. Cut into thin slices, and place in a 13- x 9-inch baking dish. Top with gravy. Bake at 350° for 30 minutes or until thoroughly heated. Serve with roasted potatoes.

1	(4½-lb.) rib-eye roast, trimmed*	2	tsp. chopped fresh or 1 tsp. dried basil
2	Tbsp. vegetable oil	2	tsp. chopped fresh or 1 tsp. dried oregano
1	(15-oz.) can tomato sauce	1	(16-oz.) package red potatoes, cut into wedges
½	cup red wine	½	tsp. salt
2	large tomatoes, chopped	¼	tsp. pepper
1	medium onion, minced	3	Tbsp. all-purpose flour
4	garlic cloves, minced	1	cup beef broth or water
1	Tbsp. salt		Garnish: chopped fresh parsley (optional)
1	Tbsp. pepper		

1. Preheat oven to 325°. Cook roast in hot oil in a large Dutch oven over medium-high heat 5 to 6 minutes or until browned on all sides.

2. Combine tomato sauce and next 8 ingredients; pour sauce mixture over roast in Dutch oven.

3. Bake, covered, at 325° for 3 hours or until roast is tender. Remove roast from Dutch oven, and keep warm; reserve drippings in Dutch oven.

4. Place potato wedges in a lightly greased 15- x 10-inch jelly-roll pan. Increase oven temperature to 450°. Bake at 450° for 30 minutes. Sprinkle with ½ tsp. salt and ¼ tsp. pepper.

5. Skim fat from drippings in Dutch oven. Whisk together flour and beef broth until smooth; add to drippings. Cook mixture, stirring constantly, over low heat 8 minutes or until thickened.

6. Cut roast into thin slices. Arrange roast and potatoes on a serving platter. Garnish, if desired. Serve with tomato gravy.

* 1 (4½-lb.) boneless beef rump roast, trimmed, may be substituted. Bake, covered, at 325° for 2 hours and 20 minutes or until tender.

AUNT MARY'S POT ROAST

makes 6 servings   prep: 10 min.   bake: 3 hr.   **pictured on page 414**

To reduce the fat in this recipe, substitute an eye of round roast for the chuck roast. Both cuts of meat become fall-apart tender when cooked with slow, moist heat. Long before the use of electricity, pioneers were using cast-iron Dutch ovens as "slow cookers."

1 (3- to 4-lb.) chuck roast	1 (0.7-oz.) envelope Italian dressing mix
1 (12-oz.) can beer	Roasted Vegetables (optional)

1. Preheat oven to 300°. Brown roast on all sides in a lightly oiled 5-qt. cast-iron Dutch oven over high heat. Remove from heat, and add beer and dressing mix.

2. Bake, covered, at 300° for 3 hours or until tender, turning once. Serve with Roasted Vegetables, if desired.

Roasted Vegetables

makes 6 servings   prep: 10 min.   cook: 45 min.

Slow roasting in a cast-iron skillet accentuates the natural sweetness of these root vegetables. If desired, you may omit the olive oil and add vegetables to the Dutch oven with the pot roast during the last hour of cooking.

1½ lb. new potatoes, cut in half	1 Tbsp. olive oil
1 (16-oz.) bag baby carrots	Salt and pepper to taste
2 medium onions, quartered	

1. Preheat oven to 300°. Toss potatoes, baby carrots, and onions with olive oil, and season to taste with salt and pepper.

2. Bake at 300° in a large cast-iron skillet for 45 minutes, stirring once.

SKILLET PEPPER STEAK AND RICE

makes 4 to 6 servings   prep: 20 min.   cook: 20 min.   **pictured on page 417**

Don't be put off by the long list of ingredients. Most items are probably already in your pantry, spice cabinet, or fridge.

[for kids]

1 (3.5-oz.) boil-in-bag white rice	½ tsp. pepper
1 (10½-oz.) can beef broth	1 lb. boneless top sirloin steak, cut into thin slices
3 Tbsp. cornstarch, divided	1 Tbsp. vegetable oil
2 Tbsp. soy sauce	2 tsp. sesame oil
1 tsp. sugar	1 green bell pepper, sliced
2 tsp. minced fresh or 1 tsp. ground ginger	1 medium-size red onion, sliced
½ tsp. garlic-chili sauce (optional)	½ (8-oz.) package sliced fresh mushrooms
½ tsp. salt	1 garlic clove, pressed

1. Prepare rice according to package directions; set aside.

2. Whisk together beef broth, 1 Tbsp. cornstarch, soy sauce, sugar, ginger, and, if desired, garlic-chili sauce; set aside.

3. Combine remaining 2 Tbsp. cornstarch, salt, and pepper; dredge steak slices in mixture.

4. Heat oils in a large skillet or wok over medium-high heat; add steak, and stir-fry 4 minutes or until browned. Add bell pepper, onion, and mushrooms; stir-fry 8 minutes or until tender. Add garlic; stir-fry 1 minute.

5. Stir in broth mixture. Bring to a boil; reduce heat, and simmer 3 to 5 minutes or until thickened. Remove from heat; stir in rice.

BEEF FAJITAS WITH PICO DE GALLO

makes 6 servings   prep: 5 min.   chill: 8 hr.   grill: 10 min.   stand: 5 min.

We tested this recipe with a George Foreman Jumbo Size Plus electric grill, which grilled all the beef called for in the recipe at one time. If you already own a smaller version of this appliance, cook the beef in batches, wrap in foil, and keep warm while the remainder cooks. Be sure to read the manufacturer's instruction book and safety guidelines first.

1 (8-oz.) bottle zesty Italian dressing	Shredded Cheddar cheese
3 Tbsp. fajita seasoning	Pico de Gallo
2 (1-lb.) flank steaks	Garnishes: lime wedges, fresh cilantro
12 (6-inch) flour tortillas, warmed	sprigs (optional)

1. Combine Italian dressing and fajita seasoning in a shallow dish or zip-top plastic bag; add steak. Cover or seal, and chill 8 hours, turning occasionally. Remove steak from marinade, discarding marinade.

2. Preheat a two-sided contact indoor electric grill according to manufacturer's instructions on HIGH. Place steaks on grill rack, close lid, and grill 10 minutes (medium-rare) or to desired degree of doneness. Remove steaks, and let stand 5 minutes.

3. Cut steaks diagonally across the grain into very thin slices, and serve with tortillas, cheese, and Pico de Gallo. Garnish, if desired.

Note: When using an outdoor gas or charcoal grill, grill steaks, covered with grill lid, over medium-high heat (350° to 400°) for 8 minutes. Turn and grill 5 more minutes or to desired degree of doneness. Proceed as directed. We tested with McCormick Fajitas Seasoning Mix.

Pico de Gallo

makes about 3 cups   prep: 25 min.   chill: 1 hr.

1 pt. grape tomatoes, chopped	1 garlic clove, pressed
1 green bell pepper, chopped	¾ tsp. salt
1 red bell pepper, chopped	½ tsp. ground cumin
1 avocado, peeled and chopped	½ tsp. lime zest
½ medium-size red onion, chopped	¼ cup fresh lime juice
½ cup chopped fresh cilantro	

1. Stir together all ingredients; cover and chill 1 hour.

TASTE OF THE SOUTH

Chicken-fried steak might just well be the national entrée of Texas. Dinner plates laden with fried steaks, potatoes, and gravy are as much a part of the Lone Star State's persona as tumbleweeds and cowboy hats. Though historians stand divided on whether the dish appeared first as a chuck-wagon creation or a takeoff on German Wiener shnitzel, all agree that is a fine way to enjoy some of the less tender cuts of beef.

The dish begins with round steak that has been pounded with a meat mallet or run through a cubing machine. Thus tenderized, it is breaded, fried, and served with cream gravy made from the pan drippings. On this last point, Texas cooks are adamant, because it separates chicken-fried steak from country-fried. "This is not brown gravy, it's cream gravy," says Annetta White of Austin's Broken Spoke restaurant. Mashed or fried potatoes on the plate are a must, but beyond that, the side dishes become a free-for-all of choices with fried okra, fried whole ears of corn, green beans, coleslaw, greens, and biscuits among them.

"At my parents' house, no vegetable except mashed potatoes goes on the plate unless Mom requires it," says Vanessa McNeil Rocchio of our Test Kitchen. Vanessa is a Texan who, as a teenager, made it her mission to find a great chicken-fried steak recipe. "My Dad wanted to have chicken-fried at home, but we didn't know how to do it," she says. "Then I visited Austin, which has lots of places that serve it, and I met someone who worked in one of the kitchens. He told me the secret is crumbled saltine crackers—they give chicken-fried steak a great crust."

One taste of Vanessa's out-of-this-world recipe, and you'll see why Texans are proud to call chicken-fried steak their own.

CHICKEN-FRIED STEAK

makes 4 servings prep: 10 min. cook: 24 min.

Because of its crunchy coating, tender inside, and peppery gravy, this recipe received our highest rating. To acheive maximum flavor, firmly push the cracker crumbs into the cube steak to fill the crevices and to keep the steak from shrinking as it cooks. One taste of this amazing dish, and you'll see why we named it one of our best-ever recipes.

¼ tsp. salt

¼ tsp. pepper

4 (4-oz.) cube steaks

38 saltine crackers (1 sleeve), crushed

1¼ cups all-purpose flour, divided

½ tsp. baking powder

2 tsp. salt, divided

1½ tsp. ground black pepper, divided

½ tsp. ground red pepper

4¾ cups milk, divided

2 large eggs

3½ cups peanut oil

Garnish: chopped fresh parsley (optional)

1. Preheat oven to 225°. Sprinkle salt and pepper evenly over steaks. Set aside.

2. Combine cracker crumbs, 1 cup flour, baking powder, 1 tsp. salt, ½ tsp. black pepper, and red pepper.

3. Whisk together ¾ cup milk and eggs. Dredge steaks in cracker crumb mixture; dip in milk mixture, and dredge in cracker mixture again.

4. Pour oil into a 12-inch skillet; heat to 360°. (Do not use a nonstick skillet.) Fry steaks 10 minutes. Turn and fry 4 to 5 more minutes or until golden brown. Remove to a wire rack on a jelly-roll pan. Keep steaks warm in a 225° oven. Carefully drain hot oil, reserving cooked bits and 1 Tbsp. drippings in skillet.

5. Whisk together remaining ¼ cup flour, 1 tsp. salt, 1 tsp. black pepper, and 4 cups milk. Pour mixture into reserved drippings in skillet; cook over medium-high heat, whisking constantly, 10 to 12 minutes or until thickened. Serve gravy with steaks and mashed potatoes. Sprinkle with parsley, if desired.

TEX-MEX SALISBURY STEAK

makes 6 servings prep: 20 min. cook: 25 min.

1　lb. ground round

½　lb. hot or mild ground pork sausage

1　small onion, chopped

1　large egg

½　cup fine, dry breadcrumbs

¼　cup mild salsa

2　Tbsp. taco seasoning mix

2　Tbsp. chopped fresh cilantro, divided

1　(2.64-oz.) package country-style gravy mix

1　(14½-oz.) can low-sodium beef broth

1　(10-oz.) can diced tomatoes with green chiles, undrained

Garnish: fresh cilantro sprigs (optional)

1. Combine first 7 ingredients and 1 Tbsp. cilantro. Shape mixture into 6 (⅓-inch-thick) patties.

2. Heat a lightly greased large nonstick skillet over medium-high heat. Add patties; reduce heat to low, cover, and cook 8 to 10 minutes on each side or until center is no longer pink. Remove from skillet. Wipe pan clean.

3. Whisk together gravy mix, broth, tomatoes with chiles, and remaining 1 Tbsp. cilantro. Cook over medium heat 1 minute or until thickened. Return patties to skillet, and cook until thoroughly heated. Garnish, if desired.

MINUTE STEAK WITH MUSHROOM GRAVY

makes 4 to 6 servings prep: 10 min. cook: 29 min.

1　(10¾-oz.) can cream of mushroom soup

½　cup buttermilk

¼　tsp. ground red pepper

1½　tsp. salt

1½　tsp. black pepper

1　to 1½ lb. cubed sirloin steaks

½　cup all-purpose flour

2　Tbsp. canola oil

1　(8-oz.) package sliced fresh mushrooms

½　tsp. dried thyme

1. Whisk together soup, buttermilk, ¼ cup water, and red pepper until smooth; set aside.

2. Sprinkle 1 tsp. salt and 1 tsp. pepper evenly over steaks. Stir together remaining ½ tsp. salt, ½ tsp. pepper, and flour in a shallow dish. Dredge steaks in flour mixture.

3. Fry steaks in hot oil in skillet over medium-high heat 2 minutes on each side. Remove steaks, reserving drippings in skillet. Add mushrooms and thyme; sauté 3 to 4 minutes or until browned.

4. Stir reserved soup mixture into mushroom mixture in skillet; cook 1 minute, stirring to loosen particles from bottom of skillet. Bring to a boil, and return steaks to skillet. Cover, reduce heat, and simmer 15 to 20 minutes or until done.

MASHED POTATO-STUFFED FLANK STEAK

makes 4 to 6 servings   prep: 25 min.   cook: 47 min.

There are so many good reasons to use stuffing in recipes. Pragmatic cooks will note that stuffing adds a bit of moisture to lean cuts of beef, pork, and poultry, and the mixture can easily stretch a meal where meat is in short supply. More whimsical cooks may employ stuffing to add an element of surprise to what might otherwise look like a plain dish.

¼	lb. andouille sausage, chopped	1	small garlic clove, minced
1	Tbsp. olive oil	1	cup instant mashed potatoes
1	small onion, chopped	1	cup hot water
1	celery rib, chopped	2	Tbsp. chopped fresh parsley
½	tsp. salt	1½	tsp. chopped fresh thyme
⅛	tsp. pepper	⅛	tsp. ground nutmeg
2	Tbsp. dry white wine or chicken broth	1	(1½-lb.) flank steak

1. Preheat oven to 425°. Cook sausage in hot oil in a skillet over medium heat 5 minutes or until browned. Remove from skillet; set aside.

2. Sauté onion and next 3 ingredients in skillet 5 minutes or until tender. Add wine and garlic; cook 2 minutes or until liquid evaporates. Remove from heat.

3. Stir together mashed potatoes and 1 cup hot water in a large bowl; stir in sausage, onion mixture, parsley, thyme, and nutmeg.

4. Place steak between 2 sheets of heavy-duty plastic wrap; flatten to ¼- to ½-inch thickness using a meat mallet or rolling pin. Spread potato mixture evenly over flank steak, leaving a ½-inch border.

5. Roll steak, jelly-roll fashion, starting with a long side; secure with string. Place on a lightly greased rack in a broiler pan.

6. Bake at 425° for 10 minutes; reduce heat to 375°. Bake 25 to 30 minutes or to desired degree of doneness.

PAN-SEARED SKIRT STEAK WITH POBLANO CHILES AND ONIONS

makes 4 to 6 servings   prep: 25 min.   broil: 10 min.   stand: 15 min.   chill: 20 min.   cook: 35 min.

This popular dish is similar to fajitas. Purchase bitter orange juice marinade in the Mexican food section of supermarkets.

3 poblano chiles	1 tsp. cracked black pepper
2 lb. skirt or flank steak	1 Tbsp. olive oil
2 cups bitter orange juice marinade or	1 medium-size red onion, sliced
apple cider vinegar	1 white onion, sliced
1 tsp. salt	2 carrots, sliced

1. Preheat oven to broil. Broil chiles on an aluminum foil-lined baking sheet 5 inches from heat 5 minutes on each side or until chiles look blistered.

2. Place chiles in a zip-top plastic freezer bag; seal and let stand 15 minutes to loosen skins. Peel chiles; remove and discard seeds. Cut chiles into thin slices, and set aside.

3. Cut steak into 4 to 6 pieces, and place the steak in an 11- x 7-inch baking dish. Pour bitter orange juice marinade over steak, and sprinkle with salt and pepper. Cover and chill 20 minutes.

4. Drain steak, discarding marinade. Heat a cast-iron skillet over medium-high heat 3 minutes; add oil. Cook steak pieces, in batches, 5 minutes on each side or until a meat thermometer inserted in steak registers 135° or to desired degree of doneness. Remove to a serving plate, and keep warm.

5. Add onions, carrots, and chiles to skillet; cook, stirring often, 10 minutes or until onions are browned. Cut steak pieces diagonally across the grain into thin strips. Spoon vegetables over steak; serve immediately.

Note: We tested with Goya Bitter Orange Marinade.

How To Roast Chiles

Roast poblano chiles over an open flame or under the broiler until they are thoroughly charred. Place the chiles in a zip-top plastic or paper bag, and seal or fold down the top. Let stand for 15 minutes; then pull off the charred skin with your fingers. Remove and discard the seeds and stems. Poblano chiles are mild, so there's no need to wear gloves.

inspirations for your table

Set up a taco bar with toppings for a quick weeknight family dinner or festive gathering with friends.

Taco Night

Set out flour and corn tortillas with a variety of toppings. Some of our favorites include carrots, avocados, mangoes, onions, queso fresco, red cabbage, jalapeños, and salsa.

SLOW-COOKER BEEF TACOS

makes 8 servings   prep: 20 min.   cook: 6 hr., 8 min.

We had stress-free nights in mind when we created this Southwestern favorite. We brown the beef before slow-cooking to add color and enhance flavor. This mixture is also great over baked potatoes with your favorite toppings.

2 lb. boneless beef chuck roast, cut into
   1-inch cubes
1 tsp. salt
1 Tbsp. vegetable oil
1 Tbsp. chili powder
1 (6-oz.) can tomato paste
2 cups beef broth
1 small white onion

1 (8-oz.) can tomato sauce
½ medium-size green bell pepper
1 tsp. ground cumin
½ tsp. pepper
Flour or corn tortillas, warmed
Toppings: shredded Cheddar or Monterey Jack
    cheese, sour cream

1. Sprinkle beef evenly with salt.
2. Cook beef, in batches, in hot oil in a Dutch oven over medium-high heat 5 to 7 minutes or until browned on all sides. Remove beef, reserving drippings in Dutch oven. Add 1 Tbsp. chili powder to Dutch oven; cook, stirring constantly, 1 minute. Stir in tomato paste, and cook, stirring constantly, 2 minutes. Add 2 cups beef broth, and stir, scraping bits from bottom of Dutch oven. Return beef to Dutch oven, and stir.
3. Place beef mixture in a 4½-qt. slow cooker. Add onion and next 4 ingredients. Cook on HIGH 4 hours or on LOW 6 hours or until beef is tender. Serve with warm tortillas and desired toppings.

BEEF-AND-SAUSAGE MEATLOAF WITH CHUNKY RED SAUCE

makes 12 servings (2 meatloaves)   prep: 15 min.   bake: 50 min.   stand: 10 min.

Serve one meatloaf for supper, and freeze the other for a meal later in the month.

1   lb. ground sirloin*

1   lb. ground pork sausage

1   sleeve multigrain saltine crackers, crushed

1   (15-oz.) can tomato sauce

1   green bell pepper, diced

½   cup diced red onion

2   large eggs, lightly beaten

Chunky Red Sauce

1. Preheat oven to 425°. Line bottom and sides of 2 (8- x 4-inch) loaf pans with aluminum foil, allowing 2 to 3 inches to extend over sides; fold foil down around sides of pan. Lightly grease foil.

2. Gently combine first 7 ingredients in a medium bowl. Shape mixture into 2 loaves. Place meatloaves in prepared pans.

3. Bake at 425° for 50 minutes or until a meat thermometer inserted into thickest portion registers 160°. Let stand 10 minutes. Remove meatloaves from pans, using foil sides as handles. Serve with Chunky Red Sauce.

* Ground chuck or lean ground beef may be substituted.

Note: If serving 1 meatloaf, let remaining cooked meatloaf stand until completely cool (about 30 minutes). Wrap tightly in plastic wrap and aluminum foil, and place in a large zip-top plastic bag. Store in refrigerator 2 to 3 days or freeze up to 1 month.

Chunky Red Sauce

makes about 3 cups   prep: 5 min.   cook: 15 min.

1   (26-oz.) jar vegetable spaghetti sauce

1   (14.5-oz.) can fire-roasted diced tomatoes*

2   tsp. dried Italian seasoning

¼   tsp. pepper

1. Stir together all ingredients in a large saucepan over medium heat. Cook, stirring frequently, 15 minutes or until thoroughly heated.

* 1 (14.5-oz.) can diced tomatoes may be substituted.

Note: We tested with Ragu Garden Combination Pasta Sauce and Hunt's Fire Roasted Diced Tomatoes.

BEEF-AND-SAUSAGE MEATLOAF WITH CHUNKY RED SAUCE ON CHEESE TOAST

makes 6 servings   prep: 15 min.   bake: 35 min.   **pictured on page 416**

1   cooked Beef-and-Sausage Meatloaf (recipe at left), chilled
1   (12-oz.) French bread loaf
1   (8-oz.) block mozzarella cheese, grated and divided

Chunky Red Sauce (recipe at left)
2   Tbsp. chopped fresh parsley

1. Preheat oven to 325°. Cut chilled meatloaf into 6 (1-inch-thick) slices. Place on an aluminum foil-lined baking sheet.

2. Bake for 30 minutes. Remove to a wire rack. Increase oven temperature to 400°.

3. Cut bread diagonally into 6 (1-inch-thick) slices. Place on an aluminum foil-lined baking sheet. Sprinkle evenly with 1 cup (4 oz.) mozzarella cheese.

4. Bake at 400° for 5 to 7 minutes or until cheese is melted and bubbly. Place 1 meatloaf slice on each piece of cheese toast. Top with desired amount of Chunky Red Sauce. Sprinkle with parsley and remaining cheese.

EASY SHREDDED BEEF OVER RICE

makes 6 to 8 servings   prep: 20 min.   cook: 4 hr.

This dish is known as ropa viejo [ROH-pah VYAY-hoh], Spanish for "old clothes." Using fajita seasoning as a rub gives it a tasty twist.

1   (4-lb.) boneless top chuck roast
2   tsp. fajita seasoning
2   Tbsp. vegetable oil

2   (14½-oz.) cans Mexican-style stewed tomatoes
4   cups hot cooked rice
2   Tbsp. chopped fresh parsley

1. Rub both sides of roast evenly with fajita seasoning.

2. Cook roast in hot oil in a large Dutch oven over medium-high heat 5 minutes or until browned on all sides.

3. Combine stewed tomatoes and 2 cups water; pour over roast in Dutch oven. Cover, reduce heat to low, and cook 4 hours or until roast is tender. Remove roast, and shred using 2 forks.

4. Skim fat from tomato liquid in Dutch oven, and discard. Stir shredded beef into tomato liquid.

5. Combine rice and parsley. Serve beef mixture over rice.

OLD-FASHIONED MEATLOAF

makes 6 to 8 servings   prep: 20 min.   cook: 7 min.   bake: 55 min.   stand: 10 min.

This recipe is a favorite at Fairfield Grocery & Market, a popular neighborhood market in Shreveport, Louisiana, that prides itself on customer service, including down-home meals that are delivered to your door.

1   Tbsp. butter
3   celery ribs, finely chopped
½   large onion, finely chopped
2   lb. lean ground beef
2   Tbsp. Worcestershire sauce, divided
½   cup Italian-seasoned breadcrumbs
⅓   cup ketchup
2   tsp. Creole seasoning

1   tsp. Greek seasoning
1   tsp. garlic powder
2   large eggs, lightly beaten
1   (8-oz.) can tomato sauce
3   Tbsp. tomato paste
1   Tbsp. ketchup
Garnish: chopped fresh flat-leaf parsley (optional)

1. Preheat oven to 350°. Melt butter in a medium nonstick skillet over medium heat; add celery and onion, and sauté 7 minutes or just until tender.

2. Stir together celery mixture, ground beef, 1 Tbsp. Worcestershire sauce, breadcrumbs, and next 5 ingredients in a large bowl. Shape into a 10- x 5-inch loaf; place on a lightly greased broiler rack. Place rack in an aluminum foil-lined broiler pan.

3. Bake at 350° for 45 minutes. Stir together remaining 1 Tbsp. Worcestershire sauce, tomato sauce, tomato paste, and 1 Tbsp. ketchup until blended; pour evenly over meatloaf, and bake 10 to 15 more minutes or until no longer pink in center. Let stand 10 minutes before serving.

Note: We tested with Tony Chachere's Original Creole Seasoning and Cavender's All Purpose Greek Seasoning.

HERB-AND-VEGGIE MEATLOAF

makes 8 servings   prep: 20 min.   cook: 6 min.   bake: 1 hr.   stand: 10 min.

For an equally flavorful, lower fat version, try the Herb-and-Veggie Turkey Loaf. Pair meatloaf with your favorite refrigerated or frozen mashed potatoes prepared with reduced-fat milk.

1   medium onion, chopped
1   tsp. minced garlic
2   tsp. canola or vegetable oil
1   cup shredded carrots
1   cup roasted garlic-and-herb pasta sauce, divided
1½ lb. extra-lean ground beef
8   oz. 50%-less-fat fresh pork sausage
1   (10-oz.) package frozen chopped spinach, thawed and drained

½   cup uncooked regular oats
2   tsp. dried Italian seasoning
1¼ tsp. salt
1   tsp. pepper
1   large egg, lightly beaten
Vegetable cooking spray
Additional roasted garlic-and-herb pasta sauce (optional)

1. Preheat oven to 350°. Sauté onion and garlic in hot oil in a large nonstick skillet over medium-high heat 3 minutes. Add carrots, and sauté 3 to 4 minutes or until onion is tender; cool slightly.
2. Combine onion mixture, ½ cup pasta sauce, beef, and next 7 ingredients in a large bowl until blended. Shape mixture into a 10- x 5-inch loaf. Place on a rack coated with cooking spray; place rack in broiler pan coated with cooking spray.
3. Bake at 350° for 45 minutes. Spread remaining ½ cup pasta sauce over loaf, and bake 10 to 15 more minutes or until a thermometer inserted into thickest portion registers 155°.
4. Cover loosely with aluminum foil, and let stand 10 minutes. Serve with additional pasta sauce, if desired.

Note: We tested with Prego Roasted Garlic-and-Herb Pasta Sauce.

Per serving: Calories 240; Fat: 12.2g (sat 4.1g, mono 3.5g, poly 0.9g); Protein 21g; Fiber 3.3g; Chol 65mg; Iron 3.4mg; Sodium 670mg; Calc 88mg

Herb-and-Veggie Turkey Loaf: Substitute 2 lb. lean ground turkey for beef and pork. Proceed with recipe as directed.

Per serving: Calories 203; Fat 5.6g (sat 1.5g, mono 1g, poly 0.6g); Protein 26g; Carb 12g; Fiber 3.3g; Chol 82mg; Iron 2.4mg; Sodium 884mg; Calc 83mg

Kids' Pool Party serves 10 to 12

Mini Sweet-and-Sour Sloppy Joes
Baby carrots and bottled Ranch dressing
Sweet potato chips   Watermelon wedges
All-Time Favorite Chocolate Chip Cookies (page 280)
*Lemonade (page 92)

*double recipe

MINI SWEET-AND-SOUR SLOPPY JOES

makes 12 sandwiches   prep: 15 min.   cook: 50 min.

Because these are child-size portions, adults may choose to eat two sandwiches.

1½ lb. extra-lean ground beef

1   cup finely chopped onion

½   cup finely chopped green bell pepper

3   (8-oz.) cans basil, garlic, and oregano tomato sauce

¼   cup cider vinegar

1   Tbsp. brown sugar

2   tsp. Worcestershire sauce

1   tsp. chili powder

¼   tsp. salt

1   (13.9-oz.) package dinner rolls, toasted

1. Cook ground beef in a large nonstick skillet coated with cooking spray over medium-high heat 10 minutes or until beef crumbles and is no longer pink. Remove meat from skillet, and drain well.

2. Sauté onion and bell pepper in skillet 5 minutes or until tender. Return meat to skillet; stir in tomato sauce and next 5 ingredients. Bring mixture to a boil; cover, reduce heat, and simmer, stirring occasionally, 30 minutes. Spoon mixture evenly into toasted dinner rolls, and serve immediately.

Note: We tested with Pepperidge Farm Soft Country Style Dinner Rolls. They're about the size of a baseball.

Per 1 sandwich: Calories 216; Fat: 6.7g (sat 2g, mono 2.2g, poly1.2g); Protein 15.8g; Fiber 1.8g; Chol 21mg; Iron 2.8mg; Sodium 506mg; Calc 31mg

southern lights

ITALIAN MEATBALLS

makes 30 meatballs (6 to 8 servings)   prep: 20 min.   cook: 35 min.   **pictured on page 420**

We adapted and scaled down this recipe from Barbara Jean's Cookbook *(Barbara Jeans LLC, 2005) by Barbara Jean Barta, owner of the Barbara Jean's Restaurant chain. Make a large batch of these, and freeze them in meal-size portions to cook during the week.*

½ lb. mild Italian sausage, casings removed

¾ lb. ground turkey

1 cup fine, dry breadcrumbs

¾ cup minced onion

4 large eggs, lightly beaten

¾ cup grated Parmesan cheese

1 Tbsp. minced garlic

½ tsp. salt

½ tsp. pepper

2 tsp. dried Italian seasoning

Marinara Sauce

Hot cooked spaghetti

Freshly grated Parmesan cheese (optional)

1. Combine sausage, ground turkey, and next 8 ingredients in a large bowl until well blended.

2. Gently shape meat mixture into 30 (1½-inch) balls.

3. Bring Marinara Sauce to a boil in a Dutch oven over medium heat, stirring occasionally; reduce heat, and simmer. Add 10 meatballs, and cook 6 to 8 minutes or until meatballs are done. Remove meatballs from sauce, and keep warm; repeat procedure with remaining meatballs.

4. Return all cooked meatballs to sauce, reduce heat to low, and cook 10 more minutes. Serve over hot cooked spaghetti, and, if desired, sprinkle with Parmesan cheese.

Marinara Sauce

makes about 6 cups   prep: 5 min.   cook: 10 min.

1 cup beef broth

½ cup dry red wine

1 (26-oz.) jar marinara sauce

1 (8-oz.) can tomato sauce with basil, garlic, and oregano

1. Stir together broth, red wine, ½ cup water, marinara sauce, and tomato sauce. Cook over medium heat, stirring occasionally, 10 minutes or until thoroughly heated.

RED WINE SHORT RIBS

makes 4 servings prep: 20 min. cook: 40 min. bake: 3 hr., 30 min. stand: 30 min.

Make this a day ahead, and chill it so you can easily remove the solidified fat from the top of the strained gravy before reheating. Serve these ribs over polenta, mashed sweet potatoes, or risotto for the ultimate comfort meal.

6 lb. beef short ribs	1 (14.5-oz.) can Italian-style diced tomatoes
½ tsp. kosher salt	2 cups dry red wine
½ tsp. freshly ground pepper	1 cup chicken broth
6 garlic cloves, pressed	1 fresh rosemary sprig
2 carrots, coarsely chopped	1 fresh thyme sprig
2 celery ribs, coarsely chopped	1 fresh oregano sprig
1 onion, coarsely chopped	

1. Preheat oven to 350°. Sprinkle ribs evenly with ½ tsp. salt and ½ tsp. pepper. Cook ribs, in batches, in a large ovenproof Dutch oven over medium-high heat 4 to 5 minutes on each side or until browned. Remove ribs to a large bowl, and drain Dutch oven.

2. Reduce heat to medium; add garlic and next 3 ingredients to Dutch oven. Cook, stirring occasionally, 6 to 7 minutes or until vegetables are tender and browned. Stir in tomatoes and next 5 ingredients. Return ribs to Dutch oven, and bring to a boil; cover tightly with heavy-duty aluminum foil and lid.

3. Bake at 350° for 3½ to 4 hours or until ribs are very tender. Remove ribs and herbs. Discard herbs; keep ribs warm.

4. Drain vegetable mixture through a fine wire-mesh strainer into a large bowl, reserving vegetable mixture. Pour gravy into an 8-cup glass measuring cup. Let stand 30 minutes, and skim fat from gravy. Add strained gravy and vegetables back to Dutch oven. Return to a boil over medium-high heat, and cook, uncovered, 20 minutes or until thickened. Serve gravy over short ribs.

OSSO BUCO

makes 8 servings   prep: 15 min.   cook: 1 hr., 15 min.   bake: 1 hr., 45 min.   **pictured on page 418**

The Itlain influence on Southern cooking can be seen in this stew-like dish. Osso bucco (AW-soh-BOO-koh) yields tender meat chunks smothered in a thick vegetable-enriched broth for a one-dish meal.

3	fresh parsley sprigs	3	large carrots, cut into ½-inch cubes
1	fresh thyme sprig	3	celery ribs, cut into ½-inch cubes
1	bay leaf	2	cups dry white wine
8	(2-inch-thick) veal shanks	4	cups hot water
½	tsp. salt	4	tsp. beef bouillon granules
1	tsp. pepper	1	Tbsp. all-purpose flour
¼	cup olive oil, divided	1	Tbsp. butter, softened
2	large onions, chopped		

1. Preheat oven to 350°. Tie together first 3 ingredients with kitchen string; set aside.

2. Rub veal with salt and pepper.

3. Brown half of veal in 1½ Tbsp. hot oil in a large skillet over medium-high heat, turning often, 5 minutes. Remove to a roasting pan; keep warm. Repeat with 1½ Tbsp. oil and remaining veal.

4. Sauté onion, carrot, and celery in remaining 1 Tbsp. hot oil in skillet until tender. Add wine; bring to a boil, and boil, stirring occasionally, until reduced by two-thirds (about 15 minutes). Add 4 cups hot water, bouillon, and herb bundle; cover and bring to a boil. Pour over veal.

5. Bake, covered, at 375° for 1 hour and 45 minutes or until veal is tender. Remove veal from pan; keep warm. Pour drippings through a wire-mesh strainer into a skillet, discarding solids. Bring to a boil, and boil until reduced by half (about 40 minutes).

6. Whisk together flour and butter until smooth; whisk into drippings. Cook, whisking constantly, 1 minute or until thickened. Serve with veal.

CREAMY LAMB CURRY

makes 6 servings   prep: 20 min.   cook: 1 hr., 15 min.

Serve this aromatic, full-flavored dish over basmati rice, a nutty-tasting long-grain variety. Look for garam masala, a fragrant spice mixture, in Indian markets or in the spice or ethnic sections of supermarkets. It's available in the McCormick Gourmet Collection. The flavor makes it worth the search.

{southern lights}

2 lb. lean boneless lamb, cut into 2-inch pieces	2 bay leaves
½ tsp. salt	1 (1-inch) cinnamon stick
1 medium onion, chopped (1 cup)	2 cups fat-free reduced-sodium chicken broth
1 (1-inch) piece fresh ginger, peeled and minced	1 (14.5-oz.) can diced tomatoes, undrained
2 garlic cloves, minced	½ cup plain nonfat yogurt
2 tsp. ground coriander	1 Tbsp. garam masala
1 tsp. ground cumin	8 fresh mint leaves, chopped
⅛ tsp. ground cloves	

1. Sprinkle lamb pieces with salt.

2. Cook lamb, in batches, in a Dutch oven coated with cooking spray over medium-high heat, stirring often, 5 minutes or until lamb is lightly browned. Remove and set aside.

3. Sauté onion and ginger in a Dutch oven coated with cooking spray over medium-high heat 1 to 2 minutes. Add garlic; cook 1 minute. Stir in coriander and next 4 ingredients. Add cooked lamb, broth, and tomatoes; bring to a boil. Cover, reduce heat, and simmer 1 hour or until lamb is tender. Remove from heat; add yogurt and garam masala, stirring until blended. Sprinkle with chopped mint leaves.

Per serving: Calories 257; Fat 11g (sat 4.5g, mono 4g, poly 0.5g); Protein 29.6g; Fiber 1.3g; Chol 100.5mg; Iron 2.4mg; Sodium 512mg; Calc 109mg

ROSEMARY-CRUSTED LAMB WITH TZATZIKI SAUCE

makes 4 servings prep: 10 min. bake: 45 min. stand: 10 min.

The Middle Eastern influence on Southern cooking can be seen in this dish that pairs well with tab-bouleh and baby carrots.

¼ cup chopped fresh rosemary

3 garlic cloves

3 Tbsp. fresh lemon juice

3 Tbsp. olive oil

1 tsp. salt

1 tsp. pepper

1 (6-lb.) leg of lamb, boned and trimmed

Tzatziki Sauce

Garnish: fresh rosemary sprigs (optional)

1. Preheat oven to 450°. Process first 6 ingredients in a food processor until smooth. Spread rosemary mixture evenly on lamb. Place on a lightly greased rack in a roasting pan.

2. Bake at 450° for 45 minutes or until a meat thermometer inserted into thickest portion registers 160°.

3. Let stand 10 minutes before slicing. Serve with Tzatziki Sauce. Garnish, if desired.

Tzatziki Sauce

makes 2½ cups prep: 20 min.

This Greek sauce can also be served as a dip or a spread for sandwiches or thinned out with good olive oil for a salad dressing.

1 (16-oz.) container plain yogurt

1 large cucumber, peeled, seeded, and diced

1 Tbsp. chopped fresh dill

1 Tbsp. chopped fresh mint

1 tsp. salt

1 tsp. lemon zest

1 garlic clove, pressed

1. Stir together all ingredients in a large bowl. Cover; chill until ready to serve.

CREAMY DIJON LAMB CHOPS

makes 4 servings prep: 15 min. cook: 13 min. bake: 15 min. stand: 5 min.

8   (2-inch-thick) lamb chops, trimmed
½   tsp. salt
¼   tsp. freshly ground pepper
1   Tbsp. olive oil
2   garlic cloves, pressed

½   cup whipping cream
⅓   cup Dijon mustard
2   Tbsp. chopped fresh thyme
1   to 2 Tbsp. chopped fresh rosemary

1. Preheat oven to 400°. Sprinkle lamb chops evenly with salt and pepper.

2. Brown chops in hot oil in a heavy skillet over medium-high heat 2 minutes on each side; place chops in a 13- x 9-inch baking dish, reserving drippings in skillet.

3. Bake at 400° for 15 minutes or until a meat thermometer inserted into thickest portion registers 150° (medium-rare). Let stand 5 minutes before serving.

4. Sauté garlic in reserved drippings over medium heat 3 minutes or until lightly browned.

5. Stir together cream and next 3 ingredients in a small bowl. Add mixture to skillet, and bring to a boil over medium heat, stirring occasionally. Reduce heat, and simmer 5 minutes. Serve with chops.

PISTACHIO-CRUSTED LAMB RACK

makes 8 servings prep: 10 min. chill: 2 hr. cook: 32 min. stand: 5 min. **pictured on page 496**

¾   cup fine, dry breadcrumbs
½   cup pistachios
2   Tbsp. chopped fresh marjoram
4   (4-rib) lamb rib roasts (12 to 16 oz. each), trimmed

¼   cup Dijon mustard
Salt and pepper to taste
¼   cup olive oil
Cranberry-Black Bean Relish

1. Process first 3 ingredients in food processor 30 seconds or until finely ground. Transfer crumb mixture to a shallow dish or pan. Brush lamb with Dijon mustard, and sprinkle with salt and pepper. Roll in crumb mixture, coating well. Chill 2 hours.

2. Preheat oven to 350°. Cook lamb, in batches, in hot oil in a large skillet over medium-high heat 1 minute on each side or until light brown. Transfer to 2 (13- x 9-inch) lightly greased baking dishes. Bake lamb at 350° for 24 minutes or until a meat thermometer inserted into thickest portion registers 135° (medium-rare), or bake 30 to 35 minutes or until a meat thermometer inserted into thickest portion registers 145° (medium).

3. Remove from oven; cover loosely with aluminum foil, and let stand 5 minutes or until thermometer registers 145° (medium-rare) or 160° (medium). Cut into chops, and serve with Cranberry-Black Bean Relish.

Cranberry-Black Bean Relish

makes 1½ cups   prep: 5 min.   chill: 2 hr.

1   cup canned black beans, rinsed and drained
½   cup dried cranberries, chopped
2   Tbsp. chopped fresh cilantro
2   Tbsp. olive oil
1   Tbsp. lime juice
1   Tbsp. honey
Salt to taste

1. Stir together all ingredients in a bowl; chill at least 2 hours.

GARLIC-AND-HERB STUFFED LEG OF LAMB

makes 8 servings   prep: 1 hr.   bake: 2 hr., 40 min.   stand: 15 min.

2   large garlic bulbs
2   Tbsp. olive oil
2½   tsp. salt, divided
2½   tsp. pepper, divided
¼   cup olive oil
1   Tbsp. fresh lemon juice
1   Tbsp. minced shallots
1   (5- to 6-lb.) leg of lamb, boned
3   Tbsp. chopped fresh or 1 tsp. dried rosemary
3   Tbsp. chopped fresh or 1 tsp. dried thyme
2   tsp. lemon zest
Garnish: fresh rosemary sprigs (optional)

1. Preheat oven to 425°. Cut off pointed ends of garlic bulbs. Place each bulb on a piece of aluminum foil; drizzle evenly with 2 Tbsp. olive oil, and sprinkle evenly with ½ tsp. salt and ½ tsp. pepper. Fold foil to seal.

2. Bake at 425° for 30 minutes; cool. Squeeze pulp from garlic cloves; mash and set aside.

3. Whisk together ¼ cup olive oil, lemon juice, and shallots; brush inside of lamb with half of oil mixture, and sprinkle with 1 tsp. salt and 1 tsp. pepper. Spread inside with mashed garlic, and sprinkle with rosemary, thyme, and lemon zest.

4. Roll up lamb, and tie with string at 1-inch intervals. Place on a rack in a roasting pan. Brush with remaining oil mixture. Sprinkle with remaining 1 tsp. salt and remaining 1 tsp. pepper.

5. Bake at 425° for 25 minutes; reduce oven temperature to 350°, and bake 1 hour and 45 minutes or until a meat thermometer inserted into thickest portion registers 145°. Let stand 15 minutes or until meat thermometer registers 150° (medium-rare). Garnish, if desired.

APPLE-SAGE STUFFED PORK CHOPS

makes 6 servings   prep: 30 min.   cook: 52 min.   stand: 25 min.   **pictured on page 494**

3   Tbsp. butter
½   cup finely chopped yellow onion
½   cup finely chopped celery
½   cup finely chopped Granny Smith apple
½   cup finely chopped fresh mushrooms
1½ cups herb stuffing mix
1   (14.5-oz.) can chicken broth
5   fresh sage leaves, finely chopped*
6   Tbsp. finely chopped fresh flat-leaf parsley,
    divided

1   tsp. salt, divided
1   tsp. ground black pepper, divided
¼   tsp. ground red pepper
6   (2-inch-thick) bone-in center-cut pork chops
¼   cup olive oil, divided
Garnishes: steamed baby carrots, pearl onions,
    chopped flat-leaf parsley (optional)

1. Melt butter in a large skillet over medium-high heat; add onion and next 3 ingredients, and sauté 10 minutes or until vegetables are tender and liquid evaporates. Remove from heat. Add stuffing mix and broth; stir until liquid is absorbed. Stir in sage, 2 Tbsp. chopped parsley, ½ tsp. salt, ½ tsp. black pepper, and ground red pepper. Let stand 20 minutes.
2. Preheat oven to 375°. Trim excess fat from each pork chop, and cut a slit in 1 side of each chop to form a pocket. Spoon stuffing mixture evenly into each pocket.
3. Combine remaining 4 Tbsp. parsley, ½ tsp. salt, and ½ tsp. black pepper. Rub both sides of stuffed pork chops evenly with 2 Tbsp. oil, and spread parsley mixture evenly over chops.
4. Cook chops in remaining 2 Tbsp. hot oil in a large nonstick skillet over medium-high heat, in batches, 2 minutes on each side or until browned. Place on a lightly greased rack in a broiler pan. Add 1 cup water to bottom of broiler pan.
5. Bake at 375° for 30 to 40 minutes. Let stand 5 minutes before serving. Garnish, if desired.

* ½ tsp. rubbed sage may be substituted.

Note: We tested with Pepperidge Farm Herb Seasoned Stuffing Mix.

JALAPEÑO-BASIL PORK CHOPS

makes 4 servings   prep: 10 min.   cook: 5 min.   stand: 30 min.   grill: 6 min.

Nothing could be easier than this time-saving recipe. The pork chops marinate for 30 minutes, about the time it takes to remove the chill for even cooking. Pair it with cheese grits and a fresh strawberry salad for a delicious dinner

1   (10-oz.) jar jalapeño pepper jelly
½   cup dry white wine
¼   cup chopped fresh basil

4   (1-inch-thick) bone-in pork loin chops
½   tsp. salt
¼   tsp. pepper

1. Preheat grill to 350° to 400° (medium-high) heat. Cook first 3 ingredients in a small saucepan over low heat, stirring often, 5 minutes or until pepper jelly melts. Remove from heat, and let mixture cool completely.

2. Pour ¾ cup pepper jelly mixture into a large zip-top plastic freezer bag, reserving remaining mixture; add pork chops, turning to coat. Seal and let stand at room temperature 30 minutes, turning pork chops occasionally.

3. Remove chops from marinade, discarding marinade. Sprinkle evenly with salt and pepper.

4. Grill, covered with grill lid, over medium-high heat (350° to 400°) 3 to 4 minutes on each side or until a meat thermometer inserted into thickest portion registers 160°. Serve with remaining pepper jelly mixture.

Jalapeño-Basil Chicken: Substitute 4 skinned and boned chicken breasts for pork chops. Prepare pepper jelly mixture, and marinate chicken as directed. Grill, covered with grill lid, over medium-high heat (350° to 400°) 4 minutes on each side or until done. Serve with remaining pepper jelly mixture.

Hot Tamales: Not Just for Texans

Mississippi isn't a likely locale for hot tamales, but for almost a century they have been just as popular as catfish in some Delta towns.

There is even a Mississippi Delta Tamale Trail, for heaven's sake. Which means that somehow this Mexican culinary tradition, mostly associated with Texas, slipped across the Mississippi River when a lot of folks weren't looking. According to local Delta legend, that's exactly what happened. In the early to mid part of the 20th century, Mexican immigrants came through the area on their way to or from field work wherever they could find it. It wasn't uncommon to find a Mexican cook peddling tamales on street corners in cities such as Greenville or Clarksdale. Soon, African-Americans looking for a cost-efficient way to make money picked up tamale making and sold the shuck-wrapped treats from their homes, from pushcarts, from tiny stands, or on street corners. Now, stands and restaurants known for their tamales are run by all ethnic groups throughout the Delta region.

Despite the Mexican roots, locals admit the tamales are sometimes different than those you'll find in Texas. Some use wax or parchment paper rather than corn shucks to wrap the tamale fillings. Rougher textured cornmeal seems to be preferred over the traditional soft corn masa used by traditional Mexican tamale makers. The filling may not be as spicy. You're likely to find ground beef chili filling the centers as well as pulled pork or chicken. And sometimes the tamale filling is eaten smothered with chili and cheese rather than with the traditional salsa.

In Texas, finely ground corn masa is still the choice in the state of heavy Mexican influence. Endless filling varieties are found throughout within the borders, and are usually served with red or green chile sauce. Fillings include pork, beef, spinach and cheese, pinto bean, black bean, and even sweet coconut-raisin-pecan, though beef and pork seem to be the most popular, says Nola McKey, of Austin. "Pedro's Tamales in Lubbock is still my favorite place to buy them, though," she says. Lucky for Nola, Pedro's ships them hot and straight to her door, so she doesn't have to make the long trek across Texas to get them.

DELTA TAMALES

makes about 24 tamales   prep: 1 hr.   soak: 1 hr.   cook: 3 hr., 15 minutes

We call for using an entire package of corn husks in this recipe because some of them will be torn or split; use the larger whole ones. Tamales can be assembled a day ahead and refrigerated until you're ready to cook them.

1 (6-oz.) package dried corn husks
Cornmeal Dough (recipe on following page)
Meat Filling (recipe on following page)
2 (15-oz.) cans tomato sauce

2 tsp. chili powder
2 tsp. ground cumin
Toppings: diced red onion, sliced jalapeño peppers

[freeze it]

1. Soak corn husks in hot water 1 hour or until softened. Drain husks, and pat dry.

2. Spread 3 Tbsp. Cornmeal Dough into a 3- x 3 ½-inch rectangle in center of 1 husk. Spoon 1 heaping Tbsp. Meat Filling down center of Cornmeal Dough rectangle.

3. Fold long sides of husk over, enclosing filling completely with Cornmeal Dough; fold bottom of husk over folded sides (leave top end open). Repeat procedure using remaining husks, Cornmeal Dough, and Meat Filling.

4. Place a 1-cup ovenproof glass measuring cup upside down in center of a Dutch oven. Stir together tomato sauce, chili powder, cumin, and 4 cups water. Pour tomato sauce mixture around measuring cup in Dutch oven.

5. Stand tamales, open end up, around measuring cup. Bring to a boil over medium-high heat. Cover, reduce heat to low, and simmer 3 hours. Using tongs, remove tamales to a serving plate. Remove measuring cup. Cook tomato mixture over medium-high heat 10 minutes or until thickened. Serve tamales with sauce and desired toppings.

Note: After cooking, the tamales with the sauce can be frozen up to 1 month. Thaw overnight in refrigerator. Microwave thawed tamales in sauce in a single layer at HIGH in 45-second intervals until hot.

Cornmeal Dough

makes 4½ cups   prep: 10 min.

1¼ cups shortening
4   cups instant corn masa mix or
     yellow cornmeal

1¾ cups warm chicken broth
1   Tbsp. salt
2   tsp. paprika

1. Beat shortening at medium speed with an electric mixer 2 to 3 minutes or until creamy.
2. Stir together corn masa mix and next 3 ingredients in a medium bowl until well blended. Gradually add corn masa mixture to shortening, beating at medium speed just until blended after each addition. Cover dough with plastic wrap until ready to use.

Meat Filling

makes about 2 cups   prep: 10 min.

1   (17-oz.) package fully cooked pork
     roast au jus
1   (10-oz.) can mild diced tomatoes and
     green chiles, drained
¾   cup barbecue sauce

1   tsp. garlic powder
1   tsp. onion powder
1   tsp. chili powder
½   tsp. ground red pepper
¼   tsp. salt

1. Rinse and drain au jus from pork roast. Shred and chop pork.
2. Stir together pork and remaining ingredients until blended.

CROWN PORK ROAST

makes 8 to 10 servings   prep: 20 min.   bake: 2 hr., 30 min.   stand: 15 min.   **pictured on page 419**

This roast makes a lot, so if you have leftovers, simply cut it into chops, and freeze in zip-top plastic bags up to three months. Pull a bag out of the freezer, and thaw in the refrigerator overnight. You can then brown the chops in a skillet to warm them.

3   Tbsp. steak seasoning

1   (11-rib) crown pork roast, trimmed and tied

1   large apple

1   cup fresh kumquats

Garnishes: fresh thyme sprigs, flat-leaf parsley, apples, pears, and kumquats

1. Preheat oven to 350°. Rub steak seasoning evenly over all sides of pork roast. Place roast in a roasting pan; position a large apple in center of roast to help hold its shape.

2. Bake pork roast at 350° for 2 hours. Top apple with 1 cup kumquats, and bake 30 more minutes or until a meat thermometer inserted between ribs 2 inches into meat registers 160°. Let pork roast stand 15 minutes or until thermometer registers 165° before slicing. Garnish, if desired.

Note: We tested with McCormick Grill Mates Montreal Steak Seasoning.

Crown Pork Roast Secrets

1. An apple inserted in the center of the roast before baking helps the roast keep its shape and lends moisture. Kumquats will be placed on top of the apple during baking for an elegant presentation.

2. Placing a meat thermometer at the right spot in the roast is essential to achieving the proper degree of doneness. Insert it 2 inches into the meat between the ribs.

TORTILLA-CRUSTED PORK

makes 6 servings   prep: 20 min.   cook: 12 min.   pictured on page 494

Let the pork sear evenly on each side to allow the coating to reach maximum crispness.

2   lb. pork tenderloin
½   cup finely crushed blue-corn tortilla chips
½   cup finely crushed tortilla chips
1   Tbsp. coarsely ground pepper
½   tsp. chili powder
½   tsp. salt

¼   tsp. ground cumin
3   Tbsp. extra virgin olive oil, divided
Pico de Gallo
Tomatillo Salsa
Garnish: fresh cilantro sprigs (optional)

1. Remove silver skin from tenderloin, leaving a thin layer of fat covering tenderloin. Cut tenderloin into 1-inch-thick medallions.

2. Combine blue-corn tortilla chips and next 5 ingredients in a bowl. Brush pork medallions with 1½ Tbsp. olive oil, and dredge in tortilla chip mixture, pressing mixture into medallions on all sides to thoroughly coat.

3. Cook pork medallions in remaining 1½ Tbsp. hot oil in a large skillet over medium heat 6 minutes on each side or until done. Serve with salsas. Garnish, if desired.

Note: Nutritional analysis does not include salsas.

Per serving: Calories 262; Fat 12.5g (sat 2.8g, mono 7.3g; poly 1.6g); Protein 32.4g; Fiber 0.6g; Chol 98mg; Iron 2mg; Sodium 262mg; Calc 21mg

Pico de Gallo

makes 3 cups   prep: 15 min.   chill: 1 hr.

Pico de Gallo is best when made the day you plan to serve it. Prepare it early the morning of the party and spoon atop a fried egg or in an omelet; just be sure to save enough for the pork.

2   medium tomatoes, seeded and diced
1   medium-size ripe avocado, diced
¼   cup diced white onion
1   serrano or jalapeño pepper, seeded and finely
    chopped

2   Tbsp. lime juice
1   Tbsp. extra virgin olive oil
Salt to taste

1. Toss together first 6 ingredients in a medium bowl. Cover; chill 1 hour. Season with salt to taste.

Per ½ cup: Calories 83; Fat 6.9g (sat 0.9g, mono 4.5g, poly 0.9g); Protein 1.2g; Fiber 2.8g; Chol 0mg; Iron 0.4mg; Sodium 5.7mg; Calc 12mg

Tomatillo Salsa

makes 3 cups   prep: 15 min.   chill: 1 hr.

Serve with tortilla chips for a quick snack.

2	cups diced tomatillos	1	jalapeño pepper, seeded and finely chopped
½	cup diced onion	1	Tbsp. lime juice
2	Tbsp. chopped fresh cilantro	½	tsp. pepper
2	Tbsp. extra virgin olive oil		Salt to taste

1. Stir together first 7 ingredients in a medium bowl. Cover and chill 1 hour. Season with salt to taste.

Per ½ cup: Calories 61; Fat 5g (sat 0.7g, mono 3.4g, poly 0.9g); Protein 0.6g; Fiber 1.2g; Iron 0.3mg; Sodium 1.2mg; Calc 6.9mg

MUSTARD-AND-WINE PORK TENDERLOIN

makes 6 to 8 servings   prep: 15 min.   chill: 24 hr.   broil: 27 min.   stand: 10 min.

Oven broilers will vary depending on your model, so you may not need to turn the tenderloin as it broils to produce even browning. Coating the pork with flour adds rich flavor and visual appeal.

2¼	lb. pork tenderloin	1	tsp. minced garlic
1¼	cups dry white wine	1	tsp. pepper, divided
1	cup chicken broth	1½	tsp. kosher salt
2	Tbsp. coarse grained mustard	½	cup all-purpose flour
1	Tbsp. chopped fresh thyme		Vegetable cooking spray

1. Remove silver skin from tenderloin, leaving a thin layer of fat covering the tenderloin.
2. Combine wine and next 4 ingredients in a zip-top plastic freezer bag; add pork and ½ tsp. pepper. Seal and chill 24 hours, turning occasionally.
3. Preheat oven to broil. Remove pork tenderloin from marinade, discarding marinade. Pat dry, and sprinkle evenly with salt and remaining ½ tsp. pepper. Dredge in flour. Place pork on a lightly greased rack in a broiler pan; coat pork evenly with cooking spray.
4. Broil 5½ inches from heat 27 to 30 minutes or until pork is browned and a meat thermometer inserted in thickest portion registers 150°, turning pork occasionally. Let stand 10 minutes.

Note: Pork tenderloin may be frozen raw in marinade up to 1 month. Thaw in refrigerator 2 days or until completely thawed. Proceed as directed.

CITRUS-AND-GARLIC PORK ROAST

makes 6 to 8 servings   prep: 15 min.   chill: 8 hr.   bake: 4 hr., 30 min.

1	(6-lb.) bone-in pork shoulder roast (Boston butt)	2	tsp. pepper
1	Tbsp. salt	2	tsp. dried oregano
3	Tbsp. chopped fresh or 1 (4-oz.) jar minced garlic	½	cup fresh lime juice
		½	cup fresh orange juice

1. Place roast in an aluminum foil-lined roasting pan. Cut 4 to 5 (1-inch-deep) slits across top of roast. Sprinkle evenly with salt.

2. Stir together garlic and next 4 ingredients. Pour mixture evenly over roast, rubbing mixture into slits. Cover and chill 8 hours.

3. Preheat oven to 325°. Bake, uncovered, at 325° for 4½ hours or until meat thermometer inserted into thickest portion registers 175°. Remove from oven, and let stand until thermometer reaches 185°.

CLASSIC BARBECUE RIBS

makes 4 to 6 servings   prep: 15 min.   cook: 6 hr.

Put these on before you leave for work, or cook them overnight and refrigerate until dinnertime. If you make this recipe a day ahead, refrigerate overnight and remove fat from the sauce before reheating. If you reheat in the microwave, use 50% power.

4	lb. bone-in country-style pork ribs	½	cup orange juice
2	tsp. salt, divided	1	Tbsp. steak sauce
1	medium onion, chopped	1	tsp. coarse-ground pepper
1	cup firmly packed light brown sugar	1	tsp. minced garlic
1	cup apple butter	½	tsp. Worcestershire sauce
1	cup ketchup		Garnish: chopped fresh parsley (optional)
½	cup lemon juice		

1. Cut ribs apart, if necessary, and trim excess fat; sprinkle 1 tsp. salt evenly over ribs.

2. Stir together remaining 1 tsp. salt, onion, and next 9 ingredients until blended. Pour half of mixture into a 5-qt. slow cooker. Place ribs in slow cooker; pour remaining mixture over ribs.

3. Cover and cook on HIGH 6 to 7 hours or until ribs are tender. Garnish, if desired.

Note: We tested with A.1. Steak Sauce.

[make ahead]

Fall Supper Club serves 6 to 8

Boston Butt With Gravy
Roasted potatoes, carrots, and onions
Fresh Tomato Biscuits (page 108)
Fruit Salad With Blackberry-Basil Vinaigrette (page 720)
Fig-Walnut Pudding (page 337)

BOSTON BUTT ROAST WITH GRAVY

makes 6 to 8 servings   prep: 20 min.   bake: 3 hr., 30 min.   stand: 10 min.   cook: 15 min.

For the ultimate in comfort food, serve with roasted potatoes, carrots, and onions.

1	(5- to 6-lb.) Boston butt pork roast, trimmed	4	garlic cloves
1½	Tbsp. salt	¼	cup hot sauce
½	Tbsp. dried Italian seasoning	2	Tbsp. butter
1	tsp. garlic powder	1	cup low-sodium beef broth
1	tsp. pepper	¼	cup red wine
6	Tbsp. all-purpose flour, divided	½	tsp. dried Italian seasoning
¼	cup white vinegar		Salt and pepper to taste
1	onion, chopped		

1. Preheat oven to 375°. Place roast in an aluminum foil-lined roasting pan. Sprinkle pork evenly with 1½ Tbsp. salt and next 3 ingredients. Sprinkle evenly with 4 Tbsp. flour. Pour 2 cups water and vinegar into the bottom of roasting pan. Add onion and garlic cloves. Drizzle pork evenly with hot sauce.

2. Bake at 375° for 3½ hours or until tender. Remove pork from roasting pan, and wrap in aluminum foil. Pour about 1 cup pan drippings into a 2-cup glass measuring cup. Let stand 10 minutes, and skim fat from drippings.

3. Melt butter in a large skillet over medium-high heat; whisk in remaining 2 Tbsp. flour, pan drippings, broth, wine, and ½ tsp. Italian seasoning. Bring to a boil, whisking constantly; reduce heat to medium, and simmer 10 minutes. Season with salt and pepper to taste. Serve gravy over sliced pork.

PORK ROAST WITH HOPPING JOHN STUFFING

makes 6 to 8 servings   prep: 30 min.   cook: 1 hr.   pictured on page 493

1 small onion, chopped	½ cup diced cooked country ham
½ medium-size green bell pepper, chopped	½ tsp. sugar
2 Tbsp. vegetable oil	½ tsp. salt
1½ cups cooked long-grain rice	1 large egg, lightly beaten
1½ cups frozen chopped collard greens, thawed	1 (2½-lb.) boneless pork loin roast
1 (15-oz.) can black-eyed peas, rinsed and drained	

1. Preheat oven to 375°. Sauté onion and bell pepper in hot oil in a large skillet over medium-high heat 5 to 7 minutes or until tender. Remove from heat. Add rice and next 5 ingredients; stir in egg. Set stuffing aside.

2. Butterfly pork loin roast by making a lengthwise cut down center of 1 flat side, cutting to within ½ inch of bottom. From bottom of cut, slice horizontally to ½ inch from left side; repeat procedure to right side. Open roast, and place between 2 sheets of heavy-duty plastic wrap; flatten to ½-inch thickness using a meat mallet or rolling pin.

3. Spoon 1½ cups stuffing evenly over roast, leaving a ½-inch border. Roll up; tie with string at 1-inch intervals. Place, seam side down, in a lightly greased 11- x 7-inch baking dish.

4. Bake at 375° for 55 to 60 minutes or until a meat thermometer inserted in center registers 160°. Reheat remaining hopping John, and serve with roast.

Tips for Stuffed Pork Loin

• Pounding the pork loin with the flat, smooth side of a meat mallet or rolling pin to a ½-inch thickness produces an even surface and allows for easier rolling of stuffed meat.

• Leave a ½-inch border on the edge of the meat to prevent stuffing from spilling out the sides. The stuffing will expand as you roll up the pork jelly-roll style.

• Using butcher's twine, tie the roast at 1½-inch intervals. The twine is available at kitchen specialty shops and at grocery stores on the cooking utensils aisle.

FIG-BALSAMIC ROASTED PORK LOIN

makes 8 to 10 servings   prep: 45 min.   bake: 1 hr., 30 min.   cook: 18 min.   stand: 15 min.

Purchase a pork loin roast, not a rolled pork loin roast (which has two loins tied together with netting). Don't trim away the entire fat cap on top of the loin; this layer prevents the meat from drying out.

½ lb. ground pork sausage

1¾ cups herb-seasoned stuffing mix

1 large ripe Bartlett pear, peeled and chopped

½ red bell pepper, finely chopped

⅓ cup chopped dried figs

½ cup hot chicken broth

1 Tbsp. minced fresh thyme

1 (4-lb.) boneless pork loin roast

1 tsp. salt

1 to 2 Tbsp. cracked pepper

1 (11.5-oz.) jar fig preserves

1 cup Madeira wine

2 Tbsp. balsamic vinegar

¼ cup butter

¼ cup all-purpose flour

Garnishes: dried figs, Bartlett pear slices, fresh parsley sprigs (optional)

1. Preheat oven to 375°. Cook sausage in a large skillet over medium-high heat, stirring often, 4 to 5 minutes or until lightly browned. Drain well. Stir together sausage, stuffing mix, and next 5 ingredients. Set aside.

2. Butterfly pork loin roast by making a lengthwise cut down center of 1 flat side, cutting to within ½ inch of the bottom. (Do not cut all the way through roast.) Open roast, forming a rectangle, and place between 2 sheets of heavy-duty plastic wrap. Flatten to ½-inch thickness using a meat mallet or rolling pin. Sprinkle evenly with salt and pepper. Spoon sausage mixture evenly over pork loin roast, leaving a ½-inch border. Roll up roast, and tie with string at 1½-inch intervals. Place roast, seam side down, in a greased shallow roasting pan.

3. Bake at 375° for 55 to 60 minutes or until a meat thermometer inserted into thickest portion registers 145°. Remove roast from pan, reserving drippings in pan.

4. Stir together fig preserves, Madeira, and balsamic vinegar. Spoon half of preserves mixture evenly over roast.

5. Bake at 375° for 20 to 30 more minutes or until meat thermometer registers 160°. Let roast stand 15 minutes before slicing.

6. Melt butter in a medium saucepan; whisk in flour until smooth. Cook, whisking constantly, 3 minutes. Whisk in reserved pan drippings and remaining fig preserves mixture, and cook over medium-high heat 5 minutes. Serve sauce with roast; garnish, if desired.

HAM WITH GARLIC AND ORANGE

makes 18 servings   prep: 15 min.   chill: 8 hr.   bake: 7 hr.   stand: 20 min.

Note that this recipe uses a fresh ham. Be sure to call your supermarket's meat department to ensure taht they carry fresh hams. If not, call a week ahead to order one.

1 (15- to 18-lb.) fresh ham (not cured or smoked)	2 tsp. dried oregano
1 Tbsp. salt	½ cup fresh lime juice
½ cup chopped fresh or 1 (4-oz.) jar minced garlic	½ cup fresh orange juice
2 tsp. pepper	

1. Preheat oven to 350°. Place ham in an aluminum foil-lined roasting pan. Cut 4 to 5 (1-inch-deep) slits across top of ham. Sprinkle evenly with salt.

2. Stir together garlic and next 4 ingredients. Pour mixture evenly over ham, rubbing mixture into slits. Cover and chill 8 hours.

3. Bake, uncovered, at 350° for 7 hours or until a meat thermometer inserted into thickest portion registers 185°. Let stand 20 minutes before slicing.

COUNTRY HAM

makes 35 to 40 servings   prep: 1 hr.   soak: 24 hr.   cook: 4 hr.

1 (12- to 14-lb.) uncooked country ham	1 Tbsp. whole cloves
2 qt. cider vinegar	Hot biscuits

1. Preheat oven to 325°. Place ham in a large container. Add water to cover, and soak 24 hours. Drain. Scrub ham 3 to 4 times in cold water with a stiff brush, and rinse well.

2. Place ham, fat side up, in a large roasting pan. Pour vinegar over ham; sprinkle with cloves. Cover with lid or aluminum foil.

3. Bake at 325° for 4 hours or until meat thermometer registers 140°. Remove from oven, and cool slightly. Slice ham, and serve with hot biscuits.

Hammin' It Up Across the South

Probably the strongest differences of opinion on the curing of country ham are found between the two Smithfields—Virginia and North Carolina—at the annual Ham and Yam Festival where the two country ham-producing cities are pitted against each other. But these aren't the only two states who disagree about the "right" way to cure a ham.

Smithfield, Virginia, claims history is on its side. The first hams of the New World were cured here, with some guidance from the local natives. The queen of England preferred the hams from Virginia, lending royal credence to their status. And, today, they are cured just the same way— left long in shank, cured in pure salt, twirled in black pepper after salting, smoked a bit with hickory, oak, and apple woods, and then left to age naturally in wooden rafters.

That doesn't bother the folks in Smithfield, North Carolina, who know that their hams are really the best. They prefer a bit of sugar in their salt cure. And they wouldn't dare put a coating of black pepper on their smoked hams. A North Carolina producer once lightheartedly claimed that the pepper coating was a Virginia tradition to cover the "sins" of the hams cured there.

Western and northern Kentucky and west Tennessee are the only other places where smoke-curing is tradition. Green hickory and sassafras are the woods of choice in Kentucky. But in the dry air of the Appalachian Mountains in eastern Tennessee and Kentucky, western Virginia, and the mountains of North Carolina, hams are never smoked. Country ham experts claim that the smoking helps in preservation in the more humid climates near the coast.

Regional differences appear in the way the hams are cooked, as well. The most common methods are baked, simmered, and fried. Some swear by simmering the ham in cola in a large container, others use fruit juice, and still other cooks like the liquid from jars of sweet pickles, or pickled pears or peaches.

Near the Virginia coast, tradition combines country ham and seafood in an array of recipes. In Kentucky, the Hot Brown sandwich is the most famous recipe featuring country ham. And in North Georgia, sliced, fried, and covered with thin red-eye gravy (made with coffee) is considered the best way to savor the salt-cured ham. But in all regions, no one denies that a stack of thin country ham slices sandwiched between two sides of a homemade biscuit can't be beat.

Ham 101

- Ham comes from the leg of the hog. You may buy them cooked, uncooked, dry cured, or wet cured.
- Cooked hams can be served directly from the refrigerator. If you'd like to serve it hot, heat it in a 350° oven to an internal temperature of 140°. At 140°, the ham will be thoroughly warmed and moist.
- Uncooked hams should be heated to an internal temperature of 160° in a 350° oven. Depending on the size, plan to cook it 18 to 25 minutes per pound.
- Dry-cured hams are rubbed with salt, sugar, and other seasonings, and then stored until the salt penetrates the meat.
- Wet-cured hams are seasoned with a brine solution, which keeps the meat moist and produces a more tender texture.

CLASSIC COLA-GLAZED HAM

makes 12 to 14 servings   prep: 10 min.   bake: 2 hr., 30 min.   stand: 15 min.

Ham is a perennial favorite that's easy to prepare. It's also a healthful choice of meat with minimal fat and great flavor.

1	(6- to 7-lb.) fully cooked, bone-in ham	1	cup spicy brown mustard
30 to 32 whole cloves		1	cup cola soft drink
1	(16-oz.) package dark brown sugar	½	cup bourbon or apple juice

1. Preheat oven to 350°. Remove skin from ham, and trim fat to ¼-inch thickness. Make ¼-inch-deep cuts in a diamond pattern, and insert cloves at 1-inch intervals. Place ham in an aluminum foil-lined 13- x 9-inch pan.

2. Stir together brown sugar and next 3 ingredients until smooth. Pour mixture evenly over ham.

3. Bake at 350° on lower oven rack for 2 hours and 30 minutes, basting with pan juices every 20 minutes. Remove ham, and let stand 15 minutes before serving.

CITRUS GLAZED HAM

makes 12 to 14 servings   prep: 10 min.   bake: 2 hr., 30 min.   stand: 15 min   **pictured on page 495**

1 (6- to 7-lb.) fully cooked, bone-in ham
30 to 32 whole cloves
1 (10-oz.) bottle orange juice-flavored soft drink
1¼ cups orange marmalade

½ cup firmly packed light brown sugar
¼ cup Dijon mustard
Garnishes: apple slices, orange slices, orange zest,
  salad greens (optional)

1. Preheat oven to 350°. Remove skin from ham, and trim fat to ¼-inch thickness. Make ¼-inch-deep cuts in a diamond pattern, and insert cloves at 1-inch intervals. Place ham in an aluminum foil-lined 13- x 9-inch pan.

2. Stir together soft drink and next 3 ingredients until smooth. Pour mixture evenly over ham.

3. Bake at 350° on lower oven rack 2 hours and 30 minutes, basting with pan juices every 20 minutes. Remove ham; let stand 15 minutes before serving. Garnish, if desired.

Note: We tested with Orangina Sparkling Citrus Beverage.

HAM STEAK WITH ORANGE GLAZE

makes 6 servings   prep: 10 min.   cook: 9 min.   pictured on page 420

Ham steak is sometimes labeled center-cut ham steak. You can purchase boneless or bone-in steak that contains a small, round, nickel-size bone.

1 (2½-lb.) package fully cooked, bone-in
  (½-inch-thick) center-cut ham steak
1 cup orange juice
1 (8-oz.) can pineapple tidbits in juice

¼ cup golden raisins
1 Tbsp. Dijon mustard
1 tsp. cornstarch
1 Tbsp. cold water

1. Rinse ham, and pat dry.

2. Cook ham in a lightly greased skillet over medium-high heat 3 to 4 minutes on each side or until thoroughly heated. Remove ham, reserving drippings in skillet.

3. Stir in orange juice, and cook 2 minutes, stirring to loosen particles from bottom of skillet. Stir in pineapple, raisins, and mustard. Stir together cornstarch and 1 Tbsp. cold water; add to orange juice mixture. Bring to a boil; cook, stirring constantly, 1 minute. Serve sauce with ham.

PASTA, RICE & GRAINS

"Tomatoes and oregano make it Italian; wine and tarragon make it French. Sour cream makes it Russian; lemon and cinnamon make it Greek. Soy sauce makes it Chinese; garlic makes it good." —Alice May Brock

Look Past the Ground Beef

Try fresh Italian sausage instead. It adds extra flavor to recipes, and you can find it in the meat case at your supermarket. If you're trying this sausage for the first time, cut through the casing lengthwise on one side of each sausage. Remove the meat, and place it in a large nonstick skillet or Dutch oven, discarding the casings. Cook the sausage over medium-high heat for a few minutes, stirring frequently, until the meat crumbles and is no longer pink.

TURKEY SPAGHETTI WITH SAUSAGE AND PEPPERS

makes 4 servings   prep: 20 min.   cook: 20 min.

Add this no-fuss weeknight staple to your family's stash of best recipes.

[freeze it]

8   oz. uncooked spaghetti
1   (1-lb.) package Italian turkey sausage
2   Tbsp. olive oil, divided
1   medium onion, cut into eighths
1   medium-size green bell pepper, cut into strips
1   medium-size red or yellow bell pepper, cut into strips

2   to 3 garlic cloves, minced
1   (28-oz.) can diced tomatoes with basil, garlic, and oregano
¼   tsp. salt
¼   tsp. pepper
½   cup grated Parmesan cheese

1. Prepare pasta according to package directions.

2. Meanwhile, remove and discard casings from sausage; cook sausage in 1 Tbsp. hot oil in a large Dutch oven over medium-high heat 8 to 10 minutes or until meat is no longer pink, breaking sausage into pieces while cooking. Remove sausage and drippings from Dutch oven, and drain well on paper towels. Discard any drippings in Dutch oven.

3. Sauté onion and next 3 ingredients in remaining 1 Tbsp. hot oil in Dutch oven over medium-high heat 5 to 6 minutes or until vegetables are crisp-tender. Stir in tomatoes, salt, and pepper; cook 4 minutes or until thoroughly heated. Stir in sausage, pasta, and cheese. Transfer mixture to a serving platter, and serve immediately.

To freeze: Prepare recipe as directed. Cool 30 minutes. Place pasta mixture in a 13- x 9-inch baking dish. Cover tightly with plastic wrap and aluminum foil. Freeze up to 2 months. Thaw in refrigerator 24 hours. Preheat oven to 350°. Remove and discard plastic wrap and aluminum foil. Cover with aluminum foil; bake at 350° for 40 to 45 minutes or until thoroughly heated.

TOMATO-HERB PASTA

makes 6 servings   prep: 30 min.   cook: 10 min.   stand: 30 min.   **pictured on page 497**

Discover how getting your family to eat healthfully doesn't have to be a chore. Sneak some nutritious alternatives past them. Carefully hidden in this tasty recipe is a bounty of wholesome ingredients your picky eaters may even grow to love. Turn this zesty side dish into a hearty entrée by adding cooked shrimp or chicken.

½   cup rice vinegar

1   Tbsp. sugar

½   medium-size red onion, thinly sliced

½   (12-oz.) package whole grain spaghetti

2   medium tomatoes, seeded and chopped

1   large cucumber, peeled and thinly sliced into half moons

4   green onions, thinly sliced

⅓   cup firmly packed fresh mint leaves, chopped

⅓   cup firmly packed fresh cilantro leaves, chopped

¼   cup fresh lime juice

2   Tbsp. canola oil

1   tsp. sugar

1   tsp. salt

½   tsp. dried crushed red pepper

¼   cup chopped peanuts

1. Whisk together vinegar and 1 Tbsp. sugar in a bowl. Add onion, and let stand 30 minutes; drain, reserving 2 Tbsp. vinegar mixture.

2. Prepare pasta according to package directions.

3. Place chopped tomatoes and next 9 ingredients in a serving bowl. Add hot cooked pasta, onion, and reserved vinegar mixture, gently tossing to combine. Sprinkle with peanuts. Serve immediately, or cover and chill up to 24 hours.

Note: We tested with Mueller's Whole Grain Spaghetti.

Per serving: Calories 219; Fat 8g (sat 0.8g, mono 4.2g, poly 2.5g); Protein 6.7g; Fiber 5.4g; Iron 1.8mg; Sodium 324mg; Calc 44mg

[southern lights]

WHITE SPAGHETTI AND MEATBALLS

makes 6 servings   prep: 30 min.   chill: 20 min   bake: 13 min.   cook: 45 min.

This may seem like a long list of ingredients, but don't be intimidated——you probably have most of them on hand already.

1½ lb. skinned and boned chicken
    breast halves, cut into chunks
1 large garlic clove
1 large egg
10 saltine crackers, finely crushed
1 tsp. Italian seasoning
Vegetable cooking spray
1 (8-oz.) package sliced fresh mushrooms
⅛ tsp. ground nutmeg

1 tsp. olive oil
1 large garlic clove, minced
2 Tbsp. all-purpose flour
½ cup dry white wine
3 cups fat-free, reduced-sodium chicken broth
1 (8-oz.) package ⅓-less-fat cream cheese
¼ tsp. ground red pepper
¼ cup chopped fresh Italian parsley
1 (8-oz.) package spaghetti

1. Process chicken and garlic clove in a food processor until ground. Stir together chicken mixture, egg, and next 2 ingredients in a large bowl. Cover and chill 20 minutes.

2. Preheat oven to 375°. Shape mixture into 1-inch balls. Place a rack coated with cooking spray in an aluminum foil-lined broiling pan. Arrange meatballs on rack; lightly spray meatballs with cooking spray.

3. Bake at 375° for 13 minutes or until golden and thoroughly cooked.

4. Sauté mushrooms and nutmeg in hot oil in a Dutch oven over medium-high heat 8 to 10 minutes or until mushrooms are tender. Add minced garlic; sauté 1 minute. Sprinkle with flour; cook, stirring constantly, 1 minute. Add wine, stirring to loosen browned particles from bottom of pan. Whisk in broth. Bring to a boil; reduce heat, and simmer, stirring occasionally, 15 minutes. Add cream cheese, whisking until smooth and sauce is thickened.

5. Add meatballs, red pepper, and parsley to sauce; simmer 10 minutes. Meanwhile, cook pasta according to package directions omitting salt and oil; drain. Serve sauce with meatballs over pasta.

Per serving: Calories 431; Fat 11.2g (sat 5.2g, mono 3.5g, poly 1.1g); Protein 40g; Fiber 1.7g; Chol 122mg; Iron 3.8mg; Sodium 629mg; Calc 78mg

CHICKEN WITH MUSHROOM SAUCE

makes 4 servings   prep: 25 min.   cook: 32 min.

4   skinned and boned chicken breasts

1½ tsp. salt, divided

¼   cup all-purpose flour

¼   tsp. pepper

½   cup milk

1   cup Italian-seasoned breadcrumbs

Olive oil

1   garlic clove, minced

12 fresh mushrooms, sliced

4   green onions, chopped

3   Tbsp. chopped fresh parsley

2   Tbsp. capers

½   cup chicken broth or water

½   cup Marsala or white wine

2   Tbsp. lemon juice

2   lemons, sliced

Hot cooked spaghetti (optional)

Tomato pasta sauce (optional)

{ freeze it }

1. Place chicken breasts between 2 sheets of heavy-duty plastic wrap; flatten to ½-inch thickness, using a meat mallet or rolling pin. Sprinkle chicken evenly with ½ tsp. salt.

2. Combine ¼ cup flour, ½ tsp. salt, and ¼ tsp. pepper in a shallow dish; dredge chicken in flour mixture, shaking off excess. Dip chicken in milk; dredge in breadcrumbs.

3. Pour olive oil to a depth of ¼ inch in a large skillet. Fry chicken, in batches, in hot oil over medium-high heat 5 to 6 minutes on each side. Remove from skillet, and drain on paper towels, reserving 2 Tbsp. drippings in pan.

4. Sauté garlic in hot drippings 20 seconds; add mushrooms, and sauté 3 minutes or until lightly browned. Add green onions, parsley, and capers; sauté 1 minute. Stir in chicken broth, next 3 ingredients, and remaining ½ tsp. salt. Bring to a boil over medium-high heat, and cook, stirring constantly, 2 minutes or until slightly thickened. Serve mushroom sauce over chicken. Serve with spaghetti topped with tomato pasta sauce, if desired.

PASTA MEXICANA

makes 8 servings prep: 10 min. cook: 10 min.

Use refrigerated pasta, not dried. We tried both kinds in this recipe and discovered a big difference in taste.

2   (9-oz.) packages refrigerated angel hair pasta   Toppings: freshly grated Parmesan cheese, sliced
¾   cup Mojo de Ajo   fresh chives

1. Cook angel hair pasta according to package directions in a Dutch oven; drain. Return pasta to Dutch oven, and toss with ¾ cup Mojo de Ajo. Serve pasta immediately with desired toppings.

Mojo de Ajo

makes about 1½ cups prep: 10 min. cool: 5 min. cook: 5 min. stand: 5 min.

Guajillo [gwah-HEE-yoh] chiles are dried peppers with a bright tangy taste and kick of heat. Find them at grocery stores and supercenters alongside other Hispanic ingredients. Cook the chiles in hot oil for just seconds to mellow out the flavor and for easy crumbling. Don't let the ¾ cup minced garlic scare you away. The flavor smooths out as it cooks.

¾   cup olive oil   5   Tbsp. fresh lime juice
3   whole guajillo chiles*   1½ tsp. salt
¾   cup bottled minced garlic

1. Heat oil in a 2-qt. saucepan over medium heat to 350°. Using tongs, submerge 1 chile into oil, and cook 5 seconds; remove and drain on paper towels. Let cool 5 minutes or until completely cool. Repeat with remaining 2 chiles. Remove and discard stems. Process remaining portion of chiles in food processor 30 seconds to 1 minute or until crumbled into small flakes.
2. Cook garlic in hot oil in same saucepan over medium heat, stirring occasionally, 3 to 4 minutes or until golden. Let stand 5 minutes.
3. Stir in chile flakes, lime juice, and salt. Store mixture in an airtight container in refrigerator up to 5 days. Allow mixture to come to room temperature before using.

* 2 Tbsp. sweet paprika may be substituted. Omit Step 1; proceed with recipe as directed, stirring in paprika with lime juice and salt in Step 3.

CHICKEN SCALOPPINE WITH SPINACH AND LINGUINE

makes 6 servings   prep: 25 min.   cook: 20 min.   **pictured on page 499**

1   lb. fresh asparagus
1   (16-oz.) package linguine
1   (9-oz.) package fresh spinach, thoroughly
    washed
¾   cup all-purpose flour
2   tsp. salt, divided
1½ tsp. pepper, divided
6   chicken cutlets (about 1½ lb.)
2   Tbsp. butter

2   Tbsp. olive oil
2   Tbsp. all-purpose flour
2½ cups chicken broth
1   Tbsp. lemon zest
3   Tbsp. fresh lemon juice
¼   cup capers, rinsed and drained
2   plum tomatoes, seeded and chopped
Grated Parmesan cheese

1. Snap off and discard tough ends of asparagus; cut asparagus in half crosswise.

2. Prepare linguine according to package directions, adding asparagus during last 2 minutes of cooking. Drain; return to pan. Stir in spinach; cover and keep warm over low heat.

3. Combine ¾ cup flour, 1½ tsp. salt, and 1 tsp. pepper in a large zip-top plastic bag. Add chicken cutlets; seal bag, and shake to lightly coat.

4. Melt 1 Tbsp. butter with 1 Tbsp. olive oil in a large nonstick skillet over medium-high heat. Cook 3 cutlets in skillet 2 to 3 minutes; turn and cook 2 to 3 minutes or until lightly browned and done. Remove from skillet. Repeat procedure with remaining 1 Tbsp. butter, 1 Tbsp. oil, and 3 cutlets. (Chicken may be kept warm in a 250° oven on a wire rack.)

5. Whisk 2 Tbsp. flour into skillet, and cook 30 seconds. Whisk in chicken broth, next 3 ingredients, and remaining ½ tsp. salt and pepper. Cook over medium-high heat 6 to 8 minutes or until slightly thickened, whisking to loosen particles from bottom of skillet. Pour over warm pasta mixture; toss to combine. Transfer to a serving dish, and sprinkle with tomatoes. Serve immediately with chicken and Parmesan cheese.

Worth the Splurge: Use Parmigiano-Reggiano cheese. Allow your guests to grate the cheese tableside right onto their plates.

LINGUINE WITH CLAM SAUCE

makes 6 servings   prep: 20 min.   cook: 25 min.

1   (12-oz.) package linguine
2   (6½-oz.) cans chopped clams
1   Tbsp. butter
¼   cup olive oil
1   (8-oz.) package sliced fresh mushrooms
3   garlic cloves, minced
⅓   cup dry white wine

2   Tbsp. chopped fresh basil
2   Tbsp. chopped fresh parsley
2   tsp. crushed Italian seasoning*
¼   tsp. freshly ground black pepper
⅛   tsp. crushed dried red pepper
Garnish: freshly grated Parmesan
      cheese (optional)

1. Cook pasta in a Dutch oven according to package directions. Drain and return to Dutch oven; set aside.

2. Drain clams, reserving juice.

3. Melt butter with oil in a large skillet over medium heat; add mushrooms and garlic, and sauté 5 minutes or until mushrooms are tender. Add clams, white wine, basil, and next 4 ingredients; cook, stirring often, 5 minutes.

4. Stir reserved clam juice into pasta in Dutch oven; cook over medium heat 5 minutes. Remove from heat; add mushroom mixture, tossing to coat. Garnish, if desired.

* 1 tsp. dried Italian seasoning may be substituted.

Note: We tested with Dean Jacob's Grinder's Fresh Italiano All Natural Seasoning.

TWO-TOMATO LINGUINE

makes 4 to 6 servings   prep: 25 min.   cook: 25 min.   **pictured on page 499**

The short 10-minute simmer time for the tomato sauce helps keep your kitchen cool. The mixture of chopped parsley, garlic, and lemon zest sprinkled over the pasta is called a gremolata.

6   Tbsp. finely chopped fresh flat-leaf parsley,
      divided
4   tsp. lemon zest, divided
1½ tsp. minced fresh garlic, divided
12 oz. uncooked linguine
1   Tbsp. olive oil

2   (14.5-oz.) cans petite diced tomatoes
½   tsp. freshly ground pepper
¼   tsp. salt
1   Tbsp. fresh lemon juice
1   yellow tomato, seeded and chopped*
Extra virgin olive oil (optional)

1. Combine 4 Tbsp. parsley, 3 tsp. lemon zest, and ½ tsp. garlic in a small bowl; set aside.

2. Cook pasta according to package directions in a large Dutch oven; drain. Return pasta to Dutch oven, and set aside.

3. Sauté remaining 1 tsp. garlic in hot oil in a large nonstick skillet over medium-high heat 1 minute or until lightly browned. Stir in petite diced tomatoes, pepper, and salt. Bring to a boil; reduce heat to medium, and simmer, stirring occasionally, 10 minutes or until slightly thickened. Stir in remaining 2 Tbsp. parsley, remaining 1 tsp. lemon zest, and lemon juice.

4. Pour tomato sauce over hot cooked pasta, and toss to combine. Top each serving evenly with chopped yellow tomatoes and parsley mixture. Drizzle each serving evenly with olive oil, if desired.

* ¾ cup yellow grape or cherry tomatoes, halved, or 1 red tomato, seeded and chopped, may be substituted.

CRAWFISH AND TASSO FETTUCCINE

makes 6 servings   prep: 15 min.   cook: 10 min.

Tasso is a spicy smoked pork or beef popular in Cajun dishes.

12	oz. uncooked fettuccine	2	cups whipping cream
3	Tbsp. butter	1	tsp. dried oregano
3	garlic cloves, minced	1	tsp. dried thyme
3	oz. tasso or smoked ham, chopped (½ cup)	¼	tsp. ground red pepper
1	cup sliced green onions	¼	tsp. freshly ground black pepper
1	cup fresh mushrooms, sliced	¼	tsp. salt
1	medium-size green bell pepper, seeded and chopped	1	lb. frozen cooked crawfish tails, thawed and drained
3	Tbsp. all-purpose flour	½	cup refrigerated shredded Parmesan cheese

1. Cook pasta according to package directions; drain and keep warm.

2. Melt butter in a skillet over medium heat; add garlic, and sauté until tender. Stir in tasso and next 3 ingredients; sauté 5 minutes.

3. Stir in flour; gradually stir in whipping cream and next 5 ingredients. Bring to a boil, and cook, stirring constantly, 1 minute or until smooth and thickened. Add crawfish tails; cook, stirring occasionally, just until thoroughly heated.

4. Pour over pasta, tossing gently to coat. Sprinkle with shredded Parmesan cheese; serve immediately.

FETTUCCINE WITH WILTED GREENS

makes 8 servings prep: 20 min. cook: 40 min.

1   (16-oz.) package fettuccine
8   chicken cutlets (about 2½ lb.)
1   tsp. salt
½   tsp. pepper
1   cup all-purpose flour
½   cup extra virgin olive oil
2   sweet onions, thinly sliced
2   (8-oz.) packages sliced fresh mushrooms

2   tsp. minced garlic
½   cup chicken broth
1   cup white wine
1   tsp. salt
1   tsp. pepper
2   (9-oz.) packages fresh spinach,
     thoroughly washed
Freshly grated Parmesan cheese

1. Cook pasta in a Dutch oven according to package directions. Drain, return to Dutch oven, and keep warm.

2. Sprinkle chicken with 1 tsp. salt and ½ tsp. pepper. Dredge in flour. Sauté chicken, in batches, in hot oil in a large skillet over medium-high heat 3 to 5 minutes on each side. Remove; keep warm.

3. Add onions, mushrooms, and garlic to skillet; sauté 5 to 7 minutes or until mushrooms are lightly browned. Stir in chicken broth and next 3 ingredients, and cook 3 to 5 minutes or until liquid is reduced by half, stirring to loosen particles from bottom of skillet.

4. Add mixture and spinach to pasta in Dutch oven; toss to coat. Cook, covered, over medium-low heat 4 to 6 minutes or until greens are wilted. Top with chicken and Parmesan cheese.

SHRIMP BOURBON

makes 8 servings prep: 30 min. cook: 14 min.

2   lb. unpeeled, medium-size raw shrimp
2   Tbsp. butter
8   large shallots, chopped
2   garlic cloves, minced
1   cup chicken broth

½   cup bourbon
1   cup half-and-half
½   tsp. ground red pepper
Hot cooked fettuccine
Shredded Parmesan cheese (optional)

1. Peel shrimp, and devein, if desired.

2. Melt butter in a Dutch oven over medium-high heat; add shallots and garlic. Sauté 3 minutes or until tender. Stir in chicken broth and next 3 ingredients. Cook, stirring occasionally, 5 minutes or until slightly thickened. Add shrimp, and cook 3 minutes or until shrimp turn pink. Remove from heat, and serve over fettuccine. Sprinkle with Parmesan cheese, if desired.

CHICKEN TETRAZZINI

makes 12 servings   prep: 10 min.   cook: 10 min.   bake: 35 min.

Freeze unbaked casserole up to 1 month, if desired. Thaw overnight in refrigerator. Let stand 30 minutes at room temperature, and bake as directed.

1 (16-oz.) package vermicelli

½ cup chicken broth

4 cups chopped cooked chicken breasts

1 (10¾-oz.) can cream of mushroom soup

1 (10¾-oz.) can cream of chicken soup

1 (10¾-oz.) can cream of celery soup

1 (8-oz.) container sour cream

1 (6-oz.) jar sliced mushrooms, drained

½ cup (2 oz.) shredded Parmesan cheese

½ tsp. salt

1 tsp. pepper

2 cups (8 oz.) shredded Cheddar cheese

[*freeze it*]

1. Preheat oven to 350°. Cook vermicelli according to package directions; drain. Return to pot, and toss with chicken broth.

2. Stir together chicken and next 8 ingredients; add vermicelli, and toss well. Spoon mixture into 2 lightly greased 11- x 7-inch baking dishes. Sprinkle evenly with Cheddar cheese.

3. Bake, covered, at 350° for 30 minutes; uncover and bake 5 more minutes or until cheese is melted and bubbly.

HAM TETRAZZINI

makes 6 to 8 servings   prep: 25 min.   cook: 15 min.   bake: 20 min.

2 (7-oz.) packages thin spaghetti, uncooked

¼ cup butter

1 (8-oz.) package sliced fresh mushrooms

6 green onions, chopped

3 garlic cloves, minced

½ tsp. salt

½ tsp. pepper

3 Tbsp. flour

2 cups half-and-half or whipping cream

2 cups (8 oz.) shredded Cheddar cheese

½ cup shredded Parmesan cheese

2 cups chopped cooked ham

1. Preheat oven to 350°. Cook pasta according to package directions. Drain and set aside.

2. Melt butter in a large skillet over medium-high heat; add sliced mushrooms, chopped green onions, and minced garlic; sauté 3 to 4 minutes or until tender. Add salt and pepper.

3. Whisk in flour gradually until blended. Gradually whisk in half-and-half until smooth. Stir in Cheddar cheese and ¼ cup Parmesan cheese until melted; stir in ham and pasta. Pour mixture into a lightly greased 13- x 9-inch baking dish. Sprinkle with remaining ¼ cup Parmesan cheese.

4. Bake at 350° for 20 to 25 minutes.

MUSHROOM-AND-FRESH PARSLEY NOODLES

makes 6 servings   prep: 10 min.   cook: 8 min.   **pictured on page 496**

1 (8-oz.) package medium egg noodles	1 (8-oz.) package sliced fresh button mushrooms*
3 chicken bouillon cubes	¼ cup finely chopped fresh parsley or basil
5 Tbsp. butter	Freshly ground pepper to taste

1. Prepare pasta according to package directions, adding chicken bouillon cubes to water.

2. Meanwhile, melt 4 Tbsp. butter in a large skillet over medium heat. Add sliced mushrooms, and sauté 5 minutes or until liquid evaporates and mushrooms are golden brown. Remove from heat. Stir in chopped parsley, noodles, and remaining 1 Tbsp. butter. Stir in pepper to taste.

* 1 (8-oz.) package assorted mushrooms, sliced, may be substituted.

SNAPPY SMOTHERED CHICKEN

makes 4 servings   prep: 10 min.   cook: 30 min.

If you prefer not to use wine, increase the milk to 1⅓ cups.

1 (8-oz.) package wide egg noodles	1 (16-oz.) package mushrooms, sliced
1 tsp. paprika	2 tsp. jarred minced garlic
1 tsp. dried thyme leaves, crumbled	1 (10¾-oz.) can cream of mushroom soup
½ tsp. salt	1 cup milk
¼ tsp. pepper	⅓ cup dry white wine (optional)
3 Tbsp. butter	1 rotisserie chicken, cut into serving pieces
1 large onion, chopped	2 Tbsp. chopped fresh parsley

1. Prepare noodles according to package directions. Keep warm.

2. Meanwhile, stir together paprika, dried thyme, salt, and pepper in a small bowl.

3. Melt butter in a large skillet over medium-high heat; add onion and mushrooms, and sauté 8 to 10 minutes or until onion is tender. Stir in garlic and paprika mixture; sauté 2 minutes. Add soup, milk, and, if desired, wine, and bring to a boil, stirring frequently. Add chicken pieces; spoon sauce over top of chicken. Reduce heat to low, and cook, covered, 10 to 15 minutes or until chicken is thoroughly heated. Stir in 1 Tbsp. parsley. Serve over hot cooked noodles. Sprinkle with remaining parsley.

VEGETABLE-BACON NOODLE TOSS

makes 4 to 6 servings prep: 20 min. cook: 20 min.

½ (16-oz.) package uncooked wide egg noodles
4 bacon slices
½ small onion, chopped
2 yellow squash, cut in half lengthwise and sliced
1 zucchini, cut in half lengthwise and sliced
2 medium tomatoes, seeded and chopped

½ cup light balsamic vinaigrette
2 Tbsp. chopped fresh flat-leaf parsley
½ tsp. salt
½ tsp. freshly ground pepper
Garnish: flat-leaf parsley sprig

[for kids]

1. Prepare egg noodles according to package directions; drain noodles, and keep warm.

2. Cook bacon in a large nonstick skillet over medium-high heat until crisp; remove bacon, and drain on paper towels, reserving 2 tsp. drippings in a small bowl. Discard remaining drippings. Wipe skillet clean with a paper towel. Crumble bacon.

3. Sauté chopped onion in hot reserved drippings over medium-high heat 5 minutes or until tender. Add squash, zucchini, and tomatoes; sauté 6 minutes or until squash and zucchini are crisp-tender. Add egg noodles, bacon, vinaigrette, and next 3 ingredients, stirring until well blended. Cook, stirring constantly, until thoroughly heated. Serve immediately. Garnish, if desired.

Note: We tested with Newman's Own Lighten Up Balsamic Vinaigrette.

PEANUT-NOODLE SALAD

makes 6 to 8 servings prep: 25 min.

2 large cucumbers
1 cup soy sauce
½ cup coconut milk
½ cup rice wine vinegar
½ cup chunky peanut butter
4 garlic cloves, minced
1 tsp. sesame oil

½ to 1 tsp. dried crushed red pepper
½ tsp. salt
1 (16-oz.) package soba noodles or angel hair pasta, cooked
1 (8-oz.) package shredded fresh carrot
6 green onions, cut diagonally into 1½-inch pieces

1. Peel cucumbers; cut in half lengthwise, removing and discarding seeds. Cut cucumber halves into half-moon-shaped slices.

2. Whisk together soy sauce and next 7 ingredients in a large bowl; add cucumber, pasta, carrot, and onions, tossing to coat. Cover and chill 8 hours, if desired.

FIRE-ROASTED SHRIMP WITH ORZO

makes 4 servings   prep: 45 min.   chill: 1 hr.   cook: 30 min.   **pictured on page 500**

pictured on page 500

1   lb. unpeeled, jumbo raw shrimp
2   tsp. hot chili-sesame oil
6   Tbsp. fresh cilantro, divided
¾   tsp. salt
1½ cups uncooked orzo
1   small carrot, chopped
1   celery rib, chopped
1   large shallot, chopped

2   garlic cloves, minced
1   tsp. canola oil
½   stalk lemongrass, diced
¼   tsp. curry powder
2   Tbsp. coconut milk
1   Tbsp. lite soy sauce
1   tsp. grated fresh ginger

1. Peel shrimp, leaving tails on; devein, if desired. Reserve shells.

2. Toss together shrimp, chili-sesame oil, 2 Tbsp. cilantro, and salt in a large bowl. Cover and chill 1 hour.

3. Cook orzo according to package directions; drain. Spoon hot orzo into 4 lightly greased 6-oz. custard cups, pressing lightly with back of a spoon. Set aside.

4. Sauté carrot and next 3 ingredients in hot canola oil over medium-high heat in a large nonstick skillet 3 minutes. Add 2 cups water; bring to a boil. Add reserved shrimp shells, lemongrass, and curry powder. Reduce heat, and simmer 20 minutes. Remove from heat; cool slightly.

5. Process shell mixture in a food processor. Pour through a fine wire-mesh strainer into a saucepan, pressing with the back of a spoon. Discard solids. Stir in coconut milk, soy sauce, ginger, and remaining cilantro; bring to a boil. Remove from heat.

6. Heat a nonstick skillet over high heat; add shrimp, and cook 3 minutes or just until shrimp turn pink.

7. Unmold orzo. Spoon coconut milk mixture around orzo. Arrange shrimp around orzo.

Note: Lemongrass, an herb that has a sour lemon flavor, is used in Asian cooking. Find it in large supermarkets and Asian markets.

[test kitchen favorite]

LEMON COUSCOUS

makes 6 servings   prep: 5 min.

10 oz. couscous, cooked

2   Tbsp. fresh lemon juice

1. Stir together couscous and lemon juice.

MEDITERRANEAN CHICKEN COUSCOUS

makes 8 servings   prep: 15 min.   cook: 3 min.   stand: 5 min.

Middle Eastern foods such as this one have come to be common across the South as folks try to eat more healthfully. No pots and pans are required for this easy, no-mess recipe. Simply use a glass measuring cup to heat the broth in the microwave, place dry couscous in the serving bowl, and then add the broth. Once the remaining ingredients are stirred in, the dish is ready to serve.

1¼ cups fat-free low-sodium chicken broth
1   (5.6-oz.) package toasted pine nut couscous
     mix
3   cups chopped cooked chicken (about
     1 rotisserie chicken)
¼   cup chopped fresh basil
1   (4-oz.) package crumbled feta cheese

1   pt. grape tomatoes, halved
1½   Tbsp. fresh lemon juice
1   tsp. lemon zest
¼   tsp. pepper
Garnish: fresh basil leaves (optional)

1. Heat broth and seasoning packet from couscous in the microwave at HIGH for 3 to 5 minutes or until broth begins to boil. Place couscous in a large bowl, and stir in broth mixture. Cover and let stand 5 minutes.

2. Fluff couscous with a fork; stir in chicken and next 6 ingredients. Serve warm or cold. Garnish, if desired.

Tip: You'll need to buy a ⅔-oz. package of fresh basil and 1 rotisserie chicken to get the right amount of basil and chicken for this recipe. Substitute 4 tsp. of dried basil if you can't find fresh.

Per 1 cup: Calories 212; Fat 6.8g (sat 3.1g, mono 1.9g, poly 1.1g); Protein 21.3g; Fiber 1.4g; Chol 58mg; Iron 1.2mg; Sodium 455mg; Calc 89mg

southern lights

TASTE OF THE SOUTH

Macaroni and Cheese

The sturdy simplicity of macaroni and cheese offers a happy reminder that no matter how rough the day has been, there is comfort to be found.

Nonetheless, there are rigorous standards for the perfect macaroni and cheese—just ask our Food staff. The custard vs. creamy debate raged at the tasting table for days, with advocates on both sides advancing their causes. This food obviously runs deep in our blood (and our waistlines).

Here are some of the other dividing lines: Bake it in a deep bowl or shallow dish? Stir in a sleeve of crumbled saltines to help give it body or not? Cheddar cheese, Velveeta, or a combination of Cheddar and American? (We all concluded that good-quality sharp and extra-sharp Cheddar give the best results to both creamy and custard-style versions.) Finally, we considered whether to put the cheese on top at the last minute or bake it the whole time to make it crusty.

The cook's style and skill, though, are the most important factors. Custard versions can be dry without enough cheese or milk-and-egg mixture, or if they're overbaked. Other cooks take a more-is-better approach, loading their recipes with extra cheese and butter, producing an oil slick of sauce. We don't mention in polite company those folks who include such foreign ingredients as mushrooms, fresh herbs, or pimiento. (Well, okay. We might allow a little pimiento.)

In the end, your mac 'n' cheese preference bakes down to what you grew up with. All the discussion and research in the world won't change the fact that your mama's recipe is the best, at least in your eyes.

CREAMY MACARONI AND CHEESE

makes 6 to 8 servings   prep: 35 min.   bake: 20 min.

½ cup butter
½ cup all-purpose flour
½ tsp. salt
½ tsp. ground black pepper
¼ tsp. ground red pepper
¼ tsp. granulated garlic
2 cups half-and-half

2 cups milk
2 (10-oz.) blocks sharp Cheddar cheese, shredded and divided
1 (10-oz.) block extra-sharp Cheddar cheese, shredded
1 (16-oz.) package elbow macaroni, cooked

1. Melt butter in a large skillet over medium-high heat. Gradually whisk in flour until smooth; cook, whisking constantly, 2 minutes. Stir in salt and next 3 ingredients. Gradually whisk in half-and-half and milk; cook, whisking constantly, 8 to 10 minutes or until thickened.
2. Stir in half of sharp Cheddar cheese. Stir in extra-sharp Cheddar cheese until smooth. Remove from heat.
3. Combine pasta and cheese mixture, and pour into a lightly greased 13- x 9-inch baking dish. Sprinkle with remaining sharp Cheddar cheese. Bake at 350° for 20 to 35 minutes.

Note: We tested with Kraft Cracker Barrel cheeses.

LAYERED MACARONI AND CHEESE

makes 8 to 10 servings   prep: 20 min.   cook: 55 min.   stand: 10 min.

1 (8-oz.) package large elbow macaroni, cooked
16 saltine crackers, finely crushed
1 tsp. salt
1 tsp. seasoned pepper
1 (8-oz.) block sharp Cheddar cheese, shredded

1 (8-oz.) block extra-sharp Cheddar cheese, shredded
6 large eggs, lightly beaten
4 cups milk

1. Preheat oven to 350°. Layer one-third each of macaroni, crackers, salt, pepper, and cheeses into a greased 13- x 9-inch baking dish. Repeat layers twice. Whisk together eggs and milk; pour over pasta. Bake at 350° for 55 to 60 minutes or until set. Let stand 10 minutes.

Note: We tested with Kraft Cracker Barrel cheeses.

FRESH TOMATO PENNE WITH OREGANO

makes 6 servings prep: 20 min. cook: 20 min.

We prefer the flavor of fresh oregano instead of dried for this recipe.

1   (16-oz.) package penne pasta
¼   lb. prosciutto, chopped
¼   cup olive oil
3   plum tomatoes, seeded and diced
4   garlic cloves, minced
1   (2-oz.) package pine nuts, lightly toasted

¼   cup chopped fresh oregano
½   tsp. dried crushed red pepper
¼   tsp. sugar
¼   tsp. freshly ground black pepper
⅛   tsp. salt
Freshly grated Parmesan cheese (optional)

1. Cook pasta according to package directions; drain and keep warm.

2. Cook prosciutto in hot oil in a large skillet over medium heat 8 minutes or until crisp. Add tomatoes and next 7 ingredients; cook, stirring often, 5 minutes or until tomatoes are tender. Toss with warm cooked pasta. Serve with Parmesan cheese, if desired.

SPICY CHICKEN PASTA

makes 4 servings prep: 10 min. cook: 8 min.

3   celery ribs, chopped
2   garlic cloves, minced
1   medium onion, chopped
½   green bell pepper, chopped
½   yellow bell pepper, chopped
3   Tbsp. olive oil

1   lb. skinned and boned chicken breasts, cubed
1   (16-oz.) jar salsa
1   Tbsp. dried parsley flakes
½   tsp. salt
¼   tsp. hot sauce
8   oz. penne pasta, cooked

1. Sauté first 5 ingredients in hot oil in a large saucepan over medium-high heat 3 to 4 minutes or until crisp-tender. Add chicken, and cook, stirring often, 3 to 4 minutes or until done. Stir in salsa; bring to a boil. Reduce heat, and simmer, stirring often, 2 minutes or until thickened. Stir in parsley, salt, and hot sauce. Serve over pasta.

{ family favorite }

PENNE WITH SPINACH AND FETA

makes 4 servings   prep: 15 min.   cook: 15 min.

1   (8-oz.) package penne pasta
5   large plum tomatoes, seeded and chopped
2   cups fresh spinach, thoroughly washed
4   green onions, chopped
2   Tbsp. olive oil
2   tsp. dried or 1 Tbsp. chopped fresh oregano

2   tsp. dried or 1 Tbsp. chopped fresh basil
½   tsp. salt
¼   tsp. pepper
1   (6-oz.) package basil-and-tomato crumbled feta cheese

1. Prepare pasta in a large Dutch oven, according to package directions; drain. Return to Dutch oven.

2. Stir in tomatoes and next 7 ingredients; cook 2 minutes over medium heat or until thoroughly heated. Top with cheese. Serve immediately.

Note: We tested with Athenos Basil & Tomato crumbled feta cheese.

SAUTÉED MUSHROOM-AND-CHEESE RAVIOLI

makes 4 to 6 servings   prep: 15 min.   cook: 22 min.

1   (25-oz.) package frozen cheese ravioli
3   Tbsp. butter
1   Tbsp. olive oil
1   (8-oz.) package sliced fresh mushrooms
¼   cup finely chopped sweet onion

½   tsp. kosher salt
½   tsp. pepper
2   Tbsp. chopped fresh parsley
2   Tbsp. grated Parmesan cheese

1. Cook ravioli according to package directions in a Dutch oven; drain and keep warm. Wipe Dutch oven clean.

2. Melt 2 Tbsp. butter with oil in Dutch oven over medium-high heat; add mushrooms and next 3 ingredients, and sauté 8 to 10 minutes or until vegetables are tender. Reduce heat to low, and stir in ravioli and remaining 1 Tbsp. butter, stirring until butter is melted. Add parsley, and toss gently to combine. Sprinkle with cheese, and serve immediately.

Note: We tested with Rosetto Cheese Ravioli.

TUSCAN PASTA WITH TOMATO-BASIL CREAM

makes 4 to 6 servings   prep: 10 min.   cook: 5 min.

This pasta favorite features chopped tomatoes and basil that freshen up a jarred sauce in just 15 minutes.

1   (20-oz.) package refrigerated four-cheese ravioli*
1   (16-oz.) jar sun-dried tomato Alfredo sauce
2   Tbsp. white wine

2   medium-size fresh tomatoes, chopped**
½   cup chopped fresh basil
⅓   cup grated Parmesan cheese
Garnish: fresh basil strips (optional)

1. Prepare pasta according to package directions.

2. Meanwhile, pour Alfredo sauce into a medium saucepan. Pour wine into sauce jar; cover tightly, and shake well. Stir wine mixture into saucepan. Stir in chopped tomatoes and ½ cup chopped basil, and cook over medium-low heat 5 minutes or until thoroughly heated. Toss with pasta, and top evenly with ⅓ cup grated Parmesan cheese. Garnish, if desired.

* 1 (13-oz.) package three-cheese tortellini may be substituted.

** 1 (14.5-oz.) can petite diced tomatoes, fully drained, may be substituted.

Note: We tested with Buitoni Four Cheese Ravioli and Classico Sun-dried Tomato Alfredo Pasta Sauce.

SPINACH-RAVIOLI LASAGNA

makes 6 to 8 servings   prep: 10 min.   bake: 35 min.

Ready in just 45 minutes, this cheesy dish is made with frozen cheese ravioli, Alfredo sauce, fresh spinach, and garnished with fresh basil.

1   (6-oz.) package fresh baby spinach, thoroughly washed
⅓   cup refrigerated pesto sauce
1   (15-oz.) jar Alfredo sauce
¼   cup vegetable broth*

1   (25-oz.) package frozen cheese-filled ravioli (do not thaw)
1   cup (4 oz.) shredded Italian six-cheese blend
Garnishes: chopped fresh basil, paprika (optional)

1. Preheat oven to 375°. Chop spinach, and toss with pesto in a medium bowl.

2. Combine Alfredo sauce and vegetable broth. Spoon one-third of Alfredo sauce mixture (about ½ cup) into a lightly greased 11- x 7-inch baking dish. Top with half of spinach mixture. Arrange half of ravioli in a single layer over spinach mixture. Repeat layers once. Top with remaining Alfredo sauce.

3. Bake at 375° for 30 minutes. Remove from oven, and sprinkle with shredded cheese. Bake 5 more minutes or until hot and bubbly. Garnish, if desired.

* Chicken broth may be substituted.

Note: We tested with Santa Barbara Original Basil Pesto and Bertolli Alfredo Sauce.

ITALIAN MEAT SAUCE

makes 10 cups   prep: 35 min.   cook: 3 hr.

1   lb. ground pork*

1   lb. ground beef

1   medium onion, diced

2   celery ribs, diced

2   small carrots, diced

3   garlic cloves, minced

1   tsp. salt

1   tsp. pepper

1   (8-oz.) package sliced fresh mushrooms

2   (15-oz.) cans tomato sauce

1   (14½-oz.) can beef broth

1   (10¾-oz.) can tomato puree

1   (6-oz.) can Italian-style tomato paste

1   Tbsp. chopped fresh thyme

1   Tbsp. chopped fresh oregano

1   Tbsp. chopped fresh basil

1   (20-oz.) package refrigerated cheese-filled
    ravioli, cooked

Garnish: chopped fresh basil (optional)

1. Cook first 8 ingredients in a large Dutch oven over medium heat, stirring until meat crumbles and is no longer pink; drain.

2. Stir in mushrooms and next 6 ingredients; simmer 3 hours. Stir in 1 Tbsp. basil just before serving; serve over ravioli. Garnish, if desired.

* 1 lb. ground beef may be substituted.

EGGPLANT PARMESAN LASAGNA

makes 8 to 10 servings   prep: 50 min.   cook: 1 hr.   bake: 35 min.   stand: 20 min.

2	(26-oz.) jars tomato, garlic, and onion pasta sauce	¼	tsp. black pepper
¼	cup chopped fresh basil	3	large eggs, lightly beaten
½	tsp. dried crushed red pepper	1	cup all-purpose flour
½	cup whipping cream	6	Tbsp. olive oil
1	cup grated Parmesan cheese	6	lasagna noodles, cooked and drained*
1	large eggplant (about 1½ lb.)	1	(15-oz.) container part-skim ricotta cheese
½	tsp. salt	2	cups (8 oz.) shredded mozzarella cheese

1. Cook first 3 ingredients in a 3½-qt. saucepan over medium-low heat 30 minutes. Remove from heat; stir in cream and Parmesan cheese. Set aside.

2. Peel eggplant, and cut crosswise into ¼-inch-thick slices. Sprinkle slices evenly with salt and black pepper. Stir together eggs and 3 Tbsp. water. Dredge eggplant in flour; dip into egg mixture, and dredge again in flour, shaking to remove excess.

3. Cook eggplant, in batches, in 1½ Tbsp. hot oil in a large nonstick skillet over medium-high heat 4 minutes on each side or until golden brown and slightly softened. Drain on paper towels. Repeat with remaining oil and eggplant, wiping skillet clean after each batch, if necessary.

4. Layer 3 lasagna noodles lengthwise in a lightly greased 13- x 9-inch baking dish. Top with one-third tomato sauce mixture and half of eggplant. Dollop half of ricotta cheese evenly on eggplant in dish; top with half of mozzarella. Repeat layers with remaining noodles, one-third sauce mixture, remaining eggplant, and remaining ricotta. Top with remaining one-third sauce mixture and mozzarella cheese.

5. Bake at 350° for 35 to 40 minutes or until golden brown. Let stand 20 minutes before serving.

* 6 no-cook lasagna noodles may be substituted. Prepare recipe as directed, reserving last half of mozzarella from top. Bake, covered, at 350° for 45 minutes. Sprinkle top with reserved cheese; bake, uncovered, for 20 more minutes or until golden brown.

Note: We tested with Bertolli Vidalia Onion With Roasted Garlic pasta sauce.

EASY LASAGNA

makes 6 to 8 servings   prep: 15 min.   bake: 55 min.   stand: 15 min.   **pictured on page 498**

Scrape the layer of solidified oil from the top of the container of pesto, and discard. Then measure the pesto.

1	lb. mild Italian sausage	2	(26-oz.) jars pasta sauce
1	(15-oz.) container part-skim ricotta cheese	9	no-boil lasagna noodles
¼	cup refrigerated ready-made pesto	4	cups (16 oz.) shredded Italian three-cheese
1	large egg, lightly beaten		blend or mozzarella cheese

1. Preheat oven to 350°. Remove and discard casings from sausage. Cook sausage in a large skillet over medium heat, stirring until meat crumbles and is no longer pink; drain.
2. Stir together ricotta cheese, pesto, and egg.
3. Spread half of 1 jar pasta sauce evenly in a lightly greased 13- x 9-inch baking dish. Layer with 3 lasagna noodles (noodles should not touch each other or sides of dish), half of ricotta mixture, half of sausage, 1 cup three-cheese blend, and remaining half of 1 jar pasta sauce. Repeat layers using 3 lasagna noodles, remaining ricotta mixture, remaining sausage, 1 cup three-cheese blend. Top with remaining 3 noodles and second jar of pasta sauce, covering noodles completely. Sprinkle evenly with remaining 2 cups three-cheese blend.
4. Bake, covered, at 350° for 40 minutes. Uncover and bake 15 more minutes or until cheese is melted and edges are lightly browned and bubbly. Let stand 15 minutes.

Note: We tested with Classico Tomato & Basil spaghetti sauce and Barilla Lasagne Oven-Ready noodles.

Staunton Grocery

There's no guessing the flavors on your plate at Staunton Grocery in Staunton, Virginia. Chef/owner Ian Boden wants you to be one with the experience, so his menu breaks it down and spells it out. One example: Crispy Pork Belly + Plums + Red Wine Reduction. No surprises— just the simple, straightforward marriage of local ingredients. Local is the backbone here. A posted chalkboard lists the sources: farmers a shout away (including a few retirees from the D.C. government scene) growing seasonal fare. You'll find your- self pondering each bite—identifying the husky mushrooms playing off the creaminess of goat cheese in the house-made gnocchi, the sweetness of a breakfast radish atop tuna sashimi, and the surprising velvety richness of that pork belly with its fruity embellishments. Mouthwatering seasonal produce shapes each menu. Fish, though brought from elsewhere, is either wild or sustainably farmed. It's fresh food with conscience, benefitting you, the farmers, and the Earth. Good intentions never tasted so fine.

105 West Beverley Street
Staunton, Virginia 24401
www.stauntongrocery.com or (540) 886-6880.

FIESTA TACO LASAGNA

makes 9 servings   prep: 15 min.   cook: 15 min.   bake: 40 min.   stand: 5 min.

No-boil lasagna noodles make this dish easy to assemble.

1   lb. lean ground beef

1   (1.25-oz.) package taco seasoning

1   (11-oz.) can yellow corn with red and green peppers, drained

1   (8-oz.) container soft onion-and-chive cream cheese

2   cups (8 oz.) shredded Cheddar-Monterey Jack cheese blend, divided

4½ cups salsa

9   no-boil lasagna noodles

Toppings: sour cream, chopped fresh cilantro

1. Preheat oven to 350°. Cook ground beef in a large skillet over medium-high heat, stirring until it crumbles and is no longer pink; drain and return to skillet. Stir in taco seasoning, corn, and ½ cup water.

2. Cook, uncovered, stirring occasionally, 5 minutes or until thickened. Add cream cheese, stirring until melted. Remove from heat, and stir in 1 cup Cheddar-Monterey Jack cheese.

3. Spread 1 cup salsa evenly in a lightly greased 13- x 9-inch baking dish. Layer with 3 lasagna noodles (noodles should not touch each other or sides of dish), 2 cups ground beef mixture, and ¾ cup salsa. Repeat layers using 3 lasagna noodles, remaining ground beef mixture, and ¾ cup salsa. Top with remaining 3 noodles and 2 cups salsa, covering noodles completely. Sprinkle evenly with remaining 1 cup Cheddar-Monterey Jack cheese.

4. Bake, covered, at 375° for 30 minutes. Uncover and bake 10 to 15 more minutes or until cheese is melted and edges are lightly browned. Let stand 5 minutes. Serve with desired toppings.

Note: We tested with Skinner Oven Ready Lasagna and Old El Paso Thick 'n Chunky salsa.

VEGETABLE MANICOTTI

makes 6 servings   prep: 25 min.   cook: 16 min.   bake: 50 min.   stand: 10 min.

2   garlic cloves, minced

3   Tbsp. olive oil

1   medium eggplant, peeled and cubed

2   medium zucchini, cut in half lengthwise and thinly sliced

1   small onion, cut in half and thinly sliced (about ½ cup)

1   (8-oz.) package sliced fresh mushrooms

½   tsp. salt

½   tsp. dried Italian seasoning

¼   tsp. pepper

2   (14.5-oz.) cans diced tomatoes with oregano and basil, undrained

1   (15-oz.) package frozen cheese-stuffed manicotti, unthawed

½   cup freshly grated Parmesan cheese

1   (16-oz.) package shredded mozzarella cheese, divided

1. Preheat oven to 350°. Sauté minced garlic in hot olive oil in a large skillet over medium heat 1 minute.

2. Stir in eggplant and next 3 ingredients; cook, stirring occasionally, 15 to 20 minutes or until vegetables are tender and liquid evaporates. Stir in salt, Italian seasoning, and pepper; add diced tomatoes, and remove mixture from heat.

3. Spoon half of vegetable mixture in bottom of a lightly greased 13- x 9-inch baking dish.

4. Layer evenly with stuffed frozen manicotti, grated Parmesan cheese, and half of mozzarella cheese; top with remaining half of vegetable mixture.

5. Bake at 375°, uncovered, for 40 minutes. Sprinkle evenly with remaining half of mozzarella cheese, and bake 10 more minutes or until cheese is melted and bubbly. Let stand 10 minutes before serving.

FLUFFY WHITE RICE

makes 4 servings   prep: 5 min.   cook: 15 min.   stand: 10 min.

Rinsing the rice reduces its starchiness, making for a fluffy, not sticky, product.

1 cup uncooked long-grain rice	1 tsp. vegetable oil

1. Bring rice, 1½ cups water, and oil to a boil in a heavy saucepan. Cover, reduce heat, and simmer 15 minutes or until done. Remove from heat, and let stand 10 minutes. Fluff with a fork.

[quick]

BRAISED RICE

makes 10 servings   cook: 20 min.

¼ cup butter	3 (14½-oz.) cans chicken broth
1 large onion, diced	½ tsp. salt
3 cups uncooked long-grain rice	½ tsp. pepper

1. Preheat oven to 350°. Melt butter in an ovenproof skillet; add onion, and sauté until tender.
2. Add rice, broth, salt, and pepper; bring to a boil. Remove from heat.
3. Bake, covered, at 350° for 20 minutes or until broth is absorbed and rice is tender. Stir with a fork, and serve.

[quick]

CURRIED RICE

makes about 3½ cups   prep: 20 min.   cook: 25 min.

1 cup uncooked long-grain white rice	Vegetable cooking spray
1 small onion, chopped	2 cups low-sodium fat-free chicken broth
1 apple, peeled and chopped	¼ tsp. salt
1 Tbsp. curry powder	¼ cup golden raisins
1 tsp. minced garlic	¼ cup sliced green onions
2 tsp. olive oil	2 Tbsp. slivered almonds, toasted

1. Sauté uncooked rice and next 4 ingredients in hot oil in a large saucepan coated with cooking spray 5 minutes. (Do not brown.) Stir in broth and salt; bring to a boil. Cover, reduce heat, and simmer 20 minutes or until liquid is absorbed. Stir in raisins, green onions, and toasted almonds.

GREEN RICE TIMBALES

makes 12 servings prep: 10 min.   cook: 3 min.   bake: 30 min.   cool: 5 min.

3   cups cooked rice

3   cups (12 oz.) shredded fontina cheese

3   cups half-and-half

4   large eggs

1½ tsp. salt

1   tsp. freshly ground pepper

2   Tbsp. butter

½   cup minced green onions

4   garlic cloves, minced

1   (10-oz.) package fresh spinach, thoroughly washed and coarsely chopped

½   cup chopped fresh parsley

Garnishes: baby carrot fans, fresh parsley sprigs (optional)

1. Preheat oven to 350°. Combine first 6 ingredients in a large bowl.

2. Melt butter in a large skillet; add green onions and garlic, and sauté 2 to 3 minutes or until tender. Add spinach; cook, stirring constantly, 1 minute or just until wilted. Stir in parsley, and add to rice mixture. Spoon into 12 lightly greased 10-oz. custard cups or individual soufflé dishes, and place in 2 (13- x 9-inch) pans. Add hot water to pans to depth of 1 inch.

3. Bake at 350° for 30 minutes or until set. Remove from water; cool on wire racks 5 minutes. Loosen edges with a knife; unmold onto a serving platter. Garnish, if desired.

SEASONED RICE MIX

makes 3 cups (4 servings) prep: 5 min.   cook: 20 min.

3   cups uncooked long-grain rice

¼   cup dried parsley flakes

2   Tbsp. chicken bouillon granules

2   tsp. onion powder

½   tsp. garlic powder

¼   tsp. dried thyme

1. Stir together all ingredients. Place 1 cup mixture into each of 3 airtight containers. Store in a cool, dry place.

2. Directions for gift card: Bring 2 cups water and 1 Tbsp. butter to a boil in a saucepan; stir in rice mix. Cover, reduce heat, and simmer 20 minutes or until liquid is absorbed.

PICADILLO RICE

makes 4 servings   prep: 15 min.   cook: 30 min.

¾ lb. lean ground beef

1 small onion, chopped

½ cup chopped green bell pepper

1 (16-oz.) can diced tomatoes

1 cup water

2 Tbsp. raisins

2 Tbsp. chopped pimiento-stuffed olives

1 tsp. chili powder

1 tsp. ground cumin

¼ tsp. salt

Dash of ground cinnamon

½ cup uncooked long-grain rice

1. Cook first 3 ingredients in a large skillet over medium heat, stirring until beef crumbles and is no longer pink. Drain well, and return mixture to skillet.

2. Stir in diced tomatoes and next 7 ingredients. Bring mixture to a boil, and stir in rice. Cover, reduce heat, and simmer 20 minutes or until rice is tender.

ORANGE RICE PILAF

makes 6 servings   prep: 15 min.   cook: 30 min.

½ cup chopped red bell pepper

6 green onions, sliced

1 Tbsp. olive oil

1½ cups uncooked long-grain white rice

3 cups chicken broth

1 Tbsp. orange zest

½ tsp. salt

¼ tsp. pepper

1. Sauté bell pepper and green onions in hot oil in a medium saucepan over medium-high heat 5 to 7 minutes or until tender. Stir in rice, and sauté 1 minute. Stir in broth, and bring to a boil. Cover, reduce heat, and simmer 20 minutes or until rice is tender. Stir in remaining ingredients.

Tip: To make ahead, cook bell pepper, green onions, and rice according to directions; refrigerate. At serving time, reheat in a microwave-safe serving dish covered loosely with plastic wrap; stir in orange zest, salt, and pepper just before serving.

make ahead

MIXED FRUIT PILAF

makes 6 servings   prep: 15 min.   cook: 30 min.   stand: 5 min.

½ cup chopped celery

¼ cup chopped onion

1 Tbsp. olive oil

1 garlic clove, minced

½ cup dried mixed fruit, chopped

1 cup apple juice

1 cup chicken broth

1 tsp. cumin seeds

1 tsp. curry powder

¼ tsp. ground allspice

1 tsp. salt

1 cup uncooked bulgur wheat

1. Sauté celery and onion in hot oil in a 3-qt. saucepan over medium-high heat 5 minutes or until onion is tender. Add garlic, and sauté 1 more minute.

2. Stir in dried fruit and next 6 ingredients. Bring to a boil; stir in bulgur wheat. Cover; reduce heat, and simmer, stirring occasionally, 15 minutes. Remove from heat, and let stand 5 minutes.

Note: Pack Mixed Fruit Pilaf in a zip-top plastic bag or waterproof container, and chill to transport to a picnic. It can safely stand at room temperature 2 hours.

HOPPIN' JOHN

makes 4 to 6 servings   soak: 8 hr.   prep: 10 min.   cook: 2 hr.   stand: 10 min.

1 cup (8 oz.) dried black-eyed peas

3 bacon slices

1 small onion, chopped

1 green bell pepper, chopped

1 cup uncooked long-grain rice

1½ tsp. salt

Garnishes: green onion pieces, tomato
    wedges (optional)

1. Place peas in a Dutch oven or large saucepan. Add water to cover 2 inches above peas; let soak 8 hours. Drain peas, discarding water.

2. Bring peas and 7 cups water to a boil over medium-high heat in Dutch oven. Reduce heat to medium, and simmer, uncovered, 1½ hours or until peas are tender.

3. Cook bacon in a large skillet 5 minutes or until crisp; remove bacon, and drain on paper towels, reserving drippings in skillet. Crumble bacon.

4. Sauté onion and bell pepper in hot drippings in skillet over medium heat 5 minutes or until tender. Add vegetable mixture, 3 cups water, rice, and salt to peas. Cook, covered, over medium heat 20 minutes or until rice is tender. Remove from heat, and let stand, covered, 10 minutes before serving. Sprinkle with crumbled bacon. Garnish, if desired.

taking sides

Hoppin' John

This timeless, good-luck combination of rice and peas is a New Year's Day must-have.

In our search for the definitive Hoppin' John recipe, we discovered lots of differences. Black-eyed peas (also known as cowpeas) are just one kind of dried peas popping up in recipes (others include regional darlings such as crowder, pink-eyed, lady, and good ol' field peas). Some recipes call for cooking the rice and peas together, while others suggest spooning the peas over a mound of hot rice. Some folks prefer a creamier, stewlike consistency over drier versions. But regardless of whether the cook uses salt pork, a ham hock, or bacon, pork is the primary flavoring agent.

Hoppin' John is one of those Southern culinary icons that seems so simple, yet upon closer inspection blooms with layers of history, lore, and tradition. The hearty combination first emerged on Lowcountry rice plantations. Abundant Carolina Gold rice and field peas re-created the rice-and-pigeon pea combination familiar to West African slaves, who were hungry for the comforting flavors of their homeland. Good

food travels fast, and soon this stick-to-your-ribs specialty made its way out of the fields and into kitchens throughout the South.

As for lore, there are as many stories regarding the origin of the name Hoppin' John as there are tributaries flowing into the Mississippi. One of the more popular theories suggests it's a Southern-ization of Hoppin' John *pois à pigeon* (pwah ah pee-ZHAN), which is French for "pigeon pea."

Tradition holds that when eaten on New Year's Day, Hoppin' John brings good luck. The rice signifies abundance for the coming year, while peas—specifically black-eyed peas—are thought to bring wealth in the form of coins. (Collard greens, a classic Hoppin' John partner, represent dollar bills.) Pork also plays an important role in the dish, and it's for more than just flavor. Hogs can't look back, so pork represents the future. This recipe gives you an authentic and soul-soothing taste of Hoppin' John in all of its delicious glory.

SKILLET HOPPIN' JOHN WITH SCALLION HOE CAKE MEDALLIONS

makes 6 servings   prep: 30 min.   cook: 35 min.   fry: 6 min.

4   turkey bacon slices, chopped

1   Tbsp. olive oil

1   medium onion, chopped

1   small red bell pepper, chopped

1½ tsp. salt, divided

½   tsp. dried thyme

¼   tsp. freshly ground pepper

⅛   tsp. dried crushed red pepper

⅛   tsp. ground chipotle chili pepper

2   cups cooked Valencia short-grain rice

1   (15-oz.) can black-eyed peas, rinsed and drained

2   cups white cornmeal

¼   cup butter, melted

2   cups boiling water

4   large scallions, finely chopped

¼   cup vegetable oil

3   Tbsp. fresh lime juice

1. Preheat oven to 250°. Cook turkey bacon in 1 Tbsp. hot oil in a large well-greased cast-iron skillet or ovenproof nonstick skillet over medium-high heat, stirring constantly, 5 minutes or until browned. Add onion; sauté 5 minutes. Add bell pepper, and sauté 5 minutes or until tender. Stir in ½ tsp. salt and next 4 ingredients until blended. Stir in rice and black-eyed peas; sauté 10 minutes or until thoroughly heated.

2. Cover skillet loosely with aluminum foil, and place in preheated oven to keep warm.

3. Combine cornmeal, butter, and remaining 1 tsp. salt in a large bowl. Gradually add 2 cups boiling water, stirring until mixture resembles thickened grits. (Batter should be soft but not too thin. Add more water if mixture becomes too firm.) Fold in finely chopped scallions.

4. Drop batter by tablespoonfuls, in batches, into ¼ cup hot oil in a large skillet over medium-high heat, and fry 3 minutes on each side or until golden, adding more oil as needed for each batch. Drain on paper towels; keep warm.

5. Remove rice mixture from oven, and stir in lime juice. Serve with hoe cakes.

Chocolate-Walnut Pie,
page 629

Blackberry Cobbler,
page 636

Apple-Gingerbread Cobbler,
page 636

Honeyed Apple-Cranberry
Fried Pies, page 638

Cream Puffs, page 641

Creamy Lemonade
Pie, page 628

Fudgy Peanut Butter
Cup Pie, page 622

X-Treme Chocolate Double-Nut
Caramel Ladyfinger Torte,
page 634

Turnip-Bacon Turnovers,
page 647

Jan's Roasted Chicken and
Jan's Roasted Potatoes,
page 655

Garlic-Herb Roasted Chicken,
page 650

Sun-dried Tomato Chicken,
page 690

Greek-Style Chicken,
page 688

Crunchy Pan-fried
Chicken, page 659

Chicken Cakes With Creole
Sauce, page 693

Chicken Enchiladas,
page 685

Spicy Curried Fried
Chicken, page 660

FRIED RICE 101

makes 4 servings prep: 10 min. cook: 10 min.

Asian cuisine, such as this Chinese favorite, has seduced Southern taste buds.

3 Tbsp. oil, divided
2 large eggs, lightly beaten
½ cup diced onion
½ cup diced bell pepper
1 cup chopped cooked meat, poultry, or shrimp

½ cup frozen sweet green peas
3 cups cooked rice
¼ cup soy sauce
1 tsp. garlic-chili sauce
Sliced green onions and chopped almonds

1. Heat 1 Tbsp. oil in a large skillet over medium-high heat; add eggs, and gently stir 1 minute or until softly scrambled. Remove eggs from skillet; chop and set aside.
2. Heat remaining 2 Tbsp. oil in skillet; add onion and bell pepper, and stir-fry 3 minutes. Add chopped cooked meat, poultry, or shrimp and peas; stir-fry 2 minutes. Add rice, soy sauce, and garlic-chili sauce; stir-fry 3 to 4 minutes or until thoroughly heated. Stir in scrambled eggs; sprinkle with green onions and almonds.

VEGGIE FRIED RICE

makes 4 servings prep: 10 min. cook: 10 min.

Try this dish for a tasty vegetarian side or light supper. Toss in leftover chicken, ham, or shrimp, and you'll have a superfast meal packed with whole grains.

1 (5.3-oz.) bag quick-cooking brown rice
1 (8-oz.) package fresh sugar snap peas
4 green onions, cut into 2-inch pieces
½ cup matchstick-cut carrots
1 Tbsp. grated fresh ginger

2 garlic cloves, minced
2 large eggs, lightly beaten
3 Tbsp. lite soy sauce
2 tsp. dark sesame oil

1. Cook rice according to package directions; drain well. Sauté peas, green onions, and carrots in a large nonstick skillet coated with cooking spray over medium-high heat 3 minutes or until crisp-tender. Add ginger and garlic; sauté 1 minute. Add rice, and cook 2 minutes or until thoroughly heated. Push rice mixture to sides of pan, making a well in center of mixture.
2. Add eggs to center of mixture, and cook, stirring occasionally, 1 to 2 minutes or until set. Stir eggs into rice mixture. Stir in soy sauce and sesame oil.

Per 1¼ cups: Calories 240; Fat 5.8g (sat 1.1g, mono 1g, poly 0.4g); Protein 9.6g; Fiber 4g; Chol 106mg; Iron 2.2mg; Sodium 439mg; Calc 92mg

TASTE OF THE SOUTH

Red Beans and Rice

After chatting with food experts and home cooks, we quickly learned that no two red beans and rice recipes are alike. "In New Orleans, you come out of the womb instinctually knowing how to cook red beans and rice. Really, only the nervous newlywed follows a recipe," says Poppy Tooker, a Louisiana native who is one of four U.S. international governors of Slow Food, an Italy-based organization dedicated to preserving world food traditions.

There's more to this dish than beans, though. For some cooks, ham hocks, andouille sausage, or bacon are a must; for others, it's pickled or salt pork.

Food writer Marcelle Bienvenu, who has collaborated with Emeril Lagasse on several cookbooks and who edits the cooking section of his Web site, says, "Some people like to serve fried pork chops with the red beans and rice; others omit the smoked sausage in the pot but serve a link of sausage with the red beans. Everyone has his or her version, depending on family traditions."

Former *Southern Living* Lifestyle Editor and New Orleans native Majella Chube Hamilton uses smoked turkey to give her red beans their characteristic flavor, while her mom, Merion Chube, sticks to smoked sausage and, sometimes, ham hocks. "It's not a seasoning I use often," Merion says, "but when I visit family in Indianapolis, I know my son-in-law and his dad like my red beans cooked with smoked ham hocks."

Nobody knows exactly when the dish was born: "Red beans have been ingrained in the New Orleans landscape for about 200 years," Poppy says. It is well known that Louis "Satchmo" Armstrong loved them. In a letter to a fellow New Orleanian, Armstrong wrote, "It really shouldn't be any problem at all for you to figure out my favorite dish. We all were brought up eating the same thing, so I will tell you: Red Beans and Rice with Ham Hocks is my birthmark." We should all be so lucky.

SPICY RED BEANS AND RICE

makes 2 qt.   soak: 8 hr.   prep: 3 min.   cook: 3 hr., 30 min.

Cooking red beans and rice on wash day Mondays is an old Louisiana custom. Families would simmer a pot of beans all day while they did laundry.

2 lb. dried red kidney beans

5 bacon slices, chopped

1 lb. smoked sausage, cut into ¼-inch-thick slices

½ lb. salt pork, quartered

6 garlic cloves, minced

5 celery ribs, sliced

2 green bell peppers, chopped

1 large onion, chopped

2 (32-oz.) containers chicken broth

1 tsp. salt

1 tsp. ground red pepper

1 tsp. black pepper

Hot cooked rice

1. Place kidney beans in a Dutch oven. Cover with water 2 inches above beans; let soak 8 hours.
Drain beans; rinse thoroughly, and drain again.
2. Sauté bacon in Dutch oven over medium-high heat 5 minutes. Add smoked sausage and salt pork; sauté 5 minutes or until sausage is golden brown. Add garlic and next 3 ingredients; sauté 5 minutes or until vegetables are tender.
3. Stir in beans, broth, salt, red pepper and black pepper; bring to a boil. Boil 15 minutes; reduce heat, and simmer, stirring occasionally, 3 hours or until beans are tender. Remove salt pork before serving. Serve over rice.

Note: For quick soaking, place kidney beans in a Dutch oven; cover with water 2 inches above beans, and bring to a boil. Boil 1 minute; cover, remove from heat, and let stand 1 hour. Drain and proceed with recipe.

RED BEANS AND SAUSAGE

makes 6 servings   prep: 15 min.   cook: 2 hr.   **pictured on page 502**

2 lb. hot hickory-smoked sausage, sliced

1 red bell pepper, finely chopped

1 green bell pepper, finely chopped

3 celery ribs, finely chopped

1 cup chopped onion

4 garlic cloves, minced

3 (15-oz.) cans red beans, drained

1 (15-oz.) can tomato sauce

1⅔ cups water

3 Tbsp. sweet pepper sauce

1 Tbsp. Worcestershire sauce

2 tsp. hot sauce

1½ cups uncooked long-grain rice

1. Cook sausage in a Dutch oven over medium-high heat about 5 minutes, stirring until sausage is browned. Remove sausage, and drain on paper towels, reserving 1 Tbsp. drippings in Dutch oven. Sauté bell peppers and next 3 ingredients in hot drippings 5 minutes or until tender.

2. Stir in red beans, tomato sauce, 1⅔ cups water, pepper sauce, Worcestershire sauce, and hot sauce. Bring to a boil; reduce heat, and simmer 15 minutes. Stir in sausage. Simmer, covered, 1½ hours.

3. Prepare rice according to package directions. Serve Red Beans and Sausage over hot cooked rice.

Note: We tested with Bush's Red Beans and Pickapeppa Sauce for sweet pepper sauce.

Final Four Chow Down serves 6

Chicken-Fried Steak Fingers With Creole Mustard Sauce (page 70)
Dirty Rice **Coleslaw from deli**
Skillet Cornbread (page 122)
Lemon Meringue Pie (page 618)

DIRTY RICE

makes 6 servings prep: 25 min. cook: 40 min.

1	lb. lean ground beef	1	tsp. salt
2	garlic cloves, minced	¼	tsp. ground red pepper
2	celery ribs, chopped (about ½ cup)	¼	tsp. ground black pepper
1	medium onion, chopped	1	Tbsp. Worcestershire sauce
1	Tbsp. chopped fresh parsley	1	cup uncooked rice
1	green bell pepper, chopped	1	(14.5-oz.) can beef broth

1. Cook ground beef and next 5 ingredients in a large skillet over medium-high heat, stirring until beef crumbles and is no longer pink.

2. Stir in salt and next 3 ingredients, stirring well. Add rice, broth, and ¾ cup water, stirring well. Bring to a boil; cover, reduce heat, and simmer 25 to 30 minutes or until rice is tender.

Per serving: Calories 267; Fat 7g (sat 2.8g, mono 3g, poly 0.4g); Protein 20g; Fiber 1.6g; Chol 28mg; Iron 3.4mg; Sodium 775mg; Calc 36mg

[*southern lights*]

TASTE OF THE SOUTH

Red Rice
It starts with bacon drippings for sautéing onions, and then comes a tomato paste-chicken broth mixture that simmers with long-grain rice to yield a side dish rich with flavor.

Steaming is the preferred method for making this South Carolina specialty, because the tomato paste tends to scorch over direct heat. Still, occasional stirring (about every 15 minutes) is a must.

RED RICE

makes 6 to 8 servings   prep: 15 min.   cook: 1 hr., 30 min.   **pictured on page 502**

9	bacon slices	
1	small onion, chopped	
1	(12-oz.) can tomato paste	
3½ cups chicken broth		

2	tsp. sugar
1	tsp. salt
½	tsp. pepper
2	cups uncooked long-grain rice

1. Cook bacon slices in a large skillet over medium-high heat until crisp. Remove bacon, and drain on paper towels, reserving 2 Tbsp. drippings in skillet. Crumble bacon, and set aside.
2. Sauté chopped onion in hot drippings in skillet over medium-high heat 3 minutes or until tender.
3. Add tomato paste to skillet, stirring until mixture is smooth. Gradually stir in 3½ cups chicken broth, stirring to loosen particles from bottom of skillet. Stir in sugar, salt, and pepper. Bring to a boil; reduce heat, and simmer, stirring occasionally, 10 minutes.
4. Combine tomato mixture and 2 cups uncooked long-grain rice in top portion of a cooktop rice steamer. Stir in crumbled bacon. Add water to bottom of steamer, and bring to a boil over high heat. (We used 4½ cups water, but amounts may vary with different steamers. Follow manufacturer's instructions.) Place the top of steamer over boiling water. Reduce heat to medium-high; cover and cook 1 hour or until rice is tender, stirring every 15 minutes.

Note: We tested with a 5½-qt. Metro cooktop rice steamer.

FANTASTIC FOOLPROOF SMOKEY JAMBALAYA

makes 4 to 6 servings   prep: 15 min.   cook: 10 min.   bake: 1 hr.   **pictured on page 501**

1 cup peeled, uncooked, medium-size fresh or frozen raw shrimp	4 Tbsp. vegetable oil
1 onion, finely chopped	1½ cups uncooked extra long-grain white rice
1 green bell pepper, finely chopped	1 cup shredded smoked pork
1 celery rib, finely chopped	2 (10½-oz.) cans beef broth
1 cup diced smoked sausage	3 Tbsp. Creole seasoning
1 cup cubed boneless, skinless chicken thighs	1 bay leaf
	Garnish: green onion tops (optional)

1. Preheat oven to 325°. If frozen, thaw shrimp according to package directions. Devein, if desired, and set aside.

2. Cook onion and next 4 ingredients in hot oil in a 4-qt. cast-iron Dutch oven over medium-high heat, stirring constantly, 10 minutes or until chicken is lightly browned. Stir in rice, 1 cup water, and next 4 ingredients. Bake, covered, at 325° for 50 minutes. (Do not remove lid or stir.)

3. Remove from oven, and stir in shrimp. Bake, covered, 10 more minutes or just until shrimp turn pink. Garnish, if desired.

JAMBALAYA

makes 6 to 8 servings   prep: 15 min.   cook: 40 min.

1 (16-oz.) package spicy hickory-smoked sausage, cut into ½-inch slices	1 (14½-oz.) can stewed tomatoes, undrained and chopped
1 large onion, chopped	1 (8-oz.) can tomato sauce
1 small green bell pepper, chopped	2 tsp. Cajun seasoning
3 garlic cloves, minced	1 tsp. hot sauce
2 cups uncooked rice	1 lb. unpeeled medium-size raw shrimp
1 (32-oz.) container chicken broth	3 Tbsp. chopped green onions

1. Brown sausage in a large Dutch oven over medium-high heat. Drain, reserving 3 Tbsp. drippings in pan. Add onion and bell pepper, and sauté 2 to 3 minutes or until tender. Add garlic, and sauté 1 more minute.

2. Add rice and chicken broth. Bring to a boil; cover, reduce heat to low, and simmer 20 minutes. Stir in tomatoes and next 3 ingredients.

3. Peel shrimp, and devein, if desired.

4. Stir in shrimp and green onions; cook 2 to 3 minutes or just until shrimp turn pink.

ROASTED GARLIC-AND-CHEESE RISOTTO

makes 8 servings   prep: 15 min.   bake: 30 min.   cook: 50 min.

Arborio rice is a short-grain, starchy rice traditionally used for risotto. Long-grain rice will not work in this recipe.

1   garlic bulb
7   shiitake mushrooms
1   tsp. butter
1   tsp. olive oil
1   medium onion, chopped
1½ cups uncooked Arborio rice
½   cup frozen corn kernels
½   cup dry white wine

7   to 8 cups fat-free reduced-sodium chicken broth, heated
1½ tsp. minced fresh or ½ tsp. dried thyme
½   tsp. salt
½   tsp. pepper
¼   tsp. rubbed sage
½   (8-oz.) package ⅓-less-fat cream cheese, softened

1. Preheat oven to 425°. Cut off pointed end of garlic; place garlic on a piece of aluminum foil. Fold foil to seal.

2. Bake at 425° for 30 minutes; cool. Squeeze pulp from garlic cloves, and chop. Set aside.

3. Remove stems from mushrooms, and discard. Thinly slice mushroom caps.

4. Melt butter with oil in a 2-qt. saucepan over medium-high heat. Add onion and mushrooms, and sauté 2 to 3 minutes. Add rice; sauté 1 minute. Stir in corn and wine; reduce heat to medium, and simmer, stirring constantly, until wine is reduced by half. Add ½ cup hot broth, and cook, stirring constantly, until liquid is absorbed. Repeat procedure with remaining hot broth, ½ cup at a time, until rice is tender. (Total cooking time is about 35 to 45 minutes.)

5. Stir in thyme and next 3 ingredients. Add cream cheese and chopped roasted garlic, stirring until blended. Serve immediately.

Per serving: Calories 243; Fat 4.7g (sat 2.2g, mono 0.8g, poly 0.5g); Protein 9.5g; Fiber 1.7g; Chol 10mg Iron 0.4mg; Sodium 301mg; Calc 40mg

QUICK COLLARD GREENS AND BEANS RISOTTO

makes 6 to 8 servings   prep: 20 min.   cook: 30 min.

1   Tbsp. salt

1   (16-oz.) package chopped fresh collard greens, thoroughly washed

1   cup chopped onion (about 1 large)

3   large garlic cloves, minced

1   Tbsp. canola oil

3   cups chicken broth

2   Tbsp. all-purpose flour

1   (15.5-oz.) can cannellini beans, rinsed and drained

½   tsp. salt

¼   tsp. freshly ground black pepper

1   (3.5-oz.) bag brown rice

½   tsp. dried crushed red pepper

¾   cup grated Parmesan cheese, divided

Garnish: ¼ cup chopped fresh parsley (optional)

1. Bring 4 qt. water to a boil in a large Dutch oven. Add 1 Tbsp. salt, and stir until dissolved. Add collard greens to Dutch oven, and cook 2 minutes or until wilted. Drain greens in colander; rinse with cold water. Drain and pat dry with paper towels. Set aside.

2. Sauté onion and garlic in hot oil in Dutch oven over medium heat 3 to 4 minutes or until tender.

3. Whisk together chicken broth and flour; add to Dutch oven, and bring to a boil. Add cannellini beans, ½ tsp. salt, pepper, and collard greens. Simmer, uncovered, 5 minutes. Reduce heat to low, and stir in rice and red pepper. Simmer, stirring frequently, 10 minutes or until greens and rice are tender. Remove from heat, and stir in ½ cup Parmesan cheese.

4. Sprinkle each serving evenly with remaining ¼ cup Parmesan cheese, and garnish, if desired. Serve immediately.

TASTE OF THE SOUTH

Grits Through the years grits have been the workhorse of the Southern table. Enlisted to fill plates when more expensive ingredients were scarce, grits also acted as a foundation for flavorful items such as gravy or over-easy eggs. However, in the past decade or so, grits have experienced a renaissance, appearing on upscale menus with peppers, cheese, and shrimp.

Yet confusion abounds over what grits actually are. Commercially produced grits are made from ground, degerminated, dried white or yellow corn kernels that have been soaked in a solution of water and lye. The only grits for purists are produced by the old-fashioned method of stone grinding with a water-turned stone. These grits retain a more natural texture and rich flavor. Stone-ground grits are sometimes labeled as "speckled heart," because the remaining germ—or heart of the kernel—looks like a tiny black fleck.

CREAMY GRITS

makes 6 servings   prep: 5 min.   cook: 45 min.

2 cups milk	1 cup whipping cream
2 cups water	¼ cup butter
1 to 1½ tsp. salt	1 to 2 tsp. freshly ground pepper
1 cup uncooked regular grits	

1. Bring first 3 ingredients to a boil in a large saucepan; gradually stir in grits. Reduce heat; simmer, stirring occasionally, 30 to 40 minutes or until thickened.

2. Stir in whipping cream, butter, and pepper; simmer, stirring occasionally, 5 minutes.

Note: For thinner grits, stir in additional milk. To lighten, use 1% milk, fat-free half-and-half for cream, and reduce butter to 2 Tbsp.

JALAPEÑO-CHEESE GRITS

makes 8 to 10 servings prep: 10 min. cook: 45 min.

2 (14½-oz.) cans chicken broth
1¾ cups uncooked quick-cooking grits
½ cup butter
1 medium onion, chopped
2 red or green jalapeño peppers, seeded and diced

1 large green bell pepper, chopped
2 cups (8 oz.) shredded sharp Cheddar cheese
2 cups (8 oz.) shredded Monterey Jack cheese
4 large eggs, lightly beaten
¼ tsp. salt

1. Preheat oven to 350°. Bring broth to a boil in a large saucepan; stir in grits. Reduce heat, and simmer, stirring occasionally, 5 minutes. Cover.

2. Melt butter in a large skillet; add onion and peppers, and sauté 5 minutes or until tender.

3. Stir in grits, Cheddar cheese, and next 3 ingredients. Pour into a lightly greased 13- x 9-inch baking dish.

4. Bake at 350° for 30 minutes or until set; serve grits immediately.

BAKED CHEESE GRITS

makes 3½ cups prep: 15 min. cook: 40 min.

⅔ cup uncooked quick-cooking grits
2 Tbsp. light margarine
2 large eggs, lightly beaten
½ (8-oz.) package light pasteurized prepared cheese loaf, cut into ½-inch pieces

¼ tsp. salt
¼ tsp. ground red pepper

1. Preheat oven to 350°. Bring 2⅔ cups water to a boil; add grits, and cook, stirring often, 5 minutes or until thickened. Remove from heat. Add margarine and next 4 ingredients, stirring until blended.

2. Spoon mixture into a 2-qt. baking dish coated with cooking spray.

3. Bake at 350° for 40 minutes or until lightly browned.

Note: Chill up to 8 hours. Let stand at room temperature 30 minutes; bake as directed.

Per serving: Calories 131; Fat 5g (sat 1.9g, mono 1.3g, poly 1g); Protein 6.3g; Fiber 0.3g; Chol 67mg; Iron 0.3mg; Sodium 389mg; Calc 101mg

STACKABLE GRITS

makes 6 servings   prep: 10 min.   cook: 19 min.   chill: 8 hr.

½ large Vidalia onion, diced
2 garlic cloves, minced
2 Tbsp. olive oil
1 (14½-oz.) can chicken broth
1 cup half-and-half
1 cup uncooked quick-cooking grits

1½ tsp. salt
½ cup (2 oz.) shredded Cheddar cheese
⅛ tsp. ground red pepper
⅛ tsp. ground nutmeg
Vegetable cooking spray

1. Sauté diced onion and minced garlic in hot oil in a 3-qt. saucepan over medium-high heat until tender. Add broth and half-and-half; bring to a boil. Gradually stir in grits and salt. Cover, reduce heat, and simmer, stirring occasionally, 10 minutes or until thickened.
2. Add cheese, pepper, and nutmeg; stir until cheese melts. Pour grits into a lightly greased 11- x 7-inch baking dish; chill 8 hours.
3. Preheat oven to broil. Invert grits onto a flat surface; cut into 12 wedges. Spray top and bottom of each wedge with cooking spray; arrange wedges on a baking sheet.
4. Broil wedges 6 inches from heat 2 minutes on each side or until golden.

PARMESAN CHEESE GRITS

makes 4 servings   prep: 5 min.   cook: 5 min.

1 cup uncooked quick-cooking grits
¾ tsp. salt

1 Tbsp. butter
1 (5-oz.) package shredded Parmesan cheese

1. Cook grits according to package directions, using 4 cups water. Stir in salt, butter, and Parmesan cheese.

EARLY-MORNING GRANOLA

makes 6 cups   prep: 15 min.   cook: 5 min.   bake: 25 min.   cool: 30 min.

Stock your pantry with this easy-to-make recipe. Store in an airtight container in a cool, dry place for up to a month.

3   cups uncooked regular oats
1   cup wheat germ
½   cup chopped pecans
½   cup sliced almonds
⅓   cup sunflower seeds
½   tsp. ground cinnamon
¼   cup honey

¼   cup maple syrup
2   Tbsp. brown sugar
2   Tbsp. vegetable oil
1   cup raisins
½   cup chopped dried apricots
½   cup chopped dried apples
Yogurt (optional)

1. Preheat oven to 350°. Combine first 6 ingredients in a large bowl, stirring well.

2. Cook honey and next 3 ingredients in a large saucepan over low heat, stirring until sugar dissolves. Stir in oat mixture.

3. Spread mixture in a lightly greased, aluminum foil-lined 15- x 10-inch jelly-roll pan.

4. Bake at 350° for 25 minutes or until golden, stirring every 5 minutes. Invert onto wax paper; let cool 30 minutes. Stir in dried fruits. Serve with yogurt, if desired.

[make ahead]

QUICK STOVETOP GRANOLA

makes 2 cups   prep: 10 min.   cook: 5 min.   cool: 20 min.

3   Tbsp. light brown sugar
1½ Tbsp. butter
1   Tbsp. honey

2   cups cranberry-vanilla trail mix nutlike cereal nuggets

1. Cook sugar and butter in a large skillet over medium-high heat, stirring often, 2 minutes or until butter is melted and sugar is dissolved. Stir in honey until blended. Stir in cereal; cook, stirring often, 2 to 3 minutes or until cereal is lightly browned. Pour mixture onto a wax paper-lined jelly-roll pan; spread in an even layer. Let cool 20 minutes. Store in an airtight container up to 1 week.

Note: We tested with Post Trail Mix Crunch Cranberry Vanilla Cereal.

[quick]

PIES & PASTRIES

"I don't think a really good pie can be made without a dozen or so children peeking over your shoulder as you stoop to look in at it every little while." —John Gould

BASIC PASTRY FOR AN 8-INCH PIE

makes 6 servings   prep: 8 min.   bake: 10 min.

1 cup all-purpose flour	⅓ cup shortening
½ tsp. salt	2 to 3 Tbsp. ice water

1. Combine flour and salt; cut in shortening with a pastry blender until mixture is crumbly. Sprinkle ice water, 1 Tbsp. at a time, evenly over surface; stir with a fork until dry ingredients are moistened. Shape into a ball; cover and chill until ready to use.
2. Roll pastry to ⅛-inch thickness on a lightly floured surface.
3. Place in pie plate; trim off excess pastry along edges. Fold edges under, and crimp. Chill. (For baked pastry shell, prick bottom and sides of pastry shell with a fork. Chill until pastry is ready to bake.)
4. Preheat oven to 450°. Bake pastry shell for 10 to 12 minutes or until golden.

BASIC PASTRY FOR A 9-INCH PIE

makes 8 servings   prep: 8 min.   bake: 10 min.

1¼ cups all-purpose flour	⅓ cup plus 1 Tbsp. shortening
½ tsp. salt	3 to 4 Tbsp. ice water

1. Combine flour and salt; cut in shortening with a pastry blender until mixture is crumbly. Sprinkle ice water, 1 Tbsp. at a time, evenly over surface; stir with a fork until dry ingredients are moistened. Shape into a ball; cover and chill until ready to use.
2. Roll pastry to ⅛-inch thickness on a lightly floured surface.
3. Follow directions for 8-inch pie (above).

BASIC PASTRY FOR A 10-INCH PIE

makes 10 servings   prep: 8 min.   cook: 10 min.

1½ cups all-purpose flour

¾ tsp. salt

½ cup shortening

4 to 5 Tbsp. ice water

1. Combine flour and salt; cut in shortening with a pastry blender until mixture is crumbly.

2. Sprinkle ice water, 1 Tbsp. at a time, evenly over surface; stir with a fork until dry ingredients are moistened. Shape into a ball; cover and chill until ready to use.

3. Roll pastry to ⅛-inch thickness on a lightly floured surface.

4. Follow directions for 8-inch pie (opposite page).

DOUBLE-CRUST PASTRY

makes 8 servings   prep: 5 min.   bake: 10 min.

Double-crust pies have both a top and bottom crust, and the filling is baked between the crusts. To make a double-crust pie, use a pastry recipe specifically for this type of pie. You can also double a recipe for a single-crust pie.

2 cups all-purpose flour

1 tsp. salt

⅔ cup plus 2 Tbsp. shortening

4 to 5 Tbsp. ice water

1. Combine flour and salt; cut in shortening with a pastry blender until mixture is crumbly.

2. Sprinkle ice water, 1 Tbsp. at a time, evenly over surface; stir with a fork until dry ingredients are moistened. Shape into a ball; chill until ready to use.

3. Follow directions for 8-inch pie (opposite page).

OIL PASTRY

makes 8 servings   prep: 6 min.   bake: 10 min.

1¼ cups all-purpose flour

½ tsp. salt

¼ cup plus 2 Tbsp. vegetable oil

3 to 4 Tbsp. ice water

1. Combine flour and salt; add oil, stirring until mixture is crumbly.

2. Sprinkle ice water, 1 Tbsp. at a time, evenly over surface, stirring quickly. Shape into a ball.

3. Roll pastry to ⅛-inch thickness on a lightly floured surface.

4. Follow directions for 8-inch pie (opposite page).

taking sides

What Makes a Real Apple Pie?

You've heard the phrase, "easy as apple pie?" Not in the South where the opinions on what make an apple pie vary from crust to spices to the type of apple.

"It's got to have a top and a bottom crust to be a real apple pie," says Teresa Sands, of Irmo, South Carolina. "My Tennessee grandmother was famous for her pastry and double crust pies, and that's what I like." In fact, Teresa's grandmother's pies were so famous that she sometimes gave them as birthday presents. And according to her, the key to a great apple pie was using Wolf River apples, purchased from an orchard in the North Carolina mountains, and just a little bit of ground cloves in the filling.

Famous for her apple dishes at Graves Mountain Lodge in Syria, Virginia, cook Margie Tyree says it's the apples and seasonings that make the pie. "It should be Rome or McIntosh apples, and the spices should be cinnamon and nutmeg," she says. She does agree, though, that a double crust pastry apple pie is the quintessential apple pie.

Lola Coston makes and sells apple pies on her family's fourth generation farm store in Hendersonville, North Carolina. She prefers the double crust versions, but her daughter, Holly Burgess, says only a crumb crust apple pie will do. "She thinks they're prettier and that the crumb crust pies are juicier," says Lola.

There is also some discrepancy as to whether serving a piece of apple pie with a wedge of Cheddar cheese is a "Yankee thing" or not. Historians tell us that this practice is from ancient times when only the wealthy ended their meals with fruit, cheese, and nuts "for digestion purposes." The practice followed some settlers to America. So, while it may still be a habit of some, most Southerners agree that, rather than cheese, apple pie should be served hot, with a big, fat scoop of vanilla ice cream.

DOUBLE APPLE PIE WITH CORNMEAL CRUST

makes 8 servings prep: 30 min. stand: 30 min. bake: 1 hr., 20 min. cool: 1 hr., 30 min.

pictured on page 503

Don't skip the apple jelly—it makes the baked pie juices taste rich. It also decreases the cloudiness that sometimes occurs with a flour-thickened apple pie filling.

2¼ lb. Granny Smith apples

2¼ lb. Braeburn apples

¼ cup all-purpose flour

2 Tbsp. apple jelly

1 Tbsp. fresh lemon juice

½ tsp. ground cinnamon

¼ tsp. salt

¼ tsp. ground nutmeg

⅓ cup sugar

Cornmeal Crust Dough (page 608)

3 Tbsp. sugar

1 Tbsp. butter, cut into pieces

1 tsp. sugar

Brandy-Caramel Sauce (page 609)

[test kitchen favorite]

1. Preheat oven to 425°. Peel and core apples; cut into ½-inch-thick wedges. Place in a large bowl. Stir in flour and next 6 ingredients. Let stand 30 minutes, gently stirring occasionally.

2. Place 1 Cornmeal Crust Dough disk on a lightly floured piece of wax paper; sprinkle dough lightly with flour. Top with another sheet of wax paper. Roll dough to about ⅛-inch thickness (about 11 inches wide).

3. Remove and discard top sheet of wax paper. Starting at 1 edge of dough, wrap dough around rolling pin, separating dough from bottom sheet of wax paper as you roll. Discard bottom sheet of wax paper. Place rolling pin over a 9-inch glass pie plate, and unroll dough over pie plate. Gently press dough into pie plate.

4. Stir apple mixture; reserve 1 Tbsp. juices. Spoon apples into crust, packing tightly and mounding in center. Pour remaining juices in bowl over apples. Sprinkle apples with 3 Tbsp. sugar; dot with butter.

5. Roll remaining Cornmeal Crust Dough disk as directed in Step 2, rolling dough to about ⅛-inch thickness (13 inches wide). Remove and discard wax paper, and place dough over filling; fold edges under, sealing to bottom crust, and crimp. Brush top of pie, excluding fluted edges, lightly with reserved 1 Tbsp. juices from apples; sprinkle with 1 tsp. sugar. Place pie on a jelly-roll pan. Cut 4 or 5 slits in top of pie for steam to escape.

6. Bake at 425° on lower oven rack 15 minutes. Reduce oven temperature to 350°; transfer pie to middle oven rack, and bake 35 minutes. Cover loosely with aluminum foil to prevent excessive browning, and bake 30 more minutes or until juices are thick and bubbly, crust is golden brown, and apples are tender when pierced with a long wooden pick through slits in crust. Remove to a wire rack. Cool 1½ to 2 hours before serving. Serve with Brandy-Caramel Sauce.

Yes, we used 4½ pounds of apples for the double apple pie (on page 607)! Use your fingers to position wedges tightly together as you form a tall stack of fruit.

Instead of brushing the top piecrust with beaten egg white or yolk or dusting the piecrust with flour, we used 1 Tbsp. of the flavorful juices that remain in the bottom of the bowl the apple mixture was in. Not only does this carry

the delicious filling flavor to the top piecrust, but it also gives the apple pie a beautiful finished look.

Cornmeal Crust Dough

makes 2 dough disks   prep: 15 min.   chill: 1 hr.

For a flaky crust, make sure the butter and shortening are cold. Our Food staff loved the flavor the apple cider brings to the crust. (Ice-cold water may be substituted.)

2⅓ cups all-purpose flour

¼ cup plain yellow cornmeal

2 Tbsp. sugar

¾ tsp. salt

¾ cup cold butter, cut into ½-inch pieces

¼ cup chilled shortening, cut into ½-inch pieces

8 to 10 Tbsp. chilled apple cider

1. Stir together first 4 ingredients in a large bowl. Cut butter and shortening into flour mixture with a pastry blender until mixture resembles small peas. Mound mixture on 1 side of bowl.
2. Drizzle 1 Tbsp. apple cider along edge of mixture in bowl. Using a fork, gently toss a small amount of flour mixture into cider just until dry ingredients are moistened; move mixture to other side of bowl. Repeat procedure with remaining cider and flour mixture.
3. Gently gather dough into 2 flat disks. Wrap in plastic wrap, and chill 1 to 24 hours.

Brandy-Caramel Sauce

makes about 2 cups prep: 5 min. cook: 4 min. cool: 10 min.

We suggest using the full amount of butter in this sauce, although half of our tasting table thought it was fine with 2 Tbsp.

1   cup whipping cream
1½ cups firmly packed brown sugar
2   Tbsp. to ¼ cup butter

2   Tbsp. brandy*
1   tsp. vanilla extract

1. Bring whipping cream to a light boil in a large saucepan over medium heat, stirring occasionally. Add sugar, and cook, stirring occasionally, 4 to 5 minutes or until sugar is dissolved and mixture is smooth. Remove from heat, and stir in butter, brandy, and vanilla. Let cool 10 minutes.

* Apple cider may be substituted.

inspirations for your taste

Quick Cornmeal Crusts

makes 2 crusts   prep: 10 min.

Unroll 1 (15-oz.) package refrigerated piecrusts as directed; place each piecrust on a surface lightly sprinkled with plain yellow cornmeal. Sprinkle top of crusts with additional cornmeal. Using a rolling pin, press cornmeal into crusts. Use immediately.

Fast Caramel Sauce

makes about 2¼ cups   prep: 5 min.

Stir together 1 (19-oz.) jar butterscotch-caramel topping, 2 Tbsp. brandy, and ⅛ tsp. salt in a microwave-safe bowl. Microwave at HIGH 1½ minutes or until warm, stirring at 30-second intervals. Serve immediately.

BUTTERMILK PIE

makes 1 (9-inch) pie   prep: 15 min.   bake: 6 min.   cook: 45 min.

This rich and custardy Southern favorite mixes up in just one bowl and will bring rave reviews from family and friends.

½   (15-oz.) package refrigerated piecrusts
½   cup butter, melted
1½ cups sugar
2   Tbsp. all-purpose flour

3   large eggs
½   cup buttermilk
2   Tbsp. vanilla extract

1. Preheat oven to 350°. Fit piecrust into a 9-inch pie plate according to package directions; fold edges under, and crimp.

2. Bake at 425° for 6 to 8 minutes or until golden; cool on a wire rack.

3. Beat butter, sugar, and flour at medium speed with an electric mixer until blended; add eggs, buttermilk, and vanilla, beating well. Pour into prepared crust.

4. Bake at 350° for 45 minutes, shielding edges with aluminum foil after 10 minutes to prevent excessive browning.

RANCHER'S BUTTERMILK PIE

makes 8 servings   prep: 15 min.   bake: 45 min.

½   (15-oz.) package refrigerated piecrusts
2   cups sugar
2   Tbsp. cornmeal
5   large eggs, lightly beaten
⅔   cup buttermilk
½   cup crushed pineapple, drained

½   cup sweetened flaked coconut
¼   cup butter, melted
2   tsp. lemon zest
2   tsp. fresh lemon juice
1   tsp. vanilla extract

1. Preheat oven to 350°. Fit piecrust into a 9-inch pie plate according to package directions; fold edges under, and crimp.

2. Combine sugar and cornmeal in a large bowl. Stir in eggs and buttermilk until combined.

3. Stir in pineapple and next 5 ingredients. Pour filling into piecrust.

4. Bake at 350° for 45 minutes or until pie is set and top is lightly browned. Serve warm, at room temperature, or cover and chill until ready to serve.

WARM APPLE-BUTTERMILK CUSTARD PIE

makes 1 (9-inch) pie   prep: 30 min.   cook: 3 min.   bake: 1 hr., 10 min.   stand: 1 hr.

The combination of a buttery fruit filling and a crumbly cinnamon topping makes this a dessert delight.

½ (15-oz.) package refrigerated piecrusts	2 Tbsp. all-purpose flour
½ cup butter, divided	1 tsp. vanilla extract
2 Granny Smith apples, peeled and sliced	¾ cup buttermilk
¾ cup granulated sugar, divided	3 Tbsp. butter, softened
¾ tsp. ground cinnamon, divided	¼ cup firmly packed light brown sugar
1⅓ cups granulated sugar	½ cup all-purpose flour
4 large eggs	

1. Preheat oven to 300°. Fit piecrust into a 9-inch pie plate according to package directions; fold edges under, and crimp. Prick bottom and sides of piecrust with a fork.

2. Melt ¼ cup butter in a large skillet over medium heat; add apple, ½ cup granulated sugar, and ½ tsp. cinnamon. Cook, stirring occasionally, 3 to 5 minutes or until apple is tender; set aside.

3. Beat ¼ cup butter and 1⅓ cups granulated sugar at medium speed with an electric mixer until creamy. Add eggs, 1 at a time, beating just until yellow disappears. Add 2 Tbsp. flour and vanilla, beating until blended. Add buttermilk, beating until smooth. Spoon apple mixture into piecrust; pour buttermilk mixture over apple mixture.

4. Bake at 300° for 30 minutes. Stir 3 Tbsp. butter, remaining ¼ cup granulated sugar, brown sugar, ½ cup flour, and remaining ¼ tsp. cinnamon until crumbly. Sprinkle over pie. Bake 40 more minutes or until a knife inserted in center comes out clean. Let pie stand 1 hour before serving.

TASTE OF THE SOUTH

Chess Pie You can't get more basic than chess pie. Remarkable in its simplicity, timeless in appeal, this is the ultimate pantry pie.

No one has ever been able to determine how chess pie came about its name, but the colorful explanations make for great table conversation.

Some say gentlemen were served this sweet pie as they retreated to a room to play chess. Others say the name was derived from Southerners' dialect: It's jes' pie (it's just pie). Yet another story suggests that the dessert is so high in sugar that it kept well in pie chests at room temperature and was therefore called "chest pie." Southern drawl slurred the name into chess pie. Or, perhaps, a lemony version of the pie was so close to the traditional English lemon curd pie, often called "cheese" pie, that chess pie became its American name.

Of course, you can get fancy with flavorings such as lemon juice. Or add a dash of nutmeg, ginger, or cinnamon. Sprinkle in some flaked coconut or toasted chopped pecans. Some believe a splash of buttermilk makes it better; others swear by a tablespoon of vinegar. To double the already-decadent richness, stir in cocoa powder.

Chess pie may be a chameleon confection, but at its heart are always the basic four ingredients—flour, butter, sugar, and eggs. And preparation is never much more than a little stirring and about half an hour in the oven.

"There are a lot of similar desserts that share the same ingredients," explains cookbook author Jeanne Volz. "That's because the South was at one time agrarian, and a farm woman had to cook with what was there—things like eggs, butter, sugar, and cornmeal. She'd put it all together and try to make something out of it, and when it was good, she'd try to remember what she did."

Mysteries of its origin aside, here are some of our favorite chess pie recipes.

CLASSIC CHESS PIE

makes 1 (9-inch) pie prep: 23 min. bake: 56 min. pictured on page 504

½ (15-oz.) package refrigerated piecrusts

2 cups sugar

2 Tbsp. cornmeal

1 Tbsp. all-purpose flour

¼ tsp. salt

½ cup butter, melted

¼ cup milk

1 Tbsp. white vinegar

½ tsp. vanilla extract

4 large eggs, lightly beaten

1. Preheat oven to 425°. Fit piecrust into a 9-inch pie plate according to package directions; fold edges under, and crimp. Line with aluminum foil; fill with pie weights or dried beans.

2. Bake at 425° for 4 to 5 minutes. Remove weights and foil; bake 2 more minutes or until golden. Cool. Reduce oven temperature to 350°.

3. Stir together sugar and next 7 ingredients until blended. Add eggs, stirring well. Pour into piecrust. Bake at 350° for 50 to 55 minutes, shielding edges with aluminum foil after 10 minutes to prevent excessive browning. Cool completely on a wire rack.

ORANGE CHESS PIE

makes 1 (9-inch) pie prep: 12 min. bake: 8 min. cook: 40 min.

1 (15-oz.) package refrigerated piecrusts

1½ cups sugar

1 Tbsp. all-purpose flour

1 Tbsp. yellow cornmeal

¼ tsp. salt

¼ cup butter, melted

¼ cup milk

2 tsp. orange zest

⅓ cup fresh orange juice

1 Tbsp. lemon juice

4 large eggs, lightly beaten

1. Preheat oven to 450°. Unfold piecrusts; stack piecrusts on a lightly floured surface. Roll into 1 (12-inch) circle. Fit piecrust into a 9-inch pie plate according to package directions; fold edges under, and crimp.

2. Bake piecrust at 450° for 8 minutes; cool on a wire rack. Reduce oven temperature to 350°.

3. Whisk together sugar and next 9 ingredients until blended. Pour into piecrust.

4. Bake at 350° for 40 to 45 minutes or until center is set, shielding edges of crust with aluminum foil after 20 minutes to prevent excessive browning. Cool on a wire rack.

COCONUT CHESS PIE

makes 1 (9-inch) pie   prep: 23 min.   bake: 56 min.

½ (15-oz.) package refrigerated piecrusts	¼ cup milk
2 cups sugar	1 Tbsp. white vinegar
2 Tbsp. cornmeal	½ tsp. vanilla extract
1 Tbsp. all-purpose flour	4 large eggs, lightly beaten
¼ tsp. salt	1 cup toasted sweetened flaked coconut
½ cup butter, melted	

1. Preheat oven to 425°. Fit piecrust into a 9-inch pie plate according to package directions; fold edges under, and crimp.

2. Line pastry with aluminum foil, and fill with pie weights or dried beans.

3. Bake at 425° for 4 to 5 minutes. Remove weights and foil; bake 2 more minutes or until golden. Cool. Reduce oven temperature to 350°.

4. Stir together sugar and next 7 ingredients until blended. Add eggs, stirring well; add coconut. Pour into piecrust.

5. Bake at 350° for 50 to 55 minutes shielding edges with aluminum foil after 10 minutes to prevent excessive browning. Cool completely on a wire rack.

LEMON CHESS PIE

makes 1 (9-inch) pie   prep: 23 min.   bake: 56 min.

½ (15-oz.) package refrigerated piecrusts	¼ cup milk
2 cups sugar	1 Tbsp. white vinegar
2 Tbsp. cornmeal	½ tsp. vanilla extract
1 Tbsp. all-purpose flour	4 large eggs
¼ tsp. salt	⅓ cup lemon juice
½ cup butter, melted	2 tsp. lemon zest

1. Preheat oven to 425°. Fit piecrust into a 9-inch pie plate according to package directions; fold edges under, and crimp.

2. Line pastry with aluminum foil, and fill with pie weights or dried beans.

3. Bake at 425° for 4 to 5 minutes. Remove weights and foil; bake 2 more minutes or until golden. Cool. Reduce oven temperature to 350°.

4. Stir together sugar and next 7 ingredients until blended. Add eggs, stirring well. Add lemon juice and lemon zest. Pour into piecrust.

5. Bake at 350° for 50 to 55 minutes, shielding edges with aluminum foil after 10 minutes to prevent excessive browning. Cool completely on a wire rack.

CHOCOLATE-PECAN CHESS PIE

makes 1 (9-inch) pie   prep: 23 min.   bake: 56 min.

½ (15-oz.) package refrigerated piecrusts	¼ cup milk
2 cups sugar	1 Tbsp. white vinegar
2 Tbsp. cornmeal	½ tsp. vanilla extract
1 Tbsp. all-purpose flour	4 large eggs, lightly beaten
¼ tsp. salt	3½ Tbsp. cocoa
½ cup butter, melted	½ cup toasted chopped pecans

1. Preheat oven to 425°. Fit piecrust into a 9-inch pie plate according to package directions; fold edges under, and crimp.

2. Line pastry with aluminum foil, and fill with pie weights or dried beans.

3. Bake at 425° for 4 to 5 minutes. Remove weights and foil; bake 2 more minutes or until golden. Cool. Reduce oven temperature to 350°.

4. Stir together sugar and next 7 ingredients until blended. Add eggs, stirring well. Stir in cocoa and pecans. Pour into piecrust.

5. Bake at 350° for 50 to 55 minutes, shielding edges with aluminum foil after 10 minutes to prevent excessive browning. Cool completely on a wire rack.

Key Lime Pie
Just as Memphis is known for barbecue and New Orleans is celebrated for gumbo, Key West is internationally famous for Key lime pie. Every restaurant in the city serves this Southern specialty.

Despite the dessert's immediate name recognition, there's certainly no shortage of theories surrounding its origin or its ingredients.

No one can pinpoint when lime pie first showed up in the Keys. Developed by early Bahamian settlers, it appears to have been around for more than 100 years. Debating the history, though, is child's play compared to the arguments that can erupt over the mechanics of the pie. Opinions differ on whether it should contain eggs or even if it should be baked—and that's just for the filling!

You could probably incite a riot discussing the topping and crust. Should the topping be made of whipped cream or meringue? Does it call for a graham cracker crust or a pastry crust?

Key West locals—"conchs," as they're called—do adhere to a few universals. First, Key lime pie is never green, but rather a natural creamy yellow. It's always made with small, round Key limes, not the large Persian limes found in grocery stores. And any Key lime pie worth its weight—and taste—is made with sweetened condensed milk. Never milk. That is because milk was unavailable in the Florida Keys until the 1930s with the opening of the Overseas Highway when tank trunks carrying ice could get to the region. And after much debate the Key Lime Pie was made Florida's official pie in 2006.

KEY LIME PIE

makes 1 (9-inch) pie prep: 30 min. bake: 35 min. chill: 8 hr.

1¼ cups graham cracker crumbs	2 egg whites
¼ cup firmly packed light brown sugar	¼ tsp. cream of tartar
⅓ cup butter, melted	2 Tbsp. granulated sugar
2 (14-oz.) cans sweetened condensed milk	Garnish: lime slices (optional)
1 cup fresh Key lime juice	

1. Preheat oven to 350°. Combine first 3 ingredients. Press into a 9-inch pie plate.

2. Bake at 350° for 10 minutes; cool. Stir together milk and lime juice until blended. Pour into crust. Reduce oven temperature to 325°.

3. Beat egg whites and cream of tartar at high speed with an electric mixer just until foamy. Add 2 Tbsp. granulated sugar, 1 Tbsp. at a time, beating until soft peaks form and sugar dissolves (2 to 4 minutes).

4. Spread meringue over filling.

5. Bake at 325° for 25 to 28 minutes. Chill 8 hours. Garnish, if desired.

LIGHTENED KEY LIME PIE

makes 1 (9-inch) pie prep: 10 min. bake: 12 min.

1 (14-oz.) can fat-free sweetened condensed milk	1 (6-oz.) reduced-fat ready-made graham cracker crust
¾ cup egg substitute	1 (8-oz.) container fat-free whipped topping, thawed
½ cup fresh Key lime juice	
2 tsp. Key lime zest (about 2 limes)	

1. Preheat oven to 350°. Process first 4 ingredients in a blender until smooth. Pour mixture into piecrust.

2. Bake at 350° for 10 to 12 minutes or until golden. Let pie cool completely, and top with whipped topping.

Per slice: Calories 290; Fat 3.7g (sat 0.5g); Protein 7.4g; Fiber 0.1g; Iron 0.4mg; Sodium 185mg; Calc 143mg

GOLDEN PEACH MERINGUE TART

makes 1 (10-inch) tart   prep: 20 min.   cook: 5 min.   bake: 30 min.

6   cups fresh peach slices*

½   cup sugar, divided

2   Tbsp. cornstarch

¼   tsp. salt

¼   to ½ tsp. ground nutmeg

1   (15-oz.) package refrigerated piecrusts

3   egg whites

¼   tsp. cream of tartar

1. Preheat oven to 450°. Bring peach, ¼ cup sugar, and next 3 ingredients to a boil in a large saucepan, stirring often. Boil 1 minute. Cool.

2. Stack piecrusts, and roll into an 11-inch circle. Fit into a 10-inch tart pan according to package directions. Trim off excess pastry along edges.

3. Bake at 450° for 10 to 12 minutes. Reduce oven temperature to 350°.

4. Pour peach mixture into tart crust.

5. Beat egg whites and cream of tartar at high speed with an electric mixer until foamy. Add remaining ¼ cup sugar, 1 Tbsp. at a time, beating until stiff peaks form and sugar dissolves (2 to 4 minutes). Spread meringue over peach filling, sealing to edge of pastry.

6. Bake at 350° for 20 to 25 minutes or just until golden brown.

* 2 (16-oz.) packages frozen peach slices, thawed, may be substituted.

LEMON MERINGUE PIE

makes 8 to 10 servings   prep: 25 min.   freeze: 10 min.   bake: 42 min.

Sealing meringue to the outer edge of crust over a hot filling ensures that the meringue topping will cook completely without shrinking.

1   (15-oz.) package refrigerated piecrusts

Lemon Meringue Pie Filling

6   egg whites

½   tsp. vanilla extract

6   Tbsp. sugar

1. Preheat oven to 425°. Unfold and stack piecrusts on a lightly floured surface. Roll into 1 (12-inch) circle. Fit piecrust into a 9-inch pie plate (about 1 inch deep); fold edges under, and crimp. Prick bottom and sides of piecrust with a fork. Freeze 10 minutes.

2. Line piecrust with parchment paper; fill with pie weights or dried beans.

3. Bake at 425° for 10 minutes. Remove weights and parchment paper; bake 12 to 15 more minutes or until crust is lightly browned. (Shield edges with aluminum foil if they brown too quickly.) Reduce oven temperature to 325°.

4. Prepare Lemon Meringue Pie Filling; pour into piecrust. Cover with plastic wrap, placing directly on filling. (Proceed immediately with next step to ensure that the meringue is spread over the pie filling while it is still warm.)

5. Beat egg whites and vanilla at high speed with an electric mixer until foamy. Add sugar, 1 Tbsp. at a time, and beat 2 to 4 minutes or until stiff peaks form and sugar dissolves.

6. Remove plastic wrap from pie, and spread meringue evenly over warm Lemon Meringue Pie Filling, sealing edges.

7. Bake at 325° for 20 to 25 minutes or until golden brown. Cool pie completely on a wire rack. Store leftovers in the refrigerator.

Lemon Meringue Pie Filling

makes enough for 1 (9-inch) pie   prep: 10 min.   cook: 10 min.

1 cup sugar	⅓ cup fresh lemon juice
¼ cup cornstarch	3 Tbsp. butter
⅛ tsp. salt	1 tsp. lemon zest
4 large egg yolks	½ tsp. vanilla extract
2 cups milk	

1. Whisk together first 3 ingredients in a heavy nonaluminum medium saucepan. Whisk together egg yolks, milk, and lemon juice in a bowl; whisk into sugar mixture in pan over medium heat. Bring to a boil, and boil, whisking constantly, 1 minute. Remove pan from heat; stir in butter, lemon zest, and vanilla until smooth.

PINEAPPLE MERINGUE PIE

makes 8 servings   prep: 20 min.   bake: 20 min.   cool: 2 hr.   cook: 8 min.   chill: 4 hr.

pictured on page 504

Pineapple, like lemon juice, is acidic and will prevent the cornstarch from thickening properly if added before the custard is cooked. Chilling the pie after it cools at room temperature further sets the filling and makes for perfect slices.

2   cups pecan shortbread cookie crumbs

1⅓ cups sweetened flaked coconut, divided

¼   cup butter, melted

2   cups milk

¼   cup cornstarch

3   large eggs, separated

1   cup sugar, divided

1   (20-oz.) can crushed pineapple, drained

1   Tbsp. butter

1   tsp. vanilla extract

1. Preheat oven to 350°. Stir together cookie crumbs, 1 cup coconut, and ¼ cup melted butter; firmly press on bottom, up sides, and onto lip of a lightly greased 9-inch pie plate.

2. Bake at 350° for 10 to 12 minutes or until lightly browned. Remove to a wire rack, and let cool 1 hour or until completely cool.

3. Whisk together milk and cornstarch in a heavy saucepan, whisking until cornstarch is dissolved. Whisk in egg yolks and ¾ cup sugar, whisking until blended. Cook over medium-low heat, whisking constantly, 8 to 10 minutes or until a chilled puddinglike thickness. (Mixture will just begin to bubble and will be thick enough to hold soft peaks when whisk is lifted.) Remove from heat; stir in pineapple, 1 Tbsp. butter, and vanilla. Spoon immediately into cooled piecrust.

4. Beat egg whites at high speed with an electric mixer until foamy. Add remaining ¼ cup sugar, 1 Tbsp. at a time, beating until stiff peaks form and sugar is dissolved. Spread meringue over hot filling, sealing edges. Sprinkle remaining ⅓ cup coconut over meringue.

5. Bake at 350° for 10 to 12 minutes or until golden brown. Remove from oven to wire rack, and let cool 1 hour or until completely cool. Chill 4 hours.

CHOCOLATE-COVERED CHERRY PIE

makes 8 servings prep: 30 min. bake: 30 min. chill: 8 hr., 15 min.

1 (12-oz. package) semisweet chocolate morsels
½ cup whipping cream
¼ cup butter, cut into pieces
1 (6-oz.) ready-made chocolate crumb piecrust
1 (21-oz.) can cherry pie filling
1 (8-oz.) package cream cheese, softened

⅓ cup powdered sugar
1 large egg
¼ tsp. almond extract
16 maraschino cherries with stems
2 cups thawed whipped topping

1. Preheat oven to 350°. Microwave chocolate morsels and cream in a glass bowl at MEDIUM (50% power) 1 to 2 minutes or until chocolate begins to melt. Whisk in butter until smooth. Let cool, whisking occasionally, 5 to 10 minutes or until a spreadable consistency.

2. Spoon half of chocolate mixture into piecrust. Cover and chill remaining chocolate mixture.

3. Spoon cherry pie filling evenly over chocolate mixture in piecrust. Place piecrust on a baking sheet, and set aside.

4. Beat cream cheese and next 3 ingredients at medium speed with an electric mixer until smooth. Pour cream cheese mixture evenly over cherry pie filling mixture. (Pie shell will be very full but will not overflow when baking.)

5. Bake at 350° for 30 minutes or until center is set. Remove from oven, and cool on a wire rack. Cover and chill 8 hours.

6. Drain maraschino cherries on paper towels; pat dry.

7. Microwave reserved chocolate mixture at MEDIUM (50% power) 1 minute. Remove from microwave; stir until spreading consistency, reheating, if necessary.

8. Dip cherries in chocolate mixture, and place on a baking sheet lined with wax paper; chill chocolate-covered cherries 15 minutes.

9. Spread remaining chocolate mixture evenly over top of pie. Spoon 8 dollops of whipped topping around outer edge of pie; place 2 chocolate-covered cherries in center of each dollop.

FUDGY PEANUT BUTTER CUP PIE

makes 10 to 12 servings   prep: 15 min.   stand: 20 min.   freeze: 2 hr., 10 min.   **pictured on page 582**

1 (1.75-qt.) container vanilla ice cream with peanut butter cups swirled with fudge

⅓ cup creamy or chunky peanut butter

1 (6-oz.) ready-made chocolate crumb piecrust

6 (0.6-oz.) peanut butter cup candies, halved

Chocolate-peanut butter shell coating

1. Allow container of ice cream to stand at room temperature 20 minutes to soften.

2. Spread peanut butter over crust; freeze 10 minutes.

3. Spread softened ice cream evenly over peanut butter in crust. Arrange peanut butter cup candy halves, cut sides down, around edges of crust. Drizzle chocolate-peanut butter shell coating evenly over ice cream.

4. Freeze at least 2 hours. Cut frozen pie with a warm knife to serve.

Note: We tested with Mayfield Moose Tracks Ice Cream, Reese's Peanut Butter Cups, and Reese's Chocolate & Peanut Butter Shell Topping.

SPIKED STRAWBERRY-LIME ICE-CREAM PIE

makes 10 to 12 servings   prep: 30 min.   bake: 10 min.   stand: 30 min.   freeze: 3 hr.

This pie will soften quickly due to the alcohol content, which lowers the freezing temperature of the ice cream.

4 cups pretzel twists

½ cup butter, melted

2 Tbsp. granulated sugar

1 (½-gal.) container premium strawberry ice cream

1 (16-oz.) container fresh strawberries (1 qt.), stemmed

½ cup powdered sugar

1 (6-oz.) can frozen limeade concentrate, partially thawed

½ cup tequila

¼ cup orange liqueur

Garnishes: lime zest curls, fresh whole strawberries, pretzels (optional)

1. Preheat oven to 350°. Process first 3 ingredients in a food processor until pretzels are finely crushed. Firmly press mixture onto bottom of a lightly greased 10-inch springform pan.

2. Bake at 350° for 10 minutes. Cool completely in pan on a wire rack.

3. Let strawberry ice cream stand at room temperature 20 minutes or until slightly softened.

4. Process strawberries and powdered sugar in food processor until pureed, stopping to scrape down sides.

5. Place ice cream in a large bowl; cut into large (3-inch) pieces. Fold strawberry mixture, limeade concentrate, tequila, and orange liqueur into ice cream until well blended. Spoon mixture into prepared crust in springform pan. Freeze 3 hours or until firm. Let stand 10 minutes at room temperature before serving. Garnish, if desired.

Note: We tested with Blue Bell Strawberry Ice Cream and Triple Sec orange liqueur.

Strawberry-Lime Ice-Cream Pie: Omit tequila and orange liqueur, and add 1 (6-oz.) can frozen orange juice concentrate, partially thawed. Proceed with recipe as directed. Let stand 15 minutes at room temperature before serving. Garnish, if desired.

FROZEN HAWAIIAN PIE

makes 16 servings   prep: 30 min.   freeze: 12 hr.   stand: 10 min.   pictured on page 581

1   (14-oz.) can sweetened condensed milk
1   (12-oz.) container frozen whipped topping, thawed
1   (20-oz.) can crushed pineapple, drained
2   Tbsp. lemon juice
½   cup mashed ripe banana (about 1 large banana)
1   large orange, peeled and sectioned

½   cup sweetened flaked coconut
½   cup chopped walnuts, toasted
½   cup maraschino cherries
2   (9-inch) ready-made graham cracker crusts
Garnishes: chopped pineapple, maraschino cherries, chopped walnuts, whipped topping, toasted coconut, fresh mint sprigs (optional)

1. Stir together condensed milk and whipped topping. Fold in pineapple and next 6 ingredients. Pour evenly into graham cracker crusts.
2. Cover and freeze 12 hours or until firm. Remove from freezer, and let stand 10 minutes before serving. Garnish, if desired.

STRAWBERRY SMOOTHIE ICE-CREAM PIE

makes 10 to 12 servings   prep: 50 min.   bake: 10 min.   stand: 35 min.   freeze: 4 hr., 30 min.

Each layer of this frozen pie has four stripes of flavor—strawberry, banana, blueberry, strawberry—layered on top of a waffle-cone crust. The waffle-cone crust idea came from Cheryl F. Rogers of Kenner, Louisiana.

[for kids]

1 (7-oz.) package waffle cones, broken into pieces
6 Tbsp. butter, melted
1 Tbsp. granulated sugar
2 (1-qt.) containers premium vanilla ice cream, divided
1 (16-oz.) container fresh strawberries (1 qt.), stemmed

¼ cup powdered sugar, divided
1 pt. fresh blueberries
2 ripe bananas
Garnishes: waffle cone pieces, fresh whole strawberries, fresh blueberries (optional)

1. Preheat oven to 350°. Process first 3 ingredients in a food processor until finely crushed. Firmly press mixture onto bottom of a lightly greased 10-inch springform pan.

2. Bake at 350° for 10 minutes. Cool completely in pan on a wire rack.

3. Let vanilla ice cream stand at room temperature 20 minutes or until slightly softened.

4. Process strawberries and 2 Tbsp. powdered sugar in a food processor until pureed, stopping to scrape down sides; remove strawberry mixture, and set aside.

5. Process blueberries and 1 Tbsp. powdered sugar in food processor until pureed, stopping to scrape down sides; set aside.

6. Mash bananas with a fork in a large bowl; stir in remaining 1 Tbsp. powdered sugar. Set aside.

7. Place 1 qt. of ice cream in a large bowl; cut into large (3-inch) pieces. Fold strawberry mixture into ice cream until blended. Freeze 30 minutes or until slightly firm.

8. Divide remaining qt. of ice cream in half, placing halves in separate bowls. Stir blueberry mixture into half and mashed banana mixture into remaining half. Place bowls in freezer.

9. Spread half of strawberry mixture evenly into prepared crust in springform pan. Place pan and remaining strawberry mixture in freezer. Freeze 30 minutes or until strawberry layer in pan is slightly firm. Spread banana mixture evenly over strawberry layer in pan; return pan to freezer, and freeze 30 minutes or until banana layer is slightly firm. Repeat procedure with blueberry mixture. Spread remaining strawberry mixture over blueberry layer in pan, and freeze 3 hours or until all layers are firm. Let pie stand at room temperature 15 minutes before serving. Garnish, if desired.

Note: We tested with Häagen-Dazs Vanilla ice cream.

COCONUT CREAM PIE

makes 6 to 8 servings prep: 10 min. cook: 10 min. stand: 30 min. chill: 30 min.

½ (15-oz.) package refrigerated piecrusts

½ cup sugar

¼ cup cornstarch

2 cups half-and-half

4 egg yolks

3 Tbsp. butter

1 cup sweetened flaked coconut

2½ tsp. vanilla extract, divided

2 cups whipping cream

⅓ cup sugar

Garnish: toasted coconut (optional)

1. Fit 1 piecrust into a 9-inch pie plate according to package directions; fold edges under, and crimp. Prick bottom and sides of piecrust with a fork. Bake according to package directions for a 1-crust pie.

2. Combine ½ cup sugar and cornstarch in a heavy saucepan. Whisk together half-and-half and egg yolks. Gradually whisk egg mixture into sugar mixture; bring to a boil over medium heat, whisking constantly. Boil 1 minute; remove from heat.

3. Stir in butter, 1 cup coconut, and 1 tsp. vanilla. Cover with plastic wrap, placing plastic wrap directly on filling in pan; let stand 30 minutes. Spoon custard mixture into prepared crust, cover and chill 30 minutes or until set.

4. Beat whipping cream at high speed with an electric mixer until foamy; gradually add ⅓ cup sugar and remaining 1½ tsp. vanilla, beating until soft peaks form. Spread or pipe whipped cream over pie filling. Garnish, if desired.

CHOCOLATE ICEBOX PIE

makes 8 servings   prep: 20 min.   cook: 8 min.   chill: 8 hr.   **pictured on page 504**

Desserts don't come any tastier than this one, topped with toasted pecans and chopped milk chocolate.

⅔ cup milk

¾ cup semisweet chocolate morsels

¼ cup cold water

2 Tbsp. cornstarch

1 (14-oz.) can sweetened condensed milk

3 large eggs, beaten

1 tsp. vanilla extract

3 Tbsp. butter

1 (6-oz.) ready-made chocolate crumb piecrust

1 cup whipping cream

¼ cup sugar

½ cup chopped pecans, toasted

1 (1.55-oz.) milk chocolate candy bar, chopped

1. Heat milk until it just begins to bubble around the edges in a 3-qt. saucepan over medium heat (do not boil). Remove from heat, and whisk in chocolate morsels until melted. Cool slightly.

2. Stir together cold water and cornstarch until dissolved.

3. Whisk cornstarch mixture, sweetened condensed milk, eggs, and vanilla into chocolate mixture. Bring to a boil over medium heat, whisking constantly. Boil 1 minute or until mixture thickens and is smooth. (Do not overcook.)

4. Remove from heat, and whisk in butter. Spoon mixture into piecrust. Cover and chill at least 8 hours.

5. Beat whipping cream at high speed with an electric mixer until foamy; gradually add sugar, beating until soft peaks form. Spread whipped cream evenly over pie filling, and sprinkle with pecans and candy bar pieces.

White House Café

For delicious Southern favorites, the White House Café in Camden, Arkansas, ranks as tops. Everyone from bikers to grandmas pull up a chair for this restaurant's hamburgers, rib-eye steaks, and chocolate cake...all Southern comfort food. Put the emphasis on the word "comfort," and you'll be giving thanks.

323 South Adams Avenue, Camden, Arkansas 71701
(870) 836-2255

CREAMY LEMONADE PIE

makes 8 servings   prep: 10 min.   freeze: 4 hr.   **pictured on page 581**

Be sure to let the cream cheese soften and to thaw the frozen whipped topping and frozen lemonade concentrate before you start preparing this recipe.

2   (5-oz.) cans evaporated milk
2   (3.4-oz.) packages lemon instant pudding
     mix
2   (8-oz.) packages cream cheese, softened
2   (3-oz.) packages cream cheese, softened

1   (12-oz.) can frozen lemonade concentrate,
     partially thawed
1   (9-inch.) ready-made graham cracker crust
Garnishes: whipped cream, fresh mint sprigs,
     lemon slices

1. Whisk together evaporated milk and pudding mix in a bowl 2 minutes or until thickened.
2. Beat cream cheeses at medium speed with an electric mixer, using whisk attachment, until fluffy. Add lemonade concentrate, beating until blended; add pudding mixture, and beat until blended.
3. Pour into crust; freeze 4 hours or until firm. Garnish, if desired.

PINK LEMONADE PIE

makes 8 servings   prep: 10 min.   freeze: 4 hr.

1   (14-oz.) can sweetened condensed milk
1   (6-oz.) can frozen pink lemonade concentrate,
     partially thawed
1   (8-oz.) container frozen whipped topping,
     thawed

1   (6-oz.) ready-made graham cracker crust
Garnishes: fresh raspberries, fresh mint sprigs
     (optional)

1. Whisk together condensed milk and lemonade concentrate in a large bowl until smooth. Fold in whipped topping.
2. Pour into crust; freeze 4 hours or until firm. Garnish, if desired.

HONEYED ORZO-PECAN PIE

makes 1 (9-inch) pie prep: 10 min.   cook: 5 min.   bake: 40 min.

Orzo, a tiny rice-shaped pasta, cooks quickly and is good in both savory and sweet dishes.

½ (15-oz.) package refrigerated piecrusts
1 cup uncooked orzo
2 large eggs
1 cup fat-free evaporated milk
½ cup firmly packed light brown sugar

½ cup honey
½ cup chopped pecans, toasted
½ cup chopped dates
Whipped cream (optional)
Chopped toasted pecans (optional)

1. Preheat oven to 350°. Fit piecrust into a 9-inch pie plate according to package directions; fold edges under, and crimp.

2. Cook orzo according to package directions; drain well.

3. Whisk together eggs and next 3 ingredients in a medium bowl. Add orzo, ½ cup chopped pecans, and dates, stirring well. Spoon orzo mixture into piecrust.

4. Bake at 350° for 40 to 45 minutes or until set; cool on a wire rack. Serve warm with whipped cream and additional chopped pecans, if desired.

CHOCOLATE-WALNUT PIE

makes 8 servings prep: 10 min.   bake: 30 min.   **pictured on page 577**

We recommend using a standard 1½-inch-deep 9-inch pie plate.

½ (15-oz.) package refrigerated piecrusts
1 cup sugar
½ cup all-purpose flour
½ cup margarine, melted

2 large eggs, lightly beaten
1 tsp. vanilla
¾ cup chopped walnuts
¾ cup semisweet chocolate morsels

1. Preheat oven to 350°. Fit piecrust into a 9-inch pie plate according to package directions; fold edges under, and crimp.

2. Stir together sugar and next 4 ingredients until well blended; stir in walnuts and chocolate. Pour filling into piecrust.

3. Bake at 350° on lowest oven rack for 30 minutes or until pie is set; cool on a wire rack.

Note: Recipe from *My Old Kentucky Homes Cookbook* as contributed to *Best of the Best From Kentucky Cookbook* (Quail Ridge Press, 1980)

[test kitchen favorite]

CHOCOLATE-BOURBON PECAN PIE

makes 8 servings   prep: 10 min.   bake: 55 min.

½ (15-oz.) package refrigerated piecrusts

1½ cups chopped pecans

1 cup (6 ounces) semisweet chocolate morsels

1 cup dark corn syrup

½ cup granulated sugar

½ cup firmly packed brown sugar

¼ cup bourbon or water

4 large eggs

¼ cup butter, melted

2 tsp. cornmeal

2 tsp. vanilla extract

½ tsp. salt

1. Preheat oven to 325°. Fit piecrust into a 9-inch deep-dish pie plate according to package directions; fold edges under, and crimp.

2. Sprinkle pecans and chocolate evenly onto bottom of piecrust; set aside.

3. Combine corn syrup and next 3 ingredients in a large saucepan, and bring to a boil over medium heat. Cook, stirring constantly, 3 minutes. Remove from heat.

4. Whisk together eggs and next 4 ingredients. Gradually whisk about one-fourth hot mixture into egg mixture; add to remaining hot mixture, whisking constantly. Pour filling into prepared piecrust.

5. Bake at 325° for 55 minutes or until set; cool on wire rack.

MOM'S PECAN PIE

makes 8 servings   prep: 10 min.   bake: 1 hr., 3 min.

1½ cups pecan pieces

3 large eggs

1 cup sugar

¾ cup light or dark corn syrup

2 Tbsp. melted butter

2 tsp. vanilla extract

½ tsp. salt

1 (9-inch) deep-dish frozen unbaked pie shell

1. Preheat oven to 350°. Spread pecans in a single layer on a baking sheet.

2. Bake at 350° for 8 to 10 minutes or until toasted.

3. Stir together eggs and next 5 ingredients; stir in pecans. Pour filling into pie shell.

4. Bake at 350° for 55 minutes or until set, shielding pie with aluminum foil after 20 minutes to prevent excessive browning. Serve warm or cold.

Note: We tested with Mrs. Smith's Deep Dish Pie Shell, found in the frozen food section.

CARAMEL-PECAN PIE

makes 8 servings   prep: 20 min.   bake: 36 min.   cook: 5 min.

½ (15-oz.) package refrigerated piecrusts

28 caramels

¼ cup butter

¾ cup sugar

2 large eggs

½ tsp. vanilla extract

¼ tsp. salt

1 cup coarsely chopped pecans, toasted

Chocolate-Dipped Pecans (optional)

1. Preheat oven to 400°. Fit piecrust into a 9-inch pie plate according to package directions; fold edges under, and crimp. Prick bottom and sides of piecrust with a fork.

2. Bake piecrust at 400° for 6 to 8 minutes or until lightly browned; cool on wire rack.

3. Combine caramels, butter, and ¼ cup water in large saucepan over medium heat. Cook, stirring constantly, 5 to 7 minutes or until caramels and butter are melted; remove from heat.

4. Stir together sugar and next 3 ingredients. Stir into caramel mixture until thoroughly combined. Stir in pecans. Pour into prepared crust.

5. Bake pie at 400° for 10 minutes. Reduce heat to 350°, and bake 20 more minutes, shielding edges of crust with aluminum foil to prevent excessive browning. Remove pie to a wire rack to cool. Top with Chocolate-Dipped Pecans, if desired.

Chocolate-Dipped Pecans

makes 20 pecans   prep: 20 min.

1 (6-oz.) package semisweet chocolate morsels

20 pecan halves, toasted

1. Microwave chocolate morsels in a microwave-safe bowl on HIGH for 1 to 1½ minutes or until melted, stirring at 30-second intervals.

2. Dip half of each pecan into melted chocolate; place on a wax paper-lined baking sheet. Let cool completely. Store in a single layer in an airtight container for up to 2 days.

PRALINE-APPLE PIE

makes 8 servings   prep: 25 min.   bake: 45 min.   cook: 5 min.   stand: 5 min.

Make this pie the morning of your gathering. After it cools, pour the luscious praline topping over the crust. If your family likes to enjoy dessert after dinner settles, put the pie in the oven when you sit down to eat your meal, and serve it warm later.

1   (15-oz.) package refrigerated piecrusts
½   cup granulated sugar
⅓   cup all-purpose flour
½   tsp. ground cinnamon
6   cups peeled, sliced Rome or other cooking apples

2   Tbsp. butter, cut up
2   tsp. lemon juice
¼   cup butter
½   cup firmly packed light brown sugar
2   Tbsp. whipping cream
½   cup chopped pecans

1. Preheat oven to 400°. Fit 1 piecrust into a 9-inch pie plate according to package directions.

2. Stir together sugar, flour, and cinnamon. Stir in apples; spoon mixture into crust. Dot with 2 Tbsp. butter; sprinkle evenly with lemon juice. Top with remaining piecrust; fold edges under, and crimp. Cut several slits in top.

3. Bake pie at 400° for 45 minutes on lower oven rack, shielding with aluminum foil after 30 minutes to prevent excessive browning. Remove from oven, and let cool.

4. Melt ¼ cup butter in a small saucepan; stir in brown sugar and whipping cream. Bring to a boil over medium heat, stirring constantly; cook 1 minute, and remove from heat. Stir in pecans, and let stand 5 minutes. Slowly drizzle mixture over pie.

GROUND PECAN TORTE

makes 10 to 12 servings   prep: 25 min.   bake: 25 min.   cool: 35 min.

Layers of raspberry preserves and a scrumptious Cream Cheese Filling atop crunchy pecan crusts make this tasty dessert irresistible.

1 cup butter, softened	1 Tbsp. lemon zest
1 cup sugar	⅓ cup cake flour
3 large eggs	Cream Cheese Filling
3 cups pecan meal	½ cup raspberry preserves

1. Beat butter and sugar at medium speed with an electric mixer until creamy. Add eggs, 1 at a time, beating just until blended after each addition; add in pecan meal and lemon zest, and beat at low speed until blended.

2. Add flour, and beat at low speed just until blended. Spread into 2 buttered and floured 9-inch round cake pans.

3. Bake at 350° for 25 to 30 minutes or until a wooden pick inserted in center comes out clean. Cool in pans on wire racks 5 minutes; remove from pans, and cool for 30 minutes. Spread half of Cream Cheese Filling on top of 1 cake layer; top evenly with half of raspberry preserves. Top with remaining cake layer; repeat procedure with remaining Cream Cheese Filling and preserves.

Note: Commercially ground pecans have a very fine texture and are often sold as pecan meal. We found this to be more economical than grinding whole or halved pecans. To make your own pecan meal, place 2½ cups pecan halves in a food processor, and pulse about 45 seconds or until pecans are finely ground.

Cream Cheese Filling

makes 1⅓ cups   prep: 5 min.

1 (8-oz.) package cream cheese, softened	1 tsp. vanilla extract
½ cup sugar	

1. Beat cream cheese at medium speed with an electric mixer until creamy; gradually add sugar and vanilla, beating well.

X-TREME CHOCOLATE DOUBLE-NUT
CARAMEL LADYFINGER TORTE

makes 12 servings   prep: 30 min.   cool: 5 min.   cook: 5 min.   chill: 1 hr.   **pictured on page 583**

1½ cups semisweet chocolate morsels

2   (3-oz.) packages ladyfingers

1   (13-oz.) jar hazelnut spread

20 caramels

2⅓ cups whipping cream, divided

1½ cups chopped pecans

⅓   cup powdered sugar

1   (8-oz.) package cream cheese, softened

2   Tbsp. crème de cacao

3   (1-oz.) semisweet chocolate baking squares

2   Tbsp. powdered sugar

1. Microwave chocolate morsels at HIGH 90 seconds or until melted, stirring at 30-second intervals; cool 5 minutes, and set aside.

2. Split ladyfingers, and stand halves around edge of a 9-inch springform pan, placing rounded sides against pan; line bottom with remaining halves. Reserve remaining ladyfingers for another use. Spread hazelnut spread evenly over ladyfingers on bottom of pan.

3. Cook caramels and ⅓ cup whipping cream in a medium saucepan over low heat, stirring constantly, just until melted. Stir in pecans until coated; spoon caramel mixture evenly over hazelnut spread.

4. Beat ⅓ cup powdered sugar and cream cheese in a medium bowl at medium speed with an electric mixer until fluffy. Add crème de cacao; beat until blended. Beat in melted morsels until blended.

5. Beat remaining 2 cups whipping cream in a medium bowl at medium speed with an electric mixer until stiff; fold into cream cheese mixture, and spoon evenly over caramel layer in pan.

6. Shave baking squares with a vegetable peeler evenly on top. Sprinkle evenly with 2 Tbsp. powdered sugar. Chill 1 hour.

Note: We tested with Nutella for hazelnut spread.

PEACH-AND-RASPBERRY CRISP

makes 8 servings prep: 20 min. cook: 5 min. bake: 25 min.

For a total indulgence, top this crisp with vanilla ice cream, and sprinkle with toasted slivered almonds.

1 (14-oz.) package frozen raspberries, thawed

2 (1-lb., 4-oz.) cans sliced peaches in heavy syrup, drained

¼ cup sugar, divided

5 Tbsp. all-purpose flour, divided

2 cups oatmeal cookie crumbs

½ cup cold butter, cut up

1 tsp. cornstarch

¼ cup powdered sugar

1. Preheat oven to 375°. Drain thawed raspberries, reserving the juice.

2. Combine peaches, 2 Tbsp. sugar, and 1 Tbsp. flour; pour into an 11- x 7-inch baking dish, and top with raspberries.

3. Combine cookie crumbs and remaining sugar and flour; cut in butter with a pastry blender or fork until mixture is crumbly. Sprinkle over fruit mixture.

4. Bake at 375° for 25 to 30 minutes or until bubbly and golden.

5. Whisk together reserved raspberry juice, cornstarch, and powdered sugar in a small saucepan over medium-high heat. Bring to a boil, and cook 1 minute. Serve with baked crisp.

PEAR CRISP

makes 4 servings prep: 15 min. bake: 25 min.

4 large ripe pears, peeled and sliced

5 Tbsp. no-calorie sweetener, granular, divided

2 Tbsp. orange juice

¼ cup all-purpose flour

2 Tbsp. butter, melted

1 tsp. pumpkin pie spice

¼ cup uncooked quick-cooking oats

¼ cup chopped pecans

2 cups fat-free, sugar-free vanilla ice cream

1. Preheat oven to 375°. Toss together pears, 1 Tbsp. no-calorie sweetener, and orange juice; spoon into a 9-inch pie plate or 4 (8-oz.) custard cups.

2. Stir together remaining 4 Tbsp. no-calorie sweetener, flour, butter, and pumpkin pie spice. Stir in oats and chopped pecans, and sprinkle evenly over pear mixture.

3. Bake at 375° for 25 to 30 minutes or until top is crisp and fruit is tender. Serve warm with vanilla ice cream.

APPLE-GINGERBREAD COBBLER

makes 8 servings   prep: 15 min.   cook: 5 min.   bake: 30 min.   **pictured on page 578**

{ for kids }

1   (14-oz.) package gingerbread mix, divided
¼   cup firmly packed light brown sugar
½   cup butter, divided

½   cup chopped pecans
2   (21-oz.) cans apple pie filling
Vanilla ice cream

1. Preheat oven to 375°. Stir together 2 cups gingerbread mix and ¾ cup water until smooth; set mixture aside.

2. Stir together remaining gingerbread mix and brown sugar; cut in ¼ cup butter until mixture is crumbly. Stir in pecans; set aside.

3. Combine apple pie filling and remaining ¼ cup butter in a large saucepan, and cook, stirring often, 5 minutes over medium heat or until thoroughly heated.

4. Spoon hot apple mixture evenly into a lightly greased 11x7-inch baking dish. Spoon gingerbread mixture evenly over hot apple mixture; sprinkle with pecan mixture.

5. Bake at 375° for 30 to 35 minutes or until set. Serve cobbler with vanilla ice cream.

BLACKBERRY COBBLER

makes 8 servings   prep: 25 min.   stand: 10 min.   bake: 1 hr.   **pictured on page 578**

8   cups fresh blackberries
2¼ cups sugar
⅓   cup all-purpose flour
1   tsp. lemon juice

Pastry, divided
¼   cup butter, cut up
Sugar (optional)
Vanilla ice cream

1. Preheat oven to 425°. Stir together first 4 ingredients; let mixture stand 10 minutes or until sugar dissolves.

2. Roll half of Pastry to ¼-inch thickness; cut into 1½-inch-wide strips. Place on a lightly greased baking sheet.

3. Bake at 425° for 10 minutes or until lightly browned. Remove to a wire rack to cool. Break strips into pieces. Reduce oven temperature to 350°.

4. Spoon half of blackberry mixture into a lightly greased 13- x 9-inch baking dish; top with pastry pieces. Spoon remaining blackberry mixture over pastry; dot with butter.

5. Roll remaining pastry to ¼-inch thickness; cut into 1-inch strips, and arrange in a lattice design over filling. Sprinkle with sugar, if desired. Place cobbler on a baking sheet.

6. Bake at 350° for 50 minutes or until golden. Serve with vanilla ice cream.

Pastry

makes pastry for 1 (13- x 9-inch) cobbler prep: 5 min.

2½ cups all-purpose flour

1¾ tsp. baking powder

¾ tsp. salt

½ cup shortening

⅔ cup milk

1. Combine first 3 ingredients in a medium bowl; cut in shortening with a pastry blender until mixture is crumbly. Add milk, stirring with a fork until dry ingredients are moistened and mixture forms a soft ball.

2. Turn dough out onto a floured surface, and knead 6 to 8 times.

DOUBLE-CHERRY CHEESECAKE COBBLER

makes 8 servings prep: 15 min. cook: 5 min. bake: 30 min. stand: 15 min.

1 (8-oz.) package cream cheese, softened

⅓ cup sugar

⅓ cup all-purpose flour

1 large egg

1 tsp. vanilla extract

¼ tsp. almond extract

1 (15-oz.) can dark sweet cherries, drained

1 (21-oz.) can cherry pie filling

¼ cup butter, melted and divided

20 vanilla wafers, crushed

1. Preheat oven to 350°. Beat cream cheese, sugar, and flour at low speed with an electric mixer; add egg and extracts, beating until smooth. Set aside.

2. Stir together cherries, cherry pie filling, and 2 Tbsp. melted butter in a large saucepan, and cook over medium heat, stirring often, 5 minutes or until thoroughly heated.

3. Spoon hot cherry mixture into a lightly greased 9-inch deep-dish pie plate. Spoon cream cheese mixture evenly over hot cherries.

4. Combine crushed vanilla wafers and remaining 2 Tbsp. melted butter. Sprinkle evenly over cream cheese mixture.

5. Bake at 350° for 30 minutes or until golden brown and set. Let cobbler stand 15 minutes before serving.

GINGER-PEAR COBBLER

makes 10 servings   prep: 45 min.   cook: 10 min.   bake: 20 min.

12 large firm Bosc pears, peeled and sliced

1   cup firmly packed light brown sugar

¼   cup all-purpose flour

¼   cup butter

½   cup chopped pecans, toasted

1   Tbsp. fresh grated ginger

1   tsp. lemon zest

1   (15-oz.) package refrigerated piecrusts

1   large egg

1   Tbsp. water

1. Toss sliced pears with brown sugar and flour.

2. Melt butter in a large skillet over medium-high heat; add pear mixture, and cook, stirring often, 10 minutes or until tender. Remove from heat, and stir in pecans, ginger, and lemon zest.

3. Spoon mixture into a lightly greased 2-qt. baking dish.

4. Preheat oven to 425°. Roll piecrusts to press out fold lines; cut into ½-inch strips. Arrange strips in a lattice design over filling. Reroll remaining strips and scraps. Cut leaf shapes from piecrust using a small 1-inch leaf-shaped cookie cutter. Use a paring knife to gently score designs in leaves, if desired. Arrange leaf shapes around inner edge of the baking dish, forming a decorative border over ends of lattice.

5. Whisk together egg and 1 Tbsp. water; brush over piecrust.

6. Bake at 425° for 20 to 25 minutes or until golden brown.

HONEYED APPLE-CRANBERRY FRIED PIES

makes 1½ dozen   prep: 25 min.   cook: 25 min.   fry: 4 min.   **pictured on page 579**

If you don't want to fry these irresistible pies, you can bake them instead. Place them on lightly greased baking sheets, and bake at 425° for 12 minutes or until golden and crispy.

2   Granny Smith apples, peeled and chopped

1   cup fresh cranberries*

½   cup sugar

2   Tbsp. honey

⅛   tsp. salt

¾   tsp. ground cinnamon, divided

1   (15-oz.) package refrigerated piecrusts

Vegetable oil

1   Tbsp. sugar

1. Cook first 5 ingredients and ½ tsp. ground cinnamon in a large saucepan over medium heat 5 minutes; reduce heat to medium-low, and cook, stirring occasionally, 20 minutes or until apples are tender. Cool completely, and drain.

2. Roll piecrusts into 12-inch circles; cut each crust into 9 (4-inch) circles.

3. Spoon 1 level Tbsp. fruit mixture onto half of each pastry circle. Moisten edges with water; fold dough over fruit mixture, pressing edges to seal. Crimp edges with a fork dipped in flour.

4. Pour oil to a depth of ½ inch into a large heavy skillet; heat to 350°. Fry pies, in batches, 2 minutes on each side. Combine 1 Tbsp. sugar and remaining ¼ tsp. cinnamon, and sprinkle over hot pies.

* Thawed frozen cranberries or dried cranberries may be substituted for fresh cranberries.

FRIED STRAWBERRY PIES

makes 18 pies   prep: 30 min.   cook: 8 min.   freeze: 1 hr.

Freeze the pies before frying to prevent the crusts from disintegrating in the hot oil.

2 cups fresh strawberries, mashed	1 (15-oz.) package refrigerated piecrusts
¾ cup sugar	Vegetable oil
¼ cup cornstarch	Powdered sugar

1. Combine first 3 ingredients in a saucepan. Bring strawberry mixture to a boil over medium heat. Cook, stirring constantly, 1 minute or until thickened. Cool completely.

2. Roll 1 piecrust to press out fold lines; cut into 9 circles with a 3-inch round cutter. Roll circles to 3½-inch diameter; moisten edges with water. Spoon 2 tsp. strawberry mixture in the center of each circle; fold over, pressing edges to seal. Repeat with remaining piecrust and strawberry mixture.

3. Place pies in a single layer on a baking sheet, and freeze at least 1 hour.

4. Pour oil to a depth of 1 inch into a large heavy skillet; heat to 350°. Fry pies, in batches, 1 minute on each side or until golden. Drain on paper towels; sprinkle with powdered sugar.

LONE STAR FRIED PIES WITH FRUIT SALSA

makes 12 servings   prep: 25 min.   chill: 10 min.   fry: 6 min.

⅓ cup orange liqueur or fresh orange juice

1 (8-oz.) package dried figs

2 tsp. orange zest

1 (15-oz.) package refrigerated piecrusts

Vegetable oil

Sifted powdered sugar

Fruit Salsa

Garnish: fresh mint sprigs (optional)

1. Cook liqueur and ¼ cup water in a small saucepan over low heat until hot.

2. Process liqueur mixture, figs, and orange zest in a food processor until smooth; set aside.

3. Roll piecrusts to press out fold lines; cut with a 4-inch round cutter.

4. Spoon 2 Tbsp. fig mixture in center of each pastry circle. Moisten edges with water; fold circles in half. Press edges with a fork to seal; place on lightly greased baking sheets. Cover; chill 10 minutes.

5. Pour oil to a depth of 3 inches into a large saucepan; heat to 400°. Fry pies, in batches, 3 minutes on each side or until golden. Drain on paper towels.

6. Place a small star shape on top of pies, and sprinkle with powdered sugar to form a design just before serving. Serve with Fruit Salsa; garnish, if desired.

Fruit Salsa

makes 3½ cups   prep: 15 min.

1 (8-oz.) can pineapple tidbits, drained

¼ cup chopped fresh strawberries

1 cup chopped cantaloupe

1 cup chopped honeydew

1 cup chopped mango

3 kiwifruit, peeled and chopped

3 Tbsp. chopped fresh mint

2 Tbsp. fresh lime juice

1. Combine all ingredients; chill.

MINI TIRAMISÙ ÉCLAIRS

makes 24 éclairs   prep: 35 min.

⅓ cup hot water

2 tsp. instant coffee granules

2 Tbsp. granulated sugar

2 (3-oz.) packages ladyfingers, split

1 (8-oz.) package mascarpone cheese*

1½ cups powdered sugar, divided

2 Tbsp. chocolate syrup

½ cup semisweet chocolate morsels

1 Tbsp. butter

1 Tbsp. whipping cream

1. Stir together first 3 ingredients until sugar is dissolved; set aside 2 Tbsp. mixture.

2. Brush cut sides of ladyfingers evenly with remaining coffee mixture.

3. Stir together mascarpone cheese, ½ cup powdered sugar, and chocolate syrup until blended. Spoon or pipe mascarpone cheese mixture evenly onto 24 cut sides of ladyfinger halves; top with remaining ladyfinger halves, cut sides down.

4. Microwave chocolate morsels, butter, and cream at HIGH 30 seconds or until melted, stirring twice. Place chocolate mixture in a small zip-top plastic freezer bag; seal bag. Snip a tiny hole in 1 corner of bag, and drizzle over éclairs. Let stand until firm.

5. Stir together reserved coffee mixture and remaining 1 cup powdered sugar, stirring until blended. Place coffee-powdered sugar mixture in a small zip-top plastic freezer bag; seal bag.

6. Snip a tiny hole in 1 corner of bag. Drizzle éclairs evenly with coffee-powdered sugar mixture. Place on a serving platter, cake stand, or in candy boxes, if desired.

* 1 (8-oz.) package cream cheese, softened, may be substituted.

CREAM PUFFS

makes 2 dozen   prep: 15 min.   cook: 25 min.   **pictured on page 580**

¾ cup water

⅓ cup butter

½ tsp. salt

¾ cup all-purpose flour

3 large eggs

Whipped cream

Fresh strawberries, sliced

1. Preheat oven to 400°. Bring first 3 ingredients to a boil in a saucepan; reduce heat to low. Add flour; beat with a wooden spoon until mixture leaves sides of pan. Remove from heat. Add eggs, 1 at a time, beating until smooth after each. Drop by teaspoonful onto buttered baking sheets.

2. Bake at 400° for 25 to 30 minutes or until lightly browned and puffed; transfer to wire racks to cool. Stuff pastry with whipped cream, and served with sliced fresh strawberries.

BOURBON-CHOCOLATE-PECAN TARTS

makes 6 tarts   prep: 15 min.   chill: 30 min.   bake: 30 min.   **pictured on page 504**

Try this wonderfully rich twist on a favorite Southern dessert.

Cream Cheese Pastry

¾ cup (4.5 oz.) semisweet chocolate morsels

3 large eggs, lightly beaten

⅓ cup sugar

3 Tbsp. firmly packed light brown sugar

1 Tbsp. all-purpose flour

¾ cup light corn syrup

¼ cup butter, melted

3 Tbsp. bourbon

2 tsp. vanilla extract

2 cups pecan halves

Garnishes: whipped cream, pecan halves,
   chopped pecans (optional)

1. Divide pastry into 6 portions, and shape each into a ball; press each into a 4½-inch tart pan. Sprinkle morsels over pastry; chill 30 minutes.

2. Preheat oven to 350°. Beat eggs and next 7 ingredients at medium speed with an electric mixer until blended. Pour into tart shells, filling each half full. Arrange pecan halves over filling; drizzle with remaining filling.

3. Bake at 350° for 30 to 35 minutes or until set; cool. Garnish, if desired.

Note: Tart filling may be baked in a 9-inch tart pan fitted with pastry crust. Prepare as directed; bake at 350° for 55 minutes or until set.

Cream Cheese Pastry

makes enough for 6 (4½-inch) tarts

1 (3-oz.) package cream cheese, softened

½ cup butter, softened

1 cup all-purpose flour

1. Beat cream cheese and butter at medium speed with an electric mixer until smooth. Add flour; beat at low speed until a soft dough forms.

Ladies' Tea serves 8

Savory Chicken Pot Pie (page 676)
Three-Tomato Salad (page 740)
Croissants
Lime-and-Macadamia Nut Tart

LIME-AND-MACADAMIA NUT TART

makes 8 servings   prep: 25 min.   bake: 7 min.   cook: 8 min.   chill: 4 hr.   cool: 15 min.

1   (5⅓-oz.) package graham crackers, crushed (about 1½ cups)
½   cup macadamia nuts, finely chopped
¼   cup sugar
6   Tbsp. butter, melted
6   large eggs
1½ Tbsp. lime zest

½   cup fresh lime juice (about 6 large limes)
1   cup sugar
6   Tbsp. butter
1   drop green liquid food coloring (optional)
1   drop yellow liquid food coloring (optional)
Garnishes: toasted macadamia nuts, lime slices, and whipped cream (optional)

1. Preheat oven to 350°. Stir together first 4 ingredients. Firmly press crumb mixture evenly on bottom and up sides of a 10-inch tart pan.

2. Bake crust at 350° for 7 to 9 minutes. Cool on a wire rack.

3. Whisk together eggs, lime zest, and fresh lime juice in a nonaluminum saucepan over low heat. Add 1 cup sugar, 6 Tbsp. melted butter, and if desired, food coloring; cook, whisking constantly, 8 minutes or until lime mixture is thickened and bubbly. Let cool 15 to 20 minutes.

4. Pour filling into prepared crust; cover and chill 4 hours or until set. Remove sides of tart pan, and garnish, if desired.

GRAPEFRUIT TART

makes 8 servings   prep: 40 min.   cook: 10 min.   bake: 10 min.   chill: 2 hr., 30 min.

Bring your meal to a scrumptious close with this gorgeous tart. It starts with a buttery shortbread crust made from commercial cookies followed by a smooth-as-silk red grapefruit custard.

1	(5.3-oz.) package pure butter shortbread	2	cups fresh red grapefruit juice
3	Tbsp. sugar	4	egg yolks
2	Tbsp. butter, melted	3	Tbsp. butter
½	cup sugar	2	tsp. grapefruit zest
6	Tbsp. cornstarch	3	red grapefruit, peeled and sectioned
⅛	tsp. salt	2	Tbsp. sugar

1. Preheat oven to 350°. Process shortbread in a blender or food processor until graham cracker crumb consistency (about 1⅓ cup crumbs).

2. Stir together shortbread crumbs, 3 Tbsp. sugar, and 2 Tbsp. melted butter in a small bowl. Press mixture lightly into a greased 9-inch tart pan.

3. Bake at 350° for 10 to 12 minutes or until lightly browned. Set aside.

4. Combine ½ cup sugar, cornstarch, and salt in a medium-size heavy saucepan. Whisk in juice and egg yolks. Cook over medium-high heat, whisking constantly, 10 to 12 minutes or until mixture thickens and boils. Remove from heat; stir in 3 Tbsp. butter and zest.

5. Pour filling into prepared tart shell. Cover surface of filling directly with plastic wrap. Chill 2½ hours.

6. Place red grapefruit sections in an 8-inch baking dish. Sprinkle with 2 Tbsp. sugar, and chill until ready to assemble. Drain grapefruit.

7. Arrange segments, with outer part of segments facing the edge, around border of tart. Arrange remaining segments around tart, slightly overlapping to cover filling completely. Serve immediately. Chill leftovers.

Note: We tested with Walkers Pure Butter Shortbread and TexaSweet Ruby Red Grapefruit.

To make ahead: Prepare the crust and filling up to 2 days ahead, but do not top with fruit. Top with grapefruit just before serving.

FRESH CHERRY TART

makes 8 to 10 servings   prep: 50 min.   bake: 6 min.   cook: 10 min.   chill: 2 hr.

1⅓ cups graham cracker crumbs

3 Tbsp. sugar

1 tsp. ground cinnamon

⅓ cup butter or margarine, melted

2½ cups fresh cherries, pitted (about 1 lb.)

⅔ cup sugar, divided

3 Tbsp. cornstarch

⅓ cup orange marmalade, divided

2 Tbsp. butter

1 (8-oz.) container soft cream cheese

1. Preheat oven to 375°. Stir together first 4 ingredients. Press into bottom and up sides of a 13- x 4-inch tart pan with removable bottom.

2. Bake at 375° for 6 minutes. Cool in pan on a wire rack.

3. Bring cherries, ⅓ cup sugar, cornstarch, and 3 Tbsp. water to a boil in a medium saucepan over medium heat, stirring constantly; boil, stirring constantly, 1 minute or until thickened and bubbly. Remove from heat; stir in 3 Tbsp. orange marmalade and 2 Tbsp. butter until melted. Cool; cover and chill at least 2 hours.

4. Stir together remaining ⅓ cup sugar, remaining orange marmalade, and cream cheese until blended. Spread evenly in crust, and top with chilled cherry mixture.

TOMATO-PESTO TART

makes 4 main-dish or 8 appetizer servings   prep: 20 min.   bake: 28 min.   cool: 15 min.

Don't miss one of our savory tarts—they're great for a weeknight supper or a festive brunch.

½ (15-oz.) package refrigerated piecrusts

2 cups (8 oz.) shredded mozzarella cheese, divided

5 plum tomatoes, sliced

½ cup mayonnaise

¼ cup grated Parmesan cheese

2 Tbsp. basil pesto

½ tsp. freshly ground pepper

3 Tbsp. chopped fresh basil

1. Preheat oven to 425°. Unfold piecrust on a lightly greased baking sheet. Roll into a 12-inch circle. Brush outer 1 inch of crust with water. Fold edges up and crimp. Prick bottom.

2. Bake at 425° for 8 to 10 minutes. Remove from oven. Sprinkle with 1 cup mozzarella cheese; let cool 15 minutes. Arrange tomato slices over cheese. Reduce oven temperature to 350°.

3. Stir together remaining 1 cup mozzarella cheese, mayonnaise, and next 3 ingredients. Spread over tomato slices. Bake at 375° for 20 to 25 minutes. Remove from oven; sprinkle with basil.

SOUTHWESTERN TART

makes 4 to 6 servings prep: 25 min.   chill: 15 min.   bake: 30 min.   cool: 10 min.

This irresistible pie tastes just as good as it looks. Take it to your next gathering, or serve it for supper tonight.

1 cup all-purpose flour	½ tsp. ground cumin
½ cup grated Parmesan cheese	1 large ripe avocado, chopped
2 Tbsp. chopped fresh cilantro, divided	1 to 2 Tbsp. fresh lime juice
½ tsp. salt, divided	½ cup sour cream
⅓ cup shortening	½ cup (2 oz.) shredded Cheddar cheese
1 (8-oz.) package cream cheese, softened	1 tomato, chopped
2 large eggs	Salsa (optional)
2 green onions, chopped	

1. Preheat oven to 450°. Combine flour, Parmesan cheese, 1 Tbsp. cilantro, and ¼ tsp. salt; cut in shortening with a pastry blender or fork until crumbly. Add ¼ cup water, 1 Tbsp. at a time, and stir with a fork until dry ingredients are moistened.

2. Shape dough into a ball, and press into a 4-inch circle over heavy-duty plastic wrap. Cover with more plastic wrap, and chill 15 minutes.

3. Roll dough, covered with plastic wrap, into an 11-inch circle. Remove plastic wrap, and fit dough into a 9-inch tart pan with removable bottom. Line pastry with aluminum foil, and fill with pie weights or dried beans.

4. Bake at 450° for 10 minutes. Remove weights and foil; bake 4 to 5 more minutes or until lightly browned. Cool on a wire rack.

5. Beat cream cheese at medium speed with an electric mixer until smooth. Add eggs, green onions, cumin, and remaining 1 Tbsp. cilantro and ¼ tsp. salt, beating until blended. Spread evenly over crust.

6. Bake at 400° for 20 minutes. Cool on a wire rack 10 minutes.

7. Toss together avocado and lime juice. Spread pie with ½ cup sour cream, and sprinkle with Cheddar cheese, avocado, and tomato. Serve with salsa, if desired.

LEEK-GOAT CHEESE TART

makes 4 servings prep: 20 min. bake: 26 min. cook: 12 min.

Be sure to lightly brown the crust in the oven for a firm shell. Then add your filling, and bake until golden.

½ (15-oz.) package refrigerated piecrusts
4 to 5 medium leeks
2 Tbsp. olive oil
3 Tbsp. whipping cream

½ tsp. salt
¼ tsp. ground white pepper
1½ Tbsp. chopped fresh tarragon
3 oz. (¾ cup) crumbled goat cheese

1. Preheat oven to 425°. Unfold piecrust, and roll into a 12-inch circle on a lightly greased baking sheet. Fold outer 2 inches of dough over, and crimp. Prick bottom of crust with a fork.
2. Bake at 425° for 8 to 10 minutes or until lightly browned. Reduce oven temperature to 375°.
3. Remove root, tough outer leaves, and tops from leeks, leaving 2 inches of dark leaves. Thinly slice leeks; rinse well, and drain.
4. Sauté leeks in hot oil in a skillet over medium heat 8 to 10 minutes or until tender. (Do not brown.) Stir in cream, salt, and pepper; cook, stirring constantly, 4 to 5 minutes or until slightly thickened. Stir in tarragon.
5. Sprinkle 2 oz. (½ cup) goat cheese on bottom of crust; top with leek mixture. Sprinkle with remaining cheese.
6. Bake at 375° for 18 to 20 minutes or until golden and bubbly.

TURNIP-BACON TURNOVERS

makes about 30 turnovers prep: 20 min. bake: 15 min. **pictured on page 584**

1 small turnip, peeled and grated
½ small onion, finely chopped
4 to 5 pieces finely chopped cooked bacon
¼ tsp. salt

¼ tsp. pepper
1 (15-oz.) package refrigerated piecrusts
2 Tbsp. butter, melted

1. Preheat oven to 375°. Combine turnip, onion, and bacon in a small bowl. Toss with salt and pepper.
2. Unfold piecrusts, and press out fold lines. Cut out 30 rounds with a 2-inch round cutter.
3. Place 1 tsp. turnip mixture on half of each round, and fold the other half over. Press edges together with a fork to seal. Place on an ungreased baking sheet; brush tops with melted butter.
4. Bake at 375° for 15 to 17 minutes or until edges are lightly browned.

POULTRY

"Nothing rekindles my spirits, gives comfort to my heart and mind, more than a visit to Mississippi...and to be regaled as I often have been, with a platter of fried chicken, field peas, collard greens, fresh corn on the cob, sliced tomatoes with French dressing...and to top it all off with a wedge of freshly baked pecan pie." —Craig Claiborne

GARLIC-HERB ROASTED CHICKEN

makes 4 to 6 servings   prep: 10 min.   bake: 1 hr., 15 min.   stand: 10 min.   **pictured on page 585**

Add additional moistness and flavor by replacing the wire roasting rack with a colorful bed of carrots and celery ribs. Tuck in a few sprigs of fresh herbs, some unpeeled whole shallots, and apple slices.

3	garlic cloves, minced	1	tsp. chopped fresh sage
2	tsp. chopped fresh thyme	1	tsp. salt
2	tsp. chopped fresh rosemary	¾	tsp. freshly ground pepper
2	tsp. chopped fresh parsley	1	(4- to 5-lb.) whole chicken

1. Preheat oven to 450°. Stir together first 7 ingredients.

2. If applicable, remove giblets from chicken, and reserve for another use. Rinse chicken, and pat dry. Gently loosen and lift skin from breast and drumsticks with fingers. (Do not totally detach skin.) Rub herb mixture evenly underneath skin. Carefully replace skin. Place chicken, breast side up, on a lightly greased wire rack in a lightly greased shallow roasting pan.

3. Bake at 450° for 30 minutes. Reduce heat to 350°, and bake 45 minutes or until a meat thermometer inserted in thigh registers 180°, covering loosely with aluminum foil to prevent excessive browning, if necessary. Let chicken stand, covered, 10 minutes before slicing.

MUSTARD BAKED CHICKEN

makes 8 servings   prep: 10 min.   chill: 30 min.   bake: 50 min.   stand: 15 min.

[for kids]

1	(4-lb.) whole chicken	1	tsp. pepper
1	Tbsp. paprika	2	Tbsp. Worcestershire sauce
1½	tsp. dry mustard	1	Tbsp. olive oil
1	tsp. salt		

1. Remove giblets and neck, and rinse chicken with cold water; pat dry. Place chicken in a large zip-top plastic freezer bag. Stir together paprika and next 5 ingredients until well blended; rub over chicken, coating evenly. Seal and chill at least 30 minutes or up to 8 hours, turning occasionally. Preheat oven to 425°. Remove chicken from marinade, discarding marinade. Place chicken in a roasting pan.

2. Bake at 425° for 50 minutes or until a meat thermometer inserted in thickest portion registers 170°. Let stand, covered, 15 minutes before slicing.

STICKY CHICKENS WITH CORNBREAD DRESSING

makes 6 servings   prep: 30 min.   chill: 8 hr.   bake: 1 hr., 45 min.   stand: 10 min.

2   (4-lb.) whole chickens
1   cup balsamic vinaigrette, divided
2   Tbsp. butter
6   green onions, chopped
½   cup chopped celery
1   (8-oz.) bag cornbread stuffing

1   (14.5-oz.) can chicken broth
½   cup chopped flat-leaf parsley
½   tsp. pepper
1   (12-oz) jar molasses
1   (2-oz.) bottle hot sauce
Garnish: flat-leaf parsley (optional)

1. Remove giblets from chickens, and reserve for another use. Rinse chickens, and pat dry; remove excess fat and skin. Place 1 chicken and ½ cup balsamic vinaigrette each in 2 large zip-top plastic freezer bags; seal and chill 8 hours, turning occasionally.

2. Preheat oven to 350°. Remove chickens from vinaigrette, discarding vinaigrette, and pat chickens dry.

3. Melt butter in a large skillet over medium heat; add chopped green onions and celery, and sauté until tender. Remove from heat. Stir in cornbread stuffing, broth, chopped parsley, and pepper. Stuff each chicken with half of mixture, and tie ends of legs together with string; tuck wing tips under. Place chickens, breast sides up, in a roasting pan.

4. Stir together molasses and hot sauce. Brush chickens evenly with about 3 Tbsp. molasses mixture.

5. Bake at 350° for 1 hour and 45 minutes or until a meat thermometer inserted in thigh registers 180° and internal temperature in center of stuffing registers 190°. Let stand 10 minutes. Garnish, if desired.

Broiling 101

This quick-cooking method will help you put together a full-flavored meal using freezer staples such as chicken, steak, or fish. Use a broiler pan, or place the meat on a rack in a baking pan so that the fat can drip off. Just watch the meat carefully, because it may brown quickly. Pay attention to the distance between the oven rack and your broiler. We measured ours at 7 and 8 inches. If your rack is closer to the broiler, the cook time will likely shorten.

BROILED HERB CHICKEN WITH LEMON-BUTTER SAUCE

makes 4 to 6 servings   prep: 10 min.   broil: 20 min.

Broiler-fryers are usually 2½ to 4 lb.; larger chickens, known as roasters, usually weigh 4 to 7 lb.

1 tsp. salt	½ tsp. paprika
1 tsp. dried oregano	¼ tsp. ground red pepper
½ tsp. garlic powder	1 (3- to 3½-lb.) broiler-fryer, cut into pieces
½ tsp. lemon pepper	Lemon-Butter Sauce

1. Preheat oven to broil. Combine first 6 ingredients.

2. Arrange chicken pieces, skin side down, on a lightly greased rack in an aluminum foil-lined roasting pan. Sprinkle chicken evenly with 2 tsp. salt mixture.

3. Broil 7 to 8 inches from heat 12 to 15 minutes or until golden brown. Turn chicken pieces, and sprinkle evenly with remaining salt mixture. Broil 8 to 10 minutes or until a meat thermometer inserted into thickest portion of white meat registers 170° and dark meat registers 180°. Serve with Lemon-Butter Sauce.

Lemon-Butter Sauce

makes about ⅓ cup   prep: 5 min.

3 Tbsp. butter, melted	2 tsp. fresh lemon juice
2 tsp. lemon zest	1 tsp. chopped fresh parsley

1. Stir together first 3 ingredients until blended. Stir in parsley.

CHIPOTLE ROASTED CHICKEN

makes 4 servings prep: 20 min. cook: 1 hr., 30 min. stand: 10 min.

Instead of carving your roast right when it's done, allow it to rest 10 to 15 minutes before slicing. This gives the meat a chance to finish cooking and enables the juices to resettle throughout the meat.

[test kitchen favorite]

1 lemon, halved	1 tsp. ground cumin
½ medium onion	1 tsp. coarse-grain salt
1 (5 lb.) roasting chicken	1 tsp. coarse-grain ground pepper
¼ cup butter, softened	1 cup chicken broth
1 canned chipotle pepper, chopped	½ cup dry white wine
¼ cup canned adobo sauce	2 Tbsp. all purpose flour

1. Preheat oven to 350°. Place 1 lemon half and onion half into chicken cavity. Squeeze remaining lemon half into chicken cavity.

2. Stir together butter, chipotle pepper, and adobo sauce. Starting at neck cavity, loosen skin from breast and drumsticks by inserting fingers and gently pushing between skin and meat. (Do not totally detach skin.) Rub half of butter mixture evenly under skin.

3. Tie ends of legs together with string; tuck wing tips under. Spread remaining half of butter mixture over chicken. Sprinkle evenly with ground cumin, salt, and pepper. Place chicken, breast side up, on a lightly greased rack in a lightly greased shallow roasting pan.

4. Bake at 450° for 30 minutes.

5. Reduce heat to 400°, and bake for 55 to 60 minutes or until a meat thermometer inserted into thigh registers 180°. Cover loosely with aluminum foil to prevent excessive browning, if necessary. Remove to a serving platter, reserving drippings in pan. Cover with foil, and let stand 10 minutes before slicing.

6. Add broth to reserved drippings in pan, stirring to loosen browned bits from bottom.

7. Whisk together pan drippings mixture, wine, and flour in a small saucepan. Cook, stirring often, over medium heat 5 minutes or until thickened. Serve with chicken.

LEMON-THYME ROASTED CHICKEN

makes 4 servings   prep: 20 min.   cook: 1 hr., 30 min.   stand: 10 min.

We start off at a higher temperature to first brown the skin and lock in juices and taste. Reducing the heat ensures that the bird cooks evenly.

1 lemon, halved	1 tsp. coarse-grain salt
½ medium onion	1 tsp. coarsely ground pepper
1 (5-lb.) roasting chicken	1 cup chicken broth
¼ cup butter, softened	½ cup dry white wine
3 garlic cloves, minced	2 Tbsp. all-purpose flour
2 tsp. chopped fresh thyme	

1. Preheat oven to 450°. Place 1 lemon half and onion half into chicken cavity. Squeeze remaining lemon half into chicken cavity.

2. Stir together butter, garlic, and thyme. Starting at neck cavity, loosen skin from breast and drumsticks by inserting fingers and gently pushing between skin and meat. (Do not totally detach skin.) Rub half of butter mixture evenly under skin.

3. Tie ends of legs together with string; tuck wing tips under. Spread remaining half of butter mixture over chicken. Sprinkle evenly with salt and pepper. Place chicken, breast side up, on a lightly greased rack in a lightly greased shallow roasting pan.

4. Bake at 450° for 30 minutes.

5. Reduce heat to 400°, and bake for 55 to 60 minutes or until a meat thermometer inserted into thigh registers 180°. Cover loosely with aluminum foil to prevent excessive browning, if necessary. Remove to a serving platter, reserving drippings in pan. Cover with foil, and let stand 10 minutes before slicing.

6. Add broth to reserved drippings in pan, stirring to loosen browned bits from bottom.

7. Whisk together pan drippings mixture, wine, and flour in a small saucepan. Cook, stirring often, over medium heat 5 minutes or until thickened. Serve with chicken.

JAN'S ROASTED CHICKEN

makes 4 servings   prep: 15 min.   cook: 1 hr., 30 min.   **pictured on page 584**

Jan Karon, best-selling author of the Mitford book series, lives on a farm in Virginia and shared two of her favorite comfort foods with us.

1	(3- to 4-lb.) whole chicken	1	Tbsp. coarsely ground pepper
3	Tbsp. olive oil, divided	3	sprigs fresh rosemary
3	garlic cloves	1	lemon, quartered
1	tsp. salt		

1. Preheat oven to 450°. Rub chicken and cavities with 2 Tbsp. olive oil, garlic cloves, salt, and pepper.

2. Tuck chicken wings under; tie legs together with string, if desired. Pour remaining 1 Tbsp. oil into a large cast-iron skillet; place chicken, breast side up, in skillet.

3. Place 1 rosemary sprig and 2 lemon quarters into neck cavity of chicken; repeat in lower cavity. Place remaining rosemary sprig underneath skin.

4. Bake at 450° for 30 minutes; reduce heat to 350°, and bake 1 hour. Serve with Jan's Roasted Potatoes.

JAN'S ROASTED POTATOES

makes 4 servings   prep: 5 min.   cook: 1 hr.   **pictured on page 584**

8 medium new potatoes, halved	1 tsp. salt
3 Tbsp. butter, melted	1 tsp. pepper

1. Preheat oven to 350°. Place potatoes on a baking sheet. Drizzle with butter; sprinkle with salt and pepper.

2. Bake potatoes at 350° for 1 hour, turning every 20 minutes.

BASIC BEER-CAN CHICKEN

makes 2 to 4 servings   prep: 10 min.   grill: 1 hr., 15 min.   stand: 5 min.

2 Tbsp. All-Purpose Barbecue Rub, divided	1 Tbsp. vegetable oil
1 (3½- to 4-lb.) whole chicken	1 (12-oz.) can beer

1. Sprinkle 1 tsp. All-Purpose Barbecue Rub inside body cavity and ½ tsp. inside neck cavity of chicken.

2. Rub oil over skin. Sprinkle with 1 Tbsp. All-Purpose Barbecue Rub, and rub over skin.

3. Pour out half of beer (about ¾ cup), leaving remaining beer in can. Make 2 additional holes in top of can. Spoon remaining 1½ tsp. rub into beer can. Beer will start to foam.

4. Place chicken upright onto the beer can, fitting can into cavity. Pull legs forward to form a tripod, allowing chicken to stand upright.

5. Light one side of the grill, heating to 300° to 350° (medium) heat; leave other side unlit. Place chicken upright over drip pan. Grill, covered with grill lid, 1 hour and 15 minutes or until golden and a meat thermometer inserted into thigh registers 180°.

6. Remove chicken from grill, and let stand 5 minutes; carefully remove can.

All-Purpose Barbecue Rub

makes about 1 cup   prep: 5 min.

¼ cup coarse salt	¼ cup sweet paprika
¼ cup firmly packed dark brown sugar	2 Tbsp. pepper

1. Combine all ingredients. Store mixture in an airtight jar, away from heat, up to 6 months.

COLA-CAN CHICKEN

makes 2 to 4 servings   prep: 20 min.   grill: 1 hr., 15 min.   stand: 5 min.

2 Tbsp. Barbecue Rub, divided	1 (12-oz.) can cola
1 (3½- to 4-lb.) whole chicken	**Cola Barbecue Sauce**
3 Tbsp. vegetable oil	

1. Sprinkle 1 tsp. Barbecue Rub inside body cavity and ½ tsp. inside neck cavity of chicken.

2. Rub oil over skin. Sprinkle with 1 Tbsp. Barbecue Rub, and rub over skin.

3. Pour out half of cola (about ¾ cup), and reserve for Cola Barbecue Sauce, leaving remaining cola in can. Make 2 additional holes in top of can. Spoon remaining 1½ tsp. rub into cola can. Cola will start to foam.

4. Place chicken upright onto the cola can, fitting can into cavity. Pull legs forward to form a tripod, allowing chicken to stand upright.

5. Light one side of the grill, heating to 300° to 350° (medium) heat; leave the other side unlit. Place chicken upright over unlit side. Grill, covered with grill lid, 1 hour and 15 minutes or until golden and a meat thermometer inserted into thigh registers 180°.

6. Remove chicken from grill, and let stand 5 minutes; carefully remove can. Serve with Cola Barbecue Sauce.

Barbecue Rub

makes 3 Tbsp.   prep: 5 min.

1 Tbsp. mild chili powder	1 tsp. ground cumin
2 tsp. salt	½ tsp. garlic powder
2 tsp. light brown sugar	¼ tsp. ground red pepper
1 tsp. pepper	

1. Combine all ingredients.

Cola Barbecue Sauce

makes about 1½ cups   prep: 15 min.   cook: 8 min.

1 Tbsp. butter	2 Tbsp. fresh lemon juice
½ small onion, minced	2 Tbsp. Worcestershire sauce
1 Tbsp. minced fresh ginger	2 Tbsp. steak sauce
1 garlic clove, minced	½ tsp. liquid smoke
¾ cup reserved cola	½ tsp. pepper
¾ cup ketchup	Salt to taste
½ tsp. lemon zest	

1. Melt butter in a heavy saucepan over medium heat. Add onion, ginger, and garlic; sauté 3 minutes or until tender.

2. Stir in reserved cola; bring mixture to a boil. Stir in ketchup and remaining ingredients; bring to a boil. Reduce heat, and simmer 5 minutes.

Note: We tested with A.1. Steak Sauce.

taking sides

How To Fry Chicken Right

Fried chicken? It's a Southern thing. But that doesn't mean everybody cooks it the same way.

Chicken pieces. Flour. Fat for frying. A big, heavy skillet. From celebrity chefs to the next-door neighbor, these are the must-haves for every cook who fries chicken. Yet not every piece of fried chicken tastes the same.

The cook's reputation comes from the subtle differences, such as the seasonings: just salt and pepper or spicy Cajun? And the fat: peanut oil, butter, or lard? Some soak the chicken in buttermilk before dredging in flour, and others dip the chicken in a thick batter of flour and milk or beer before sizzling it in hot oil. Many cooks simply roll the pieces in flour and fry. Some remove the skin. Most don't. Some skillet-fry, some deep-fry.

No matter the method, it's messy. Grease splatters. Flour flies. But the crunchy goodness makes it all worthwhile.

PICNIC FRIED CHICKEN

makes 6 servings   prep: 20 min.   cook: 20 min.   **pictured on back cover**

2 (2-lb.) whole chickens, cut up	2 Tbsp. salt
2 cups milk	2 tsp. pepper
1 large egg	3 cups shortening
2 cups all-purpose flour	2 tsp. salt

1. Rinse chicken with cold water; pat dry, and set aside.

2. Whisk together milk and egg in a bowl. Combine flour, 2 Tbsp. salt, and pepper in a zip-top plastic freezer bag.

3. Dip 2 chicken pieces in milk mixture. Place in plastic bag; seal and shake to coat. Remove chicken; repeat procedure with remaining pieces.

4. Melt shortening in a Dutch oven over medium heat; heat to 350°. Fry chicken, in batches, 10 minutes on each side or until done and golden brown. Drain on paper towels. Sprinkle evenly with 2 tsp. salt.

CRUNCHY PAN-FRIED CHICKEN

makes 4 servings   prep: 10 min.   cook: 6 min.   **pictured on page 588**

pictured on page 588

½ cup self-rising cornmeal mix

½ cup seasoned fine, dry breadcrumbs

½ tsp. pepper

4 boneless, skinless chicken breasts

1 large egg, beaten

¼ cup vegetable oil

1. Combine first 3 ingredients in a shallow dish. Dip chicken in egg, and dredge in cornmeal mixture.

2. Cook chicken in hot oil in a large skillet over medium-high heat 3 to 5 minutes on each side or until done.

VIRGINIA PAN-FRIED CHICKEN

makes 4 to 6 servings   prep: 40 min.   chill: 8 hr.   cook: 20 min.

2 qt. cold water

½ cup kosher salt or coarse-grain sea salt

1 (3½-lb.) whole chicken, cut up

1 qt. buttermilk

¾ cup all-purpose flour

2 Tbsp. cornstarch

2 Tbsp. potato starch*

¾ tsp. fine-grain sea salt or salt

¼ tsp. freshly ground pepper

1 lb. lard

½ cup unsalted butter

4 slices bacon

1. Combine water and kosher salt in a large bowl; add chicken. Cover and refrigerate 4 to 8 hours. Drain chicken, and pat dry; rinse bowl.

2. Return chicken to bowl; add buttermilk. Cover and refrigerate 4 to 8 hours.

3. Drain chicken on a wire rack; discard buttermilk.

4. Combine flour and next 4 ingredients in a zip-top plastic freezer bag; add 2 pieces of chicken. Seal and shake to coat. Remove chicken; repeat procedure with remaining chicken pieces.

5. Place lard, unsalted butter, and bacon evenly in 2 large cast-iron or heavy skillets; heat to 350°. Remove and discard bacon.

6. Add chicken, skin side down (fat will come halfway up sides of chicken). Cook over medium-high heat 10 to 12 minutes on each side or until chicken is done. Drain on paper towels.

* We tested with Manischewitz Potato Starch, but all-purpose flour may be substituted.

Note: Coarse-grain sea salt may be crushed in a zip-top plastic freezer bag with a rolling pin to use for fine-grain sea salt.

CAJUN FRIED CHICKEN

makes 12 servings   prep: 40 min.   cook: 36 min.

3 (3-lb.) whole chickens   1½ gal. peanut oil
3 Tbsp. Cajun seasoning

1. Remove giblets and necks, and rinse chicken with cold water. Drain cavities well; pat dry.
Rub inside and outside of chickens with seasoning; set aside.
2. Pour oil into a deep propane turkey fryer; heat to 350° according to manufacturer's instructions over medium-low flame. Place 1 chicken on fryer rod; carefully lower into hot oil. Fry
12 minutes or until a meat thermometer registers 180°. (Keep oil temperature at 350°.)
3. Remove from oil, and drain. Repeat for 2 remaining chickens. Cool slightly before serving.

SPICY CURRIED FRIED CHICKEN

makes 4 servings   prep: 15 min.   chill: 3 hr.   stand: 30 min.   fry: 1 hr., 5 min.   **pictured on page 588**

*The wings cook more quickly than larger pieces, so we recommend that you cook them first. While we
normally fry at 375°, this recipe requires a lower temperature to keep the chicken from overbrowning.*

1   (3½-lb.) cut-up whole chicken   1½ tsp. garam masala
Spicy Yogurt Marinade   1   tsp. coarsely ground pepper
1½ cups all-purpose baking mix   Canola oil
⅓   cup sesame seeds   Minted Mango Dipping Sauce

1. Place chicken in a 13- x 9-inch baking dish; pour Spicy Yogurt Marinade over chicken, turning to coat. Cover and chill at least 3 hours or overnight, turning occasionally.
2. Remove chicken from marinade, and place on a wire rack on an aluminum foil-lined baking
sheet; let stand 10 minutes.
3. Stir together baking mix and next 3 ingredients in a large bowl; toss chicken in mixture until
coated, shaking off excess. Repeat coating process. Return chicken to rack; let stand 15 minutes.
4. Preheat oven to 200°. Pour oil to a depth of 1 inch in a large heavy skillet; heat to 350°.
(Temperature will reduce as chicken is added. For best results, keep temperature between 300°
and 325°.) Fry wings 6 minutes; turn and cook 6 more minutes. Remove wings to a rack on an
aluminum foil-lined baking sheet. Keep warm in a 200° oven. Fry remaining chicken, 2 pieces at
a time, skin sides down, 6 minutes; turn and cook 6 more minutes. Turn pieces; cover and cook
6 minutes or until done, turning during last 3 minutes for even browning, if necessary. (Chicken

Chicken-and-
Pot Pie, page 6.

King Ranch Chicken
Casserole, page 684

Bourbon-Cranberry
Turkey Tenderloin,
page 701

Oven-Barbecued Turkey Drumsticks, page 703

Toasted Pecan, Cranberry, and Gorgonzola Turkey Burgers, page 704

Grilled Peach-and-Mozzarella
Salad, page 722

Avocado Fruit Salad,
page 719

Apple-Pe
B

Tomato and Watermelon
Salad, page 740

Fried Okra Salad,
page 734

Fruit Salad With Blackberry-Basil
Vinaigrette, page 720

Peanutty Coleslaw,
page 732

Succotash Salad,
page 725

New Potato Salad With
Feta Cheese, page 729

Raspberry-Tomato
Aspic, page 724

672

pieces will be very dark.) Remove to a wire rack; let stand 5 minutes. Serve with Minted Mango Dipping Sauce.

Spicy Curried Fried Shrimp: Substitute 2 lb. peeled and deveined jumbo shrimp for chicken; proceed as directed. Fry shrimp, in batches, at 350° for 3 minutes or until golden; drain on paper towels.

Spicy Yogurt Marinade

makes about 2 cups prep: 10 min.

You can make this marinade up to 1 day ahead and store it in the fridge.

2 cups plain yogurt	2 garlic cloves, minced
6 Tbsp. chopped fresh cilantro	1½ tsp. ground ginger
4 tsp. red curry powder	1 tsp. salt
1 Tbsp. lemon zest	

1. Stir together all ingredients in a medium bowl.

Minted Mango Dipping Sauce

makes about 1 cup prep: 5 min.

1. Stir together 1 (9-oz.) jar mango chutney (about ¾ cup), 3 Tbsp. fresh lime juice, and 1 Tbsp. chopped fresh mint.

FRIED CHICKEN LIVERS

makes 4 to 5 servings prep: 5 min. cook: 4 min.

1 lb. chicken livers	1 tsp. pepper
2 cups all-purpose flour	1 cup buttermilk
1½ tsp. seasoned salt	Vegetable oil

1. Pierce chicken livers several times with a fork.

2. Combine flour, salt, and pepper in a shallow dish; dredge livers in flour mixture. Dip livers into buttermilk, and dredge in flour mixture again.

3. Pour oil to a depth of 2 inches into a Dutch oven or electric fryer; heat to 365°. Cook chicken livers, a few at a time, 4 to 5 minutes or until golden brown. Serve immediately.

ALMOND-CRUSTED CHICKEN

makes 5 servings   prep: 10 min.   cook: 8 min.

Jamaican jerk seasoning offers the sweet-spicy flavors of thyme, allspice, and crushed red pepper.

¼ cup almonds, coarsely chopped

½ cup fine, dry breadcrumbs

2 tsp. Jamaican jerk seasoning

¼ tsp. kosher salt

1 tsp. lime zest

1½ lb. skinned and boned chicken breast cutlets

1 Tbsp. olive oil, divided

1. Process first 5 ingredients in a food processor or blender 45 seconds or until finely ground. Place almond mixture in a shallow bowl.

2. Brush chicken evenly with ½ Tbsp. olive oil. Dredge chicken in almond mixture.

3. Cook chicken in remaining ½ Tbsp. hot olive oil in a nonstick skillet over medium-high heat 4 minutes on each side or until done.

Calories 245; Fat: 7.7g (sat 1g, mono 4.1g, poly 1.3g); Protein 33.8g; Fiber 1.1g; Chol 79mg; Iron 1.7mg; Sodium 402mg; Calc 53mg

CRISPY OVEN-FRIED DRUMSTICKS

makes 4 servings   prep: 15 min.   bake: 25 min.

3 cups cornflake cereal, crushed

⅓ cup grated Parmesan cheese

½ tsp. salt

¼ to ½ tsp. ground red pepper

¼ tsp. freshly ground black pepper

¾ cup fat-free buttermilk

8 chicken drumsticks (about 2 lb.), skinned

Vegetable cooking spray

1. Preheat oven to 425°. Combine first 5 ingredients in a large zip-top plastic freezer bag; seal and shake well to combine.

2. Pour buttermilk into a shallow bowl. Dip 2 drumsticks in buttermilk, and place in bag. Seal and shake well, coating drumsticks completely. Place drumsticks on an aluminum foil-lined baking sheet coated with cooking spray. Repeat procedure with remaining drumsticks. Sprinkle remaining cornflake mixture evenly over drumsticks on baking sheet. Lightly coat with vegetable cooking spray.

3. Bake at 425° for 25 to 30 minutes or until drumsticks are well browned and done. Serve immediately.

Per 2 drumsticks: Calories 324; Fat: 7.8g (sat 2.6g, mono 2.4g, poly 1.5g); Protein 40.7g; Fiber 1g; Chol 137mg; Iron 5.9mg; Sodium 790mg; Calc 150mg

[southern lights]

MAW-MAW'S CHICKEN PIE

makes 8 servings   prep: 15 min.   bake: 40 min.

This simple recipe gives rise to a golden cakelike crust that won rave reviews at the tasting table. Try replacing a portion of the chicken with an equal amount of frozen, thawed vegetables, or stir a cup of shredded cheese into the soup mixture. We especially enjoyed the pie with broccoli and Cheddar cheese.

4   cups chopped cooked chicken
1   (10¾-oz.) can cream of chicken soup, undiluted
1½ cups chicken broth
2   Tbsp. cornstarch

1½ cups self-rising flour
1   cup buttermilk
½   cup butter, melted

1. Preheat oven to 400°. Place chopped chicken in a lightly greased 12- x 8-inch baking dish. Whisk together soup, broth, and cornstarch; pour mixture evenly over chicken.
2. Whisk together flour, buttermilk, and butter; spoon batter evenly over chicken mixture.
3. Bake at 400° for 40 minutes or until crust is golden brown.

CHICKEN-AND-EGG POT PIE

makes 4 to 6 servings   prep: 20 min.   bake: 33 min.   **pictured on page 661**

Let leftover chicken, turkey, or roast beef give you a jump on dinner.

2   cups chopped cooked chicken
2   hard-cooked eggs, chopped
1   (15¼-oz.) can whole kernel corn, rinsed and drained
1   (15¼-oz.) can sweet green peas, rinsed and drained

1   (10¾-oz.) can cream of chicken soup, undiluted
1   cup (4 oz.) shredded Cheddar cheese
1   (2-oz.) jar diced pimiento, drained
¼   tsp. pepper
2   (8-oz.) cans refrigerated crescent roll dough, divided

1. Preheat oven to 350°. Stir together first 8 ingredients in a large bowl until blended.
2. Unroll 1 can crescent roll dough, and press into a lightly greased 9-inch square baking dish.
3. Bake at 350° for 15 minutes. Remove from oven; spoon chicken mixture over crescent roll dough in dish.
4. Unroll remaining can roll dough; roll into a 9-inch square. Place over chicken mixture, pressing edges of top and bottom crusts to dish to seal. Bake 18 to 20 more minutes or until golden.

inspirations for your taste

SAVORY CHICKEN POT PIE

makes 8 servings   prep: 20 min.   cook: 16 min.   stand: 15 min.   bake: 30 min.

To round out your meal, add a bagged salad and a loaf of crusty bread.

1 small sweet potato	3 cups chicken broth
12 boneless, skinless chicken thighs, cut into bite-size pieces	1 (10¾-oz.) can cream of mushroom soup
½ tsp. seasoned salt	1 (16-oz.) package frozen peas and carrots, thawed
⅓ cup chopped onion	1 Tbsp. fresh lemon juice
1 tsp. vegetable oil	½ tsp. freshly ground pepper
¼ cup butter	½ (15-oz.) package refrigerated piecrusts
⅓ cup all-purpose flour	

1. Pierce sweet potato several times with a fork. Place in microwave oven, and cover with a damp paper towel. Microwave at HIGH 3 minutes or until done. Let stand 5 minutes; peel and dice. Set aside.

2. Sprinkle chicken evenly with seasoned salt. Sauté chicken and onion in hot oil in a Dutch oven over medium-high heat 5 to 8 minutes or until done. Remove chicken and onion.

3. Melt butter in Dutch oven over medium-high heat; whisk in flour, chicken broth, and soup. Reduce heat to medium-low, and cook, stirring occasionally, 3 to 4 minutes or until thickened. Stir in cooked chicken and onion, sweet potato, peas and carrots, lemon juice, and pepper.

Cook, stirring often, 5 minutes or until thoroughly heated. Spoon chicken mixture into a lightly greased 13- x 9-inch baking dish.

4. Roll piecrust into a 13- x 9-inch rectangle; fit over chicken mixture in baking dish. Cut several slits in top of crust for steam to escape.

5. Bake at 400° for 30 to 35 minutes or until crust is golden brown and filling is thoroughly heated. Let stand 10 minutes before serving.

CHICKEN-AND-CORNBREAD CASSEROLE

makes 6 servings   prep: 20 min.   cook: 7 min.   bake: 40 min.

Pick up a deli-roasted chicken if you don't have 3½ cups of chopped chicken on hand. It yields just enough meat for this recipe.

2 celery ribs, chopped	1 large egg, lightly beaten
½ medium onion, chopped	1 (4.5-oz.) jar sliced mushrooms, drained
1 Tbsp. vegetable oil	¼ tsp. dried crushed red pepper
3 cups packed crumbled cornbread	¼ tsp. salt
1 Tbsp. poultry seasoning	2 Tbsp. butter, melted
3½ cups chopped cooked chicken	1 cup (4 oz.) shredded sharp Cheddar cheese
1¼ cups low-sodium chicken broth	Garnish: chopped fresh parsley (optional)
1 cup sour cream	

1. Preheat oven to 350°. Sauté celery and onion in hot oil in a medium skillet over medium-high heat 7 minutes or until vegetables are tender; set aside.

2. Combine cornbread and poultry seasoning in a large bowl.

3. Layer half of cornbread mixture on bottom of a lightly greased 11- x 7-inch baking dish.

4. Combine onion mixture, chicken, and next 6 ingredients in a bowl. Spoon mixture evenly over top of cornbread mixture in dish. Top evenly with remaining half of cornbread mixture, and drizzle with melted butter.

5. Bake, covered, at 350° for 30 minutes or until bubbly. Remove from oven, and top with cheese. Bake, uncovered, 10 more minutes or until cheese is golden. Garnish, if desired.

So Many Ways To Make Dumplings!

Slick, fluffy, sad, happy. Who knew there were so many ways to describe the cooked dough in chicken and dumplings?

"I was shocked," said East Tennessean Cathy Riddle. "I had cooked up a pot of chicken and dumplings, and one of my coworkers came in and said, 'oh, you make sad dumplings.' Then she told me that slick, chewy dumplings are 'sad' and the fluffy ones are 'happy,'" she recalls.

The slick ones are biscuit or pastry dough rolled out in thin strips. For the doughy, fluffy kind, biscuit dough is dropped into the broth like drop biscuits. But cooks in a hurry have been known to make dumplings from frozen or canned biscuits, tortilla strips, or the handy dandy dumpling strips found in the frozen food section. And though the doughy kind have been labeled "Yankee dumplings" by some, any true Southerner would be happy to accept a bowlful of either type.

CHICKEN AND DUMPLINGS

makes 4 to 6 servings   prep: 15 min.   cook: 25 min.   **pictured on page 661**

We used a deli-roasted chicken for this recipe. One chicken yields about 3 cups.

1   (32-oz.) container low-sodium chicken broth
1   (14 ½-oz.) can low-sodium chicken broth
3   cups shredded cooked chicken (about 1½ lb.)
1   (10 ¾-oz.) can reduced-fat cream of celery soup

¼   tsp. poultry seasoning
1   (10.2-oz.) can refrigerated jumbo buttermilk
    biscuits

1. Stir together first 5 ingredients in a Dutch oven over medium-high heat; bring to a boil. Reduce heat to low; simmer, stirring occasionally, 15 minutes.

2. Place biscuits on a lightly floured surface. Roll or pat each biscuit to ⅛-inch thickness; cut into ½-inch-wide strips.

3. Return broth mixture to a low boil over medium-high heat. Drop strips, 1 at a time, into boiling broth. Reduce heat to low; simmer 10 minutes, stirring occasionally to prevent dumplings from sticking.

CHICKEN-AND-SAUSAGE CREOLE

makes 6 servings   prep: 15 min.   cook: 30 min.

1 cup uncooked long-grain rice
2 (14-oz.) cans low-sodium fat-free chicken
   broth, divided
½ lb. smoked sausage, cut into ½-inch rounds
1 medium-size yellow onion, chopped
   (about 2 cups)
1 cup chopped celery
1 green bell pepper, chopped

2 garlic cloves, minced
3 cups chopped cooked chicken
1 (14½-oz.) can diced tomatoes
2 tsp. chopped fresh parsley
1 tsp. salt
⅛ tsp. ground red pepper
2 bay leaves

1. Prepare rice according to package directions, substituting 2 cups broth for water.
2. Sauté sausage and next 4 ingredients in a lightly greased Dutch oven over medium-high heat
5 minutes or until vegetables are tender. Stir in remaining broth, chicken, and next 5 ingredients. Bring to a boil over medium-high heat. Reduce heat to low; simmer, stirring occasionally,
20 minutes. Remove and discard bay leaves, and serve over hot cooked rice.

BEER-SMOTHERED CHICKEN

makes 4 servings   prep: 15 min.   cook: 1 hr., 20 min.   stand: 5 min.

4 chicken leg-thigh quarters (about 2 lb.),
   separated
½ cup all-purpose flour
2 garlic cloves, minced
¼ cup vegetable oil
1 small onion, diced
½ medium-size green bell pepper, diced

2 (12-oz.) bottles nonalcoholic beer
1 (6-oz.) jar sliced mushrooms, drained
¼ cup lite soy sauce
1 (10¾-oz.) can cream of celery soup
1 cup whipping cream
Hot cooked rice

1. Place chicken in a large zip-top plastic freezer bag; add flour, and seal. Shake to coat.
2. Sauté garlic in hot oil in a large skillet. Add chicken, and fry, in batches, 5 minutes on each
side or until golden brown. Remove chicken, reserving drippings in skillet. Sauté onion and bell
pepper in drippings 5 minutes or until tender; add chicken, beer, mushrooms, and soy sauce.
3. Cook over medium heat for 30 minutes. Stir in soup; cook, stirring occasionally, 30 more
minutes. Add whipping cream; cook until thoroughly heated. Let stand 5 minutes. Serve over
hot cooked rice.

CHICKEN-AND-RICE

makes 4 servings   prep: 10 min.   cook: 22 min.

1½ lb. boneless, skinless chicken breasts
2   (8.8-oz.) pouches ready-to-serve long-grain rice
4   bacon slices, diced
½   cup chopped onion

½   cup frozen green peas, thawed*
1   (4-oz.) can sliced mushrooms, drained
¾   tsp. salt
¼   tsp. pepper
Garnish: fresh parsley sprigs (optional)

1. Cut chicken into ¼-inch slices, and set aside.

2. Heat rice according to package directions; set aside.

3. Sauté bacon in a large skillet over medium-high heat 8 minutes or until crisp; remove bacon with a slotted spoon, reserving 1 Tbsp. drippings in skillet.

4. Sauté onion in hot drippings in skillet 3 minutes or until tender. Stir in chicken, and sauté 8 minutes or until chicken is done. Stir in rice, bacon, peas, and next 3 ingredients; cook, stirring occasionally, 3 minutes or until thoroughly heated. Garnish, if desired.

* 4 oz. (about 1 heaping cup) snow peas may be substituted for green peas. Microwave snow peas and ¼ cup water in a microwave-safe bowl 2 minutes before adding to chicken mixture. Proceed with recipe as directed.

Note: We tested with Uncle Ben's Original Long Grain Ready Rice.

SWEET-AND-SOUR CHICKEN AND RICE

makes 8 servings   prep: 20 min.   cook: 1 hr.

Skinned and boned chicken thighs contain a little more fat than breast meat, but they are very nutritious and boast lots of flavor and moisture.

½   tsp. salt
½   tsp. pepper
2   lb. skinned and boned chicken thighs
1   small onion, diced
1   medium-size red bell pepper, chopped

2   garlic cloves, minced
1   cup uncooked long grain rice
1   cup sweet-and-sour dressing
1   cup low-sodium fat-free chicken broth
2   green onions, chopped

1. Sprinkle salt and pepper evenly over chicken thighs.

2. Brown chicken in a Dutch oven coated with cooking spray over medium-high heat 2 to 3 minutes on each side or until browned. Remove chicken from pan, and set aside.

3. Add onion, bell pepper, and garlic to Dutch oven coated with cooking spray; sauté 5 minutes. Add rice; sauté 2 minutes or until rice is opaque. Stir in dressing and broth. Add chicken pieces; bring to a boil. Cover, reduce heat, and simmer 45 minutes or until liquid is absorbed and chicken is done. Sprinkle with green onions.

Note: We tested with Old Dutch Sweet & Sour Dressing.

Calories 289; Fat 5g (sat 1.3g, mono 1.4g, poly 1.2g); Protein 25g; Fiber 1.2g; Chol 95mg; Iron 2.4mg; Sodium 739mg; Calc 31mg

ISLAND CHICKEN AND RICE

makes 6 servings   prep: 15 min.   cook: 1 hr.   stand: 5 min.

This is a one-pot meal cooked with coconut milk and topped with macadamia nuts.

4½ lb. chicken pieces

1½ tsp. salt, divided

¾ tsp. pepper, divided

1 Tbsp. vegetable oil

1 Tbsp. butter

1 small onion, chopped

1 cup uncooked long-grain rice

2 garlic cloves, pressed

1 (14-oz.) can chicken broth

1 (13.5-oz.) can coconut milk

¾ cup unsweetened pineapple juice

¼ tsp. dried crushed red pepper

4 green onions, chopped

1 (3.5-oz.) jar macadamia nuts, toasted and chopped

Garnish: fresh pineapple slices (optional)

1. Sprinkle 4½ lb. chicken pieces evenly with 1 tsp. salt and ½ tsp. pepper.

2. Brown chicken in hot oil in a large skillet over medium-high heat 8 to 10 minutes on each side. Remove chicken from skillet, and drain, reserving 1 Tbsp. drippings in skillet.

3. Add butter to skillet, and melt, stirring to loosen particles from bottom of skillet; add chopped onion, and sauté 4 minutes. Add long-grain rice, and sauté 4 minutes; add garlic, and sauté 1 minute. Stir in chicken broth and next 3 ingredients; return chicken to skillet. Sprinkle with remaining ½ tsp. salt and ¼ tsp. pepper; bring to a boil. Cover, reduce heat to low, and simmer 35 minutes or until rice is tender.

4. Uncover, fluff rice with a fork, and let stand 5 minutes before serving. Sprinkle evenly with green onions and nuts. Garnish, if desired.

Note: We tested with Foster Farms Pick of the Chick (3 thighs, 3 breasts, 3 legs) for chicken pieces.

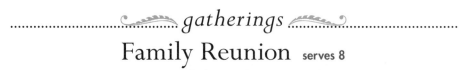

Family Reunion serves 8

Creamy Chicken-and-Rice Casserole

*Green Bean-and-Red Bell Pepper Toss (page 844)

*Suffolk Waldorf Salad (page 715)

Honey-Oatmeal Wheat Bread (page 140)

Dark Chocolate Bundt Cake (page 210)

*double recipe

CREAMY CHICKEN-AND-RICE CASSEROLE

makes 8 servings   prep: 30 min.   cook: 10 min.   bake: 30 min.

We lightened this dish by using fat-free soup and sour cream instead of regular and by replacing lots of regular Cheddar with a smaller portion of reduced-fat Cheddar.

[southern lights]

1   (5-oz.) package long-grain and wild rice mix

1   tsp. salt-free herb-and-spice seasoning

4   (6-oz.) skinless, boneless chicken breasts, cut into small pieces

1   small sweet onion, chopped

1   (10¾-oz.) can fat-free cream of mushroom soup, undiluted

1   (8-oz.) can sliced water chestnuts, drained

1   (8-oz.) container nonfat sour cream

1   (7-oz.) jar roasted red bell peppers, drained and chopped

½   tsp. pepper

1   cup (4 oz.) shredded reduced-fat sharp Cheddar cheese

1. Preheat oven to 350°. Cook rice mix according to package directions, omitting fat.

2. Sprinkle seasoning evenly over chicken pieces.

3. Cook chicken in a large nonstick skillet coated with cooking spray over medium-high heat 10 minutes or until chicken is done, stirring often.

4. Stir together chicken, rice, onion, and next 5 ingredients in a bowl. Spoon into an 11- x 7-inch baking dish coated with cooking spray. Sprinkle with cheese.

5. Bake at 350° for 30 minutes or until bubbly around edges.

Note: We tested with Mrs. Dash salt-free herb-and-spice seasoning.

Per serving: Calories 268; Fat 5g (sat 2.4g, mono 0.8g, poly 0.3g) Protein 28g; Fiber 1.8g; Chol 59mg; Iron 7mg; Sodium 784mg; Calc 209mg

Rare

"**S**oul food is the fabric of Atlanta," explains Lorenzo Wyche, creator of the restaurant Rare. "For lack of a better term, it's comfort food, the food we grew up with at Sunday dinner. But we challenge the palate a little bit." Ready for that challenge, we kick back, cozy on upholstered "beds," watching vintage cartoons projected on a blank wall (no sound, just memories). The food begins to arrive. First and favorite—lobster mac and cheese, creamy with white Cheddar béchamel. Next: a BLT salad, featuring lightly fried green tomatoes. Then teeny versions of chicken and waffles; Jamaican jerk-spiced tilapia; and pot stickers filled with collard greens, wild mushrooms, and fresh ginger. The concept is tapas, a series of small plates you share.

The music builds as the hours pass; Betty Boop replaces Popeye. The place fills up, the music grows even louder—but people come for the food. "The menu is the story here," says Lorenzo, waving a hand at the bounty. So dig in.

554 Piedmont Avenue NE.
Atlanta, Georgia 30308
www.rareatl.com or (404) 549-9024.

KING RANCH CHICKEN CASSEROLE

makes 8 to 10 servings   prep: 30 min.   cook: 1 hr., 19 min.   cool: 30 min.
bake: 55 min.   stand: 10 min.   **pictured on page 662**

1 (4½- to 5-lb.) whole chicken	1 (10¾-oz.) can cream of chicken soup
2 celery ribs, cut into 3 pieces each	2 (10-oz.) cans diced tomatoes and green chiles,
2 carrots, cut into 3 pieces each	drained
2½ to 3 tsp. salt	1 tsp. dried oregano
2 Tbsp. butter	1 tsp. ground cumin
1 medium onion, chopped	1 tsp. Mexican-style chili powder*
1 medium-size green bell pepper, chopped	3 cups grated sharp Cheddar cheese
1 garlic clove, pressed	12 (6-inch) fajita-size corn tortillas, cut into
1 (10¾-oz.) can cream of mushroom soup	½-inch strips

1. If applicable, remove giblets from chicken, and reserve for another use. Rinse chicken.

2. Place chicken, celery, carrots, and salt in a large Dutch oven with water to cover. Bring to a boil over medium-high heat; reduce heat to low. Cover and simmer 50 minutes to 1 hour or until chicken is done. Remove from heat. Remove chicken from broth; cool 30 minutes. Remove and reserve ¾ cup cooking liquid. Strain any remaining cooking liquid; reserve for another use.

3. Preheat oven to 350°. Melt butter in a large skillet over medium-high heat. Add onion, and sauté 6 to 7 minutes or until tender. Add bell pepper and garlic, and sauté 3 to 4 minutes. Stir in reserved ¾ cup cooking liquid, cream of mushroom soup, and next 5 ingredients. Cook, stirring occasionally, 8 minutes.

4. Skin and bone chicken; shred meat into bite-size pieces. Layer half of chicken in a lightly greased 13- x 9-inch baking dish. Top with half of soup mixture and 1 cup Cheddar cheese. Cover with half of corn tortilla strips. Repeat layers once. Top with remaining 1 cup cheese.

5. Bake at 350° for 55 minutes to 1 hour or until bubbly. Let stand 10 minutes before serving.

* 1 tsp. chili powder and ⅛ tsp. ground red pepper may be substituted for Mexican-style chili powder.

Lightened King Ranch Chicken Casserole: Reduce butter to 1 Tbsp. Substitute reduced-fat cream of mushroom and cream of chicken soup for regular and 2% reduced-fat cheese for regular. Prepare recipe as directed through Step 4. Bake, covered, at 350° for 50 minutes; uncover and bake for 10 to 15 minutes or until bubbly. Let stand 10 minutes before serving.

Note: We tested with Cracker Barrel 2% Milk Natural Sharp Cheddar Cheese.

Quick-and-Easy King Ranch Chicken Casserole: Substitute 1 (2-lb.) skinned, boned, and shredded deli-roasted chicken for whole chicken, 3 cups coarsely crumbled lime-flavored white corn tortilla chips for corn tortillas, and ¾ cup chicken broth for cooking liquid. Omit celery, carrots, and salt. Prepare recipe as directed, beginning with Step 3.

CHICKEN ENCHILADAS

makes 4 servings   prep: 15 min.   cook: 30 min.   **pictured on page 588**

Substitute leftover roast beef or your favorite shredded barbecued pork as a tasty alternative to chicken.

3   cups chopped cooked chicken
2   cups (8 oz.) shredded Monterey Jack cheese
     with peppers
½   cup sour cream
1   (4.5-oz.) can chopped green chiles, drained
⅓   cup chopped fresh cilantro

8   (8-inch) flour tortillas
Vegetable cooking spray
1   (8-oz.) container sour cream
1   (8-oz.) jar tomatillo salsa
Toppings: diced tomatoes, chopped avocado,
     chopped green onions, sliced ripe olives

1. Preheat oven to 350°. Stir together first 5 ingredients. Spoon chicken mixture evenly down center of each tortilla, and roll up. Arrange seam side down in a lightly greased 13- x 9-inch baking dish.
2. Coat tortillas with cooking spray.
3. Bake at 350° for 30 minutes or until golden brown.
4. Stir together 8-oz. container sour cream and salsa. Spoon over hot enchiladas; sprinkle with desired toppings.

MARGARITA-MARINATED CHICKEN WITH MANGO SALSA

makes 6 servings   prep: 10 min.   chill: 2 hr.   grill: 12 min.

2   large limes
2   cups liquid margarita mix
1   cup vegetable oil
1   cup chopped fresh cilantro
2   tsp. salt
½   tsp. ground red pepper

3   Tbsp. tequila (optional)
6   boneless, skinless chicken breasts
2   cups uncooked long-grain rice
Cooking spray for grilling
Mango Salsa
Garnish: fresh cilantro sprig (optional)

1. Cut limes in half. Squeeze juice into a shallow dish or large zip-top plastic freezer bag; add squeezed lime halves to juice. Add margarita mix, next 4 ingredients, and, if desired, tequila. Whisk (or seal bag and shake) to blend. Add chicken; cover or seal, and chill at least 2 hours or up to 6 hours. Remove chicken from marinade, discarding marinade. Set chicken aside.
2. Prepare rice according to package directions; keep warm.
3. Coat cold food grate with grilling spray; place on grill. Preheat grill to 300° to 350° (medium) heat. Place chicken on grate.
4. Grill chicken, covered with grill lid, 6 minutes on each side or until done. Serve over hot cooked rice. Serve with Mango Salsa, and garnish, if desired.

Mango Salsa

makes about 2½ cups   prep: 10 min.

2   mangoes, peeled
2   avocados, peeled
1   red bell pepper
½   red onion

1   Tbsp. chopped fresh cilantro
1   Tbsp. vegetable oil
Juice of 1 large lime (about 1 Tbsp.)

1. Chop mangoes, avocados, red bell pepper, and red onion; place in a medium bowl. Add chopped cilantro, oil, and lime juice. Chill, if desired.

CHICKEN WITH GREEN OLIVES

makes 4 to 6 servings   prep: 25 min.   cook: 1 hr.

This recipe came to us from Giuliano Hazan, whose cookbook Every Night Italian *(Scribner, 2000), promises easy recipes for fresh, healthy food. His approach to cooking—few ingredients, simple directions, quick results, and impressive tastes—yielded this family favorite.*

5 anchovy fillets

1½ cups (8 oz.) green olives, slivered and divided

3 lb. chicken legs, thighs, and wings

½ tsp. salt

½ tsp. pepper

2 Tbsp. olive oil

4 garlic cloves, peeled and crushed

½ cup dry white wine

3 Tbsp. red wine vinegar

3 Tbsp. lemon juice

3 Tbsp. finely chopped fresh flat-leaf parsley

1. Process anchovy fillets and ¾ cup green olives in a food processor until chopped, stopping to scrape down sides; set aside.

2. Sprinkle chicken with salt and pepper. Brown chicken on all sides in hot oil in a large skillet over medium-high heat. Remove chicken, reserving 2 tsp. drippings in skillet; add garlic, and sauté 1 minute. Add white wine and vinegar; cook 2 minutes stirring to loosen browned particles. Stir in anchovy mixture and 2 Tbsp. water.

3. Return chicken to skillet, turning to coat pieces in sauce.

4. Cook, covered, over medium-low heat 45 minutes or until chicken is tender. (Stir in additional water, if needed.)

5. Add 3 Tbsp. lemon juice, parsley, and remaining ¾ cup green olives; cook 1 to 2 more minutes. Serve immediately.

GREEK-STYLE CHICKEN

makes 4 servings   prep: 20 min.   cook: 20 min.   bake: 30 min.   **pictured on page 587**

pictured on page 587

½   tsp. salt

½   tsp. pepper

1½   tsp. Greek seasoning

4   (6- to 8-oz.) boneless, skinless chicken breasts

2   Tbsp. olive oil

1   medium-size red bell pepper, chopped

1   small onion, thinly sliced

½   cup dry white wine

½   cup chicken broth

16   small pitted ripe black olives

Hot cooked rice

Chopped fresh flat-leaf parsley

Garnish: fresh flat-leaf parsley sprig

1. Preheat oven to 350°. Combine first 3 ingredients; sprinkle evenly over chicken.

2. Cook chicken in hot oil in a large ovenproof skillet over medium-high heat 5 minutes on each side or until browned. Remove chicken.

3. Add bell pepper and onion to skillet; sauté 5 minutes or until tender. Stir in wine and broth, stirring to loosen particles from bottom of pan. Stir in olives. Return chicken to skillet.

4. Bring to a boil. Remove skillet from heat.

5. Bake, covered, at 350° for 30 minutes or until chicken is done. Combine rice and chopped parsley. Serve chicken over rice. Garnish, if desired.

QUICK CHICKEN STIR-FRY

makes 4 to 6 servings   prep: 20 min.   stand: 30 min.   cook: 9 min.

4   boneless, skinless chicken breasts

1   (14-oz.) can reduced-sodium chicken broth

2   Tbsp. lite soy sauce

1   to 2 Tbsp. chili-garlic paste

2   Tbsp. cornstarch

1   Tbsp. brown sugar

1   Tbsp. grated fresh ginger

2   Tbsp. vegetable oil

2   cups packaged matchstick carrots

1   red bell pepper, cut into slices

1   green bell pepper, cut into slices

2   green onions, sliced

Hot cooked rice

1. Cut chicken into ¼-inch-thick strips; place in a shallow dish.

2. Whisk together chicken broth and next 5 ingredients in a small bowl. Pour half of broth mixture over chicken, reserving remaining broth mixture. Turn chicken to coat, and let stand 30 minutes.

3. Heat 2 Tbsp. oil in a wok or large skillet over medium-high heat 2 minutes. Remove chicken from marinade, discarding marinade. Add chicken to wok, and stir-fry 3 to 5 minutes or until lightly browned. Add carrots, bell peppers, and green onions, and stir-fry 3 to 4 minutes. Add reserved broth mixture, and cook 1 minute or until thickened. Serve over hot cooked rice.

CHAMPAGNE CHICKEN AND MUSHROOMS

makes 6 servings   prep: 30 min.   stand: 15 min.   cook: 50 min.

Champagne lends this dish delicate flavor, but you could use white wine also. Ask your butcher to bone the chicken breasts, which offer the best results, or use skinned and boned breasts.

½ cup all-purpose flour	2 (3.5-oz.) packages shiitake mushrooms, stems removed and sliced
1 tsp. salt	
½ tsp. pepper	3 garlic cloves, minced
6 skin-on, boneless chicken breasts	2 cups Champagne or sparkling wine
2 Tbsp. unsalted butter	2 tsp. chopped fresh thyme
2 Tbsp. olive oil	½ cup whipping cream
½ cup minced shallots (about 3 medium)	Salt and pepper to taste

1. Stir together first 3 ingredients in a shallow bowl. Dredge chicken in flour mixture; place on a wire rack. Let stand 15 minutes. Dredge chicken in flour mixture again; return to rack.

2. Melt butter with olive oil in a large skillet over medium heat. Cook chicken, in batches, 5 minutes on each side or until golden brown. Remove chicken to a plate.

3. Add shallots to skillet; cook, stirring often, 2 minutes or until golden brown. Add mushrooms and garlic, and cook, stirring often, 10 minutes or until mushrooms are tender.

4. Stir in Champagne and thyme; bring to a boil, stirring to loosen browned particles from bottom of skillet. Reduce heat, and return chicken to skillet. Cover and simmer 10 minutes or until done.

5. Transfer chicken to a serving platter. Stir cream into mushroom mixture. Cook 5 to 6 minutes or until thickened. Add salt and pepper to taste. Serve sauce immediately over chicken.

SUN-DRIED TOMATO CHICKEN

makes 6 servings   prep: 10 min.   bake: 1 hr.   **pictured on page 586**

1   (4-lb.) package chicken pieces (3 breasts,
    4 thighs, 3 legs)
1   cup sun-dried tomato vinaigrette with roasted
    red pepper dressing

½   tsp. coarsely ground pepper
Toppings: chopped sun-dried tomatoes, sliced
    fresh basil

1. Preheat oven to 400°. Arrange chicken pieces in a single layer in a lightly greased 13- x 9-inch baking dish. Pour dressing evenly over chicken pieces, and sprinkle with ground pepper.
2. Bake, uncovered, at 400° for 1 hour or until done, basting every 15 minutes. Sprinkle baked chicken with desired toppings.

Note: We tested with Good Seasons Sun Dried Tomato Vinaigrette With Roasted Red Peppers dressing.

Sun-dried Tomato Chicken Breasts: Substitute 6 skinned and boned chicken breasts for chicken pieces. Prepare recipe as directed, decreasing bake time to 30 minutes.

QUICK CHICKEN PICCATA

makes 4 servings   prep: 20 min.   cook: 10 min.

1   lb. boneless, skinless chicken breasts
½   tsp. salt
½   tsp. pepper
½   cup Italian-seasoned breadcrumbs
2   Tbsp. olive oil

¼   cup chicken broth
3   Tbsp. fresh lemon juice
2   Tbsp. butter
2   Tbsp. chopped fresh parsley
1   (12-oz.) package cooked noodles

1. Cut each chicken breast in half horizontally. Place chicken between 2 sheets of heavy-duty plastic wrap; flatten to ¼-inch thickness, using a rolling pin or the flat side of a meat mallet.
2. Sprinkle chicken evenly with salt and pepper; lightly dredge in breadcrumbs.
3. Cook half of chicken in 1 Tbsp. hot oil in a large nonstick skillet over medium-high heat 2 minutes on each side or until golden brown and done. Remove chicken to a serving platter, and cover with aluminum foil. Repeat procedure with remaining chicken and 1 Tbsp. olive oil.
4. Add broth and lemon juice to skillet, and cook, stirring to loosen particles from bottom of skillet, until sauce is slightly thickened. Remove from heat; add butter and parsley, stirring until butter melts. Pour sauce over chicken, and serve over warm noodles.

{family favorite}

BASIL CHICKEN PARMIGIANA

makes 8 servings   prep: 25 min.   cook: 4 min. per batch   bake: 20 min.

[*southern lights*]

8 oz. uncooked whole wheat rotini	1 Tbsp. olive oil
4 (6-oz.) boneless, skinless chicken breasts	1 (26-oz.) jar low-fat pasta sauce
⅔ cup Italian-seasoned breadcrumbs	¼ cup sliced fresh basil
½ cup grated Parmesan cheese, divided	1 cup (4 oz.) shredded low-fat mozzarella cheese
½ cup egg substitute	2 Tbsp. minced fresh flat-leaf parsley

1. Preheat oven to 350°. Prepare pasta according to package directions, omitting salt and oil. Drain and keep warm.

2. Cut each chicken breast into 2 pieces. Place each piece between 2 sheets of heavy-duty plastic wrap; flatten to ¼-inch thickness using a meat mallet or rolling pin.

3. Combine ⅔ cup breadcrumbs and ¼ cup Parmesan cheese. Dip chicken in egg substitute, and dredge in breadcrumb mixture.

4. Brown chicken, in batches, in hot oil in a large nonstick skillet over medium-high heat, 1 to 2 minutes on each side; remove chicken from skillet.

5. Stir together pasta sauce and basil; spoon half of sauce into an 11- x 7- inch baking dish.

6. Arrange chicken in an even layer over sauce; pour remaining sauce over chicken. Sprinkle evenly with mozzarella cheese and remaining ¼ cup Parmesan cheese.

7. Bake at 350° for 20 minutes or until mozzarella cheese is lightly browned and sauce is bubbly around edges. Remove from oven, and sprinkle with 2 Tbsp. parsley. Serve chicken over hot cooked pasta.

Per 1 chicken breast and ½ cup pasta: Calories 337; Fat 8g (sat 2.9g, mono 2.2g, poly 0.8g); Protein 33.8g; Fiber 4g; Chol 61mg; Iron 2.8mg; Sodium 732mg; Calc 364mg

CHICKEN SCALOPPINE WITH LINGUINE ALFREDO

makes 4 servings   prep: 5 min.   cook: 6 min.

The secret to sautéing thinly sliced cutlets is to have both the pan and the oil hot enough to sear the meat—the food should hiss as soon as it hits the pan.

½ cup all-purpose flour

1 tsp. salt

¾ tsp. seasoned pepper

1½ lb. chicken cutlets

2 Tbsp. olive oil

1 cup white wine

Garnish: fresh parsley sprig (optional)

Linguine Alfredo

1. Combine first 3 ingredients in a shallow dish; dredge chicken cutlets in flour mixture.

2. Cook chicken in hot oil in a large skillet over medium-high heat 1 to 2 minutes on each side or until done. Remove from skillet, and keep warm.

3. Add wine to skillet; cook 1 to 2 minutes or until liquid is reduced by half, stirring to loosen particles from bottom of skillet.

4. Arrange cutlets on a serving platter, and drizzle with sauce. Garnish, if desired. Serve with Linguine Alfredo.

Linguine Alfredo

makes 4 servings   prep: 5 min.   cook: 3 min.

1 (10-oz.) container light refrigerated Alfredo sauce

½ cup fresh parsley

½ cup white wine

3 Tbsp. reduced-fat sour cream

1 garlic clove, sliced

1 (8-oz.) package refrigerated linguine

1. Process first 5 ingredients in a blender or food processor until smooth, stopping to scrape down sides.

2. Prepare linguine according to package directions; drain and return to pot. Stir in Alfredo sauce mixture, and serve immediately.

Note: We tested with Buitoni Light Alfredo Sauce.

CHICKEN CAKES WITH CREOLE SAUCE

makes 8 servings   prep: 20 min.   cook: 12 min.   chill: 15 min.   **pictured on page 588**

We reduced the oil and butter in the original recipe and substituted light mayonnaise for the full-fat version.

½	medium-size red bell pepper, diced	1	large egg, lightly beaten
4	green onions, thinly sliced	2	Tbsp. light mayonnaise
1	garlic clove, pressed	1	Tbsp. Creole mustard
3	cups chopped cooked chicken breast	1	tsp. Creole seasoning
1	cup soft breadcrumbs		Creole Sauce

1. Sauté first 3 ingredients in a nonstick skillet coated with cooking spray 4 minutes or until vegetables are tender. Wipe skillet clean.

2. Stir together bell pepper mixture, chicken, and next 5 ingredients in a bowl. Shape chicken mixture into 8 (3½-inch) patties. Cover and chill 15 minutes.

3. Cook patties, in 2 batches, in skillet coated with cooking spray over medium heat 3 minutes on each side or until golden. Serve immediately with Creole Sauce.

Calories 123; Fat: 6.6g (sat 1g, mono 0.3g, poly 0.1g); Protein 3.8g; Fiber 1.9g; Chol 33mg; Iron 0.8mg; Sodium 370mg; Calc 55mg

Creole Sauce

makes 1¼ cups   prep: 5 min.

½	cup light mayonnaise	2	garlic cloves, pressed
½	cup plain nonfat yogurt	1	Tbsp. chopped fresh parsley
3	green onions, sliced	¼	tsp. ground red pepper
2	Tbsp. Creole mustard		

1. Stir together all ingredients until well blended.

Per 2 Tbsp.: Calories 55; Fat 4g (sat 0.6g); Protein 1.1g; Carb 3.3g; Fiber 0.6g; Chol 4.4mg; Iron 0.2mg; Sodium 154mg; Calc 34mg

GARLIC-AND-HERB-STUFFED CHICKEN BREASTS

makes 4 servings   prep: 15 min.   cook: 10 min.   bake: 20 min.

This simple stuffed chicken recipe serves only four, but it can easily be doubled for a larger crowd.

[southern lights]

4	(6-oz.) boneless, skinless chicken breasts	½	cup Italian-seasoned breadcrumbs
1	(8-oz.) container light buttery-garlic-and-herb spreadable cheese	½	cup whole wheat cracker crumbs
		¼	tsp. salt
2	egg whites	¼	tsp. pepper
¼	cup nonfat buttermilk	2	tsp. olive oil

1. Preheat oven to 400°. Place chicken between 2 sheets of heavy-duty plastic wrap, and flatten to a ¼-inch thickness using a meat mallet or rolling pin.

2. Spread cheese evenly over 1 side of each chicken breast. Fold short ends of each chicken breast over center, covering cheese, and secure with wooden picks.

3. Whisk together egg whites and buttermilk in a small bowl. Combine breadcrumbs and next 3 ingredients in a shallow dish. Dip chicken in egg white mixture, and dredge in breadcrumb mixture.

4. Cook chicken breasts in hot oil in a large nonstick skillet 4 to 5 minutes on each side or until chicken breasts are browned. Place chicken on a wire rack, and place wire rack in a jelly-roll pan.

5. Bake at 400° for 20 minutes or until a meat thermometer inserted into the thickest portion of chicken breast registers 170°.

Note: We tested with Alouette Light Garlic & Herbs Spreadable Cheese and Neva Betta Whole Wheat Crackers.

Per serving; Calories 392; Fat 14g (sat 6.2g, mono 2.7g, poly 1.3g); Protein 47.8g; Fiber 1.3g; Chol 129mg; Iron 1.8mg; Sodium 660mg; Calc 93mg

SOUTHERN-STUFFED ROSEMARY CHICKEN

makes 8 servings   prep: 25 min.   bake: 20 min.   cook: 10 min.

2 (6-oz.) packages cornbread stuffing mix

1 large egg, lightly beaten

½ cup finely chopped pecans, toasted

8 boneless, skinless chicken breasts

¼ cup olive oil, divided

1 Tbsp. chopped fresh rosemary

1 tsp. salt

½ tsp. pepper

¼ cup grated Parmesan cheese

1 (8-oz.) package sliced fresh mushrooms

4 green onions, sliced

1 (10¾-oz.) can reduced-fat cream of chicken soup

1 cup chicken broth

Garnish: fresh rosemary sprigs (optional)

1. Preheat oven to 400°. Prepare stuffing mix according to package directions, and let cool. Stir in egg and pecans.

2. Butterfly chicken breasts by making a lengthwise cut in 1 side, cutting to but not through the opposite side; unfold. Spoon stuffing mixture evenly down center of one side of each butterflied chicken breast; fold opposite side over stuffing, and place in a lightly greased baking dish. Stir together 3 Tbsp. olive oil and chopped rosemary; brush evenly over chicken. Sprinkle chicken evenly with salt, pepper, and Parmesan cheese.

3. Bake chicken, uncovered, at 400° for 20 minutes or until done.

4. Sauté mushrooms and onions in remaining 1 Tbsp. oil in a large skillet over medium-high heat 5 minutes or until tender; stir in soup and chicken broth. Reduce heat, and simmer, stirring often, 5 minutes or until thoroughly heated. Spoon mushroom mixture evenly over chicken; garnish, if desired.

Note: We tested with Stove Top Cornbread Stuffing Mix.

SOUTHERN-FRIED STUFFED CHICKEN WITH ROASTED RED PEPPER-AND-VIDALIA ONION GRAVY

makes 4 servings prep: 25 min. cook: 10 min.

4   oz. cream cheese, softened

1   cup dry chicken-flavored stuffing mix

½   cup (2 oz.) finely shredded Romano cheese

½   cup chopped Vidalia onion

¼   cup minced fresh basil

4   large skin-on, boneless chicken breasts

4   bacon slices

1   large egg

1   cup milk

1   cup all-purpose baking mix

2   tsp. Creole seasoning

1   tsp. black pepper

Canola oil

Roasted Red Pepper-and-Vidalia Onion Gravy

1. Stir together first 5 ingredients in a medium bowl. Set aside.

2. Place chicken, skin side down, between 2 sheets of heavy-duty plastic wrap; flatten to ¼-inch thickness, using a mallet or rolling pin.

3. Spread one-fourth of cream cheese mixture on skinless side of each chicken breast half; top with 1 piece of bacon. Roll up chicken, jelly-roll fashion, lifting skin and tucking roll under skin.

4. Whisk together egg and milk in a bowl. Combine baking mix, Creole seasoning, and pepper in a shallow dish. Dip chicken rolls in egg mixture; dredge in baking mix mixture.

5. Pour oil to a depth of 2 inches in a large skillet; heat to 350°. Fry chicken rolls, in batches, 10 to 12 minutes or until dark brown and done, turning chicken rolls often. Drain on a wire rack over paper towels.

6. Spoon ¼ cup Roasted Red Pepper-and-Vidalia Onion Gravy on each of 4 serving plates; top each with 1 chicken roll. Drizzle with remaining gravy.

Roasted Red Pepper-and-Vidalia Onion Gravy

makes 3 cups prep: 20 min. stand: 10 min. cook: 35 min.

1   large Vidalia onion, halved vertically

1   large red bell pepper, halved and seeded

1   Tbsp. olive oil

¼   tsp. kosher salt

3   Tbsp. butter

3   Tbsp. all-purpose flour

2   cups chicken broth

2   tsp. Creole seasoning

2   Tbsp. minced fresh basil

Black pepper to taste

1. Preheat oven to broil. Dice 1 onion half; set aside.

2. Cut remaining onion half into slices. Place onion slices and bell pepper halves, cut sides down, on a baking sheet lined with nonstick aluminum foil; drizzle with oil, and sprinkle with salt.

3. Broil 5 inches from heat about 10 minutes or until bell pepper looks blistered. Place bell pepper halves in a zip-top plastic freezer bag; seal and let stand 10 minutes to loosen skin. Peel bell pepper halves, and dice one half. Reserve diced bell pepper and remaining half. Dice roasted onion, and set aside.

4. Melt butter in a large skillet over medium-high heat. Add reserved diced raw onion, and sauté 10 minutes or until onion begins to brown. Stir in flour; cook, stirring constantly, 5 minutes, or until flour mixture is caramel-colored. Stir in chicken broth and Creole seasoning. Reduce heat to medium, and cook, stirring constantly, until thickened.

5. Process gravy mixture and reserved bell pepper half in a blender until smooth, stopping to scrape down sides.

6. Combine gravy mixture, reserved diced roasted bell pepper, diced roasted onion, basil, and black pepper.

CHICKEN SAUSAGE WITH FENNEL

makes 4 servings   prep: 10 min.   cook: 20 min.

4	boneless, skinless chicken breasts	½	tsp. dried crushed red pepper
1	small onion, minced	¼	tsp. ground nutmeg
3	Tbsp. fine, dry breadcrumbs	4	hoagie rolls, split
1	Tbsp. fennel seeds	¼	cup Dijon mustard
1	tsp. salt		Red onion slices
1	tsp. garlic powder		Plum tomato slices
1	tsp. onion powder		Leaf lettuce

1. Pulse chicken in a food processor 6 times or until ground. Add onion and next 7 ingredients; process 2 minutes. Shape into 8 patties.

2. Cook patties in a lightly greased nonstick skillet 5 minutes on each side or until done.

3. Spread cut sides of rolls evenly with mustard. Place onion and tomato on bottom halves; top each with 2 sausage patties and lettuce. Cover with top halves.

Note: To grill sausage, coat cold food grate with cooking spray; place on grill. Preheat grill to 300° to 350° (medium) heat. Grill patties, covered with grill lid, 5 minutes on each side or until done.

gatherings

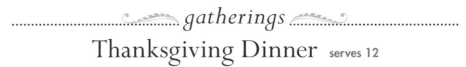

Thanksgiving Dinner serves 12

Roast Turkey With Sage and Thyme

Sausage Dressing (page 850)

***Roasted Apples and Sweet Potatoes** (page 873)

Broccoli-and-Cauliflower Gratin (page 847) ***Layered Macaroni and Cheese** (page 561)

Yeast rolls from frozen dough (such as Sister Schubert's)

Shortcut Carrot Cake (page 219)

*double recipe

ROAST TURKEY WITH SAGE AND THYME

makes 12 servings prep: 30 min. cook: 2 hr., 45 min. stand: 20 min.

- 1 (14-lb.) frozen whole turkey, thawed*
- ¼ cup butter, softened and divided
- ½ tsp. salt
- ½ tsp. pepper
- ¼ cup fresh sage leaves
- 4 fresh thyme sprigs
- 1 pear or apple, halved
- 2 celery ribs, halved
- 1 large onion, halved
- 2 garlic cloves, peeled
- Garnishes: flat-leaf parsley, pecans, Seckel pears, muscadines, fresh sage leaves, fresh thyme sprigs (optional)

1. Preheat oven to 325°. Remove giblets and neck from turkey; discard. Rinse turkey with cold water; pat dry. Loosen skin from turkey breast without totally detaching skin.

2. Stir together 2 Tbsp. butter, salt, and pepper; rub evenly over turkey breast under skin. Carefully place sage leaves and thyme sprigs evenly on each side of breast under skin. Replace skin.

3. Place pear halves, celery ribs, onion halves, and garlic cloves inside cavity. Place turkey, breast side up, on a lightly greased wire rack in an aluminum foil-lined shallow roasting pan. Rub entire turkey evenly with remaining 2 Tbsp. butter.

4. Bake at 325° for 2 hours and 45 minutes to 3 hours and 30 minutes or until a meat thermometer inserted into thigh registers 180°, basting turkey every 30 minutes with pan drippings. (Prevent overcooking turkey by checking for doneness after 2 hours.) Remove turkey from roasting pan, and let stand 20 minutes before slicing. Garnish, if desired.

* 1 (14-lb.) whole fresh turkey may be substituted.

HICKORY-SMOKED BOURBON TURKEY

makes 12 to 14 servings   prep: 30 min.   chill: 48 hr.   soak: 30 min.   cook: 6 hr.   stand: 15 min.

1   (11-lb.) whole turkey, thawed
2   cups maple syrup
1   cup bourbon
1   Tbsp. pickling spice
Hickory wood chunks
1   large carrot, scraped

1   celery rib
1   medium onion, peeled and halved
1   lemon
1   Tbsp. salt
2   tsp. pepper
Garnishes: mixed greens, lemon wedges (optional)

1. Remove giblets and neck from turkey; reserve for another use, if desired. Rinse turkey thoroughly with cold water, and pat dry.

2. Add water to a large stockpot, filling half full; stir in maple syrup, bourbon, and pickling spice. Add turkey and, if needed, additional water to cover. Cover and chill turkey 2 days.

3. Soak hickory wood chunks in fresh water at least 30 minutes. Prepare smoker according to manufacturer's directions, bringing internal temperature to 225° to 250°; maintain temperature for 15 to 20 minutes.

4. Remove turkey from water, discarding water mixture; pat dry. Cut carrot and celery in half crosswise. Stuff cavity of turkey with carrot, celery, and onion. Pierce lemon with a fork; place in neck cavity.

5. Combine salt and pepper; rub mixture over turkey. Fold wings under, and tie legs together with string, if desired.

6. Drain wood chunks, and place on coals. Place water pan in smoker, and add water to depth of fill line. Place turkey in center of lower cooking grate; cover with smoker lid. Smoke turkey, maintaining temperature inside smoker between 225° and 250°, for 6 hours or until a meat thermometer inserted into thickest portion of turkey thigh registers 180°, adding additional water, charcoal, and wood chunks as needed. Remove from smoker, and let stand 15 minutes before slicing. Garnish, if desired.

DEEP-FRIED TURKEY

makes 20 servings   prep: 40 min.   cook: 1 hr.

1   (12- to 15-lb.) turkey
2   Tbsp. ground red pepper (optional)
4   to 5 gal. vegetable oil

Garnishes: fresh sage, parsley, thyme sprigs, kumquats with leaves (optional)

1. Remove giblets and neck from turkey; reserve for another use; Rinse turkey with cold water. Drain cavity well; pat dry with paper towels. Place turkey on fryer rod; allow all liquid to drain from cavity (20 to 30 minutes). Rub outside of turkey with red pepper, if desired.
2. Pour oil into a deep propane turkey fryer 10 to 12 inches from top; heat to 375° over a medium-low flame according to manufacturer's instructions. Carefully lower turkey into hot oil with rod attachment.
3. Fry 1 hour or until a meat thermometer inserted in turkey breast registers 170°. (Keep oil temperature at 340°.) Remove turkey from oil; drain and cool slightly before slicing. Garnish, if desired.

CITRUS-ROSEMARY TURKEY BREAST

makes 8 servings   prep: 20 min.   cook: 2 hr., 30 min.   stand: 10 min.

3   Tbsp. butter, softened and divided
3   garlic cloves, minced
1   (6-lb.) bone-in turkey breast
1   tsp. salt
1   tsp. pepper
1   large orange, sliced

1   large lemon, sliced
4   fresh rosemary sprigs
4   fresh sage leaves
1   tsp. seasoned pepper
1   onion, quartered
2   cups chicken broth

1. Preheat oven to 350°. Stir together 2 Tbsp. butter and garlic. Loosen skin from turkey without detaching it; sprinkle salt and pepper under skin. Rub 2 Tbsp. garlic mixture over meat. Place fruit slices, rosemary, and sage under skin; replace skin.
2. Rub remaining 1 Tbsp. butter over skin; sprinkle with 1 tsp. seasoned pepper. Place turkey breast on a lightly greased rack in a broiling pan. Add onion and chicken broth.
3. Bake at 350° for 1 hour and 30 minutes, basting every 30 minutes. Shield with foil, and bake 1 more hour or until a meat thermometer inserted into thickest breast portion registers 170°. Let stand 10 minutes before slicing. Serve with pan juices.

BOURBON-CRANBERRY TURKEY TENDERLOIN

makes 8 to 10 servings   prep: 15 min.   cook: 15 min.   stand: 1 hr., 15 min.   grill: 20 min.

pictured on page 663

1   (16-oz.) can whole-berry cranberry sauce
⅓   cup firmly packed brown sugar
⅔   cup bourbon
2   Tbsp. orange zest

4   lb. turkey tenderloins
1½ tsp. salt
1   Tbsp. coarsely ground pepper
Garnish: grilled orange slices

1. Preheat grill to 350° to 400° (medium-high) heat. Bring first 4 ingredients to a boil in a saucepan over medium-high heat; reduce heat to medium-low, and simmer 10 minutes or until mixture thickens slightly. Remove from heat, and let stand 30 minutes or to room temperature. Remove ½ cup cranberry mixture; reserve remaining mixture.

2. Rinse tenderloins, and pat dry with paper towels. Brush with ¼ cup cranberry mixture, and let stand at room temperature 30 minutes. Sprinkle with salt and pepper.

3. Grill, 10 to 12 minutes on each side or until a meat thermometer inserted in thickest portion registers 165°, basting occasionally with ¼ cup cranberry mixture. Remove from heat, and let stand 15 minutes before slicing. Serve with reserved cranberry mixture.

Bourbon-Cranberry Roasted Turkey: Substitute 1 (14-lb.) whole fresh turkey for tenderloins. Remove giblets and neck; reserve for another use. Rinse turkey with cold water. Drain cavity well; pat dry with paper towels. Let turkey stand at room temperature 30 minutes. Meanwhile, prepare cranberry mixture as directed in Step 1. Place turkey, breast side up, on a lightly greased wire rack in a roasting pan. If desired, tie ends of legs together with kitchen string; tuck wing tips under. Brush with 2 Tbsp. melted butter, and sprinkle with salt and pepper. Bake at 325° for 3½ hours or until a meat thermometer inserted in thickest portion of thigh registers 170°, brushing with ½ cup cranberry mixture during the last 30 minutes of roasting. (If turkey starts to brown too much, cover loosely with aluminum foil.) Let turkey stand 15 minutes before carving. Serve with reserved cranberry mixture.

NUTTY TURKEY CUTLETS

makes 4 servings   prep: 10 min.   cook: 6 min.

Substitute pork or chicken cutlets for turkey.

[quick]

¾ cup fine, dry breadcrumbs

½ cup pecans

¾ tsp. salt

¾ tsp. pepper

1 (1-lb.) package boneless turkey cutlets

½ cup all-purpose flour

2 large eggs, lightly beaten

3 Tbsp. olive oil

Garnish: chopped fresh parsley (optional)

1. Process breadcrumbs and pecans in a food processor or blender 10 to 15 seconds or until finely ground.

2. Sprinkle ½ tsp. salt and ½ tsp. pepper over cutlets. Combine flour and remaining salt and pepper in a shallow dish or pie plate. Dredge turkey cutlets in flour mixture; dip in eggs, and dredge in breadcrumb mixture.

3. Sauté cutlets in hot oil in a large skillet over medium-high heat 3 minutes on each side or until golden. Remove from skillet, and serve immediately. Garnish, if desired.

OVEN-BARBECUED TURKEY DRUMSTICKS

makes 4 servings   prep: 15 min.   cook: 10 min.   bake: 1 hr., 30 min.   **pictured on page 664**

Turkey drumsticks are a favorite with kids. For family suppers, plan on one drumstick for two youngsters and a drumstick apiece for teenagers or adults.

1½ cups ketchup	2 garlic cloves, pressed
½ cup lite soy sauce	1 bay leaf
¼ cup firmly packed brown sugar	2 tsp. hot sauce
2 tsp. Worcestershire sauce	4 fresh turkey drumsticks (about 3 lb.)

1. Preheat oven to 350°. Stir together first 7 ingredients in a 1-qt. saucepan over medium-high heat. Bring to a boil; reduce heat to low, and simmer, stirring occasionally, 10 minutes.
2. Place drumsticks in an 11- x 7-inch baking dish. Pour 1 cup ketchup mixture evenly over drumsticks. Bake, covered, at 350° for 1 hour; uncover, top with remaining 1 cup sauce, and bake 30 more minutes or until fork-tender.

Note: To make ketchup sauce ahead, prepare as directed in Step 1. Cool sauce, pour into a 1-qt. airtight container, and chill for up to 2 days.

HERB-BLEND TURKEY BURGERS

makes 4 servings   prep: 10 min.   grill: 10 min.

1 lb. lean ground turkey	⅛ tsp. salt
¼ cup chopped fresh basil	4 kaiser rolls, split
2 tsp. lemon zest	Shredded spinach leaves
¾ tsp. minced garlic	Tomato slices

1. Preheat grill to 350° to 400° (medium-high) heat. Combine first 5 ingredients in a large bowl until blended. (Do not overwork meat mixture.) Shape mixture into 4 (5-inch) patties.
2. Grill, covered with grill lid, 5 to 6 minutes on each side or until done.
3. Scoop out soft centers from bottom half of rolls, leaving ¼-inch-thick shells. Place burgers in shells; top evenly with spinach and tomato slices, and cover with roll tops.

TOASTED PECAN, CRANBERRY, AND GORGONZOLA TURKEY BURGERS

makes 6 servings   prep: 15 min.   bake: 8 min.   cook: 12 min.   **pictured on page 664**

Make the Cranberry Mustard right after you warm the buns.

6   honey wheat hamburger buns
½   cup coarsely chopped pecans
1½ lb. lean ground turkey
⅔   cup crumbled Gorgonzola cheese
1   tsp. onion powder

1   tsp. garlic salt
½   tsp. pepper
Cranberry Mustard
2   cups fresh baby spinach

1. Preheat oven to 350°. Wrap buns in aluminum foil; place pecans on a baking sheet.

2. Bake buns and pecans at 350° for 8 minutes. Remove pecans from oven, and set aside; leave hamburger buns in oven.

3. Combine ground turkey and next 4 ingredients in a large bowl. Shape into 6 (¾-inch-thick) patties.

4. Cook patties in a large skillet coated with cooking spray over medium heat 6 minutes on each side or until done.

5. Remove buns from oven. Spread 2 heaping tsp. Cranberry Mustard on each side of bun halves. Arrange half of spinach leaves evenly on bottom halves; top with turkey patties, toasted pecans, remaining spinach leaves, and remaining bun halves. Serve with remaining Cranberry Mustard, if desired.

Cranberry Mustard

makes about ¾ cup   prep: 5 min.

½   cup whole-berry cranberry sauce
⅓   cup Dijon mustard

⅛   tsp. dried crushed red pepper

1. Stir together all ingredients.

KENTUCKY HOT BROWN CORNBREAD SKILLET

makes 4 servings   prep: 15 min.   bake: 16 min.   cook: 4 min.

1   (6-oz.) package country or buttermilk
     cornbread mix
½   cup canned French fried onions
½   cup milk
1   large egg, lightly beaten
¼   cup butter
3   Tbsp. all-purpose flour
2   cups milk
1   tsp. Worcestershire sauce

½   tsp. salt
¼   tsp. ground red pepper
¼   tsp. freshly ground black pepper
1½   cups freshly grated Parmesan cheese, divided
2   cups chopped cooked turkey
1   cup real bacon pieces, divided
1   large tomato, sliced*
Chopped fresh parsley (optional)
Freshly grated Parmesan cheese (optional)

1. Preheat oven to 425°. Generously grease a 10-inch cast-iron skillet, and heat in a 425° oven 5 minutes.

2. Stir together cornbread mix and next 3 ingredients, and spoon evenly into hot skillet.

3. Bake at 425° for 8 to 10 minutes or just until light golden brown and set.

4. Melt butter in a medium saucepan over medium heat. Whisk in flour, and cook, whisking constantly, 1 minute. Gradually whisk in 2 cups milk, and cook, whisking constantly, 3 to 5 minutes or until mixture is smooth and thickened. Stir in Worcestershire sauce, next 3 ingredients, and ½ cup grated Parmesan cheese until blended. Remove from heat, and keep warm.

5. Spoon turkey evenly over cooked cornbread mixture in skillet, and top with warm Parmesan sauce. Sprinkle with remaining 1 cup Parmesan cheese and ½ cup bacon pieces.

6. Bake at 425° for 8 to 12 minutes or until bubbly and lightly browned. Top with tomato slices and remaining ½ cup bacon pieces. Sprinkle with parsley and Parmesan cheese, if desired. Serve immediately.

* 2 cups quartered grape tomatoes may be substituted.

CORNISH HENS WITH SAVORY-SWEET STUFFING

makes 2 servings   prep: 20 min.   bake: 1 hr., 30 min.   stand: 5 min.

2   (1½- to 1¾-lb.) Cornish game hens
1½ tsp. salt, divided
½   tsp. pepper, divided
1   Granny Smith or Golden Delicious apple
1   cup butternut squash, peeled, seeded, and cut into ½-inch cubes
1   cup coarsely chopped fennel, white part only
¼   cup dried cranberries
1   medium shallot, coarsely chopped
1   tsp. olive oil

1. Preheat oven to 350°. Rinse hens with cold water; pat dry with paper towels.

2. Combine 1 tsp. salt and ¼ tsp. pepper. Sprinkle cavities and outside of hens evenly with salt mixture. Set hens aside.

3. Peel apple, and cut into 1-inch cubes.

4. Combine apple, remaining ½ tsp. salt, remaining ¼ tsp. pepper, squash, and next 4 ingredients in a medium bowl, tossing to coat.

5. Stuff hen cavities with apple mixture; place extra mixture in a lightly greased 11- x 7-inch baking dish. Place hens on top of apple mixture; cover tightly with aluminum foil.

6. Bake at 350° for 45 minutes; remove foil, and bake 45 more minutes or until meat juices run clear and a meat thermometer inserted into thigh registers 180° and internal temperature in center of stuffing registers 165°. Remove from oven; let stand 5 minutes before serving.

CORNISH HENS WITH SPICY PECAN-CORNBREAD STUFFING

makes 8 servings   prep: 15 min.   cook: 55 min.

Spicy Pecan-Cornbread Stuffing
8   (1 to 1½-lb.) Cornish hens
Skewers
Melted butter

1. Preheat oven to 450°. Spoon about 1 cup Spicy Pecan-Cornbread Stuffing into each hen; close opening with skewers. Place hens, breast side up, in a roasting pan. Brush with butter.

2. Bake, covered, at 450° for 5 minutes. Reduce heat to 350°, and bake 50 more minutes or until a meat thermometer inserted in stuffing registers 165°. Remove skewers, and serve.

Spicy Pecan-Cornbread Stuffing

makes 8 servings   prep: 20 min.   bake: 40 min.   cook: 8 min.

10 bacon slices	1½ cups Spicy Pecans
1⅓ cups yellow cornmeal	1 large onion, diced
1⅓ cups all-purpose flour	2 Tbsp. vegetable oil
2 tsp. baking powder	3 celery ribs, diced
1 tsp. garlic powder	1 red bell pepper, chopped
¾ tsp. baking soda	¾ cup diced mushrooms
½ tsp. salt	2 tsp. dried thyme
½ to 2 cups chicken broth	2 tsp. dried sage
2 large eggs	3 or 4 large eggs, lightly beaten
2 Tbsp. butter	

1. Preheat oven to 400°. Cook bacon in a 9-inch cast-iron skillet until crisp. Remove bacon; drain on paper towels. Reserve 2 Tbsp. drippings in skillet. Keep skillet warm. Crumble bacon.
2. Combine cornmeal and next 5 ingredients in a large bowl. Whisk together broth, 2 eggs, and butter; add to dry ingredients, stirring just until moistened. Pour into hot skillet with drippings.
3. Bake at 400° for 25 minutes or until golden around edges. Crumble cornbread onto a baking sheet; reduce over temperature to 350°, and bake, stirring occasionally, 15 minutes or until lightly toasted. Transfer cornbread to a large bowl, and stir in crumbled bacon and Spicy Pecans.
4. Sauté diced onion in hot oil in a large skillet over medium-high heat 5 minutes or until tender. Add diced celery, chopped bell pepper, and diced mushrooms, and cook 3 minutes; stir in thyme and sage. Stir vegetable mixture into cornbread mixture; stir in lightly beaten eggs.

Spicy Pecans

makes 1½ cups   prep: 10 min.   cook: 8 min.   bake: 8 min.

2 Tbsp. brown sugar	½ tsp. chili powder
2 Tbsp. orange juice concentrate	¼ tsp. pepper
1½ Tbsp. butter	1½ cups coarsely chopped pecans
½ tsp. salt	

1. Preheat oven to 350°. Cook first 6 ingredients in a skillet over medium-high heat, stirring until brown sugar dissolves. Remove from heat, and stir in pecans. Transfer to a lightly greased baking sheet. Bake at 350° for 8 minutes or until toasted. Cool; store in an airtight container.

SALADS & DRESSINGS

"It's difficult to think anything but pleasant thoughts while eating a homegrown tomato." —Lewis Grizzard

LANNY'S SALAD WITH CANDIED PUMPKIN SEEDS

makes 8 servings   prep: 5 min.

Use a fork to crumble queso fresco, which adds an authentic flavor experience to this salad. If sweet baby greens are not available, substitute Bibb or Boston lettuce. Chef Lanny Lancarte, II of Lanny's Alta Cocina Mexicana in Fort Worth, Texas, created this recipe.

2   (5-oz.) bags sweet baby greens, thoroughly washed

Citrus-Cumin Dressing

1   cup crumbled queso fresco (about 4 oz.)

¾   cup Candied Pumpkin Seeds

1. Toss greens with Citrus-Cumin Dressing; arrange on a serving platter. Sprinkle evenly with queso fresco and Candied Pumpkin Seeds. Serve immediately.

Note: We tested with Fresh Express Sweet Baby Greens.

Candied Pumpkin Seeds

makes about 4¾ cups   prep: 10 min.   cook: 8 min.   bake: 6 min.   cool: 30 min.

Health food stores, Hispanic markets, and specialty grocery stores carry pumpkin seeds. Toast in a skillet until puffed, but watch them closely and don't brown or they will taste burned.

2   cups raw pumpkin seeds*

½   cup granulated sugar

½   cup firmly packed light brown sugar

1   Tbsp. paprika

¾   tsp. salt

3   Tbsp. fresh orange juice

1. Preheat oven to 350°. Cook pumpkin seeds in a medium nonstick skillet over medium heat, stirring often, 8 to 10 minutes or until puffed. (Do not brown.) Transfer to a medium bowl.
2. Combine granulated sugar and next 3 ingredients.
3. Toss pumpkin seeds with orange juice. Stir pumpkin seeds into sugar mixture, tossing to coat. Spread in a single layer on a parchment paper-lined jelly-roll pan.
4. Bake at 350° for 6 minutes, stirring once. Cool in pan on a wire rack 30 minutes. Store in an airtight container up to 2 days.

* 2 cups pecan halves may be substituted. Cook as directed in Step 1 until lightly toasted. (Pecans will not puff.)

Citrus-Cumin Dressing

makes ½ cup prep: 10 min.

3   Tbsp. fresh orange juice
2   Tbsp. fresh lemon juice
½   tsp. sugar
½   tsp. ground cumin

¼   tsp. salt
¼   tsp. pepper
⅓   cup olive oil

1. Whisk together first 6 ingredients in a small bowl; add oil in a slow, steady stream, whisking constantly until smooth. Use immediately, or cover and chill up to 3 days. Whisk before serving.

TEXAS PECAN-AND-AVOCADO SALAD

makes 8 servings prep: 15 min.

1   head Bibb lettuce
2   avocados, thinly sliced
1   red bell pepper, thinly sliced

1   yellow bell pepper, thinly sliced
½   cup chopped toasted pecans
Tangy Dijon Dressing

1. Arrange lettuce leaves on a serving platter. Top evenly with avocados and bell pepper slices; sprinkle with pecans. Drizzle with desired amount of dressing.

Tangy Dijon Dressing

makes about ⅔ cup prep: 5 min.

⅓   cup olive oil
2   Tbsp. lemon juice
1   Tbsp. sugar

2   tsp. Dijon mustard
⅛   tsp. salt
⅛   tsp. pepper

1. Whisk together olive oil, lemon juice, 2 Tbsp. water, and next 4 ingredients. Store in an airtight container in the refrigerator up to 1 week.

GARDEN SALAD WITH TARRAGON-MUSTARD VINAIGRETTE

makes 6 servings   prep: 15 min.

This quick side salad requires just a few staple ingredients and some fresh herbs. The dressing also tastes great tossed with diced roasted sweet potatoes.

8   cups torn green leaf and red leaf lettuce

2   Tbsp. fresh minced chives

1   Tbsp. fresh minced tarragon

Tarragon-Mustard Vinaigrette

1. Toss together lettuce, chives, and tarragon in a large bowl. Drizzle with Tarragon-Mustard Vinaigrette just before serving.

Tarragon-Mustard Vinaigrette

makes about ¼ cup   prep: 10 min.

1   Tbsp. fresh lemon juice

1   Tbsp. Dijon mustard

½   tsp. salt

3   Tbsp. extra virgin olive oil

2   tsp. finely chopped fresh tarragon*

1. Whisk together first 3 ingredients in a small bowl until blended. Add oil in a slow, steady stream, whisking vigorously until well blended. Stir in fresh tarragon.

* Fresh basil or flat-leaf parsley may be substituted.

Make Your Own Vinaigrette

A simple vinaigrette requires very few ingredients and features fresh, seasonal herbs. The secret is to balance the acidic ingredient, emulsifier, and oil. In Tarragon-Mustard Vinaigrette, lemon juice is used as the acid and mustard as the emulsifier. By slowly whisking in the olive oil, the flavors disperse throughout the vinaigrette. Create your own flavor profile by using the proportion 1 part acid to 2 parts oil. Try balsamic vinegar or apple cider vinegar for the acid; flavored mustard for the emulsifier; any fresh herb such as parsley, basil, or rosemary; and canola oil or olive oil. You'll find these are a cinch to make and will keep in an airtight container in the refrigerator up to one week.

SOUTHERN SPINACH SALAD WITH CHEESE GRITS CROUTONS AND VIDALIA ONION-BALSAMIC VINAIGRETTE

makes 4 servings   prep: 10 min.   cook: 5 min.   chill: 2 hr.   fry: 20 min.

1   (14-oz.) can chicken broth

½   cup uncooked quick-cooking grits

1   (3-oz.) package cream cheese, cubed

½   cup grated Parmesan cheese

½   cup all-purpose flour

2   Tbsp. butter

2   Tbsp. olive oil

1   (6-oz.) bag baby spinach, thoroughly washed

1   cup cherry or grape tomatoes, halved

Vidalia Onion-Balsamic Vinaigrette

6   bacon slices, cooked and crumbled

1. Bring chicken broth to a boil over medium-high heat in a medium saucepan. Gradually stir in grits; reduce heat to low, and simmer, stirring constantly, 5 minutes or until thickened. Remove from heat. Stir in cream cheese and Parmesan cheese until melted.

2. Pour grits mixture into an 8-inch square pan coated with cooking spray; spread evenly. Chill 2 hours or until firm.

3. Cut grits into 1-inch cubes with a wet knife. Dredge cubes in flour.

4. Melt 1 Tbsp. butter in a large skillet over medium heat; add 1 Tbsp. oil. Fry half of cubes in hot olive oil and butter 10 minutes, turning once to lightly brown. Repeat procedure with remaining cubes, 1 Tbsp. butter, and 1 Tbsp. oil.

5. Place baby spinach in a large serving bowl; add halved cherry tomatoes. Drizzle Vidalia Onion-Balsamic Vinaigrette evenly over salad, and toss to coat. Add grits croutons, and sprinkle evenly with crumbled bacon.

Vidalia Onion-Balsamic Vinaigrette

makes about 1 cup   prep: 10 min.

2   Tbsp. balsamic vinegar

2   Tbsp. honey

1   tsp. Dijon mustard

½   tsp. salt

¼   tsp. pepper

3   Tbsp. finely chopped Vidalia onion

4   Tbsp. olive oil

1. Stir together first 5 ingredients in a small bowl; stir in onion. Whisk in olive oil, 1 Tbsp. at a time, until well blended.

TANGY FETA DRESSING OVER ICEBERG

makes 4 servings   prep: 10 min.

½   cup mayonnaise

½   (4-oz.) package crumbled feta cheese

2   Tbsp. chopped fresh parsley

1   to 2 Tbsp. fresh lemon juice

Pepper to taste

5   cups shredded iceberg lettuce

1. Stir together mayonnaise, feta cheese, parsley, and lemon juice. Stir in pepper to taste. Spoon dressing over lettuce.

TOMATO-FETA LETTUCE SALAD

makes 4 servings   prep: 15 min.   chill: 1 hr.

If you make this salad a day ahead, add 1 extra chopped tomato just before serving. Oil-cured ripe black olives are sold on the pickle aisle.

¼   cup Greek dressing

2   Tbsp. chopped fresh parsley

1   (4-oz.) package feta cheese

6   plum tomatoes, chopped

½   cup sliced oil-cured ripe black olives

¼   cup chopped red onion

1   small head iceberg lettuce

1   small head romaine lettuce

1. Stir together dressing and parsley.

2. Break feta cheese into small pieces. Do not crumble. Stir in feta, tomato, olives, and red onion. Cover and chill at least 1 hour or up to 2 days.

3. Tear lettuces into bite-size pieces; toss together. Arrange lettuces evenly on 4 serving plates, and top evenly with chilled tomato mixture. Serve immediately.

Note: We tested with Ken's Steak House Greek dressing.

APPLE-PEAR SALAD WITH LEMON-POPPYSEED DRESSING

makes 6 to 8 servings prep: 10 min. **pictured on page 667**

If desired, an equal amount of shredded Swiss cheese may be substituted for shaved.

1 (16-oz.) package romaine lettuce, thoroughly washed
1 (6-oz.) block Swiss cheese, shaved
1 cup roasted, salted cashews
½ cup sweetened dried cranberries
1 large apple, thinly sliced
1 large pear, thinly sliced
   Lemon-Poppy Seed Dressing

1. Toss together first 6 ingredients in a large bowl; serve with Lemon-Poppy Seed Dressing

Lemon-Poppy Seed Dressing

makes 1¼ cups prep: 10 min.

⅔ cup light olive oil
½ cup sugar
⅓ cup fresh lemon juice
1½ Tbsp. poppy seeds
2 tsp. finely chopped onion
1 tsp. Dijon mustard
½ tsp. salt

1. Process all ingredients in a blender until smooth. Store in an airtight container in the refrigerator up to 1 week; serve at room temperature.

SUFFOLK WALDORF SALAD

makes 6 servings prep: 10 min. chill: 30 min.

We've updated this classic with dried cherries and spinach in place of raisins and lettuce. Apples are key, but make sure you use a crisp snacking variety such as the heart-shaped Gala.

⅓ cup light mayonnaise
2 Tbsp. peanut butter
1 tsp. lemon juice
2 large Gala apples, chopped
1 celery rib, chopped
¼ cup dried cherries, chopped
1 cup spinach leaves
¼ cup pecans, chopped

1. Whisk together first 3 ingredients in a large bowl. Stir in apples, celery, and cherries; toss to coat. Cover and chill 30 minutes. Arrange spinach leaves on a serving platter; top with chilled apple mixture, and sprinkle evenly with pecans.

MUSHROOM, APPLE, AND GOAT CHEESE SALAD

makes 6 to 8 servings   prep: 20 min.   bake: 8 min.   cook: 6 min.   cool: 15 min.

If you receive candied or spiced nuts as a holiday gift, try them on this salad for a special touch. To splurge, use a variety of mushrooms such as shiitake, portobello, oyster, or enoki. Often grocers carry a gourmet mushroom mix. Standard white mushrooms will yield tasty results too.

½   cup walnut halves
1   Tbsp. butter
1   lb. assorted mushrooms, trimmed and coarsely chopped

Honey-Balsamic Vinaigrette, divided
1   (4-oz.) package arugula, thoroughly washed
1   large Cameo apple, thinly sliced
3   oz. goat cheese, crumbled

1. Preheat oven to 350°. Place walnuts in a single layer on a baking sheet.

2. Bake at 350° for 8 to 10 minutes or until toasted.

3. Melt butter in a large skillet over medium-high heat; add mushrooms, and sauté 6 minutes or until tender. Stir in 2 Tbsp. Honey-Balsamic Vinaigrette. Remove from heat, and let cool 15 minutes.

4. Toss together arugula, apple, mushrooms, and desired amount of Honey-Balsamic Vinaigrette. Transfer to a serving dish, and sprinkle with toasted walnuts and goat cheese.

Honey-Balsamic Vinaigrette

makes about 1 cup   prep: 10 min.

Make this vinaigrette up to two days ahead, and refrigerate in an airtight container. Allow it to come to room temperature, and whisk before serving.

½   cup olive oil
⅓   cup balsamic vinegar
1   Tbsp. chopped fresh parsley

1   Tbsp. chopped fresh thyme
2   Tbsp. honey
Salt and pepper to taste

1. Whisk together first 5 ingredients until blended. Whisk in salt and pepper to taste.

FIELD GREENS WITH ROASTED BACON-WRAPPED PEARS

makes 4 servings   prep: 15 min.   bake: 10 min.

Drizzled with the sweet-sharp taste of Apple-Ginger Vinaigrette, this salad highlights the savory side of fall fruits.

12 ready-to-serve bacon slices

3 large pears, peeled and quartered

6 cups mixed salad greens

⅔ cup pecans, toasted

⅔ cup shaved Parmesan cheese

Apple-Ginger Vinaigrette

1. Preheat oven to 350°. Wrap 1 slice of bacon around each pear quarter, and secure with a wooden pick. Place pear quarters on a wire rack in a 15- x 10-inch jelly-roll pan.

2. Bake pears at 350° for 10 minutes.

3. Arrange salad greens on 4 serving plates, and sprinkle evenly with pecans and Parmesan cheese. Place 3 pear quarters on each salad, and serve with Apple-Ginger Vinaigrette.

Note: We tested with Oscar Mayer Ready to Serve Bacon.

Apple-Ginger Vinaigrette

makes about 2 cups   prep: 10 min.

½ cup apple jelly, melted

⅓ cup cider vinegar

1 Tbsp. Dijon mustard

2 Tbsp. light brown sugar

2 Tbsp. chopped fresh chives

2 tsp. grated ginger

¼ tsp. salt

1 cup vegetable oil

1. Whisk together first 7 ingredients; gradually whisk in oil until well blended.

Cinco de Mayo Celebration serves 12

*Citrus-Avocado Salad With Tex-Mex Vinaigrette

*Tortilla-Crusted Pork (page 534)

Spanish rice **Smashed Pinto Beans** (page 841)

Flour tortillas

Sugar-and-Spice Fruit Tamales (page 350)

*double recipe

CITRUS-AVOCADO SALAD WITH TEX-MEX VINAIGRETTE

makes 6 to 8 servings prep: 10 min.

Two bags of any lettuce blend can be substituted for Bibb lettuce. Pomegranate seeds add a unique crunch.

3	heads Bibb lettuce, torn	**Tex-Mex Vinaigrette**
2	avocados, sliced	**Garnishes: pomegranate seeds, fresh cilantro**
1	(24-oz.) jar refrigerated orange and grapefruit sections, drained	**sprigs (optional)**

1. Combine first 3 ingredients in a salad bowl. Toss with Tex-Mex Vinaigrette. Garnish, if desired. Serve immediately.

Note: We tested with Del Monte SunFresh Citrus Salad for orange and grapefruit sections.

Tex-Mex Vinaigrette

makes ⅔ cup prep: 10 min.

½	cup fresh orange juice	½	tsp. salt
¼	cup fresh lime juice	½	tsp. pepper
1	tsp. brown sugar	⅓	cup olive oil
½	tsp. ground cumin		

1. Combine first 6 ingredients in a small bowl. Whisk in oil in a slow, steady stream, whisking until smooth. Use immediately, or cover and chill up to 3 days. Whisk before serving.

AVOCADO FRUIT SALAD

makes 6 cups   prep: 15 min.   chill: 1 hr.   **pictured on page 666**

You can prepare this salad a day ahead, but don't cut up the avocado or add garnishes until just before you serve it.

1 (24-oz.) jar refrigerated orange and grapefruit sections, rinsed, drained, and patted dry

1 (24-oz.) jar refrigerated tropical mixed fruit in light syrup, rinsed, drained, and patted dry

2 cups cubed fresh cantaloupe

1 medium-size ripe avocado, halved and cut into chunks

¼ cup chopped fresh mint

2 Tbsp. lime juice

Garnishes: light sour cream, crushed pistachios (optional)

1. Toss together first 6 ingredients. Cover and chill 1 hour. Garnish, if desired.

Note: We tested with Del Monte SunFresh Citrus Salad and Del Monte SunFresh Tropical Mixed Fruit in Light Syrup With Passion Fruit Juice.

Note: Nutritional analysis does not include garnish.

Per 1 cup: Calories 166; Fat 4.7g (sat 0.7g, mono 2.8g, poly 0.6g); Protein 1.9g; Fiber 3.5g; Iron 1.3mg; Sodium 33mg; Calc 66mg

How To Remove Pomegranate Seeds

First, cut off the crown of the pomegranate. Then, using a small paring knife, score the outer layer of skin into sections. Working with the pomegranate fully submerged in a large bowl of water, break apart sections along scored lines. Roll out the seeds with your fingers. (The seeds will sink to the bottom, while the white membrane will float to the top.) Remove and discard the membrane with a slotted spoon. Pour the seed mixture through a fine wire-mesh strainer. Pat seeds dry with paper towels.

FRUIT SALAD WITH BLACKBERRY-BASIL VINAIGRETTE

makes 6 servings   prep: 10 min.   **pictured on page 669**

Look for refrigerated jars of sliced mango and pink grapefruit segments in the produce section of the supermarket.

test kitchen favorite

8   cups gourmet mixed salad greens
1½ cups sliced mango
1½ cups pink grapefruit segments
1½ cups sliced fresh strawberries

1   cup fresh blackberries
1   large avocado, sliced
Blackberry-Basil Vinaigrette

1. Place salad greens and next 5 ingredients in a large bowl, and gently toss. Serve immediately with Blackberry-Basil Vinaigrette.

Blackberry-Basil Vinaigrette

makes 1 cup   prep: 5 min.

½   (10-oz.) jar seedless blackberry preserves
¼   cup red wine vinegar
6   fresh basil leaves
1   garlic clove, sliced

½   tsp. salt
½   tsp. seasoned pepper
¾   cup vegetable oil

1. Pulse blackberry preserves, red wine vinegar, and next 4 ingredients in a blender 2 or 3 times until blended. With blender running, pour vegetable oil through food chute in a slow, steady stream; process until smooth.

NEW AMBROSIA WITH BUTTERMILK-COCONUT DRESSING

makes 6 servings   prep: 30 min.   chill: 1 hr.

Matt Lee and Ted Lee in their cookbook, The Lee Bros. Southern Cookbook *(W.W. Norton & Co., 2006), created this recipe.*

2   large ruby red grapefruit, peeled and sectioned
2   large navel oranges, peeled and sectioned
3   celery ribs, chopped (about ¾ cup)
2   large avocados, cut into 1-inch cubes
1   large cucumber, peeled, seeded, and chopped (about 1½ cups)

1   jalapeño pepper, seeded and minced
½   cup chopped fresh basil
Buttermilk-Coconut Dressing
1   (5-oz.) package arugula, thoroughly washed
Garnish: toasted sweetened flaked coconut

1. Combine first 7 ingredients in a large bowl. Pour Buttermilk-Coconut Dressing over grapefruit mixture, tossing to coat. Cover and chill 1 hour.

2. Arrange arugula evenly on 6 salad plates. Toss grapefruit mixture, and place on arugula using a slotted spoon. Garnish, if desired.

Buttermilk-Coconut Dressing

makes about 1 cup   prep: 10 min.

1   garlic clove
1   tsp. kosher salt
⅔   cup buttermilk
2   Tbsp. fresh lime juice

1   Tbsp. plus 1 tsp. finely chopped fresh tarragon
1   Tbsp. plus 1 tsp. sweetened shredded coconut
1   Tbsp. extra virgin olive oil
½   tsp. freshly ground pepper

1. Place peeled garlic clove on a cutting board with salt. Smash garlic and salt together using flat side of a knife to make a paste.

2. Whisk together smashed garlic and remaining ingredients. Cover and chill until ready to use.

GRILLED PEACH-AND-MOZZARELLA SALAD

makes 4 servings   prep: 25 min.   grill: 10 min.   **pictured on page 665**

5   peaches (not white)

3   green onions, sliced

¼   cup chopped fresh cilantro

3   Tbsp. honey

1   tsp. salt

1   tsp. lime zest

½   cup fresh lime juice

¾   tsp. ground cumin

¾   tsp. chili powder

1½ Tbsp. tequila (optional)

⅓   cup olive oil

1   (6-oz.) package watercress or baby arugula, thoroughly washed

¾   lb. fresh mozzarella, cut into 16 (¼-inch) slices

Garnish: fresh cilantro sprigs

1. Peel and chop 1 peach. Cut remaining 4 peaches into 28 (¼-inch-thick) rounds, cutting through stem and bottom ends. (Cut peaches inward from sides, cutting each side just until you reach the pit. Discard pits.) Process chopped peach, green onions, next 7 ingredients, and, if desired, tequila in a food processor 10 to 15 seconds or until smooth. Add oil, and pulse 3 to 4 times or until thoroughly combined.

2. Coat cold cooking grate of grill with cooking spray, and place on grill. Preheat grill to 350° to 400° (medium-high) heat. Brush both sides of peach rounds with ⅓ cup peach dressing. Grill peach rounds, covered with grill lid, 3 to 5 minutes on each side or until grill marks appear.

3. Arrange watercress evenly on 4 plates. Alternately layer 4 grilled peach rounds and 4 cheese slices over watercress on each plate. Top each with 3 more peach rounds. Drizzle with remaining peach dressing. Garnish, if desired.

Grilled Peach-and-Feta Salad: Preheat oven to 350°. Arrange ¼ cup pecans, chopped, in a single layer in a shallow pan. Bake 8 to 10 minutes or until toasted and fragrant, stirring after 5 minutes. Reduce peaches from 5 to 4, and reduce salt to ½ tsp. Substitute 8 cups loosely packed Bibb lettuce leaves (about 6 oz.; 1 to 2 heads of lettuce) for watercress and ¼ cup crumbled feta cheese for mozzarella cheese. Peel and chop 1 peach. Cut each of remaining 3 peaches into 8 wedges. Proceed with recipe as directed in Steps 2 through 4, decreasing grilling time for peach wedges to 2 to 3 minutes on each side or until grill marks appear. Divide Bibb lettuce and 4 cooked bacon slices, halved crosswise, among 4 plates or shallow bowls. Top with grilled peach wedges. Sprinkle with feta cheese and pecans. Serve with dressing. Makes 4 servings; Prep: 25 min., Bake: 10 min., Grill: 6 min.

Note: You can also use a grill pan to get those beautiful grill marks on the peaches.

PICKLED PEACH SALAD

makes 6 to 8 servings   prep: 10 min.   cook: 5 min.   chill: 8 hr.

1   (25.5-oz.) jar spiced pickled peaches*
1   (3-oz.) package lemon-flavored gelatin
½   cup orange juice
1   (15-oz.) jar pitted Royal Ann cherries in light syrup, drained

1   cup chopped pecans
Bibb lettuce leaves (optional)
1   cup whipping cream
1   Tbsp. mayonnaise
Garnish: fresh cranberries (optional)

1. Drain pickled peaches, reserving 1 cup liquid in a saucepan. Coarsely chop peaches.

2. Bring reserved 1 cup liquid to a boil; remove from heat. Stir in gelatin, stirring 2 minutes or until gelatin dissolves. Stir in orange juice and ½ cup water. Stir in chopped pickled peaches, cherries, and pecans.

3. Spoon mixture into a lightly greased 4½-cup ring mold. Cover and chill 8 hours or until firm. Unmold salad onto Bibb lettuce leaves, if desired, or onto a platter or serving dish.

4. Beat whipping cream at high speed with an electric mixer until soft peaks form; fold in mayonnaise. Serve salad with whipped cream mixture. Garnish, if desired.

* 2 (15-oz.) cans harvest spice sliced peaches may be substituted for spiced pickled peaches. Proceed as directed, using a 5½-cup mold.

Note: We tested with Oregon Fruit Products Pitted Light Sweet Royal Anne Cherries in Light Syrup.

make ahead

RASPBERRY-TOMATO ASPIC

makes 10 servings   prep: 15 min.   cook: 5 min.   stand: 1 min.   chill: 8 hr.   **pictured on page 672**

Laced with rosemary and mint, this aspic offers a unique blend of sweet-and-savory flavors that pairs perfectly with Chicken or Shrimp Salad.

make ahead

1⅔ cups tomato juice

2 Tbsp. sugar

2 Tbsp. finely chopped fresh mint

2 Tbsp. red wine vinegar

2 Tbsp. fresh lemon juice

½ bay leaf

⅛ tsp. crushed dried rosemary

1 envelope unflavored gelatin

½ cup cold water

1 (3-oz.) package raspberry-flavored gelatin

Garnishes: fresh mint sprigs, lemon slices

Chicken or Shrimp Salad

1. Bring tomato juice and next 6 ingredients to a boil in a large saucepan; reduce heat, and simmer 5 minutes. Pour tomato juice mixture through a wire-mesh strainer into a large mixing bowl, discarding solids.

2. Sprinkle unflavored gelatin over ½ cup cold water; let stand 1 minute. Stir softened gelatin mixture into tomato juice mixture, stirring until gelatin dissolves.

3. Prepare raspberry-flavored gelatin according to package directions; do not chill. Add to tomato juice mixture, stirring until combined. Pour mixture into 10 (6-oz.) punch cups; chill 8 hours or until firm. Garnish, if desired. Serve with Chicken or Shrimp Salad.

Chicken Salad

makes 10 servings   prep: 15 min.

6 cups chopped cooked chicken

1¼ cups mayonnaise

6 thinly sliced green onions

3 celery ribs, diced

Salt and pepper to taste

¼ cup chopped pecans (optional)

1. Stir together chicken, mayonnaise, sliced green onions, celery, and salt and pepper to taste. Sprinkle with chopped pecans, if desired.

Shrimp Salad

makes 10 servings   prep: 15 min.

6   cups chopped cooked shrimp

1¼ cups mayonnaise

6   thinly sliced green onions

3   celery ribs, diced

3   tsp. lemon zest

½   tsp. ground red pepper

Salt and black pepper to taste

1. Stir together shrimp, mayonnaise, green onions, celery, lemon zest, red pepper, and salt and pepper to taste.

SUCCOTASH SALAD

makes 6 servings   prep: 20 min.   cook: 23 min.   pictured on page 670

1   cup fresh butter beans

2   cups fresh corn kernels (3 large ears)

3   Tbsp. canola oil, divided

2   Tbsp. fresh lemon juice

3   Tbsp. chopped fresh chives

½   tsp. hot sauce

¼   tsp. salt

¼   tsp. pepper

1. Cook butter beans in boiling salted water to cover 20 minutes or until tender; drain.

2. Sauté corn in 1 Tbsp. hot oil in a small skillet over medium-high heat 2 to 3 minutes or until crisp-tender.

3. Whisk together lemon juice, next 4 ingredients, and remaining 2 Tbsp. oil in a large bowl; stir in butter beans and corn. Serve immediately, or cover and chill up to 3 days.

Per serving: Calories 239; Fat 8.2g (sat 0.6g, mono 4.4g, poly 2.5g); Protein 9.1g; Fiber 8.7g; Iron 2.2mg; Sodium 112mg; Calc 30mg

southern lights

HAM-AND-FIELD PEA SALAD

makes 8 servings   prep: 20 min.   cool: 1 hr.   chill: 8 hr.   cook: 4 min.

Combining a variety of field peas, such as black-eyed peas, speckled butter beans, and lady peas, gives additional color and texture to this tasty salad. We stirred in bits of sautéed ham just before serving, but it's equally good without.

3 cups fresh or frozen assorted field peas	¼ cup vegetable oil
¼ cup sugar	1 green bell pepper, diced
¼ cup cider vinegar	½ small red onion, diced
2 garlic cloves, minced	1 celery rib, diced
1 tsp. hot sauce	1 cup chopped ham
¾ tsp. salt	1 tsp. vegetable oil
¾ tsp. pepper	

1. Prepare peas according to package directions; drain and let cool 1 hour.

2. Whisk together sugar and next 5 ingredients in a large bowl. Add ¼ cup oil in a slow, steady stream, whisking constantly until smooth. Add cooked field peas, bell pepper, onion, and celery, tossing to coat; cover and chill 8 hours.

3. Sauté ham in 1 tsp. hot oil in a small skillet over medium-high heat 4 to 5 minutes or until lightly browned. Stir into pea mixture just before serving.

FRESH CORN SALAD

makes 6 cups   prep: 15 min.   cook: 3 min.   chill: 2 hr.

This recipe doubles easily for a crowd.

5 large ears white corn	½ tsp. pepper
¼ cup sugar	1 medium-size red onion, diced
¼ cup cider vinegar	1 medium-size red bell pepper, diced
¼ cup olive oil	¼ cup coarsely chopped fresh parsley
½ tsp. salt	

1. Cook corn in boiling salted water in a large stockpot 3 to 4 minutes; drain. Plunge corn into ice water to stop the cooking process; drain. Cut kernels from cobs.

2. Whisk together ¼ cup sugar and next 4 ingredients in a large bowl; add corn, onion, bell pepper, and parsley, tossing to coat. Cover and chill at least 2 hours.

This dish unites two of summer's grandest flavors. And it's quick and delicious.

Tomato-Cucumber Salad

makes 4 servings   prep: 10 min.

Stir together 1 seedless cucumber, sliced; ½ small onion, thinly sliced; and 2 cups small vine-ripened tomatoes, cut into quarters. Add ¼ cup olive oil-and-vinegar dressing, ½ tsp. lemon zest, 1 Tbsp. lemon juice, and salt and pepper to taste. Toss to coat.

Tip: Grape or cherry tomatoes, halved, may be substituted.

Note: We tested with Campari tomatoes and Newman's Own Olive Oil & Vinegar Dressing.

TOASTED PECAN-AND-BROCCOLI SALAD

makes 10 servings   prep: 15 min.   bake: 6 min.   chill: 2 hr.

Serve this yummy salad alongside beef or chicken for a sweet and tangy side.

⅓ cup chopped pecans

1 cup light mayonnaise

⅓ cup sugar

2 Tbsp. cider vinegar

1½ lb. fresh broccoli florets, chopped*

¼ cup chopped red onion

⅓ cup sweetened dried cranberries or raisins

4 cooked reduced-fat bacon slices, crumbled

1. Preheat oven to 350°. Place chopped pecans in a single layer in a shallow pan.

2. Bake at 350° for 6 to 8 minutes or until lightly toasted, stirring occasionally.

3. Stir together mayonnaise, sugar, and vinegar in a large bowl; add broccoli, onion, and cranberries, gently tossing to coat. Cover and chill 2 hours. Sprinkle with bacon and pecans just before serving.

* 2 (12-oz.) packages fresh broccoli slaw may be substituted.

Per ¾ cup: Calories 175; Fat 11g (sat 1.5g, mono 5.6g, poly 3.3g); Protein 3.8g; Fiber 2.6g; Chol 12mg; Iron 0.8mg; Sodium 266mg; Calc 38mg

southern lights

In Praise of Potato Salad

If there is one salad that shows up at every Southern food event, it's got to be potato salad. Tangy or sweet, chilled or warm, with mustard or without, no gathering is complete without it.

If you want to see every type of potato salad Southerners love spread out on the same table, just take a look at the buffet at your next church picnic, family reunion, or neighborhood potluck. You'll probably find several bowls of famous Southern-style, with cubed potatoes and chopped hard-cooked eggs in a creamy mayonnaise dressing with sweet pickle relish and tangy mustard stirred in. About the only difference in Southern- and American-style is the mustard,

though personal preference dictates whether to include onions, pickle relish or chopped sweet pickles, and crunchy fresh celery or celery salt.

In Texas, potato salad is as much a "must" with beef barbecue as coleslaw is in other areas of the South. But in central Texas, where German influence is strong, it's German potato salad that the locals crave. Served warm, it's more tangy than sweet and coated in a traditional vinegar-bacon dressing.

BACON-AND-SWEET POTATO SALAD

makes 8 to 10 servings   prep: 30 min.   cook: 50 min.   stand: 15 min.

Kentucky native Stephen Barber was inspired by his Southern roots to create this flavor-packed salad.

3 large eggs	1 Tbsp. mustard seeds
1 lb. sweet potatoes, peeled and cut into chunks	1 tsp. dried crushed red pepper
2 tsp. salt, divided	¼ cup canola oil
2 lb. red potatoes, quartered	¼ tsp. black pepper
6 bacon slices, diced	1 bunch green onions, chopped (about 1 cup)
1 large red onion, chopped	¼ cup chopped fresh parsley
¾ cup cider vinegar	Salt and black pepper to taste (optional)

1. Place eggs in a single layer in a stainless steel saucepan. (Do not use nonstick.) Add water to a depth of 3 inches. Bring to a boil; cover, remove from heat, and let stand 15 minutes.

2. Drain immediately, and return eggs to pan. Fill pan with cold water and ice. Tap each egg firmly on the counter until cracks form all over the shell. Peel under cold running water. Chop eggs.

3. Bring sweet potatoes, ½ tsp. salt, and water to cover to a boil in a Dutch oven. Cook 10 minutes; add red potatoes, and cook 15 minutes or until tender. Drain.

4. Cook bacon in a large skillet over medium-high heat 8 to 10 minutes or until crisp; remove bacon, and drain on paper towels, reserving 1 Tbsp. drippings in skillet.

5. Sauté red onion in hot drippings 8 minutes or until tender. Reduce heat to low, and whisk in vinegar, mustard seeds, and red pepper; cook 2 minutes, whisking occasionally. Whisk in canola oil, pepper, and remaining 1½ tsp. salt.

6. Pour hot vinegar mixture over potatoes. Add eggs, bacon, green onions, and parsley, stirring gently to combine. Season with salt and pepper to taste, if desired.

NEW POTATO SALAD WITH FETA CHEESE

makes 6 servings   prep: 10 min.   cook: 30 min.   chill: 2 hr.   **pictured on page 671**

At six servings, this salad is an ample main dish. As a side dish, it will serve 8 to 10.

3 lb. small new potatoes	1 bunch green onions, sliced
⅔ cup olive oil	1 (4-oz.) package crumbled garlic-and-herb
½ cup fresh lemon juice	feta cheese
1 tsp. Dijon mustard	¼ cup chopped fresh parsley
1 tsp. salt	Mixed salad greens (optional)
¾ tsp. pepper	

1. Bring potatoes and water to cover to a boil, and cook 25 minutes or just until tender; drain well. Cool slightly, and cut into wedges.

2. Whisk together oil and next 4 ingredients in a large bowl; add potatoes, green onions, and feta cheese, tossing to coat. Cover and chill at least 2 hours or up to 8 hours. Sprinkle with parsley before serving. Serve over mixed salad greens, if desired.

CILANTRO POTATO SALAD

makes 8 servings   prep: 20 min.   cook: 15 min.   chill: 4 hr.

Canned green chiles add extra zest to this picnic favorite.

3   lb. red potatoes

2   tsp. salt, divided

1   cup mayonnaise

1   (4.5-oz.) can chopped green chiles

⅓   cup chopped fresh cilantro

3   green onions, chopped

2   Tbsp. fresh lime juice (about 2 limes)

1   garlic clove, minced

½   tsp. pepper

4   slices maple bacon, cooked and crumbled

Garnish: chopped fresh cilantro (optional)

1. Cook potatoes and 1 tsp. salt in boiling water to cover in a large Dutch oven 15 minutes or until fork-tender. Drain and cool. Cut potatoes into quarters.

2. Stir together mayonnaise, next 6 ingredients, and remaining 1 tsp. salt in a large bowl; add potatoes, and toss to coat. Cover and chill at least 4 hours. Stir in bacon just before serving; garnish, if desired.

SOUTHERN-STYLE POTATO SALAD

makes 8 servings   prep: 25 min.   cook: 40 min.

You can substitute light mayonnaise and sour cream with good results.

4   lb. potatoes (about 4 large)

3   hard-cooked eggs, grated

1   cup mayonnaise

½   cup sour cream

¼   cup celery, finely chopped

2   Tbsp. onion, finely chopped

2   Tbsp. sweet pickle relish

1   Tbsp. mustard

1   tsp. salt

½   tsp. freshly ground pepper

½   lb. bacon, cooked and crumbled

Garnishes: chopped fresh parsley (optional)

1. Cook potatoes in boiling water to cover 40 minutes or until tender; drain and cool. Peel potatoes, and cut into 1-inch cubes.

2. Stir together potatoes and eggs.

3. Stir together mayonnaise and next 7 ingredients; gently stir into potato mixture. Cover and chill. Sprinkle with bacon just before serving. Garnish, if desired.

GREEN BEAN-AND-NEW POTATO SALAD

makes 8 servings   prep: 10 min.   cook: 24 min.

This may be prepared the night before and stored in the refrigerator.

2 lb. new red potatoes, quartered	2 lb. thin fresh green beans, trimmed
1 tsp. salt	Rosemary Vinaigrette
2 Tbsp. salt	

1. Bring new potatoes, 1 tsp. salt, and water to cover to a boil in a Dutch oven; cook 18 to 20 minutes or until potatoes are tender. Drain and let cool.

2. Bring 2 qt. water and 2 Tbsp. salt to a boil in a Dutch oven; add beans. Cook 6 minutes or until crisp-tender; drain. Plunge beans into ice water to stop the cooking process; drain.

3. Combine green beans and potatoes in a large bowl. Pour Rosemary Vinaigrette over green bean mixture, tossing to coat. Cover and chill until ready to serve.

Rosemary Vinaigrette

makes 1⅓ cups   prep: 5 min.

Store dressing in an airtight container in the refrigerator up to two days.

½ cup white balsamic vinegar	1 Tbsp. Dijon mustard
¼ cup honey	½ tsp. salt
2 garlic cloves	Freshly ground pepper to taste
2 Tbsp. chopped fresh rosemary leaves	½ cup extra virgin olive oil
¼ medium-size red onion	

1. Process balsamic vinegar and next 7 ingredients in a blender or food processor 15 to 20 seconds, stopping to scrape down sides. With blender or processor running, gradually add olive oil in a slow, steady stream; process until smooth.

CREAMY SWEET SLAW

makes 8 servings   prep: 20 min.

1	large cabbage, shredded*	¼	cup white vinegar
4	celery ribs, chopped	¾	cup mayonnaise
1	small green bell pepper, finely chopped	⅓	cup evaporated milk
1	(2-oz.) jar diced pimiento, drained	1	tsp. salt
½	cup sugar	½	tsp. pepper

1. Combine cabbage and next 3 ingredients in a large bowl.

2. Stir together ½ cup sugar, ¼ cup vinegar, and next 4 ingredients; spoon over cabbage mixture, tossing to coat.

* 2 (10-oz.) bags angel hair cabbage may be substituted for shredded cabbage.

PEANUTTY COLESLAW

makes 6 servings   prep: 15 min.   chill: 1 hr.   **pictured on page 670**

Wasabi paste can be purchased in the Asian section of most supermarkets. If you prefer a creamy coleslaw, double the amount of dressing.

½	cup chopped fresh cilantro	1	tsp. grated fresh ginger
¼	cup chopped green onions	2	tsp. wasabi paste
3	Tbsp. white vinegar	½	tsp. salt
1	Tbsp. sesame oil	½	tsp. pepper
2	Tbsp. mayonnaise	1	(16-oz.) package shredded coleslaw mix
1	tsp. sugar	¾	cup lightly salted peanuts

1. Whisk together first 10 ingredients in a large bowl; add coleslaw mix, stirring to coat. Cover and chill 1 hour; stir in peanuts just before serving.

The Scoop on Slaw

Whether you're spooning it onto a barbecue sandwich or serving it alongside fried chicken or fish, everyone has their favorite version of crunchy coleslaw, and usually that's the only one that will do.

In North Carolina you have your choice of colors. Will it be red—the Lexington-style sweet-tart vinegar-based coleslaw with a bit of sugar and ketchup? Or maybe Eastern North Carolina yellow slaw with sweet pickles and a mayo-mustard blend? Or, creamy white mayo slaw with a touch of sweetness?

Though North Carolina is rather regionally defined, elsewhere in the South, there's no telling which kind of slaw will wind up on your plate. It might be soaked in clear, tangy vinaigrette dressing, or so thick with mayo that you can hardly see the cabbage. The cabbage could be chopped fine enough to sip through a straw, shredded thin as angel hair, or into thick, long crunchy strands. The only thing Southern slaws have in common? Cabbage.

BROCCOLI SLAW

makes 8 servings   prep: 20 min.

This is a terrific dish to take to a potluck after a busy day because you can make it the night before. We love the fresh taste.

1   (12-oz.) package fresh broccoli slaw
1   cup red seedless grapes, halved
1   Granny Smith apple, diced
1   cup Vidalia onion dressing or poppy seed dressing

2   oranges, peeled and sectioned
Toasted chopped pecans (optional)

1. Stir together first 5 ingredients in a large bowl. Top with chopped pecans, if desired.

[*make ahead*]

FRIED OKRA SALAD

makes 6 servings   prep: 20 min.   cook: 2 min.   **pictured on page 668**

1½ cups self-rising yellow cornmeal

1   tsp. salt

1   lb. fresh okra

1½ cups buttermilk

Peanut oil

1   head Bibb lettuce

1   large tomato, chopped (about 1 cup)

1   medium-size sweet onion, thinly sliced
     (about ¾ cup)

1   medium-size green bell pepper, chopped

Lemon Dressing

3   bacon slices, cooked and crumbled

1. Combine cornmeal and salt. Dip okra in buttermilk; dredge in cornmeal mixture.

2. Pour peanut oil to a depth of 2 inches into a Dutch oven or deep cast-iron skillet; heat to 375°. Fry okra, in batches, 2 minutes or until golden, turning once. Drain on a wire rack over paper towels.

3. Arrange lettuce leaves on a serving platter; top with tomato, onion slices, and bell pepper.

4. Add Lemon Dressing, tossing to coat. Top with fried okra, and sprinkle with crumbled bacon. Serve immediately.

Lemon Dressing

makes ¾ cup   prep: 5 min.

This also makes a tangy dipping sauce for steamed artichokes or asparagus.

¼   cup fresh lemon juice

3   Tbsp. chopped fresh basil

1   tsp. salt

1   tsp. paprika

½   tsp. pepper

¼   cup olive oil

1. Combine first 5 ingredients in a bowl. Add oil, whisking until combined.

610 Magnolia

A request from Edward Lee at 610 Magnolia: "Trust us."

Trust comes easily as the plates come from his tiny kitchen in Louisville. The six courses form a montage of foods as diverse as the chef himself. Born in Brooklyn of Korean parents, he trained in New York and Europe. His approach is new to the South yet takes us forward.

Edward's emphasis is natural, fresh, and diverse, so the menu changes weekly. There is only one seating nightly, and reservations are required; but the table is yours for the night to enjoy a three-, four-, or six course meal.

A few years back, Edward stopped by Louisville for the Kentucky Derby but ended up in the kitchen at 610 Magnolia instead. Now chef/owner, he savors the South for one major reason: "Southern cuisine is the only thing I consider to be truly American," he says. "Food is a journey. That's what I try to infuse into my cooking. It has roots now in the South, and everything from there is open game. No rules."

610 West Magnolia Avenue
Louisville, Kentucky 40208
www.610magnolia.com or (502) 636-0783.

LAYERED BLT SALAD

makes 8 servings   prep: 20 min.   chill 2 hr.

1 (8-oz.) container sour cream	¼ tsp. garlic powder
1 cup mayonnaise	1 large head iceberg lettuce, torn (about 4 cups)
1 Tbsp. lemon juice	1 (32-oz.) package thick bacon slices, cooked and
1 tsp. dried basil	crumbled
½ tsp. salt	6 plum tomatoes, thinly sliced
½ tsp. pepper	3 cups large croutons

1. Stir together first 7 ingredients until well blended.

2. Layer lettuce, bacon, and tomato in a 13- x 9-inch baking dish. Spread mayonnaise mixture evenly over tomato, sealing to edge of dish. Cover and chill salad at least 2 hours.

3. Sprinkle with croutons, and serve immediately.

taking sides

Mayonnaise Fans Fight for Their Favorites

Over the last century, three Southern brands of mayonnaise have had faithful followers throughout the region. One can never be too picky about the main ingredient for deviled eggs, potato salad, coleslaw, and tomato sandwiches.

Almost 100 years ago, production of Duke's mayonnaise cranked up in Greenville, South Carolina. It's still there today, and fans such as Bonita Voigt, of Mt. Pleasant, South Carolina, have never wavered in loyal support. "Being an ol' Southern girl, I was born and raised on Duke's," she says. "BLT sandwiches, peanut butter and banana sandwiches, chicken salad, and the ambrosia of the gods—'tater salad, were all made with the goodness of Duke's."

The Richmond company who makes Duke's also owns Bama, another Southern favorite. Then there is Blue Plate Mayonnaise, a New Orleans claim to fame. Melanie Amos of Norcross, Georgia, claims allegiance to Bama. "It was always my favorite," she says. "I love the texture. Very creamy and with a touch of lemon taste."

LAYERED CORNBREAD-AND-TURKEY SALAD

makes 6 to 8 servings   prep: 25 min.   chill: 2 hr.   **pictured on page 747**

This salad is just as scrumptious with chopped cooked chicken.

1   (15-oz.) bottle roasted-garlic dressing
½   cup buttermilk
1   head romaine lettuce, shredded
1½ cups chopped smoked turkey (about ½ lb.)
8   oz. crumbled feta cheese

1   (12-oz.) jar roasted red bell peppers, drained and chopped
2   cups crumbled cornbread
8   bacon slices, cooked and crumbled
5   green onions, chopped

1. Stir together dressing and buttermilk, blending well.
2. Layer a 3-qt. glass bowl with half each of lettuce and next 6 ingredients; top with half of dressing. Repeat layers with remaining ingredients and dressing. Cover and chill 2 hours.

Note: We tested with T. Marzetti Roasted Garlic Italian Vinaigrette Dressing.

HOT TOMATO SALAD

makes 5 cups   prep: 15 min.   chill: 2 hr.

4   yellow banana peppers
2   green banana peppers
2   jalapeño peppers
4   to 5 large tomatoes
2   garlic cloves, minced
1   Tbsp. chopped fresh basil
1   Tbsp. chopped fresh parsley
1   tsp. chopped fresh rosemary

1   tsp. chopped fresh oregano
2   oz. smoked Cheddar cheese, cubed (optional)
½   cup olive oil
1   Tbsp. lemon juice
1   tsp. salt
½   tsp. pepper
2   tsp. sugar (optional)
Garnish: fresh basil sprig (optional)

1. Remove and discard seeds from peppers and tomatoes. Dice peppers and tomatoes; place in a large bowl. Toss in garlic, herbs, and, if desired, cheese.
2. Stir together oil, next 3 ingredients, and, if desired, sugar; add to tomato mixture, tossing to coat. Cover and chill 2 to 4 hours. Serve with a slotted spoon. Garnish, if desired.

Mom's Back-to-School Lunch Party serves 6

Cantaloupe Soup (page 881)
Peppery Turkey-and-Brie Panini (page 797)
Green Bean-and-Tomato Pasta Salad
Easy Tiramisù (page 355)

GREEN BEAN-AND-TOMATO PASTA SALAD

makes 6 servings prep: 20 min. cook: 10 min.

½ (16-oz.) package rotini pasta

½ lb. fresh green beans, trimmed and cut into
     1½-inch pieces

1 cup cherry tomatoes, halved

½ cup Basil-Honey-Garlic Vinaigrette

¼ cup chopped red onion

1. Bring a large Dutch oven of salted water to a boil over medium-high heat. Add pasta, and cook 5 minutes. Add green beans, and cook 5 to 6 minutes or until pasta is tender but still firm to the bite and green beans are tender. Drain and rinse with cold water; place in a large bowl.
2. Add tomatoes, vinaigrette, and onion, tossing to coat. Serve immediately, or cover and chill up to 2 hours.

Basil-Honey-Garlic Vinaigrette

makes 1 cup prep: 10 min.

1 garlic clove

½ tsp. salt

½ cup extra virgin olive oil

⅓ cup balsamic vinegar

2 Tbsp. chopped fresh basil

2 Tbsp. honey

½ tsp. freshly ground pepper

1. Smash garlic and salt together using flat side of knife to make a paste.
2. Whisk together garlic paste, oil, and remaining ingredients until blended.

Kitchen Express: Whisk together ½ cup bottled balsamic vinaigrette, 1 Tbsp. chopped fresh basil, and 1 Tbsp. honey until blended. Makes about ½ cup.

Note: We tested with Newman's Own Balsamic Vinaigrette.

TOMATO NAPOLEON

makes 4 servings   prep: 30 min.   chill: 1 hr.

Two top rated recipes combine for this scrumptious Southern salad.

8   oz. fresh mozzarella cheese, cut into 8 slices
¾   cup Fresh Tomato Dressing
3   large tomatoes, each cut into 4 slices

1   tsp. salt
1   tsp. pepper
24   fresh basil leaves, shredded

1. Place cheese in a shallow dish. Pour Fresh Tomato Dressing over cheese; cover and chill 1 hour. Remove cheese slices, reserving Tomato Dressing marinade.
2. Sprinkle tomato slices evenly with salt and pepper.
3. Place 1 tomato slice on each of 4 salad plates; top each with 1 cheese slice and 2 shredded basil leaves. Repeat with tomato slice, cheese slice, and basil. Top with remaining tomato slice and basil. Drizzle evenly with reserved Fresh Tomato Dressing marinade.

Fresh Tomato Dressing

makes 4 cups   prep: 20 min.   stand: 1 hr.   chill: 8 hr.

1   cup olive oil
½   cup balsamic vinegar
3   garlic cloves, sliced
1   Tbsp. sugar

1   Tbsp. salt
1   tsp. pepper
4   large tomatoes, peeled and chopped
2   Tbsp. fresh thyme leaves or 4 thyme sprigs

1. Whisk together first 6 ingredients in a large glass bowl. Stir in tomato and fresh thyme.
2. Cover and let stand at room temperature 1 hour, stirring occasionally. Cover and chill 8 hours.

Note: Dressing may be stored in refrigerator up to 1 month. Stir additional fresh chopped tomato into dressing after each use.

[test kitchen favorite]

THREE-TOMATO SALAD

makes 8 servings   prep: 10 min.   stand: 3 hr.

You can use all red tomatoes, such as a combination of cherry, plum, and beefsteak. But add other varieties and colors, when available, for a beautiful presentation.

½	cup olive oil	1	large yellow or red tomato, sliced
3	Tbsp. red wine vinegar	2	plum tomatoes, cut into wedges
2	tsp. dried Italian seasoning	1	pt. cherry tomatoes, cut in half
1	tsp. sugar	16	green leaf lettuce leaves
1	tsp. salt		Salt and pepper to taste
½	tsp. pepper		

1. Whisk together olive oil, red wine vinegar, and next 4 ingredients. Place tomatoes in a 2-qt. baking dish, and pour olive oil mixture over tomatoes. Cover and let stand 3 hours.
2. Place 2 lettuce leaves on each of 8 salad plates, and divide tomato mixture evenly among plates. Season with salt and pepper to taste.

TOMATO-AND-WATERMELON SALAD

makes 4 to 6 servings   prep: 20 min.   stand: 15 min.   chill: 2 hr.   **pictured on page 667**

This refreshing dish is adapted from Seasoned in the South: Recipes From Crook's Corner and From Home *(Algonquin Books, 2006) by Bill Smith.*

5	cups (¾-inch) seeded watermelon cubes	½	cup red wine vinegar
1½	lb. ripe tomatoes, cut into ¾-inch cubes	¼	cup extra virgin olive oil
3	tsp. sugar		Romaine lettuce leaves (optional)
½	tsp. salt		Cracked black pepper to taste
1	small red onion, quartered and thinly sliced		

1. Combine watermelon and tomatoes in a large bowl; sprinkle with sugar and salt, tossing to coat. Let stand 15 minutes.
2. Stir in onion, vinegar, and oil. Cover and chill 2 hours. Serve chilled with lettuce leaves, if desired. Sprinkle with cracked black pepper to taste.

[test kitchen favorite]

inspirations for your taste

This tasty salad doubles as a main dish or side.

Tomato-Basil-Asparagus Salad

makes 4 main-dish servings or 8 side-dish servings   prep: 10 min.   cook: 14 min.   chill: 1 hr.

Cook 16 ounces pasta according to package directions; add 1 pound asparagus cut into 2-inch pieces during the last 2 minutes of cooking time. Drain pasta, and rinse under cool water. Stir together 1 cup lemon vinaigrette and 1 ounce chopped fresh basil; pour ¾ cup dressing mixture over pasta mixture. Stir in 1 pint grape tomatoes halved and salt and pepper to taste. Cover and chill 1 hour. Toss pasta mixture with remaining ¼ cup dressing before serving. Garnish with fresh basil, if desired.

LEMON-TARRAGON CHICKEN SALAD

makes 4 to 6 servings   prep: 20 min.   bake: 5 min.   cool: 15 min.

When fresh tarragon isn't available, substitute 1½ tsp. dried crushed tarragon.

½   cup chopped pecans

¾   cup mayonnaise

1   Tbsp. chopped fresh tarragon

1   tsp. lemon zest

1   Tbsp. fresh lemon juice

1   tsp. salt

½   tsp. freshly ground pepper

3   cups chopped cooked chicken

2   celery ribs, finely chopped

½   small sweet onion, finely chopped

2   cups seedless red grapes, cut in half (optional)

Garnish: halved lemon slices (optional)

1. Preheat oven to 350°. Arrange pecans in a single layer on a baking sheet.

2. Bake at 350° for 5 to 7 minutes or until lightly toasted. Cool pecans on a wire rack 15 minutes or until completely cool.

3. Whisk together mayonnaise and next 5 ingredients in a large bowl; stir in pecans, chicken, celery, and onion just until blended. Stir in grape halves, if desired. Garnish, if desired.

GRILLED CHICKEN-AND-ARTICHOKE SALAD

makes 4 servings   prep: 20 min.   chill: 2 hr.   grill: 10 min.   stand: 15 min.   cook: 4 min.

1½ lb. skinned and boned chicken breasts
½ cup light Italian dressing
2 Tbsp. sesame seeds
1 (14-oz.) can artichoke hearts, drained and quartered

⅓ cup mayonnaise
2 Tbsp. chopped fresh basil
2 Tbsp. sesame oil
½ tsp. salt

1. Place chicken and dressing in a zip-top plastic freezer bag; seal and chill 2 hours, turning occasionally. Remove chicken from marinade, discarding marinade.

2. Preheat grill to 350° to 400° (medium-high) heat. Grill chicken, covered with grill lid, 5 to 7 minutes each side or until done. Remove from grill, and let stand 15 minutes; coarsely chop.

3. Heat sesame seeds in a small nonstick skillet over medium-low heat, stirring often, 4 minutes or until toasted.

4. Stir together grilled chicken, sesame seeds, artichoke hearts, and remaining ingredients in a large bowl just until blended.

SOUTHERN-STYLE COBB SALAD

makes 6 servings   prep: 30 min.

½ to 1 lb. fresh sugar snap peas
2 heads iceberg lettuce
3 hard-cooked eggs
4 plum tomatoes
1 large avocado
1 bunch fresh watercress, torn

2 skinned and boned chicken breasts, cooked and sliced
12 bacon slices, cooked and crumbled
Blue Cheese-Buttermilk Dressing
Freshly ground pepper
Garnish: edible flowers

1. Cook peas in boiling water to cover 2 to 3 minutes; drain. Plunge into ice water to stop the cooking process; drain and set aside.

2. Cut iceberg lettuce into 6 wedges. Coarsely chop eggs. Remove and discard pulp from tomatoes, and cut into thin strips. Dice avocado.

3. Arrange watercress evenly on 6 salad plates. Top with peas, chopped eggs, tomato strips, avocado, and chicken; sprinkle with bacon. Place a lettuce wedge on each plate. Drizzle with Blue Cheese-Buttermilk Dressing; sprinkle with pepper. Garnish, if desired.

Blue Cheese-Buttermilk Dressing

makes 1¾ cups   prep: 5 min.

1   (4-oz.) package crumbled blue cheese
1   cup nonfat buttermilk
½   to ⅔ cup reduced-fat mayonnaise
3   to 4 Tbsp. lemon juice
1   garlic clove, minced

1. Stir together all ingredients in a bowl. Serve over salad.

HOT AND CRUSTY CHICKEN SALAD

makes 8 servings   prep: 15 min.   cook: 35 min.

½   cup slivered almonds
4   cups chopped cooked chicken
2   cups sliced celery
¼   cup chopped onion
¼   cup chopped pimiento, drained
1   (4.5-oz) jar sliced mushrooms, drained
1   (8-oz.) can sliced water chestnuts, drained
¼   tsp. salt
½   tsp. pepper
2   cups (8 oz.) shredded Cheddar cheese, divided
1   cup mayonnaise
½   cup sour cream
3   Tbsp. lemon juice
1   cup crushed potato chips
1   cup shredded Parmesan cheese

1. Preheat oven to 350°. Bake almonds in a shallow pan 5 to 10 minutes or until toasted.
2. Stir together almonds, chicken, and next 7 ingredients in a large bowl.
3. Stir together 1 cup Cheddar cheese, mayonnaise, sour cream, and lemon juice until blended; stir into chicken mixture.
4. Spoon into a lightly greased 13- x 9-inch baking dish; sprinkle with remaining 1 cup Cheddar cheese, crushed potato chips, and Parmesan cheese.
5. Bake at 350° for 30 minutes or until thoroughly heated.

MAIN DISH TURKEY SALAD WITH CRANBERRY VINAIGRETTE AND GARLIC CROUTONS

makes 4 servings prep: 15 min. **pictured on page 746**

1 head romaine lettuce, torn
2 cups coarsely chopped cooked turkey
4 bacon slices, cooked and crumbled
1 medium-size Granny Smith or Braeburn apple, thinly sliced

1 cup Garlic Croutons
Cranberry Vinaigrette

1. Toss together first 4 ingredients in a large serving bowl. Top salad with Garlic Croutons, and serve with Cranberry Vinaigrette.

Garlic Croutons

makes about 3 cups prep: 10 min. cook: 2 min. bake: 20 min.

¼ cup butter
2 large garlic cloves, pressed
¾ tsp. ground red pepper

4 large dinner yeast rolls, cubed (about 3¼ cups cubes)

1. Preheat oven to 300°. Melt butter in a large nonstick skillet over medium-high heat. Add garlic and red pepper; sauté 30 seconds. Remove from heat; stir in bread cubes until evenly coated.
2. Spread bread cubes in an even layer on a lightly greased aluminum foil-lined jelly-roll pan.
3. Bake at 300° for 20 to 25 minutes or until browned and crisp, stirring occasionally. Spread in a single layer on wax paper to cool completely. Store in an airtight container up to 1 week.

Cranberry Vinaigrette

makes about 1 cup prep: 10 min.

½ cup whole-berry cranberry sauce
2 Tbsp. balsamic vinegar
½ tsp. orange zest
2 Tbsp. fresh orange juice

1½ tsp. Dijon mustard
½ tsp. honey
⅛ tsp. salt
¼ cup olive oil

1. Stir together first 7 ingredients until blended. Stir in olive oil, 1 Tbsp. at a time, until well blended.

Pork Tenderloin-and-Tomato
Salad, page 759

Calypso Steak Salad, page 757

Main Dish Turkey Salad With
Cranberry Vinaigrette and
Garlic Croutons, page 744

Layered Cornbread-
and-Turkey Salad,
page 737

Peanut Chicken
Pitas, page 777

Toasted Club Sandwiches,
page 771

Fish ...
pa...

Meatloaf Sandwich,
page 781

Fried Fish
Sandwiches,
page 786

Muffuletta Calzones,
page 794

Egg Salad Club Sandwiches,
page 769

Lightened Hot
Browns, page 778

Muffuletta, page 793

Anytime Turkey Gravy,
page 814

Easy Redeye Gravy,
page 816

White Barbecue Sauce,
page 809

Cider Vinegar Barbecue
Sauce, page 810

Peppery Barbecue
Sauce, page 809

Lemon Curd, page 822

Toasted Pecan-
Caramel Sauce,
page 822

Easiest Pepper Jelly,
page 820

CALYPSO STEAK SALAD

makes 4 servings prep: 20 min. grill: 8 min. stand: 10 min. **pictured on page 746**

To make the salsa mixture ahead, just cover and chill up to 8 hours. Let stand at room temperature about 20 minutes, while steaks marinate in lime juice mixture.

1½ lb. beef strip steaks

1½ tsp. lime zest, divided

3   Tbsp. fresh lime juice, divided

1   (8-oz.) can pineapple tidbits, drained

½   cup peach-mango salsa*

⅓   cup diced red onion

⅓   cup diced green bell pepper

¼   cup chopped fresh cilantro

½   tsp. salt

1   tsp. Jamaican jerk seasoning

1   head romaine lettuce

Garnish: chopped fresh cilantro (optional)

1. Preheat grill to 350° to 400° (medium-high) heat. Place strip steaks in a shallow dish, and add 1 tsp. lime zest and 1½ Tbsp. lime juice, turning to coat.

2. Stir together pineapple, next 5 ingredients, remaining ½ tsp. lime zest, and remaining 1½ Tbsp. lime juice until blended.

3. Remove steaks from lime juice mixture, discarding juice. Sprinkle steaks evenly with 1 tsp. Jamaican jerk seasoning.

4. Grill steaks, covered with grill lid, 4 to 5 minutes on each side or to desired degree of doneness. Let steaks stand 10 minutes, and cut into thin strips.

5. Arrange lettuce leaves on a serving platter, and top with sliced steak and salsa mixture. Garnish, if desired.

* ½ cup salsa may be substituted.

Note: We tested with Desert Pepper Trading Company Peach Mango Salsa.

ASIAN BEEF SALAD

makes 8 servings   prep: 15 min.   chill: 1 hr.   grill: 10 min.   stand: 5 min.

No grill available? Cook the beef in a grill skillet on the cooktop. Napa cabbage may be called Chinese cabbage in some grocery stores.

¼ cup teriyaki sauce

2 Tbsp. olive oil

2 (1-lb.) flank steaks

1 (1¾-lb.) napa cabbage, chopped

1 large head romaine lettuce, chopped

2 large tomatoes, cut into wedges

2 cucumbers, thinly sliced

½ small red onion, thinly sliced

½ cup loosely packed fresh cilantro

Soy-Sesame Dressing

1. Preheat grill to 350° to 400° (medium-high) heat. Combine teriyaki sauce and oil in a shallow dish or large zip-top plastic freezer bag; add steaks, turning to coat. Cover or seal, and chill 1 hour, turning steaks occasionally.

2. Remove steaks from marinade, discarding marinade.

3. Grill steaks, covered with grill lid, 5 to 7 minutes on each side or to desired degree of doneness. Let stand 5 minutes; cut diagonally across the grain into thin slices.

4. Toss steak slices, cabbage, and next 5 ingredients together; drizzle with desired amount of Soy-Sesame Dressing, tossing gently to coat.

Soy-Sesame Dressing

makes ¾ cup   prep: 5 min.

Sesame oil lends a nutty flavor. Use the higher amount of Asian garlic-chili sauce for a spicier dressing. Store dressing in the refrigerator up to 1 week.

¼ cup fresh lime juice

1 Tbsp. light brown sugar

3 Tbsp. olive oil

3 Tbsp. sesame oil

2 Tbsp. lite soy sauce

1 to 2 tsp. Asian garlic-chili sauce

1. Whisk together all ingredients.

PORK TENDERLOIN-AND-TOMATO SALAD

makes 4 servings   prep: 15 min.   cook: 20 min.   bake: 15 min.   stand: 10 min.   **pictured on page 745**

Save the crumbled bacon from the dressing to scatter over the salad.

1   (1-lb.) pork tenderloin
1   Tbsp. coarsely ground pepper
¾   tsp. salt
2   Tbsp. olive oil

1   (5-oz.) package spring mix, thoroughly washed
3   large tomatoes, cut into ½-inch-thick slices
Warm Bacon Vinaigrette
Garnish: cooked and crumbled bacon (optional)

1. Preheat oven to 400°. Remove silver skin from tenderloin, leaving a thin layer of fat.
2. Preheat oven to 400°. Rub pepper and salt over pork. Cook pork in hot oil in a large skillet over medium-high heat 5 minutes on all sides or until browned. Transfer to a 13- x 9-inch pan.
3. Bake at 400° for 15 minutes or until a meat thermometer inserted into thickest portion registers 155°. Let stand 10 to 12 minutes or until thermometer registers 160°.
4. Cut pork into ¼-inch-thick slices. Divide greens among 4 plates; arrange tomato slices and pork over greens. Serve immediately with Warm Bacon Vinaigrette. Garnish, if desired.

Warm Bacon Vinaigrette

makes about 1½ cups   prep: 10 min.   cook: 12 min.

4   bacon slices
4   Tbsp. minced shallot
2   Tbsp. minced garlic
3   Tbsp. brown sugar
6   Tbsp. orange juice

5   Tbsp. balsamic vinegar
3   Tbsp. coarse-grained mustard
⅓   cup olive oil
½   tsp. salt

1. Cook bacon in a large skillet over medium-high heat 8 to 10 minutes or until crisp; remove bacon, and drain on paper towels, reserving 2 Tbsp. drippings in skillet. Crumble bacon, and reserve for another use.
2. Cook shallots and garlic in hot drippings over medium heat, stirring occasionally, 3 minutes or until tender. Add brown sugar, and cook, stirring constantly, 1 minute or until sugar is dissolved.
3. Process shallot mixture, orange juice, and next 4 ingredients in a blender until combined.

GRILLED SHRIMP, ORANGE, AND WATERMELON SALAD WITH PEPPERED PEANUTS IN A ZESTY CITRUS DRESSING

makes 4 servings   prep: 1 hr.   bake: 10 min.   cook: 2 min.   grill: 4 min.

If using wooden skewers, soak them in water for at least 30 minutes to prevent them from burning.

½ cup coarsely chopped dry-roasted peanuts

½ tsp. canola oil

½ tsp. sugar

½ tsp. pepper

¼ tsp. salt

2 cups fully cooked, frozen, shelled edamame (green soybeans), thawed*

16 unpeeled, jumbo raw shrimp

4 metal or wooden skewers

5 oranges, divided

½ cup hoisin sauce

½ cup fresh lime juice

2 garlic cloves, minced

1 tsp. minced fresh ginger

Salt and pepper to taste

6 cups loosely packed torn red leaf lettuce

2 (4-oz.) bags watercress, stems removed

2 lb. red seedless watermelon, peeled and cut into ½-inch cubes (about 4 cups)

4 green onions, thinly sliced

¼ cup chopped fresh cilantro

¼ cup chopped fresh basil

1. Preheat oven to 400°. Toss together first 5 ingredients in a small bowl; spread peanut mixture in a single layer on a baking sheet.

2. Bake at 400° for 10 to 12 minutes, stirring once. Cool.

3. Coat cold cooking grate with cooking spray, and place on grill. Preheat grill to 350° to 400° (medium-high) heat.

4. Cook edamame in boiling water to cover 2 minutes or until crisp-tender; drain. Plunge into ice water to stop the cooking process; drain and set aside.

5. Peel shrimp, leaving tails on; devein, if desired. Thread 4 shrimp onto each skewer. Set aside.

6. Peel 4 oranges, and cut each into 6 (½-inch-thick) slices; set slices aside.

7. Grate remaining orange to equal ½ tsp. orange zest in a small bowl; squeeze juice from orange into bowl. Add hoisin sauce and next 3 ingredients to bowl, and stir until blended. Remove 2 Tbsp. citrus dressing, and brush evenly on shrimp. Reserve remaining dressing.

8. Place shrimp skewers on grate, and grill 2 minutes on each side or just until done. Sprinkle with salt and pepper to taste.

9. Arrange lettuce and watercress on 4 serving plates, and top evenly with edamame, orange slices, watermelon, and green onions. Top each salad with 4 shrimp. Sprinkle evenly with cilantro, basil, and peanut mixture; drizzle with reserved citrus dressing.

* 2 cups uncooked fresh green shelled soybeans may be substituted for frozen. Boil soybeans in lightly salted water to cover 15 to 20 minutes or until crisp-tender; drain. Plunge into ice water to stop the cooking process; drain. Proceed with recipe as directed.

Note: Nutritional analysis does not include added salt to taste.

Per serving: Calories 504; Fat 18g (sat 2g, mono 6.4g, poly 6.6g); Protein 27g; Fiber 13.4g; Chol 44mg; Iron 5.3mg; Sodium 764mg; Calc 363mg

GRILLED SHRIMP-AND-GREEN BEAN SALAD

makes 4 to 6 servings prep: 30 min. soak: 30 min. cook: 4 min. chill: 15 min. grill: 4 min.

8 (12-inch) wooden skewers	6 cooked bacon slices, crumbled
1½ lb. fresh green beans, trimmed	1⅓ cups shredded Parmesan cheese
2 lb. peeled, medium-size raw shrimp	¾ cup chopped roasted, salted almonds
Basil Vinaigrette, divided	Cornbread (optional)

1. Preheat grill to 350° to 400° (medium-high) heat. Soak wooden skewers in water to cover 30 minutes.

2. Cook green beans in boiling salted water to cover 4 minutes or until crisp-tender; drain. Plunge into ice water to stop the cooking process; drain, pat dry, and place in a large bowl.

3. Combine shrimp and ¾ cup Basil Vinaigrette in a large zip-top plastic freezer bag; seal and chill 15 minutes, turning occasionally. Remove shrimp from marinade, discarding marinade. Thread shrimp onto skewers.

4. Grill, covered with grill lid, 2 minutes on each side or just until shrimp turn pink. Remove from skewers; toss with beans, bacon, cheese, almonds, and remaining ¾ cup Basil Vinaigrette. Serve over hot cornbread, if desired.

Basil Vinaigrette

makes about 1½ cups prep: 10 min.

½ cup balsamic vinegar	1 Tbsp. brown sugar
½ cup chopped fresh basil	1 tsp. seasoned pepper
4 large shallots, minced	½ tsp. salt
3 garlic cloves, minced	1 cup olive oil

1. Whisk together balsamic vinegar and next 6 ingredients in a small bowl until blended; gradually add olive oil, whisking constantly until blended.

CRUNCHY TUNA-AND-ALMOND SALAD

makes 6 servings prep: 10 min.

Use crackers, Melba toast, or bagel chips to scoop this curry-kissed salad, or try it between two slices of multigrain bread.

¾ cup light mayonnaise

1 tsp. lemon zest

1 Tbsp. fresh lemon juice

½ tsp. curry powder

⅛ tsp. garlic powder

1 (13-oz.) can solid white tuna in spring water, drained and flaked

½ (10-oz.) package frozen peas, thawed

2 celery ribs, chopped

¼ tsp. salt

⅛ tsp. pepper

1 (10-oz.) package mixed salad greens

¼ cup slivered almonds, toasted

½ cup chow mein noodles

1. Stir together first 5 ingredients in a large bowl until blended. Add tuna and next 4 ingredients; toss gently to coat. Serve over greens. Sprinkle with almonds and noodles.

FRESH PEACH-BASIL VINAIGRETTE

makes about 1¼ cups prep: 10 min.

Serve over a colorful variety of tomatoes from the local farmers market.

⅓ cup white balsamic vinegar

1 garlic clove, minced

2 Tbsp. brown sugar

¼ tsp. freshly ground pepper

⅛ tsp. salt

2 Tbsp. olive oil

1 large peach, chopped

1½ Tbsp. chopped fresh basil

1. Whisk together first 5 ingredients until sugar is dissolved. Whisk in olive oil. Stir in chopped peach and basil. Serve immediately.

Per 1 Tbsp.: Calories 23; Fat 1.4g (sat 0.2g, mono 1g, poly 0.2g); Protein 0.1g; Fiber 0.1g; Iron 0.1mg; Sodium 16mg; Calc 2mg

CREAMY GARLIC SALAD DRESSING

makes about 1 cup   prep: 5 min.   chill: 1 hr.

1   tsp. salt

3   garlic cloves, minced

½   cup mayonnaise

3   Tbsp. white vinegar

3   Tbsp. oil

1. Combine salt and garlic in a small bowl, pressing with the back of a spoon to form a paste.

2. Whisk in mayonnaise and remaining ingredients. Cover and chill 1 hour.

HONEY-MUSTARD DRESSING

makes 2 cups   prep: 5 min.

1   (8-oz.) container light sour cream

¼   cup reduced-fat mayonnaise

½   cup honey

2   Tbsp. stone-ground mustard

2   Tbsp. Dijon mustard

2   Tbsp. lemon juice

1. Stir together all ingredients; cover and chill up to 3 days.

BUTTERMILK-GARLIC DRESSING

makes ½ cup   prep: 5 min.

½   cup buttermilk

2   Tbsp. mayonnaise

1   garlic clove, pressed

Salt and pepper to taste

1. Whisk together all ingredients. Cover and chill until ready to serve.

SANDWICHES

"Call me All-American, but I love ham and cheese sandwiches. And not just any old ham and cheese sandwich....My mother's is the best. I've tried many times to make these sandwiches on my own, but it's never the same." —Andy Roddick

GRILLED PIMIENTO CHEESE

makes 4 servings   prep: 25 min.   cook: 6 min. per batch

To save time, purchase prepared pimiento cheese.

¾ cup mayonnaise, divided

1   (2-oz.) jar diced pimiento, drained

½ tsp. Worcestershire sauce

⅛ tsp. Cajun seasoning

Pinch of granulated garlic

⅛ tsp. ground black pepper

¼ tsp. hot sauce

1   (10-oz.) block Cheddar cheese, shredded

8   slices whole grain white bread

1. Stir together ½ cup mayonnaise and next 6 ingredients; gently stir in cheese. Cover and chill up to 3 days, if desired.

2. Spread remaining ¼ cup mayonnaise evenly on 1 side of each bread slice. Place 4 bread slices, mayonnaise sides down, on wax paper.

3. Spread cheese mixture evenly on top of 4 bread slices on wax paper; top with remaining bread slices, mayonnaise sides up.

4. Cook sandwiches, in batches, on a hot griddle or in a large nonstick skillet over medium heat 3 minutes on each side or until golden brown and cheese melts.

Note: We tested with Sara Lee Whole Grain White Bread.

Grill It Up Golden

An electric griddle allows you to cook more sandwiches at a time. Test Kitchen professional Angela Sellers says, "The secret is to preheat your griddle or skillet to a medium temperature." The results are perfectly melted cheese and crispy, golden crusts every time.

Pimiento Cheese

Highbrow enough for sandwiches sold at the Masters golf tournament and downhome enough for a kid's lunch box, pimiento cheese is right at home at any occasion. It's just that not everyone is of like mind when you talk about how to make it.

For almost 100 years, Southerners have relished one of the region's truly original creations with crackers, on celery, and spread on soft white sandwich bread. Pimiento cheese requires only three basic ingredients—sharp Cheddar, mayonnaise, and pimiento. Some blend it smooth and others coarsely grate the cheese to leave it chunky. But the main recipe differences lie in the extras cooks have added to personalize their own, such as hot sauce, mustard, sugar, cream cheese, garlic, lemon juice, ground red pepper, Worcestershire sauce, grated onion, and sweet pickle relish. And if you're as crazy about pimiento cheese as *Southern Living* Executive Editor Scott Jones is, you'll find dozens of ways to add it to burgers, hot dogs, baked potatoes, or deviled eggs. Or maybe grilled in a sandwich with tomato slices and crispy bacon.

PESTO-CRUSTED GRILLED CHEESE

makes 4 servings   prep: 15 min.   cook: 6 min. per batch

⅓   cup mayonnaise
2   Tbsp. jarred pesto sauce
8   sourdough bread slices
4   (1-oz.) fontina cheese slices

1   (12-oz.) jar roasted red bell peppers, drained and chopped
4   (1-oz.) Cheddar cheese slices

1. Stir together mayonnaise and pesto sauce. Spread evenly on 1 side of each sourdough bread slice. Place 4 bread slices, pesto sides down, on wax paper.
2. Layer 4 bread slices on wax paper each with 1 fontina cheese slice, bell peppers, and 1 Cheddar cheese slice; top with remaining bread slices, pesto sides up.
3. Cook sandwiches, in batches, on a hot griddle or in a nonstick skillet over medium heat, gently pressing with a spatula, 3 minutes on each side or until golden brown and cheese melts.

Cut bread for this sandwich into heart or other desired shape before filling with chocolate and cooking.

Grilled Chocolate Sweetheart

makes 1 serving   prep: 5 min.   cook: 2 min.

Place 2 (0.375-oz.) good-quality chocolate squares between 2 white bread slices; brush both sides of sandwich with 1½ tsp. melted butter. Cook in a hot nonstick skillet over medium-high heat 30 to 60 seconds on each side or until chocolate is melted and bread is golden brown. Dust with powdered sugar. Garnish with raspberries, if desired.

Note: We tested with thin squares that would melt quickly and evenly, such as Ghirardelli 60% Cacao Squares Dark Chocolate, Ghirardelli Milk Chocolate With Caramelized Almonds Squares, and Lindt Excellence 70% Cocoa Dark Chocolate Extra Fine Squares.

ITALIAN CHEESE BITES

makes 8 appetizer servings   prep: 15 min.   cook: 6 min. per batch

This four-ingredient favorite closely resembles the richness of fried cheese sticks. We visited our supermarket bakery for a presliced Italian bread loaf.

½ cup butter, softened
½ cup freshly grated Parmesan cheese
16 Italian bread slices

16 provolone cheese slices
Marinara sauce

1. Stir together butter and Parmesan cheese; spread on 1 side of each bread slice. Place 8 bread slices, buttered sides down, on wax paper.
2. Layer 8 bread slices on wax paper each with 2 provolone cheese slices, and top with remaining bread slices, buttered sides up.
3. Cook sandwiches, in batches, on a hot griddle or in a nonstick skillet over medium heat, gently pressing with a spatula, 3 minutes on each side or until golden brown and cheese melts. Cut each sandwich into fourths, and serve with marinara sauce for dipping.

EGG SALAD CLUB SANDWICHES

makes 4 servings   prep: 25 min.   **pictured on page 752**

For a checkerboard effect, you can use both white and wheat breads. If you want to serve only the salad, just omit the bread, spinach, and ⅓ cup mayonnaise.

⅔ cup mayonnaise, divided
4   large hard-cooked eggs, chopped
1   celery rib, diced
4   bacon slices, cooked and crumbled
¼   cup chopped fresh chives
1   Tbsp. minced sweet onion

¼   tsp. seasoned salt
½   tsp. freshly ground pepper
12 very thin white or wheat sandwich bread slices, lightly toasted
1   cup firmly packed fresh spinach

Garnish: whole fresh chives

1. Stir together ⅓ cup mayonnaise and next 7 ingredients.
2. Spread remaining ⅓ cup mayonnaise evenly over 1 side of each bread slice. Spread 4 bread slices, mayonnaise side up, evenly with half of egg salad. Top evenly with half of spinach and 4 bread slices.
3. Repeat procedure with remaining egg salad, spinach, and bread slices. Cut each sandwich into quarters; garnish, if desired.

SWEET-PICKLE EGG SALAD CLUB

makes 4 servings   prep: 25 min.

If your favorite egg salad recipe seems a little wet, stir in 2 tablespoons of instant potato flakes.

⅔ cup mayonnaise, divided
4   large hard-cooked eggs, chopped
1   celery rib, diced
2   Tbsp. instant potato flakes
1   Tbsp. sweet pickle relish
1   Tbsp. minced sweet onion

¼   tsp. seasoned salt
½   tsp. freshly ground pepper
12 very thin white or wheat sandwich bread slices, lightly toasted
1   cup firmly packed spinach

1. Stir together ⅓ cup mayonnaise and next 7 ingredients.
2. Spread remaining ⅓ cup mayonnaise evenly over 1 side of each bread slice. Spread 4 bread slices, mayonnaise side up, evenly with half of egg salad. Top evenly with half of spinach and 4 bread slices.
3. Repeat procedure with remaining egg salad, spinach, and bread slices. Cut each sandwich into quarters.

SHRIMP-EGG SALAD CLUB

makes 4 servings   prep: 25 min.

⅔ cup mayonnaise, divided

4 large hard-cooked eggs, chopped

1 celery rib

⅔ cup finely chopped boiled shrimp

½ tsp. lemon zest

¼ tsp. ground red pepper

¼ cup chopped fresh chives

1 Tbsp. minced sweet onion

¼ tsp. seasoned salt

½ tsp. freshly ground pepper

12 very thin white or wheat sandwich bread slices, lightly toasted

1 cup firmly packed fresh spinach

Garnish: whole fresh chives (optional)

1. Stir together ⅓ cup mayonnaise and next 9 ingredients.

2. Spread remaining ⅓ cup mayonnaise evenly over 1 side of each bread slice. Spread 4 bread slices, mayonnaise side up, evenly with half of egg salad. Top evenly with half of spinach and 4 bread slices.

3. Repeat procedure with remaining egg salad, spinach, and bread slices. Cut each sandwich into quarters; garnish, if desired.

TOMATO-EGG SANDWICHES

makes 12 appetizer servings   prep: 20 min.

The day before serving, combine the first 4 ingredients; cover and chill. Boil eggs, peel, and slice; cover and chill. Slice the tomatoes and toast the bread just before assembling the sandwiches.

1 (8-oz.) package cream cheese, softened

1 (9-oz.) jar horseradish sauce

1 small onion, grated (about ¼ cup)

1 (1-oz.) package Ranch dressing mix

12 white sandwich bread slices, toasted

12 whole wheat sandwich bread slices, toasted

24 tomato slices (about 6 medium-size ripe tomatoes)

48 hard-cooked egg slices (about 8 large eggs)

Chopped fresh dill

Freshly ground pepper

1. Beat cream cheese and next 3 ingredients at medium speed with an electric mixer until blended; set aside.

2. Cut 24 rounds from toasted bread using a 3-inch cutter. (Select a cutter close to the size of the tomato slices.) Reserve bread trimmings for another use, if desired.

3. Spread 1 side of each round evenly with cream cheese mixture; top with 1 tomato slice and 2 egg slices. Sprinkle evenly with dill and pepper.

[make ahead]

FRIED GREEN TOMATO SANDWICHES

makes 8 servings prep: 20 min.

1 cup fine, dry breadcrumbs
2 Tbsp. grated Parmesan cheese
½ tsp. salt
Dash of ground red pepper
4 large green tomatoes, cut into ¼-inch-thick
   slices
2 large eggs, lightly beaten

¼ cup butter
8 lettuce leaves
1 large sweet onion, thinly sliced
1 (16-oz.) package bacon, cooked
8 sandwich rolls, split
⅓ cup Ranch dressing

1. Stir together first 4 ingredients in a shallow bowl.

2. Dip tomato slices in egg, and dredge in breadcrumb mixture.

3. Melt butter in a large skillet over medium heat. Cook tomatoes, in batches, 2 minutes on each side or until golden. Drain on a wire rack over paper towels.

4. Layer lettuce, onion, fried green tomatoes, and bacon evenly on bottom half of each roll.

5. Drizzle evenly with dressing. Cover with tops of rolls. Serve immediately.

Note: We tested with Pepperidge Farm Sandwich Rolls.

TOASTED CLUB SANDWICHES

makes 4 servings prep: 15 min. **pictured on page 749**

¾ cup mayonnaise
2 Tbsp. yellow mustard
12 sourdough bread slices, toasted
8 (1-oz.) slices deli ham
8 (1-oz.) slices deli turkey breast

16 fully cooked bacon slices
8 (¾-oz.) Swiss cheese slices
16 plum tomato slices
4 iceberg lettuce leaves, halved

1. Stir together mayonnaise and yellow mustard in a small bowl. Spread mayonnaise mixture evenly onto 1 side of toasted bread slices. Layer 4 bread slices, mayonnaise sides up, with 1 slice ham, 1 slice turkey, 2 bacon slices, 1 Swiss cheese slice, 2 tomato slices, and ½ lettuce leaf. Top each with 1 bread slice, mayonnaise side down; layer with remaining ham, turkey, bacon, cheese, and lettuce. Top with remaining 4 bread slices, mayonnaise sides down. Cut each sandwich into quarters, and, if desired, secure with wooden picks.

Note: We tested with Pepperidge Farm Sourdough Bread.

MELTED AVOCADO CLUB

makes 4 sandwiches   prep: 20 min.   cook: 12 min.

2 ripe avocados, mashed	½ lb. thinly sliced deli ham
1 Tbsp. fresh lime juice	½ lb. thinly sliced deli roast beef
1 Tbsp. mayonnaise	4 tomato slices
1 Tbsp. yellow mustard	8 bacon slices, cooked
⅛ tsp. ground red pepper	¼ lb. provolone cheese slices
8 whole wheat bread slices	3 Tbsp. butter, softened and divided

1. Stir together first 5 ingredients. Spread avocado mixture evenly onto 1 side of 4 bread slices. Top each evenly with ham, next 4 ingredients, and remaining bread slices. Spread butter on both sides of each sandwich.

2. Cook sandwiches in a nonstick skillet or on a griddle over medium heat 6 minutes on each side or until golden.

Amazing Avocados

• To effortlessly pit an avocado, slice all the way around the pit and through both ends of the avocado with a large knife. Then twist the halves in opposite directions, and pull them apart. If the avocado flesh is firm, tap the pit sharply with the knife, and twist the blade to lift out the pit. For those with softer flesh, gently squeeze the outside of the avocado, and remove the pit with your fingers.

• Two varieties are widely available: Hass (from California and Mexico) and Florida (also sold as Fuerte). Smaller Hass avocados have bumpy, dark green skin and a vibrant, buttery flesh. Florida ones are larger with almost smooth, emerald-green skin and a firm, mild flesh.

• Hass avocados contain about 30% more fat than Florida ones, but both are filled with monounsaturated fat, which boosts HDL (good cholesterol) levels. The creamy flesh of the higher fat Hass is ideal for mashing or pureeing for guacamole or salad dressing; Florida's mild, firm flesh is perfect for dicing and slicing for sandwiches and salsa.

COBB CLUBS

makes 4 servings   prep: 25 min.

4   hoagie rolls, split and lightly toasted
1   cup blue cheese dressing
¾   lb. thinly sliced cooked turkey
4   (1-oz.) sharp Cheddar cheese slices
1   large avocado, thinly sliced

8   bacon slices, cooked
4   plum tomatoes, sliced
3   cups shredded leaf lettuce
¼   cup olive oil vinaigrette

1. Spread cut sides of each hoagie roll with dressing.

2. Layer bottom halves of rolls evenly with turkey and next 5 ingredients; drizzle with vinaigrette. Cover with top halves of rolls.

Note: We tested with Newman's Own Olive Oil & Vinegar Dressing.

STEAK-AND-ONION SANDWICHES

makes 6 sandwiches   prep: 15 min.   chill: 1 hr.   grill: 10 min.

1   large yellow onion, coarsely chopped
2   large garlic cloves, coarsely chopped
½   cup lemon juice
2   Tbsp. canola oil
½   tsp. salt
1½ tsp. freshly ground pepper

2   (1¼-lb.) flank steaks
1   cup light mayonnaise
¼   cup salsa, drained
12 light rye bread slices
2   avocados, peeled and thinly sliced

1. Pulse onion and garlic in a food processor until finely chopped. Add juice and next 3 ingredients; pulse 2 times or until blended.

2. Place steaks in a large shallow dish or zip-top plastic freezer bag, and pour onion mixture over steaks. Cover or seal bag, and chill 1 hour, turning occasionally.

3. Preheat grill to 350° to 400° (medium-high) heat. Remove steaks from marinade, discarding mariade.

4. Grill, covered with grill lid, 5 minutes on each side or to desired degree of doneness. Cut across grain into thin slices.

5. Stir together mayonnaise and salsa; spread evenly on 1 side of each bread slice. Arrange steak evenly on half of bread slices; top with avocado slices and remaining bread slices.

PANHANDLE SANDWICHES

makes 4 servings   prep: 15 min.   bake: 5 min.

½ cup butter, softened

4 green onions, diced

2 Tbsp. yellow mustard

2 tsp. Worcestershire sauce

4 (6-inch) French bread loaves, split

4 Monterey Jack cheese slices

8 Baked Glazed Ham slices

1. Preheat oven to 350 °. Stir together first 4 ingredients.

2. Spread butter mixture evenly over cut sides of bread.

3. Cut cheese slices in half; place 2 halves evenly on bottom halves of bread. Top with ham slices and tops of bread. Wrap each sandwich in aluminum foil.

4. Bake sandwiches at 350° for 5 minutes or until thoroughly heated and cheese melts.

Note: Sandwiches may be prepared ahead and frozen. Bake at 350° for 40 minutes.

Baked Glazed Ham

makes 16 servings   prep: 10 min.   cook: 1 hr., 30 min.   stand: 15 min.

2 Tbsp. sugar

1 Tbsp. paprika

1 Tbsp. chili powder

1 tsp. ground cumin

¾ tsp. ground cinnamon

½ tsp. ground cloves

1 (8-lb.) smoked fully cooked ham half, trimmed

1 (12-oz.) can cola soft drink

1 (8-oz.) jar plum or apricot preserves

⅓ cup orange juice

1. Preheat oven to 325°. Combine first 6 ingredients. Score fat on ham in a diamond pattern. Sprinkle ham with sugar mixture, and place in a lightly greased shallow roasting pan. Pour cola into pan.

2. Bake, covered, at 325° for 1 hour. Uncover and bake 15 more minutes. Stir together preserves and orange juice. Spoon ¾ cup glaze over ham, and bake 15 more minutes or until a meat thermometer inserted into thickest portion registers 140°. Let stand 15 minutes before slicing. Serve with remaining glaze.

taking sides

How Do You Make a Peanut Butter Sandwich? Let Me Count the Ways!

Gather any group of kids in your kitchen to make a peanut butter sandwich for the fastest way to learn that jelly isn't the only thing to team with the famous Southern spread on a sandwich.

It's not just the kids that are drawn to the creamy spread that the South made famous. Remember Elvis and his famed fried peanut butter and banana sandwich? Then there's former *Southern Living* Executive Food Editor Susan Dosier, of Charlotte, who has a mighty reputation as a peanut butter connoisseur. As a purist, her favorite sandwich is just plain peanut butter—and lots of it—on whole wheat bread. "But if I change that up," she says, "I like to drizzle honey over the peanut butter and add apple slices."

South Carolinian Elizabeth Orr says peanut butter and honey has been her choice of sandwich since she was a child. Never jelly. But the honey and peanut butter have to be stirred together. Others argue that it's best mixed with marshmallow crème, maple syrup, or raisins, or to pair crunchy peanut butter and slices of banana on soft Sunbeam bread to savor with a tall glass of cold milk. On the weirder side, it's not uncommon to find folks who enjoy their peanut butter with bacon, potato chips, pickles, grated carrot, and even stranger combinations.

Caroline Lowery of Florence, Alabama, has a hard time believing that at one time she didn't like peanut butter and jelly sandwiches, though they were a staple of many of her friends' diets. "One day when I was little I went to the park on a picnic with my family," she recalls. "My Aunt Teresa had rolled white bread slices really flat with a rolling pin and then spread the squished bread with a mixture of pb&j before rolling it up tightly for my cousins to eat. It looked kind of like a cigar. From that day on, I had to have 'peanut butter and jelly roll-ups' whenever we made sandwiches. It became a family tradition for my brother and me. We still love them!"

TOMATO, SWISS, AND BACON SANDWICHES

makes 4 sandwiches   prep: 10 min.   cook: 6 min.

8   Canadian bacon slices
3   Tbsp. light mayonnaise
½   tsp. fresh dill
8   multigrain sandwich bread slices
1   large tomato, cut into 8 slices

¼   tsp. salt
½   tsp. freshly ground pepper
4   (⅔-oz.) slices reduced-fat Swiss cheese
4   iceberg lettuce leaves

1. Cook bacon in a skillet coated with cooking spray over medium heat 3 minutes on each side or until browned. Drain on paper towels.

2. Combine mayonnaise and dill; spread mayonnaise evenly on 1 side of 4 bread slices. Top evenly with bacon slices and tomato slices; sprinkle with salt and pepper. Top evenly with cheese and lettuce. Cover with remaining bread slices.

Note: Canadian bacon is similar to lean ham. It has less fat and cholesterol than bacon.

Per serving: Calories 330; Fat 14g (sat 5g, mono 2.6g, poly 0.9g); Protein 23g; Fiber 4.1g; Chol 46mg; Iron 2.5mg; Sodium 1316mg; Calc 228mg

CHICKEN SALAD CROISSANTS

makes 20 sandwiches   prep: 15 min.   chill: 30 min.

Tarragon adds a fresh flair to this Southern favorite. If desired, prepare the chicken salad two days ahead, and then assemble the sandwiches the morning of the party.

1   cup mayonnaise
1   cup sour cream
1   tsp. salt
1   tsp. pepper
¼   to ½ tsp. fresh tarragon
3   cups chopped cooked chicken

1   cup seedless green or red grapes
¾   cup pecans, toasted and coarsely chopped
20   croissants
Red leaf lettuce
Fresh tarragon sprigs

1. Stir together mayonnaise and next 4 ingredients in a large bowl. Add chicken, grapes, and chopped pecans, tossing to coat. Cover and chill at least 30 minutes.

2. Cut a slit horizontally on 1 side of each croissant; fill evenly with lettuce and chicken salad. Skewer sandwiches with fresh tarragon sprigs to hold together.

ᑐ᠁᠁ inspirations for your taste ᑐ᠁᠁

Peanut butter sandwiches take a bum rap. Because they're easy to make and easier to eat, some people think that they just can't be healthy. We've come up with a version that proves those folks wrong.

PB & GOOD—Peanut Butter Sandwich Variations

The monounsaturated fat in peanut butter and most nuts can, in fact, help lower cholesterol. Instead of heaping on lots of jelly, start with a wholesome bread and your favorite peanut butter, and then add nutritious ingredients such as the following:

- shredded carrots
- chopped apples
- sliced bananas
- chopped mixed nuts
- dried cranberries
- raisins
- low-fat granola cereal
- honey granola cereal

Tip: Don't like whole wheat bread? Consider using white wheat, a white bread with all the nutrients of wheat.

PEANUT CHICKEN PITAS

makes 8 servings   prep: 15 min.   **pictured on page 748**

1   romaine lettuce heart, chopped
1¼ cups chopped cooked chicken breast
¾   cup frozen snow peas, thawed and trimmed
¼   cup shredded carrot

¼   cup chopped roasted lightly salted peanuts
½   cup light sesame-ginger dressing
8   (1-oz.) mini whole wheat pita rounds, halved

1. Combine chopped lettuce and next 4 ingredients in a large bowl. Drizzle with sesame-ginger dressing; toss to combine. Fill each pita half evenly with mixture.

Note: We tested with Newman's Own Low Fat Sesame Ginger Dressing and Toufayan Bakeries Hearth Baked Whole Wheat Pitettes Pita Bread.

Per serving: Calories 166; Fat: 4g (sat 0.6g, mono 1.4g, poly 1g) Protein 11.9g; Fiber 3.2g; Chol 19mg; Iron 2mg; Sodium 383mg; Calc 47mg

SPICY BUFFALO CHICKEN SANDWICHES

makes 6 servings   prep: 10 min.   bake: 8 min.

3   Tbsp. butter, melted

½   cup buffalo-style hot sauce, divided

6   hoagie rolls, split

⅓   cup refrigerated blue cheese dressing

½   tsp. Creole seasoning

1½ cups matchstick-cut carrots

1½ cups diagonally sliced celery

¼   cup finely chopped onion (optional)

12 large deli-fried chicken strips (about 1¼ lb.)

1   (4-oz.) package crumbled blue cheese

Buffalo-style hot sauce (optional)

1. Preheat oven to 350°. Stir together butter and 2 tsp. hot sauce. Brush cut sides of rolls evenly with mixture. Place, cut sides up, on a baking sheet.

2. Bake at 350° for 8 to 10 minutes or until toasted.

3. Stir together blue cheese dressing, 2 tsp. to 3 tsp. hot sauce, and Creole seasoning. Add carrots, celery, and, if desired, onion; toss to coat.

4. Arrange chicken on bottom halves of rolls; drizzle evenly with remaining hot sauce. Layer chicken evenly with carrot mixture and crumbled blue cheese. Top with remaining roll halves. Serve with additional hot sauce, if desired.

Note: We tested with Frank's Red Hot Buffalo Wing Sauce, Marzetti The Ultimate Blue Cheese refrigerated dressing, and Zatarain's Creole Seasoning.

LIGHTENED HOT BROWNS

makes 4 servings   prep: 15 min.   broil: 4 min.   **pictured on page 753**

Originally created at the Brown Hotel in Louisville, Kentucky, this open-faced knife-and-fork sandwich boasts turkey, crisp bacon, and a rich cheese sauce.

8   (1-oz.) rye, wheat, or white bread slices,
    toasted

¾   lb. sliced deli-roasted turkey breast

Parmesan Cheese Sauce

¼   cup freshly shredded Parmesan cheese

4   cooked reduced-fat bacon slices, crumbled

3   plum tomatoes, sliced

1. Preheat oven to broil. Arrange desired bread slices on an aluminum foil-lined 15- x 10-inch jelly-roll pan. Top evenly with turkey and Parmesan Cheese Sauce; sprinkle with Parmesan cheese.

2. Broil 6 inches from heat 4 to 6 minutes or until bubbly and lightly browned; remove from oven. Top with crumbled bacon and tomato slices; serve immediately.

Club-Style Lightened Hot Browns With Caramelized Onions: Melt 2 Tbsp. butter in a medium skillet over medium heat. Add 1 large sweet onion, sliced, and ¼ tsp. salt. Cook, stirring often, 15 to 20 minutes or until onions are caramel colored. Place desired bread slices on jelly-roll pan, and layer with ¼ lb. each of sliced deli-roasted turkey, roast beef, and ham. Top with Parmesan Cheese Sauce and onions; sprinkle with Parmesan cheese. Broil as directed. Top with crumbled bacon and tomato slices; serve immediately.

Southwestern Lightened Hot Browns: Substitute 4 (2-inch-thick) square cornbread slices, halved and toasted, for bread. Place on jelly-roll pan, and top with turkey, Spicy Cheese Sauce, and 1 (4.5-oz) can chopped green chiles, drained. Substitute shredded Mexican four-cheese blend for Parmesan cheese, and sprinkle over sandwiches; broil as directed. Top with crumbled bacon and tomato slices; serve immediately.

Parmesan Cheese Sauce

makes about 1¼ cups   prep: 5 min.   cook: 5 min.

This creamy sauce is also great over steamed veggies and multigrain pasta.

1½ **Tbsp. butter**	¼ **tsp. salt**
2 **Tbsp. flour**	¼ **tsp. pepper**
1 **cup 1% low-fat milk**	**Paprika**
½ **cup freshly graated Parmesan cheese**	

1. Melt butter in a medium skillet over medium-high heat. Sprinkle flour into melted butter, whisking constantly. Cook, whisking constantly, 30 seconds to 1 minute or until mixture is golden and lumpy.
2. Gradually whisk in milk, and bring to a boil. Cook, whisking constantly, 1 to 2 minutes, or until thickened.
3. Add Parmesan cheese, salt, pepper, and a pinch of paprika, whisking until smooth. Remove from heat, and use immediately.

Spicy Cheese Sauce: Prepare Parmesan Cheese Sauce as directed, and whisk in 1 tsp. hot sauce.

SLAW REUBENS

makes 2 servings   prep: 10 min.   cook: 4 min.

2   cups shredded coleslaw mix

5   Tbsp. Thousand Island dressing, divided

1   Tbsp. white vinegar

¼   tsp. freshly ground pepper

1   tsp. spicy brown mustard

4   slices rye or pumpernickel bread

1   (7-oz.) package shaved roast beef

½   Granny Smith apple, cored and thinly sliced

2   (1-oz.) Swiss cheese slices

2   Tbsp. butter, melted

1. Stir together coleslaw mix, 2 Tbsp. Thousand Island dressing, vinegar, and pepper in a medium bowl.

2. Stir together spicy brown mustard and remaining 3 Tbsp. Thousand Island dressing; spread mixture evenly on 1 side of bread slices. Top 2 bread slices evenly with beef; top each with half of apple slices and 1 cheese slice. Divide slaw mixture evenly over cheese. Top with remaining bread slices, dressing mixture sides down. Brush both sides of sandwiches evenly with melted butter.

3. Cook sandwiches in a large lightly greased nonstick skillet over medium-high heat 2 minutes on each side or until golden. Serve immediately.

GRILLED CHEESE MEATLOAF SANDWICHES

makes 4 servings   prep: 5 min.   cook: 4 min.

{ family favorite }

¼   cup butter, melted

8   hearty white bread slices

12 American cheese slices

8   (½-inch-thick) cold meatloaf slices

Garnish: sweet gherkin pickles (optional)

1. Preheat electric griddle to 350° or a nonstick skillet over medium-high heat.

2. Brush butter evenly on 1 side of each bread slice. Place 4 bread slices on griddle or in skillet, buttered side down. Top each with 1½ slices cheese, 2 meatloaf slices, and an additional 1½ slices cheese (total of 3 cheese slices on each sandwich). Top with remaining bread slices, buttered side up.

3. Cook 4 to 5 minutes on each side or until golden. Serve immediately. Garnish, if desired.

MEATLOAF SANDWICH

makes 4 servings prep: 20 min. cook: 8 min. bake: 1 hr., 10 min. pictured on page 750

1 (16-oz.) Italian or sourdough bread loaf	1½ cups (6 oz.) shredded Cheddar cheese, divided
2½ Tbsp. butter, divided	1 lb. lean ground beef
1 small onion, chopped	½ cup dry red wine or beef broth
½ (8-oz.) package sliced fresh mushrooms	1 tsp. garlic salt
1 large egg	¼ tsp. dried thyme
6 to 7 Tbsp. ketchup, divided	2 to 3 Tbsp. mayonnaise

1. Preheat oven to 350°. Cut bread loaf in half lengthwise. Scoop out bread, leaving ¼-inch-thick shells. Tear reserved bread into pieces, and measure 1½ cups, reserving remaining bread pieces for another use. Set bread shells and 1½ cups breadcrumbs aside.

2. Melt 1½ Tbsp. butter in a large skillet over medium heat; add chopped onion and mushrooms, and sauté 8 minutes or until tender.

3. Stir together egg and 2 Tbsp. ketchup in a large bowl. Add onion mixture, 1½ cups breadcrumbs, ½ cup cheese, ground beef, and next 3 ingredients, blending well. Shape mixture into a 6- to 7-inch loaf. Place on a lightly greased rack in a roasting pan.

4. Bake at 350° for 1 hour or until done.

5. Spread bottom bread shell with mayonnaise; top with meatloaf. Top with remaining ketchup; sprinkle with remaining 1 cup cheese. Top with remaining bread half. Melt remaining 1 Tbsp. butter; brush over bread top. Wrap in aluminum foil.

6. Bake at 350° for 10 to 15 minutes or until heated.

Make It Great

Mince (very finely chop) the bell pepper and onion. Large pieces will cause the meatloaf to break apart.

• Don't take a shortcut and substitute dry breadcrumbs for soft, or the loaf will be dry. To make soft breadcrumbs, pulse about 8 slices of white sandwich bread in a food processor until finely crumbled (makes 4 cups).

• For the least shrinkage and nice slices, we tested with lean ground beef that was specifically labeled 93% lean and 7% fat.

CHIMICHURRI CHEESESTEAKS

makes 4 to 6 servings prep: 20 min.   cook: 15 min.   grill: 20 min.

These sandwiches are perfect for a quick and easy dinner.

2   cups packed fresh flat-leaf parsley leaves (about 2 bunches)
4   garlic cloves, chopped
¼   cup lemon juice
2   Tbsp. extra virgin olive oil
1¾ tsp. salt, divided
1¼ tsp. pepper, divided

4   cups thinly sliced sweet onion (about 2)
2   vegetable oil
1½ lb. beef boneless chuck-eye steaks (¾ to 1 inch thick)
4   to 6 center split deli rolls
¼   lb. thinly sliced provolone cheese

1. Preheat grill to 350° to 400° (medium-high) heat. Pulse parsley and garlic in a blender or food processor just until finely chopped. (Do not puree.) Remove to a medium bowl; stir in lemon juice, olive oil, ¾ tsp. salt, and ¾ tsp. pepper. Set aside.

2. Cook onion and ½ tsp. salt in hot vegetable oil over medium-high heat, stirring often, 15 minutes or until onions are golden brown and tender.

3. Sprinkle steaks evenly with remaining ½ tsp. salt and remaining ½ tsp. pepper.

4. Grill steaks, covered with grill lid, 7 to 10 minutes on each side or to desired degree of doneness.

5. Grill cut sides of deli rolls during the last few minutes of cooking steaks. Remove steaks and rolls.

6. Cut steaks into thin slices. Spread parsley mixture evenly on cut sides of bread; place steak slices and onion evenly on bottom bread halves, and top each evenly with cheese and remaining bread halves. Wrap each sandwich in foil. Grill, covered with grill lid, 3 to 4 minutes or until cheese melts.

Backyard Get-Together serves 6

Szechuan Burgers With Cllantro Slaw

French Fries (page 865)

Iced tea   **Key Lime Frozen Yogurt** (page 364)

SZECHUAN BURGERS WITH CILANTRO SLAW

makes 6 servings   prep: 20 min.   chill: 30 min.   grill: 10 min.

Southerners love Asian food and they love to grill, to it's no surprise to find inspired burgers like these sizzling in the South year round

⅓ cup cucumber Ranch dressing

2 Tbsp. minced fresh cilantro

2 tsp. orange juice

1 tsp. kosher salt, divided

1½ cups loosely packed shredded coleslaw mix

½ cup diced green onions

1 Tbsp. black sesame seed

1½ lb. ground chicken breast

¼ cup Asian toasted sesame dressing

2 tsp. minced garlic

1½ tsp. Szechwan seasoning

6 sesame seed hamburger buns

1. Whisk together first 3 ingredients and ¼ tsp. salt in a large bowl. Stir in coleslaw mix, green onions, and sesame seeds. Cover and chill at least 30 minutes or up to 2 hours.

2. Coat a cold cooking grate with cooking spray, and place grate on grill. Preheat grill to 300° to 350° (medium) heat.

3. Combine ground chicken, next 3 ingredients, and remaining ¾ tsp. salt in a large bowl until blended. Shape chicken mixture into 6 (¾-inch-thick) patties.

4. Grill patties, covered with grill lid, 5 minutes on each side or until done. Grill hamburger buns, cut sides down, 1 to 2 minutes or until lightly toasted.

5. Place 1 burger on top of each bottom bun; top evenly with coleslaw mixture and tops of buns.

TURKEY CHEESEBURGERS WITH ROSEMARY ONIONS

makes 6 servings   prep: 10 min.   chill: 30 min.   cook: 22 min.   broil: 3 min.

As Southerners tend toward healthier meals, you'll often find turkey in place of beef within the the bun. Rosemary and goat cheese kick up the flavor.

[southern lights]

1 (20-oz.) package lean ground turkey breast
1 large egg, lightly beaten
1 tsp. salt
½ tsp. freshly ground pepper
1½ Tbsp. butter, divided
1 large sweet onion, halved and sliced

1 tsp. chopped fresh or dried rosemary
1 (4-oz.) package goat cheese, sliced*
6 (1.5-oz.) whole grain white hamburger buns
Toppings: lettuce leaves, Dijon mustard, tomato
   slices

1. Gently combine first 4 ingredients. Shape mixture into 6 thin patties; cover and chill 30 minutes.

2. Melt 1 Tbsp. butter in a nonstick skillet over medium-high heat; add onion and rosemary, and sauté 10 minutes or until onion is tender and golden. Remove onion mixture from skillet.

3. Preheat oven to broil. Melt remaining ½ Tbsp. butter in same skillet over medium heat. Cook patties 6 minutes on each side or until no longer pink in center. Place on an aluminum foil-lined baking sheet or broiler pan coated with cooking spray.

4. Top each patty evenly with onion mixture and 1 cheese slice. Broil 6 inches from heat 3 to 5 minutes or until cheese is lightly browned. Serve on hamburger buns with desired toppings.

* 4 oz. blue cheese, Gorgonzola cheese, or Swiss cheese may be substituted.

Note: Nutritional analysis does not include toppings.

Per serving: Calories 320; Fat 10.5g (sat 5.7g, mono 2g, poly 0.8g); Protein 30.8g; Fiber 1.4g; Chol 89mg; Iron 2.3mg; Sodium 783mg; Calc 138mg

FISH SANDWICHES

makes 4 servings   prep: 15 min.   **pictured on page 750**

Use steamed, poached, or baked fish in this sandwich. It's a great way to use leftover grilled fish too. Any firm white fish, such as tilapia, snapper, or grouper, works well.

2	lb. firm white fish, cooked	¼	tsp. pepper
¼	tsp. lemon zest	½	cup Basil Mayonnaise
¼	cup fresh lemon juice	4	French bread rolls, split
2	Tbsp. olive oil	4	romaine lettuce leaves
¼	tsp. salt	¼	cup thinly sliced red onion

1. Flake fish in a medium bowl. Add ¼ tsp. lemon zest, ¼ cup lemon juice, 2 Tbsp. olive oil, ¼ tsp. salt, and ¼ tsp. pepper, tossing gently to coat.

2. Spread Basil Mayonnaise evenly on cut sides of rolls. Place lettuce and fish on bottom halves of rolls; top with onion, and cover with roll tops.

Basil Mayonnaise

makes 1½ cups   prep. 10 min.

1	cup light mayonnaise	1	Tbsp. fresh lemon juice
1	tsp. lemon zest	1	cup loosely packed fresh basil leaves

1. Process all ingredients in a food processor or blender until smooth, stopping to scrape down sides. Store in an airtight container in the refrigerator up to 1 week.

Garlic-Chili Mayonnaise: Omit lemon zest and basil. Substitute fresh lime juice for lemon juice. Stir together mayonnaise, juice, and 2 Tbsp. Asian garlic-chili sauce. Makes about 1 cup.

FRIED FISH SANDWICHES

makes 4 servings   prep: 20 min.   fry: 4 min. per batch   **pictured on page 750**

2   lb. grouper, mahi-mahi, cod, or halibut fillets
2   tsp. Greek seasoning, divided
1½   tsp. salt, divided
1   tsp. freshly ground pepper, divided
2¼   cups all-purpose flour
¼   cup yellow cornmeal
2   tsp. baking powder

2   cups cold beer
1   large egg, lightly beaten
Vegetable oil
4   sesame seed hamburger buns
Tartar sauce or mayonnaise
4   green leaf lettuce leaves
4   tomato slices

1. Cut fish into 3-inch strips. Sprinkle evenly with 1 tsp. Greek seasoning, 1 tsp. salt, and ½ tsp. pepper.

2. Combine flour, cornmeal, baking powder, remaining 1 tsp. Greek seasoning, ½ tsp. salt, and ½ tsp. pepper; stir well. Add 2 cups cold beer and egg, stirring until thoroughly blended and smooth.

3. Pour oil to a depth of 2 to 3 inches into a Dutch oven; heat to 375°.

4. Dip fish strips into batter, coating both sides well; shake off excess. Fry fish, in batches, 2 minutes on each side or until golden (do not crowd pan). Drain on paper towels.

5. Spread top half of each bun evenly with tartar sauce. Place 1 lettuce leaf and 1 tomato slice on bottom half of each bun; top each with 2 fried fish strips and top halves of buns.

GRILLED-TUNA SANDWICHES

makes 4 sandwiches   prep: 10 min.   grill: 12 min.

4   (½-inch-thick) tuna steaks (about 1 lb.)
2   Tbsp. olive oil, divided
½   tsp. salt
½   tsp. pepper
8   slices sourdough bread
¼   tsp. ground red pepper (optional)

¼   cup finely chopped green onions
¼   cup mayonnaise
2   Tbsp. fresh lime juice
2   tsp. prepared horseradish
1   large tomato, thinly sliced
1   ripe avocado, sliced

1. Preheat grill to 350° to 400° (medium-high) heat. Rub tuna with 1 Tbsp. olive oil, and sprinkle salt and pepper evenly on both sides of tuna.

2. Grill, covered with grill lid, 5 minutes on each side or until tuna reaches desired degree of doneness.

3. Brush bread slices with remaining 1 Tbsp. olive oil, and grill 1 minute on each side or until golden.

4. Flake tuna; combine with ground red pepper, if desired, and next 4 ingredients. Spread tuna mixture evenly on 1 side each of 4 bread slices; top with tomato and avocado slices. Cover with remaining 4 bread slices.

Note: The tuna steaks may be broiled, if desired.

CUMIN-DUSTED CATFISH SANDWICHES

makes 4 servings   prep: 10 min.   grill: 6 min.

Thin fillets of mild, firm-textured fish, such as cod, tilapia, perch, or orange roughy, may be substituted. If the grilled fillets hang over the sides of the bun, break them in half to stack on the bun. You may also serve remaining halves on the side.

1 cup mayonnaise	2 tsp. ground cumin
3 Tbsp. orange juice	4 (6-oz.) catfish fillets
1 to 2 tsp. minced canned chipotle chiles in adobo sauce	Vegetable cooking spray
	4 whole wheat buns, split and toasted
1½ tsp. salt, divided	Tomato slices, shredded lettuce
¼ cup self-rising cornmeal	

1. Preheat grill to 350° to 400° (medium-high) heat. Stir together first 3 ingredients and ½ tsp. salt. Set aside.

2. Combine cornmeal, cumin, and remaining 1 tsp. salt. Rinse fish, and dredge in cornmeal mixture. Spray fish evenly with cooking spray.

3. Grill fish, covered with grill lid, 3 to 4 minutes on each side or just until fish begins to flake with a fork.

4. Serve on buns with mayonnaise mixture, tomato slices, and shredded lettuce.

CATFISH PO'BOYS

makes **4 servings**   chill: 1 hr.   bake: 10 min.

½ cup mayonnaise	1 large egg
2 Tbsp. sweet pickle relish	3 Tbsp. mayonnaise
2 Tbsp. instant minced onion	2 (8-oz.) catfish fillets, cut in half crosswise
2 tsp. lemon juice	4 hoagie rolls, split
¼ tsp. ground red pepper	2 cups shredded lettuce
½ cup fine, dry breadcrumbs	8 tomato slices
1 to 2 Tbsp. Creole seasoning	

1. Combine mayonnaise and next 4 ingredients, stirring well; cover with plastic wrap, and chill 1 hour.

2. Preheat oven to 425°. Combine breadcrumbs and Creole seasoning in a shallow dish. Combine egg and 3 Tbsp. mayonnaise, stirring well. Dip fillets in egg mixture, and dredge in breadcrumb mixture; place on a lightly greased baking sheet.

3. Bake at 425° for 10 minutes or until fish flakes with a fork.

4. Spread chilled mayonnaise mixture on cut sides of rolls; top with fillets, lettuce, and tomato. Cover with roll tops. Serve immediately.

DRESSED MINI OYSTER PO'BOYS

makes **4 to 6 servings**   prep: 30 min.   cook: 3 min. per batch

To save time, purchase premade coleslaw. Selects are fairly large shucked oysters—the perfect size for frying.

1¼ cups self-rising cornmeal	1 (10-oz.) package shredded cabbage
2 Tbsp. Creole seasoning	2 Tbsp. ketchup
2 (8-oz.) containers fresh Select oysters, drained	1 Tbsp. prepared horseradish
Peanut or vegetable oil	1 tsp. Creole seasoning
1 cup mayonnaise, divided	¾ tsp. paprika
2 Tbsp. white vinegar	12 French bread rolls, split and toasted
2 Tbsp. Dijon mustard	Garnish: lemon wedges (optional)

1. Combine cornmeal and 2 Tbsp. Creole seasoning. Dredge oysters in cornmeal mixture.

2. Pour oil to a depth of 1 inch into a Dutch oven; heat to 375°.

3. Fry oysters, in 3 batches, 3 to 4 minutes or until golden. Drain oysters on paper towels.

4. Stir together ½ cup mayonnaise, vinegar, and mustard. Stir in cabbage; set slaw aside.

5. Stir together remaining ½ cup mayonnaise, ketchup, and next 3 ingredients in a small bowl.

6. Spread cut sides of French bread rolls with ketchup mixture; place oysters and slaw evenly on bottom halves of each roll. Cover with tops. Serve po'boys immediately. Garnish, if desired.

FRIED BUFFALO OYSTER PO'BOYS

makes 4 servings   prep: 20 min.   chill: 2 hr.   fry: 3 min. per batch

2 pt. fresh Select oysters, drained	½ tsp. dry mustard
2 cups buttermilk	½ tsp. salt
1 cup all-purpose flour	½ tsp. ground black pepper
½ cup yellow cornmeal	Vegetable oil
1 Tbsp. paprika	4 French bread rolls
1½ tsp. garlic powder	¼ cup mayonnaise
1½ tsp. dried oregano	1 cup shredded iceberg lettuce
1½ tsp. ground red pepper	

1. Combine oysters and buttermilk in a large shallow dish or zip-top plastic freezer bag. Cover or seal, and chill at least 2 hours. Drain oysters well.

2. Combine flour and next 8 ingredients. Dredge oysters in flour mixture, shaking off excess.

3. Pour oil to a depth of 1 inch in a Dutch oven; heat to 370°.

4. Fry oysters, in batches, 3 minutes or until golden. Drain on paper towels.

5. Split rolls. Spread 1 Tbsp. mayonnaise evenly on cut sides of rolls. Place ¼ cup lettuce and one-fourth of oysters on bottom halves of rolls; cover with roll tops.

DRESSED OYSTER PO'BOYS

makes 4 sandwiches   prep: 30 min.   cook: 6 min.

1¼ cups self-rising cornmeal

2   Tbsp. Creole seasoning

2   (12-oz.) containers fresh Select oysters, drained

Peanut or vegetable oil

1   cup mayonnaise, divided

2   Tbsp. white vinegar

2   Tbsp. Dijon mustard

1   (10-oz.) package finely shredded cabbage

2   Tbsp. ketchup

1   Tbsp. prepared horseradish

1   tsp. Creole seasoning

¾   tsp. paprika

4   French bread rolls, split and toasted

1. Combine cornmeal and Creole seasoning; dredge oysters in mixture.

2. Pour oil to a depth of 2 inches into a Dutch oven; heat to 375°. Fry oysters, in 3 batches, 2 to 3 minutes or until golden. Drain on wire racks.

3. Stir together ½ cup mayonnaise, vinegar, and mustard. Stir in cabbage; set slaw aside.

4. Stir together remaining ½ cup mayonnaise, ketchup, and next 3 ingredients.

5. Spread cut sides of rolls with mayonnaise mixture. Place oysters and slaw evenly on bottom halves of rolls; cover with roll tops.

ZESTY FISH PO'BOYS

makes 4 servings   prep: 20 min.   **pictured on page 750**

2   (11-oz.) packages frozen breaded fish fillets

2   (12-inch) French bread loaves

1   cup regular or light mayonnaise

3   Tbsp. lemon juice

1   Tbsp. Creole mustard

1   Tbsp. sweet pickle relish

1   tsp. chopped fresh or ½ tsp. dried parsley

¼   tsp. dried tarragon

½   tsp. hot sauce

4   lettuce leaves

1. Bake fish fillets according to package directions. Set aside, and keep warm.

2. Cut bread in half crosswise. Split each half lengthwise, and toast.

3. Stir together mayonnaise and next 6 ingredients. Spread mixture evenly over cut sides of bread halves. Place lettuce and fish on bottom bread halves; top with remaining bread halves. Serve immediately.

Note: We tested with Gorton's Southern Fried Country Style Breaded Fish Fillets.

FRIED GREEN TOMATO PO'BOYS

makes 3 servings   prep: 20 min.   fry: 4 min. per batch   broil: 2 min.

2	cups self-rising flour	9	slices fully cooked bacon
3	Tbsp. Cajun seasoning	3	center split deli rolls
2	cups canola oil	6	Tbsp. mayonnaise
3	large green tomatoes, cut into ¼-inch-thick slices	1	ripe avocado, sliced
1	cup buttermilk	1½	cups shredded iceberg lettuce
			Hot sauce (optional)

1. Preheat oven to broil. Combine flour and Cajun seasoning in a shallow dish.

2. Heat oil in a large nonstick skillet over medium-high heat to 360°. Dip tomato slices into buttermilk, and dredge in flour mixture. Fry tomatoes, in batches, 2 minutes on each side or until golden. Drain on a wire rack over paper towels; set aside.

3. Heat bacon according to package directions; keep warm.

4. Split rolls, and arrange, split sides up, on a baking sheet. Broil 5 inches from heat 2 minutes or until lightly toasted; remove from oven.

5. Spread cut sides of rolls with mayonnaise; place fried green tomatoes on bottom roll halves. Top evenly with bacon, avocado, and lettuce; sprinkle with hot sauce, if desired. Top with remaining roll halves, and serve immediately.

TASTE OF THE SOUTH

Muffuletta Olive salad and a crusty round loaf are the hallmarks of this New Orleans favorite.

Take a bite of a well-prepared muffuletta, and you'll know why these large, round sandwiches remain enduring standards of the New Orleans food scene. Filled with layers of salami, ham, cheese, and olive salad, muffulettas are the cold-cut competitors of the po'boys. The flavors are bold, and the servings are generous.

Muffuletta lovers are divided on whether they prefer the sandwiches warm or cold, but they find them a taste delight either way. The crusty Italian bread offers a mouth-boggling chew and soothes the garlicky, salty intensity of the olive salad and salami in the filling.

Who created the first muffuletta is a matter of dispute, but food critic and historian Gene Bourg uncovered a likely scenario. He interviewed elderly Sicilians who lived in the French Quarter for many years. "They told me vendors used to sell them on the streets as did Italian groceries," he says. The name refers to the shape of the bread. 'Muffulett' means 'little muffin.' Italian bakers made muffuletta loaves and sold them to Italian delis. The delis then wrapped the sandwiches in the same paper the bread came in so the sandwich took on the name."

You'll find many places to enjoy a muffuletta in New Orleans, but two favorites reside on Decatur Street. Lines begin to form outside Central Grocery by midmorning. Luigi's Fine Food, two doors down, offers an excellent sandwich without the wait. Or try the warm muffuletta at Napoleon House Bar & Café at 500 Chartres Street. If the Big Easy isn't in your travel plans, don't despair. Read on for our favorite muffuletta.

MUFFULETTA

makes 4 servings   prep: 10 min.   **pictured on page 753**

1 (10-inch) round Italian bread loaf	½ lb. sliced cooked ham
2 cups Olive Salad	6 Swiss cheese slices
½ lb. sliced hard salami	6 thin provolone cheese slices

1. Cut bread loaf in half horizontally; scoop out soft bread from both halves, leaving a 1-inch-thick shell. Reserve soft bread centers for another use, if desired.

2. Spoon 1 cup Olive Salad evenly into bottom bread shell; top with salami, ham, cheeses, and remaining 1 cup Olive Salad. Cover with bread top, and cut crosswise into wedges or quarters.

Olive Salad

makes 6 cups   prep: 15 min.   chill: 8 hr.

1 (1-qt.) jar mixed pickled vegetables	½ cup olive oil
1 red onion, quartered	1½ tsp. dried parsley flakes
1 (16-oz.) jar pitted green olives, drained	1 tsp. dried oregano
1 (6-oz.) can medium pitted ripe black olives, drained	1 tsp. dried basil
	½ tsp. ground black pepper
¼ cup sliced pepperoncini salad peppers	1 (7-oz.) jar roasted red bell peppers, drained
2 Tbsp. capers	and coarsely chopped (optional)
1 Tbsp. minced garlic	

1. Drain pickled vegetables, reserving ¼ cup liquid.

2. Pulse pickled vegetables 4 times in a food processor or until coarsely chopped; pour into a large bowl. Pulse onion 4 times in food processor or until coarsely chopped; add to pickled vegetables in bowl. Pulse olives and salad peppers in food processor 4 times or until coarsely chopped; add to vegetable mixture. Stir in capers, next 6 ingredients, reserved ¼ cup pickled vegetable liquid, and, if desired, chopped red bell peppers. Cover and chill 8 hours. Chill leftover mixture up to 2 weeks.

Note: We used mixed pickled vegetables that contained cauliflower, onions, carrots, peppers, and celery.

Kick off your next gathering with easy and innovative bite-size delights.

Muffuletta on a Stick

makes 24 servings   prep: 30 min.   chill: 30 min.

Layer 1 slice each of deli-style smoked ham, provolone cheese, and Genoa salami; tightly roll up, and slice into 4 equal pieces. Repeat procedure 5 times. Thread 24 (4-inch) wooden skewers with 1 each of pepperoncini salad pepper, meat-and-cheese roll, 1½ inch-long roasted red bell pepper, large pitted ripe black olive, another 1½-inch-long roasted red bell pepper, and pimiento-stuffed Spanish olive. Place in a 13- x 9-inch dish. Whisk together 1 (8-oz.) bottle olive oil-and-vinegar dressing and ½ tsp. dried Italian seasoning; pour over skewers, and chill 30 minutes.

MUFFULETTA CALZONES

makes 4 servings   prep: 20 min.   bake: 20 min.   **pictured on page 751**

2   Tbsp. olive oil, divided
1   cup jarred mixed pickled vegetables, rinsed and finely chopped
1   (7-oz.) package shredded provolone-Italian cheese blend

8   thin slices Genoa salami, chopped (about ⅛ lb.)
½   cup diced cooked ham
¼   cup sliced pimiento-stuffed Spanish olives
1   lb. bakery pizza dough
2   Tbsp. grated Parmesan cheese

1. Preheat oven to 425°. Stir together 1 Tbsp. oil, pickled vegetables, and next 4 ingredients.
2. Place dough on a lightly floured surface. Cut dough into 4 equal pieces. Roll each piece into a 7-inch circle.
3. Place 2 dough circles on a lightly greased baking sheet. Spoon vegetable mixture evenly on top of circles, mounding mixture on dough and leaving a 1-inch border. Moisten edges of dough with water, and top with remaining 2 dough circles. Press and crimp edges to seal. Cut small slits on tops to allow steam to escape. Brush with remaining 1 Tbsp. olive oil, and sprinkle with Parmesan cheese.
4. Bake at 425° for 20 to 24 minutes or until golden brown.

OVEN-GRILLED LOADED TURKEY MELTS

makes 4 sandwiches   prep: 30 min.   cook: 20 min.

2	ripe avocados, peeled and mashed	4	tomato slices
2	Tbsp. mayonnaise	4	sliced red onion rings
1	tsp. garlic powder	8	bacon slices, cooked
8	bread slices	¼	lb. smoked mozzarella cheese slices
1	lb. thinly sliced deli turkey	3	Tbsp. butter, softened

1. Preheat oven to 400°. Stir together avocado, mayonnaise, and garlic powder. Spread avocado mixture on 1 side of 4 bread slices. Top evenly with turkey, tomato, onion, bacon, cheese, and remaining bread slices.

2. Spread half of butter on 1 side of each sandwich. Place buttered sandwiches on a baking sheet. Place a second baking sheet on top of sandwiches. Bake at 400° for 20 minutes or until golden.

CUBAN GRILLS

makes 4 servings   prep: 15 min.   cook: 8 min. per batch

This twist on the classic Cuban sandwich so popular in South Florida uses corn tortillas instead of crusty bread. Look for thinly sliced roasted pork in the deli section of your grocery store.

8	(5-inch) corn tortillas	8	thin slices deli ham
1	Tbsp. butter, melted	8	thin slices deli roasted pork
2	Tbsp. honey mustard	12	dill pickle chips
8	baby Swiss cheese slices	2	Tbsp. hot mustard

1. Brush 1 side of each tortilla with melted butter. Place 4 tortillas, buttered sides down, on wax paper.

2. Spread honey mustard evenly over 4 tortillas on wax paper. Layer each tortilla with 1 cheese slice, 2 ham slices, and 2 pork slices; top with 3 pickle chips and 1 cheese slice. Spread hot mustard evenly on 1 side of 4 remaining tortillas, and place, mustard sides down, over layered tortillas.

3. Cook sandwiches, in batches, on a hot griddle or in a nonstick skillet over medium heat, gently pressing with a spatula, 4 minutes on each side or until golden brown and cheese melts.

HOT BROWN PANINI

makes 8 servings   prep: 20 min.   cook: 2 min. per batch

This richly delicious sandwich was inspired by reader Julie Morgan's recipe for a Kentucky classic.

2   Tbsp. melted butter
16 (½-inch-thick) Italian bread slices
1   cup (4 oz.) shredded Swiss cheese, divided
3   cups chopped cooked chicken or turkey

4   plum tomatoes, sliced
3   cups warm White Cheese Sauce, divided
13 cooked bacon slices, crumbled

1. Preheat a panini press. Brush melted butter evenly on 1 side of 16 bread slices. Place, butter sides down, on wax paper.

2. Sprinkle 1 Tbsp. Swiss cheese on top of each of 8 bread slices; top evenly with chicken, tomato slices, and 1 cup warm White Cheese Sauce. Sprinkle with bacon and remaining cheese, and top with remaining bread slices, butter sides up.

3. Cook sandwiches, in batches, in panini press 2 to 3 minutes or until golden brown. Serve with remaining 2 cups warm White Cheese Sauce for dipping.

White Cheese Sauce

makes 3 cups   prep: 10 min.   cook: 10 min.

¼   cup butter
¼   cup all-purpose flour
3½ cups milk
1   cup (4 oz.) shredded Swiss cheese

1   cup grated Parmesan cheese
½   tsp. salt
¼   tsp. ground red pepper

1. Melt butter in a heavy saucepan over low heat; whisk in flour until smooth. Cook 1 minute, whisking constantly. Gradually whisk in milk; cook over medium heat, whisking constantly, until mixture is thickened and bubbly. Whisk in Swiss and Parmesan cheeses, salt, and red pepper, whisking until cheeses are melted and sauce is smooth.

PEPPERY TURKEY-AND-BRIE PANINI

makes 8 servings   prep: 10 min.   cook: 2 min. per batch

1 (15-oz.) Brie round

16 multigrain sourdough bread slices

2 lb. thinly sliced smoked turkey

½ cup red pepper jelly

2 Tbsp. melted butter

1. Preheat a panini press. Trim and discard rind from Brie. Cut Brie into ½-inch-thick slices. Layer 8 bread slices evenly with turkey and Brie.

2. Spread 1 Tbsp. pepper jelly on 1 side of each remaining 8 bread slices; place, jelly sides down, onto Brie. Brush sandwiches with melted butter.

3. Cook sandwiches, in batches, in a panini press 2 to 3 minutes or until golden brown.

Note: We tested with Braswell's Red Pepper Jelly.

CRISPY GINGER-AND-GARLIC ASIAN TURKEY LETTUCE WRAPS

makes 4 to 5 servings   prep: 15 min.   cook: 13 min.

½ cup finely chopped carrots

1 (20-oz.) package lean ground turkey

1 cup chopped shiitake mushrooms

1 (8-oz.) can water chestnuts, drained and chopped

3 garlic cloves, minced

2 Tbsp. minced fresh ginger

⅓ cup teriyaki sauce

3 Tbsp. creamy peanut butter

1 Tbsp. sesame oil

1 Tbsp. rice vinegar

¼ cup hoisin sauce

½ cup sliced green onions

1 head iceberg lettuce, separated into leaves

Hoisin sauce (optional)

1. Cook carrots and ½ cup water in a large nonstick skillet over high heat, stirring occasionally, 3 to 5 minutes or until carrots are softened and water is evaporated. Remove from skillet.

2. Reduce heat to medium. Cook turkey in skillet about 5 minutes, stirring until turkey crumbles and is no longer pink. Add carrots, mushrooms, and next 8 ingredients. Increase heat to medium-high, and cook, stirring constantly, 4 minutes. Add green onions, and cook, stirring constantly, 1 minute. Spoon mixture evenly onto lettuce leaves; roll up. Serve with hoisin sauce, if desired.

[for kids]

GREEK CHICKEN ROLLUPS

makes 4 to 6 servings   prep: 20 min.   grill: 12 min.   stand: 10 min.

3 to 4 skinned and boned chicken breasts	1 cup Low-Cal Dilled Yogurt Dressing
1 Tbsp. olive oil	1 cucumber, thinly sliced
1 to 2 tsp. Greek seasoning	4 plum tomatoes, thinly sliced
4 to 6 slices Italian herb flatbread*	6 green leaf lettuce leaves

1. Preheat grill to 350° to 400° (medium-high) heat. Brush chicken breasts with oil, and sprinkle evenly with Greek seasoning.

2. Grill chicken breasts, covered with grill lid, 6 to 8 minutes on each side or until chicken is done. Let chicken stand 10 minutes; cut into ¼-inch-thick slices.

3. Place sliced chicken down center of warmed flatbread slices. Top with Low-Cal Dilled Yogurt Dressing, cucumber, tomato slices, and lettuce; roll up. Serve immediately.

* Pita bread rounds may be substituted for flatbread. Line warmed pita rounds with Low-Cal Dilled Yogurt Dressing, lettuce, tomato slices, and cucumber slices. Fill with sliced chicken, and serve immediately.

Low-Cal Dilled Yogurt Dressing

makes 1½ cups   prep: 10 min.   chill: 1 hr.

1 cup plain nonfat yogurt	¼ tsp. dry mustard
½ small onion, chopped	¼ tsp. minced garlic
2 Tbsp. chopped fresh or 2 tsp. dried dill	¼ cup fat-free mayonnaise

1. Process yogurt and next 4 ingredients in a blender or food processor until smooth, stopping to scrape down sides. Whisk in mayonnaise. Cover and chill 1 hour.

12 Bones Smokehouse

Blueberry-chipotle ribs—blasphemy or bliss? It's hard to imagine the traditional Southern favorite tweaked to such fruity/spicy terms, yet the taste is terrific. Tom Montgomery's attempt in the we-do-them-our-way South has turned into triumph at the restaurant called 12 Bones Smokehouse. "Fruit is a natural pairing with pork on any level," he explains. "You can use orange or blueberry or peach." The restaurant also uses local beers in the kitchen and on the menu. "We'll trade brewers a rack of ribs for beer and make a sauce," says Sabra Kelley, Tom's wife and co-owner.

She also points out a menu of sides so divine that a vegetarian can eat heartily—especially the jalapeño cheese grits, corn pudding, and mashed sweet potatoes. There's diversity in the sauces too (tomato, jalapeño, mustard, and vinegar); though, honestly, the baby back ribs need no adornment. Lines to get in form early and run deep into the parking lot here. There's no doubt why.

5 Riverside Drive
Ashville, North Carolina 28801
www.12bones.com or (828) 253-4499

3578 Sweeten Creek Road
Arden, North Carolina 28704
www.12bones.com or (828) 687-1395

CLUB WRAPS

makes 4 servings prep: 25 min.

½ cup creamy mustard-mayonnaise blend

4 (10-inch) flour tortillas

½ lb. thinly sliced smoked turkey

½ lb. thinly sliced honey ham

1 cup (4 oz.) shredded smoked provolone or mozzarella cheese

2 cups shredded leaf lettuce

2 medium tomatoes, seeded and chopped

½ small red onion, diced

8 bacon slices, cooked and crumbled

½ tsp. salt

½ tsp. pepper

1. Spread mustard-mayonnaise blend evenly over 1 side of each tortilla, leaving a ½-inch border. Layer turkey and next 6 ingredients evenly over tortillas; sprinkle with salt and pepper.

2. Roll up tortillas; cut in half diagonally, and secure with wooden picks.

DEBATE BARBECUE SANDWICHES

makes 20 servings prep: 10 min. cook: 8 hr.

A former member of our Test Kitchen staff reported that her mother-in-law sold these sandwiches at her son's debate team events to pay for his travel.

1 (3-lb.) boneless pork loin roast, trimmed

1 (18-oz.) bottle barbecue sauce

¼ cup firmly packed brown sugar

2 Tbsp. Worcestershire sauce

1 to 2 Tbsp. hot sauce

1 tsp. salt

1 tsp. pepper

Hamburger buns

Coleslaw

1. Place roast in a 4-qt. slow cooker; add 1 cup water.

2. Cook, covered, at HIGH 7 hours or until meat is tender; stir with a fork, shredding meat.

3. Add barbecue sauce and next 5 ingredients; reduce setting to LOW, and cook, covered, 1 hour. Serve barbecue on buns with coleslaw.

BBQ PORK QUESADILLA TORTA

makes 4 to 6 servings prep: 10 min. bake: 15 min.

½ lb. (about 2 cups) chopped barbecued pork

1 (15-oz.) can black beans, rinsed and drained

½ cup barbecue sauce

4 (10-inch) burrito-size flour tortillas

1 cup seeded, diced plum tomatoes (about 2 large)

2 green onions, finely chopped

2 cups (8 oz.) shredded Mexican-style cheese blend

Avocado Mash

Toppings: sour cream, barbecue sauce

Garnish: fresh cilantro sprigs (optional)

1. Preheat oven to 400°. Stir together barbecued pork, black beans, and ½ cup barbecue sauce in a medium bowl.

2. Place 1 tortilla in a lightly greased 10-inch springform pan, and spread with one-third pork mixture. Sprinkle with one-third each of tomatoes, green onions, and cheese. Repeat layers twice. Top with remaining tortilla, and gently press. Cover pan with aluminum foil.

3. Bake at 400° for 15 to 20 minutes or until golden brown. Remove sides of pan, and cut into wedges. Serve with Avocado Mash and desired toppings. Garnish, if desired.

BBQ Beef Quesadilla Torta: Substitute 2 cups chopped barbecued beef for pork, and proceed with recipe as directed.

BBQ Chicken Quesadilla Torta: Substitute 2 cups chopped barbecued chicken for pork, and proceed with recipe as directed.

Avocado Mash

makes ¾ cup prep: 10 min.

2 medium-size ripe avocados, peeled and coarsely chopped

2 Tbsp. chopped fresh cilantro

1 Tbsp. fresh lime juice

½ tsp. pepper

¼ tsp. salt

1. Mash together avocados and remaining ingredients with a fork or potato masher just until mixture is chunky.

CHICKEN SALAD CRESCENT ROLLS

makes 8 rolls   prep: 10 min.   bake: 10 min.

1   (8-oz.) can refrigerated crescent rolls
1   cup your favorite chicken salad

2   Tbsp. poppy seeds

1. Preheat oven to 375°. Unroll crescent rolls; separate each dough portion along center and diagonal perforations, forming 8 triangles. Spoon 2 Tbsp. of your favorite chicken salad on the wide end of each triangle. Starting at the wide end of each triangle, roll dough over chicken salad, pinching edges to seal.
2. Place rolls, seam sides down, on a lightly greased baking sheet. Sprinkle tops of rolls evenly with poppy seeds. (Seeds will stick to rolls without a binder; you don't need to brush with egg.) Bake at 375° for 10 to 12 minutes or until golden brown.

ROASTED RED PEPPER SANDWICHES

makes 4 servings   prep: 20 min.

Prepare these sandwiches up to six hours ahead. For a heartier option, add turkey, chicken, or prosciutto.

1   (16.5-oz.) jar roasted red bell peppers, drained
1   garlic clove, minced
1   (9-inch) deli-loaf ciabatta or focaccia bread, sliced lengthwise

¼   cup refrigerated olive tapenade
1   (5.3-oz.) container goat cheese
1½ cups arugula

1. Toss together red peppers and garlic in a small bowl.
2. Spread cut side of top half of bread evenly with tapenade and cut side of bottom half evenly with goat cheese. Layer red pepper mixture and arugula over goat cheese. Place top half of bread, tapenade side down, onto red pepper and arugula layers. Cut into 4 pieces.

CURRIED CHICKEN SALAD TEA SANDWICHES

makes about 25 servings   prep: 1 hr.

4   cups finely chopped cooked chicken
3   (8-oz.) packages cream cheese, softened
¾   cup dried cranberries, chopped
½   cup sweetened flaked coconut, toasted
6   green onions, minced
2   celery ribs, diced

1   (2¼-oz.) package slivered almonds, toasted
1   Tbsp. curry powder
1   Tbsp. freshly grated ginger
½   tsp. salt
½   tsp. pepper
48 whole-grain bread slices

1. Stir together first 11 ingredients. Spread mixture evenly on 1 side each of 24 bread slices; top with remaining 24 bread slices. Trim crusts from sandwiches; cut each sandwich into 4 rectangles with a serrated knife.

HAM-AND-PINEAPPLE SLAW SANDWICHES

makes 4 servings   prep: 10 min.

2   cups chopped cooked ham
3   cups shredded cabbage
1   (8-oz.) can pineapple tidbits
⅔   cup mayonnaise

1   cup (4 oz.) shredded Cheddar cheese
½   tsp. salt
½   tsp. pepper
4   French sandwich rolls

1. Combine first 7 ingredients, stirring gently. Spoon onto bottoms of rolls; cover with tops, and serve immediately.

SAUCES, CONDIMENTS & EXTRAS

"On a hot day in Virginia, I know nothing more comforting than a fine spiced pickle, brought up trout-like from the sparkling depths of the aromatic jar below the stairs of Aunt Sally's cellar." —Thomas Jefferson

CHEDDAR CHEESE SAUCE

makes 2 cups   prep: 2 min.   cook: 10 min.

2   Tbsp. butter
2   Tbsp all-purpose flour
1   cup milk
1   cup (4 oz.) shredded Cheddar cheese

¼   tsp. salt
Dash of ground white pepper
¼   tsp. dry mustard

1. Melt butter in a heavy saucepan over low heat; whisk in flour until smooth. Cook 1 minute, whisking constantly. Gradually whisk in milk; cook over medium heat, whisking constantly, until mixture is thickened. Whisk in cheese, salt, and remaining ingredients, whisking until cheese is melted and sauce is smooth.

TASSO HOLLANDAISE

makes 3 cups   prep: 10 min.   cook: 12 min.

Chef Tory McPhail of Commander's Palace, New Orleans, Louisiana, created this recipe.

8   egg yolks
¼   cup fresh lemon juice
2   Tbsp. white wine
2   cups butter, melted

½   tsp. salt
⅛   tsp. ground red pepper
½   cup finely chopped tasso ham (about 6 oz.)*

1. Whisk yolks in top of a double boiler; gradually whisk in lemon juice and wine. Place over hot water (do not boil). Add butter, ⅓ cup at a time, whisking until smooth; whisk in salt and red pepper. Cook, whisking constantly, 10 minutes or until thickened and a thermometer registers 160°. Stir in tasso. Serve immediately.

* ½ cup diced, cooked andouille sausage may be substituted.

Kitchen Express: Prepare 2 (0.9-oz.) packages hollandaise sauce mix according to package directions; stir in tasso. We tested with Knorr Hollandaise Sauce Mix.

HORSERADISH SAUCE

makes about 1 cup prep: 5 min.

1   cup mayonnaise
1   Tbsp. cream-style horseradish

1   Tbsp. Creole mustard

1. Stir together mayonnaise, horseradish, and Creole mustard.

[quick]

TANGY GARLIC TARTAR SAUCE

makes about 2¼ cups prep: 10 min.   chill: 2 hr.

2   cups mayonnaise*
1   (3.5-oz.) jar capers, drained

3   garlic cloves, pressed
¼   cup Dijon mustard

1. Combine all ingredients in a blender; process until smooth, stopping once to scrape down sides. Cover and chill 2 hours before serving. Store in an airtight container in refrigerator up to 3 days.

* Light mayonnaise may be substituted.

[make ahead]

SMOKY RÉMOULADE SAUCE

makes about 2 cups prep: 10 min.   chill: 2 hr.

2   cups mayonnaise
¼   cup Creole mustard
2   large garlic cloves, pressed
2   Tbsp. chopped fresh parsley

1   Tbsp. fresh lemon juice
2¼ tsp. smoked paprika*
¾   tsp. ground red pepper

1. Whisk together all ingredients until blended. Cover and chill 2 hours before serving. Store in an airtight container in refrigerator up to 3 days.

* Regular paprika may be substituted.

[make ahead]

TEX-MEX MAYONNAISE

makes 1¼ cups   prep: 15 min.   chill: 3 hr.

A dollop of this mayonnaise adds zesty flavor to sandwiches, raw vegetables, or even grilled burgers.

1 cup mayonnaise	½ tsp. onion powder
2 Tbsp. ketchup	½ tsp. garlic powder
2 Tbsp. lime juice	½ tsp. hot sauce
2 Tbsp. milk	½ tsp. Worcestershire sauce
2 to 3 tsp. chili powder	¼ tsp. lemon pepper
1 tsp. ground red pepper	

1. Combine all ingredients in a bowl. Cover and chill at least 3 hours.

BÉARNAISE MAYONNAISE

makes 1 cup   prep: 20 min.   cook: 5 min.

Spread your choice of these mayonnaise variations over hard rolls with sliced roast beef, on hamburgers, or on tomato sandwiches.

⅓ cup dry white wine	2 Tbsp. chopped fresh tarragon
1 Tbsp. white wine vinegar	1 tsp. lemon zest
2 shallots, minced	⅛ tsp. pepper
1 cup mayonnaise	Garnish: fresh tarragon sprig (optional)

1. Cook first 3 ingredients over medium-high heat 5 minutes or until liquid is reduced to 1 Tbsp. Remove from heat, and cool.

2. Stir together mayonnaise and next 3 ingredients; stir in wine reduction. Cover and chill up to 7 days. Garnish, if desired.

Tomato-Basil Mayonnaise: Stir together 1 cup mayonnaise, 2 Tbsp. tomato paste, and 2 Tbsp. chopped basil until blended.

Gremolata Mayonnaise: Stir together 1 cup mayonnaise, 2 Tbsp. chopped fresh parsley, 2 Tbsp. lemon zest, and 1 garlic clove, pressed.

CREAMY MUSTARD SAUCE

makes ½ cup   prep: 5 min.

½   cup sour cream
2   tsp. whole grain mustard

1   tsp. brown sugar
Salt and pepper to tast

1. Stir together sour cream, mustard, brown sugar, and salt and pepper to taste in a bowl.

[quick]

WHITE BARBECUE SAUCE

makes 2 cups   prep: 5 min.   pictured on page 755

If you prefer a thicker sauce, omit the water.

1½ cups mayonnaise
¼   cup water
¼   cup white wine vinegar
1   Tbsp. coarsely ground pepper
1   Tbsp. Creole mustard

1   tsp. salt
1   tsp. sugar
2   garlic cloves, minced
2   tsp. prepared horseradish

1. Whisk together all ingredients until blended. Store in the refrigerator up to 1 week.

[make ahead]

PEPPERY BARBECUE SAUCE

makes 6 cups   prep: 10 min.   pictured on page 755

2   cups firmly packed brown sugar
2   Tbsp. pepper
1   to 1½ tsp. salt
4   garlic cloves, minced
4   cups ketchup

1   cup white vinegar
2   Tbsp. vegetable oil
2   Tbsp. prepared mustard
2   Tbsp. Worcestershire sauce
2   Tbsp. hot sauce

1. Stir together all ingredients. Pour into hot sterilized jars, and seal. Store in refrigerator up to 1 month.

[make ahead]

CIDER VINEGAR BARBECUE SAUCE

makes 2 cups prep: 10 min. cook: 7 min. **pictured on page 755**

This sauce is often referred to as Lexington Style Dip, but there are many variations. Most folks can't resist adding their own touch.

quick

1½ cups cider vinegar

⅓ cup firmly packed brown sugar

¼ cup ketchup

1 Tbsp. hot sauce

1 tsp. browning and seasoning sauce

½ tsp. salt

½ tsp. onion powder

½ tsp. pepper

½ tsp. Worcestershire sauce

1. Stir together all ingredients in a medium saucepan; cook over medium heat, stirring constantly, 7 minutes or until sugar dissolves. Cover and chill sauce until ready to serve. Serve with pork.

Note: We tested with Texas Pete Hot Sauce and Kitchen Bouquet Browning & Seasoning Sauce.

COLLARD GREEN PESTO

makes 4 cups prep: 15 min. cook: 4 min.

Refrigerate leftovers up to one week. Cover tightly with plastic wrap to keep pesto a vibrant green.

quick

5 cups packaged fresh collard greens, washed, trimmed, and chopped

3 garlic cloves

¼ cup pecans

½ cup olive oil

⅓ cup grated Parmesan cheese

½ tsp. salt

1. Cook greens in boiling water to cover 3½ to 4 minutes or until tender; drain. Plunge into ice water to stop the cooking process; drain well.

2. Process garlic and pecans in a food processor until finely ground. Add greens, oil, cheese, salt, and ¼ cup water; process 2 to 3 seconds or until smooth, stopping to scrape down sides. (Mixture will be thick.)

SPICY PEACH KETCHUP

makes 2 cups   prep: 10 min.   chill: 2 hr.

1   cup ketchup
½   cup thick-and-spicy barbecue sauce

½   cup peach preserves

1. Stir together all ingredients until blended. Cover and chill 2 hours.

make ahead

CUMBERLAND SAUCE

makes about 4 cups   prep: 15 min.   cook: 25 min.

This sauce has a great depth of flavor. It's delicious with pork and turkey and can be used as a glaze for ham.

2½ cups port wine, divided
1   (10½-oz.) jar red currant jelly
3   Tbsp. light brown sugar
2   Tbsp. orange zest
⅔   cup fresh orange juice

1½ Tbsp. grated fresh ginger
2   tsp. dry mustard
¼   tsp. salt
¼   tsp. ground red pepper
2½ Tbsp. cornstarch

1. Bring 2 cups wine and next 8 ingredients to a boil in a large saucepan, stirring constantly; reduce heat, and simmer, stirring often, 20 minutes.
2. Stir together remaining ½ cup wine and cornstarch until smooth. Stir into hot mixture; bring to a boil over medium heat. Boil, stirring constantly, 1 minute. Remove from heat, and cool. Pour into hot sterilized jars, and seal. Store in refrigerator up to 1 month.

make ahead

VIDALIA ONION SAUCE

makes about 3 cups   prep: 5 min.   cook: 25 min.

2   baby Vidalia onions, sliced
1   Tbsp. olive oil
2   cups whipping cream

¼   tsp. salt
¼   tsp. pepper

1. Sauté onion in a large skillet in hot oil over medium-high heat 10 minutes or until tender; stir in whipping cream. Reduce heat, and simmer 15 minutes or until liquid is reduced by half. Stir in salt and pepper.

GINGERED JEZEBEL SAUCE

makes 1¼ cups cook: 2 min.

Ginger replaces dry mustard in this version of jezebel sauce.

⅔ cup pineapple preserves

⅓ cup apple jelly

2 Tbsp. prepared horseradish

1 Tbsp. grated fresh ginger

1. Microwave pineapple preserves and apple jelly in a glass bowl at HIGH 2 minutes or until melted. Stir in remaining ingredients.

CRANBERRY-KEY LIME SAUCE

makes about 4 cups prep: 10 min.

While at the beach, former Assistant Test Kitchen Director James Schend was inspired to slightly depart from Ursula Ann Mazzolini's original recipe and use Key limes (peel and all) instead of an orange. Now you have two super choices.

1 (12-oz.) bag fresh cranberries*

4 Key limes

1 cup sugar

¼ cup fresh mint leaves

2 Tbsp. orange liqueur or fresh orange juice

1. Pulse all ingredients in a food processor 10 to 12 times or until finely chopped, stopping to scrape down sides. Cover and chill until ready to serve. Store in an airtight container in refrigerator up to 2 weeks.

* 1 (12-oz.) bag frozen cranberries, thawed, may be substituted.

Note: Key limes are smaller, a bit more round, and have a thinner skin than Persian limes.

Cranberry-Orange Sauce: Substitute 1 medium unpeeled orange for 4 Key limes. Proceed with recipe as directed. Thin-skinned oranges, such as Valencia or Indian River, work best in this recipe.

MUSCADINE SAUCE

makes 5 (1-pt.) jars   prep: 45 min.   cook: 2 hr., 45 min.   process: 20 min.

Jennie Hart Robinson of Fort Valley, Georgia, uses muscadines from the farm. "This is a sauce, not a jelly. It will have some run to it," Jennie says. "Don't overcook it, or it won't come out of the jar."

5　lb. muscadine grapes, halved*	1　Tbsp. ground cinnamon
9　cups sugar	1　Tbsp. ground allspice
2　cups cider vinegar	1　tsp. ground cloves

1. Squeeze pulp from grape halves into a bowl, reserving skins.

2. Bring skins to a boil in a large saucepan over medium-high heat. Cover, reduce heat to medium, and cook, stirring occasionally, 15 minutes or until tender.

3. Bring pulp to a boil in a saucepan; reduce heat to medium, and cook 20 minutes or until seeds separate from pulp. Pour mixture through a wire-mesh strainer into saucepan containing skins, discarding solids. Add sugar, and cook, stirring occasionally, over medium heat, 2 hours or until thickened. Stir in vinegar and next 3 ingredients. Cook 10 to 15 minutes or until a candy thermometer registers 225° to 230°.

4. Ladle hot mixture into hot sterilized pt.-size jars, filling to ½ inch from top. Remove air bubbles; wipe jar rims. Cover at once with metal lids, and screw on bands.

5. Process in boiling-water bath 20 minutes. Serve with turkey, biscuits, or toast.

* 5 lb. of seedless red grapes may be substituted. Crush whole grapes slightly. Bring to a boil; reduce heat, and simmer 20 minutes. Strain mixture into a saucepan, discarding solids. Stir in sugar, and proceed as directed.

CREAM GRAVY

makes ¾ cup   prep: 5 min.   cook: 5 min.

Serve with vegetables, pasta, or chicken. If you have drippings from fried chicken or other meat, you can substitute those for the butter.

1   cup milk
1   (¼-inch-thick) onion slice
1   fresh parsley sprig
2   Tbsp. butter
2   Tbsp. all-purpose flour

2   Tbsp. whipping cream
⅛   tsp. salt
⅛   tsp. ground white pepper
Dash of ground nutmeg

1. Bring first 3 ingredients to a boil, and remove from heat. Pour milk mixture through a wire-mesh strainer into a small bowl, reserving the hot milk and discarding solids.

2. Melt butter in a large skillet over low heat; whisk in flour until smooth. Cook, whisking constantly, 1 minute. Gradually whisk in reserved hot milk, and cook, whisking constantly, over medium heat, until thickened and bubbly. Whisk in whipping cream and remaining ingredients.

ANYTIME TURKEY GRAVY

makes about 2½ cups   prep: 15 min.   cook: 1 hr., 7 min.   **pictured on page 754**

2½ lb. dark meat turkey pieces (wings and necks)
2   Tbsp. vegetable oil
1   medium onion, chopped
2   celery ribs, chopped
1   (49.5-oz.) can chicken broth
½   cup chopped fresh parsley

⅓   cup butter
⅓   cup all-purpose flour
½   tsp. freshly ground pepper
½   tsp. poultry seasoning
¼   tsp. rubbed sage

1. Cook turkey pieces in hot oil in a Dutch oven over medium-high heat 6 to 8 minutes on each side or until lightly browned. Add onion and celery, and sauté 4 minutes. Gradually stir in chicken broth, stirring to loosen particles from bottom of skillet; stir in parsley. Bring to a boil; cover, reduce heat to medium-low, and simmer, stirring occasionally, 30 minutes. Pour mixture through a wire-mesh strainer into a large bowl, discarding solids.

2. Melt butter in Dutch oven over medium heat; whisk in flour, and cook, whisking constantly, 1 to 2 minutes or until mixture is golden and smooth. Gradually whisk in broth mixture; increase heat to medium-high, and bring to a boil. Reduce heat to medium, and simmer, stirring occasionally, 15 to 20 minutes or to desired thickness. Stir in remaining ingredients.

[quick]

GIBLET GRAVY

makes 4 cups   prep: 10 min.   cook: 1 hr., 5 min.

We used egg yolks and flour as thickeners in this luscious recipe.

Giblets and neck from 1 turkey
½ cup butter
1   small onion, chopped
1   celery rib, chopped
1   carrot, chopped
¼   cup all-purpose flour

2   egg yolks
½   cup half-and-half
½   tsp. salt
½   tsp. pepper
½   tsp. poultry seasoning
Garnish: fresh parsley sprig (optional)

1. Bring giblets, neck, and 4 cups water to a boil in a medium saucepan over medium heat. Cover, reduce heat, and simmer 45 minutes or until tender. Drain, reserving broth. Chop giblets and neck meat, and set aside.

2. Melt butter in a large skillet over medium heat; add chopped vegetables, and sauté 5 minutes. Add flour, stirring until smooth. Add reserved broth; cook, stirring constantly, 10 minutes or until thickened. Reduce heat to low. Remove vegetables using a handheld, wire-mesh strainer, and discard, leaving gravy in skillet.

3. Whisk together egg yolks and half-and-half. Gradually stir about one-fourth of hot gravy into yolk mixture; add to remaining hot gravy. Add giblets and neck meat; cook, stirring constantly, 4 to 5 minutes or until a thermometer registers 160°. Stir in salt, pepper, and seasoning. Serve immediately. Garnish, if desired.

EASY REDEYE GRAVY

makes 6 servings   prep: 10 min.   cook: 10 min.   **pictured on page 755**

This recipe was a special treat for reader Melody Lee of Dothan, Alabama, during childhood visits to her grandmother's farm.

6	frozen biscuits	1½ Tbsp.	brown sugar
2	Tbsp. butter	⅛ to ¼ tsp.	salt
6	biscuit-size country ham slices	⅛ tsp.	freshly ground pepper
1	Tbsp. all-purpose flour	¼ tsp.	hot sauce (optional)
1	cup strong brewed coffee		

1. Prepare frozen biscuits according to package directions.

2. Meanwhile, melt butter in large skillet over medium-high heat. Add ham, and cook 3 minutes on each side or until lightly browned; remove ham.

3. Add flour to skillet; cook, whisking constantly, 1 minute. Add brewed coffee, brown sugar, and ½ cup water. Cook, whisking constantly, 3 minutes or until thickened; return ham slices to skillet. Stir in salt, pepper, and, if desired, hot sauce.

4. Split warm biscuits in half. Top bottom halves with ham slices. Pour gravy over ham; cover with remaining biscuit halves. Serve immediately.

Note: We tested with White Lily Southern Style and Buttermilk Frozen Biscuit Dough.

FRESH PEACH SALSA

makes about 4 cups   prep: 20 min.   cook: 10 min.

1	large sweet onion, chopped	6	large firm peaches, peeled and chopped
1	jalapeño pepper, seeded and minced	¼	cup fresh lemon juice
¼	cup sugar	¼	tsp. salt
2	Tbsp. grated fresh ginger	2	Tbsp. chopped fresh cilantro
2	Tbsp. olive oil		

1. Sauté first 4 ingredients in hot oil in a large skillet over medium heat 5 minutes or until onion is tender. Stir in peaches and remaining ingredients, and cook, stirring gently, 5 minutes. Serve warm or at room temperature. Store leftovers in an airtight container in the refrigerator up to 2 days.

PICKLED ONION AND CUCUMBER

makes 2 gal.   prep: 25 min.   chill: 24 hr.

5   lb. sweet onions, thinly sliced and separated
    into rings
8   medium cucumbers, thinly sliced

1   gal. white vinegar (5% acidity)
2   tsp. pepper
1   tsp. salt

1. Stir together all ingredients in a large bowl; cover and chill 24 hours. Store in refrigerator up to 2 weeks.

GREEN TOMATO PICKLES

makes 7 pt.   prep: 45 min.   stand: 4 hr.   cook: 30 min.   process: 10 min.   **pictured on page 830**

5   lb. green tomatoes, chopped
1   large onion, chopped
2   Tbsp. pickling salt
1½ cups firmly packed brown sugar
2   cups cider vinegar (5% acidity)

2   tsp. mustard seeds
2   tsp. whole allspice
2   tsp. celery seeds
1½ tsp. whole cloves

1. Sprinkle tomato and onion with pickling salt; let stand 4 to 6 hours. Drain and pat dry with paper towels; set aside.
2. Combine brown sugar and vinegar in a Dutch oven; cook over medium heat, stirring constantly, until sugar dissolves.
3. Place mustard seeds and next 3 ingredients on 6-inch square of cheesecloth; tie with string. Add spice bag, tomato, onion, and 3 cups water to vinegar mixture.
4. Bring to a boil, stirring constantly; reduce heat, and simmer, stirring occasionally, 25 minutes or until tomato and onion are tender. Remove and discard spice bag.
5. Pour hot mixture into hot jars, filling to ½ inch from top. Remove air bubbles; wipe jar rims. Cover at once with metal lids, and screw on bands.
6. Process in boiling-water bath 10 minutes.

CHOWCHOW

makes 5½ pt.   prep: 2 hr.   chill 8 hr.   cook: 8 min.   process: 15 min.   **pictured on page 831**

For more heat, add chopped jalapeño to the vegetables.

5	green bell peppers	3	cups sugar
5	red bell peppers	2	cups white vinegar (5% acidity)
2	large green tomatoes	1	cup water
2	large onions	1	Tbsp. mustard seeds
½	small cabbage	1½	tsp. celery seeds
¼	cup pickling salt	¾	tsp. turmeric

1. Chop first 5 ingredients.

2. Stir together chopped vegetables and salt in a large Dutch oven. Cover and chill 8 hours.

3. Rinse and drain; return mixture to Dutch oven. Stir in sugar and remaining ingredients.

4. Bring to a boil; reduce heat, and simmer 3 minutes.

5. Pack hot mixture into hot jars, filling to ½ inch from top. Remove air bubbles; wipe jar rims. Cover at once with metal lids, and screw on bands.

6. Process in boiling-water bath 15 minutes.

WATERMELON RIND PICKLES

makes 5 (12-oz.) jars   prep: 1 hr., 30 min.   stand: 8 hr.   cook: 1 hr., 25 min.   process: 10 min.

1	large watermelon, quartered	9	cups sugar
¾	cup salt	3	cups white vinegar (5% acidity)
2	qt. ice cubes	1	lemon, thinly sliced
1	Tbsp. whole cloves	5	(3-inch) cinnamon sticks
1	Tbsp. whole allspice		

1. Peel watermelon; remove pulp, and reserve for another use. Cut rind into 1-inch cubes; reserve 12 cups rind cubes in a large container.

2. Stir together salt and 3 qt. water; pour over rind. Add ice; cover and let stand 8 hours. Rinse well, and drain.

3. Cook rind and water to cover in a Dutch oven over high heat 10 minutes or until tender. Drain.

4. Place cloves and allspice on a 3-inch square of cheesecloth; tie with a string.

5. Stir together sugar, vinegar, and 3 cups water; add spice bag, and bring to a boil. Boil 5 minutes, and pour over rind. Stir in lemon slices. Cover and let stand 8 hours.

6. Bring rind and syrup mixture to a boil; reduce heat, and simmer, stirring occasionally, 1 hour. Discard spice bag.

7. Pack rind mixture into hot jars, filling ½ inch from top. Add 1 cinnamon stick to each jar. Remove air bubbles; wipe jar rims. Cover at once with metal lids, and screw on bands.

8. Process in boiling-water bath 10 minutes.

FIG PRESERVES

makes 4 qt.   prep: 10 min.   stand: 8 hr.   cook: 2 hr.   process: 15 min.

2 qt. fresh figs (about 4 lb.)	8 cups sugar

1. Layer figs and sugar in a Dutch oven. Cover and let stand 8 hours.

2. Cook over medium heat 2 hours, stirring occasionally, until syrup thickens and figs are clear.

3. Pack hot figs into hot jars, filling to ½ inch from top. Cover fruit with boiling syrup, filling to ½ inch from top. Remove air bubbles; wipe jar rims. Cover at once with metal lids, and screw on bands.

4. Process in boiling-water bath 15 minutes. Cool completely, and chill, if desired.

OVEN APPLE BUTTER

makes 3 cups   prep: 25 min.   cook: 30 min.   bake: 4 hr., 30 min.

8 Granny Smith apples, peeled and diced	1 cup sugar
1 cup apple juice	1 tsp. ground cinnamon

1. Cook diced apple and juice in a Dutch oven over medium heat 30 minutes or until apple is tender. Stir until apple is mashed. Stir in sugar and cinnamon. Pour apple mixture into a lightly greased 11- x 7-inch baking dish.

2. Bake at 275° for 4½ hours, stirring every hour, or until spreading consistency. Cover and chill until ready to serve.

Spiced Oven Apple Butter: Increase cinnamon to 2 tsp. and add ½ tsp. ground cloves and ¼ tsp. ground allspice.

CRANBERRY CONSERVE

makes 4 cups   prep: 10 min.   cook 30 min.   chill 30 hr.

{ make ahead }

4 cups cranberries

1 cup water

1 orange

1 cup raisins

2½ cups sugar

½ cup finely chopped pecansd

1. Combine cranberries and 1 cup water in a large saucepan; bring to a boil. Cover, reduce heat, and simmer 6 to 8 minutes or until cranberry skins pop.

2. Grate rind of orange; peel, seed, and dice orange. Stir together cranberries, orange, grated rind, raisins, sugar, and pecans. Cook over low heat, stirring often, 20 minutes or until mixture thickens. Remove from heat, and cool. Chill at least 3 hours..

EASIEST PEPPER JELLY

makes 1 cup   prep: 5 min.   cook: 5 min.   chill: 8 hr.   **pictured on page 756**

{ make ahead }

½ cup apple jelly

½ cup orange marmalade

1 tsp. apple cider vinegar

1 Tbsp. seeded and chopped jalapeño pepper

1 Tbsp. chopped green onion

1. Stir together all ingredients in a large saucepan over low heat until jelly and marmalade are melted and mixture is blended. Cool. Cover and chill 8 hours.

GRANNY SMITH APPLE FREEZER JAM

makes about 3½ cups   prep: 15 min.   stand: 20 min.

Pair this jam with some peanut butter for a mighty fine sandwich.

5 cups coarsely chopped, unpeeled Granny Smith apples (about 5 medium apples or 1½ lb.)

1 cup sugar

½ cup pasteurized apple juice

1 (1.59-oz.) envelope freezer jam pectin

1. Pulse chopped apples in food processor 10 times or until finely chopped. Place in a medium bowl. Stir in sugar and juice; let stand 15 minutes.

2. Gradually stir in pectin. Stir for 3 minutes; let stand 5 minutes.

3. Spoon fruit mixture into sterilized canning jars, filling to ½ inch from top; wipe jar rims. Cover with metal lids, and screw on bands. Place in freezer.

GREEN TOMATO-BLUEBERRY JAM

makes 5 pt. prep: 35 min. cook: 10 min. process: 10 min. **pictured on page 829**

5   cups fresh blueberries, stemmed*
4   large green tomatoes, coarsely chopped
    (about 4 lb.)
5   cups sugar

3   (1.75-oz.) packages fruit pectin
¼   cup lemon juice
2   tsp. ground cinnamon
½   tsp. ground nutmeg

1. Pulse blueberries and chopped tomato in a blender or food processor 3 or 4 times or until mixture is almost smooth.

2. Cook blueberry mixture, 1½ cups water, and sugar in a Dutch oven over medium heat, stirring constantly, until sugar dissolves.

3. Stir in fruit pectin and remaining ingredients. Bring to a boil; cook, stirring constantly, 5 minutes or until mixture thickens.

4. Pour hot mixture into hot jars, filling to ¼ inch from top. Remove air bubbles; wipe jar rims. Cover at once with metal lids, and screw on bands. Process in boiling-water bath 10 minutes.

* 5 cups frozen blueberries, thawed, may be substituted.

Note: We tested with Sure-Jell Premium Fruit Pectin.

FLAVORED VINEGARS

makes 2 to 3 cups prep: 25 min. stand: 30 min.

Fresh herbs
Garlic cloves, crushed
Unpeeled fruit slices
Orange zest
Whole peppercorns

Whole cloves
Cinnamon sticks
2   to 3 cups white vinegar (5% acidity)
¼   tsp. salt

1. Fill sterilized glass bottles with desired fresh herb sprigs, garlic, fruit, orange zest, peppercorns, cloves, and/or cinnamon sticks. Bring 2 to 3 cups of white vinegar (depending on bottle size) and ¼ tsp. salt to a boil in a medium saucepan. Remove from heat, and pour into prepared bottles. Let stand 30 minutes at room temperature. Cover opening tightly with plastic wrap or bottle top; refrigerate for at least a week before using.

Note: Use these combinations in dressings, or serve alongside oil as bread dippers: rosemary-garlic vinegar, rosemary-pear-lemon vinegar, and lemon-garlic-thyme-peppercorn vinegar.

[make ahead]

TOASTED PECAN-CARAMEL SAUCE

makes about ¾ cup   prep: 10 min.   bake: 8 min.   cook: 12 min.   **pictured on page 755**

¼ cup chopped pecans
¾ cup sugar
1 tsp. light corn syrup

½ cup evaporated milk
1½ tsp. butter

1. Preheat oven to 350°. Bake pecans in a single layer in a shallow pan 8 to 10 minutes or until toasted and fragrant.
2. Sprinkle sugar in an even layer in a small saucepan. Stir together syrup and ⅓ cup water, and pour over sugar in saucepan. Cook, without stirring, over medium-high heat 12 to 14 minutes or until sugar is dissolved and mixture is golden.
3. Remove from heat. Gradually whisk in evaporated milk. (Mixture will bubble.) Stir in butter and toasted pecans.

Per 4½ tsp.: Calories 119; Fat 3.4g (sat 0.7g, mono 1.7g, poly 0.8g); Protein 1.6g; Fiber 0.4g;
Chol 3mg; Iron 0.1mg; Sodium 24mg; Calc 50mg

LEMON CURD

makes about 1⅓ cups   prep: 10 min.   cook: 15 min.   chill: 3 hr.   **pictured on page 755**

This melt-in-your-mouth soft custard is a traditional English favorite.

1 cup sugar
1 Tbsp. lemon zest
1 cup fresh lemon juice

4 eggs yolks, lightly beaten
½ cup butter, cubed

1. Bring sugar, zest, and juice to a boil in a heavy nonaluminum 3½-qt. saucepan over medium-high heat. Remove from heat, and gradually whisk about one-fourth hot juice mixture into egg yolks; add egg yolk mixture to remaining hot juice mixture, whisking constantly until well blended.
2. Place saucepan over medium heat, and cook, whisking constantly, at least 10 or up to 12 minutes. (Mixture will be a pudding-like thickness.)
3. Add butter, in 6 batches, whisking constantly until butter melts and mixture is well blended after each addition. Remove from heat, and pour mixture through a wire-mesh strainer into a bowl. Place plastic wrap directly on warm curd (to prevent a film from forming); chill 3 hours.

Lime Curd: Substitute lime zest and lime juice for lemon zest and lemon juice. Proceed with recipe as directed.

CUSTARD SAUCE

makes 2 cups   prep: 10 min.   cook: 10 min.

6   egg yolks
⅔   cup sugar, divided
2   cups milk

1   Tbsp. brandy
1   tsp. vanilla extract

quick

1. Whisk together egg yolks and ⅓ cup sugar in a large bowl 3 minutes or until blended.
2. Bring milk and remaining ⅓ cup sugar to a boil in a medium saucepan, whisking constantly.
3. Stir about one-fourth of hot milk mixture gradually into yolks; add to remaining hot mixture, stirring constantly. Cook over medium-low heat, stirring constantly, 10 minutes or until custard is thick enough to coat back of a wooden spoon. Remove from heat. Pour through a fine wire-mesh strainer into a bowl. Stir in brandy and vanilla.

VANILLA BEAN HARD SAUCE

makes 1⅔ cups   prep: 6 min.   cook: 5 min.

1   whole vanilla bean, split lengthwise
2   cups sifted powdered sugar

1   cup butter, softened

1. Scrape tiny vanilla bean seeds into sugar; stir well. Combine vanilla sugar and butter in a bowl. Beat at medium speed with an electric mixer until blended. Transfer to a serving dish.

ULTIMATE FUDGE SAUCE

makes 2½ cups   prep: 6 min.   cook: 5 min.

1   cup heavy whipping cream
¾   cup sugar
8   oz. unsweetened chocolate, finely chopped
⅓   cup corn syrup

¼   cup unsalted butter
1½   tsp. vanilla extract
⅛   tsp. salt

1. Combine whipping cream and sugar in a heavy saucepan. Place over medium heat, and cook, stirring constantly, until sugar dissolves. Stir in chocolate, corn syrup, and butter. Cook over medium-low heat, stirring occasionally, until chocolate melts and all ingredients are blended. Remove from heat; stir in vanilla and salt. Let cool to room temperature. Transfer sauce to jars with tight-fitting lids. Store in refrigerator. To serve, spoon sauce into a microwave-safe bowl, and microwave at HIGH for 20-second intervals or until pourable.

SIDE DISHES

"Southerners can't stand to eat alone. If we're going to cook a mess of greens we want to eat them with a mess of people." —Julia Reed

LEMON ROASTED ASPARAGUS

makes 8 servings   prep: 10 min.   bake: 15 min.

Round out your weeknight meal with this fast favorite.

{quick}

2	lb. fresh asparagus	¼	cup olive oil
3	garlic cloves, minced	¾	tsp. salt
¼	cup lemon juice	¼	tsp. pepper

1. Preheat oven to 400°. Snap off and discard tough ends of asparagus; place asparagus on a lightly greased baking sheet. Whisk together remaining ingredients; drizzle mixture over asparagus, tossing to coat.

2. Bake at 400° for 15 minutes or to desired degree of tenderness, turning once after 8 minutes.

ASPARAGUS WITH GARLIC CREAM

makes 16 to 20 appetizer servings   prep: 20 min.   chill: 8 hr.   cook: 3 min.

Serve this tasty dish as an appetizer or as a side dish alongside pork or poultry.

{make ahead}

1	(8-oz.) container sour cream	2	garlic cloves, minced
2	Tbsp. milk	¼	tsp. salt
1	Tbsp. white wine vinegar	¼	tsp. freshly ground pepper
1	Tbsp. olive oil	2	lb. fresh asparagus

1. Stir together first 7 ingredients. Cover and chill 8 hours.

2. Snap off tough ends of asparagus. Cook in boiling water to cover 3 minutes or until crisp-tender; drain. Plunge asparagus into ice water to stop the cooking process; drain. Chill 8 hours, if desired. Serve with garlic cream.

BARBECUE BEANS

makes 10 servings prep: 25 min.   cook: 1 hr.   chill: 8 hr.

When we ran this recipe in 1994, it called for 10 pieces of bacon. It's still good that way, but you can also use half of the bacon or use turkey bacon and still get great results.

½ medium onion, chopped
½ lb. ground beef (optional)
10 bacon slices, cooked and crumbled
⅔ cup firmly packed brown sugar
¾ cup barbecue sauce
1 (15-oz.) can kidney beans, rinsed and drained

1 (15-oz.) can butter beans, rinsed and drained
1 (15-oz.) can pork and beans, undrained
2 Tbsp. molasses
2 tsp. Dijon mustard
½ tsp. salt
½ tsp. pepper
½ tsp. chili powder

1. Cook onion and, if desired, ground beef in a Dutch oven, stirring until meat crumbles and is no longer pink; drain. Stir in bacon and remaining ingredients, and spoon into a lightly greased 2½-qt. baking dish. Chill 8 hours, if desired.

2. Preheat oven to 350°. Bake bean mixture at 350° for 1 hour, stirring once.

Very Clean Veggies

You may have noticed that our recipes utilizing bagged salad greens call for them to be "thoroughly washed." We added this phrase to our editing style after outbreaks of E. coli in spinach and salad. While rinsing under running water offers some protection against unsafe bacteria, we offer some better suggestions.

Make a solution of 1⅓ cups 3% hydrogen peroxide and 2⅔ cups distilled water, and keep it in a spray bottle in the kitchen. Spritz the greens with the solution, rinse with running water, and then spin or pat them dry. Replace the solution once a week. It's an effective, budget-friendly solution to both expensive vegetable cleaners and to bleach, which the processors use.

The peroxide solution works well on other vegetables, too, but a good old-fashioned vegetable brush (used only for cleaning produce) and distilled water are good weapons against harmful bacteria.

SLOW-COOKER BLACK BEANS

makes 8 cups   prep: 15 min.   soak: 8 hr.   cook: 5 hr., 18 min.

You will have to soak this Southwestern favorite overnight before you begin, but the effort yields great results.

1   (16-oz.) package dried black beans
2   bacon slices
1   large sweet onion, diced (about 2 cups)
2   celery ribs, diced (about ½ cup)
3   garlic cloves, chopped
2   cups diced cooked ham

½   tsp. ground cumin
¼   tsp. coarsely ground black pepper
¼   tsp. ground red pepper
1   (32-oz.) container low-sodium fat-free chicken broth

1. Rinse and sort beans according to package directions. Place beans in a 6-qt. slow cooker. Add water 2 inches above beans; let soak 8 hours. Drain and rinse. Return beans to slow cooker.

2. Cook bacon in a large skillet over medium-high heat 4 to 5 minutes or until crisp; remove bacon, and drain on paper towels, reserving 2 Tbsp. drippings in skillet. Crumble bacon; add to slow cooker.

3. Sauté onion, celery, and garlic in hot drippings 7 to 8 minutes or until tender. Reduce heat to medium, and stir in ham, cumin, and ground peppers. Sauté 5 minutes or until thoroughly heated. Stir in ½ cup chicken broth, and cook 2 minutes, stirring to loosen particles from bottom of skillet; add mixture to slow cooker. Stir in remaining chicken broth and 1 cup water.

4. Cover and cook on HIGH 5 hours or LOW 8 hours or until beans are tender.

Green Tomato-Blueberry Jam,
page 821

Green Tomato Pickles,
page 817

Chowchow, page 818

Buttery Dijon Deviled Eggs, page 871

Buttermilk Fried Corn, page 848

Butterbeans and Bacon,
page 843

Easy Sweet Potato Casserole,
page 866

Browned Butter Mashed
Potatoes, page 863

835

Fried Pecan Okra,
page 855

Creamy Baked Sweet Onions,
page 858

Caramelized Onion-and-Pecan
Brussels Sprouts, page 847

Sage Cornbread Dressing,
page 850

Pot Likker Soup,
page 884

Lamb Soup With Spring
Vegetables, page 892

Chunky Beef Chili,
page 908

Peppered Beef Soup,
page 893

Shrimp-Tasso-Andouille Sausage
Gumbo, page 898

Golden Oyster Stew,
page 901

SMASHED PINTO BEANS

makes 14 servings   prep: 15 min.   cook: 20 min.

Keep these slightly spicy, fiber-rich beans on hand for quick breakfast burritos or soft veggie tacos.

1 medium onion, chopped	1 cup beef broth
1 tsp. olive oil	1 Tbsp. hot sauce
2 garlic cloves, minced	¼ tsp. salt
½ cup tomato sauce	¼ tsp. ground cumin
2 (15-oz.) cans pinto beans, rinsed and drained	½ tsp. pepper
	1 to 2 Tbsp. red wine vinegar

1. Sauté chopped onion in hot olive oil in a Dutch oven over medium-high heat 5 minutes or until onion is tender. Add minced garlic, and sauté 1 minute. Stir in tomato sauce and remaining ingredients.

2. Bring to a boil; reduce heat, and simmer 8 minutes.

3. Mash bean mixture with a potato masher until thickened, leaving some beans whole.

Per ¼ cup: Calories 47; Fat 0.7g (sat 0.1g, mono 0.3g, poly 0.3g) Protein 2.9g; Fiber 2.5g; Iron 0.6mg; Sodium 171mg; Calc 17mg

HEARTY BAKED BEANS

makes 6 to 8 servings   prep: 30 min.   cook: 3 hr.

3 bacon slices, chopped	⅓ cup molasses
1 large onion, chopped	⅓ cup ketchup
2 garlic cloves, minced	2½ Tbsp. prepared mustard
3 (16-oz.) cans pinto beans, drained	½ medium-size green bell pepper, chopped
⅓ cup firmly packed brown sugar	

1. Cook bacon slices in a large skillet until crisp; remove bacon, reserving drippings in pan.

2. Sauté onion and garlic in reserved drippings until tender.

3. Combine bacon slices, onion mixture, beans, and remaining ingredients in a slow cooker.

4. Cover and cook on HIGH for 2½ to 3 hours or on LOW for 5 to 6 hours.

southern lights

make ahead

taking sides

Knowing Beans Across the South

Some Southern food preferences don't have regional boundaries. But if you traveled across the South blindfolded, you probably could tell where you were just by the type of beans you're served.

Remember this song? "Juu-st a bowl of butter be-eans...Paass the cornbread, if you ple-ease. I don't want no collard greens. All I want is a bo-owl of butter beans!" If you're singing that song, then it's likely you're from the deeper South, where butter beans, a smaller, creamier version of lima beans, are king. You'd have to go a lot farther north—to Kentucky—to find the spot where lima beans are preferred.

In Louisiana it's red beans, as in spicy red beans and rice, one of the area's most famous culinary traditions. From there, head to Key West to find red beans again, where they are common in the Caribbean-style dishes—also with a bit of heat. But in the Spanish-influenced areas of Florida, black beans and yellow rice is a staple combo. Black beans are beloved in Texas areas of Spanish influence as well, in addition to cowboy pinto beans, famously served with cornbread.

East Kentuckian Betsy Fannin claims that pinto beans, more commonly known in her area as "soup beans," are favored throughout Appalachia. "A typical meal here is soup beans, fried potatoes, and cornbread," she

says. "But once green beans are ready for picking, they are the preferred bean of summer."

Travel throughout the Appalachians, and signs inviting visitors to soup bean fund-raiser suppers at churches and schools are common. Some say sliced onions also are a must with the bowls of light brown beans. Though revered today as flavorful tradition, in earlier days they were the inexpensive protein source that helped poor mountain folks survive.

Green beans are the universal Southern bean, welcomed throughout the South in summer, just as Betsy claims they do in Kentucky. And, of course, there are black-eyed peas, which really are a variety of bean introduced by African-Americans and adopted by Southerners everywhere.

What mostly unites the Southern regions where beans are concerned is the seasonings, which vary little when cooking beans of any size, shape, or color. Though some health-conscious cooks simmer beans in flavored broth these days, traditional flavorings include ham hocks, bacon or bacon drippings, and salt.

BUTTERBEANS AND BACON

makes 6 servings   prep: 20 min.   cook: 1 hr., 30 min.   **pictured on page 833**

Cooked beans freeze beautifully, so you can make a double batch to enjoy later.

3   thick-cut bacon slices, chopped

1   cup diced onion (1 medium onion)

3   garlic cloves, minced

1   bay leaf

¾   cup chopped green bell pepper

2   plum tomatoes, seeded and chopped (optional)

1   (32-oz.) container chicken broth

4   cups fresh or thawed frozen butterbeans

½   tsp. salt

1   tsp. pepper

1   tsp. Worcestershire sauce

½   tsp. hot sauce

[freeze it]

1. Cook bacon in a skillet over medium heat, stirring often, 8 minutes or until crisp. Remove bacon, and drain on paper towels, reserving drippings in skillet. Add onion, garlic, and bay leaf; cook, stirring often, 3 minutes or until onion is tender.

2. Add bell pepper; cook, stirring often, 3 minutes. Add tomatoes, if desired, and cook, stirring often, 3 minutes.

3. Add chicken broth and butterbeans; bring to a boil. Cover, reduce heat, and simmer, stirring occasionally, 30 minutes.

4. Uncover and simmer 30 minutes, stirring often. Stir in salt and next 3 ingredients. Cook, stirring often, 5 minutes. Remove and discard bay leaf. Sprinkle with cooked bacon.

HOME-STYLE LIMA BEANS

makes 6 to 8 servings   prep: 10 min.   cook: 2 hr., 10 min.

5   bacon slices, diced

1   small onion, minced

½   cup firmly packed brown sugar

1   (16-oz.) package frozen baby lima beans

¼   cup butter

2   teaspoons salt

1   teaspoon cracked pepper

1. Cook bacon and onion in a large Dutch oven over medium heat 5 to 7 minutes. Add brown sugar, and cook, stirring occasionally, 1 to 2 minutes or until sugar is dissolved. Stir in lima beans and butter until butter is melted and beans are thoroughly coated. Stir in 12 cups water.

2. Bring to a boil over medium-high heat; reduce heat to low, and simmer, stirring occasionally, 2 hours or until beans are very tender and liquid is thickened and just below top of beans. Stir in salt and pepper.

GREEN BEAN-AND-RED BELL PEPPER TOSS

makes 6 to 8 servings   prep: 10 min.   cook: 5 min.

Substitute 1 lb. trimmed green beans for the slender French beans.

2   Tbsp. butter
2   (8-oz.) packages French green beans
1   red bell pepper, cut into thin strips
3   shallots, sliced

2   garlic cloves, minced
½   tsp. salt
⅛   tsp. ground red pepper

1. Melt butter in a large Dutch oven over medium-high heat. Add green beans, bell pepper strips, and remaining ingredients, tossing to coat. Add ¼ cup water.

2. Cook, covered, 4 to 6 minutes; uncover and cook, stirring often, 1 to 2 more minutes or until water is evaporated and beans are crisp-tender.

Sugar Snap Peas-and-Red Bell Pepper Toss: Substitute 1 lb. trimmed sugar snap peas for green beans. Proceed as directed.

MARINATED DILL GREEN BEANS

makes 2 cups   prep: 10 min.   cook: 8 min.   chill: 3 hr.

Choose beans that are crisp and blemish free.

½   lb. small fresh green beans
¼   cup olive oil
2   Tbsp. rice or white wine vinegar
1   tsp. lemon zest
1   tsp. chopped fresh dill

½   tsp. salt
¼   tsp. pepper
½   medium onion, thinly sliced
1   garlic clove

1. Cook beans in boiling water to cover 3 to 5 minutes or until crisp-tender; drain. Plunge into ice water to stop the cooking process; drain and set aside.

2. Heat oil and next 5 ingredients in a saucepan over medium heat.

3. Combine beans, onion, and garlic; drizzle with warm vinaigrette, tossing to coat. Cover and chill at least 3 hours. Discard garlic clove.

TANGY GREEN BEANS WITH PIMIENTO

makes 6 servings   prep: 10 min.   cook: 20 min.

A sweet-sour dressing gives this side dish irresistible flavor appeal.

1½ lb. green beans, trimmed	¼ cup red wine vinegar
3 bacon slices	1 tsp. sugar
1 large onion, chopped	½ tsp. salt
3 garlic cloves, minced	½ tsp. pepper
1 (2-oz.) jar diced pimiento, drained	½ tsp. cumin seeds

1. Cook green beans in boiling water to cover 4 to 5 minutes. Drain and plunge beans into ice water to stop the cooking process; drain and set aside.

2. Cook bacon in a large skillet until crisp; remove bacon, and drain on paper towels, reserving 2 Tbsp. drippings in skillet. Crumble bacon, and set aside.

3. Sauté onion and garlic in hot bacon drippings over medium-high heat until tender. Stir in pimiento and next 5 ingredients. Stir in green beans; reduce heat, cover, and simmer 5 minutes. Sprinkle with bacon.

THYME-SCENTED GREEN BEANS WITH SMOKED ALMONDS

makes 4 servings   prep: 15 min.   cook: 10 min.

1 lb. fresh green beans, trimmed	¼ tsp. salt
1 Tbsp. light butter	¼ tsp. pepper
1 tsp. dried thyme*	1 Tbsp. chopped smoked almonds*

1. Arrange green beans in a steamer basket over boiling water. Cover and steam 6 minutes or until crisp-tender.

2. Melt butter in a large skillet over medium heat. Stir in green beans, thyme, salt, and pepper; cook until thoroughly heated. Sprinkle beans with almonds.

* 1 to 2 Tbsp. chopped fresh thyme may be substituted for the dried thyme, and 1 Tbsp. chopped toasted almonds may be substituted for the smoked almonds.

Note: Smoked almonds may be found in the snack section of the supermarket.

Per serving: Calories 76; Fat 3.7g (sat 2g, mono 0.5g, poly 1g); Protein 3g; Fiber 3g; Chol 5mg; Iron 3.5mg; Sodium 196mg; Calc 80mg

BROCCOLI WITH PIMIENTO CHEESE SAUCE

makes 6 to 8 servings   prep: 15 min.   cook: 25 min.

2 lb. fresh broccoli, cut into spears

Pimiento Cheese Sauce

1 cup soft white breadcrumbs

2 Tbsp. butter, melted

⅓ cup shredded Parmesan cheese

1. Preheat oven to 375°. Arrange broccoli in a steamer basket over boiling water. Cover and steam 5 minutes or until crisp-tender.

2. Arrange broccoli in a lightly greased 11- x 7-inch baking dish. Pour Pimiento Cheese Sauce evenly over broccoli.

3. Combine breadcrumbs, melted butter, and Parmesan cheese; sprinkle evenly over cheese sauce.

4. Bake at 375° for 20 minutes or until thoroughly heated.

Pimiento Cheese Sauce

makes 3½ cups   prep: 5 min.   cook: 7 min.

¼ cup butter

¼ cup all-purpose flour

2 cups milk

¼ tsp. salt

1 tsp. Worcestershire sauce

2 cups (8 oz.) shredded sharp Cheddar cheese

1 (4-oz.) jar diced pimiento, drained

1. Melt butter in a heavy saucepan over medium heat; add flour, stirring until smooth. Cook, stirring constantly, 1 minute.

2. Add milk gradually; cook, stirring constantly, until mixture is thickened and bubbly. Stir in salt and remaining ingredients.

BROCCOLI-AND-CAULIFLOWER GRATIN

makes 8 servings   prep: 15 min.   cook: 26 min.

2 (16-oz.) packages fresh broccoli and cauliflower
   florets
1½ cups reduced-fat mayonnaise
1 cup (4 oz.) shredded reduced-fat Cheddar
   cheese

1 (3-oz.) package shredded Parmesan cheese
4 green onions, sliced
2 Tbsp. Dijon mustard
¼ tsp. ground red pepper
3 Tbsp. Italian-seasoned breadcrumbs

1. Preheat oven to 350°. Arrange florets in a steamer basket over boiling water. Cover and steam for 6 to 8 minutes or until crisp-tender. Drain well.

2. Arrange florets in a lightly greased 2-qt. baking dish.

3. Stir together mayonnaise and next 5 ingredients. Spoon over florets, and sprinkle with breadcrumbs.

4. Bake at 350° for 20 to 25 minutes or until golden.

CARAMELIZED ONION-AND-PECAN
BRUSSELS SPROUTS

makes 8 servings   prep: 15 min.   chill: 8 hr.   cook: 23 min.   **pictured on page 837**

1 large onion
1 lb. brussels sprouts
¼ cup butter

1 cup pecan pieces
1 tsp. salt
½ tsp. pepper

1. Cut onion in half, and thinly slice. Cut brussels sprouts in half, and cut each half crosswise into thin slices. Place vegetables in separate plastic bags; seal and chill 8 hours.

2. Melt butter in a large heavy skillet over medium-high heat; add pecans, and sauté 5 minutes or until toasted. Remove pecans from skillet. Add onion; cook, stirring often, 15 minutes or until caramel colored. Add pecans and brussels sprouts, and cook 3 minutes or until heated. Sprinkle with salt and pepper.

PEPPER JELLY-GLAZED CARROTS

makes 6 servings   prep: 5 min.   cook: 11 min.

1   (2-lb.) package baby carrots
1   (10½-oz.) can condensed chicken broth, undiluted

2   Tbsp. butter
1   (10½-oz.) jar red pepper jelly

1. Combine carrots and chicken broth in a skillet over medium-high heat. Bring to a boil, and cook, stirring often, 6 to 8 minutes or until carrots are crisp-tender and broth is reduced to ¼ cup.

2. Stir in butter and red pepper jelly, and cook, stirring constantly, 5 minutes or until mixture is thickened and glazes carrots.

CAULIFLOWER IN BROWNED BUTTER

makes 4 to 6 servings   prep: 5 min.   cook: 3 min.

¼   cup butter
1   head cauliflower, separated into florets, cooked

1   to 2 tsp. minced roasted garlic
½   tsp. salt

1. Heat butter in a large skillet over medium heat 1 to 2 minutes or until lightly browned. Add cauliflower, garlic, and salt. Cook, stirring gently, 2 to 3 minutes or until thoroughly heated.

BUTTERMILK FRIED CORN

makes 2 cups   prep: 15 min.   stand: 30 min.   cook: 15 min.   **pictured on page 832**

2   cups fresh corn kernels
1½ cups buttermilk
⅔   cup all-purpose flour
⅔   cup cornmeal

1   tsp. salt
½   tsp. pepper
Corn oil

[test kitchen favorite]

1. Combine corn kernels and buttermilk in large bowl; let stand 30 minutes. Drain.

2. Combine flour and next 3 ingredients in large zip-top plastic freezer bag. Add corn to flour mixture, a small amount at a time, and shake bag to coat corn.

3. Pour oil to a depth of 1 inch in a Dutch oven; heat to 375°. Fry corn, a small amount at a time, in hot oil 2 minutes or until golden. Drain on paper towels. Serve as a side dish, or sprinkle on salads, soups, or casseroles.

GRILLED CORN AND SQUASH

makes 6 to 8 servings   prep: 25 min.   grill: 20 min.

4   ears fresh corn

4   medium-size yellow squash

½   medium-size sweet onion

Vegetable cooking spray

3   poblano chile peppers

1   garlic clove, pressed

2   Tbsp. chopped fresh basil

1   Tbsp. chopped fresh oregano

½   tsp. salt

½   tsp. ground cumin

1. Preheat grill to 350° to 400° (medium-high) heat. Remove husks from corn; cut squash in half lengthwise, and cut onion into ¼-inch-thick slices. Coat corn, squash, and onion with cooking spray, and set aside.

2. Grill chile peppers, covered with grill lid, 5 minutes on each side.

3. Grill corn and onion, covered, over medium-high heat 4 minutes on each side.

4. Grill squash, cut sides down, covered, over medium-high heat 5 minutes; turn squash, and grill 2 more minutes.

5. Cut corn kernels from cob. Chop vegetables, discarding chile pepper seeds; place corn kernels and vegetables in a large bowl. Toss with remaining ingredients.

Grilled Corn-and-Squash Quesadillas: Spoon 1 recipe Grilled Corn and Squash evenly on half of 12 (8-inch) flour tortillas, and sprinkle each portion with 2 cups (8 oz.) shredded Monterey Jack cheese. Fold tortillas over filling. Cook, in batches, on a hot, lightly greased griddle or nonstick skillet 2 to 3 minutes on each side or until lightly browned. Serve immediately. Makes 12 servings. Prep: 5 min.; Cook: 6 min. per batch.

SAGE CORNBREAD DRESSING

makes 8 to 10 servings   prep: 35 min.   cool: 30 min.   cook: 10 min.   bake: 45 min.

pictured on page 837

Use all three cups of broth if you like a really moist dressing.

[freeze it]

2   (6-oz.) packages buttermilk cornbread mix
⅓   cup butter
1   cup chopped celery
½   cup chopped onion
1   Tbsp. chopped fresh or 1½ tsp. dried sage
½   tsp. pepper

¼   tsp. salt
4   white bread slices, cut into ½-inch cubes
     (about 2 cups)
2½ to 3 cups chicken broth
2   large eggs, lightly beaten
Garnish: fresh sage leaves (optional)

1. Prepare cornbread according to package directions for a double recipe. Let cool 30 minutes; crumble into a large bowl.

2. Melt ⅓ cup butter in a large skillet over medium heat; add chopped celery and onion, and sauté 10 to 12 minutes or until tender. Stir in sage, pepper, and salt. Stir celery mixture and bread cubes into crumbled cornbread in bowl, stirring gently until blended. Add chicken broth and eggs, and gently stir until moistened. Spoon mixture into a lightly greased 11- x 7-inch baking dish.

3. Preheat oven to 350°. Bake at 350° for 45 to 50 minutes or until golden brown. Garnish, if desired.

Note: We tested with Martha White Cotton Country Cornbread mix. To make ahead, prepare recipe as directed through Step 2. Cover with plastic wrap; cover with heavy-duty aluminum foil or container lid. Freeze unbaked dressing up to three months, if desired. Thaw in refrigerator 24 hours. Let stand at room temperature 30 minutes. Bake, uncovered, at 350° for 1 hour and 10 minutes to 1 hour and 15 minutes or until golden.

Sausage Dressing: Prepare recipe as directed through Step 1. Omit ⅓ cup butter. Cook 1 (16-oz.) package pork sausage in a large skillet over medium-high heat, stirring often, 10 to 12 minutes or until meat crumbles and is no longer pink. Remove cooked sausage from skillet using a slotted spoon, and drain, reserving 2 tsp. drippings in skillet. Add chopped celery and onion, and sauté 10 to 12 minutes or until vegetables are tender; stir in sage, pepper, and salt. Stir in cooked sausage. Proceed with recipe as directed. Follow make-ahead directions, if desired.

Oyster Dressing: Prepare recipe as directed through Step 2, gently stirring 1 (12-oz.) container fresh oysters, drained, into cornbread mixture. Proceed with recipe as directed, increasing bake time to 50 to 55 minutes or until golden. Follow make-ahead directions, if desired.

taking sides

Defining Dressing

Hardly a Thanksgiving table in the South is without cornbread dressing, along with turkey and gravy. But the discrepancy comes when cooks reveal their recipes.

Each recipe for cornbread dressing pretty much starts the same way: crumbled cornbread, eggs, onions, celery, perhaps bell pepper. Either turkey or chicken stock or broth, sage, salt, pepper, maybe poultry seasoning. But from there, the many faces of Southern cornbread dressing take on their own personalities. Despite some regional leanings, most are based on "what my mama always made."

The smorgasbord of ingredients in the cornbread dressing recipes of Southern cooks reads like a culinary encyclopedia. Ground beef, ground pork, sausage, bacon, chopped chicken, chicken livers and gizzards, oysters. White bread slices, whole wheat bread, biscuits, crackers, cooked rice, or stuffing mix, in addition to crumbled cornbread, that is. Fresh mushrooms, pimiento, chopped hard-cooked egg, chopped apple, pecans, walnuts, dried apricots, raisins. Even cans of cream of chicken, celery, and/or mushroom soup, or cans of chicken à la king.

Instructions vary as well. "Mix enough broth until mixture is like soup…or cake batter…or just enough to moisten." Or the ever famous, "until it looks right." Should the baked result be dry (like bread) or wet-moist (like bread pudding)? Again, personal preference steps in.

"I hate the soggy stuff that feels like it weighs 10 tons!" Julie McDonald of Powder Springs, Georgia, says with strong conviction. "I make my dressing like my mama did, with only cornbread, no other bread, and it's dry, but still a bit moist."

Laneyl Owens of Indian Springs, Alabama, disagrees and says she wants her dressing wet. "I like it moister because it seems to last better as leftovers," she says. Adding white bread, or sometimes crackers, as her mother-in-law does, is tradition in her family.

In McRae, Georgia, Sandy Bennett splits the difference. "Wet in the center and crusted all around the outer edges," she says, as she describes the perfect cornbread dressing. "Mixed with biscuits makes the best dressing. However, NO gizzards will grace my table or my mom's!"

TASTE OF THE SOUTH

Turnip Greens There are several fundamentals of preparing a pot of greens. Most agree that turnip greens are best during the peak season, typically October through February.

The first step is washing them—a time-consuming task, but it's well worth the trouble. To ease the removal of dirt and grit from the leaves, we recommend chopping the greens first and then soaking them. It's best to soak and rinse the leaves four to five times. The result is perfectly clean greens.

Choosing the proper seasoning, however, can be a touchy subject in the South. Some argue that it's better to add salt pork to the pot, while others insist on ham hocks. Some cooks opt to embellish their greens with other ingredients, such as chicken broth, bacon, garlic, onions, and even wine, although purists prefer to keep it simple.

SOUTHERN TURNIP GREENS AND HAM HOCKS

makes 8 to 10 servings   prep: 30 min.   cook: 2 hr., 15 min.

We simmered the ham hocks for about 2 hours until the meat easily pulled away from the bones. If you want to save time, just simmer 30 to 45 minutes to release the flavor.

1¾ lb. ham hocks, rinsed

2   bunches fresh turnip greens with roots
    (about 10 lb.)

1   Tbsp. sugar

1. Bring ham hocks and 2 qt. water to a boil in an 8-qt. Dutch oven. Reduce heat, and simmer 1½ to 2 hours or until meat is tender.
2. Remove and discard stems and discolored spots from greens. Chop greens, and wash thoroughly; drain. Peel turnip roots, and cut in half.
3. Add greens, roots, and sugar to Dutch oven; bring to a boil. Reduce heat; cover and simmer 45 to 60 minutes or until greens and roots are tender.

WILTED GREENS AND RED BEANS

makes 4 to 6 servings   prep: 15 min.   cook: 22 min.

2   (1-lb.) packages fresh turnip greens
¼   cup diced country ham
1   Tbsp. olive or canola oil
1   (15¼-oz.) can red kidney beans, rinsed and drained

2   Tbsp. red wine vinegar
2   tsp. granulated or brown sugar
Pepper sauce (optional)

1. Remove and discard stems from greens. Tear into ½-inch pieces.

2. Sauté ham in hot oil in a large skillet over high heat 2 minutes or until browned. Add greens, beans, and vinegar; cook, stirring often, 15 to 20 minutes or until greens are tender.

3. Sprinkle with sugar. Serve with pepper sauce, if desired.

UPTOWN COLLARDS

makes 8 to 10 servings   prep: 30 min.   cook: 45 min.

7   lb. fresh collards
1   medium onion, quartered
1   cup dry white wine

1   Tbsp. sugar
1   Tbsp. bacon drippings
1   red bell pepper, diced

1. Remove and discard stems from greens. Wash leaves thoroughly, and cut into 1-inch-wide strips; set aside.

2. Pulse onion in a food processor 3 or 4 times or until minced.

3. Bring onion, 1 cup water, and next 3 ingredients to a boil in a Dutch oven. Add greens and bell pepper; cook, covered, over medium heat 45 minutes to 1 hour or until greens are tender.

TASTE OF THE SOUTH

Fried Okra
Deep-fat frying, a no-no today, isn't the problem when serving fried okra. The main concern is fending off the folks waiting to eat the crispy morsels.

Louis Van Dyke of Blue Willow Inn in Social Circle, Georgia, credits his mother for his fried okra recipe. His mother left him and his wife, Billie, a legacy of recipes that yield all the tasty dishes savored at the inn's restaurant. "We use only fresh okra for frying," he says. "It's cut, dipped in buttermilk and egg, salted and peppered, dredged in cornmeal, and then deep-fried."

When talking about the vegetable, Louis laughs and admits, "Fried okra and okra cooked in soup are the only ways I like it. No boiled or steamed okra for me."

Clearly, okra connoisseurs are like pound cake lovers—everyone has their favorite recipe. If bacon drippings aren't used, try adding them. We did here, and it made this even better.

FRIED OKRA

makes 4 servings   prep: 12 min.   chill: 45 min.   cook: 4 min.

1 lb. fresh okra	1 tsp. salt
2 cups buttermilk	¼ tsp. ground red pepper
1 cup self-rising cornmeal	Vegetable oil
1 cup self-rising flour	¼ cup bacon drippings

1. Cut off and discard tip and stem ends from okra; cut okra into ½-inch-thick slices. Stir into buttermilk; cover and chill 45 minutes.

2. Combine cornmeal and next 3 ingredients in a bowl. Remove okra from buttermilk with a slotted spoon, and discard buttermilk. Dredge okra, in batches, in the cornmeal mixture.

3. Pour oil to a depth of 2 inches into a Dutch oven or cast-iron skillet; add bacon drippings, and heat to 375°. Fry okra, in batches, 4 minutes or until golden; drain on paper towels.

Fried Okra Pods: Trim stem end, but do not trim tips or slice okra. Proceed as directed.

FRIED PECAN OKRA

makes 6 to 8 servings   prep: 10 min.   bake: 10 min.   fry: 5 min. per batch

pictured on page 836

1 cup pecans	2 large eggs
1½ cups all-purpose baking mix	½ cup milk
1 tsp. salt	2 (16-oz.) packages frozen whole okra, thawed
½ tsp. pepper	Peanut oil

1. Preheat oven to 350°. Bake pecans in a single layer in a shallow pan 10 minutes or until lightly toasted and fragrant, stirring occasionally.

2. Process pecans, baking mix, and next 2 ingredients in a food processor until pecans are finely ground. Place pecan mixture in a large bowl. Whisk together eggs and milk in a medium bowl. Dip okra in egg mixture; dredge in pecan mixture, gently pressing pecan mixture onto okra to adhere.

3. Pour oil to a depth of 2 inches into a Dutch oven or cast-iron skillet; heat to 350°. Fry okra, in batches, turning once, 5 to 6 minutes or until golden; drain on paper towels.

Note: We tested with Bisquick Original All-Purpose Baking Mix.

FRIED OKRA AND GREEN TOMATOES

makes 8 servings   prep: 20 min.   cook: 8 min. per batch

1 cup buttermilk	1 pound fresh okra, sliced
1 large egg	2 or 3 green tomatoes, cut into ½-inch pieces
1½ cups cornmeal	Vegetable oil
⅛ tsp. salt	Salt
¼ tsp. pepper	

1. Whisk together buttermilk and egg. Combine cornmeal, ⅛ tsp. salt, and pepper. Dip okra and tomato, in batches, into buttermilk mixture; coat in cornmeal mixture.

2. Pour oil to a depth of 3 inches into a Dutch oven; heat to 375°. Fry okra and tomato, in batches, 4 minutes on each side or until golden. (Turning too soon will cause breading to fall off.) Drain on paper towel; sprinkle with salt.

OKRA AND TOMATOES

makes 8 servings   prep: 25 min.   cook: 20 min. pictured on back cover

Juicy, summer-ripe tomatoes make this dish shine. You can use a large can of San Marzano tomatoes, chopped, as an out-of-season option.

4	bacon slices	1	tsp. salt
1	large sweet onion, chopped	1	tsp. pepper
3	large tomatoes, chopped	1	garlic clove, minced
1	lb. fresh okra, chopped		Hot cooked rice

1. Cook bacon in a large skillet or Dutch oven over medium heat until crisp. Remove and crumble bacon; reserve 2 Tbsp. drippings in skillet.

2. Sauté onion in hot drippings over medium-high heat 5 minutes or until tencer. Stir in tomatoes and next 4 ingredients. Reduce heat, and cook, stirring often 10 minutes or until okra is tender. Serve over rice, and sprinkle with bacon.

CROWDER PEA SUCCOTASH

makes 8 servings   prep: 20 min.   cook: 8 min.

½	large onion, finely diced	½	cup reserved Crowder Peas liquid
1	green bell pepper, finely diced	½	cup sliced green onions
1	red bell pepper, finely diced	1	Tbsp. fresh thyme leaves, finely chopped
3	Tbsp. olive oil	½	tsp. salt
2	cups fresh or frozen corn kernels		Garnish: fresh thyme sprig (optional)
	Crowder Peas (recipe facing page)		

1. Sauté onion and bell peppers in hot oil in a large skillet over medium heat 5 to 7 minutes or until tender. Stir in corn and Crowder Peas; cook 2 minutes or until thoroughly heated.

2. Stir in ½ cup reserved Crowder Peas liquid, green onions, chopped thyme, and salt; cook 1 to 2 minutes or until thoroughly heated. Garnish, if desired. Serve immediately.

CROWDER PEAS

makes 4 servings   prep: 15 min.   cook: 30 min.   stand: 30 min.

Freeze the flavorful leftover cooking liquid to use in soup or to cook rice.

½ large onion, cut in half

½ medium carrot, cut in half lengthwise

2 celery ribs, cut into 2-inch pieces

2 garlic cloves, peeled and cut in half

1 Tbsp. olive oil

2 Tbsp. jarred ham base

2 cups fresh or frozen crowder peas

2 fresh thyme sprigs

½ tsp. salt

½ tsp. pepper

1. Cook first 4 ingredients in hot oil in a Dutch oven over medium-high heat, stirring often, 5 minutes. Stir in ham base and 4 cups water until well blended. Add peas, thyme, salt, and pepper, and bring mixture to a boil. Reduce heat to low, and simmer 20 minutes or until peas are done. Remove from heat; cool 30 minutes.

2. Drain peas, reserving cooking liquid for another use. Remove and discard onion, carrots, celery, and thyme sprigs.

Note: We tested with Superior Touch Better Than Bouillon Ham Base.

PEPPERY PEAS O' PLENTY

makes 4 to 6 servings   prep: 15 min.   cook: 40 min.

4 hickory-smoked bacon slices

1 large onion, chopped

1 cup frozen black-eyed peas

1 cup frozen purple hull peas

1 cup frozen crowder peas

1 cup frozen butter peas

1 cup frozen field peas with snaps

1 (32-oz.) container chicken broth

1 Tbsp. Asian garlic-chili sauce

¾ to 1 tsp. salt

1 Tbsp. freshly ground pepper

1. Cook bacon in a Dutch oven until crisp; remove bacon, and drain on paper towels, reserving drippings in pan. Crumble bacon.

2. Sauté onion in hot drippings in Dutch oven over medium-high heat 8 minutes or until translucent. Add black-eyed peas and next 8 ingredients, and cook 20 to 25 minutes, uncovered. Top with crumbled bacon.

Note: We tested with Bryan Sweet Hickory Smoked Bacon and A Taste of Thai Garlic Chili Pepper Sauce.

HEARTY BLACK-EYED PEAS

makes 8 servings   prep: 20 min.   cook: 1 hr.

1 (16-oz.) package dried black-eyed peas
1 medium onion, chopped
½ tsp. pepper
¾ tsp. salt

1 (1-lb.) ham steak, cut into ½-inch cubes,
   or 1 ham hock
4 whole jalapeño peppers (optional)

1. Bring black-eyed peas, 4 cups water, onion, pepper, salt, ham, and, if desired, jalapeños to a boil in a Dutch oven; cover, reduce heat, and simmer 1 hour or until peas are tender.

CREAMY BAKED SWEET ONIONS

makes 4 servings   prep: 30 min.   cook: 10 min.   bake: 30 min.   **pictured on page 836**

2 (10-oz.) packages cipollini boiler onions,
   unpeeled*
2 Tbsp. butter
2 Tbsp. all-purpose flour
1½ cups milk
1½ cups (6 oz.) shredded sharp white Cheddar
   cheese

1 tsp. hot sauce
¼ tsp. salt
⅛ tsp. ground white pepper
¼ cup crushed round buttery crackers
1 Tbsp. melted butter

1. Preheat oven to 350°. Cook onions in a large saucepan in boiling water to cover 5 to 7 minutes. Drain, cool slightly, and peel. Place in a lightly greased 8-inch square baking dish.
2. Melt 2 Tbsp. butter in a heavy saucepan over medium heat; whisk in flour until smooth, and cook, whisking constantly, 1 minute. Gradually whisk in milk, and cook, whisking constantly, 1 minute or until thickened and bubbly. Add cheese, hot sauce, salt, and ground white pepper, and whisk 2 minutes or until cheese is melted. Pour mixture over onions in dish.
3. Stir together crushed crackers and 1 Tbsp. melted butter; sprinkle over top of casserole.
4. Bake at 350° for 25 to 30 minutes or until bubbly.

* 20 oz. sweet onions, peeled and cut into wedges, may be substituted. Omit boiling onions in Step 1; peel and place in baking dish as directed.

CRISPY "FRIED" ONION RINGS

makes 3 servings   prep: 20 min.   cook: 6 min.   bake: 6 min.

1   **large sweet onion**
½   **cup low-fat buttermilk**
1   **egg white**
½   **cup all-purpose flour**

2   **Tbsp. olive oil**
½   **tsp. coarse kosher salt**

1. Preheat oven to 400°. Cut onion into ¼-inch-thick slices, and separate into rings. Select largest 12 rings, reserving remaining onion slices for another use.

2. Whisk together buttermilk and egg white in a small bowl until blended.

3. Dredge onion rings in flour; dip into buttermilk mixture, coating well. Dredge again in flour, and place on a baking sheet.

4. Heat 2 tsp. oil in a 10-inch skillet over medium-high heat. Tilt pan to coat bottom of skillet. Add 4 onion rings to skillet, and cook 1 minute on each side or until golden. Wipe skillet clean. Repeat procedure twice with remaining onion rings and oil. Place fried onion rings on an aluminum foil-lined baking sheet coated with cooking spray.

5. Bake at 400° for 3 minutes. Turn onion rings, and bake 3 more minutes. Remove from oven, and sprinkle with salt. Serve immediately.

Per serving (4 onion rings): Calories 119; Fat 5.9g (sat 0.9g, mono 4.1g, poly 0.7g); Protein 3.1g; Fiber 1g; Chol 1mg; Iron 0.6mg; Sodium 345mg; Calc 24mg

Onion Rings Step-by-Step:

Follow these simple steps for fantastic "fried" onion rings.

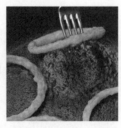

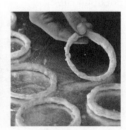

1. Using a sharp knife, cut onion into thin slices, and separate into rings.

2. Dredge onion rings in flour, and dip into buttermilk mixture; then dredge again in flour.

3. Cooking the rings in oil for a short time gives them a fried flavor without the calories.

4. Finish up the rings by baking them at 400° for 3 minutes on each side.

～inspirations for your taste～

We recommend only Vidalia or Texas Sweets for this recipe. Be sure to use a microwave-safe lid only; plastic wrap will melt.

Vidalia Onion Side Dish

makes 2 servings   prep: 5 min.   cook: 8 min.

Peel 2 medium onions, and cut a thin slice from bottom and top of each one. Scoop out a 1-inch-deep hole from the top of each onion. Place onions, top sides up, in a 2-qt. microwave-safe dish with a lid. Add 1 beef bouillon cube and ½ Tbsp. butter to shallow hole in each onion; cover with lid. Microwave, covered, at HIGH for 8 to 10 minutes or until onion is tender. Garnish each serving with fresh parsley sprig and pepper, if desired.

Note: If you'd rather grill, preheat grill to 400° to 450° (high) heat. Wrap each filled-and-topped onion in heavy-duty aluminum foil (or a double layer of regular aluminum foil). Grill, covered with grill lid, 15 to 20 minutes or until tender. Let stand 10 minutes.

VIDALIA ONION SOUFFLÉ

makes 8 servings   prep: 30 min.   cook: 35 min.

2   Tbsp. butter

5   medium Vidalia or sweet onions, chopped
    (about 4 cups)

2   cups fresh bread cubes (about 10 slices, crusts
    removed)

1   (15-oz.) can fat-free evaporated milk

3   large eggs, lightly beaten

1¼ cups (5 oz.) shredded Parmesan cheese

1   tsp. salt

1. Preheat oven to 350°. Melt butter in a large skillet over medium heat; add chopped onions, and sauté 10 to 15 minutes or until tender.

2. Place onions and bread cubes in a large bowl. Stir in milk, eggs, 1 cup cheese, and salt.

3. Pour into a lightly greased 1½-qt. soufflé or baking dish. Sprinkle with remaining ¼ cup cheese.

4. Bake at 350° for 25 minutes or until set.

SKILLET GRITS WITH SEASONED VEGETABLES

makes 6 to 8 servings   prep: 10 min.   cook: 20 min.

This is a robust, meatless recipe that you can prep in advance. Start by cooking the vegetables. If you make the vegetables a day ahead, cook them a few minutes less to ensure they don't overcook when they're reheated.

1 (32-oz.) container vegetable broth	1 cup (4 oz.) shredded Cheddar cheese
3 Tbsp. butter	⅓ cup (1.5 oz.) shredded Parmesan cheese
1 tsp. salt	½ tsp. pepper
1½ cups uncooked regular grits	**Seasoned Vegetables**

1. Bring first 3 ingredients to a boil in a large saucepan over medium-high heat. Gradually whisk in grits, and return to a boil. Reduce heat to medium-low, and simmer, stirring occasionally, 10 to 12 minutes or until thickened.

2. Whisk in cheeses and pepper until cheeses are melted. Spoon Seasoned Vegetables evenly over grits, and serve immediately.

Seasoned Vegetables

makes 6 to 8 servings   prep: 20 min.   cook: 25 min.

This recipe is similar to a ragoût, a thick, well-seasoned stew. We served the richly flavored vegetables over grits; you can also try them over rice or egg noodles.

1 medium onion, chopped	1 medium zucchini, chopped
2 garlic cloves, minced	1 (14-oz.) can vegetable broth
2 Tbsp. olive oil	1 tsp. salt
4 carrots, chopped	1 tsp. dried thyme
3 small red potatoes, diced	½ tsp. pepper
2 small turnips (about ½ lb.), peeled and chopped	1 tsp. cornstarch
2 celery ribs, diced	

1. Sauté onion and garlic in hot oil in a large skillet over medium heat 5 minutes or until caramelized. Add carrots and next 4 ingredients, and sauté 12 to 15 minutes or until vegetables are tender. Increase heat to medium-high; stir in vegetable broth and next 3 ingredients. Bring to a boil. Reduce heat to medium-low, and simmer, stirring occasionally, 5 minutes.

2. Whisk together cornstarch and 1 Tbsp. water until smooth. Whisk into vegetable mixture in skillet, and cook, stirring constantly, 3 to 5 minutes or until thickened.

ROASTED BABY VEGETABLES

makes 8 servings   prep: 20 min.   bake: 30 min.

For even roasting, all vegetables should be cut to about the same size. Put them in the oven when you take out the roast.

1 lb. baby beets with tops	1 lb. baby carrots
¼ cup olive oil, divided	2 medium-size sweet potatoes (about 1½ lb.),
1½ Tbsp. chopped fresh rosemary	peeled and cut into 1-inch pieces
1 tsp. coarse-grained sea salt, divided	1¼ lb. turnips, peeled and cut into eighths
¼ tsp. pepper, divided	Garnish: fresh rosemary sprigs (optional)
8 shallots	

1. Preheat oven to 450°. Cut tops from beets, leaving 1-inch stems. Peel beets, and cut into quarters. Place on a 12-inch square of aluminum foil. Drizzle with 1 Tbsp. olive oil; sprinkle with rosemary, ¼ tsp. salt, and ⅛ tsp. pepper. Fold up foil sides, forming a bowl.

2. Place foil bowl in 1 end of a large roasting pan; set aside.

3. Peel shallots; cut in half lengthwise.

4. Toss together shallots, carrots, potatoes, turnips, remaining 3 Tbsp. oil, remaining ¾ tsp. salt, and remaining ⅛ tsp. pepper. Place in remaining end of roasting pan.

5. Bake at 450° for 30 to 40 minutes or until tender.

POTATO-HORSERADISH GRATIN WITH CARAMELIZED ONIONS

makes 8 servings   prep: 1 hr., 25 min.   cook: 1 hr., 10 min.   stand: 10 min.

2½ lb. medium-size baking potatoes	2 large onions, thinly sliced
1 tsp. salt, divided	1 tsp. sugar
1 tsp. pepper, divided	1 Tbsp. balsamic vinegar
2 cups half-and-half	1 cup (4 oz.) shredded Swiss cheese
½ cup cream-style horseradish	¼ cup chopped fresh parsley, divided
¼ cup butter	

1. Preheat oven to 400°. Cook potatoes in boiling water to cover 20 minutes or until almost tender. Drain and cool slightly. Peel potatoes, and cut into ¼-inch-thick slices. Arrange potato slices in a lightly greased 13- x 9-inch baking dish. Sprinkle with ½ tsp. salt and ½ tsp. pepper.

2. Stir together half-and-half and horseradish, and pour over potato.

[*test kitchen favorite*]

3. Bake, covered, at 400° for 40 minutes.

4. Melt butter in a large skillet over medium heat. Add onion, remaining ½ tsp. salt, and remaining ½ tsp. pepper; cook, stirring occasionally, 20 minutes. Add sugar, and cook, stirring occasionally, 5 to 8 minutes or until onion is caramel colored.

5. Stir in vinegar, and cook 2 minutes or until liquid evaporates. Remove from heat, and cool 5 minutes. Fold in cheese and 2 Tbsp. parsley.

6. Uncover potato; top with onion mixture. Reduce temperature to 350°.

7. Bake at 350° for 30 minutes. Let stand 5 minutes; sprinkle with remaining 2 Tbsp. parsley.

BROWNED BUTTER MASHED POTATOES

makes 6 to 8 servings   prep: 15 min.   cook: 29 min.   **pictured on page 835**

Also, try tossing browned butter with steamed vegetables, or drizzle it over warm, crusty French bread.

¾   **cup butter**

4   **lb. Yukon gold potatoes, peeled and cut into 2-inch pieces**

1   **Tbsp. salt, divided**

¾   **cup buttermilk**

½   **cup milk**

¼   **tsp. pepper**

Garnishes: fresh parsley, rosemary, and thyme sprigs

1. Cook butter in a 2-qt. heavy saucepan over medium heat, stirring constantly, 6 to 8 minutes or just until butter begins to turn golden brown. Immediately remove pan from heat, and pour butter into a small bowl. (Butter will continue to darken if left in saucepan.) Remove and reserve 1 to 2 Tbsp. browned butter.

2. Bring potatoes, 2 tsp. salt, and water to cover to a boil in a large Dutch oven over medium-high heat; boil 20 minutes or until tender. Drain. Reduce heat to low. Return potatoes to Dutch oven, and cook, stirring occasionally, 3 to 5 minutes or until potatoes are dry.

3. Mash potatoes with a potato masher to desired consistency. Stir in remaining browned butter, buttermilk, milk, pepper, and remaining 1 tsp. salt, stirring just until blended.

4. Transfer to a serving dish. Drizzle with reserved 1 to 2 Tbsp. browned butter. Garnish, if desired.

Note: To make ahead, prepare recipe as directed through Step 3. Place in a lightly greased 2½-qt. ovenproof serving dish; cover and chill up to 2 days. Let stand at room temperature 30 minutes. Bake, uncovered, at 350° for 35 to 40 minutes or until thoroughly heated. Drizzle with reserved brown butter, and garnish, if desired.

make ahead

Mash 'Em Up!

It's hard to believe cooks have so many varied opinions on how to mash potatoes. Lumpy or smooth? Skin on or off? The techniques are endless!

Do people really care how potatoes are mashed? Oh, you bet! If you don't believe it, just check out the comments on the Web site www.seriouseats.com.

There are the cooks who want them smooth and creamy. Then there are those who say to leave 'em lumpy. But the real difference of opinion lies in how to mash them. Instruments of choice include a ricer, a food mill, an electric mixer, the whisk attachment on a standing mixer, a fork, and even a fork bent just for mashing potatoes.

However, true traditionalists stick to the hand-held mashers passed down through the family. Wrote one person on the Web site, "About 20 years ago I got a masher from a yard sale I still use, and it has a wooden handle held on with a rubber band."

BUTTERMILK-GARLIC MASHED POTATOES

makes 4 servings   prep: 10 min.   cook: 6 min.

Buttermilk replaces some of the butter in these potatoes with outstanding results.

2 **Tbsp. butter**	½ **tsp. salt**
3 **garlic cloves, chopped**	½ **tsp. pepper**
2 **cups buttermilk**	1 **(22-oz.) package frozen mashed potatoes**
⅔ **cup milk**	

1. Melt butter in a Dutch oven over medium heat; add garlic, and sauté 1 minute. Add buttermilk and next 3 ingredients. Cook, stirring constantly, 5 minutes or until thoroughly heated. Stir in potatoes until smooth.

Note: We tested with Ore-Ida Steam N' Mash Potatoes.

FRENCH FRIES

makes 4 to 6 servings   prep: 30 min.   cook: 5 min. per batch

4   lb. russet or Idaho potatoes, peeled   Salt to taste
Vegetable oil

1. Cut potatoes into ¼-inch-wide strips.

2. Pour vegetable oil to a depth of 4 inches in a Dutch oven, and heat to 325°. Fry potato strips, in batches, until lightly golden, but not brown, 4 to 5 minutes per batch. Drain strips on paper towels.

3. Heat oil to 375°. Fry strips, in small batches, until golden brown and crisp, 1 to 2 minutes per batch. Drain on paper towels. Sprinkle with salt, and serve immediately.

Note: We tested with Wesson Vegetable Oil.

Crinkle-Cut Fries: Cut potatoes into ½-inch-wide strips with a waffle cutter. Fry as directed.

Waffle Chips: Cut potatoes into ¼-inch-thick slices with a waffle cutter. Fry as directed.

SOUTHWEST TWICE-BAKED NEW POTATOES

makes 6 servings   prep: 25 min.   bake: 1 hr., 5 min.

A small melon baller is perfect for scooping out the potato pulp.

2   lb. medium-size new potatoes   2   Tbsp. buttermilk
1   Tbsp. canola oil   ½   tsp. pepper
½   cup shredded Cheddar cheese   ½   tsp. salt
2   Tbsp. sour cream   1   (4.5-oz.) can diced green chiles, drained
1   Tbsp. melted butter   Garnish: paprika (optional)

1. Preheat oven to 350°. Cut a thin slice from the bottom of each potato to form a flat base; brush potatoes evenly with oil, and place on a baking sheet.

2. Bake at 350° for 45 minutes or until tender. Remove from oven, and let cool slightly.

3. Cut a thin slice from the top of each potato. Carefully scoop out potato pulp into a bowl, leaving shells intact. Add shredded Cheddar cheese and next 5 ingredients to potato pulp in bowl, and beat at medium speed with an electric mixer until smooth and creamy. Stir in green chiles. Spoon mixture evenly into each potato shell, and place on baking sheet.

4. Bake potatoes at 350° for 20 minutes or just until lightly browned. Garnish, if desired.

taking sides

Keeping the Holidays Sweet

Do you recall a Thanksgiving menu without a sweet potato casserole? Pumpkin-colored and sweet as dessert, it's the topping that has some Southerners defending tradition.

So there are some new-fangled ways to put sweet potatoes on the table—mashed and spooned into orange halves, roasted for a salad, or slipped onto kabobs. But when the holidays roll around and it's time to set a table of tradition, it's the splattered recipes for sweet potato casserole, sometimes called sweet potato "SUE flay," that fly out of family cookbooks .

What does it take to avoid a family mutiny?

Tiny marshmallows on top, browned to perfection? Or a crispy cover of sugar, butter, and chopped pecans?

"Marshmallows are for roasting, not for using in recipes," say some. "It's not the same without the marshmallows," whine others. What's a Southern cook to do? Daniela Jordan of Atlanta has solved the dilemma. "I make mine with BOTH," she declares, "and everybody is happy!"

EASY SWEET POTATO CASSEROLE

makes 8 to 10 servings   prep: 10 min.   bake: 40 min.   **pictured on page 834**

3 (40-oz.) cans cut sweet potatoes in syrup, drained	1¼ tsp. vanilla extract
1¼ cups granulated sugar	½ tsp. salt
½ cup butter, softened	1¼ cups firmly packed brown sugar
½ cup milk	1¼ cups finely chopped pecans
2 large eggs	½ cup all-purpose flour
	⅓ cup butter, melted

1. Preheat oven to 350°. Beat sweet potatoes and next 6 ingredients at medium speed with an electric mixer until smooth. Spoon potato mixture into a lightly greased 13- x 9-inch baking dish. Combine 1¼ cups brown sugar and next 3 ingredients. Sprinkle evenly over top of sweet potato mixture.

2. Bake at 350° for 40 to 45 minutes.

SPINACH SOUFFLÉ

makes 4 to 6 servings   prep: 15 min.   cook: 5 min.   bake: 33 min.   stand: 5 min.

1   (10-oz.) package frozen chopped spinach, thawed

2   Tbsp. butter

1   medium onion, chopped (about ¾ cup)

2   garlic cloves, minced

3   large eggs

2   Tbsp. all-purpose flour

½   tsp. salt

¼   tsp. ground nutmeg

¼   tsp. pepper

1   cup milk

1   cup freshly grated Parmesan or Romano cheese

1. Preheat oven to 350°. Drain spinach well, pressing between paper towels to remove all excess liquid.

2. Melt butter in a large skillet over medium heat; add onion and garlic, and sauté 5 minutes or until garlic is lightly browned and onions are tender. Remove from heat, and stir in spinach until well blended; cool.

3. Whisk together eggs and next 4 ingredients in a large bowl. Whisk in milk and Parmesan cheese; stir in spinach mixture, and pour into a lightly greased 8-inch square baking dish.

4. Bake at 350° for 33 to 35 minutes or until set. Let stand 5 minutes before serving.

SAUTÉED GARLIC SPINACH

makes 4 servings   prep: 5 min.   cook: 4 min.

1 tsp. olive oil

1 garlic clove, pressed

1 (10-oz) bag fresh spinach, thoroughly washed

Salt and pepper to taste

1. Heat olive oil in a nonstick skillet over medium-high heat. Sauté garlic in hot oil 30 seconds. Add spinach to skillet, and cook 2 to 3 minutes or until spinach is wilted. Sprinkle with salt and pepper to taste. Serve spinach with a slotted spoon or tongs.

FRIED GREEN TOMATOES

makes 4 to 6 servings   prep: 20 min.   cook: 4 min.

Full of fresh, tangy flavor, these delectable tomatoes are crusty on the outside and juicy on the inside. If your family has a large appetite, you may want to double this recipe.

1	large egg, lightly beaten	½	tsp. pepper
½	cup buttermilk	3	medium-size green tomatoes, cut into
½	cup all-purpose flour, divided		⅓-inch slices
½	cup cornmeal		Vegetable oil
1	tsp. salt		Salt to taste

1. Combine egg and buttermilk; set aside.

2. Combine ¼ cup all-purpose flour, cornmeal, 1 tsp. salt, and pepper in a shallow bowl or pan.

3. Dredge tomato slices in remaining ¼ cup flour; dip in egg mixture, and dredge in cornmeal mixture.

4. Pour oil to a depth of ¼ to ½ inch in a large cast-iron skillet; heat to 375°. Drop tomatoes, in batches, into hot oil, and cook 2 minutes on each side or until golden. Drain on paper towels or a rack. Sprinkle hot tomatoes with salt to taste.

ROSEMARY-ROASTED CHERRY TOMATOES

makes 4 servings   prep: 5 min.   bake: 15 min.

Fragrant rosemary boosts the flavor of these juicy tomatoes. If you can't find cherry tomatoes, winter tomatoes, such as plum, are a terrific substitute.

2	pt. cherry tomatoes	2	garlic cloves, minced
1	tsp. olive oil	¼	tsp. salt
1½	tsp. chopped fresh rosemary	¼	tsp. pepper

1. Preheat oven to 425°. Combine first 6 ingredients in a zip-top plastic freezer bag. Gently shake until tomatoes are well coated. Transfer to an aluminum foil-lined jelly-roll pan coated with cooking spray.

2. Bake at 425°, stirring occasionally, 15 minutes or until tomatoes begin to burst.

Per ¾ cup: Calories 44; Fat 1.6g (sat 0.2g, mono 0.9g, poly 0.3g); Protein 1.4g; Fiber 1.7g; Iron 0.7mg; Sodium 161mg; Calc 12mg

MARINATED TOMATOES WITH BASIL AND BALSAMIC VINEGAR

makes 12 servings   prep: 20 min.   stand: 30 min.   chill: 30 min.

Soaking onion slices in ice water before assembling a dish makes them milder. It's a great trick to use for onions that are added to tuna, egg, or chicken salad.

1   small red onion, thinly sliced
4   cups ice water
¾   cup balsamic vinegar
¼   cup olive oil
2   tsp. sugar
½   tsp. salt

½   tsp. pepper
2   garlic cloves, minced
½   to 1 cup chopped fresh basil
6   tomatoes, thinly sliced
    Parmesan cheese curls (optional)
    French bread (optional)

1. Combine onion slices and 4 cups ice water in a large bowl; let stand 30 minutes. Drain and pat dry with paper towels.

2. Whisk together vinegar, olive oil, 2 Tbsp. water, and next 4 ingredients. Stir in basil.

3. Layer half of tomato slices in a shallow dish. Top with half of onion slices. Drizzle with half of dressing. Repeat with remaining tomato slices, onion slices, and dressing. Cover and chill 30 minutes.

4. Sprinkle with Parmesan cheese curls, if desired, and serve with bread, if desired. Serve at room temperature.

Note: Recipe may be prepared up to three hours ahead.

Per serving: Calories 88; Fat 5g (sat 0.7g, mono 3.6g, poly 0.6g); Protein 0.9g; Fiber 1.2g; Chol 0mg; Iron 0.6mg; Sodium 108mg; Calc 12mg

15-MINUTE EGGS

Eggs

1. Place eggs in a single layer in a saucepan. Add water to a depth of 3 inches, and bring to a rolling boil.

2. When water boils, cover and remove from heat. Let eggs stand 15 minutes.

3. Drain and return eggs to pan. Fill with cold water and ice; let eggs stand for a few minutes to cool. Crack shells on all sides on your countertop or other work surface. Peel eggs under cold running water, starting at the large end.

SPECIAL DEVILED EGGS

makes 2 dozen   prep: 15 min.

To hard-cook eggs, place in a large pot and cover with cold water. Boil for 1 minute, and remove from heat. Cover and let stand 15 minutes.

[*quick*]

1 dozen large hard-cooked eggs, peeled	2 tsp. sugar
5 bacon slices, cooked and crumbled	2 tsp. honey mustard
½ cup finely shredded Swiss cheese	1½ tsp. freshly ground pepper
¼ cup plus 1 Tbsp. mayonnaise	¼ tsp. salt
2½ Tbsp. cider vinegar	Finely chopped green onions or chives (optional)

1. Cut eggs in half lengthwise; carefully remove yolks, keeping egg white halves intact, and place in a bowl. Set egg whites aside.

2. Mash yolks until smooth. Add bacon and next 7 ingredients; stir until blended.

3. Spoon yolk mixture evenly into egg white halves. Sprinkle with green onions, if desired.

SAVORY DEVILED EGGS

makes 2 dozen   prep: 20 min.

Serve these tasty snacks as soon as you make them, or refrigerate them up to 24 hours.

[*make ahead*]

1 dozen large hard-cooked eggs, peeled	½ cup olive oil
2 garlic cloves, minced	Salt and pepper to taste
3 Tbsp. chopped black olives	Hot sauce to taste
1 tsp. lemon zest	Garnish: chopped fresh parsley (optional)

1. Slice eggs in half lengthwise; carefully remove yolks, keeping egg white halves intact. Process yolks, garlic, olives, and lemon zest in a food processor until combined, stopping to scrape down sides. With food processor running, gradually pour olive oil through food chute in a slow, steady stream, processing until mixture thickens. Stir in salt, pepper, and hot sauce to taste.

2. Spoon yolk mixture evenly into egg white halves. Garnish, if desired.

BUTTERY DIJON DEVILED EGGS

makes 2 dozen prep: 15 min. chill: 1 hr. **pictured on page 832**

1 dozen large hard-cooked eggs, peeled

¼ cup butter, softened

¼ cup mayonnaise

1 Tbsp. Dijon mustard

1 tsp. fresh lemon juice

¼ tsp. ground red pepper

Salt to taste

Ground white pepper to taste

Paprika (optional)

1. Slice eggs in half lengthwise; carefully remove yolks, keeping egg white halves intact. Mash yolks; stir in butter and next 4 ingredients. Stir in salt and white pepper to taste. Spoon or pipe yolk mixture evenly into egg white halves. Sprinkle with paprika, if desired. Cover and chill at least 1 hour or until ready to serve.

BARBECUE DEVILED EGGS

makes 12 servings prep: 30 min. cook: 6 min. stand: 15 min.

12 large eggs

¼ cup mayonnaise

⅓ cup finely chopped smoked pork

1 Tbsp. Dijon mustard

¼ tsp. salt

½ tsp. pepper

⅛ tsp. hot sauce

Garnish: paprika (optional)

1. Place eggs in a single layer in a large saucepan; add water to a depth of 3 inches. Bring to a boil; cover, remove from heat, and let stand 15 minutes.

2. Drain and fill pan with cold water and ice. Tap each egg firmly on the counter until cracks form all over the shell. Peel under cold running water.

3. Cut eggs in half lengthwise, and carefully remove yolks, keeping egg white halves intact. Mash yolks with mayonnaise. Stir in pork and next 4 ingredients; blend well.

4. Spoon yolk mixture evenly into egg white halves. Garnish, if desired.

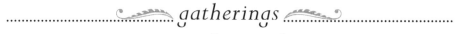

Picnic in the Park serves 12

*Dressed-up Salsa (page 52) **with tortilla chips**
*Greek Chicken Rollups (page 798)
South-of-the-Border Deviled Eggs
Carrot and celery sticks   Red seedless grapes
Fried Strawberry Pies (page 639)

*double recipe

SOUTH-OF-THE-BORDER DEVILED EGGS

makes 12 servings   prep: 25 min.   chill: 1 hr.

1 dozen large hard-cooked eggs, peeled	2 Tbsp. mayonnaise
1 small ripe avocado, peeled and coarsely chopped	1 Tbsp. dry Ranch dressing mix
2 green onions, finely chopped	½ tsp. chili powder (optional)
2 Tbsp. sweet pickle juice	½ cup mild salsa

1. Slice eggs in half lengthwise; carefully remove yolks, keeping egg white halves intact.

2. Mash together yolks and avocado in a medium bowl. Stir in green onions and next 3 ingredients until smooth. Spoon yolk mixture evenly into egg white halves. Sprinkle evenly with chili powder, if desired. Cover and chill at least 1 hour or up to 24 hours. Dollop with salsa just before serving.

ROASTED APPLES AND SWEET POTATOES

makes 4 servings   prep: 20 min.   bake: 30 min.

This oven-roasted side is flavored with a hint of orange. If you'd like your apples crisp rather than tender, you can bake them for a little less time.

3 lb. sweet potatoes (about 5 medium-size sweet potatoes), peeled	2 Tbsp. light brown sugar
2 large Granny Smith apples, peeled	1 tsp. orange zest
2 Tbsp. butter, melted	1 tsp. kosher salt
	½ tsp. coarsely ground pepper

1. Preheat oven to 400°. Cut peeled sweet potatoes into 1-inch cubes. Cut peeled apples into ½-inch-thick slices.

2. Stir together melted butter, brown sugar, and orange zest in a large zip-top plastic freezer bag until blended. Add cubed sweet potatoes and sliced apples. Seal bag, and toss to coat.

3. Place potato mixture in a single layer in a lightly greased aluminum foil-lined 15- x 10-inch jelly-roll pan. Sprinkle with salt and pepper.

4. Bake at 400° for 30 to 35 minutes or until potatoes and apples are tender and lightly browned.

PEAR-GOAT CHEESE TARTS

makes 12 tarts   prep: 20 min.   bake: 16 min.   cool: 2 min.

Leftover tarts are great for breakfast the next morning.

1 (15-oz.) package refrigerator piecrusts	2 Tbsp. honey
2 (4-oz.) packages goat cheese, crumbled	½ tsp. dried thyme
1 to 2 ripe pears, chopped	

1. Preheat oven to 375°. Unfold piecrusts, and cut each in half; cut each half into 3 pieces. Place 1 piece into a lightly greased muffin cup in a muffin pan. Fold and press pastry piece to form a cup shape. Repeat procedure with remaining pastry pieces.

2. Bake at 375° for 8 minutes or until edges of pastries are lightly browned. Remove pan to a wire rack.

3. Stir together goat cheese and next 3 ingredients. Spoon evenly into pastry shells.

4. Bake at 375° for 8 to 10 minutes or until thoroughly heated. Remove to a wire rack, and let cool 2 minutes.

SOUPS & STEWS

"As the days grow short, some faces grow long. But not mine.
Every autumn, when the wind turns cold and darkness comes early,
I am suddenly happy. It's time to start making soup again."

—Leslie Newman

Try our suggestions to turn your next bowl of tomato soup into the very best you've ever had.

Dressed-up Tomato Soup

makes about 11 cups   prep: 5 min.   cook: 10 min.

Pulse 1 (28-oz.) can Italian-seasoned diced tomatoes in a food processor 3 to 4 times or until finely diced. Stir together tomatoes; 1 (26-oz.) can tomato soup, undiluted; 1 (32-oz.) container chicken broth; and ½ tsp. freshly ground pepper in a Dutch oven. Cook over medium heat, stirring occasionally, 10 minutes or until thoroughly heated. To serve, top with a dollop of sour cream and sprinkle with chopped fresh parsley. Other tasty toppings include chopped fresh basil, chopped fresh chives, chopped fresh rosemary, croutons, freshly grated Parmesan cheese, and lemon zest.

Note: We tested with Progresso Diced Tomatoes With Italian Herbs.

CHILLED STRAWBERRY SOUP

makes about 5 cups   prep: 10 min.   chill: 2 hr.

Garnish this creamy milk shake of a soup with chopped strawberries for added appeal.

1   (16-oz.) container fresh strawberries, sliced
2   cups half-and-half
1¼ cups sour cream

¾   cup powdered sugar
2   Tbsp. white balsamic vinegar

1. Process strawberries in a food processor until smooth, stopping to scrape down sides as needed; pour into a large bowl. Whisk in half-and-half and remaining ingredients. Cover and chill at least 2 hours or up to 3 days. Stir just before serving.

Lightened Chilled Strawberry Soup: Substitute 2 cups fat-free half-and-half and 1¼ cups light sour cream for regular. Proceed with recipe as directed.

ROASTED RED PEPPER SOUP WITH PESTO CROUTONS

makes about 6 cups   prep: 20 min.   bake: 16 min.   cook: 13 min.   cool: 10 min.

Serve this company-worthy starter hot or cold. If you serve the soup cold, stir in an extra ¼ tsp. salt.

¼   cup refrigerated pesto, at room temperature
6   sourdough bread slices
1   Tbsp. butter
1   Tbsp. olive oil
1   garlic clove, minced
1   shallot, finely chopped
1   Tbsp. tomato paste
1   (15-oz.) jar roasted red bell peppers, rinsed
    and drained

4   cups low-sodium chicken broth
¼   cup half-and-half
1   Tbsp. chopped fresh parsley
Salt and pepper to taste
Garnishes: fresh flat-leaf parsley sprigs, shaved
    Parmesan cheese (optional)

1. Preheat oven to 350°. Spread pesto on 1 side of each bread slice. Cut each bread slice into ½- to 1-inch cubes. Place bread cubes in a single layer on a lightly greased aluminum foil-lined jelly-roll pan.

2. Bake at 350° for 16 to 20 minutes or until golden, turning once after 10 minutes. Remove from oven, and let cool.

3. Melt butter with oil in a large Dutch oven over medium-high heat. Add garlic and shallot, and cook, stirring constantly, 2 minutes or until vegetables are tender. Add tomato paste, and cook, stirring constantly, 1 minute. Stir in bell peppers and chicken broth; bring to a boil. Reduce heat to medium, and simmer, stirring occasionally, 5 minutes. Remove from heat; let cool 10 minutes.

4. Process red pepper mixture, in batches, in a blender or food processor 8 to 10 seconds until smooth, stopping to scrape down sides. Return red pepper mixture to Dutch oven; stir in half-and-half and parsley, and cook over medium heat 5 minutes or until thoroughly heated. Season with salt and pepper to taste.

5. Ladle soup into 6 bowls; top with croutons. Garnish, if desired.

CHILLED CUCUMBER SOUP

makes about 8 cups   prep: 20 min.   chill: 2 hr.

[make ahead]

4	cucumbers, peeled, seeded, and chopped (about 3 lb.)	¼	cup chopped fresh parsley
3	cups buttermilk	3	Tbsp. fresh lemon juice
1	(8-oz.) container plain yogurt	2	Tbsp. chopped fresh dill
2	green onions, chopped	1½	tsp. salt
		½	tsp. pepper

1. Process all ingredients, in batches, in a food processor until smooth, stopping to scrape down sides as needed. Transfer to a serving bowl; cover and chill 2 hours.

RED PEPPER-AND-PEAR SOUP

makes 7 cups   prep: 15 min.   cook: 33 min.   cool: 20 min.

Enjoy the tangy blend of red bell peppers, carrots, shallots, and pears in this tasty soup.

[southern lights]

2	Tbsp. butter	½	tsp. dried crushed red pepper
2	tsp. olive oil	½	tsp. ground black pepper
3	large red bell peppers, sliced	¼	tsp. salt
2	carrots, sliced		Dash of ground red pepper
2	shallots, sliced		Garnishes: thinly sliced fresh pears, plain yogurt,
2	Anjou pears, peeled and sliced		chopped fresh chives (optional)
1	(32-oz.) container fat-free chicken broth		

1. Melt butter with oil in a Dutch oven over medium heat; add bell pepper and next 3 ingredients, and sauté 8 to 10 minutes or until tender.

2. Stir in chicken broth and next 4 ingredients. Bring to a boil; cover, reduce heat to low, and simmer 25 to 30 minutes. Let cool 20 minutes.

3. Process soup, in batches, in a food processor until smooth, stopping to scrape down sides. Return to Dutch oven, and keep warm until ready to serve. Garnish, if desired.

Note: To make ahead, let soup cool, and store in an airtight container in refrigerator up to two days. Reheat in a saucepan over medium-low heat, stirring often.

Note: Nutritional analysis does not include garnishes.

Per 1 cup: Calories 103; Fat 5.2g (sat 2.3g, mono 1.9g, poly 0.4g); Protein 1.9g; Fiber 3.6g; Chol 9mg; Iron 0.7mg; Sodium 654mg; Calc 24mg

SAFFRON BUTTERNUT SQUASH SOUP

makes about 4 to 6 cups   prep: 25 min.   cook: 36 min.

Only a small amount of saffron is needed to add a distinctive robust flavor and vibrant orange-red color to soups and sauces. Even if it isn't available, you'll still get great results.

1 large leek	⅛ tsp. ground cinnamon
4 Tbsp. butter	⅛ tsp. ground nutmeg
1 pinch saffron threads	⅛ tsp. ground red pepper
1 cup dry white wine	¼ cup whipping cream
3 lb. butternut squash, peeled, seeded, and chopped	½ tsp. salt
	¼ tsp. ground black pepper
2 carrots, peeled and diced	Garnish: crushed almond biscotti
1 (32-oz.) container chicken broth	(optional)

1. Cut and discard green top from leek; cut white portion into slices.

2. Melt butter in a Dutch oven over medium heat; add leek slices and saffron, and sauté 5 minutes or until leek slices are tender. Add white wine, and cook 1 to 2 minutes. Add squash and next 5 ingredients, and bring to a boil. Reduce heat, and simmer, uncovered, 20 minutes or until squash and carrots are tender. Remove from heat, and let cool slightly.

3. Process squash mixture, in batches, in a blender or food processor until smooth, stopping to scrape down sides. (A handheld immersion blender may also be used.)

4. Return squash mixture to Dutch oven. Add cream, salt, and pepper; simmer 10 to 15 minutes or until thickened. Garnish, if desired.

WILDEST RICE SOUP

makes 10 cups   prep: 25 min.   cook: 20 min.

1   (6.2-oz.) package long-grain and wild rice mix
1   lb. bacon, diced
2   cups chopped fresh mushrooms
1   large onion, diced
3¾ cups half-and-half

2½ cups chicken broth
2   (10¾-oz.) cans cream of potato soup, undiluted
1   (8-oz.) loaf pasteurized prepared cheese product, cubed

1. Cook wild rice mix according to package directions, omitting seasoning packet; set aside.
2. Cook bacon in a Dutch oven until crisp; remove bacon, and drain on paper towels, reserving 2 Tbsp. drippings in Dutch oven.
3. Sauté mushrooms and onion in drippings until tender; stir in rice mix, bacon, half-and-half, and remaining ingredients. Cook over medium-low heat, stirring constantly, until soup is thoroughly heated and cheese melts.

Note: To lighten, decrease bacon to ¼ lb., reserve 2 tsp. drippings and use fat-free half-and-half, fat-free chicken broth, reduced-fat cream of potato soup, and light cheese product.

FRENCH ONION SOUP

makes 6 cups   prep: 20 min.   cook: 50 min.   broil: 3 min.

¼   cup butter
5   medium-size white onions, thinly sliced (about 3 lb.)
1   (32-oz.) container chicken broth
2   (10½-oz.) cans beef consommé, undiluted
¼   cup dry white wine

3   sprigs fresh thyme
2   sprigs fresh parsley
Salt and freshly ground pepper to taste
6   (¾-inch-thick) French baguette slices
6   (1-oz.) Swiss cheese slices

1. Melt butter in a Dutch oven over medium-high heat; add onions, and cook, stirring often, 30 to 40 minutes or until golden brown.
2. Add chicken broth and next 4 ingredients; bring to a boil. Reduce heat, and simmer, stirring occasionally, 20 minutes. Remove and discard herbs. Add salt and pepper to taste.
3. Ladle into 6 ovenproof bowls; top with bread and cheese slices. Broil, 5½ inches from heat, 3 minutes or until cheese is browned and bubbly.

{ family favorite }

Try these yummies. They'll be great with your next bowl of soup.

Parmesan-Parsley Biscuit Flatbreads

makes 8 servings   prep: 15 min.   bake: 10 min.

Preheat oven to 400°. Separate 1 (16.3-oz.) can refrigerated jumbo biscuits into individual rounds. Pour 2 Tbsp. olive oil onto a baking sheet. Dip both sides of each biscuit round in oil, and arrange on baking sheet. Using fingertips, press each biscuit into a 4-inch free-form flat circle. Sprinkle each flattened biscuit with 1 Tbsp. freshly grated Parmesan cheese, 1½ tsp. chopped fresh parsley, and a pinch of kosher salt and freshly ground pepper. Bake at 400° for 10 to 12 minutes or until golden brown. Cut into strips.

Rosemary-Garlic Biscuit Flatbreads: Omit the Parmesan cheese and parsley; prepare the recipe as directed. Sprinkle the biscuits evenly with 2 tsp. chopped fresh rosemary and 2 minced garlic cloves.

Note: We tested with Pillsbury Grands! Homestyle Buttermilk refrigerated biscuits.

CANTALOUPE SOUP

makes about 8 cups   prep: 15 min.   chill: 3 hr.

1 large cantaloupe, chopped	½ tsp. ground cinnamon
3 cups orange juice	¼ tsp. salt
1½ tsp. fresh lime juice	

1. Process all ingredients, in batches, in a blender until smooth, stopping to scrape down sides as needed.

2. Transfer to a large bowl. Cover and chill at least 3 hours or up to 3 days. Stir just before serving.

[make ahead]

SPICY CHICKEN-VEGETABLE SOUP

makes 12 cups   prep: 30 min.   cook: 40 min.

1 (2½- to 3-lb.) whole chicken	2 zucchini, chopped
3 bay leaves	2 carrots, sliced
1 Tbsp. salt	1 large green bell pepper, chopped
1 Tbsp. ground cumin	1 medium onion, chopped
1 tsp. pepper	1 (15½-oz.) can chickpeas, rinsed and drained
1 fresh basil sprig	**Tomato Rice**
4 whole cloves	Toppings: chopped fresh cilantro, chopped green
4 garlic cloves	onions, minced jalapeño pepper, coarsely
1 Tbsp. dried oregano	chopped tomato, chopped avocado

{family favorite}

1. Combine 2½ qt. water, chicken, and next 5 ingredients in a large stockpot; bring to a boil, skimming surface to remove excess foam.

2. Process whole cloves, garlic, and oregano in a food processor until finely chopped.

3. Add garlic mixture to broth, and cook, stirring occasionally, 35 minutes or until chicken is done. Remove chicken from broth, and cool. Skim fat from broth, and set broth aside.

4. Skin and bone chicken; shred chicken, and set aside.

5. Add zucchini and next 4 ingredients to broth; bring to a boil, and cook 5 minutes. Add chicken. Serve with Tomato Rice and desired toppings.

Tomato Rice

makes 1½ cups   prep: 10 min.   soak: 5 min.   cook: 25 min.

¾ cup long-grain rice	1 large garlic clove, minced
1 tsp. lemon juice	1 Tbsp. chicken base*
1 cup hot water	1 cup hot water
2 Tbsp. olive oil	1 tsp. ground cumin
2 tomatoes, chopped	½ tsp. salt
1 medium-size green bell pepper, chopped	½ tsp. pepper

1. Soak rice in lemon juice and 1 cup hot water 5 minutes; drain.

2. Sauté rice in hot oil in a large saucepan over medium-high heat 10 minutes or until golden. Stir in tomato, bell pepper, and garlic.

3. Stir together chicken base and remaining ingredients; stir into rice mixture. Cover, reduce heat, and simmer 15 minutes or until liquid evaporates (do not uncover while rice is cooking).

* Chicken base, a highly concentrated paste made from chicken stock, may be found with broth and bouillon in supermarkets.

CHUNKY VEGETABLE SOUP

makes 35 cups   prep: 10 min.   cook: 35 min.

This recipe makes almost 2 gal. If you have extra, freeze meal-size portions in zip-top plastic freezer bags. Fold top edge down, and place in a large glass measuring cup to stabilize the bag while filling. Seal the bag, removing as much air as possible; label and freeze up to 3 months. Thaw soup in the refrigerator.

2   lb. ground chuck
1   small sweet onion, chopped
1   tsp. salt
½   tsp. pepper
3   (14-oz.) cans low-sodium beef broth
3   (29-oz.) cans mixed vegetables with potatoes, rinsed and drained
3   (14½-oz.) cans diced new potatoes, rinsed and drained

1   (15-oz.) can sweet peas with mushrooms and pearl onions, rinsed and drained
2   (26-oz.) jars tomato, herbs, and spices pasta sauce
1   (14½-oz.) can diced tomatoes with sweet onion

freeze it

1. Cook ground chuck and onion, in batches, in a large Dutch oven over medium-high heat, stirring until meat crumbles and is no longer pink. Drain well, and return to Dutch oven. Stir in salt, pepper, and beef broth; bring to a boil.
2. Stir in mixed vegetables and remaining ingredients. Bring to a boil; cover, reduce heat, and simmer at least 20 minutes or until thoroughly heated.

Note: We tested with Classico Organic Tomato, Herbs & Spices Pasta Sauce.

POT LIKKER SOUP

makes 10 cups   prep: 20 min.   cook: 4 hr.   cool: 30 min.   chill: 8 hr.   **pictured on page 838**

This soup would be wonderful alongside a bowl of hoppin' John. Cooking the ham hocks the day before and chilling the broth overnight will allow you to skim the fat easily.

2   (1-lb.) smoked ham hocks
1   medium onion, chopped
1   medium carrot, diced
1   Tbsp. vegetable oil
1   garlic clove, chopped
½   cup dry white wine
½   tsp. salt

¼   tsp. dried crushed red pepper
1   (14.5-oz.) can vegetable broth
½   (16-oz.) package fresh collard greens, washed
     and trimmed
Cornbread Croutons

1. Bring ham hocks and 8 cups water to a boil in a Dutch oven over medium-high heat. Boil 5 minutes; drain. Reserve hocks; wipe Dutch oven clean.

2. Sauté onion and carrot in hot oil in Dutch oven over medium heat 4 to 5 minutes or until tender; add garlic, and cook 1 minute. Add wine; cook, stirring occasionally, 2 minutes or until wine is reduced by half.

3. Add hocks, 8 cups water, salt, and crushed red pepper to onion mixture, and bring to a boil. Cover, reduce heat to low, and simmer 3 hours or until ham hocks are tender.

4. Remove hocks, and let cool 30 minutes. Remove meat from bones; discard bones. Transfer meat to an airtight container; cover and chill. Cover Dutch oven with lid, and chill soup 8 hours.

5. Skim and discard fat from soup in Dutch oven. Stir in meat and vegetable broth.

6. Bring mixture to a boil. Gradually stir in collards. Reduce heat, and simmer, stirring occasionally, 45 to 50 minutes or until collards are tender. Serve with Cornbread Croutons.

Kitchen Express Pot Likker Soup: Omit ham hocks and salt. Prepare recipe as directed in Step 2, sautéing ½ lb. smoked boneless pork loin, chopped with onion and carrot. Stir in 2 Tbsp. jarred ham soup base, broth, 8 cups water, and red pepper. Bring to a boil. Gradually stir in collards; reduce heat, and simmer 45 minutes or until collards are tender. Prep: 20 min. Cook: 53 min.

Cornbread Croutons

makes: 6 to 8 servings   prep: 10 min.   bake: 45 min.   cool: 1 hr.

2 Tbsp. bacon drippings or vegetable oil	1 large egg
1 cup self-rising white cornmeal mix	½ tsp. salt, divided
1 cup buttermilk	½ tsp. pepper, divided

1. Preheat oven to 450°. Coat bottom and sides of an 8-inch square pan with bacon drippings; heat in oven 5 minutes.

2. Whisk together 1 cup cornmeal mix, buttermilk, egg, ¼ tsp. salt, and ¼ tsp. pepper; pour batter into hot pan.

3. Bake at 450° for 15 to 17 minutes or until lightly browned. Turn out onto a wire rack; cool completely (about 30 minutes). Reduce oven temperature to 325°.

4. Cut cornbread into 1½-inch squares. Place on a baking sheet; sprinkle with remaining salt and pepper.

5. Bake at 325° for 30 to 35 minutes or until crisp and lightly browned. Remove to a wire rack; cool completely (about 30 minutes). Store in an airtight container up to 1 day.

OKRA SOUP

makes 18 cups   prep: 25 min.   cook: 4 hr.   cool: 15 min.

1 (2½- to 3-lb.) boneless chuck roast, trimmed	2 (14.5-oz.) cans diced tomatoes
1 tsp. salt	¼ cup sugar
1 tsp. pepper	2½ to 3 tsp. salt
2 Tbsp. vegetable oil	1 tsp. pepper
2 medium onions, chopped	2½ tsp. hot sauce
2 celery ribs, chopped	½ tsp. Worcestershire sauce
2 (16-oz.) bags frozen okra	3 beef bouillon cubes

1. Sprinkle roast with 1 tsp. salt and 1 tsp. pepper.

2. Brown roast on all sides in hot oil in a Dutch oven over medium-high heat. Add 12 cups water, and bring to a boil; cover, reduce heat to low, and simmer 2 hours.

3. Remove roast from broth, reserving broth; cool 15 minutes. Shred roast, and return to broth.

4. Add onions and remaining ingredients to broth; cover and cook over low heat, stirring occasionally, 2 hours.

POTATO, BEAN, AND YOGURT SOUP

makes 8½ cups   prep: 20 min.   cook: 27 min.   stand: 10 min.

Try packing this soup warm or cold in an insulated container. The soup will retain its temperature (up to 4 hours hot; 6 hours cold), making it easy to store at your desk. The container's lid can double as a serving dish.

{southern lights}

6   cups diced red potatoes (about 4 medium potatoes)
1   cup chopped celery
1   cup grated carrot
2   Tbsp. extra virgin olive oil
1   (16-oz.) can navy beans, rinsed and drained

1½ tsp. salt
1   tsp. dried dill weed
1   tsp. garlic powder
6   cups low-sodium chicken or vegetable broth
½   cup fat-free plain yogurt
Freshly ground pepper to taste

1. Sauté first 3 ingredients in hot oil in a Dutch oven over medium heat 5 minutes. Add navy beans and next 3 ingredients, and cook, stirring often, 2 to 3 minutes. Add broth, and bring to a boil; reduce heat to low, and simmer, stirring occasionally, 20 to 30 minutes. Remove from heat; let stand 10 minutes.

2. Transfer about 4 cups potato mixture to a food processor or blender using a slotted spoon. Process 30 seconds or until smooth, stopping to scrape down sides. Return pureed mixture to Dutch oven, stirring until blended. Stir in yogurt; season with pepper to taste. Serve warm or cold. Store in refrigerator up to 1 week.

Per 1½ cups: Calories 305; Fat 6.7g (sat 1.2g, mono 4.3g, poly 1g); Protein 14.9g; Fiber 7.1g; Chol 0.4mg; Iron: 3.2mg; Sodium: 773mg; Calcium: 98mg

TORTILLA SOUP

makes 22 cups prep: 45 min. grill: 32 min. cook: 1 hr., 15 min.

We offer the option for preparing this dish partway and then refrigerating up to three days or freezing up to three months.

Mesquite chips

8 skinned and boned chicken breasts

16 medium tomatoes (about 8½ lb.)

2 large onions, peeled and cut into eighths

1 Tbsp. vegetable oil

2 poblano chile peppers

3 garlic cloves, minced

2 (10-oz.) packages 6-inch corn tortillas, cut into thin strips and divided

5 (14½-oz.) cans chicken broth

4 (14½-oz.) cans beef broth

1 (8-oz.) can tomato sauce

1 Tbsp. ground cumin

1 Tbsp. chili powder

1 bay leaf

½ tsp. salt

½ tsp. ground red pepper

½ cup vegetable oil

2 cups (8 oz.) shredded colby-Monterey Jack cheese blend

1 avocado, peeled and diced

1. Preheat grill to 350° to 400° (medium-high) heat. Wrap mesquite chips in heavy-duty aluminum foil; punch holes in top of foil. (Soak chips if using charcoal grill.) Place on coals.

2. Grill chicken, covered with grill lid, 6 minutes on each side or until done. Remove chicken; chop and set aside.

3. Place tomatoes and onion on a large piece of heavy-duty aluminum foil. Brush with 1 Tbsp. oil; fold foil to seal. Place on food rack. Grill, covered, 10 minutes. Place chile peppers on food rack with foil-wrapped vegetables, and grill, covered, 10 minutes.

4. Peel peppers, remove seeds, and chop.

5. Process one-third tomato and onion mixture in a food processor until smooth. Press through a wire-mesh strainer into a bowl, discarding solids; transfer to a Dutch oven. Repeat procedure twice with remaining tomato and onion mixture. Stir in chopped peppers and garlic.

6. Add half of tortilla strips and next 8 ingredients to tomato mixture. Bring to a boil. Cover, reduce heat, and simmer 30 minutes. Stir in chicken. Refrigerate up to 3 days, or freeze up to 3 months, if desired. Thaw in refrigerator overnight.

7. Pour ½ cup oil into a large skillet. Fry remaining tortilla strips in hot oil until crisp. Drain on paper towels.

8. Top servings with crisp tortilla strips, cheese, and avocado.

Winter Scrapbooking Party serves 8

*Grilled Pimiento Cheese Sandwiches (page 766)

Ham-and-Bean Soup

Apple wedges

Pound Cake Banana Pudding (page 338)

*double recipe

HAM-AND-BEAN SOUP

makes 8 cups prep: 15 min.   cook: 56 min.

This is a great way to use leftover ham. You'll need about 2 cups to replace the ham steak. Don't forget to toss in the bone for added flavor.

1 (16-oz.) lean ham steak	½ tsp. pepper
2 Tbsp. olive oil	2 (15-oz.) cans navy beans, drained
1 large onion, diced	2 (15-oz.) cans cannellini beans, drained
1 bunch green onions, chopped	1 (15½-oz.) can black-eyed peas, drained
2 large carrots, diced	4 large Yukon gold potatoes, peeled and diced
2 celery ribs, diced	(about 2 lb.)
1 Tbsp. jarred ham-flavored soup base	Garnish: Fall Potato Leaves (optional)

1. Trim fat from ham steak; coarsely chop ham. Reserve bone.

2. Cook ham in hot oil in a Dutch oven over medium-high heat, stirring often, 6 to 8 minutes or until browned. Add diced onion, and next 5 ingredients, and sauté 5 minutes or until onion is tender.

3. Stir in reserved ham bone, navy beans, and next 3 ingredients; add water to cover. Bring to a boil; cover, reduce heat to low, and cook, stirring occasionally, 45 minutes. Remove and discard bone before serving. Garnish, if desired.

Ham-and-Bean Soup With Fresh Spinach: Prepare recipe as directed, stirring in 1 (5-oz.) package fresh baby spinach, thoroughly washed, just before serving.

Fall Potato Leaves

makes about 20 leaves   prep: 15 min.   cook: 2 min. per batch

1   large sweet potato (about 12 oz.)
1   large Yukon gold potato (about 8 oz.)

½   cup canola oil
Kosher salt to taste

1. Cut potatoes into ⅛-inch-thick slices, placing slices in a large bowl of ice water as you work to prevent discoloration.

2. Cut potato slices into leaves, using assorted 2- to 3-inch leaf-shaped cutters. Return leaves to ice water until ready to use.

3. Drain potato leaves, and dry well with paper towels. Cook potato leaves, in batches, in hot oil in a large skillet over medium-high heat 1 minute on each side or until golden brown. Season with salt to taste.

Note: To make ahead, prepare recipe as directed; place cooked leaves in a single layer in a jelly-roll pan. Freeze on pan until firm, and transfer to a zip-top plastic freezer bag. To reheat, place leaves in a single layer on a lightly greased baking sheet. Preheat oven to 350°, and bake 8 to 10 minutes or until thoroughly heated.

HOT BROWN SOUP

makes 5 cups   prep: 10 min   cook: 15 min.

¼   cup butter
¼   cup minced onion
¼   cup all-purpose flour
½   tsp. garlic salt
⅛   tsp. hot sauce
4   cups milk

1   cup (4 oz.) shredded sharp Cheddar cheese
½   cup chopped cooked ham
½   cup chopped cooked turkey
Toppings: crumbled bacon, chopped tomato,
      chopped fresh parsley

quick

1. Melt butter in a Dutch oven over medium heat. Add onion; sauté until tender. Add flour, garlic salt, and hot sauce; cook, stirring constantly, 1 minute. Gradually stir in milk; cook until thickened and bubbly. Reduce heat; stir in cheese until melted. Add ham and turkey; cook, stirring occasionally, until heated. (Do not boil.) Serve with desired toppings.

TURKEY SOUP WITH CORNBREAD DRESSING DUMPLINGS

makes about 16 cups   prep: 20 min.   cook: 45 min.

1   Tbsp. butter

1   large sweet onion, diced (about 1½ cups)

1   garlic clove, minced

1   celery rib, diced

2½ qt. chicken broth

3   cups chopped cooked turkey

1   cup frozen green peas

3   carrots, sliced

2   medium potatoes, peeled and diced

1   tsp. pepper

Cornbread Dressing Dumpling Dough

1. Melt butter in a large 8-qt. stockpot. Add onion, garlic, and celery; sauté over medium-high heat 3 minutes. Add chicken broth and next 5 ingredients. Bring to a boil; reduce heat, and simmer 20 minutes, stirring occasionally.

2. Drop Cornbread Dressing Dumpling Dough by tablespoonfuls into simmering soup. Cook 5 minutes. Cover and cook 15 more minutes or until dumplings are done.

Cornbread Dressing Dumpling Dough

makes about 1½ cups dough   prep: 10 min.   cook: 3 min.

2   Tbsp. butter

1   celery rib, diced

½   small sweet onion, diced (about ¼ cup)

½   tsp. rubbed sage

¾   cup cornmeal

½   cup all-purpose flour

1   tsp. baking powder

1   tsp. seasoned pepper

½   tsp. salt

1   large egg, lightly beaten

⅓   cup milk

1. Melt butter in a small skillet. Add celery, onion, and sage; sauté over medium-high heat 3 minutes.

2. Combine cornmeal and next 4 ingredients in a medium bowl; add egg, milk, and celery mixture, stirring until dry ingredients are moistened.

Highlands Bar and Grill

Close your eyes, and imagine Gulf shrimp pan-roasted with oysters or perhaps served with a grilled asparagus salad. Or creamy grits against a bite of pork tenderloin sweetened with a touch of fresh peach relish.

Using commonplace, seasonal ingredients flavored with traditions from France, Italy, and the Mediterranean, this chef makes palates sing. Frank Stitt and his wife, Pardis, operate four restaurants with distinctive personalities and cuisines. Luscious foods, complemented by gracious service and extraordinary attention to detail, make each place a fabulous experience.

The signature appetizer at Highlands is the stone-ground baked grits. "It epitomizes the humble Southern ingredients, jazzed up with wild mushrooms, sherry vinegar, thyme, and Parmesan in a buttery sauce," Frank says. "In a similar way, the Parmesan soufflé at Bottega is the signature appetizer there. It has a lighter, but rich, luscious Parmesan custard done in an almost identical way as the grits."

2011 11th Ave S,
Birmingham, Alabama 35205;
(205) 939-1400 or
www.highlandsbarandgrill.com

LAMB SOUP WITH SPRING VEGETABLES

makes 6 cups   prep: 20 min.   cook: 2 hr., 37 min.   **pictured on page 839**

This soup is delicious with lots of hot bread. The Citrus-Mint Gremolata brightens up the whole dish, so you may want to make a double batch and serve some on the side for guests to use as they please.

3 lb. boneless lamb shoulder, cubed
1 tsp. salt
1 tsp. pepper
2 Tbsp. all-purpose flour
1 Tbsp. olive oil
5 garlic cloves, chopped
1½ cups dry white wine
2 cups beef broth

½ cup orange juice
2 Tbsp. chopped fresh rosemary
2 Tbsp. chopped fresh thyme
1 lb. baby carrots
1 (16-oz.) bag frozen whole pearl onions, unthawed
½ lb. fresh green beans, trimmed
Citrus-Mint Gremolata

1. Sprinkle lamb evenly with salt, pepper, and flour. Cook lamb in hot oil in a large Dutch oven, stirring constantly, over medium-high heat 5 to 7 minutes or until browned. Add garlic, and sauté 2 minutes.

2. Add wine, and cook, stirring occasionally, 5 minutes. Stir in beef broth and next 3 ingredients, and bring to a boil. Reduce heat to low, cover, and simmer, stirring occasionally, 2 hours.

3. Stir in baby carrots and pearl onions; cook, uncovered, 10 minutes. Add green beans, and cook 15 minutes. Serve hot with Citrus-Mint Gremolata.

Citrus-Mint Gremolata

makes about ¼ cup   prep: 10 min.

Gremolata is an Italian garnish of parsley, lemon, and garlic usually used to sprinkle over veal shanks or other meat and pasta dishes. Here, we've replaced the garlic and parsley with mint and toasted pine nuts for a fresh update.

2 Tbsp. pine nuts, toasted
2 Tbsp. chopped fresh mint

1 Tbsp. lemon zest

1. Combine all ingredients in a small bowl.

PEPPERED BEEF SOUP

makes 12 cups   prep: 20 min.   cook: 7 hr., 8 min.   **pictured on page 840**

Freeze leftovers in an airtight container up to three months. Add a bit of canned broth when reheating to reach desired consistency.

freeze it

1 (4-lb.) sirloin tip beef roast	2 Tbsp. balsamic vinegar
½ cup all-purpose flour	2 Tbsp. Worcestershire sauce
2 Tbsp. canola oil	2 Tbsp. dried parsley flakes
1 medium-size red onion, thinly sliced	1 Tbsp. beef bouillon granules
6 garlic cloves, minced	1½ to 3 tsp. freshly ground pepper
2 large baking potatoes, peeled and diced	4 bay leaves
1 (16-oz.) package baby carrots	Salt to taste
2 (12-oz.) bottles lager beer*	Toasted Bread Bowls, optional

1. Rinse roast, and pat dry. Cut a 1-inch-deep cavity in the shape of an "X" on top of roast. (Do not cut all the way through roast.) Dredge roast in flour; shake off excess. Cook roast in hot oil in a Dutch oven over medium-high heat 1 to 2 minutes on each side or until lightly browned.
2. Place roast in a 6-qt. slow cooker. Stuff cavity with sliced red onion and minced garlic; top roast with potatoes and baby carrots. Pour beer, balsamic vinegar, and Worcestershire sauce into slow cooker. Sprinkle with parsley, bouillon, and ground pepper. Add bay leaves to liquid in slow cooker.
3. Cover and cook on LOW 7 to 8 hours or until fork-tender. Shred roast using 2 forks. Season with salt to taste. Discard bay leaves. Serve in Toasted Bread Bowls, if desired.

* 3 cups low-sodium beef broth may be substituted.

Toasted Bread Bowls

makes 6 bowls   prep: 10 min.   bake: 8 min.

6 (5- to 6-inch) artisan bread rounds*	2 Tbsp. grated Parmesan cheese
Vegetable cooking spray	

1. Preheat oven to 350°. Cut ½ to 1½ inches from top of each bread round; scoop out center, leaving a ½-inch-thick shell. Reserve soft centers for another use. Lightly coat bread shells and, if desired, cut sides of tops, with cooking spray. Place, cut sides up, on baking sheets. Sprinkle with cheese. Bake at 350° for 8 to 10 minutes or until toasted.

* 6 (4-inch) hoagie rolls may be substituted.

TASTE OF THE SOUTH

She-Crab Soup

She-Crab Soup A culinary icon of Charleston, South Carolina, she-crab soup was traditionally a rich combination of cream crabmeat, roe (eggs), and a splash of sherry. The meat from a female crab is said to be sweeter, but it was the addition of her red-orange roe that created the dish's depth of flavor and beautiful pale color and resulted in the name "she-crab" soup.

These days, roe is not harvested in an ecological effort to preserve the supply of crabs. Is it still she-crab soup if there's no roe? Yes—and no. The heart of the recipe remains the same. But when you can, try it made with roe, and savor every precious spoonful.

You'll find some variations, but purists know that the basic recipe is the true Southern tradition. Fresh crabmeat is essential. For all of you lucky enough to catch your own crabs, you'll need about a dozen. If you remove the shell of the female crab and discover what looks like a mass of tiny red-orange beads inside, you've struck gold—I mean roe. Remove it carefully; stir it into the soup with the crabmeat. (Note: Female crabs with roe on the outside must be returned to the water.)

Whether your crabmeat is from crabs you caught yourself or from the supermarket, enjoy a taste of the region.

SHE-CRAB SOUP

makes about 6 cups   prep: 10 min.   cook: 1 hr., 20 min.

1 qt. whipping cream	⅓ cup all-purpose flour
⅛ tsp. salt	2 Tbsp. lemon juice
⅛ tsp. pepper	¼ tsp. ground nutmeg
2 fish bouillon cubes	1 lb. fresh crabmeat
2 cups boiling water	Garnish: chopped parsley
¼ cup unsalted butter	⅓ cup sherry (optional)

1. Combine first 3 ingredients in a heavy saucepan; bring to a boil over medium heat. Reduce heat, and simmer 1 hour. Set aside.

2. Stir together fish bouillon cubes and 2 cups boiling water until bouillon dissolves.

3. Melt butter in a large heavy saucepan over low heat; add flour, stirring until smooth. Cook 1 minute, stirring constantly. Gradually add hot fish broth; cook over medium heat until thickened. Stir in cream mixture, and cook until thoroughly heated. Add lemon juice, nutmeg, and crabmeat. Ladle into individual serving bowls. Garnish, if desired. Add a spoonful of sherry to each serving, if desired.

Note: We tested with Knorr Fish Bouillon. Use good-quality sherry, not cooking sherry.

Blue Crabs 101

If you're lucky enough to get the meat from fresh crabs, keep these tips in mind:

• For steamed crabs, combine ¼ cup plus 2 Tbsp. pickling spice, ¼ cup plus 2 Tbsp. Old Bay seasoning, 3 Tbsp. pickling spice, 2 Tbsp. celery seeds, and 1 Tbsp. crushed red pepper flakes. Bring 1 cup water and 1 cup vinegar to a boil in a stockpot. Place a rack in stockpot. Add 1 dozen live crabs; sprinkle with seasoning. Cover and cook for 20 to 25 minutes or until crabs turn bright red. Rinse with cold water; drain well.

• To get to the cooked meat, twist off crab legs and claws. Crack claws; remove meat with a small fork. Next, remove the apron, or tail flap, from the underside; discard. Insert thumb under shell by apron hinge; remove top shell. Pull away the gray gills; discard them along with internal organs. Break the body; remove meat from pockets. Pick through meat to remove all shell fragments.

STONE CRAB BISQUE

makes 8 cups   prep: 20 min.   cook: 15 min.

½ cup butter, divided

½ cup finely chopped onion

½ cup finely chopped green bell pepper

2 green onions, finely chopped

¼ cup chopped fresh parsley

1 (8-oz.) package fresh mushrooms, chopped

¼ cup all-purpose flour

2 cups milk

2 tsp. salt

¼ tsp. pepper

1 tsp. hot sauce

3 cups half-and-half

2½ cups stone crab claw meat (22 medium claws)*

¼ cup dry sherry

1. Melt ¼ cup butter in a Dutch oven over medium-high heat; add onion and next 4 ingredients, and cook, stirring constantly, 5 minutes or until tender. Remove from skillet; set aside.

2. Melt remaining ¼ cup butter in Dutch oven over low heat; add flour, stirring until smooth. Cook 1 minute, stirring constantly. Gradually stir in milk. Cook over medium heat, stirring constantly, until thickened and bubbly.

3. Stir in onion mixture, salt, and next 3 ingredients. Bring to a boil, stirring constantly; reduce heat, and stir in crab claw meat. Simmer 5 minutes, stirring often. Stir in sherry.

* 2½ cups flaked back-fin crabmeat may be substituted.

Note: Stone crab is in season October 15 to May 15. You can mail-order it from Joe's Stone Crab in Miami Beach, www.joesstonecrab.com or 1-800-780-2722. The medium stone crab claws comes in orders of six. Market prices vary, so call for specific prices. There's an additional charge for packing and shipping.

OYSTER-AND-ARTICHOKE SOUP

makes about 8 cups   prep: 5 min.   cook: 10 min.

1 (12-oz.) container fresh oysters

1 (14½-oz.) can chicken broth

3 Tbsp. butter

½ cup minced celery

¼ cup sliced green onions

3 Tbsp. all-purpose flour

½ tsp. dried thyme

⅛ tsp. ground red pepper

2 cups half-and-half

1 (14-oz.) can quartered artichoke hearts, drained

2 bay leaves

1. Drain oysters, reserving liquid; add broth to liquid to equal 2 cups.

2. Melt butter in a saucepan; add celery and green onions, and sauté until tender. Stir in flour, thyme, and pepper; cook, stirring constantly, 3 to 5 minutes or until golden. Gradually stir in broth mixture and half-and-half; add artichoke hearts and bay leaves.

3. Cook soup over medium heat, stirring occasionally, until thickened and bubbly (do not boil). Stir in oysters; cook, stirring occasionally, 2 to 3 minutes or until oysters begin to curl.

CORN-AND-CRAB CHOWDER

makes 10 cups   prep: 20 min.   cook: 50 min.

This chowder is worth the splurge to buy fresh crabmeat, but it's just as good with fresh shrimp. You can store it in an airtight container in the coldest part of your refrigerator up to 24 hours.

6 bacon slices	1 lb. fresh lump crabmeat, drained and picked*
2 celery ribs, diced	1 cup whipping cream
1 medium-size green bell pepper, diced	¼ cup chopped fresh cilantro
1 medium onion, diced	½ tsp. salt
1 jalapeño pepper, seeded and diced	¼ tsp. pepper
1 (32-oz.) container chicken broth	Oyster crackers
3 Tbsp. all-purpose flour	Garnish: chopped fresh cilantro (optional)
3 cups fresh corn kernels (6 ears)	

1. Cook bacon in a Dutch oven over medium heat 8 to 10 minutes or until crisp; remove bacon, and drain on paper towels, reserving 2 Tbsp. drippings in Dutch oven. Crumble bacon.

2. Sauté celery and next 3 ingredients in hot drippings 5 to 6 minutes or until tender.

3. Whisk together broth and flour until smooth. Add to celery mixture. Stir in corn. Bring to a boil; reduce heat, and simmer, stirring occasionally, 30 minutes. Gently stir in crabmeat and next 4 ingredients; cook 4 to 5 minutes or until thoroughly heated. Serve warm with crumbled bacon and oyster crackers. Garnish, if desired.

* 1 lb. peeled cooked shrimp or chopped cooked chicken may be substituted.

CHICKEN-TASSO-ANDOUILLE SAUSAGE GUMBO

makes 20 cups   prep: 45 min.   cook: 3 hr., 33 min.

Tasso is a spicy smoked cut of pork or beef popular in many Cajun dishes.

4   lb. skinned and boned chicken thighs

1   lb. andouille or smoked sausage

1   lb. tasso or smoked ham

1   cup vegetable oil

1   cup all-purpose flour

4   medium onions, chopped

2   large green bell peppers, chopped

2   large celery ribs, chopped

4   large garlic cloves, minced

4   (32-oz.) boxes chicken broth

1½ tsp. dried thyme

1   tsp. black pepper

½   tsp. ground red pepper

⅓   cup chopped fresh parsley

Hot cooked rice

Garnishes: sliced green onions, filé powder

1. Cut first 3 ingredients into bite-size pieces. Place in a large Dutch oven over medium heat, and cook, stirring often, 20 minutes or until browned. Drain on paper towels. Wipe out Dutch oven with paper towels.

2. Heat oil in Dutch oven over medium heat; gradually whisk in flour, and cook, whisking constantly, 25 minutes or until mixture is a dark mahogany.

3. Stir in onions and next 3 ingredients; cook, stirring often, 18 to 20 minutes or until tender. Gradually add broth. Stir in chicken, sausage, tasso, thyme, and black and red ground peppers.

4. Bring mixture to a boil over medium-high heat. Reduce heat to medium-low, and simmer, stirring occasionally, 2½ to 3 hours. Stir in parsley. Remove from heat; serve over hot cooked rice. Garnish, if desired.

Shrimp-Tasso-Andouille Sausage Gumbo: Omit chicken thighs and proceed with Steps 1, 2, and 3. Proceed with Step 4, stirring in 4 lb. medium-size raw shrimp, peeled and, if desired, deveined, the last 15 minutes of cooking. Pictured on page 840.

Creole Gumbo vs. Cajun Gumbo

What isn't different? That's the true question concerning the varieties of Creole and Cajun styles of gumbo. The variations on these two types of gumbo are as diverse as the ethnic roots found in Louisiana and the number of families who enjoy gumbo.

First, let's look at the similarities between Creole and Cajun gumbos; the list is shorter. Both use the famous Louisiana culinary holy trinity—onion, celery, and bell pepper. Both are traditionally served with rice. Both include two or more types of meat or seafood. Each version is a mixture of many ingredients, born of an attempt to try to stretch food resources on hand to feed a large family. There the similarities end.

Creole style, formed through a blend of European and African influence, is found in areas around New Orleans. You'll recognize this style because it's chock-full of seafood, plentiful in the area; tomatoes, a signature ingredient in anything Creole; and okra, the secret for thickening the hearty stew rather than a roux, which is a must in Cajun gumbo. If a Creole gumbo does start with a roux, it's usually thinner than that used in the Cajun version. One or more types of seafood—oysters, crab, shrimp, but not usually finfish—grace the dish. Along with the seafood, there may be chicken and even some sausage or ham for extra seasoning.

In southwest Louisiana, where Cajun style rules, it's likely you won't find okra in the gumbo. Instead, a dark, slow-cooked roux made of flour and fat is the traditional thickener. And it's spicier. Meats reflect the local terrain—chicken, duck, squirrel, rabbit, and perhaps some sausage or ham for seasoning.

Sausage or ham for either gumbo style is likely to be tasso, a spicy, smoked ham, or spicy andouille sausage. Filé powder, made of ground sassafras leaves, is another thickener, mostly associated with Creole gumbo, and is either stirred in right before serving or sprinkled on top for a unique flavor kick.

Two other gumbo versions often are tied to Mardi Gras season, including gumbo z'herbes, a stew of several different types of greens and made without meat when served during Lent. Chicken gumbo is part of Cajun Mardi Gras tradition where it's enjoyed as part of a jovial community meal. Perhaps at this festive celebration of loud, boisterous Cajuns is where the saying "gumbo ya ya," meaning "everybody talks at once," was born.

SHRIMP-CRAB GUMBO

makes 20 cups prep: 35 min. cook: 3 hr., 50 min.

Here's a gumbo recipe for a crowd. You'll need a deep pot for cooking. There are two things to remember before you tackle gumbo: Allow plenty of time; neither a roux nor gumbo can be rushed. And keep a wooden spoon handy for stirring the roux and the gumbo occasionally to prevent it from sticking.

1½ cups vegetable oil

2 cups all-purpose flour

9 (14-oz.) cans chicken broth

2½ cups chopped onion

1 cup chopped green onions

½ cup chopped celery

2 garlic cloves, chopped

1 (10-oz.) can diced tomatoes with green chiles

1 (8-oz.) can tomato sauce

3 lb. unpeeled, medium-size fresh shrimp

1 (16-oz.) container lump crabmeat

½ cup chopped fresh parsley

1 Tbsp. filé powder (optional)

10 cups hot cooked rice

1. Heat oil in a large stockpot over medium heat; gradually whisk in flour, and cook, whisking constantly, until flour is a dark mahogany (about 30 minutes).

2. Stir in chicken broth and next 6 ingredients; bring to a boil. Reduce heat, and simmer, stirring occasionally, 3 hours.

3. Peel shrimp, and devein, if desired. Add shrimp to broth mixture; cook, stirring often, 15 minutes or just until shrimp turn pink. Stir in crabmeat and parsley. Remove from heat; stir in filé powder, if desired. Serve over hot cooked rice.

The Secret To Gumbo

• Two ingredients—flour and oil—make a roux. The slow-cooked blend contributes a rich depth of flavor to Creole and Cajun dishes and is the heart of every real gumbo.

• Plan to spend from 30 to 40 minutes whisking the precious thickener, depending on the size of your pot and the temperature. You can't rush that nutty flavor. If the heat is high, the roux will burn, and then you'll need to start over.

• Store roux in an airtight container in the refrigerator up to two weeks. Any time you want gumbo, you'll be a step ahead of the game.

GOLDEN OYSTER STEW

makes 6 cups   prep: 15 min.   cook: 25 min.   **pictured on page 840**

Oyster liquor is the liquid found in the container with shucked oysters (or inside the shell of whole oysters). Drain the oysters before cooking so you can pick out bits of shell before adding the mollusks to your recipe. If the liquor seems especially gritty, line the colander with a coffee filter.

2 Tbsp. butter	1 (10¾-oz.) can cream of potato soup, undiluted
½ cup chopped onion	1 (2-oz.) jar diced pimiento, undrained
½ cup sliced celery	¼ tsp. salt
1 (8-oz.) package sliced fresh mushrooms	¼ tsp. pepper
2 Tbsp. all-purpose flour	¼ tsp. hot sauce
2 cups milk	1 (12-oz.) container standard oysters, undrained
1 cup (4 oz.) shredded sharp Cheddar cheese	Saltines or oyster crackers (optional)

1. Melt butter in a Dutch oven over medium heat; add onion and celery, and cook, stirring occasionally, 8 minutes or until tender. Add mushrooms, and cook, stirring occasionally, 5 minutes. Add flour, and cook, stirring constantly, 1 minute.

2. Gradually stir in 2 cups milk; cook, stirring often, 5 minutes or until mixture is thickened and bubbly.

3. Reduce heat to low, and stir in cheese and next 5 ingredients. Cook, stirring often, 3 minutes or until cheese melts and mixture is hot.

4. Add oysters and oyster liquor, and simmer 3 minutes or just until edges of oysters begin to curl. Serve with crackers, if desired.

Note: To make ahead, prepare the stew through Step 3. Freeze the mixture in a large zip-top plastic freezer bag for up to two months. Thaw in the refrigerator overnight. Heat in a Dutch oven over medium-low heat 10 minutes or until thoroughly heated. Proceed with recipe as directed in Step 4.

HARVEST BEEF STEW

makes 8 cups   prep: 20 min.   cook: 4 hr., 51 min.

2½ lb. beef stew meat (about 1-inch pieces)

1½ tsp. salt

¼ tsp. freshly ground pepper

¼ cup all-purpose flour

4 Tbsp. olive oil

1 (6-oz.) can tomato paste

1 (14.5-oz.) can beef broth

1 cup chopped celery

1 cup chopped sweet onion

3 garlic cloves, crushed

1 small butternut squash (about 1 lb.), peeled, seeded, and chopped

Hot cooked mashed potatoes (optional)

Garnish: fresh parsley sprigs (optional)

1. Rinse beef stew meat, and pat dry. Sprinkle with salt and pepper; toss in flour, shaking off excess.

2. Cook half of beef in 2 Tbsp. hot oil in a Dutch oven over medium-high heat, stirring occasionally, 10 minutes or until browned. Repeat procedure with remaining beef and oil. Stir in tomato paste; cook 1 minute. Add broth, and stir to loosen particles from bottom of Dutch oven. Transfer mixture to a 6-qt. slow cooker.

3. Stir in celery, onion, and garlic. Top with butternut squash. (Do not stir.) Cover and cook on LOW 4½ hours or until meat is tender. Serve over hot cooked mashed potatoes, if desired. Garnish, if desired.

BARBECUE STEW

makes 8 cups   prep: 15 min.   bake: 1 hr., 30 min.   cook: 30 min.

1 (3-lb.) boneless pork loin roast

1 Tbsp. barbecue seasoning

1 (18-oz.) bottle smoky mesquite barbecue sauce

1 (14-oz.) can chicken broth

1 (32-oz.) container chicken broth

2 (16-oz.) bags frozen vegetable soup mix

2 (14.5-oz.) cans fire-roasted diced tomatoes*

1 cup frozen whole kernel corn

½ tsp. salt

1 (24-oz.) package frozen olive oil, rosemary, and garlic oven fries

1 (22-oz.) package frozen sweet potato fries

1. Preheat oven to 350°. Rinse and pat roast dry. Rub barbecue seasoning over roast. Place in an aluminum foil-lined 13- x 9-inch pan. Pour barbecue sauce and 1 (14-oz.) can chicken broth over roast. Cover tightly with aluminum foil.

2. Bake at 350° for 1½ hours or until fork-tender. Remove roast from pan, reserving drippings in pan. Shred roast with 2 forks.

3. Carefully pour drippings into a Dutch oven. Add shredded pork, 1 (32-oz.) container chicken broth, and next 4 ingredients. Bring to a boil over medium-high heat; reduce heat to medium-low, and simmer, stirring occasionally, 30 minutes.

4. Meanwhile, prepare oven fries and sweet potato fries according to package directions; serve with stew.

* 2 (14.5-oz.) cans diced tomatoes may be substituted.

Note: We tested with McCormick Grill Mates Barbecue Seasoning; Alexia Olive Oil, Rosemary & Garlic Oven Fries; and Alexia Sweet Potato Julienne Fries.

To make ahead: Prepare recipe through Step 3. Store in an airtight container in refrigerator up to four days. Reheat in a large Dutch oven while the oven preheats to cook fries.

PORK-AND-GREENS STEW

makes 6 to 8 cups   prep: 20 min.   cook: 2 hr., 30 min.

Amber beer may easily be substituted for Oktoberfest.

1   (3½- to 4-lb.) boneless pork shoulder roast, trimmed
1   tsp. salt
1   tsp. pepper
2   (12-oz.) bottles Oktoberfest beer
2   (10½-oz.) cans condensed chicken broth, undiluted

1   large sweet onion, chopped
1   (16-oz.) package frozen chopped turnip greens, thawed
1   (15-oz.) can white hominy, rinsed and drained

1. Cut pork into 3-inch pieces; sprinkle evenly with salt and pepper, and place in a large Dutch oven. Stir in beer, broth, and onion. Bring to a boil over medium-high heat; cover, reduce heat to low, and simmer 1½ to 2 hours or until pork shreds easily with a fork.
2. Remove pork, and shred with 2 forks. Skim fat from surface of broth in Dutch oven.
3. Return pork to Dutch oven, and stir in greens and hominy. Bring to a boil; reduce heat, and simmer 20 minutes or until greens are tender.

Note: We tested with Saint Arnold Oktoberfest beer.

Georgia Says Brunswick Stew, Kentucky Claims It's Called Burgoo

Though Kentucky burgoo is almost identical to Brunswick stew, after centuries of dispute, it's Virginians and Georgians who can't seem to agree.

A sign near Brunswick, Georgia, proclaims the local coastal area to be the birthplace of Brunswick stew. In central Virginia's Brunswick County, a marker gives a long history of the camp-style stew and takes credit for being the first state to dish it up—thereby throwing a little dig at Georgia. The disagreement doesn't stop with a couple of signs, though. Years of competition at festivals have brought the two sides together to continue the "stew war," but the origin of the disputed stew is yet to be declared.

In Kentucky, a large camp-style pot of meat, vegetables, and seasonings is cooked up practically the same way as Brunswick stew and with the same ingredients. The main difference is that burgoo usually contains mutton, as well as other meats, as a nod to sheep that were once plentiful there. In the early days both Brunswick stew and burgoo contained a mixture of meat that hunters caught in the woods. Squirrel was the star of the stews in those days. Today, Brunswick stew is more likely to include pork, beef, and chicken.

But the community-style pot-stirring camaraderie still is part of the allure of both stews. In fact, stew-making is a popular fund-raiser for churches and civic groups. The stewmasters are usually men, and there is no shortage of tall tales and laughter as the stew is simmered and stirred. Potatoes, onions, corn, tomatoes, and butter beans cook with the meat and seasonings. Then, as tradition dictates, the stews, both Brunswick-style and burgoo, are served as a critical side to a hearty plate of barbecue.

BRUNSWICK STEW

makes 8 to 10 cups   prep: 5 min.   cook: 30 min.

3   cups chicken broth
2   cups chopped cooked chicken
1   (24-oz.) container barbecued shredded pork
1   (16-oz.) package frozen vegetable gumbo
    mixture

1   (10-oz.) package frozen corn
½   (10-oz.) package frozen petite lima beans
½   cup ketchup

1. Bring all ingredients to a boil in a Dutch oven over medium-high heat, stirring often. Cover, reduce heat to low, and simmer, stirring occasionally, 25 minutes or until thoroughly heated.

KENTUCKY BURGOO

makes 24 cups   prep: 20 min.   cook: 5 hr.

1   (3- to 4-lb.) whole chicken
1   (2-lb.) beef chuck roast
2   lb. pork loin chops, trimmed
5   qt. water
1   dressed rabbit (optional)
1   lb. tomatoes
5   potatoes
5   celery ribs
4   carrots
2   onions
2   green bell peppers
1   small cabbage

2   cups frozen whole kernel corn
1   cup frozen baby lima beans
1   cup frozen English peas
3   garlic cloves, minced
8   cups beef broth
1   (32-oz.) bottle ketchup
2   cups dry red wine
1   (10-oz.) bottle Worcestershire sauce
¼   cup white vinegar
1   Tbsp. salt
1   Tbsp. pepper
1   Tbsp. dried thyme

1. Bring first 4 ingredients and, if desired, rabbit to a boil in a large heavy stockpot. Cover, reduce heat, and simmer 1 hour or until tender. Remove meats, reserving liquid in stockpot; skin, bone, and shred meats, and return to pot.

2. Chop tomatoes and next 5 ingredients; shred cabbage. Add chopped vegetables, corn, and next 11 ingredients to meats; cook over low heat, stirring often, 4 hours.

CHUNKY BEEF CHILI

makes 9 cups prep: 25 min. cook: 1 hr., 45 min. **pictured on page 840**

If you've had spices longer than a year, it might be time to replace them. Seasonings tend to dull in flavor the longer they sit on the shelf. Always store them in a cool, dry place. Make a big batch of this recipe and freeze individual servings for later. Just thaw and reheat, and use the leftovers for chunky tacos, meaty baked potatoes, or smothered hamburgers and hot dogs.

[make ahead]

4 lb. boneless chuck roast, cut into ½-inch pieces	1 tsp. ground cumin
2 Tbsp. chili powder	1 tsp. paprika
2 (6-oz.) cans tomato paste	1 tsp. onion powder
1 (32-oz.) container beef broth	½ tsp. ground black pepper
2 (8-oz.) cans tomato sauce	¼ tsp. ground red pepper
2 tsp. granulated garlic	Cornbread sticks (optional)
1 tsp. salt	Toppings: crushed tortilla chips, sour cream,
1 tsp. ground oregano	shredded cheese, chopped onion

1. Brown meat, in batches, in a Dutch oven over medium-high heat. Remove meat, reserving drippings in Dutch oven. Add chili powder to Dutch oven; cook, stirring constantly, 2 minutes. Stir in tomato paste; cook 5 minutes.

2. Return beef to Dutch oven. Stir in beef broth and next 9 ingredients; bring to a boil. Reduce heat to low, and simmer, uncovered, stirring occasionally, 1½ hours or until beef is tender. Serve with cornbread sticks, if desired, and desired toppings.

MEATY BLACK BEAN CHILI

makes 8 cups prep: 10 min. cook: 20 min.

3 (15-oz.) cans black beans	1 (14-oz.) can low-sodium fat-free chicken broth
1 large sweet onion, chopped	2 (14.5-oz.) cans petite diced tomatoes with
1 lb. ground round	jalapeños
4 tsp. chili powder	Toppings: sour cream, shredded Cheddar cheese,
1 tsp. ground cumin	lime wedges, sliced jalapeño peppers, chopped
½ tsp. pepper	fresh cilantro, chopped tomatoes, corn chips
¼ tsp. salt	

1. Rinse and drain 2 cans black beans. (Do not drain third can.)

2. Sauté chopped onion and ground round in a large Dutch oven over medium heat 10 minutes or until meat is no longer pink. Stir in chili powder and next 3 ingredients; sauté 1 minute. Stir in drained and undrained beans, chicken broth, and diced tomatoes. Bring to a boil over medium-high heat; cover, reduce heat to low, and simmer 10 minutes. Serve chili with desired toppings.

PLAYOFF CHILI

makes about 7 cups   prep: 25 min.   cook: 2 hr., 15 min.

1   lb. ground beef
1   lb. ground pork
1   large white onion, chopped
1   large green bell pepper, seeded and chopped
1   large red bell pepper, seeded and chopped
2   garlic cloves, minced
1   (14½-oz.) can diced tomatoes with green chiles
1   (12-oz.) bottle beer
1   (8-oz.) can tomato sauce
1   Tbsp. chili powder
1   tsp. ground cumin

1   tsp. sugar
1   tsp. salt
½   tsp. ground red pepper
½   tsp. black pepper
½   tsp. dried oregano
1   (16-oz.) can kidney beans, rinsed and drained
1   (16-oz.) can black beans, rinsed and drained
14 (1¼-oz.) bags corn chips
Garnishes: chopped onion, shredded Cheddar cheese, sour cream (optional)

1. Cook ground beef and next 5 ingredients in a Dutch oven over medium heat 10 minutes or until meat crumbles and is no longer pink. Stir in diced tomatoes with green chiles and next 9 ingredients, and bring to a boil. Cover, reduce heat to low, and simmer 1 hour and 45 minutes, stirring every 20 minutes. Add kidney beans and black beans; cover and cook 15 minutes.
2. Cut corn chip bags open at one long side. Spoon ½ cup chili on chips in each bag. Garnish, if desired.

Note: Chili may be frozen in a zip-top plastic freezer bag up to three months. We tested with Fritos Brand Original Corn Chips.

Do You Know Beans About Chili?

If you prefer any type of chili other than the kind with beef chunks and no beans, just keep it to yourself when you're around Texans. They'll get hotter than a habanero to hear that someone's adulterated their revered bowl of red.

"Anyone who knows beans about chili knows there ain't no beans in chili!" Or, so say Texans when they boldly explain what constitutes—or not—an authentic bowl of Texas chili. The "no bean" rule probably stemmed from the cowboy trail days when beef was plentiful at the beginning of the cattle drive, but as the meat ran out, the cook added beans to the thick stew to stretch it through the remaining days. The traditional bowl of red, adapted from the influence of Mexican stew, instead features chunks of tender beef in a dark brown gravy, more like a Mexican mole sauce, and is seasoned with spicy chilies, cumin, and oregano. Adding beans is a sin of the worst kind.

As chili popularity spread, the seasonings became milder to meet Anglo tastes and sometimes the side order of beans was dumped into the meaty stew. Now, throughout the region you have to read the menu closely to figure out what you'll be getting if you decide to order chili. The meat could be sausage, chicken, turkey, ham, pork, or even seafood. Other ingredients that would make a chili purist swear include zucchini, eggplant, oranges, cashews, and even tofu.

Outside Texas, beans are relished in chili, and chopped onion, shredded cheese, and sour cream may be served as toppings. Beans and rice are served as sides for traditionalists along with tortillas or cornbread. Saltines or oyster crackers are common accompaniments.

If you want to get a complete picture of just how serious a chili fan can be, check out any one of the chili cooking competitions held throughout the South. Or even better, take in the granddaddy of them all, the annual Terlingua International Chili Championship in West Texas. The competition is stiff, the cooks are serious, and the chili sampling is the best on earth.

SMOKY CHICKEN CHILI

makes 9 cups   prep: 15 min.   cook: 1 hr., 15 min.

Pick up smoked chicken from your favorite barbecue restaurant to make this dish, or use a barbecue-flavored rotisserie chicken from your local supermarket.

2   poblano chile peppers, chopped

1   large red bell pepper, chopped

1   medium-size sweet onion, chopped

3   garlic cloves, minced

2   Tbsp. olive oil

2   (14½-oz.) cans zesty chili-style diced tomatoes

3   cups shredded or chopped smoked chicken
    (about 1 lb.)

1   (16-oz.) can navy beans

1   (15-oz.) can black beans, rinsed and drained

1   (12-oz.) can beer*

1   (1.25-oz.) envelope white chicken chili
    seasoning mix

Toppings: shredded Cheddar cheese, chopped
    fresh cilantro, sour cream, lime wedges, baby
    corn, sliced black olives, chopped red onion,
    tortilla chips

1. Sauté first 4 ingredients in hot oil in a large Dutch oven over medium-high heat 8 minutes or until vegetables are tender. Stir in diced tomatoes and next 5 ingredients. Bring to a boil over medium-high heat. Reduce heat to low, and simmer, stirring occasionally, 1 hour. Serve with desired toppings.

* 1½ cups low-sodium chicken broth may be substituted.

WHITE BEAN CHILI

makes 8 cups   prep: 10 min.   cook: 30 min.

1½ lb. boneless, skinless chicken breasts, chopped

2   Tbsp. olive oil

4   (16-oz.) cans navy beans, undrained

4   (4.5-oz.) cans chopped green chiles, undrained

1   cup chicken broth

1   (1.25-oz.) envelope white chicken chili
    seasoning mix

Toppings: chopped fresh cilantro, shredded
    Monterey Jack cheese, chopped tomatoes,
    chopped avocado

1. Sauté chicken in hot oil in a large Dutch oven over medium-high heat 8 minutes or until done.
2. Stir in beans and next 3 ingredients; bring to a boil over medium-high heat, stirring occasionally. Cover, reduce heat to low, and simmer, stirring occasionally, 15 minutes. Serve with desired toppings.

metric equivalents

The recipes that appear in this cookbook use the standard U.S. method for measuring liquid and dry or solid ingredients (teaspoons, tablespoons, and cups). The information in the following charts is provided to help cooks outside the United States successfully use these recipes. All equivalents are approximate.

Metric Equivalents for Different Types of Ingredients

A standard cup measure of a dry or solid ingredient will vary in weight depending on the type of ingredient. A standard cup of liquid is the same volume for any type of liquid. Use the following chart when converting standard cup measures to grams (weight) or milliliters (volume).

Standard Cup	Fine Powder (ex. flour)	Grain (ex. rice)	Granular (ex. sugar)	Liquid Solids (ex. butter)	Liquid (ex. milk)
1	140 g	150 g	190 g	200 g	240 ml
¾	105 g	113 g	143 g	150 g	180 ml
⅔	93 g	100 g	125 g	133 g	160 ml
½	70 g	75 g	95 g	100 g	120 ml
⅓	47 g	50 g	63 g	67 g	80 ml
¼	35 g	38 g	48 g	50 g	60 ml
⅛	18 g	19 g	24 g	25 g	30 ml

Useful Equivalents for Dry Ingredients by Weight

(To convert ounces to grams, multiply the number of ounces by 30.)

1 oz	=	⅟₁₆ lb	=	30 g
4 oz	=	¼ lb	=	120 g
8 oz	=	½ lb	=	240 g
12 oz	=	¾ lb	=	360 g
16 oz	=	1 lb	=	480 g

Useful Equivalents for Length

(To convert inches to centimeters, multiply the number of inches by 2.5.)

1 in				=	2.5 cm			
6 in	=	½ ft		=	15 cm			
12 in	=	1 ft		=	30 cm			
36 in	=	3 ft	=	1 yd	=	90 cm		
40 in				=	100 cm	=	1 m	

Useful Equivalents for Liquid Ingredients by Volume

¼ tsp					=	1 ml	
½ tsp					=	2 ml	
1 tsp					=	5 ml	
3 tsp	=	1 Tbsp		=	½ fl oz =	15 ml	
		2 Tbsp	= ⅛ cup	=	1 fl oz =	30 ml	
		4 Tbsp	= ¼ cup	=	2 fl oz =	60 ml	
		5⅓ Tbsp	= ⅓ cup	=	3 fl oz =	80 ml	
		8 Tbsp	= ½ cup	=	4 fl oz =	120 ml	
		10⅔ Tbsp	= ⅔ cup	=	5 fl oz =	160 ml	
		12 Tbsp	= ¾ cup	=	6 fl oz =	180 ml	
		16 Tbsp	= 1 cup	=	8 fl oz =	240 ml	
		1 pt	= 2 cups	=	16 fl oz =	480 ml	
		1 qt	= 4 cups	=	32 fl oz =	960 ml	
					33 fl oz =	1000 ml	= 1 l

Useful Equivalents for Cooking/Oven Temperatures

	Fahrenheit	Celsius	Gas Mark
Freeze water	32° F	0° C	
Room temperature	68° F	20° C	
Boil water	212° F	100° C	
Bake	325° F	160° C	3
	350° F	180° C	4
	375° F	190° C	5
	400° F	200° C	6
	425° F	220° C	7
	450° F	230° C	8
Broil			Grill

RECIPE INDEX

SUBJECT INDEX

Southern Living

MAMA'S WAY or YOUR WAY?
Quick and classic takes on warm apple dumplings

MADE BY SOUTHERN HANDS
GORGEOUS GIFTS & FINDS FOR FALL

Each issue of SOUTHERN LIVING celebrates the best of the South and helps you cultivate your own Southern Style. In every issue, you'll discover:

- More than 50 delicious, kitchen-tested recipes
- Travel guides to your favorite Southern destinations
- Decorating tips from our interior design experts
- Regional gardening advice for all seasons

6 FREE ISSUES R.S.V.P.

YES! Please send me 6 issues of *Southern Living* absolutely FREE! If I like them, I'll receive 13 more for a total of 19 monthly issues at the special low rate of just $16. If I don't enjoy the magazine, there's no obligation. I'll simply return your acknowledgment marked "cancel" and owe nothing. The cancellation is effective immediately, and the 6 issues are mine to keep — FREE — no matter what I decide!

Name   (Please Print)

Address

City   State   Zip

E-mail

☐ Payment enclosed.   ☐ Bill me later.

Southern Living

Southern Living

Make the most of your life in the South!

GREAT SOUTHERN DRIVES Explore the best Southern back roads. Complete with a map featuring "not-to-be-missed" sites along the way plus a "Playlist" of songs for each memorable journey.

MADE BY SOUTHERN HANDS Be the first to know about stylish new items, from jewelry and home décor to food and dishware — all made in the South, only by Southerners.

HALF-HOUR HOSTESS Simple secrets to cutting your preparation time so you can always plan the perfect party for every occasion.

MAMA'S WAY OR YOUR WAY? Updates to the recipes you loved as a kid that will have your friends and family asking for seconds — and thirds!

 PERF AND MAIL

Subscribe Now!